THE COLD WAR:
THE GREAT POWERS AND THEIR ALLIES

The Postwar World
General Editors: A.J. Nicholls and Martin S. Alexander

As distance puts events into perspective, and as evidence accumulates, it begins to be possible to form an objective historical view of our recent past. *The Postwar World* is an ambitious new series providing a scholarly but readable account of the way our world has been shaped in the crowded years since the Second World War. Some volumes will deal with regions, or even single nations, others with important themes; all will be written by expert historians drawing on the latest scholarship as well as their own research and judgements. The series should be particularly welcome to students, but it is designed also for the general reader with an interest in contemporary history.

International Relations Since 1945
A History in Two Volumes

The Cold War:
The Great Powers and
their Allies

J.P.D. Dunbabin

Longman
London and New York

LONGMAN GROUP UK LIMITED,
Longman House, Burnt Mill,
Harlow, Essex CM20 2JE, England
and Associated Companies throughout the world

*Published in the United States of America
by Longman Publishing, New York*

© Longman Group Limited 1994

First published 1994

ISBN 0 582 22866 2 CSD
ISBN 0 582 49365 X PPR

British Library Cataloguing-in-Publication Data
A catalogue record for this book is
available from the British Library

Library of Congress Cataloging-in-Publication Data
Dunbabin, J.P.D.
    International relations since 1945 : a history in two volumes /
  J.P.D. Dunbabin.
      p. cm. – (The Postwar world)
    Includes bibliographical references and indexes.
    Contents: 1. The cold war : the great powers and their allies –
  2. The post-imperial age : the great powers and the wider world.
    ISBN 0-582-22866-2 (v. 1). – ISBN 0-582-22719-4 (v. 2). – ISBN
  0-582-49355-X (pbk. : v. 1). – ISBN 0-582-22720-8 (pbk. : v. 2)
    1. Cold War. 2. World politics–1945- 3. Great powers.
  I. Title. II. Series.
  D843.D774 1994
  909.82'5–dc20   93-28429
                                                              CIP

Set by 7.00 in 10/12 New Baskerville
Produced by Longman Singapore Publishers (Pte) Ltd.
Printed in Singapore

Contents

Abbreviations

ABM	Anti-ballistic missile
ALCM	Air-launched cruise missile
ARVN	South Vietnamese army
ASEAN	Association of South-East Asian Nations
BBC	British Broadcasting Corporation
CAP	Common Agricultural Policy (European Community)
CCP	Chinese Communist Party
CDU	Christian Democratic Union (West Germany)
CIA	Central Intelligence Agency (USA)
CMEA	Council for Mutual Economic Assistance (Communist countries). Colloquially known as 'Comecon'
CND	Campaign for Nuclear Disarmament (UK)
Comecon	Council for Mutual Economic Assistance (Communist countries). *See* CMEA
COSVN	American term for 'Vietcong' headquarters, situated just over the border in Cambodia
CPSU	Communist Party of the Soviet Union
CSCE	Conference on Security and Cooperation in Europe
DC	Christian Democratic Party (Italy)
DDR	German Democratic Republic (East Germany)
DEFCON	United States Defence Condition – numbered stages of preparedness
DRV	Democratic Republic of Vietnam (North Vietnam)
EC	European Community
ECSC	European Coal and Steel Community
ecu	European Currency Unit
EDC	European Defence Community
EEC	European Economic Community

EFTA	European Free Trade Association
EMS	European Monetary System
EPU	European Payments Union
ERM	Exchange Rate Mechanism (of the EMS)
Euratom	European Atomic Energy Community
FBI	Federal Bureau of Investigation (USA)
FDP	Free Democratic Party (West Germany)
FLN	National Liberation Front (Algeria)
FNLA	National Front for the Liberation of Angola
FO	Foreign Office (Britain)
FRUS	*Foreign Relations of the United States*
G7	USA, Japan, Germany, France, UK, Italy, Canada. The group of the seven leading OECD members
GATT	General Agreement on Tariffs and Trade
GDP	Gross domestic product
GLCM	Ground-launched cruise missile
GNP	Gross national product
HSP	Hungarian Socialist Party (reconstituted in Oct 1989 from the Hungarian Socialist Workers (Communist Party))
IAEA	International Atomic Energy Agency
ICBM	Inter-continental ballistic missile
IISS	International Institute for Strategic Studies
IMF	International Monetary Fund
INF	Intermediate range nuclear force
IPC	Iraq Petroleum Company
IRBM	Intermediate range ballistic missile
ITT	International Telephone and Telegraph
JCS	Joint Chiefs of Staff (USA)
KGB	State Security Committee – Soviet secret police
KMT	Kuomintang (Nationalist Party) (China)
KOR	Committee for the Defence of Workers (Poland)
KPD	Communist Party of Germany – merged, in the Soviet zone, with SPD to create the SED
MAD	Mutual Assured Destruction
MBFR	Mutual and Balanced Force Reductions
MIRV	Multiple independently targeted re-entry vehicle
MPLA	Popular Movement for the Liberation of Angola
MRP	Popular Republican Movement (France)
MSI	Italian Social Movement – neo-fascist political party (Italy)
NATO	North Atlantic Treaty Organisation

NLF	National Liberation Front (South Vietnam)
NOP	Nuclear operations plan
NSC	National Security Council (USA)
NSF	National Salvation Front (Romania)
OAS	Secret army organisation of settler resistance in Algeria
OAU	Organisation of African Unity
OECD	Organisation for Economic Co-operation and Development
OEEC	Organisation for European Economic Cooperation
OPEC	Organisation of Petroleum Exporting Countries
PCF	French Communist Party
PCI	Italian Communist Party
PDS	Democratic Party of the Left (Italy – the former PCI)
PKI	Communist Party of Indonesia
PLO	Palestine Liberation Organisation
PS	Socialist Party (France). *See* also SFIO
PRO	Public Record Office (Britain)
RIIA	Royal Institute of International Affairs
SAC	Strategic Air Command (USA)
SACEUR	Supreme Allied Commander Europe (NATO)
SALT	Strategic Arms Limitation Talks (or Treaty)
SDI	Strategic Defense Initiative (pejoratively known as 'Star Wars')
SEATO	South-East Asia Treaty Organisation
SED	Socialist Unity Party of Germany (East Germany)
SFIO	French Socialist Party, reconstituted in 1969 as the Parti Socialiste (PS)
SIOP	Single Integrated Operations Plan (US)
SIPRI	Stockholm International Peace Research Institute
SLBM	Submarine-launched ballistic missile
SPD	Social Democratic Party of Germany (West Germany)
START	Strategic Arms Reduction Talks (or Treaty)
UAR	United Arab Republic (Egypt and Syria; later just Egypt)
UK	United Kingdom (of Great Britain and Northern Ireland)
UN	United Nations
UNITA	National Union for the Total Independence of Angola

UNRRA	United Nations Relief and Rehabilitation Administration
US or USA	United States of America
USSR	Union of Soviet Socialist Republics
WEU	Western European Union

Preface

'I know that it will be said by many, That I might have been more pleasing to the Reader if I had written the Story of mine own times . . ... To this I answer that whosoever in writing a modern History shall follow truth too near the heels, it may haply strike out his teeth.'

Fortunately the enterprise is no longer so dangerous as in Sir Walter Raleigh's time. My thanks are due in the first instance to the series editors for suggesting that I undertake it, and more particularly to Tony Nicholls for many helpful comments and suggestions; also to Longman both for accepting and producing the book and for important advice as to its structure and coverage. Responsibility for mistakes, of course, rests with me.

I am naturally greatly indebted to Oxford libraries and colleagues. Of the libraries, the Bodleian must have pride of place; but I should like to take this opportunity of thanking my former pupil, Andrew Peacock, for gifts that have made my college library far more useful, in this context, than one would a priori have expected. As for colleagues, it would be invidious to single out any of the living; but I owe much to both Alastair Buchan and Hedley Bull. The tragedy of Hedley's early death is of special relevance to this project. For it was originally hoped that he would accompany my narrative with a companion, and more analytical, volume; it is a great loss that he was not able to do so.

Beyond Oxford, I have (particularly in the mid-1980s, when British libraries were going through a bad phase) benefited from hospitality, talks, seminars, libraries and bookshops, especially in North America. My thanks are due to: the Canadian Institute of International Affairs; the libraries of the University of Toronto and of McMaster University; the Woodrow Wilson Center; the Library of

Congress; the Hoover Institution; the libraries of Stanford University and of the University of California, Berkeley; and to Princeton University (at which time my wife was at the Institute of Advanced Study). On two of these journeys I enjoyed support as a British Academy/Leverhulme Foundation Visiting Professor; otherwise the current politics of academic funding compel me to add, work for this book was done on the basis of salaries and sabbatical leave from my college and university (in that order of magnitude).

My greatest debt, though, is to my wife Jean, for more than I can easily record, and to my daughters Bridget and Penny – at least the latter will not be able to say of this, as of my more domestic academic writing, that it is just 'the history of the garden wall'.

St. Edmund Hall, Oxford

Author's Note

All told, this book is quite long. For ease of reading and handling, it has been divided into two volumes, the first covering the Cold War, the second other major developments (like, for instance, decolonisation, the rise of the Rim of Asia, the Arab-Israeli dispute, or the evolution of the international monetary system) that, though they were certainly influenced by East-West rivalry, were essentially separate and autonomous. Save in its treatment of Western Europe (and of Yugoslavia), the first volume does not seek to go beyond the end of the USSR in 1991, and so excludes the wars of succession and the partial revival of the nineteenth century 'Great Game' in Central Asia and the Caucasus. The second volume has no such natural terminal point; many of its stories are still unfolding, and important developments (sometimes, indeed, dramatic transformations) are dealt with down to the summer of 1993. Naturally the author would prefer people to buy both volumes; but each is meant to be capable of standing on its own, covering one or more of the major themes of post-war international history. To make this possible a few (though very few) topics, like the Korean and Vietnam wars, figure in both, albeit in a somewhat different context.

Two other points should be noted. Most Chinese names are rendered according to the *pinyin* phonetic system commended by the People's Republic in 1979, but for the Kuomintang and pre-communist names the old transliterated spelling is retained: thus Mao Zedong, but Chiang Kai-shek. Secondly, where the seasons of the year are used to give a general idea of date (as in 'the summer of 1993' above), they refer to the seasons of the northern hemisphere.

Editorial Foreword

The aim of this series is to describe and analyse the history of the World since 1945. History, like time, does not stand still. What seemed to many of us only recently to be 'current affairs', or the stuff of political speculation, has now become material for historians. The editors feel that it is time for a series of books which will offer the public judicious and scholarly, but at the same time readable, accounts of the way in which our present-day world was shaped by the years after the end of the Second World War. The period since 1945 has seen political events and socio-economic developments of enormous significance for the human race, as important as anything which happened before Hitler's death or the bombing of Hiroshima. Ideologies have waxed and waned, the industrialised economies have boomed and bust, empires have collapsed, new nations have emerged and sometimes themselves fallen into decline. While we can be thankful that no major armed conflict has occurred between the so-called superpowers, there have been many other wars, and terrorism has become an international plague. Although the position of ethnic minorities has dramatically improved in some countries, it has worsened in others. Nearly everywhere the status of women has become an issue which politicians have been unable to avoid. These are only some of the developments we hope will be illuminated by this series as it unfolds.

The books in the series will not follow any set pattern; they will vary in length according to the needs of the subject. Some will deal with regions, or even single nations, and others with themes. Not all of them will begin in 1945, and the terminal date may similarly vary; once again, the time-span chosen will be appropriate to the question under discussion. All the books, however, will be written by expert historians drawing on the latest fruits of scholarship, as well as their own expertise and judgement. The series should be particularly welcome to students, but it is designed also for the general reader with an interest in contemporary history. We hope that the books will stimulate scholarly discussion and encourage specialists to look beyond their own particular interests to engage in wider controversies. History, and particularly the history of the recent past, is neither 'bunk' nor an intellectual form of stamp-collecting, but an indispensable part of an educated person's approach to life. If it is not written by historians it will be written by others of a less discriminating and more polemical disposition. The editors are confident that this series will help to ensure the victory of the historical approach, with consequential benefits for its readers.

A.J. Nicholls
Martin S. Alexander

PART I
Introduction

CHAPTER ONE

The Cold War: an Overview

Soviet–American rivalry has dominated postwar international relations, and has drawn into its orbit many initially unconnected issues (like the Arab–Israeli dispute, in which both countries initially supported Israel) – so much so, indeed, that commentators often spoke rather glibly of a 'bipolar world'. Once firmly established, the system proved deep-rooted and slower to change than observers (at optimistic moments) often hoped. One development that *might* have ended the Cold War would have been the emergence of a new external challenge great enough to give the USSR and the USA overriding common interests. Something like this has indeed happened in other contexts: early in the twentieth century the challenge of Imperial Germany did much to end Franco-British rivalry, while Franco-German reconciliation after the Second World War was helped by the perceived Soviet threat. But the emergence of new Powers does not necessarily drive old ones into the arms of their former enemies: both Hitler and Stalin hoped in vain that Britain would so respond to the rise of the United States. Since 1945 only two Powers have so far emerged with a fraction of this capacity for realignment – Japan and China. Japan now has the world's second largest economy, and its trade imbalance with the USA has strained relations and could eventually have serious consequences. The Japanese challenge is purely economic, however, and Japan has thus far been happy to adopt a relatively low profile in international politics. China is the world's most populous country. In the early 1960s its official position was extremely militant; both superpowers were sufficiently concerned as to what it might do with nuclear weapons for there to have been at least some discussion of joint action to stop it developing them. A decade later it was the USSR that worried about China's long-term intentions and its capabilities should the West be foolish enough to help it modernise. One of Kissinger's aides has argued that Brezhnev's détente policy was largely directed at isolating China: hence 'the many overtures . . . attempting to lure us into arrangements whereby we would acquiesce in China's destruction. When it became clear that we would not go along with this, . . . Brezhnev's interest in détente may have flagged as well'.[1]

Although no individual Power emerged capable of bringing about a Soviet–American realignment, theoretically a coalition might have done so. The 1950s saw the growth of a 'non-aligned movement' (anxious both to keep out of East–West quarrels and to stop them monopolising the political agenda) and of an overlapping Afro-Asian one. In the 1960s much of Latin America, too, was drawn into the so-called 'Group of 77', which sought reforms of the international economic system. Its high point came in 1974–5 when, encouraged by the 1973 success of the Organisation of Petroleum Exporting Countries (OPEC) in raising the price of oil, it demanded the negotiation of a New International Economic Order. To some commentators 'North–South' issues seemed to have eclipsed 'East–West' ones – one 1976 article is subtitled 'From Nonalignment to International Class War' – and though the communist world, economically far less important than the industrialised Western states, managed to stand largely on the sidelines, it did share some interests with the other 'Northern' countries. But the 'South', though not wholly unsuccessful, proved unable to keep its demands at the centre of 'Northern' consciousness; nor, with the occasional exception of OPEC, has it appeared to the North as a serious threat. New issues did not render East–West antagonism obsolete; so it worked itself out according to its own intrinsic dynamics.

ORIGINS OF THE COLD WAR

The chief developments can be briefly stated. From 1945 to 1947 East–West relations steadily deteriorated, with regular meetings of the Four Power Council of Foreign Ministers ceasing after

---

1. Henry Kissinger, *Years of Upheaval* (1982) (hereafter *Memoirs* ii) p. 1,173 – paraphrasing W.G. Hyland, *Soviet–American Relations: A New Cold War?* (Santa Monica, Calif., 1981) pp. 26–8

December 1947. By then the political geography of Europe had largely assumed the shape it was to keep till 1989, with communist rule installed in the East (a process rounded off by the February 1948 take-over of Czechoslovakia and the defeat in 1949 of the communist rising in Greece), while the USA offered economic Marshall Aid to reconstruct the West. It was, however, still unclear quite where this would leave Germany and Austria, which had from 1945 been jointly occupied by the USSR, USA, UK and France. In 1948 the latter three moved to create their own West German state, despite the 1948–9 Soviet blockade of West Berlin. This state, and its Eastern counterpart the German Democratic Republic (DDR), came into existence in 1949; but it was not until 1955 that it became certain that West Germany would be militarily integrated into the Western NATO alliance, to prevent which the USSR *might* have been prepared to accept a united but neutral liberal-democratic Germany. When the USSR failed to gain its point, it withdrew from Austria (which it had previously been holding as a hostage). Thereafter the demarcation between East and West in Europe was not seriously at issue, though from 1958 to 1962 the USSR caused major crises by threatening to squeeze West Berlin, chiefly in order to force the Western recognition of the DDR that did not in fact come for another decade.

EAST AND SOUTH-EAST ASIA

The initial crises of the Cold War had concerned Turkey and Iran; but Eastern Asia had been largely uninvolved, even though the 1946–9 civil war led to China becoming communist. The United States did, however, decide in 1949 to try to stop communism spreading down into French Indo-China. The Korean War then had the effect of extending 'containment' throughout East Asia. In Korea, as in Germany, postwar occupation had hardened into the creation of a communist and a non-communist state. In 1950 the former (with Soviet fore-knowledge) invaded the latter in the expectation of securing rapid unification. This was prevented by US and 'United Nations' intervention. The victorious UN forces overran North Korea, but were driven out by China, which itself sought to push south but was held roughly along the prewar demarcation line. Fighting stopped in 1953, but the border has remained ever since both tense and rigidly sealed. Meanwhile in

Indo-China Chinese aid had by 1954 enabled communist insurgents to defeat the French in a 'war of national liberation'. The Geneva conference then partitioned Vietnam between communist North and non-communist South; after a brief intermission local, but Northern-assisted and controlled, insurrection broke out in the South, and would have overthrown it had not US combat troops intervened in 1965. The Vietnam War, like the Korean, was, in the first instance, a civil one. But the USA had, since 1949, expected the fall to communism of one South-East Asian country to lead to the destabilisation and collapse of its neighbours, like a row of dominoes; hence US intervention (with the support of South Korean, Australian and New Zealand, but not West European, troops). In the event North Vietnam (which came to receive war material and economic assistance from both the USSR and China) outlasted the USA and in 1975 overran South Vietnam. This triumph was accompanied by communist take-overs in Laos and Cambodia (which had been sucked into the Vietnam War), but *not* in any other putative 'domino'. Korea and Vietnam had seen the only actual 'East–West' fighting. But the containment of China also gave rise to two of the most alarming postwar crises, those of 1954–5 and 1958 over offshore islands held by the US-supported Kuomintang 'Republic of China', which had regrouped on Taiwan; at least in the first, there was a measurable chance of the USA using atomic weapons. It can, therefore, be argued that the Cold War was considerably more intense in Eastern Asia than in Europe.

KHRUSHCHEV

Specific crises apart, East–West fears were at their greatest between the outbreak of the Korean War in 1950 (which destroyed Western confidence that the USSR would not seek to expand by force) and Stalin's death in 1953. Stalin's successors sought a détente, and the ensuing years saw useful East–West agreements (the Korean armistice, the Geneva conference on Indo-China, and Austrian independence) culminating in the largely atmospheric 1955 Geneva summit conference. But if Soviet leaders, and notably Khrushchev, were determined to avoid nuclear war and genuinely anxious to improve East–West relations up to a point, they were still determined to out-compete the West. In this Khrushchev looked partly to what he hoped would prove the manifest attractiveness of the communist system, and partly to the influencing of the newly emergent Third World states away from the 'imperialist camp', whether by economic and military aid or by support for 'wars of national liberation'. Indeed the summer of 1955 saw both the summit conference (with its 'spirit of Geneva') and the Egyptian arms deal whereby the USSR first gained an entrée into the Arab world. From 1956 to 1958 the struggle for influence in that world was very much at the centre of the East–West stage (even though, confusingly, both the USSR and the USA condemned the November 1956 British-French-Israeli attack on Egypt – 'Suez').

From Khrushchev onwards, East–West relations were set in a mixture of competition and cooperation. As we have seen, the two trends were not necessarily in phase, and, of course, crises could come out of the blue as a result of the actions of third parties. US–Soviet relations were good in 1973, but Sadat's attack on Israel first forced the superpowers into competitive resupply of their respective Middle Eastern clients and then led to a distinctly tense moment when the USA signalled (through a heightened defence posture) that it would not allow Soviet troops into the Canal zone, even as part of a non-partisan force designed to effect a cease-fire. By and large, though, it can be argued that East–West relations did broadly move in successive cycles of détente and renewed antagonism. The first such cycle started with Stalin's death in 1953 and came to a sticky end with the 1956 Soviet repression of the Hungarian uprising. However, 1957 saw propaganda proposals for a halt to nuclear testing. By mid-1958 these had expanded into serious negotiations in Geneva, admittedly overshadowed by major crises over the Middle East and the Chinese offshore islands, but leading at least to a test moratorium that autumn. Khrushchev then raised the diplomatic temperature with his 'ultimatum' over Berlin, but this led to (inconclusive) negotiations, to his 1959 tour of the United States and to loose talk of the 'spirit of Camp David'. Relations were, however, blighted in 1960 when Khrushchev (infuriated, he says, by Eisenhower's refusal to apologise for aerial espionage) aborted the Paris summit. In 1961–2 Khrushchev pushed hard on several fronts, a process that ended with the alarming confrontation over the clandestine Soviet introduction of missiles into Cuba. This over, both Khrushchev and Kennedy markedly softened their stance. One result was the successful conclusion of a Test Ban treaty, another the installation of a 'hot-line' teleprinter link between Washington and Moscow – probably an over-hyped development, but one indicating acceptance of a certain joint responsibility (or 'adversary partnership') in controlling world affairs to prevent the ultimate disaster of nuclear war.

JOHNSON AND NIXON

The post-Cuba détente did not exactly end: nuclear negotiations continued and culminated in 1968 with joint US–Soviet sponsorship of a Nuclear Non-Proliferation Treaty; President Johnson seems to have been anxious for continued good relations with the USSR. However, Khrushchev's successors thought that he had been altogether too soft, thereby jeopardising Soviet influence in North Korea and North Vietnam. They also saw the escalation of the Vietnam War as an arrogant use of the USA's power and, though (professedly) ready to negotiate over it, were distinctly cool towards Johnson personally. By 1968, however, they had decided to negotiate over anti-ballistic missiles (ABMs); their intervention in Czechoslovakia made them all the more eager, so as to direct attention elsewhere.

Nixon was less enthusiastic: initially he judged the USSR by its (un)readiness to pressure North Vietnam into winding down the Indo-China war, but in 1970 he decided seriously to pursue a summit. Several threads here came together. One was domestic, the constraints placed on his ability to act in the foreign and defence fields by mounting US rejection of 'Vietnam' and the policies that had led to it. Another was Chinese. In the 1950s Sino-American hostility may have worked against détente: the Chinese thought that Khrushchev should be taking a much tougher line, and this *may* have been a factor in his 1960 decision to do so. After the Cuban missile crisis, the USSR as well as the USA worried over China; Kennedy at least hoped that this might lead to joint action. Khrushchev's fall put paid to any such ideas, but, after a brief interlude, Sino-Soviet relations continued to worsen, and by 1968–9 China was so alarmed as to welcome US overtures. Under Nixon, these were forthcoming. One motive for Brezhnev's pursuit of détente was to preclude the emergence of a hostile American–Chinese alignment and instead draw the USA into joint management of the Chinese problem. Another thread was *Ostpolitik*. The 1960s had seen first France and then West Germany seek openings in Eastern Europe. In 1969–70 the USSR and West

Germany managed to improve their hitherto very antagonistic relations, and West Germany agreed both to accept Germany's 1945 borders and to recognise the DDR. The USA was suspicious, but it could not risk alienating Bonn by opposing this process, and was able to integrate it into its own dealings with Moscow by negotiating a definitive settlement of the Berlin question. Lastly both the USA and the USSR had good reason to seek an ABM agreement.

The upshot was the conclusion, at the 1972 Moscow summit, of a Strategic Arms Limitation Treaty (SALT I), flanked by a wide range of commercial and cultural agreements. This was, from the American viewpoint, by far the most ambitious détente to date, for, instead of directly containing the Soviet Union, the USA sought to provide it with a place and stake in the existing international system such that it would not risk losing these advantages by hostile or adventurous behaviour. But whereas the accompanying US–Chinese and *Ostpolitik* détentes had lasting results, the 'Moscow' US–Soviet détente progressively came unstuck as neither country achieved from it what it had hoped. What remained was a continuing nuclear arms race (only mildly curbed by the SALT I and II treaties) and Soviet conventional arms build-up, and a Soviet readiness to take up opportunities for the spread of communism in the Third World (which seemed the more alarming since the USSR now had, for the first time, a global military reach). That several such opportunities emerged from 1975 onwards may, of course, have been fortuitous; equally the 'Moscow' détente might never have transpired had take-over plots by the Soviet-oriented Egyptian security apparatus or the communist coup in the Sudan succeeded in 1971.

CARTER AND REAGAN

Be that as it may, East–West relations worsened dramatically in 1979–81. President Carter was shocked by the Soviet invasion of Afghanistan and declared himself ready to fight for US interests in the Gulf. His successor, Reagan, saw the Marxist Sandinista take-over in Nicaragua as part of a Soviet–Cuban challenge in Central America, a whole new area of the Cold War. He also imposed sanctions on the USSR and Poland in response to the 1981 repression of the non-communist Polish movement, Solidarity. And he denounced the Soviet Union as the 'evil empire' with such vigour that people were soon talking of a 'new Cold War'. How cold it was is debatable. Of the antagonism of the early 1980s there can be no doubt. But low-level functional cooperation continued; delegations travelled abroad from communist countries, and Westerners were readily allowed through the 'iron curtain'. During the original Cold War East–West relations had largely dried up, and the border resembled that between North and South Korea. Now it did not. It is tempting to argue that, though there had certainly been ups and downs in East–West relations, these had been only cycles in an improving trend line. But this is not necessarily so; at least some Western circles feared that the Soviet Union might capitalise on its perceived military superiority to secure real gains in Western Europe.[2] More seriously Andropov is said to have declared at a 1981 KGB conference that the West was actively preparing for nuclear war. Many Soviet experts were sceptical. But for the next three years Soviet intelligence was repeatedly ordered to watch for specific pointers to the launching of a surprise nuclear attack; during a November 1983 NATO exercise, fears were expressed that US preparations for one might actually have started.[3]

These fears may have encouraged the USSR to seek better relations, as after the Cuban missile crisis. Another factor will have been the failure of its hopes that NATO moves to deploy cruise and Pershing missiles would produce a revulsion of feeling in Western Europe. The proposed deployment did indeed generate 'peace' movements and accusations that the USA meant to fight a nuclear war in Europe; left-wing sentiment rose in the British Labour and German Social Democrat parties, and both (in Opposition) broke with the NATO defence consensus that they had upheld when in office. In both countries, however, elections in 1983 returned conservative governments, and later that year deployment of missiles went ahead. The immediate Soviet reaction was to pull out of nuclear arms limitation talks. But in 1984 both sides moderated their language, Gromyko held discussions with the US leadership, and (following Reagan's re-election) steps were taken to resume negotiations.

2. C.-C. Schweitzer (ed), *The Changing Western Analysis of the Soviet Threat* (1990) esp. chaps 5, 16

3. Christopher Andrew and Oleg Gordievsky, *KGB: The Inside Story of its Foreign Operations from Lenin to Gorbachev* (1990) pp. 488–507. Gordievsky was then a KGB agent in London; his communication of these fears to British intelligence may have been *one* reason for the subsequent toning down of American and British language about the Soviet Union

GORBACHEV AND THE END OF THE COLD WAR

In December 1984 Gorbachev visited London to enlist Mrs. Thatcher's advocacy with President Reagan; in July 1985 (shortly after his accession to the Soviet leadership) he and Reagan met in Geneva. The summit proved a striking success and opened up the prospect of a new détente. But there was, at this stage, no sign of anything more; relations were again strained for much of 1986, and though Gorbachev was obviously an impressively flexible bargainer, Soviet tactics still seemed largely aimed at putting the United States in the wrong on the issue of ABM research ('Star Wars'). Clearly important changes were on foot in the USSR, but the jamming of BBC broadcasts did not stop till January 1987, that of Deutsche Welle not till December 1988. In mid-1987 US Defense Secretary Weinberger could still maintain that

> much as the new Soviet leadership would like to convince the world otherwise the Soviet Union is not just another member of the community of nations: it is a tightly-controlled, totalitarian state whose values are alien to free societies, whose military might is a constant threat to our survival, and whose goal is still to conquer all who do not support its communist policies.

In any case, as the former German Chancellor Helmut Schmidt warned in 1988, Gorbachev might well fail and the USSR revert to an 'aggressive and expansionist' strategy.[4]

The pace at which suspicions faded varied considerably. Public opinion probably took the lead: by 1988 Gorbachev was at least as well regarded in Western Europe as Reagan, while polls in early 1989 showed that 80 per cent of West Germans felt no threat from the East and that very few Soviet citizens feared Western intentions (though 90 per cent believed themselves threatened by their own *nomenklatura*). Some Western politicians (notably the German Foreign Minister Genscher) were more attuned to the new mood than others. By June 1988 Reagan was himself speculating that 'Quite possibly we are beginning to break down the barriers of the post-war era, entering a new era of history, a time of lasting change in the Soviet Union'. The Moscow summit from which he was returning had been a success; but his call to 'tear down the Berlin

---

4. *Keesing's Record of World Events* (London) (hereafter *Keesing's;* formerly *Keesing's Contemporary Archives* (Keynsham, Bristol)), 35012, 37094; Schweitzer, *Changing Analysis of the Soviet Threat* pp. 46, 91

Wall' still seemed unrealistic and propagandistic. In November 1989 the Wall did come down, and communist rule in Eastern Europe collapsed. The Soviet Union took all this in its stride, and in 1990 showed itself ready to accept German reunification and to agree a phased withdrawal of its troops. The year concluded with a treaty reducing conventional armed forces in Europe to equal ceilings for East and West, thus on paper abolishing any special Soviet threat, together with a joint declaration affirming that its signatories 'are no longer adversaries'.[5] Meanwhile the USA, UK and France had removed substantial forces from Europe for use against Iraq in a UN operation that enjoyed (slightly uneasy) Soviet support. The world was indeed changed. But not completely: for the USSR sought to evade the Conventional Forces in Europe treaty by (inter alia) relabelling its excess tanks as Naval units, while in 1991 its Prime Minister 'revealed' a Western plan to flood it with banknotes, thus creating hyperinflation and so bringing to power the 'advocates of swift privatisation' at fire-sale prices.[6] Such attitudes underline the extent to which the ending of the Cold War was dependent on the internal transformation of the Soviet Union, a process that resumed at breakneck speed after the collapse of a reactionary coup attempt in August 1991.

5. Schweitzer, *Changing Analysis of the Soviet Threat* pp. 262, 284; *Keesing's*, 36060, 37838

6. *The Independent,* 19 Jan. 1991 p. 13 and 11 Feb. 1991 p. 8 (also 24 Oct. 1989 p. 1 – admitted Soviet breach of ABM treaty – and 25 July 1991 p. 1 – East European claims of breach of INF treaty); *Keesing's*, 38012

CHAPTER TWO

The Domestic Background in the Soviet Union and the United States

Gorbachev once talked of the 'organic tie between each state's foreign and domestic policies. . . . A change in the domestic policy inevitably leads to changes in the attitude to international issues'.[1] That the sources of foreign policy are to be found primarily in internal affairs has been claimed also for many other countries. Thus one school sees the *primat der innenpolitik* as the key to German foreign policy since Bismarck, while decolonisation is as clearly linked with developments in the metropolis as in the dependencies: 'we British', one Commonwealth Secretary declared, 'have lost the will to govern'.[2] But however important the general domestic origins of foreign policy, we have space here only for a brief survey of those internal developments that had a significant bearing on the international behaviour of the two superpowers.

THE SOVIET UNION AFTER 1945

At the end of the Second World War Stalin faced two obvious internal problems, the satisfaction or containment of the aspirations it had unleashed among its subjects, and the reconstruction of a devastated land. From the outset he had recognised that people were more likely to fight for Russia than for communism; so tsarist

1. Mikhail Gorbachev, *Perestroika* (paperback edn, 1988) p.132
2. Sir Roy Welensky, *Welensky's 4000 Days* (1964) p.319

heroes and military practices were reinvoked, the Orthodox Church was allowed to revive, and ideological control by the Communist Party relaxed. The final German surrender brought spontaneous pro-Allied demonstrations in Moscow and wild rejoicing by a populace that hoped for better things than the 1930s. Much of the country, though, had been occupied by the Germans, much of the army exposed to foreign influences either as prisoners or as a victorious force in richer lands. Stalin was pathologically suspicious of all such contacts: former Soviet prisoners were often simply reassigned to Siberia, and by 1948 at least 20 per cent of the Soviet administration in Germany is supposed to have been arrested. Nor were Stalin's fears always groundless: Ukrainian guerrilla resistance to Soviet reoccupation ran at a high level for years, while its Lithuanian counterpart killed some 20,000 Soviet troops in 1944–8; equally the 1940–1 deportations were resumed, and by 1949 a quarter of the population of the Baltic states had been removed, to be replaced by Great Russians.[3]

It is therefore unsurprising that a major postwar theme was the restressing of socialist ideology, of the uniqueness of Soviet Russia, and of the threat from outside; already by August 1945 people were being reminded of 'the basic fact that our country remains the only socialist state in the world. . . . The victory achieved does not mean that all dangers to our state structure and social order have disappeared'. This theme was driven home during the February 1946 'election', the distinctiveness of the USSR, the correctness of prewar policies, and the need to resume economic growth interrupted by the German attack constituting the chief themes of Stalin's and Molotov's addresses.[4] Later that year Zhdanov embarked on an ideological clamp-down and literary purge. Of course none of this necessarily precluded continued cooperation with the Soviet Union's former allies: official policy in the 1970s combined détente in inter-state relations with enhanced ideological struggle and a clamp-down on domestic dissidents. But in the aftermath of war the Soviet regime found it essential to lower the iron curtain again as quickly as possible, and at least convenient to generate an atmosphere of external threat. The process did not make dealing with the Russians any easier for foreigners; even during the war this had been hard enough, and it may be no

3. R.W. Pethybridge, *A History of Postwar Russia* (1966) pp.66–7; N. Tolstoy, *Stalin's Secret War* (1981) pp.266, 354
4. Pethybridge, *Postwar Russia* p. 70; *New York Times*, 10 Feb. 1946 p.30 (Stalin's speech); W.G. Hahn, *Postwar Soviet Politics* (1982) pp.21–3

accident that the people most pessimistic about Soviet intentions were men like Kennan and Harriman, who had had most experience of trying.

The war had left the USSR devastated. The human casualties were enormous – upwards of 20 million – though a hostile writer argues that at least half were self-inflicted.[5] It is not clear how deeply Stalin felt such things. But there can be no doubt as to the importance he set on economic recovery, the keynote of his February 1946 speech being the need to produce

> 50,000,000 tons of pig iron per year, 60,000,000 tons of steel, 500,000,000 tons of coal and 60,000,000 tons of oil.
>
> Only under such conditions will our country be insured against any eventuality. Perhaps three new Five-Year Plans will be required to achieve this, if not more. But it can be done and we must do it.

By his own standards he succeeded, taking 'national income' by 1950 to about 173 per cent of its 1940 level. Agriculture, however, had not quite recovered to prewar levels; 'real wages' reached 1928 levels only in 1952; and in 1953 agricultural production *per capita* was still well below that of 1913.[6]

The need for economic recovery might have pulled Soviet policy in a number of ways. One possible source of assistance was the United States. The USSR did show an interest in securing an American loan, though not at the price of making political concessions; it probably viewed US reluctance to lend as a hostile act. Lend-Lease was formally cut off at the end of the war; in fact the USSR received another $492 million over the next eighteen months from deliveries in the pipeline and UNRRA (United Nations Relief and Rehabilitation Administration) humanitarian aid,[7] but this was relatively small and uncertain. Much more dependable was the extraction of resources from areas under Soviet military control. Stalin saw no reason why the Red Army should not loot and generally compensate itself for its earlier sufferings, and there was a continuum between such individual enterprise and organised economic transfer. In the circumstances no very reliable figures can be produced; but the USSR may well have extracted from East Germany the $10 billion reparations for which it pressed so hard, as well as acquiring significant sums from the rest of

---

5. Tolstoy, *Stalin's Secret War* pp.280–4

6. *Cambridge Encyclopedia of Russia and the Soviet Union* (Cambridge, 1982) p.335; R.A. Medvedev, *Let History Judge* (1972) p.486

7. G. Lundestad, *The American Non-Policy towards Eastern Europe 1943–1947* (Oslo, 1975) esp. pp.393, 395

Eastern Europe.[8] Similar processes were at work in the Far East, where the Red Army remained in Manchuria, despite US pressure, till it had removed some $860 million of industrial equipment,[9] then left.

This 'dismantling' was agreed to be the simplest way of collecting reparations. But it was often done in so hasty and haphazard a way that the equipment removed could never be fitted together again. Experience showed that it was more efficient to leave equipment in place and appropriate a share in the production. All along the Soviets had forced on the East European countries they had liberated unequal trade treaties and 'joint–stock' Soviet–local companies. The practice was soon extended to East Germany, and became so habitual that Stalin automatically sought to apply it to China after the communist victory there. At first there was little the host nations could do about it. But the urgent, generally overriding, pursuit of Soviet economic self-interest inevitably undermined the belief in the identity of interests between local communists and the USSR that Stalin had promoted so successfully in the 1930s; the Yugoslav Djilas records in his chapter on 'Disappointments' the peculiarly hard-nosed approach in 1948 of the Soviet Trade Minister Mikoyan, while Khrushchev comments on similar friction between Stalin and Mao.[10]

Politically there are two themes in the Soviet Union's immediately postwar development. One was Stalin's encouragement of competition between his subordinates, shifting his support whenever any of them seemed to be becoming too powerful. The other was that, in this process, it was almost invariably the hardest line that won. In 1946–7 Zhdanov re-established himself, at Malenkov's expense, as Stalin's second in command by stressing the revival of ideology in both party and cultural work. The year 1947 saw extensive debate between people looking to Russian and Soviet inspiration in science and philosophy and those who saw value in

8. J. Barber, *The Decision to Divide Germany* (Durham, NC, 1978) p.101 accepts the East German estimate of $4.3 billion reparations. But D.H. Aldcroft puts 'reparations, dismantlings, and occupation costs' from Eastern Europe as a whole at $14 billion – $19 billion, with two-thirds coming from East Germany (*The European Economy 1914–1980*, 1980 p.228); part of the discrepancy comes from the use of different prices and conversion rates. The USSR also gained $300 million reparations from Finland, plus the labour for many years of millions of prisoners and deportees

9. Replacement cost c.$2 billion: R.L. Garthoff (ed.) *Sino–Soviet Military Relations* (New York, 1966) p.74

10. M. Djilas, *Conversations with Stalin* (paperback edn, 1969) pp.129–30; N.S. Khrushchev, *Khrushchev Remembers* i, tr. Strobe Talbot (paperback edn, 1971) pp. 426–7

Western experience and writings; with Stalin's personal support the scientist Lysenko established that there were distinct capitalist and socialist biologies. Zhdanov may have been slightly damaged by Lysenko's triumph, but his declining power was probably more due to alcoholism. Following his death in 1948 a coalition of Malenkov and the police chief Beria moved sharply to downgrade his supporters and, in 1949–50, take over his Leningrad power base through purges and executions (the so-called 'Leningrad affair'). Stalin seems to have become increasingly worried by Malenkov and Beria, whom he checked first by recalling Khrushchev to Moscow, then more directly by ousting Beria from the control of the police, downgrading his associates, and discovering a secessionist plot in Beria's own district of Georgia. This 'Mingrelian Affair' appears to have been the prelude to a major purge that began to unroll in 1953 when it was revealed that Jewish doctors had been systematically poisoning high Soviet leaders from Zhdanov onwards. Since Stalin fortunately died at this point we cannot tell how far matters would have gone. But he appears to have had two targets – unwanted political colleagues, and Jews in general. Stalin had always been anti-Semitic, but in his old age this trait became worse. He had not been pleased by his daughter's marriage to a Jew or by the Jewish Anti-Fascist Committee's wartime suggestion that the Crimea become a Jewish Soviet Republic. The crucial turning-point may have been the tumultuous reception given in 1948 both publicly and privately to the first Israeli ambassador, Golda Meir, which showed much of the Jewish population to be alarmingly committed (and anxious to emigrate) to Israel. Executions, arrests and counter-propaganda followed immediately; 'Zionist conspiracy' became a count in purges in Eastern Europe; by 1953 the process was about to spread back to the Soviet Union.

DE-STALINISATION AND KHRUSHCHEV'S REFORMS 1953–64

Altogether Stalin left an unhappy society, and there was quite a wide measure of agreement among his successors as to what to do about it. The arrest and execution of top leaders was discontinued, at least after the elimination of Beria and his allies in 1953–4. The 'Gulag' prison labour camps, which may have contained between 10 million and 13 million people in 1953, were gradually wound down, a process encouraged by large-scale prison revolts.[11] Khrushchev says that Beria first suggested doing so, but in such a way that he would control the process. Indeed much of politics revolved around control over the admission of past excesses and the rehabilitation of their victims: Khrushchev was the most successful practitioner, using Malenkov's involvement in the Leningrad affair to force him from the Chairmanship of the Council of Ministers in 1955, and proceeding next year to an exposure of Stalin's crimes in the 'Secret Speech' to the Twentieth Party Congress. The speech was acquired and published by the US Central Intelligence Agency (CIA), and had extensive repercussions abroad. Nevertheless Khrushchev remained attracted to 'de-Stalinisation', and reverted to it as a political weapon in the 1960s; this led him to sanction the publication of disturbing works like Solzhenitsyn's *One Day in the Life of Ivan Denisovich* (1962), and such episodes did much to encourage 'dissident' writers on or beyond the fringes of the Communist Party.

Stalin's economic policy had been geared towards military strength, not welfare. It could be relaxed in two ways, by increasing agricultural production, and by tilting industry from defence and producer to consumer goods. Both Malenkov and Beria initially favoured the latter. Khrushchev affected not to, siding with the military and the 'steel-eaters' until he had obtained unchallenged supremacy in 1957. Then he moved against the army. Marshal Zhukov (who had afforded him valuable support against both Beria and the 1957 'Anti-Party Group') was now dismissed. Khrushchev embarked enthusiastically on a policy (parallel to that followed in the USA and UK at the same time) of relying on the nuclear deterrent and reducing the more expensive conventional forces; cuts of one-third were endorsed in 1960 and drew a round-robin of protest 'from the marshals of all military forces', which, together with growing international tension in 1961, induced him to desist. The Army was not the prime mover in his 1964 downfall, but it appears to have been sympathetic to the plotters.[12]

Khrushchev had always been an agricultural specialist; after

11. Most of the releases (perhaps 7 million–8 million) did not come until 1956–7. In 1977 leaked official figures gave a total of 1.7 million prisoners, 10,000 of them political (though some dissidents will also have been held on criminal charges or in psychiatric hospitals). This total probably fell; in 1986 Gorbachev began what had by late 1988 developed into a general release of political and religious prisoners: R.A. Medvedev and Z.A. Medvedev, *Khrushchev, the Years in Power* (Oxford, 1977) pp. 19–20; *Cambridge Encyclopedia of Russia* p. 391; *Keesing's*, 35470–3, 36490

12. R. Medvedev, *Khrushchev* (Oxford, 1982) pp.136–7, 183, 235; Medvedev and Medvedev, *Khrushchev, the Years in Power* p.150

Stalin's death he was constantly seeking new ways of remedying Soviet agricultural deficiencies. The most spectacular was his 'Virgin Lands Campaign' of 1954–6, the planting of 35 million hectares of steppe land in Central Asia; he was initially rewarded by good grain yields, but soil erosion has been a serious problem and, as the area is liable to drought, harvests fluctuate markedly. It was therefore only a partial solution, and so Khrushchev was always looking at others: the 1958 sale to collective farms of equipment previously held by machine tractor stations, the 1960s insistence on planting maize in all environments, the relocation of research institutes in the countryside, and the restoration to power of Lysenko. Many of these proved failures, some were unpopular: officials were upset by sudden banishment from the big cities, scientists infuriated by Lysenko's return after his post-Stalin eclipse. Politically the most damaging was the sudden decision in 1962 to split the Communist Party, at most levels, into agricultural and industrial sections, whose First Secretaries often found themselves competing instead of possessed of their traditional primacy over a distinct territorial area. It would be wrong to say that all this was to no avail – agricultural production rose considerably. But, with rising living standards, so did demand; indeed demand increased exponentially since greater affluence led to greater demand for meat, whose production now needed feed grain as an input. Probably none of this would have bothered Stalin, who had acquiesced in rural famine in 1932–3 and 1946. Khrushchev, however, began to import grain on a significant scale in 1963, and his successors went on doing so. Since the USA is the world's chief exporter, this has sometimes had political as well as economic consequences.

Agriculture provides a good illustration of Khrushchev's general style, which was still that of an early revolutionary militant. He perceived, often correctly, that something was wrong, but sought to cure it through simplistic crash programmes and institutional changes. His colleagues disliked these (and later termed them 'harebrained schemes'). They also disliked his growing tendency to concentrate power in his own hands, to take decisions without consultation, and to rely on a family and personal clientele.[13] More generally Khrushchev appears to have antagonised most politically important sectors of Soviet society. We have noted the Army; ideologically, Khrushchev's renewed attacks on Stalinism threatened to get out of hand; above all he had weakened the position of the

13. *Keesing's*, 20389–90; Medvedev, *Khrushchev* chap. 21

local Secretaries who preponderated in the party's Central Committee and had been his firm supporters in 1957, while his insistence that one-quarter to one-third of each party body be renewed at each election gave him the ability to shake up, reassign or drop the whole of the official class (towards which he is supposed to have felt a certain populist hostility).

BREZHNEV'S POLICIES OF STABILITY 1964–82

This view of Khrushchev's deficiencies seems to have dominated the Brezhnev era. The Central Committee meeting that confirmed Khrushchev's retirement in 1964 also resolved that the two chief offices, of First Secretary and of Chairman of the Council of Ministers, should not again be combined. As after Stalin's death, the principle of 'collective leadership' was emphasised, and Brezhnev's own emergence to pre-eminence was considerably slower than either Stalin's or Khrushchev's: in 1970 Nasser was appalled at the delays imposed by the Soviet leadership's mutual consultation on, and counter-signature of, even minor documents; and it was not until 1971 that messages to the US administration went out in Brezhnev's name rather than Kosygin's.[14] There is, too, some evidence that initially the collective leadership was distinctly weak. Both Suslov (in 1965 and perhaps 1969) and Shelepin (in 1965 and 1967) seem to have bid for power as rival hardliners; in 1968 Brezhnev managed to convince a leading Czech politician that if he had not intervened in Czechoslovakia he would have been toppled by a hardline Army-dominated coalition; and Marshal Grechko explained to Nasser in 1970 that he could now be more assertive since the civilians had been unable to manage the Czechs and had had to get him to do so.[15] Even when Brezhnev became clearly predominant in the 1970s, he preferred to cultivate and coopt, rather than dictate to, the great bureaucratic interests, a process symbolised by the 1973 elevation to the Politburo of Andropov of the KGB,

14. M. Heikal, *The Road to Ramadan* (1975) p.96; Henry Kissinger, *White House Years* (1979) (hereafter *Memoirs* i) p.527
15. Z. Medvedev, *Andropov* (Oxford, 1983) pp.49–57; A. Brown and M. Kaser (eds), *The Soviet Union since the Fall of Khrushchev* (1978 edn) pp.251–2; J. Radvanyi, *Delusion and Reality* (South Bend, Ind., 1978) pp.232–6; Z. Mlynar, *Night Frost in Prague* (1980) pp.158–68; 'Lord Trevelyan recalls Gamal Abdul Nasser', *The [London] Times Saturday Review*, 19 Feb. 1977 p.33

Grechko the Defence Minister, and the long-standing diplomat and Foreign Minister, Gromyko.

This conciliation of established interests appears to have had a number of implications for foreign policy. The clearest is that the USSR embarked in the Brezhnev years on a prolonged military build-up. Some increase in defence spending was no doubt inevitable: in the USA, too, Eisenhower's policy of concentrating on cheap nuclear airpower was abandoned by Kennedy; and the USSR had a further stimulus in its humiliation over the Cuban missile crisis. But the sustained scale of the increase was to puzzle Western observers, and may be due largely to the revived power of a 'military-industrial complex'. The build-up proved important, both for its effect on Western opinion, and because it provided the USSR – arguably for the first time in history – with the means of projecting power at a considerable distance from its homeland. Stalin could intervene in Eastern Europe and Manchuria, but not in most of the Third World; in 1975–6 Soviet airlifts enabled Cuban troops to install a government in Angola, and in 1977–8 to repel a Somali invasion and rescue the Ethiopian revolution.

Another aspect of Brezhnev's conciliation of interests was his cautious middle-of-the-road domestic policy. This had many dimensions. Khrushchev's persecution of the Orthodox Church was called off. Minimum wages were raised, and the condition of peasants (unaccountably neglected by Khrushchev in his later years) was much improved; in 1974 they were even accorded passports permitting internal travel. Prices remained fairly effectively frozen. This must have provided reassurance against a recurrence of the 1962 strikes (and shootings) and against any replication in the USSR of the far more serious Polish disturbances in and after 1970; it also seems to have confined 'dissent' to the intelligentsia as opposed to the workers. But it had an economic cost: rising wages and stable prices increased demand at a rate faster than the rigid economic and distributional system could cope with; the result was rationing by shortages rather than by 'market-clearing' prices.

One possible response to such problems is economic reform; in the 1960s economic reforms, some quite far-reaching, were carried out in most East European countries. They were debated in the Soviet Union too, but the reforms that Kosygin introduced in 1965 were markedly more cautious. Even they were not fully carried through, with events in Czechoslovakia convincing the Soviet leadership that there could all too easily be a link between economic reform and the loss of political control; the lesson was reinforced in 1970 when price increases generated riots that led to the fall of the Polish leader Gomulka.

Another possible remedy, one that bypassed the risks inherent in changing the system of economic management, was the easing of bottlenecks and the acquisition of technology through imports. This process began in the 1960s with grain imports and the construction by Fiat of a major car factory. Its high point came with the flowering of détente, a policy particularly linked with Brezhnev, in the early 1970s. But there were disappointments: the United States would concede 'most favoured nation' tariff status only on politically unacceptable terms; and the Soviet economic system did not always find it easy to assimilate, let alone update, imported technology. Still the 1970s were marked by a sharp rise in the prices of the USSR's chief exports, oil and gold; this, plus appreciable borrowing, greatly expanded its capacity to purchase abroad.

If the alleviation of internal difficulties was one aim of détente, détente nevertheless cut across another of Brezhnev's policies, the curbing of political and cultural dissidence that had been uncorked by Khrushchev's later attacks on Stalin. The dissidents sought Western support and addressed themselves as much to a Western as to a Soviet audience. Here as elsewhere Brezhnev followed the middle of the road: in 1965 Shelepin pushed for a crackdown and the KGB urged the arrest of a thousand Moscow intellectuals;[16] the leadership settled on show trials for two, Sinyavsky and Daniel. This was probably not enough, and may even have proved counter-productive: the dissident network and its journal, *The Chronicle of Current Events*, reached its peak in the later 1960s. Further arrests and dismissals followed, but it was from 1973 onwards that repression became markedly more severe, notwithstanding the potentially embarrassing 'human rights basket' of the 1975 Helsinki Agreements that – in other respects – represented a major achievement of Brezhnev's détente policy. In 1980 the previously untouchable Academician Sakharov was assigned to compulsory residence in Gorki (in response to his protest against the Afghanistan intervention), while the Olympic Games provided an occasion for the deportation from Moscow of many other dissidents.

The most obvious link between internal dissent and external relations lay through the repudiation of the Soviet Union by many Jews and their desire to emigrate to either Israel or the USA. This

16. Brown and Kaser, *The Soviet Union since Khrushchev* pp. 251–2

desire was not new, but it appears to have been reactivated by the combination of renewed anti-Semitism after the 1967 Arab–Israeli War and of the advent of détente. Jewish emigration rose from 400 in 1968 to 35,000 in 1973. This may have owed something to pressure from the Nixon administration, but such pressure was transmitted in private; publicly Nixon was vulnerable to charges of disinterest in the fate of dissidents, especially given the increase in Soviet internal repression that we have already noted. Congressmen like Senator Jackson attempted, with encouragement from Sakharov and at first successfully, to do better by linking trade concessions to further Soviet liberalisation of emigration. In 1974 this backfired: amendments to the Trade Act made the Soviet acquisition of 'most favoured nation' status precarious and established a congressional veto over most official loans to the USSR; this led the Soviet Union to withdraw from its 1972 trade agreement with the USA – and to cut emigration.[17] Human rights in the USSR, détente and 'congressional oversight' had fused together as issues in *American* domestic politics. Matters were then taken a step further with the advent of President Carter, who sought in 1977 to distance himself from Kissinger's geopolitics and to emphasise his nation's 'old dream' of human liberty. Carter's human rights policy was not simply anti-Soviet: it applied to, and irritated, friendly Latin American regimes; nor was such ideological competition incompatible with the official Soviet definition of détente. But the USSR did not take kindly to actions that Brezhnev termed 'direct interference in our internal affairs'.[18] This distaste was reinforced by Carter's initial handling of Strategic Arms Limitation Talks. The Soviet leadership seems to have taken a very low view both of Carter personally and of his ability to deliver congressional ratification of any agreement. Accordingly it showed no disposition in 1979 to heed his warnings not to intervene in Afghanistan.

When Brezhnev died in 1982 East–West relations were at a low ebb. Given Brezhnev's personal association with policies of détente, this must represent something of a political failure. In other respects he had, by his own standards, been not unsuccessful, for he had kept the Soviet system running without the horrors of Stalin or the often counter-productive upheavals of the Khrushchev era.

17. Kissinger, *Memoirs* ii pp.249–55, 985–98; *Keesing's*, 26850–1, 26993–5. Similar Congressional pressure had led in 1911 to the abrogation of a commercial treaty with *tsarist* Russia in retaliation for its treatment of Jews – and to a worsening of that treatment
18. *Keesing's*, 28773 ff

Soviet military power and global reach had grown impressively. If the Soviet people did not in 1980 have the highest living standard in the world (as Khrushchev had promised in 1961), per capita consumption had roughly tripled since 1950.[19]

CORRUPTION, STAGNATION AND ATTEMPTS AT REFORM

The Brezhnev regime, however, is now portrayed not as a period of success, but rather as the 'era of stagnation', symbolised by the collapse of Brezhnev's own health and intellect after his strokes of 1975 and 1978. In his last years there came into the open two problems that have had an enormous influence on subsequent political developments, corruption and economic slowdown. Corruption certainly did not start with Brezhnev, but his policy of allowing the official classes security of tenure left them more scope to exploit their positions for personal gain. Brezhnev's own family and associates were guilty; in 1982 the former KGB chief, Yuri Andropov, was able to turn this to political advantage, driving some to suicide and arresting others in a series of bizarre scandals.[20]

More seriously,

> The country began [more especially in the later 1970s] to lose momentum. Economic failures became more frequent. Difficulties began to accumulate . . . and unresolved problems to multiply.
>
> . . . [Since 1972] the national income growth rates had declined by half and by the beginning of the eighties had fallen to a level close to economic stagnation. A country that was once quickly closing on the world's most advanced nations began to lose one position after another. Moreover, the gap in the efficiency of production, quality of products, scientific and technological development, . . . and the use of advanced techniques began to widen, and not to our advantage.[21]

Figures are disputed, but there is general agreement as to the phenomenon. The leadership was not prepared to cut expenditure accordingly; and it would seem that the proportion of the budget covered by printing money rose from 20 per cent in 1970 to 30 per cent in 1982. This in turn led to a situation in which people had

19. Paul Dibb, *The Soviet Union: The Incomplete Superpower* (Basingstoke, 1988 edn) pp.70–1
20. Medvedev, *Andropov* chap. 9
21. Gorbachev, *Perestroika* pp.18–19

more money than there were goods to purchase. Since official prices did not rise accordingly, this meant that goods were snapped up as soon as they appeared in the shops (rationing by queuing or shortages), or that they were diverted from official to more remunerative black or private markets (corruption). Brezhnev's successors were ready (on their appointments) to admit that things were wrong: Andropov observed that there were 'many problems in the economy' and that he had 'no ready recipes to solve them', Chernenko that 'The system of our economic management, the whole of our economic machinery needs to be seriously restructured'.[22]

This was more easily said than done. Andropov, the ex-KGB chief, is said to have had his liberal side, but seems to have relied chiefly on the punishment of corrupt, and retirement of incompetent, officials, combined with a crack-down on 'moonlighting' and a general tightening of labour discipline (including the round-up of people queuing or patronising the public baths, to see if they were skiving off work). Within a little over a year he was dead. Brezhnev had not wanted Andropov to succeed him, and had almost managed to pass the General Secretaryship on to his right-hand man Chernenko. On Andropov's death in 1984, Chernenko took over. This might have led to a return to Brezhnevite ways, but Chernenko, too, was gravely ill, and died in March 1985. Again the succession had been contested; in the event the Politburo chose the young and energetic Gorbachev. He had been Andropov's protégé, and would clearly resume the attempt to shake the system up. Few, however, can have expected him to act as vigorously as he did, or with such extraordinary consequences.[23]

GORBACHEV'S FIRST FIVE YEARS 1985–90

It is too early to reach a balanced judgement on his rule; one can perhaps describe its effects by adapting a celebrated political joke of the Brezhnev era. This likened the USSR to a train proceeding

22. Dibb, *The Incomplete Superpower* chap. 3; Judy Shelton, *The Coming Soviet Crash* (New York, 1989) chaps 1, 2

23. N.A.D. Macrae, *The 2024 Report: A Concise History of the Future, 1974–2024* (1984) had already forecast that economic problems would bring to the USSR Liberal political reconstruction, the shedding of its peripheral nationalities, and close cooperation with the USA in the management of international relations

towards communism. It stopped; so Stalin shot the driver, and it went on. Next time it stopped, Khrushchev rehabilitated him, and progress was resumed. It then stopped again; so Brezhnev drew the curtains and said, 'Let's pretend it's moving'. Later Gorbachev undrew them again, and the passengers – realising they had got nowhere – rioted and pulled the train to pieces.

As Andropov's protégé, Gorbachev believed in honesty and discipline. Investigations into corruption were resumed, as was the reshuffling of politicians and administrators. 'To do something better', Gorbachev preached, 'you must work an extra bit harder. I like this phrase: working an *extra bit harder*'. To cut absenteeism and accidents, the new regime drastically reduced the availability of vodka – with unfortunate results, as people turned to lethal home brewing, while the state lost an important source of revenue. Gorbachev effected a fundamental change in Soviet journalism – 'glasnost' (openness) – inter alia as a guarantee that officialdom would not simply ignore reforming edicts from above. For he was conscious of the possibility that the *apparat* (administrative system of the Communist Party) would destroy him as it had Khrushchev. 'Between the people which wants changes . . . and the leadership that promotes them', he is supposed to have told a group of writers, 'stands the managerial state of the party *apparat* and the ministries, which does not want changes as it does not want to abandon its rights and privileges. Take Gosplan. For our Gosplan there exists no authority, no General Secretary, no Central Committee. Its officials do what they please.' The chief remedy lay in criticism, self-criticism, and above all in 'openness'.

Gorbachev saw glasnost as constructive. The press would go after 'loafers, profit-seekers, time-servers, suppressors of criticism, and demagogues'; but it would thereby 'actively help those who are selflessly working for perestroika [reform and restructuring of the economy]' and 'uphold the fundamental values of socialism' – 'Glasnost is aimed at strengthening our society'.[24] It probably had the opposite effect. For with encouragement from above, most of the old media controls were relaxed; and a multitude of small groups sprang up among the intelligentsia, the nucleus of a civil society distinct from the state. The new journalism was to investigate current mistakes and abuses, and did so with vigour. Also, after considerable hesitation, Gorbachev decided to 'expose the faults of the previous Soviet leaders'. Khrushchev, of course, had attacked

---

24. Gorbachev, *Perestroika* pp.29–30, 78–9; *La Repubblica*, 7 Oct. 1986 p.13

Stalin too, but chiefly for deviating from a correct policy into violence against Party members; Gorbachev allowed discussion of the liquidation of the kulaks (rich peasants working for personal profit) and the famines that had accompanied the creation of the USSR's collective agriculture. The idea came to spread that the Soviet Union had lost its way not in the 'period of stagnation' but far far earlier – some were even prepared to say from the very beginning.

Such ideas, of course, would have been less tempting had the contemporary USSR not been doing very badly. In Brezhnev's last decade it had benefited from a great rise in the price of its principal export, oil. In a little over a year after Gorbachev's accession the price of oil roughly halved and the volume of Soviet sales had to be reduced to prevent worse. A further blow was the fall of the dollars these sales brought in by about one-third *vis-à-vis* the marks and yens in which most Soviet imports from the West were priced; accordingly hard currency debt rose from $25 billion in 1985 to $55 billion in 1989.[25] There was further bad luck: in 1986 illegal experiments (conducted when safety systems were shut off) led the nuclear power station at Chernobyl to blow up. At first the authorities sought to hush up the calamity (which was first announced by Scandinavian scientists). The attempt, the general incompetence with which the disaster was handled, and the cavalier official attitude to the victims, all did a good deal to radicalise opinion in the most contaminated republics, Byelorussia and the Ukraine. It also eventually led to the closure of similar nuclear plants, thus creating major power shortages. In 1988 Soviet incompetence was again demonstrated by the slowness in getting aid to the victims of a serious earthquake in Armenia, a republic already disaffected over a border dispute with neighbouring Azerbaijan.

None of this can realistically be blamed on Gorbachev. But it can be argued that his new style and advocacy of perestroika raised public expectations that it would be dangerous to disappoint. Disappoint them he did, partly at least because he seemed to have very little feel for economics. Here there is an instructive contrast with China. After Mao's death, Deng Xiaoping permitted only very limited political change, but he returned agriculture to family

---

25. Shelton, *The Coming Soviet Crash* p. xv; *Keesing's*, 37419. Oil and currency price movements are discussed further in Dunbabin, vol. 2, *The Post-Imperial Age* chaps 14, 20

farms, raised prices and lifted controls. With industry, he was less drastic but still more adventurous than his Soviet counterparts; he provided the conditions in which foreign capital was happy to invest in the 'Special Economic Zones'. As a result China's per capita income doubled (admittedly from a very low level) between 1977 and 1987.[26] The process was not without problems: inflation and an upsurge of democratic aspirations led in 1989 to political crackdown and renewed stress on 'socialism'. It was, though, probably safer than Gorbachev's approach of talking about reform but, in the economic field, doing very little to implement it. Agriculture he left largely untouched, chiefly (it seems) because he had socialist scruples about private landownership, but also, perhaps, because Russian peasants are no longer keen to return to private farming. Elsewhere 1987 saw some half-hearted changes, designed to permit the formation of cooperatives (especially in the service sector) and to encourage joint industrial ventures with foreign companies. They were not followed through, however, and the new bodies were mostly still bound by the need to obtain permits and allocations from a hostile bureaucracy. One way of doing so was through bribery and crime; the USSR had long been corrupt, but a side-effect of perestroika has been the mushrooming of what came to be perceived as an all-pervasive 'mafia'. Meanwhile the official economy continued to create money via the budget deficit (first officially admitted to in 1988). Production was now probably falling, though we have no reliable figures; and the monetary overhang increased demand for consumer goods. By 1989, despite emergency imports, there were shortages and rationing; all the more reason for goods to disappear from the official shops, resurfacing (at a price) on the black market. By November Gorbachev was admitting that 'we have temporarily lost control of some levers of economic management', and by 1990 he was discreetly soliciting foreign economic aid.[27]

The year 1987 saw speculation about political resistance to Gorbachev; in the spring of 1988 there was an attack on perestroika as anti-socialist that was probably inspired by one of his senior colleagues, Ligachev. That summer Gorbachev proposed a new constitution in which a revivified parliament would elect an executive President (himself), claiming that the new structure

26. World Bank figures – *The Independent*, 8 July 1991 p.21

27. Gail Sheehy, *Gorbachev* (1991) *passim*; Padma Desai, *Perestroika in Perspective: The Design and Dilemmas of Soviet Reform* (1989) esp. chaps 3–5; *Keesing's*, esp. 36767–9, 36827, 37419, 37629

would be better able to resist bureaucratic pressure and that the absence of political reform had been one reason for the failure of Khrushchev's and Kosygin's attempts at economic reform.[28] What he envisaged was very much 'guided democracy', since candidate nomination remained subject to controls and since one-third of the new Congress of Peoples Deputies was to be chosen not by the electorate but by official bodies. But the prospect did provide a stimulus for the emergence, in some areas, of independent political activity; voting was genuinely secret; a number of substantial figures (like the Leningrad First Secretary) were defeated; and the celebrated critic of establishment perquisites, Boris Yeltsin, whom Gorbachev had dismissed with some brutality in 1987, was triumphantly returned for Moscow. All this, Ligachev is supposed to have warned, constituted a dangerous precedent. The Congress itself (and the Supreme Soviet it elected) proved broadly, though not entirely, amenable to Gorbachev's wishes; but it proved the forum for a quite unprecedented degree of open debate, regularly broadcast on television, and so widened the bounds of political possibility.

THE UNRAVELLING OF THE SOVIET UNION

Early 1990 saw further free elections for local and republican soviets. Arguably these constituted the watershed in the refashioning of the old Soviet Union. In the Baltic republics – which Stalin had brutally annexed – they were won by nationalist Popular Fronts. In March 1990 Lithuania proclaimed its independence, to which Gorbachev responded by blockading it and cutting off its oil supplies as a deterrent. After some months a *modus vivendi* was reached, with the USSR restoring supplies and Lithuania agreeing to negotiate on independence. But the deterrent did not work: Lithuania was followed (rather more circumspectly) by Estonia, Latvia, Georgia, Armenia and Moldova, which became grey areas – occupied but only partly controlled by the USSR. The other republics, comprising the vast majority of Soviet territory and population, did not seek full independence, but they rapidly came to constitute alternative political centres: in May 1990 Yeltsin was chosen President of the vast Russian Republic, and a year later confirmed in office by direct elections, thus acquiring greater

28. *Keesing's*, 36111–16

democratic legitimacy than his (by now less popular) rival Gorbachev. The republics also pressed strongly for devolution, asserting the primacy of their own legislation over all-Union laws. This made it difficult to settle a USSR budget for 1991; even when one was agreed on paper, the republics still held back their contributions, paying only one-third of what was due in the first quarter of 1991 and so ending any hope of staunching the deficit.

By late 1990 the Soviet Union was in deep trouble. Parts of it were trying to secede. The food distribution system had broken down (and/or been sabotaged by communist functionaries anxious to prove the failure of reform). Gorbachev, one of his former spokesmen cuttingly remarked, had been awarded the Nobel Prize for Peace, not Economics. Talk was now of the need for fundamental systemic change. In August 1990 Gorbachev and Yeltsin had jointly commissioned experts to 'draft a concept for the transition to a market economy'. The result was a highly ambitious 500-day programme, which Yeltsin endorsed but Gorbachev did not. Instead he decided to weave it together with one prepared by his unreconstructed Prime Minister; the result was unconvincing, and retained far more scope for central planning. In December the liberal Foreign Minister, Shevardnadze, suddenly resigned, warning of the 'onset of dictatorship'. Whether through fear of a coup or as a desperate measure to hold the country together, Gorbachev reconstructed his government with old-style apparatchiks. These turned back to blaming Soviet troubles on Western conspiracy, enhancing the role of the KGB and the army, and justifying the seizure of buildings and killing of civilians by special forces in Lithuania and Latvia. None of this did the economy any good; indeed April saw massive (and partly political) strikes, while overall production is said to have fallen by 10 per cent in the first half of 1991. Such pressures may have nudged Gorbachev back to a more liberal course; in late April he agreed with representatives of the non-seceding republics to negotiate a new Union Treaty enhancing their role, which would be followed by a new federal constitution and multi-party elections. Mid-summer saw talk of a new economic reform programme that would be submitted to the July 1991 G7 summit meeting of the seven chief capitalist states in the hope of securing their financial or at least technical assistance – though again Gorbachev finally balked at any thorough-going displacement of centralised control from his all-Union government and nothing came of it. He did, however, proceed with negotiations for the new Union Treaty.

The day before he and the Republican Presidents were to sign it and so end the traditional Soviet structure, Gorbachev was arrested while still on holiday. In Moscow a 'Committee of National Emergency' (including the head of the KGB, the Defence Minister, the Prime Minister and the Vice-President) assumed power on a platform of discipline, law and order, and proposed to return the country to the ideas of 1985 – that is to controlled reform within the old system. But both the KGB and the armed forces were split. Elements of the former tipped off Yeltsin, who managed to evade arrest and reach the Russian Parliament building. From there he defied the coup and drew a crowd of sympathisers to defend him. Incredibly, too, telecommunications were not cut and he was able both to issue decrees as President of Russia and appeal for support at home and abroad. The army could quite easily have moved in and arrested him, but it was not prepared to do so; indeed the air force contemplated bombing the coup leaders in the Kremlin. So after three tense days the coup suddenly collapsed, unleashing a reaction in which crowds destroyed first the statue of the founder of the secret police, then those of Lenin and other symbols of communist power. Yeltsin was the man of the hour; though Gorbachev was brought back to Moscow with honour, he fluffed things badly by continuing to stress the need to keep the USSR together as before and by seeking to protect the Communist Party from post-coup punishment. In any case it was obvious that, since he had recently placed the coup's ring-leaders in office, he had at the least shown poor political judgement. Yeltsin seized the opportunity, banning the Communist Party within Russia, and recognising the independence of the Baltic states. The other Republics, even those whose leaders had kept quiet during the coup, followed suit, also declaring their own formal independence. Gorbachev continued to proclaim the need to stay together with a significant authority (himself) at the centre. But he steadily lost ground. In December 1991 Russia, Belarus and the Ukraine agreed to constitute a 'Commonwealth of Independent States'. The other Republics (bar Georgia, and, of course, the now fully sovereign Baltic states) joined and so put an end to the Soviet Union. Yeltsin then pushed Gorbachev into formally resigning, and himself took over the Kremlin – and many of Gorbachev's problems.

Some American hawks have contended that it was Reagan's defence build-up that forced the USSR to recognise that it was not economically strong enough to compete and so to seek more friendly relations. Things are not so simple. In the 1970s – well before Reagan's build-up – Shevardnadze and Gorbachev had been meeting, noting the absurdities of the Soviet system, and concluding that 'we just couldn't go on like this'. When they heard the news of the 1979 invasion of Afghanistan they 'agreed it was a fatal error that would cost the country dearly'. Nor, Shevardnadze claims, were they alone. 'The invasion produced a strong negative action. . . . Whereas only a few people protested about the sending of troops into Prague in 1968, after 1979 the majority condemned the Afghan adventure, either directly or indirectly'.[29] It may therefore be taken that Gorbachev had long contemplated significant changes in foreign (as in domestic) policy, and that he knew what he was doing when in June 1985 he insisted on replacing the unreconstructed Gromyko as Foreign Minister by Shevardnadze. Shevardnadze felt, as he declared publicly in 1990, that 'by squandering a quarter of our budget on military expenditure, we have ruined the country'. Although in *Perestroika* Gorbachev implored the Americans to rid themselves of 'Hopes of using any advantages in technology or advanced equipment so as to gain superiority over our country' and of 'the belief that the economic system of the Soviet Union is about to crumble', in practice Shevardnadze did see it as one of his functions 'to secure by political means the favourable external conditions needed to bring about change inside the country'.[30] While the USSR clearly did not feel it had to make any and every concession – even in 1991 it is rumoured to have turned down a Japanese offer of $26 billion aid in exchange for the cession of four small disputed islands[31] – its leadership probably was operating in the Gorbachev era from a position of perceived financial weakness. But then another leadership might have felt differently. Many people saw Shevardnadze's concessions as quite unnecessary, indeed treasonable. It is entirely possible that had (say) Grishin rather than Gorbachev succeeded Chernenko, the traditional Soviet system could have been maintained, both at home and abroad, for a good deal longer.

29. E. Shevardnadze, *The Future Belongs to Freedom* (1991) pp.23–6, 121

30. ibid. pp.52, 54; *The Independent*, 4 July 1990 p. 9; *Perestroika* pp.10–11

31. *Keesing's*, 38148. Admittedly Gorbachev probably faced constraints over the islands – Defence Minister Yazov said publicly that 'Gorbachev cannot decide on this alone' (*Daily Telegraph*, 20 Aug. 1991 p.4). Nor had anything come, by late 1993, of subsequent Japanese attempts to settle with Yeltsin. The question of the islands is treated more fully in *The Post-Imperial Age* chap. 7

THE POLITICAL CONTEXT OF US FOREIGN POLICY

With hindsight, we can now see that the United States was, in most respects, always by far the stronger of the two 'superpowers'. Since 1945 it has, if we judge by recent Soviet standards, encountered neither economic slump nor political upheaval. Its polity has altered in details but not in essence; and the most important change, the ending of legally enforced racial segregation in the South, has had relatively little direct impact on international relations. Many aspects of US domestic politics, though, do affect foreign affairs; Speaker Tip O'Neill, indeed, went so far as to claim that *all* politics were local politics. At a trivial level, Nixon had been befriended by Pepsicola, so (when he promoted détente) it was Pepsi, not Coca-Cola, that was chosen to manufacture in the USSR. Business politics are not always so innocent: ITT (a conglomerate with substantial interests in Chile) used its privileged access to the Nixon administration to urge intervention, though it seems that the 'de-stabilisation' of Allende was probably decided on for other reasons. Equally politicians may launch foreign policy initiatives primarily, or even exclusively, for their domestic effect: the congressional initiative to cut off funds for the CIA's Angola intervention in 1975 was taken to boost a senator facing a difficult primary.[32]

Moves like these may be important, but they can succeed only in conjunction with two other phenomena – lobbies and public opinion. Kissinger remarks that

> Israel affects our decisions through inspiration, persistence, and a judicious, not always subtle or discrete, influence on our domestic policy.
> . . . [Ambassador] Dinitz was brilliant at mobilizing media and Congressional pressures but much too wise to make his prowess explicit. Listening to him, one could only be astonished how it had happened that so many normally individualistic Americans had come spontaneously to the conclusion that we were not doing enough for Israel.[33]

Admirably organised as it may be, probably the chief advantage of the Israeli lobby has, till recently, been the absence of countervailing power, chiefly because the USA has a sizable (and active) Jewish population but a very small Arab one. For the same reason,

32. T.M. Franck and E. Weisband, *Foreign Policy by Congress* (New York, 1979) pp. 514 ff
33. *Memoirs* ii pp.484–5

though Turkey is larger and more important than Greece, the Greek lobby is easily the stronger in Congress – a factor that led (despite executive displeasure) to the suspension of arms sales to Turkey after its 1974 Cyprus intervention.

Lobbies change, but slowly. The ebb and flow of public opinion is more rapid, and constitutes the climate within which politicians must operate. Among the currents influential since the Second World War (and often long before it), one would include the following six forces.

First, 'internationalism' (in the eyes of its detractors, 'globalism'), that is the acceptance of Kennan's ringing call for the United States to create abroad

> the impression of a country which . . . is coping successfully with the problems of its internal life and with the responsibilities of a World Power, and which has a spiritual vitality capable of holding its own among the major ideological currents of the time . . . [with] gratitude to a Providence which, by providing the American people with this implacable challenge, has made their entire security as a nation dependent on their . . . accepting the responsibilities of moral and political leadership that history plainly intended them to bear.[34]

Second, a residual 'isolationism', the feeling that the United States has dangerously over-extended itself by meddling where no major national interests were at stake, frequently on behalf of ungrateful allies or disreputable clients. Initially this contained a marked anti-European component – President Washington's advice to steer clear of European quarrels was still widely cherished – and sometimes also a feeling that the USA should put 'Asia first'. Ironically it is this milieu that has produced the most warlike demands, in the belief that, if the worst came to the worst, the United States should not let itself be bogged down but go all out for quick and complete success; as General MacArthur put it, 'there is no substitute for victory'. In other contexts, though, Asian entanglements may seem no more attractive than European, indeed less since they have actually resulted in fighting.

Third, populist suspicion of the 'eastern establishment' – when things appear to go wrong, it is natural to blame people at the top. This is true of all countries, but perhaps particularly of the United States, where there are substantial geographical differences of interest, where important 'ethnic' groups feel they have not yet been fully accepted and resent what is (or was till very recently)

34. X, 'The Sources of Soviet Conduct', *Foreign Affairs* xxv (1947) pp.581–2

perceived as a WASP (White Anglo Saxon Protestant) upper class, and where political rhetoric is unrestrained by a tradition of deference. Such suspicions are usually voiced by political insurgents like Senator Joseph McCarthy or Governor Wallace, but they are felt much more widely: Presidents Johnson and Nixon both believed that they had been destroyed by the eastern establishment. In prewar days this 'establishment' used to be portrayed as reactionary: sometimes it still is, but since the New Deal it is just as likely to be denounced as 'ultra-liberal' or simply as out of touch with the rest of the country.

Fourth, trust or distrust of the presidency as an institution: as the twentieth century wore on, the power of the presidency increased in domestic and still more in foreign affairs. Liberals and 'internationalists' initially supported this process; Truman managed also to secure support for his foreign policy even though he was often dealing with a Republican Congress. The USA has a strong bipartisan tradition: without it no President could assemble the two-thirds majorities in the Senate that are needed for the ratification of treaties and many could not even secure confirmation of their Cabinet appointments. Congress has often been reluctant to push its powers too far, especially in foreign or security matters. However, US institutions do not display self-restraint indefinitely; and though the catalyst for renewed self-assertion is often political, the process has a certain rhythm. President Wilson took the USA into war in 1917. Congress rejected his peace treaty, and later – in the 1930s – passed Neutrality (and other) Acts to prevent any repetition. They did not succeed. The Roosevelt and Truman administrations were very active in foreign affairs. Opponents later accused them of 'betraying' to communism both Eastern Europe and China, especially at the Yalta conference; the result was much investigative activism on the part of congressional committees, and the promotion of a constitutional amendment to block the growing presidential tendency to evade congressional scrutiny by concluding 'executive agreements' not treaties. This (Bricker) Amendment failed and things quietened down under Eisenhower. The 1960s again saw the current set towards a strong presidency. But it went abruptly into reverse in 1968 as disenchantment set in with the consequence, the Vietnam War. Domestically, too, Congress saw its position as endangered, notably by Nixon's attempts to control public spending, which threatened the congressional trump card, the power of the purse. For most of Nixon's presidency the two were at daggers drawn. Congress seized the opportunity of his decline and fall to settle constitutional disputes, both domestic and foreign, by legislation in its own favour. So much so that commentators began to describe *Foreign Policy by Congress* (1979), only to see the pendulum then again swing back towards the presidency.

Fifth, fashions of economic thinking – another cycle (though one not peculiar to the USA) is that which runs between 'Big Government' (a readiness to spend money to tackle problems, occasionally even just to stimulate the economy) and concern that such an approach ('throwing money at problems') is both ineffective per se and, in the long run, risks economic decline and national bankruptcy. These two attitudes encourage widely different policies both domestically and in terms of defence.

The sixth influential topic is civil rights; probably the most remarkable development of postwar US history is the abandonment of the legally imposed racial segregation general in the South since the 1890s. The theme is chiefly domestic, its main impact on foreign affairs coming indirectly from the turmoil of the later 1960s to which it was a contributory factor. But we may note that President Carter, a symbol of the 'New South's' acceptance of desegregation, appointed as his UN Ambassador the black Georgian Congressman, Andy Young. Young not only reversed his predecessor's denunciations of the UN Afro-Asian majority, but also displayed a highly visible profile in Africa, sympathetic to liberation movements but simultaneously confident that the capitalist system would enable blacks in South Africa to replicate the achievements of their brothers in the American Deep South. (Interestingly Young's downfall came at the hands of the Jewish lobby, after he had too openly met with the Palestine Liberation Organisation.)

COMMITMENT OF THE US TO INTERNATIONAL LEADERSHIP

So much for the setting. The years after 1945 marked the triumph of the 'internationalists' beyond their expectations and probably beyond their intentions. This can (I think should) be explained primarily as a response to external developments. But it can also be seen as internally generated, by endemic American anti-communism, by the nature of the US economy, and by the style of the men at the top. This last is scarcely contentious. There were, of course, differences of both policy and temperament. But, as compared (say) with the British leadership of the 1930s, the Americans, backed by vastly greater resources, were glad that 'the center of power is in Washington', that 'the buck stops here', and confident that they could do a better job than either their American predecessors after the First World War or their British ones between the wars.

Economic determinism is never easy to prove, disprove or even define. The USA pushed, as it had done since the mid-1930s, for open non-discriminatory trade as the economic system most likely to promote peace and prosperity. As the only major economy undamaged by the war, it was the country best placed to take advantage of that trade, which might also serve to prise open areas under British (or Russian) political control. So US political and economic interests largely coincided. Also in the rare cases (like Saudi Arabian oil) where the principle of the Open Door worked against US interests, it suddenly seemed less attractive. To go further and to contend, with one school of historians, that the USA was pushed by economic needs into a neo-imperialist world role is to make a considerable jump. Objectively the United States was, and remains, much less trade-dependent than such earlier Great Powers as Britain, Germany or Japan.[35] Although it bought limited but important quantities of raw materials, the world hunger for dollars would have made these easy to come by, however isolationist American foreign policy. Subjectively, though, some important men perceived things differently; Eisenhower wrote in 1951 that

> From my viewpoint, foreign policy is, or should be, based primarily on one consideration . . . the need for the U.S. to obtain certain raw materials to sustain its economy and, when possible, to preserve profitable foreign markets for our surpluses. Out of this need grows the necessity for making certain that those areas of the world in which essential raw materials are produced are not only accessible to us, but their populations and governments are willing to trade with us on a friendly basis.[36]

But this was probably a minority view. In January 1945 the US Treasury had suggested lending the Soviet Union $10 billion, to be

---

35. In 1945–50 foreign trade accounted for only 3–5% of its GNP, while as late as 1950 the book value of US investments abroad (mostly in the Americas) was only about 4% of GNP

36. Blanche W. Cook, *The Declassified Eisenhower* (New York, 1981) pp.112–3

repaid with supplies of strategic raw materials.[37] Most Americans did not feel it worth extending cheap credits to secure these, and rejected the argument (voiced inter alia by Molotov) that the stimulus of Soviet orders was needed to counteract the post-hostilities slump in military spending. Congress was not Keynesian, and believed (correctly) that the US economy had many domestic sources of dynamism. So there was no Soviet loan, and only rather grudging lending to Western Europe until the onset of the Cold War. This did bring massive disbursements of Marshall Aid; people campaigning for such aid naturally used all available arguments, including the contention that Western European recovery was essential for American prosperity. But Marshall Aid was clearly a consequence of the Cold War, not a deliberate solution to *American* economic problems. As the intensity of the Cold War declined, so did the volume of aid. The argument that aid is in the long-term economic interests of rich countries is still deployed, but at present to little practical effect.

However, even if the USA does not seem to have been under any overriding economic pressure to espouse 'internationalism' in the 1940s, it could still be contended that big business elements favouring it had disproportionate political weight. The Democrats were definitely not the party of Business. But, under Truman, the US State and Defense Departments, unlike the more partisan domestic departments, did draw heavily on investment bankers and corporate attorneys. The case of the Republicans is clearer. Traditionally the Grand Old Party had leaned towards isolation; in the 1950s important (often midwestern) elements were, if not strictly isolationist, at least unilateralist – notably Senator Taft (the preferred candidate of the machine) and insurgents like General MacArthur and Senators McCarthy and Bricker. One reason why Eisenhower accepted nomination in 1952 was to preserve both the party and foreign policy from Taft. In doing so he relied on the more eastern, liberal and big business wing of the party; it was his Defense Secretary who thought 'what was good for our country was good for General Motors, and vice versa'.

Anyway, whatever the reasons, the 'internationalists' triumphed, and US foreign policy has remained essentially within the para-meters established by Truman. This decision for permanent involvement generated new institutions: a real peacetime army in

---

37. W. Taubman, *Stalin's American Policy: From Entente to Detente to Cold War* (New York, 1982) pp.85–8

place of the token force that had sufficed since Independence; within government, the National Security Council (NSC) and the Central Intelligence Agency (1947); outside it, a plethora of think-tanks starting with the US Air Force's RAND Corporation; and, in the universities, for the first time a sustained tradition of thinking about foreign and defence affairs. Indeed there emerged a 'new profession, that of "military intellectual" '; Kennedy brought in its practitioners to reformulate military strategy, and since then the most eminent have 'stalked through the corridors of the Pentagon and the State Department' like 'Jesuits through the courts of Madrid and Vienna' during the Counter-Reformation. Two of them, Kissinger and Brzezinski, were at the hub of foreign policy-making from 1969 to 1981. In his Farewell Address Eisenhower warned of the 'conjunction of an immense military establishment and a large arms industry. . . . We must guard against the acquisition of unwarranted influence, whether sought or unsought, by the military-industrial complex'. In subsequent years of disillusion this warning was to be seized on and probably exaggerated; both the diffusion of the US political process and the unplanned nature of its economy provide at least some safeguards against the degree of entrenchment that existed in the USSR. But, in American terms, the internationalists' early successes certainly created an important and enduring constituency.

ANTI-COMMUNISM AND McCARTHYISM 1946–57

One of the ways that the internationalists sold their policies in the later 1940s was by invoking anti-communism. This had deep roots: 1919–20 had seen a Red Scare. Later, however, and more particularly during the Second World War, the communists had, by following a popular front policy, made some progress both in intellectual circles and among the newer trade unions. In 1945–6 such relationships broke down very rapidly (on both sides).[38] The National Chamber of Commerce went after the communists (whom it blamed for post-war union militancy) in a campaign assisted by the Federal Bureau of Investigation (FBI), much of the press, and the Catholic Church (which not only disliked communism on principle but also reacted strongly to the persecution of Catholics in

---

38. Stalin abandoned the policy and had the American party leadership purged

Eastern Europe). Such anti-communism played a role in the Republican triumph in the 1946 mid-term elections. The resultant 1947 Taft-Hartley Act regulating trade unions also required their officials to renounce communism on oath: this formed a backdrop to the campaign, launched that year with catholic assistance, to exclude communists completely from union leadership. Anti-communism was, therefore, an autonomous force. The Truman administration not only shared the sentiment, but also invoked it in order to mobilise support for policies (like massive foreign aid) that would in any other circumstances have been unpopular. Such considerations influenced the wording of the speech that became known as the 'Truman Doctrine'; one writer notes 'the growing tendency [thereafter] to place the U.S.–Soviet conflict on an ideological basis, rather than as a great power clash, the way the State department had always seen the issue'.[39]

Initially this served the administration well. It got its policies through Congress. In 1948, when Wallace's anti-containment candidature threatened to draw off leftist votes and so hand the elections to the Republicans, it sought successfully 'to identify and isolate him in the public mind with the Communists'.[40] But anti-communism could cut both ways. Late in 1948 the Hiss case spotlighted the presence of communist espionage in the upper bureaucracy. In 1949 the USSR detonated its first nuclear explosion, much sooner than expected and partly as a result of the treason of Western scientists. Then the USA's protégé Chiang Kai-shek collapsed, and China went communist. 1950 saw the Korean War; that autumn US troops were badly mauled by Chinese intervention, and the administration's refusal to license direct retaliation against China seemed to many unnatural. Americans have often been given to conspiracy theories; enterprising politicians, like Senator McCarthy, jumped in to explain these disasters by alleging massive penetration of the upper echelons of government and society by communists and fellow-travellers, and to launch inquisitorial congressional hearings to winkle them out. There was some resistance, but to no avail. Truman's comparatively restrained attitude only confirmed suspicions that he and Acheson were also communist agents. More usually liberals (including the Supreme Court) either ducked for cover or sought to establish anti-

39. B. Rubin, *The Great Powers in the Middle East 1941–1947* (1980) pp.224–8
40. R. Griffith and A. Theoharis (eds), *The Specter* (New York, 1974) p.278 – quoting Clark Clifford

communist credentials by moving similar legislation (occasionally in the hope that Truman would veto it). Matters did not immediately mend with the advent of Eisenhower, despite his choice of the anti-communist crusader Nixon for Vice-President. But there had been a distinct partisan element in McCarthyism, and most (though not all) Republicans were less ready to attack Eisenhower and Dulles. Also, like other waves of hysteria, this one blew itself out in the mid-1950s.

McCarthyism drew on a wide range of traditions. We have already noted anti-communism, hatred of the 'eastern establish-ment' that dominated the State Department, and congressional concern at presidential activism. The other components were distaste for European entanglements (General MacArthur always maintained that his military plans leaked to China via the UK), and the 'China lobby'. Missionary activity and diplomatic protection had long given China, or rather a particular image of China, a peculiar place in American affections. In the late 1940s disillusion set in with Chiang Kai-shek, and (even after the promulgation of the supposedly 'universalist' Truman Doctrine) nobody urged US inter-vention to save him. But, irrationally, the administration was to be bitterly blamed for the 'loss' of China (which may have hardened its response next year to the invasion of South Korea). 'Red China's' subsequent intervention in the Korean War established it in American eyes as worse even than the USSR.

The consequences of the McCarthyist wave are diffuse. Undoubtedly one of the considerations determining the way that Nixon disengaged from Vietnam was the fear that an immediate scuttle, as distinct from fighting on to an 'honorable peace', would replicate the 'loss of China' in again unleashing right-wing hysteria at home. More generally 'anti-communism' has remained strong. Nixon believed that his earlier 'communist-baiting' record gave him more latitude to move towards détente than would have been available to other Presidents. But détente withered. This was due, no doubt, primarily to external reasons, but also to the remobili-sation of anti-communist suspicion by such bodies as the Committee on the Present Danger. More debatable is the contention that McCarthyism led directly to Vietnam: first, by driving out of the State Department the officials who knew about China and were thus implicated in its 'loss', and who *might* successfully have warned of the dangers of involvement in South-East Asia; second, by destroying any leftist tradition in the universities, leaving the Cold War liberal orthodoxy unchallenged; and third, by so blackening the image of Red China that policy-makers in the 1960s felt that, even if the USSR was (with the disintegration of monolithic 'international communism') now becoming more accommodating, China was still unregenerately expansionist and needing to be taught a lesson.

During the 1952 election campaign Eisenhower sensed that support for the Korean War was ebbing as a result of its prolonged and bloody deadlock. After his election he moved rapidly to end it. What really brought the communists to resume the stalled cease-fire negotiations we do not know, but Eisenhower thought it was his hints that he might both expand the war and use nuclear weapons. This success confirmed his belief in the effectiveness of the deterrent. Another reason for the adoption of a policy of 'massive retaliation' was economic. Eisenhower believed strongly in a balanced budget as essential to the nation's long-term economic health. He was therefore attracted to an emphasis on air-power as giving the 'biggest bang for the buck'. It also enabled him to placate isolationist sentiment by promising 'no more land wars in Asia'. The administration remained fervently anti-communist – Secretary of State Dulles equated neutralism with sin – but it operated by forming defence pacts and seeking local allies who would provide ground troops fairly cheaply, backed by US aid and air-power. Whatever the theoretical merits of these policies, in Eisenhower's day they largely worked. At home, too, he enjoyed much success in calming the passions that had raged earlier in the decade. In retrospect some have come to see his years as golden.

US POLICIES IN THE 1960s

By the end of Eisenhower's presidency, however, opinion-makers had become disenchanted. Eisenhower was too ill; he played too much golf; his economy-minded vetoes and clashes with a Democratic Congress in 1960 reduced things to a deadlock. Moreover the launching of Sputnik (the first earth satellite) in 1957 came as a great shock; the Soviets seemed to have closed the technological gap, and this early prowess with rockets prompted (erroneous) talk of a missile gap in the USA's disfavour. The USA even seemed to be lagging economically: in 1961 Khrushchev undertook to outproduce it within ten years. Kennedy responded to this mood by promising change, movement and a 'New Frontier'.

In the tradition of the New Deal, he was prepared to spend money; this had important repercussions on defence. Having campaigned on the missile gap, he pushed though a rapid expansion of American inter-continental ballistic missiles (ICBMs). Kennedy also increased conventional forces. For he had assimilated the intellectuals' criticism that to rely solely on 'massive retaliation' left no response appropriate for an intermediate challenge; and, being sensitive to the importance of the Third World, he believed that most challenges would come in the form of 'brush-fire', generally guerrilla, wars for which nuclear weapons were quite inappropriate. This did not necessarily commit him to armed intervention: he was distinctly cautious over Laos. But Kennedy's defence posture provided both the means and the rationale for an escalating involvement in Vietnam.

Domestically, too, the United States changed. The economy revived, but new and more self-critical examination revealed the extent of continuing poverty. Demands for black civil rights in the South swelled to the point where the issue could no longer be ignored in Washington. Whether Kennedy could have handled things we shall never know. After his assassination in November 1963, Lyndon Johnson sought a place in history by delivering a Great Society that would end discrimination and abolish poverty. His early successes were remarkable, but after 1966 domestic developments fused with opposition to the Vietnam War to produce a series of catastrophes. Black protest evolved from the non-violent southern civil rights march to the northern urban riot: there were 164 disturbances in the 'long, hot summer' of 1967, and outbreaks in 110 cities after Martin Luther King's murder in 1968. The Vietnam War radicalised much of the intelligentsia, produced violent demonstrations, street battles outside the Democratic Nominating Convention in 1968, and widespread campus disruptions the following year. Initially the war enjoyed overwhelming public support, but by early 1968 the New Hampshire primary showed that this had been massively eroded. The war also distorted the economy: Johnson's heart was with the Great Society, and he would not trim it just because he was fighting in Vietnam. Nor (till 1968) did he raise taxes – the 1964 tax cuts had been one of his triumphs. The result was not only impressive economic growth, but also an unpopular inflation and a sharp deterioration in the US balance of payments – the product both of rising military expenditure abroad and of increased imports.

The most immediate repercussions were naturally felt in

Indo-China. In 1968 Johnson for the first time rejected requests for additional troops, then ended the bombing of North Vietnam and began the attempts to negotiate that dragged on till a settlement was suddenly reached in January 1973. Kissinger tells us that 'No meeting with the North Vietnamese was complete without a recitation of the statements of our domestic opposition which they cited as an essential component in the "balance of forces" '.[41] Equally Nixon's strategy was dominated by the need to reduce direct US military involvement at a rate fast enough to preempt a congressional cut-off of funds.

Vietnam heightened suspicion of the 'military–industrial complex' and led to pressure to trim defence spending. Some reduction was natural as US involvement there declined. In any case, with the completion of 'Minuteman' deployment in 1967, the USA believed that it had enough ICBMs. But it became increasingly difficult to assemble support for new weapons systems; nearly two decades later 'Minuteman' still had no successor. The defence budget was squeezed to make room for welfare spending that continued to rise in the wake of the Great Society: on one calculation defence fell from a 1968 peak of $116 billion (constant 1970 dollars) to a 1976 trough of $80 billion.[42] In the Soviet Union, as we have seen, domestic pressures after 1964 were rather for expansion. At the end of the 1970s the USA suddenly became alarmed by the consequences for the relative strength of the two powers, and altered course abruptly.

Two other consequences of the US malaise of the late 1960s are more nebulous, but perhaps equally far-reaching. First, the Vietnam War was as unpopular in Western Europe as at home; together with American domestic violence, it greatly tarnished the United States' international image, especially with the younger generation. Second, the decline in the American trade surplus reduced US capacity to underwrite the Bretton Woods monetary system that had, in effect, made the dollar the international standard of value. In 1968 and 1969 capital movements mastered this process, but they went into reverse in 1970; in 1971, faced with unacceptably high foreign claims on the remaining US stock of gold, Nixon suspended the dollar's convertibility into gold. This had the effect, albeit unintended, of inaugurating a far less stable era of floating

41. Kissinger, *Memoirs* i pp. 1041, 444, ii pp.327, 329
42. International Institute for Strategic Studies (IISS), *The Military Balance 1979–80* (London, 1979) p.93

exchange rates. In both cases the causes of change lay deeper than the US domestic developments of the 1960s, but these certainly speeded things up.

NIXON'S 'IMPERIAL PRESIDENCY' 1969–74, AND ITS EFFECTS IN THE LATER 1970s

In 1953 President Eisenhower had taken over a country engaged in an Asian land war and marked by internal turmoil; in his first term he succeeded in calming things down. Nixon (Eisenhower's former Vice-President) sought to emulate him – not entirely unsuccessfully (riots and domestic conflict over Vietnam both slowly died away). But Nixon was not an eirenic individual, and he got badly across a Congress that had started to reassert itself even before his election. He felt surrounded by 'enemies', and retreated into the White House, governing through aides and institutions within his Executive Office rather than through the ordinary bureaucracy. Again this was not new, but Nixon went far further than his predecessors – sometimes, as in foreign policy, with remarkable success. However the 'plumbers' he assembled (partly because the FBI withheld cooperation) to stop the political 'leaking' of documents proved a disaster: some were caught bugging the Watergate headquarters of the Democratic National Committee. In most other countries, possibly even in the USA at another time, things would have been hushed up. But throughout 1973–4 Nixon's cover-up was prised open by the press, the courts, and congressional investigation. In the process many nasty things came to light; the defence that they were by no means unprecedented cut little ice. In August 1974 Nixon resigned to avoid impeachment.

The episode was a great blow to the 'imperial presidency'. Congress felt obliged to probe matters about which it had preferred not (publicly) to know too much – notably the CIA, which temporarily ceased to be a *secret* service. Congress also followed the Case Act, 1972 (compelling the registration of 'executive agreements') with the War Powers Act, 1973 (restricting presidential ability to commit troops abroad); it cut off funds for US air action in, and halved defence and economic aid to, Indo-China. Nor was it only the presidency that was weakened; internal reform fragmented the power of congressional committee chairmen, with the result that, though Congress could – and did – continue to *stop* things, nobody seemed able to assemble enough votes to get anything positive through. The election of President Carter did not help. His chief recommendation had been that he was an outsider, clean and uncorrupted by Washington; when he got there, he lacked the necessary empathy with Congress, and (like Nixon) retreated into a circle of White House advisers. Harmony was not restored till after the 1980 elections.

Obviously the institutional rivalries and weaknesses of the 1970s had a considerable impact. Thus Nixon would have preferred the forceful Connally for his successor, but had to settle for the emollient Ford. More concretely, he responded to the 1973 OPEC oil price rise with a grandiose 'Project Independence' for self-sufficiency by 1980; but the necessary legislation did not come through until 1978–80 (and even then on a reduced scale). Some observers expected Watergate to have catastrophic international consequences: 'You are the anchor of the whole non-Communist world,' said Lee Kuan Yew privately,[43] 'and because of righteous indignation this anchor is slithering in the mud'. In fact Watergate did not prevent Kissinger from bringing off further spectacular coups, while President Carter managed to steer through the Senate an unpopular settlement of the Panama Canal question (though not the SALT II treaty) and also to mediate peace between Egypt and Israel. But Kissinger claims that 'the collapse of our executive authority as a result of Watergate, the erosion of the leadership structure in the Congress, the isolationism born of the frustrations of Vietnam, and an emerging pattern of geopolitical abdication' left Nixon too indecisive to hold Hanoi to the 1973 Indo-China cease-fire agreement, precluded other initiatives, and prevented 'the establishment of the balance of incentives and penalties that might have preempted several crises and in the long run given us a genuine period of [Soviet] restraint'.[44] Kissinger is probably too ready to treat Watergate as an alibi for all his foreign policy failures, but his analysis is not without substance.

The current of 'isolationism' or 'geopolitical abdication' seemed to be in the ascendant with the election of President Carter on a platform that included the withdrawal of US troops from South Korea. Admittedly he was later persuaded that this would prove disastrous, but, during the first crisis of his administration, he kept a low profile, citing Vietnam and declaring that 'We do not intend

---

43. Kissinger, *Memoirs* ii p.124
44. Kissinger, *Memoirs* ii pp. 5 ff and chap. viii, i pp.1143–4

to get militarily involved, unless our own security is directly threatened'. So in 1977 and 1978 the lead in preserving Zaïre from invasion was left to Morocco and France. However, times change. By 1979 Carter had already announced the creation of a 'Rapid Deployment Force' for use, if necessary, outside Europe. That December Soviet intervention in Afghanistan produced a 'dramatic change in my own opinion of what the Soviet Union's ultimate goals are'. Carter determined to make the Soviets 'pay for their unwarranted aggression' and imposed sanctions, including a ban on grain sales that had to be dropped in 1981 as a result of pressure from US farmers.[45]

REAGAN'S LEGACY 1981–9

Carter lost the 1980 elections (largely through his inability to procure the release from Iran of American hostages). The new President, Ronald Reagan, seemed to ride a wave of conservative or reactionary sentiment; in his early years he used it to move the country his own way, much as Roosevelt and Johnson had done before him. This included a not unsuccessful attempt to restore public confidence in the American dream, and his speeches were full of uplift: 'In this blessed land, there is always a better tomorrow' (1985 Inaugural), and 'As the global democratic revolution has put totalitarianism on the defensive, we have left behind the days of retreat – America is again a vigorous leader of the free world. . . . No legacy would make me prouder than leaving in place a bipartisan consensus that prevents a paralysis of American power from ever occurring again' (1988 State of the Union). Reagan fits the general postwar rule that Presidents who began hostile to the USSR end with good relations, and vice versa; he can only be regarded as fortunate in foreign affairs.

However, Reagan left an unhappy fiscal legacy. The federal deficit was already intractable when he took office, but it soon got worse. With the collapse of détente, defence spending had already been increased both by President Carter and by Congress. Since the new administration overlooked this when it upped the defence

---

45. *Europa*, iv (8 May 1977) p. iv – issued with *The Times*, 3 May 1977; Raymond L. Garthoff, *Detente and Confrontation: American–Soviet Relations from Nixon to Reagan* (Washington, DC, 1985) pp. 950 ff, 1034

budget, it found itself committed to a rise of 10 per cent per year in real terms; Defense Secretary Weinberger stopped all attempts to row back when the mistake was discovered. The budget for 1982 was also intended to effect a complete overhaul of federal finances, cutting both taxes and (non-defence) expenditure. Something along these lines was indeed carried through Congress in the teeth of liberal Democrat opposition: politically a remarkable achievement, but one that only added up economically on the most optimistic of assumptions. The budget's 'Rosy Scenario' did not materialise, but its mistakes could not be corrected. The President managed to defend the defence spending and tax cuts against renewed liberal attack, but not to carry off-setting reductions in other (domestic) programmes. By 1985 legislation had to be enacted to bring the $172 billion deficit back into balance by 1991, if necessary through automatic cuts entailing equal political sacrifices by the President and his congressional opponents. But this only encouraged fiscal sleight-of-hand that enabled politicians to avert the need for these sacrifices. So the US budget is little easier to follow than the Soviet; in July 1991, however, the White House put the current deficit at $348 billion.[46]

The economic effects were not perhaps too serious. In the early 1980s the US economy was in marked recession as the Federal Reserve squeezed out inflation through high interest rates. (By raising the international value of the dollar, in which most debts were denominated, this had the side-effect of pushing many Third World countries into insolvency and forcing them to seek accommodations with their creditors.) But the United States recovered strongly, helped by a growing propensity to consume and (to a lesser extent) by the Keynesian stimulus of the deficit. The boom continued to the end of the 1980s, when it made a fairly soft landing. Again Reagan had been lucky. However, the expansion sucked in imports; although this helped the rest of the world, and especially the rapidly growing countries of the Pacific Basin, it resulted in a large US balance of payments deficit ($153 billion in 1987 and still over $100 billion per year in late 1989). This was financed by foreign investment (chiefly British and Japanese), and converted the United States, at least on paper, into the world's largest debtor. Given the size of the US economy and the world's orientation towards the dollar, this did not carry the implications of

46. David Stockman, *The Triumph of Politics* (paperback edn, 1986) esp. pp. 113–15, 298–320; *Keesing's*, 32901–6, 34094–5; *The Independent*, 17 July 1991 p.8

(say) Brazilian or Soviet international debt. But it gave vogue, at least in academic circles, to the thesis (enunciated in 1987 by Paul Kennedy's *The Rise and Fall of the Great Powers*) that the USA was following the pattern of its predecessors and moving into decline as a result of 'imperial overstretch' and high military expenditure. The process was, however, at least temporarily interrupted by the sudden collapse of the only obvious challenger, the USSR.

The 1980s not only enhanced the United States' international primacy, but also left it with problems and rekindled economic protectionism. Before the 1930s this had been the hallmark of the Republican Party. It began to appeal to organised labour in the 1970s. By the 1980s it had many Democratic adherents – notably House Majority Leader Gephardt, who sought in 1989 to correct the trade deficit by crude mandatory legislation. Republican administrations continued to endorse free trade. But under congressional and public pressure, they came to take an increasingly hard line in attacking what they saw as foreign protectionist practices hampering US exports. A striking example was the demand, made in the context of 1990–2 GATT (General Agreement on Tariffs and Trade) negotiations, for the substantial abandonment of the European Community's Common Agricultural Policy. But most demands are directed at Japan, the country with the largest surplus on trade with the USA; the issue has generated an intensity of feeling that puts at risk one of the greatest successes of postwar US foreign policy, the reorientation of Japan towards friendly interdependence across the Pacific. Much therefore hangs on the success of the 'Uraguay round' of GATT negotiations launched in 1986. After an exceedingly rocky course, this was finally brought to an agreed conclusion in December 1993. If it is ratified, the way of multi-lateral trade, which the USA has seen since the Second World War as underpinning the international system, remains open, even promising. But there is growing talk of regional trade blocs as an alternative. One, the North American Free Trade Area, would seem ready-made for a more isolationist USA – though it is a measure of the extent of US protectionist feeling, and of fears of Mexican cheap labour competition, that in 1993 the administration was only just able to secure its congressional ratification, mostly by Republican votes.

PART II

East–West Relations 1945–91

Part 4

CHAPTER THREE

The First Phases of the Cold War 1945–50

RIVAL INTERPRETATIONS

If the course of Soviet–American rivalry is reasonably clear, there is less agreement as to its origins. Broadly there are three main approaches.

First, it was the natural outcome of a situation where there were now only two first-class Powers, both ideological, both vigorous, expansive and drawn into the power vacuums created by the defeat of Germany and Japan, the exhaustion of most of Europe and the decline of the British Empire.

Second, Stalin's wartime and postwar policy was expansionist. Had the United States, then clearly the stronger power, moved at a sufficiently early stage in the war to restrain him, he *might* have accommodated himself to such constraint as he had accepted the status quo for most of the interwar period. But he was first apparently given a green light by the West so that his power, opportunities and appetite all grew, then, at the end of the war, criticised and interfered with, but for a goodish time not effectively countered. Only gradually did the USA come to see the need to organise a rival coalition, not to contest the gains that the Soviet Union had already made, but to 'contain' it by preventing further expansion.

Third, others see the real expansionist power in the United States, which (for instance) monopolised the occupation of Japan, excluded the USSR from influence in Italy, and soon gave up trying to work with it in Germany. Although acting unilaterally in its own sphere, the United States would not accord Stalin the right to do likewise in his: for it misperceived as expansionist moves that sought only to secure for the USSR (after its catastrophic experience of two major wars with Germany) a limited defensive glacis; also the United States was itself constrained by 'universalist' ideology (or economic interest) to foster in Eastern Europe and elsewhere a political and social system incompatible with Soviet security.

Each of these interpretations can, and generally does, have political implications. The first was initially put forward – as a prophecy – by Hitler, who saw himself as 'Europe's last hope' of coalescing into a super-state that would dominate the world in the future as in the past. Nowadays, those who argue that the Cold War was inevitable usually claim that neither side was really 'to blame'. But the interpretation does fit naturally with the reviving view that 'Europe' has interests of its own, distinct from those of external superpowers.

The second interpretation, that the USSR was expansionist and had to be contained, was the official view of the NATO alliance, and was almost unchallenged until the 1960s. Politicians like Churchill and Eden sought in their memoirs to prove they had perceived the need to contain Soviet expansion fairly early in the war, but were thwarted by Roosevelt's naivety and the general US inexperience in foreign affairs. Opportunities were therefore missed and costs unnecessarily incurred, but eventually the Truman administration came to see the light.

In the 1960s this 'orthodox' view of the Cold War came under 'revisionist' attack. One inspiration was a European 'Gaullist' recognition that the US 'hegemony', like the Soviet, imposed constraints, and that the institutions of the postwar Western world, drawn up at the height of US power, have been well adapted to the spread of American business, economic and cultural influence – as, indeed, the Soviets had always maintained.[1] But the principal motor of revisionism was a domestic disenchantment that became increasingly strident as the Vietnam War turned sour. American 'universalism' and the 'arrogance of power' had led to worldwide involvement, often on behalf of very shady clients and with disastrous consequences both for the local population and for the domestic society of the United States. And all for no good reason, since there either never had been a threat to the USA, or (if there had) it had come about only because the USA had first taken the

1. The Marshall Plan, Zhdanov explained in 1947, 'amounts in essence to a scheme to create a bloc of states bound by obligations to the United States, and to grant American credits to European countries as a recompense for their renunciation of economic, and then of political, independence' – Royal Institute of International Affairs (RIIA), *Documents on International Affairs 1947–8* p.130

offensive. Such views are basically isolationist, though now sometimes cast in a loosely Marxist guise.

The standard interpretations of the Cold War, then, differ
widely. But they have more in common than meets the eye. First,
they tend to be primarily concerned with the behaviour of the
Soviet Union and the United States and to pass over the wishes
and/or actions of lesser countries; this makes the picture easier to
draw, but leaves out quite a lot. Second, it is generally agreed that
Stalin intended to control much of Eastern Europe;[2] Cold War
historians tend to condemn this, revisionists to regard it as legitimate in the light of Soviet security interests. Third, most authors
(of whatever persuasion) concentrate chiefly on the American
evidence, which is usually so copious that the problem is to tell the
wood from the trees.[3] (Another focus has come to the fore, at least
for the 1940s and 1950s, with the digestion of the British
documents now available under the thirty-year rule.) But many
authors either derive Stalin's calculations and motives from his
actions or impute to him what they themselves regard as the natural
responses to American actions. This is not satisfactory, but since
Soviet archives are still not really open, the only (though I believe
preferable) alternative is to employ rather dubious anecdotal evidence. The problem is not peculiar to our period: did Stalin in the
1930s genuinely seek an antifascist alliance only to be rebuffed by
the West (the official Soviet line), or was his preference (as
defectors like Krivitsky tell us) always for a Nazi–Soviet Pact, which
he sought in 1935 and 1937 and finally obtained in 1939? But, since
the USSR played a greater role in postwar than in interwar politics,
we are the more hampered by our ignorance.

GEOPOLITICAL AND IDEOLOGICAL ORIGINS

With the defeat of the Reich [declared Hitler in April 1945] and
pending the emergence of the Asiatic, the African, and perhaps the

---

2. Stalin is alleged to have said, 'Any freely elected government in these countries
will be an anti-Soviet government, and we cannot allow that' – Harold F. Gosnell,
Truman's Crises (Westport, Conn., 1980) p. 239, citing R.S. Kirkendall (ed.) *The
Truman Period as a Research Field* (Columbia, Miss., 1967) p. 47

3. The striking exception relates to Roosevelt's own ideas about foreign policy:
just as he never set out (perhaps because he never decided) how far he meant in
1940–1 to go in helping Britain, so he never made it clear how he intended to
handle Stalin after the war

South American nationalisms, there will remain in the world only two Great Powers capable of confronting each other – the United States and Soviet Russia. The laws of both history and geography will compel these two powers to a trial of strength, either military or in the fields of economics and ideology. These same laws make it inevitable that both Powers should become enemies of Europe. And it is equally certain that both these Powers will sooner or later find it desirable to seek the support of the sole surviving great nation in Europe, the German people.[4]

To a considerable extent Hitler was right. True the 'laws of history' do not *compel* struggle between two preponderant Powers: after the First World War the British Empire and the United States found themselves pre-eminent, but, despite some forebodings, managed to settle their differences with no more than minor verbal bickering. They did, however, have much in common; and US aspirations, if strongly pressed, were then fairly limited. In other circumstances rivalries – like those between Rome and Carthage, Habsburg and Valois, France and Britain, and (despite, it is interesting to note, a good deal of reluctance on both sides) Britain and Germany – have run through much of history. Soviet–American antagonism can be seen as a sequel on a global scale.

By the 'laws of geography' Hitler would have understood the view (derived from Mackinder and Haushofer) on which he had himself acted, that control of the area between Central Europe and the Caucasus would, in the long run, carry with it dominance of the world. As he knew to his cost, the United States had twice intervened to prevent the establishment of such control. Already in 1900 Theodore Roosevelt had written privately that 'If England should fail to preserve the European balance of power, the United States would be forced to step in and re-establish it'. Franklin Roosevelt deployed similar arguments in public:

At this moment [December 1940], the forces of the states that are leagued against all peoples who live in freedom are being held away from our shores. . . . [But] If Great Britain goes down, the Axis powers will control the continents of Europe, Asia, Africa, Australasia, and the high seas – and they will be in a position to bring enormous military and naval resources against this hemisphere.[5]

Should the Soviet Union ever be perceived as mounting another

---

4. A. Hitler, *The Testament of Adolf Hitler* (1961 edn, n. pl.) p. 107
5. George E. Mowry, *The Era of Theodore Roosevelt* (paperback edn, 1962) p.148; US State Department, *Peace and War: United States Foreign Policy 1931–1941* (Washington, DC, 1943) pp.599–600

threat beyond the power of Britain to contain, it would be wholly in character for the United States to step in again.

Such a threat was perceived in the later 1940s, the United States did step in, and the clash did assume an ideological form. That it should have done so on the Soviet side is unsurprising. The USSR saw itself as a Marxist-Leninist state, the 'socialist motherland', and the director of the world communist movement. In accordance with Marxist doctrine it represented capitalist states as always hostile (even if not always immediately dangerous). US ideology is less systematised than Soviet, but it too is strong. As expressed in, for instance, the Declaration of Independence or the inscription on the Statue of Liberty, it was not necessarily for export. But a universalist strain accompanied the USA on to the world scene; Woodrow Wilson's Fourteen Points and the League Covenant sought to set the tone of international politics. Similarly when Roosevelt responded to the Axis challenge he did so in language remarkably like that of the Cold War – 'the Axis not merely admits but proclaims that there can be no ultimate peace between their philosophy of government and our philosophy of government' – and followed up with the Atlantic Charter and the Yalta Declaration on Liberated Europe. Certainly he did not mean to quarrel with Stalin; some say that, had he lived, he could have avoided doing so. But the ideological materials for a quarrel were there: Stalin's regime did not afford any of the Four Freedoms (of speech and worship, from want and fear) for whose early attainment 'everywhere in the world' Roosevelt had called in his 1941 Inaugural.[6] If a quarrel came, the United States was, on past form, as likely as the Soviet Union to conduct it in an ideological fashion.

THE NON-ADOPTION OF A FIRM ANGLO–AMERICAN LINE TOWARDS THE USSR BEFORE 1945

The view that the Cold War might have been avoided had a firm line been taken with the Soviet Union early on need not detain us long. There is indeed dispute as to whether, during the war, anybody ever seriously advocated such a policy. Perhaps, as Carlton argues,[7] Churchill did. But it would have required US backing; and

6. US State Department, *Peace and War*, esp. pp.600–1, 603, 611
7. David Carlton, *Anthony Eden* (1981) chap. vii

in late 1943 Roosevelt veered away and appeared, at the Teheran conference, closer to Stalin than Churchill. Thereafter, while still making some suspicious noises, Churchill's primary concern – in the continued absence of tangible US support for any alternative course – was to salvage Greece at the price of conceding Russian dominance over much of the rest of south-east Europe and making the least bad bargain he could over Poland. Be that as it may, there had been no concerted attempt to be firm with Stalin before the end of fighting in Europe. So what effect it would have had must remain speculative,[8] though no more so than the 'revisionist' contention that all would have been well had not Roosevelt died in 1945 and Truman abandoned his Russian policy. For what it is worth, we should note the view of Litvinov (then a Deputy Foreign Minister) that things should have been sorted out much earlier. In October 1944 he was worried that Britain and the USSR were organising against each other and that it would not be possible 'to agree on a common program for Germany':

> diplomacy might have been able to do something to avoid it if we had made our purposes clear to the British and if we had made clear the limits of our needs, but it is now too late, suspicions are rife on both sides.

By the following June he had drifted further into dissidence:

> Why did you Americans wait till right now to begin opposing us in the Balkans and Eastern Europe? You should have done this three years ago. Now it's too late and your complaints only arouse suspicion here.[9]

STALIN'S POLICY TOWARDS EASTERN EUROPE, AND US REACTIONS 1945–6

In 1939 Stalin and Hitler reached an explicit spheres of influence agreement. By June 1941 this had obviously broken down. We are

8. One possible consequence would have been a separate Soviet–German peace, but obstacles to this may have arisen more on the German than the Soviet side – H.W. Koch, 'Russo-German "Peace Feelers", 1942–44', *Journal of Contemporary History* x (1975). Even had Stalin continued in the European war, he might not subsequently have entered that against Japan (as Roosevelt, though not Truman) strongly hoped he would

9. V. Mastny, 'The Cassandra in the Commissariat: Maxim Litvinov and the Cold War', *Foreign Affairs* liv (1975–6), esp. pp.371, 373. Litvinov had already been devastatingly frank in private about Soviet foreign policy once before, in 1938: Tolstoy, *Stalin's Secret War* p.76

not here concerned with German ambitions and motivations, but Stalin's conduct is relevant: he was, in some respects, to repeat it in his later dealings with the West. He did not intend to attack Hitler; indeed he was very slow to recognise that Hitler was turning on him. But equally Stalin went beyond the 1939 Pact to follow a forward policy of minor territorial gains in Eastern Europe that threw Romania into the arms of Germany, and that made impossible the general alliance Germany *appeared* to be seeking in November 1940. The primary points of friction were, first, Stalin's refusal to limit himself to the recovery of ex-Russian Bessarabia, and his occupation of Northern and designs on Southern Bukovina (uncomfortably close to the Romanian oil that Germany so badly needed); second, determined Soviet pressure for another round of war with Finland, which might jeopardise German nickel and iron-ore supplies and which Germany would not allow until the conclusion of the main European war; and third, insistence on the inclusion of Bulgaria within the Soviet security zone and on a Soviet base commanding the Black Sea outlets. All Russian advances, made or aspired to, can be related to an idea of enhancing Soviet security in a dangerous world, the 'defensive' motivation that has been seen as underlying all Stalin's actions during the Cold War. In practice none had this effect; all were militarily indefensible in 1941. But Stalin seems not to have appreciated the offence they caused in Berlin, and was in January 1941 apparently surprised by German disinclination to pursue further the political discussions of early November.[10]

After the German invasion, Stalin presented his new partner, Britain, with demands for another agreement. 'A declaration I regard as algebra, but an agreement as practical arithmetic. I do not wish to decry algebra, but I prefer practical arithmetic.' He suggested a secret protocol (like that in the 1939 Pact) recognising the USSR's 1941 frontiers and according it bases in Finland and Romania, offered in exchange support for British bases in Western Europe, and floated far-reaching ideas about the general peace settlement. Britain and the USA, however, never explicitly concluded such a deal. They showed themselves alarmingly prone to general declarations, like the Atlantic Charter and the 'Declaration on Liberated Europe'. But they may also have

---

10. H.W. Koch, 'Hitler's Programme and the Genesis of Operation "Barbarossa"', *Historical Journal.* xxvi (1983); R.J. Sontag and J.S. Beddie (eds), *Nazi–Soviet Relations 1939–1941* (Washington, DC, Department of State, 1948)

accepted, slowly and informally, a Soviet sphere in Eastern Europe – reading between the lines, the Soviets, and much revisionist historiography, saw Yalta as such an agreement.

The most explicit deal related to the Balkans, where Churchill informally traded Soviet preponderance in Romania and Bulgaria for British in Greece. The Americans always deprecated spheres of influence, but, as Roosevelt privately told Senators concerned with events in Poland,

> the idea kept coming up because the occupying forces had the power in the areas where their arms were present and each knew that the other could not force things to an issue. He stated that the Russians had the power in Eastern Europe, that it was obviously impossible to have a break with them and that, therefore, the only practicable course was to use what influence we had to ameliorate the situation.

Hitherto Roosevelt had in fact conspicuously failed to attempt this over Poland. At Yalta he tried for a genuine coalition government, but settled for a limited expansion of the 'Lublin Committee' whose support derived almost entirely from the Red Army. The new 'Provisional Government of National Unity' should hold 'free and unfettered elections as soon as possible', but Stalin was allowed to rebuff any proposals for their external supervision. Privately Roosevelt accepted that 'this is so elastic that the Russians can stretch it all the way from Yalta to Washington without technically breaking it'.[11] In the last resort, then, neither Roosevelt nor (later) Truman, nor therefore the British, were prepared to contest Soviet doings in Poland. But the Cold War cannot be understood without remembering that some of these left a very nasty taste – notably the hampering of any Western assistance to the anti-German Warsaw Rising of 1944,[12] and the arrest in 1945 of leading figures of the Polish Home Army who had been brought to Moscow to discuss the broadening of the Provisional Government. Hitler had been less perturbed by the, in fact far more violent, way in which Stalin had consolidated his sphere of influence in 1939–40.

That Stalin would seek so to consolidate his sphere was inevitable. The 'Sovietisation' of captured areas had been assumed in army writings of the interwar period, and implemented in

11. R. Dallek, *Franklin D. Roosevelt and American Foreign Policy 1932–1945* (New York, 1979) pp.507–8, 513–16

12. The rising was admittedly anti-communist in seeking to present the advancing Red Army with the fait accompli of 'London' Polish control of the capital, but the Soviet reaction – to leave the Germans to crush it – was of a piece with their response to both the Slovak national rising of 1944 and the Prague one of 1945

1939–40.[13] At all times Stalin maintained a lively sense of the distinctiveness of the socialist and capitalist worlds – 'They will never accept the idea that so great a space [as the USSR] should be red, never, never' (1944) – and in 1945 he declared that 'This war is not as in the past; whoever occupies a territory also imposes on it his own social system. Everyone imposes his own system as far as his army has power to do so. It cannot be otherwise.'[14] This was not to prove literally true; as we shall see there were uncertainties and exceptions at the margin. But the Red Army, unlike the US Army, conducted its operations (and especially the winter sweep up the Danube in 1944–5) with postwar considerations very much in mind. The period 1945–7 saw the transfer of all political power to the communists throughout Eastern Europe, bar Czechoslovakia (1948), Finland,[15] and Greece. Only in Yugoslavia and Albania can *indigenous* communists be said to have gained power through their own resources, a fact that was to influence these countries' later evolution. The Russians always stressed the dominant contribution of the Red Army:

> Even though the French and Italian CPs [Communist Parties] have so far achieved less success than the CPY[ugoslavia], this is not due to any special qualities of the CPY, but mainly because . . . . the Soviet army came to the aid of the Yugoslav people, liberated Belgrade and in this way created the conditions which were necessary for the CPY to achieve

13. P.H. Vigor, *The Soviet View of War, Peace and Neutrality* (1975) pp.115–6
14. M. Djilas, *Conversations with Stalin* (paperback edn, 1969) pp.62, 90
15. Finland is unique in that, although within the Soviet security sphere, it succeeded in maintaining a liberal political and economic system subject only to self-censorship and very occasional Soviet intervention in its internal politics. Such a compromise between Soviet security needs and local freedom (which gave rise to the term 'Finlandisation') was never permanently secured elsewhere in Eastern Europe. The reasons for Finland's success were obscure even to participants – Djilas records a 1948 exchange between Zhdanov, who, impressed by Finnish industry, regretted not having occupied the country, and Molotov, who described Finland as 'a peanut' (*Conversations with Stalin* p. 120). In 1944 Finland had not lain on a strategic axis, and the USSR (which had bitter experience of Finnish resistance) was content to conclude an armistice that allowed the Red Army to concentrate elsewhere and left to Finland the task of driving out the Germans. Thereafter Finland enjoyed considerable, if tacit, US sympathy, but followed a policy of close friendship with the USSR, abstaining from participation in the Marshall Plan, and in 1948 concluding a Security Treaty with the USSR. This may have been one factor leading the USSR to acquiesce in the exclusion (at much the same time) of the Finnish Communist Party from the coalition government after it had been shown to have planned a coup. Another was perhaps fear that a take-over of Finland would throw Sweden into the arms of the USA

power. Unfortunately the Soviet army did not and could not render such assistance to the French and Italian CPs.[16]

For a very brief period in the summer of 1945 the Americans may have hoped to contest this drift of events in Romania and Bulgaria. The war was now over, and with it the Red Army's need for absolute acquiescence in its rear. Also US Secretary of State Byrnes felt that the mere existence of the atom bomb might make the Russians 'more manageable' on Eastern Europe.[17] At Potsdam the Americans took a tougher line on Romania and Hungary than on Poland, and no agreements were reached. In August 1945 Truman pronounced that Bulgaria, Romania and Hungary were not to be in the sphere of interest of any one power; Byrnes told the US representative in Bucharest to let it be known 'that this Govt. hopes to see established in Rumania, through the efforts of the Rumanians themselves, and if necessary with the assistance of the three Allied Govts as provided in the Crimea Declaration on Liberated Europe, a more representative regime'. Encouraged, the King of Romania sought the resignation of the government imposed on him by Vyshinski immediately after Yalta, and appealed to the Big Three for help in constituting a more representative one. But the Prime Minister refused to resign, and by 25 August Byrnes drew back: 'We hope no action will be taken which might seem to give ground for Soviet suspicion that crisis was brought about by "Anglo–American intervention". . . . We do not think that any advice or assurances should be given to the King.'

Thereafter Byrnes sought not to challenge Soviet pre-eminence in Eastern Europe, only to humanise it. At the London Foreign Ministers' meeting in September, he found it 'impossible to believe that a temporary Roumanian government could not be formed which would be both friendly to the Soviet Union and also representative of the people'; when he met resistance from Molotov he suggested that the Polish model (of a government expanded to include one-third non-communists) 'gave the various parties . . . adequate representation'. No agreement was reached in London,

16. Letter of the CPSU to the CPY, 4 May 1948 (RIIA, *Documents . . . 1947–8* p.383). Khrushchev allegedly said the same to the last great world conference of communist parties in 1960: 'What did we do in the people's democracies? We helped the communists take power'; and 'if the soviet army had reached Paris we could today be eating at comrade Thorez' table, if it had arrived in Italy we could dine at Rome with comrades Togliatti and Longo': Karel Kaplan, 'Il piano di Stalin', *Panorama* (Milan), 26 April 1977 p.174

17. G. Herken, *The Winning Weapon: The Atomic Bomb and the Cold War 1945–50* (New York, 1980) pp.43–5

but at Moscow in December Byrnes undertook to recognise the Romanian and Bulgarian governments if they were broadened to include two opposition politicians. Truman exploded: 'those two police states. I am not going to agree to the recognition of those governments unless they are radically changed'; although recognition for Romania followed fairly quickly, that for Bulgaria did not come until late 1947, after the entry into force of the peace treaty (and one week after the execution of the leading opposition politician).[18]

By late 1945 the Americans had already abandoned any serious hopes of altering things in these countries. What they worried about was how many more were to follow. Potsdam, Truman reflected in January 1946, 'would go down in history as a bad conference. Yet . . . nothing more could have been done because they were confronted with so many accomplished facts before they started.' Or, as he had put it the previous month, the Russians

> confront us with an acknowledged fact and then there is little we can do. 'Now they have 500,000 men in Bulgaria and some day they are going to move down and take the Black Sea straits and that will be an accomplished fact again. There's only one thing they understand'.
> 'Divisions?' Ross asked.
> The President nodded and added that we can't send any divisions over to prevent them moving from Bulgaria. 'I don't know what we're going to do.'[19]

TURKEY, IRAN, AND OTHER SOVIET INITIATIVES

What Truman in fact decided to do was to engage US prestige in preventing further Soviet expansion into the Middle East. This attempted Soviet expansion beyond anything that had been accepted at Yalta did much to draw the United States into the Cold War, just as Stalin's efforts to go beyond the Nazi–Soviet Pact had upset Germany in 1940. In a way Stalin was unlucky. Northern Iran and the Straits were long-standing Russian interests, but the area had not previously been of much concern to the Americans.

---

18. Lundestad, *American Non-Policy towards Eastern Europe* pp. 233–47; W. Taubman, *Stalin's American Policy: From Entente to Detente to Cold War* (New York, 1982) p.126

19. Herken, *Winning Weapon* pp. 354, 79

Truman, however, was a history buff, with an interest in the Middle East from Alexander the Great onwards and a strong sense of its strategic importance.[20] Also, in the case of Iran, the credibility of the United Nations, in which the USA had invested a lot of political capital, was at risk.

In November 1940 Stalin sought to enlist Bulgaria in a joint attack on, and partition of, European Turkey; the Turks also claimed that Soviet agents had been stirring up minorities in eastern Turkey and Iran by dangling before them the prospect of a separate state.[21] In 1945 the USSR was again in a position to take up these threads, in March denouncing its non-aggression treaty with Turkey and in June intimating its terms for conceding a new one: not only the revision of the 1936 Montreux Convention governing the Black Sea Straits (which Britain and the USA, at the Potsdam conference, showed themselves ready to accept), but also the cession of Kars and Ardahan,[22] and the realignment of the Bulgarian frontier. For the next year press and radio campaigns, and overbearing Soviet representatives in Turkey, reinforced (and expanded) these demands. They were, in themselves, quite unacceptable to Turkey, but were also viewed as a preliminary to bringing 'Turkey "like Poland" under direct Soviet influence'. They thus reawakened all Turkey's old historic fears and its leaders turned for aid to the United States, voicing sentiments that were to become the typical rhetoric of the Cold War: 'The Soviets have gone mad, they dream of world domination. They are crossing you and Britain at many points: Bornholm, Trieste, Albania, Greece, Turkey, Iran. Where they find a weak point they exploit it' (Prime Minister Saracoglu, July 1945). Given these convictions Turkey kept its large army mobilised, a burden beyond its economic capacity to sustain indefinitely. In 1946 the USA offered gestures of naval support: in February the *Missouri* was sent to Istanbul, ostensibly to return the ashes of a former Turkish ambassador. In August the Soviet Union demanded a new regime for the Straits, whose defence should become a matter for the Black Sea powers jointly. The United States (with Britain and France) encouraged Turkey to reject this demand, and dispatched its latest aircraft carrier to the

20. Joseph M. Jones, *The Fifteen Weeks* (New York, 1955) p.66
21. US State Department, *Foreign Relations of the United States* (hereafter *FRUS*) 1941 i pp.336, also pp.288, 334–5
22. A strategic area conquered by Russia in 1877–8; its recovery by Turkey after the First World War, at a time when the destruction of independence in the Caucasus was a mutual Turkish and Bolshevik interest, was confirmed by treaty in 1921

area, Truman remarking 'that we might as well find out whether the Russians [were] bent on world conquest now as in five or ten years'. There were no further Soviet demands, but tension remained high and, by the end of the year, the US was privately questioning Turkey's capacity to hold out indefinitely.[23]

Geographically adjacent to eastern Turkey was northern Iran. In 1941 the USSR and Britain had jointly occupied Iran; a smaller US presence followed, and in 1943 the USA obtained a promise that they would all withdraw their troops within six months of the end of the war. In late 1945 the Soviets showed no signs of keeping to this, and repulsed Western attempts to discuss the question. But precisely what they wanted is unclear. On the one hand they created the communist Tudeh Party to operate in Iran proper, and conducted troop movements that appeared to threaten Teheran. They also exploited genuine national cleavages by establishing in the far north a Kurdish and an Azerbaijani republic (the latter run by a long-standing Comintern official). Finally they demanded an oil concession analogous to that enjoyed by Britain in the south. Iran's response was both to negotiate with the Soviet Union – where Prime Minister Quavam was ominously told, 'We don't care what U.S. and Britain think and are not afraid of them' – and to enlist US support for complaints to the United Nations. This support was readily forthcoming, as Truman took the Soviet refusal to evacuate very seriously, and it thwarted Soviet attempts to dodge or shelve the issue at the UN. But Soviet troop withdrawal was more probably due to progress in direct negotiations: Quavam eventually promised a joint oil company, broadened his government to include Tudeh and Azerbaijani representatives, and recognised the autonomous government of Azerbaijan. Iran gradually left the international limelight. But by the summer there were fears that, as in Eastern Europe, the communists would come to control its government. The growth of the Tudeh Party led not only to strikes in the southern oil fields – and demonstrative British troop deployments across the river in Iraq – but also to serious trouble (conceivably fanned by the British) with the southern tribes. Partly as a result, the Shah and Quavam decided in October to swing against the Soviets, dismissing the Tudeh ministers, applying to the USA for financial aid, and finally, in December, suppressing the autonomous

23. Rubin, *The Great Powers in the Middle East 1941–47* chap. 10; R. Jervis and J. Snyder (eds) *Dominoes and Bandwagons: Strategic Beliefs and Great Power Competition in the Eurasian Rimland* (New York, 1991) chap. 3; W. Millis (ed.) *The Forrestal Diaries* (1952) p.193

republics in the north. The Russian oil concession was over-whelmingly rejected by a nationalist Parliament.[24]

In Turkey and Iran the USSR was clearly prepared to press quite hard, but ultimately to draw back when checked. The episodes are important in the drift to Cold War, but they are only two among a wide range of Soviet actions and demands: in Asia the annexation of its satellite Tannu-Tuva, the taking (agreed at Yalta) from Japan of south Sakhalin and the Kuriles, from China the recovery of the Manchurian railway and a naval base at Port Arthur; in Africa a bid for a UN trusteeship over Libya (which alarmed the British); in the East Mediterranean a threat to withhold approval for the transfer of the Dodecanese to Greece unless the latter conceded bases on the islands; a request to Norway for the cession of Bear Island and for bases in Spitzbergen; and insistence on liberating, and for a year maintaining a military presence on, the Danish Baltic island of Bornholm. Sometimes it is clear what the Soviet Union wanted: its reluctance to evacuate Manchuria alarmed the USA in early 1946, but as soon as the province's (ex-Japanese) industry had been thoroughly looted, the Red Army withdrew; the wish to help the Chinese communists (by securing them Japanese arms) had been a purely secondary consideration. Sometimes it may be presumed, as in the case of Libya, that the Soviet demand represented primarily a bargaining chip. Elsewhere the probability must be that Stalin was seeking to take what he could without being quite sure, in each case, how much that would be. To Chiang Kai-shek's son (who had been educated in the USSR until 1937), he explained in December 1945 'that it was his intention to strengthen himself everywhere that he could in the domination of his adjacent areas and to attain as many strategic positions as was possible at this time. In this he referred to Eastern Europe and other areas.'[25]

---

24. The whole episode closely parallels events in 1920–1, when the Red Army established the Gilan Republic by the south Caspian, but withdrew in early 1921 following a treaty that appeared to give the USSR a privileged position in Iran as a whole. By the year's end a certain strong nationalist had grasped power and suppressed Gilan: G. Lenczowski, *The Middle East in World Affairs* (Ithaca, NY, 1980 edn) chap. 5; Rubin, *Great Powers in the Middle East* chap.ix; Jervis and Snyder, *Dominoes and Bandwagons* pp. 56–60, 75–7; K. Roosevelt, *Countercoup: The Struggle for the Control of Iran* (New York, 1979) pp. 51 ff, 112

25. For Greece, see P.E. Moseley, *The Kremlin in World Politics* (1960) p. 231; for Norway, J.F. Byrnes, *Speaking Frankly* (1947) pp. 292–3; for Stalin's explanation, W. Averell Harriman and E. Abel, *Special Envoy to Churchill and Stalin* (1976) p. 540. It should be added that the US military were also very keen, at this time, on collecting as many bases as possible; the chief restraint on their appetite was financial

THE COMMUNIST TAKE-OVER OF HUNGARY AND CZECHOSLOVAKIA

In Eastern Europe itself, Stalin's commitment to dominating Poland, Romania and Bulgaria could, by 1945, probably have been shaken only by war. In Hungary the USSR seemed to aspire to pre-eminence of influence, and Molotov haggled for a revision of Churchill's percentages deal to that effect. But the government installed in 1944 represented a wide spectrum; in November 1945 it held free elections which the Smallholders won comfortably, thereafter assuming the premiership in a continued coalition. At this time the communist leader, Rakosi, sought to discourage all talk of a take-over, while explaining that 'if the situation changes – and in years the situation will change – then the line will change too', Stalin foreseeing a communist take-over in ten to fifteen years. The delay was apparently known at the top of the party as the 'Polish trade-off'. Hungary, then, was less important to the USSR than Poland (or Romania-Bulgaria), and it is just possible that a resolute display of Western interest might have kept it from going the same way.[26] In the event the pace hotted up in mid-1946: the Soviet occupation authorities began to squeeze the Smallholders in the name of anti-fascism or by the discovery of conspiracies, dissolving organisations and forcing resignations. The term 'salami tactics' was originally coined to describe this take-over, which was completed within a year.

Czechoslovakia was a rather special case. President-in-exile Beneš concluded a deal with Moscow that effectively 'Finlandised' the country; it consistently endorsed Soviet foreign policy, but internally a communist-led coalition government continued to operate a more or less liberal political system until 1948. The communist leader, Gottwald, was later to say that 'We prepared [the] February 1948 [take-over] from 1945 on and particularly from 1947'. In May 1946 the communists gained 38 per cent of the votes; initially they looked to achieving an absolute majority, and with it full power, at the next elections – a distinctive road to socialism endorsed by Stalin that August. This electoral strategy was never abandoned.[27]

26. Taubman, *Stalin's American Policy* p. 78; M. Charlton, *The Eagle and the Small Birds: Crisis in the Soviet Empire from Yalta to Solidarity* (1984) p. 67

27. Both communists and non-communists expected to do well at the 1948 elections (a communist poll in January forecast 55%). Gottwald himself doubted whether the communists would get 45%, though he did look also to using independently elected Socialist fellow travellers: Karel Kaplan, *The Short March: The Communist Takeover in Czechoslovakia 1945–1948* (1987) pp. 106, 115n., 148–9

But from mid-1947 one wing of the party came to doubt its wisdom and to look instead to their control of the security forces and to extra-parliamentary action – a process encouraged when the Czechs were rebuked, at the first meeting of Cominform (see p. 93), for having overvalued the parliamentary approach and so let slip the right moment for seizing power. The non-communist parties were disunited, and also handicapped by their belief that communist participation in government was a guarantee of Czech alignment with the USSR and hence a protection against direct Soviet intervention. Nevertheless some communists feared that they might be excluded from government as in France and Italy. As a political crisis mounted in February 1948 over the partisan behaviour of the police, the Soviet ambassador pushed Gottwald to take decisive action and invited him to turn for military help to the USSR. Gottwald declined, confident that the communists were fully in control of the situation. This indeed soon proved to be the case: anti-communist ministers precipitated a crisis by resigning, and the communists pressured Beneš into appointing a new government that rapidly established their monopoly of power.[28]

STALIN'S HOPES FOR POSTWAR GERMANY AND EUROPE; HIS PURSUIT OF TOO MANY PERIPHERAL GAINS

More important than Hungary and Czechoslovakia was Germany. One defector has claimed that in 1944–6 the prospects of 'sovietising' were hotly debated in Moscow. Malenkov was pessimistic, and in 1944 'the Politburo had no confidence in the possibility of successfully sovietizing even those parts of Germany occupied by Soviet troops. It was considered probable that the United States and Great Britain would insist on conditions of peace under which the sovietization of Germany would be impossible.' This provided an added reason for the rapid dismantlement of German industry, even at the cost of gross inefficiency: 'If we can't ship it out, it's better to destroy it, so that the Germans won't have it' (July 1945). By the autumn Malenkov's position had weakened. Mikoyan, on pragmatic grounds, pushed for a prolonged occu-

28. Kaplan, *The Short March* esp. pp. 14–15, 75–7, 105, 123–4, 138, 175–85. Soviet anxiety to afford military help may have stemmed from fears of US counter-intervention: *Khrushchev Remembers* ii p. 189

pation and the economic exploitation *in situ* of the Soviet zone, while Zhdanov who 'was chiefly interested in the political aspects of the question' joined in urging Sovietisation.[29] There is some more general support for this view: according to Khrushchev, Stalin often spoke of Eisenhower's generosity in allowing the Russians to reach Berlin first; had he not done so 'the question of Germany might have been decided differently and our own position turned out quite a bit worse'.[30]

Whatever may have been their earlier fears, Stalin, Molotov and Zhdanov sounded quite optimistic when they briefed the future East German leadership in early June 1945:

> Perspective – there will be two Germanies, the 'unity of the Allies' notwithstanding [trotz aller Einheit der Verbündeten]
> . . . Secure the unity of Germany through a united KPD-united Central Committee, united Party of the working classes, in the centre of things a united Party
> . . . SPD very split – majority of members for unity [with the KPD].[31]

In March–April 1945 the German communists had been told to concentrate on a bourgeois-democratic transformation of the country within the context of a broad undifferentiated anti-fascist movement; now they were warned against 'anti-fascist committees' as there was a danger that these would act spontaneously:

> Character of the anti-fascist struggle: Completion of the bourgeois-democratic revolution; bourgeois-democratic government; break the power of the landed aristocracy; eliminate the rest of feudalism.

Accordingly in June–July 1945 communist activists learned that political parties of many hues were to be set up and land reform hurried forward. Later the pace of change accelerated; in November they were suddenly ordered to bring about the (previously downplayed) merger of the Communist and Socialist parties, which was achieved in April 1946.[32] That spring, according to the Yugoslav leader Djilas, Stalin was saying 'that all Germany must be ours, that is, Soviet, Communist'.

Obviously a united communist Germany would have been an enormous gain – with considerable implications for Western Europe. Djilas suspects that it represented more wishful thinking

---

29. R. Slusser (ed.) *Soviet Economic Policy in Postwar Germany: A Collection of Papers by Former Soviet Officials* (New York, 1953) esp. pp. 19, 41–2, 46–7, 52

30. *Khrushchev Remembers* i pp. 194–5

31. Pieck's notes: *Frankfurter Allgemeine Zeitung*, 30 March 1991, p. 6

32. ibid; W. Leonhard, *Child of the Revolution* (1957) pp. 280–3, 326–8, 341–2, 350–4

than detailed planning, but that the Russians had been brought to it 'by their hopes for the economic and political dissolution of Western Europe'.[33] These hopes would seem to have been of long standing and widely held in Kremlin circles.[34] But they were inevitably rather vague. In 1945 the Soviet economist Varga forecast a two-to-three year upsurge in the capitalist world, followed by a second slump; many have speculated that Stalin shared these views (which would also have been widely accepted in the West), and certainly Stalin catechised Western visitors in 1946–7 on economic prospects[35]. In August 1946 he is also alleged to have approached Harold Laski (whose importance in the Labour Party it would have been natural for him to exaggerate) and privately suggested Soviet concessions in exchange for Anglo–Soviet collaboration, a free hand for the USSR on the continent, and the peaceful bringing of all Europe to socialism on an anti-American basis, albeit possibly by routes other than that the USSR had taken. The alternative course, which he said was favoured by Molotov, was a harsh policy of confrontation with an Anglo–American bloc, leading to the consolidation of zones of influence and the partition of Germany. This was, of course, what eventually happened. But the idea of attracting Western Europe into the Soviet fold seems to have died hard. The same source claims that in January 1949 Stalin told the inaugural meeting of Comecon that

> Europe will follow. . . . If we supply primary products to all the European countries, the American diktat to Europe will explode. . . . We must elaborate plans and projections for ten years. There can be no revolutionary movements in western Europe if the workers are afraid of being without coal, cotton and other primary products if their country breaks with America. We must eliminate this fear and then they will go forward with courage.[36]

But if Stalin hoped for gains through the internal dissolution of

---

33. Djilas, *Conversations with Stalin* p. 191. The more sceptical Litvinov privately remarked in June that since 'each side wants a unified Germany – under its control', the country would 'obviously be broken into two': Taubman, *Stalin's American Policy* p. 153

34. For 1940 hopes that the current war would generate revolution and the Bolshevisation of all Europe, see R.C. Raack, 'Stalin's Plans for World War II', *Journal of Contemporary History* xxvi (1991) pp. 219–20. For Khrushchev's confirmation that Stalin and his circle entertained similar hopes after the war, see the quotation on pp.93–4 from N.S. Khrushchev, *Khrushchev Remembers. The Glasnost Tapes* (hereafter *Khrushchev Remembers* iii), tr. J.L. Schechter with V.V. Luchkov (Boston, Mass., 1990) pp.100–1

35. Taubman, *Stalin's American Policy* pp.87, 135–9

36. Kaplan, 'Il piano di Stalin', esp. pp.174–7, 182

Western Europe, it seems most unlikely that he looked to achieve them by war. In 1948 the USSR explained that it could have gained Trieste for Yugoslavia only by seizing it and starting a war with the Anglo-Americans – but 'Yugoslav comrades could not fail to realise that after such a hard war the USSR could not enter another'.[37] By then Soviet armed forces had (though this was not realised in the West) been reduced to 2.8 million – as compared to the United States' 1.4 million – and the looting of East Germany included the reduction to single track of railways that would have been strategic in any war.[38] There is, too, no reason to doubt that Stalin took the atom bomb seriously – 'That is a powerful thing, powerful' – which is why he had been seeking to develop it since 1941 and devoted such resources to uranium mining in the Erzgebirge. Indeed, if we are to believe what he told Chiang Ching-Kuo in 1945, 'it was the Soviet Government's intention to industrialise Siberia during the next fifty years. During that period he considered that there was no chance that the United States would want war and this would give him time to strengthen his weak position in the East'.[39]

War, admittedly, might come sooner: in April 1945 Stalin was talking of a German recovery in twelve to fifteen years, which was why it was so important to secure Slav unity, and added, 'The war will soon be over. We shall recover in fifteen or twenty years, and then we'll have another go at it'. The time-scale is much the same as that of the 'three new Five-Year Plans . . . if not more' which he said, in his celebrated February 1946 speech, would be needed to insure our country against 'any eventualities'. It may well have governed communist tactics outside Stalin's immediate sphere of control. The French leader Thorez was reportedly told in September 1946 that

> The international situation is favorable in general to the interests of the Soviet Union but the latter is not in the position at the present juncture of European affairs to draw the greatest possible benefit therefrom. The Soviet Union is not prepared for war and its military preparation will not be completed for a number of years. Hence, the necessity to *gain time* and to avoid situations of a highly dangerous nature while

37. RIIA, *Documents 1947–9* p. 369
38. German railways, Slusser, *Soviet Economic Policy in Post-war Germany* pp. 32–3. The official *History of the Joint Chiefs of Staff [JCS]* (typescript, National Archives, Washington, DC) gives the most recent estimate of Soviet military strength in 1946 as 4.75 million (ii p. 22) and provides figures for the USA (i p. 238, ii p. 561). For the Soviet 1948 figure, a claim by Khrushchev, see M. McCauley, *The Soviet Union since 1917* (1981) pp. 151–2
39. Djilas, *Conversations with Stalin* p. 119; Harriman, *Envoy to Churchill and Stalin* p. 540

endeavoring to maintain and even consolidate positions already acquired. The policy and tactics of the French Communist Party must follow *closely in line with this perspective* . . .

Because the Soviet Union is in the position of having to avoid during a relatively long period participation in a major war, it follows that the French Communist Party should not advance too rapidly and above all must not endeavor to seize power by force since to do so would probably precipitate an international conflict from which the Soviet Union could hardly emerge victorious. The eyes of the United States and England are directed towards France and should the French communists become too openly aggressive, they would bring about a major crisis which might too deeply involve the Soviet Union.[40]

There never was a crisis that 'too deeply' involved the USSR. Equally it is clear that Stalin was not quite careful enough. Very possibly because he had been more successful in Eastern Europe than he had originally expected, he was tempted to try for minor gains elsewhere. We have noted how the USA was drawn into the eastern Mediterranean by pressure on Iran and Turkey, and Khrushchev is supposed to have cited the Dardanelles episode as an illustration of the way Stalin's opportunism 'helped the capitalists to organise resistance and reinforce their positions'.[41] The question of Greece is also instructive. This had been in the British sphere, and in 1944 the local communists were not encouraged (perhaps even discouraged) from seizing power. When they did rebel in December, Stalin acquiesced in their suppression by the British. The rebellion alarmed moderate Greek opinion: it not only secured a royalist victory at the 1946 elections (internationally supervised, but boycotted by the communists[42]) and plebiscite, but also triggered an unpleasant rightist reaction. In late 1946, capitalising on the fear and distaste that this engendered, the communists rose again, with prospects that sometimes seemed promising. They were supported chiefly by Yugoslavia and its then satellite Albania, but also by Bulgaria, where Soviet control was paramount. The USSR did nothing to stop the fighting, and effectively hampered UN attempts to supervise the Greek borders. To the anger of some Greek communists, however, it never formally recognised the insurgent government, and never provided aid commensurate with that reaching Athens from the Anglo-Americans. By 1948 Stalin was coming to believe it had all been a mistake:

40. Djilas, *Conversations with Stalin* pp. 90–1; *FRUS*, 1946 v pp. 472–3
41. Kaplan, 'Il piano di Stalin' p. 189
42. Had they participated, Allied observers thought they might have got 15% of the vote; subsequent research based on this report increases the estimate to 20–25%: E. Nicolacopoulos, *Parties and Elections in Greece* (Athens, 1988)

they have no prospect of success at all. What, do you think that Great
Britain and the United States – the United States, the most powerful
state in the world – will permit you to break their line of communication in the Mediterranean? Nonsense . . . The uprising . . .
must be stopped, and as quickly as possible.[43]

(It did, however, last a further year, with Bulgarian – and some
Romanian – assistance continuing to the end.) Finally, to complete
the argument, we may mention one further probe that turned out
disastrously – North Korea's 1950 attempt, with Stalin's blessing, to
reunite the peninsula by force. This had the effect both of
deepening US involvement in the Far East and of greatly
simplifying its construction of alliances with Japan and Germany.

WESTERN BELIEFS, VALUES AND FOREIGN POLICY EXPECTATIONS

From a Western perspective, the chief themes of the Cold War must
be the growing perception of the existence of a challenge from
Soviet expansionism and the involvement of the United States in
resisting it, at first chiefly by diplomatic and economic means but
eventually also by military alliances and interventions. The arena
was initially the 'northern tier' of the Middle East and Europe, but
in 1950 it spread also to East and South-East Asia. An account of
this length must focus chiefly on the United States, but it should
not be concluded that the evolution of American perceptions was
unique, or that the USA was always the originator of a confrontational line. We have already noted the Cold War language
with which Turkey sought to enlist support against the Soviet
demands of 1945–6; similarly Iran's decision to break with the
communists in late 1946 was made very largely on its own.[44] It has
also been claimed 'that a drive to sustain Britain's own world role
and to contain Soviet power underscored British policy even before
the declaration and implementation of containment by successive
United States' governments'. Which was very much what Henry
Wallace contended in the September 1946 speech that led to his
dismissal from the US Cabinet:

> to make Britain the key to our foreign policy would be . . . the height
> of folly. . . . We must not let British balance-of-power manipulations

43. Djilas, *Conversations with Stalin* pp. 140–1, 102–3
44. The US ambassador wished to encourage it, but was restrained by Acheson:
Jervis and Schneider, *Dominoes and Bandwagons* pp. 76–7

determine whether and when the U.S.A. gets into war. Make no mistake about it – British imperialistic policy in the Near East, combined with Russian retaliation, would lead the U.S.A. straight to war unless we have a clearly defined . . . policy of our own. . . . To prevent war and ensure our survival in a stable world, it is essential that we look abroad through our own American eyes and not through the eyes of either the British Foreign Office or a pro-British and anti-Russian press.[45]

It would, however, be absurd to maintain that the USA was simply bounced into an 'entangling alliance.' We described earlier (pp. 33–42) some of the domestic currents that made for a Cold War policy; at a more detailed level, some important developments and initiatives can be attributed at least in part to domestic bureaucratic politics.[46] There were also, in 1945, a number of widely spread attitudes that did much to influence the subsequent evolution of US foreign policy. First, once fighting was over, the public insisted on demobilisation on a first-in-first-out basis. This had devastating effects on efficiency: two months after Japan's surrender most units are supposed to have lost 50–75 per cent of their combat value.[47] Effectively the USA reverted to the 'offshore' naval and air-power it had been before 1941. Nor, despite its continuing concern to preserve its nuclear monopoly, did it build its nuclear arsenal with any urgency: in July–August 1945 one bomb was tested, two dropped on Japan with the intention that a third should follow by the end of the month if there were no surrender; in April 1947 the USA had no bombs actually assembled for use.[48]

45. Ann Deighton (ed.) *Britain and the First Cold War* (1990) p. 4, and chaps 2, 3, 5, 9; *Keesing's*, 8151

46. The abrupt cutting-off of Lend-Lease in 1945 was largely due to its administrator's determination to honour his earlier promises to Congress; the language of the Truman Doctrine was that needed to induce Congress to authorise financial aid to Greece and Turkey; one historian maintains that 'The Marshall Plan . . . grew out of a continuing bureaucratic struggle between the Army and the State Department'; Clay's March 1948 retraction of his earlier insistence that the USSR did not intend war was a move to help the military gain appropriations; the new strategy of NSC–68 (rearmament and the universalisation of containment) was, inter alia, a way to bypass Truman's freezing of defence spending and the inter-service feuding that this occasioned

47. *History of the JCS*, i pp. 212, 214

48. Two more bombs were tested in 1946. In April 1947 the stockpile contained about twelve bombs, none assembled and some probably inoperable. New 'shaped' high-explosive charges (necessary as triggers) were devised later that month, which facilitated assembly, but the real increase did not come till a crash programme was ordered after the Berlin Blockade. By 1953 the US arsenal was apparently 1600, while the USSR is not believed to have had any operationally deployed: Herken, *Winning Weapon* pp. 197, 199; D. Yergin, *Shattered Peace: The Origins of the Cold War and National Security State* (paperback edn, Harmondsworth, 1980) pp.266, 465–6; *History of the JCS*, i pp.294–5; S.E. Ambrose, *Eisenhower the President* (1984) p.93

The USA was certainly not in the business of crude 'nuclear blackmail'; and the Joint Chiefs of Staff did not in fact believe that the Soviet Union could be conquered, even given the use of nuclear weapons.[49]

At the same time Truman felt, when he took over, that agreements with the USSR had so far been 'a one-way street and that could not continue; we could not, of course, expect to get 100 percent of what we wanted but . . . on important matters he felt we should be able to get 85 percent'. In this he was fairly representative, polls suggesting that more people criticised US diplomacy over the next couple of years as too soft than as too hard, the commonest view in September 1945 being that keeping on friendly terms with the Soviet Union was important 'but not so important that we should make too many concessions to her'.[50] There were reasons, ranging from the *prestige* of the possession of nuclear weapons to Russia's supposed need for financial assistance, why US leaders believed in mid-1945 that they had a strong hand. Although one can cite many acts of American appeasement over Eastern Europe, the *concept* of appeasement, as opposed to principled firmness, had been widely discredited by the events of the 1930s.

Another attitude was a disinclination, particularly prevalent in the Congress, to allow the rest of the world to cash blank cheques on Uncle Sam. This was not a specifically anti-Russian sentiment. In 1945–6 congressional consent for a loan to the UK was secured only with difficulty and through British undertakings as to the adoption of convertibility and the elimination of discriminatory tariffs that the USSR would never have given. The Soviet request for a loan in 1945 was initially stalled to enhance American bargaining power, but the US administration would not have found it easy to meet even had it wanted to. This general American attitude remained very relevant to the topics of reparations and of German currency: Washington believed that in the 1920s the cost of reparations had actually been met by the USA, and would not contemplate any Soviet (or French) moves that threatened to repeat the experience.

49. *History of the JCS.*, esp. i chap. 4, ii chaps 9, 10. The appreciation that the USSR could not be conquered dates from 1944 (i pp. 14–16), but subsequently the use of nuclear weapons was only expected to hamper Soviet overrunning of Western Europe and the Middle East and assist their eventual recovery

50. Truman, *FRUS*, 1945 v p. 233; Hadley Cantril (with Mildred Strunk), *Public Opinion 1935–1946* (Princeton, NJ, 1951) esp. pp. 962–4; see also George H. Quester, 'Origins of the Cold War: Some Clues from Public Opinion', *Political Science Quarterly*, xciii (1978–9)

Unfortunately experience soon taught the Russians that by far the best way of collecting reparations was to take over German factories and appropriate their production – which they simply did, disregarding the Potsdam agreement that the first claim (never even nearly met) on current production should be to cover the costs of the imports necessary to keep Germany fed. Their absolute insistence on this policy put the Soviets firmly in the wrong with the USA (and with Britain, which, being itself insolvent, resented still more having to finance its occupation zone).

Finally, during and after the Second World War, as earlier in 1919, the United States attached great importance to the United Nations and sought to make it a major actor in world politics. There were many strands to this approach, ranging from real enthusiasm for a new type of international relations to a belief that only through the UN would American public opinion consent to play a continuing role in world affairs and a comfortable knowledge that the UN was likely to vote the right way. Americans accordingly overreacted to the USSR's frequent use of its veto, and other defensive tactics in a body in which the socialist states were in a small minority. More justifiably, the reassertion by Soviet leaders (and its pointing up by US observers) of Marxist views of the fundamental cleavages and antagonisms between capitalist and socialist states occasioned genuine dismay, as did the disregard for the UN Charter and the Yalta Declaration on Liberated Europe evinced in the socialisation of Eastern Europe. Linked with the UN in a rather curious way was the question of the atom bomb. It was generally felt (especially in Congress) that the USA should preserve its monopoly, acting as the UN's 'trustee' at least until agreement was reached for conferring on the UN exclusive and veto-proof control of the production and use of fissionable material. Understandably such an enhancement of UN capabilities had no attractions for a Soviet Union that was vigorously developing its own bomb. But discoveries of its espionage activities to that end were initially disturbing, and by the end of the decade were a major contributor to the McCarthyite climate of opinion. The rejection of the Baruch Plan, and other Soviet actions emasculating the UN, were ill-received and ultimately led not only the USA but also other Western countries (notably Britain, Canada and France) to a determination to go it alone, outside either a UN or a Four Power framework.

BYRNES' 1945 APPROACH TO NEGOTIATING WITH THE USSR AND TRUMAN'S RESPONSE

East–West relations cooled progressively after the Second World War, but they did not just suddenly freeze. Negotiations, indeed, were incessant until the Council of Foreign Ministers meeting of December 1947, spasmodic for another eighteen months. If anything, however, negotiations – though not always unsuccessful – generally tended to worsen the atmosphere. This was due mostly, no doubt, to substantive differences between East and West, but also to a Soviet negotiating style that has irritated others besides Westerners; Mao Zedong once compared prising concessions out of Stalin in 1950 to getting 'a piece of meat from the mouth of a tiger'.[51] Soviet technique was, perhaps after an initial warmth, to pile on the pressure and retract earlier concessions until it became clear that nothing more could be obtained; positions might then be suddenly abandoned and settlement reached in a euphoric atmosphere (though not necessarily implemented thereafter). A risk inherent in this approach was that the other side might give up in disgust before the Soviets judged the time ripe for a settlement: Hitler may have done so when Molotov proved stubborn in November 1940, Marshall probably did before the March–April 1947 Moscow Council at which Stalin appeared at his most forthcoming over Germany.

Perhaps the most successful Western negotiator was Truman's first Secretary of State, Byrnes, who was initially in the Rooseveltian tradition of reluctance to 'gang up against' the Russians and readiness to deal over the head of the UK. He had been largely instrumental in securing a package settlement at the Potsdam summit (July–August 1945) – substantial acceptance of the USSR's unilateral gift of north-west Silesia[52] to Poland in exchange for Soviet acceptance of most of his ideas on German reparations and agreement on procedures for discussing peace treaties. Peace treaties were broached at the London Council of Foreign Ministers (September–October 1945). Here Molotov appeared both stubborn and irritating, a posture to which the US interest in Romania and Bulgaria (noted above) may have contributed. But the Russians clearly expected Byrnes to 'start trading'. That was indeed his

---

51. D. Wilson, *Mao: The People's Emperor* (1979) p. 266
52. Strictly, the land between the two rivers Neisse (which included Breslau and Leignitz)

intention, but one blocked by a Republican member of his delegation, John Foster Dulles.[53] Immediately after the conference's failure, however, Truman sought to reopen the dialogue, sending Ambassador Harriman to Stalin with a personal letter – which, however, made no reference to Japan. Stalin complained about the way in which the USA had so far monopolised occupation policy there. But he was not disposed to push the Japanese question too far: it had, as he hinted, useful parallels with the Soviet position in Eastern Europe; instead he suggested that the USSR might after all do better to stand aside and adopt 'a policy of isolation'. Quite what this meant he did not define. But Harriman took it to be one of unilateral action, with no reliance on the Western Powers for either economic or military aid;[54] some have seen it as a significant turning-point. The meeting ended amicably, with Stalin's consent to a peace conference, though without agreement on who should attend.

But the atmosphere that autumn in Moscow was chilly; Litvinov secretly told Harriman that the USA could now do nothing to improve relations, and the general party line accused the United States of nuclear blackmail in the Balkans. Harriman, indeed, accepted the view that the hardening of the Soviet position stemmed partly from the bomb's having suddenly revived traditional feelings of insecurity. Perhaps for this reason Byrnes sought to use proposals for sharing scientific nuclear information to secure another package deal. This was to be a centre-piece of the Three Power Foreign Ministers' meeting which he arranged (with minimal consultation of Britain) for December 1945 in Moscow. Agreements were indeed concluded: there should, as the USA wished, be a UN Atomic Energy Commission to control nuclear weapons and materials and share knowledge, though, as the USSR insisted, it should report to the Security Council, not the veto-proof General Assembly; a consultative Allied Council should be established in Tokyo, but General MacArthur's decisions would be 'controlling'; the Romanian and Bulgarian governments should be recognised after they had taken in two more non-communists and given assurances of their intention to hold free elections; and the composition and date of a peace conference was fixed.

Byrnes clearly regarded this as a great success. Truman did not. He resented the high-handed way in which Byrnes had bypassed

53. Yergin, *Shattered Peace* pp. 127, 129–30
54. Harriman, *Envoy to Churchill and Stalin* pp. 510–16

instructions and held back information. Truman had also been lobbied by influential senators, again partly as a result of Byrnes's style but largely because they feared that, to secure an agreement, he was giving way on vital nuclear safeguards. Truman also deplored the omission in the final communiqué of all reference to 'Iran or any other place where the Soviets were on the march. We had gained only an empty promise of further talks.' Bevin had in fact asked awkward questions on Iran at the conference, but Byrnes had settled over his head. When Byrnes got back to Washington, Truman finally plucked up courage to tell him off. Thereafter, though he did not abandon (nor Truman wish him to) his search for bargains, his line was distinctly tougher. In September, when Commerce Secretary Wallace publicly protested, Byrnes (now supported by Senators Vandenberg and Connally) secured his dismissal.

THE BARUCH PLAN, AND THE EUROPEAN PEACE TREATIES 1946–7

On the diplomatic level 1946, like 1945, saw only limited progress, but no catastrophic break. What appeared to be the major event were the UN discussions on atomic energy. Many people (including Acheson, who was not usually a dove) believed that the USA could share with the USSR both scientific information and fissionable material so treated as to remove its weapons potential, while giving the UN a monopoly of bombs and the materials from which they could be made. The dangers were obvious, and the US plan hardened in the course of bureaucratic infighting. As melo-dramatically presented – 'We are here to make a choice between the quick and the dead' – by Baruch in June, it insisted on prior safeguards. Only when all countries had allowed surveys and controls of their reserves, mining and processing of nuclear materials would the USA surrender its stockpile; to promote confidence there should be 'condign punishment' for infractions, and the UN's Atomic Development Authority should not be subject to veto. There can never have been any prospect of Stalin opening his country to such detailed inspection; nor could he have had any interest in suspending his own nuclear programme to leave a US monopoly in the transitional phase, a UN one thereafter. The Soviet counter-proposal, an initial uninspected sharing of scientific information and establishment of safeguards that would be subject to veto, was even less convincing. Baruch settled down to playing subsequent negotiations for the propaganda value of the USSR's rejection of a plan that would have so enhanced the UN's standing and ability to maintain peace.[55]

Although the Baruch Plan failed, negotiations over the Italian and East European peace treaties, while excruciatingly slow, eventually succeeded. Byrnes had a shrewd sense of timing, and his apparent readiness to abandon proceedings brought Molotov suddenly to reverse his position on a number of occasions. But it cannot be said that the treaties (formally signed in early 1947) mattered very greatly: the human rights clauses of the East European treaties were not adhered to, nor did the restrictions on Italian armed forces last. If anything, the enhanced legitimacy that the treaties conferred on Romania, Bulgaria and Hungary probably facilitated the final extinction, in 1947, of non-communist politics. What mattered a good deal more were US perceptions of a Soviet challenge and of the appropriate response, and the way in which the Powers handled the most important country that they (in theory) jointly occupied, Germany.

KENNAN'S LONG TELEGRAM 1946

As we have seen, by December 1945 Truman despaired of Bulgaria, anticipated a Soviet move to take the Black Sea Straits and create another 'accomplished fact', but did not know how to respond. To some extent the question was resolved *ambulando*. Strong diplomatic pressure appeared to secure Soviet evacuation of northern Iran, diplomatic support and naval demonstrations to sustain Turkey. But 1946 also saw the emergence of a coherent rationale for US action, containment. At the end of February 1946 Kennan, from the Moscow Embassy, dispatched his celebrated 'Long Telegram', deriving Soviet behaviour and hostility from internal and ideological causes, and arguing that it was responsive not to appeals or cajolery but only to external constraint:

> It does not take unnecessary risks. Impervious to logic of reason, it is highly sensitive to logic of force. For this reason it can easily withdraw – and usually does – when strong resistance is encountered at any point.

55. Herken, *Winning Weapon* chaps 8, 9

Thus, if the adversary has sufficient force and makes clear his readiness to use it, he rarely has to do so. If situations are properly handled there need be no prestige-engaging show-downs.

Further, 'World communism is like a malignant parasite that feeds only on diseased tissue'. One should, therefore, deny it opportunities by affording a more positive leadership to a war-torn Europe.

Kennan's Telegram enjoyed enormous success in official Washington, largely because it expressed clearly and cogently attitudes that many people from the President down were instinctively coming to adopt. However, it still left some questions unresolved. Should the United States resist all Soviet expansion, or only expansion in certain areas? How far should the USA go in resisting expansion? How, in practice, should it provide Europe with 'a much more constructive picture of the sort of world we would like to see than we have put forward in the past'? Answers to the first two questions were slow to emerge. By September 1946, after wide consultations, the presidential aide Clark Clifford was recommending that,

> If we find it impossible to enlist Soviet cooperation in the solution of world problems, we should be prepared to join with the British and other Western countries in an attempt to build up a world of our own which will pursue its own objectives and will recognise the Soviet orbit with which conflict is not predestined but with which we cannot pursue common aims.

Accordingly

> the United States should support and assist all democratic countries which are in any way menaced or endangered by the U.S.S.R. Providing military support in case of attack is a last resort; a more effective barrier to communism is strong economic support.

Truman's immediate reaction was to tell Clifford to lock his report up, as publicity 'could have an exceedingly unfortunate impact on our efforts to try to develop some relationship with the Soviet Union'. But he was probably already in general sympathy with its approach; and, in the course of 1947, the USA came to act along the lines that Clifford suggested.[56]

---

56. Kennan's telegram, *FRUS*, 1946 vi pp. 707–9; Clifford's report, Arthur Krock, *Memoirs. Sixty Years on the Firing Line*, (New York, 1968), esp. pp. 476, 479; Truman's reaction, Yergin, *Shattered Peace* p. 245

BRITISH WITHDRAWAL FROM GREECE AND TURKEY – THE TRUMAN DOCTRINE 1947

Two external stimuli brought it to do so, developments in the Balkans and in Germany/Western Europe. We have already seen that Soviet pressure led Turkey to keep its army mobilised at considerable expense. Further west Tito, despite much British aid during the war, was looking to advance his interests by a tough and ultra-communist line. In 1945 New Zealand forces had excluded the Yugoslavs from Trieste, an Italian port with a Slav hinterland; in 1946 Yugoslavia and the USSR pushed hard, though unavailingly, for it in connection with the Italian peace treaty, Yugoslavia reinforcing its pressure by shooting down two US supply planes en route for Austria.[57] To the south, Yugoslavia (or its satellite Albania) mined the Corfu channel, blowing up two British warships. Later both backed a communist rising in a Greece that was in no shape economically to sustain the necessary military counter-measures. Greece, like Turkey, was in the British Middle Eastern sphere, and had in 1945–6 cost Britain some £132 million.[58] It had for some time been the target of a search for economies; and in February 1947 Bevin was brought to concede the sudden termination of aid to both Greece and Turkey.

Bevin had feared that too many withdrawals – the same month saw a fuel crisis and massive industrial shutdowns, the dumping on to the UN of the Palestine problem, and the announcement of Britain's intention to quit India in 1948 – would make the USA feel that Britain was no longer worth supporting. In fact the decision over Greece and Turkey had the opposite effect. The US administration soon resolved on assistance, but it then had to secure approval of what some Congressmen saw as pulling British chestnuts out of the fire. Restrained advocacy by the new US Secretary of State, Marshall, fell flat, so Acheson went over the top: not since Rome and Carthage had there been such a polarisation of power, and it was further exacerbated by an unbridgeable ideological chasm. Initial Soviet successes would spread by contagion, like apples in a barrel infected by one rotten one (the better-known 1950s metaphor was like a row of dominoes), until eventually even the United States was threatened. Aid for Greece and Turkey was

---

57. This action apparently pleased the Russians, though Molotov also warned Yugoslavia not to go too far: Djilas, *Conversations with Stalin* p. 102

58. K.O. Morgan, *Labour in Power* (Oxford, 1984) pp. 252–3

not therefore a matter of bailing out the British but of building US security by strengthening free peoples against communist aggression and subversion. Impressed, Senator Vandenberg promised Truman support if he would publicly make the same plea to the Congress.

The result was the 'Truman Doctrine' of 12 March 1947, a request for $400 million for Greece and Turkey, buttressed by the potentially universalist prescription

> I believe it must be the policy of the United States to support free peoples who are resisting attempted subjugation by armed minorities or by outside pressures.
> I believe that we must assist free peoples to work out their own destinies in their own way.
> I believe that our help should be primarily through economic and financial aid which is essential to economic stability and orderly political processes.[59]

This Doctrine is often represented as a turning-point, but perhaps its significance can be exaggerated. It might have torpedoed the important Council of Foreign Ministers meeting then being held in Moscow, but does not in fact seem to have upset Stalin. It did not commit the United States to military intervention. Although the reference to free peoples resisting attempted subjugation was very broad, Acheson repeatedly explained to Congressmen that it was *not* meant either to encompass China or to sanction attempts to roll back Soviet control of Eastern Europe. It was, however, intended to pave the way for a further expansion of US aid to Western Europe: there had from the outset been acceptance that, though Greece and Turkey were the most urgent cases, they were not alone, and committees were set up in early March to study other countries in similar circumstances. On his return from what had proved an unsuccessful conference in Moscow, Marshall assigned this top priority.

THE GERMAN QUESTION 1945–7

The 1947 Moscow conference, too, is sometimes seen as a turning-point where a deal on Germany was missed. It would never have been easy to work the arrangements agreed in 1945 at Potsdam. Germany was to be treated as a single economic unit, and

---

59. RIIA, *Documents 1947–8* pp. 2–7 (esp. p. 6)

all-German administrative bodies were accordingly to be created. Overall policy was to be determined by a Four Power Control Council, subject to a veto and including a France that had not been admitted to the Potsdam conference and disliked some of its policies. But actual control in each zone lay with the occupying Power. Each Power should look primarily to its own zone for reparations for itself and/or its clients, and these should be taken by dismantling industrial plant surplus to the productive capacity the Four Powers adjudged appropriate for Germany as a whole; that determined, the first charge on actual production (and one that was not to be met for several years) was to be the financing of the imports of food and raw materials necessary to provide the German people with a low but acceptable standard of living. However, the Russians also held out for, and secured, agreement that 15 per cent of the equipment dismantled in the Western zones should be traded for food and raw materials from the East, 10 per cent dispatched East as simple reparations; but the total figure of which these were percentages could not be known until after the permissible production capacity for Germany had been determined. Basically these reparations provisions represented Soviet concessions (alleviated by some Western counter-concessions) in a package deal arranged by Byrnes at Potsdam that was in other respects (the Polish frontier) favourable to the Soviet Union; some of the pitfalls they might occasion had in fact been foreseen.[60]

Four Power control did not necessarily have to lead to partition. In Austria the Soviets installed a coalition government presided over by a distinguished but very elderly Socialist. The Anglo-Americans were reluctant to recognise this, fearing a repetition of East European developments, but did so against a token reconstruction and a promise of free elections. These were held in November

60. The USSR would have liked $10 billion (or at least $8 billion) reparations, at least $2 billion of which should have come from the Ruhr, which it would have liked to see under joint Four Power control. Britain would not allow such control. Byrnes suggested that attempts to put an agreed value on the material the USSR had already stripped from its zone would only lead to trouble, and that it would therefore be best if each Power collected reparations from its own zone (by his calculations the 50% – Molotov said 42% – of German wealth that was located in the Soviet zone would cover the 50% share of total reparations that the USSR sought); but the USSR insisted on receiving some reparations from the Western zones. That the financing of necessary imports should be the first charge on German production was to satisfy the absolute US and British refusal again to provide Germany with money so that it might pay reparations. These should therefore come from capital equipment, the limitation of which would also reduce the danger of Germany again emerging as a threat to its neighbours

1945, the communists polling only 5 per cent and being relegated to a minor portfolio. A universally recognised government with authority throughout the country was thus in place; and in 1946 it secured (with British assistance) revision of the Control agreement so that laws could be vetoed only by the joint action of all the occupying Powers, hence substantial self-government. (However, full independence was postponed until 1955 by a mixture of Soviet concern for economic advantage and the deteriorating international situation.) By contrast, in Germany, the government that concluded the surrender was extinguished almost immediately (as was not the case in Japan or Italy). No new one was ever appointed. It might, of course, have developed out of the all-German administrative bodies agreed at Potsdam. But France vetoed them when its wish to detach from Germany the Saar, Rhineland and Ruhr fell on deaf ears in the autumn of 1945. The USA regretted this, but did not pressurise France (then in a very shaky political condition); the Soviet Union theoretically supported a unified German state, but in practice wobbled on the issue of all-German bodies and might have blocked them if France had not.

By early 1946 there were already private doubts in both the USA and Britain as to whether it was either possible or desirable to work out with the USSR a solution for Germany within a Four Power framework; events that year certainly made such an outcome less likely. Agreement was reached in March, without too much difficulty, on the maximum level of industrial production to be permitted (about half that of 1938). This should have unlocked the door to the determination of which plants should be dismantled for reparations and to the drawing up of an import-export programme for the whole of Germany; but progress on the first was slow, on the second non-existent. The US response in May was to suspend reparations deliveries as a lever to force France and the USSR to resume Four Power cooperation. They also determined, when the moment was right, to offer to merge their zone with the British.

Britain, too, was moving towards a harder line. Whitehall had been concerned about the Soviets from a very early date; ministers took rather longer to be convinced. In March 1946 Bevin still favoured controlling the Ruhr through an international holding company with Soviet participation. But by May he felt that 'the danger of Russia has become certainly as great as, and possibly even greater than, that of a revived Germany. The worst situation of all would be a revived Germany in league with or dominated by Russia'. Against this background, he put to the Cabinet the question of whether 'we should continue to work towards a unified . . . Germany or . . . towards a West German State or States which would be more amenable to our influence'. The latter course

> would mean an irreparable breach with the Russians, who would go all out to destroy our policy in western Germany and turn the population against us. This task would not be too difficult in an industrial area in a period of acute food shortage. They would, no doubt, also redouble their attacks on us in all other parts of the world, and the prospect of U.N.O. continuing in such circumstances would be slender.
> . . . The Americans are probably not yet ready for this. . . . In any case one could not count on continued American support even if they came to agree to it. But full American support would be essential.

For this and other reasons, Bevin did not favour such a drastic course, and sought, at the forthcoming Council of Foreign Ministers session in Paris, the best of both worlds, 'development along [very loose] federal lines' that would not 'exclude the possibility of splitting Germany into two parts'. Meanwhile it would be necessary 'to apply the economic principles of Potsdam to the western zones even if the Russians refuse to collaborate, . . . to foster the solidarity of the western zones . . . [and] to act in the fullest collaboration with the Americans'. Lastly, if it was ever decided 'to abandon the idea of a united Germany, . . . it would be most important to ensure that responsibility for the break was put squarely on the Russians'.[61]

The Foreign Ministers made progress on several issues, but not on Germany. In July 1946 Bevin brought matters to a head by insisting on the full implementation of economic unity, with reparations subordinated to the elimination of the trade deficit that had to be met exclusively by Britain and the USA; otherwise the UK would go it alone and so organise its occupation zone that no further liability fell on the British taxpayer. Molotov responded with an unyielding statement that the USSR would continue to collect reparations from current production and would not send food from its zone west. At this point Byrnes made his offer to merge the US zone economically with any other. Britain agreed in late July to accept, and 'Bizonia' came into effect in January 1947. It would, the British realised, have important political implications: for if

> our reforms are given some time to operate German opinion of the Western powers is likely to change for the better. The French are unlikely to stand out of the arrangements for the unification of the two

61. 'Policy Towards Germany', 3 May 1946 (Public Record Office, Cab 129/9)

zones for long, and a temporary split between Eastern and Western Germany will be complete. The long term result . . . , given some kind of economic recovery, may well be that the Western zones are regarded by the Germans as 'Germany' and the Eastern zone as the lost provinces. A westward orientation of the Western zones might thus be effected, and a German desire stimulated for a Germany unified on our principles.[62]

The year 1946 also saw the start of the process, foretold by Hitler, whereby both the USSR and the USA would appeal for the allegiance of the German people. The USSR had certain initial advantages. It was at first markedly more successful in restoring economic life in its zone; also this being more agricultural and the Russians unwilling to send food west, they were able to feed their Germans better – General Clay observed that 'there is no choice between becoming a communist on 1500 calories and a believer in democracy on 1000'.[63] The Russians also played up to national sentiments. They allowed their political party to question the new border with Poland; in May 1946 Marshal Sokolovsky asserted (incorrectly) that the dismantling and removal of German industry had ended; at the Foreign Ministers' Council Molotov stressed the desirability of a united German state, free to develop its civilian industry beyond the currently approved levels, while implying that the West sought to agrarianise the country,[64] dismember it and detach the Ruhr. This invited retaliation in kind, which came with Byrnes's Stuttgart speech in September: Byrnes favoured German retention of the Ruhr (though not the Saar), gave only partial support to Polish annexations in the East, promised to help the Germans win back to 'an honorable place among the free and peace-loving nations', and, most importantly, promised that, as long as an occupation force was required, the US Army would form part of it – thus scotching rumours that while the Soviets would remain indefinitely, the Americans would soon go home.[65] Voting soon showed that, in this competition, the Russians were the less popular. In March 1946 a Socialist Party (SPD) referendum in the Western

---

62. Anne Deighton, *The Impossible Peace: Britain, the Division of Germany and the Origins of the Cold War* (Oxford, 1990) p. 134 and chaps 3–5

63. W. Krieger, 'Was General Clay a Revisionist? Strategic Aspects of the United States' Occupation of Germany', *Journal of Contemporary History* xviii (1983) p. 172. In Austria the Russians, at one point, deliberately obstructed the passage of food to the western sectors of Vienna

64. A reference to the Morgenthau Plan to reduce Germany to a 'pastoral' state, which had been official US-British policy for some months in 1944–5

65. Beate Ruhm von Oppen (ed.) *Documents on Germany under Occupation 1945–1954*, (1955) pp. 144 ff. (Molotov, 10 July 1946), pp. 152 ff (Byrnes, Stuttgart)

sectors of Berlin went heavily against Soviet-sponsored proposals to merge with the Communist Party. The merger still went ahead in (but only in) eastern Germany. However, though the new Socialist Unity Party (SED) secured a plurality in the Soviet zone in October, it gained only an embarrassing 20 per cent (to the SPD's 49 per cent) in Berlin. The Western Powers had contributed little to this result, beyond supervising the Berlin elections, but it was clearly encouraging for those who wished to go it alone.

Yet if 1946 saw growing division and disharmony on the ground in Germany, it did not necessarily close the door to an agreed peace treaty. In September 1945 Byrnes floated the idea of a twenty-five year Four Power Treaty to guarantee German demilitarisation; Molotov appeared to welcome it, as did Stalin in December. A draft was therefore submitted to Molotov in February, but he responded negatively in April. Byrnes then put it to him as something of a test question:

> it might serve as a reinsurance against any Soviet fears of a renewed attack by Germany and thus remove any element of doubt of the United States bearing its full share in safeguarding the peace [a course it had repudiated in 1920]. He said, frankly, there were many people in the United States who were unable to understand the exact aim of the Soviet Union – whether it was a search for security or expansionism. Such a treaty . . . and also the similar treaty suggested for Japan . . . would effectively take care of the question of security.

Molotov stalled; this may well have been a factor in Byrnes's private confession in May 1946 that 'he had almost given up hope for a united Germany' and come to think the Western zones could become a viable country. German questions did come before the Council of Foreign Ministers in July. As he admitted privately to Byrnes, Molotov was not ready to negotiate (hence, no doubt, the propaganda); but when asked what the Soviet Union really wanted, replied what it had asked at Yalta, $10 billion in reparations and Four Power control of the Ruhr. The picture we get from Djilas and Litvinov suggests that there may have been more, but Byrnes believed him, and some scholars have wondered whether a deal could not have been obtained on these terms.[66]

Agreement was reached in December 1946 to proceed with discussion of a peace treaty; there were some signs of greater Soviet warmth (perhaps not unconnected with the conclusion of the other peace treaties), and this persisted in the initial phases of the

66. *FRUS*, 1945 ii p. 268, 1946, ii pp. 146–7; Yergin, *Shattered Peace* pp. 225–6; James F. Byrnes, *Speaking Frankly* (1947) pp. 171–4, 194

Moscow Foreign Ministers' Conference in March 1947, despite the enunciation of the 'Truman Doctrine' on the 12th. But though some Americans (notably Clay) were hopeful of a deal, the general approach was pessimistic in the extreme; in late February a US State Department briefing ran that Marshall, the new (and tired) Secretary of State, 'is going to Moscow knowing in advance that nothing would be decided there for the peace of the world. . . . Our experience with them has proved by now that it is impossible to negotiate with them. It is either to yield to them or tell them no'.[67] In the event few concessions were made by *any* of the four parties, and both the USSR and the USA sought to reopen questions they had tacitly conceded at Potsdam. France was alone in seeking to detach the Rhine and Ruhr and also in wishing to give German coal deliveries abroad priority over the level of German industrial production, but was now prepared to concede central administrative agencies. There was, however, no agreement on who should run these. The Western Powers favoured representatives of the *Länder* (states), which they also insisted on entrenching within a new German constitution; the Russians preferring the re-establishment of Weimar (bar its presidential powers) though ready to refer the question to a plebiscite.

The conference therefore failed, and we cannot know what (beyond trouble with France) would have followed had the USA and UK sought agreement by substantially accepting the Soviet position. Probably nothing but further acrimony: the Soviets would not have found it easy to open up their zone, in which they had so far behaved unilaterally and for whose 'socialisation' – already begun through the process of land reform – there was (as we have seen) a good deal of Politburo support.[68] Nor, given the past record of Four Power control over Germany, would Four Power control over the Ruhr have been easy; Byrnes (and the British) saw it as 'an effective way of destroying the industries [there] . . ., which, properly supervised, are vital to an economically healthy Europe'.[69] But it can be argued that acceptance of the Soviet position would have been a reasonable price to pay for the installation

67. Yergin, *Shattered Peace* p. 297. Actually Marshall did show some flexibility over the Soviet desire for reparations from current production, but both Truman and Bevin proved discouraging and a meeting with Stalin finally disillusioned him

68. One illustration of the Soviet difficulty in making even minor concessions was Stalin's refusal (in an otherwise friendly talk with Bevin) to permit the emigration of the handful of women who had married Britons during the war

69. Byrnes, *Speaking Frankly* p. 194

of an elected all-German government. In this connection it is worth noting that, admittedly within a Western framework, a supranational Ruhr authority was ultimately conceded to French pressure. Although Anglo-American distaste for subsidising Germany while the Russians extracted reparations from it is understandable, the USA was just coming to the point of proposing the even larger politico-economic subventions of the Marshall Plan. Finally, nobody can determine what would have been the effect on the international system of a united Germany had one emerged from the Moscow conference. The necessity for watching it might have preserved a degree of East–West cooperation. Equally it might have sought to play East off against West in pursuit of national revival. Instead the next two decades were to see the increasing integration of the Soviet zone into the 'socialist camp' (effected largely by force), of the Western zones into a West European and North Atlantic world. This latter process was due largely to their perceived need for protection against the Soviet Union, but also to the ascendance of Adenauer's CDU (Christian Democratic Union) over the more nationalist SPD, an ascendance that would (for reasons of past electoral geography) have been unlikely had the inhabitants of the Soviet zone also been able to vote in 1949.

MARSHALL AID AND THE DIVISION OF EUROPE

Towards the end of the Moscow conference Stalin had tried to soothe Marshall – differences had occurred before only to be compromised eventually, there was no need to be desperate, etc. – but the attempt was counter-productive. Marshall was deeply impressed by 'Stalin's seeming indifference to what was happening in Germany' and concluded that he felt 'the best way to advance Soviet interests was to let matters drift'. Marshall was already under pressure from Bevin to increase the permitted level of Bizone production, and 'All the way back to Washington, . . . [he] talked of the importance of finding some initiative to prevent the complete breakdown of Western Europe'.[70] The initiative was to be an increase of American aid, rendered the more urgent as UNRRA (under which e.g. Italy had received $589 million) was about to come to an end. State Department planning had, as we have seen,

---

70. Taubman, *Stalin's American Policy* p. 158 (quoting Bohlen)

been in progress since March; the ground was prepared by a speech of Acheson's in May that estimated that Europe would need $5 billion per year for several years; at Harvard in June 1947 Marshall professed readiness to assist 'the revival of a working economy in the world so as to permit the emergence of political and social conditions in which free institutions can exist'; should the Europeans draw up a programme to that end, the United States would support it 'so far as it may be practical for us to do so'. It was a deliberately low-key launch, but the State Department was under no illusions as to the effect it could have in dividing Europe.

In fact the division of Europe was already proceeding very fast. In January 1947 Mikolajczyk's Peasant Party was crushed in Polish elections that Khrushchev admits were rigged – he enjoyed the joke, 'What sort of box is this? You drop Mikolajczyk in, but get Gomulka out'.[71] In Hungary a round of arrests, starting in December 1946, and the 'revelations' of conspiracy they produced, emasculated the Smallholders Party, whose secretary was interned in February; the screw was tightened again after the failure of the Moscow conference, and the Prime Minister persuaded to retire into exile in late May 1947. The opposite process occurred in Belgium, and in France and Italy, both of which had large Communist parties. Neither had tried to seize power at the Liberation, the French PCF believing itself too weak, the Italian PCI feeling that at best it could only take over in the north and that this would destroy national unity and entrench a reactionary regime in the south. So both embarked on what they envisaged as a long period of coalition government, within which they naturally sought to push their fortunes but not too dramatically; we have seen that in September 1946 Stalin apparently endorsed such an approach in France. Nevertheless many people were suspicious, and the difficulties of working with the communists increased over time, seriously hampering the conduct of economic policy. Early in May 1947 the communists were dismissed from the French government after unwisely voting against its (increasingly unpopular) incomes policy. At the end of the month an Italian political crisis was ended by the formation of an almost exclusively Christian Democrat (DC) government. In both cases the communists, who had believed themselves indispensable, were taken by surprise and went quietly, though the French government had feared a coup and prepared against it. The initiative in shedding the communists appears to

71. *Khrushchev Remembers*, ii p. 174; Kaplan, 'Il piano di Stalin' p. 174

have been local, taken by socialist ministers in France, by the DC Premier de Gasperi in Italy.[72] The US ambassadors offered private encouragement (in the French case even assistance in contingency planning). Equally de Gasperi used the threat (that if his new government failed, the only alternative would be one of the far left) to extract from the USA financial aid,[73] and a departure from its previously neutral stance on internal Italian politics.[74]

After Marshall's speech Bevin and Bidault sought a European conference to draw up the recovery programme he had called for, and carefully invited Molotov to Paris in late June 1947 to discuss the joint issuing of invitations. Molotov was to tell Djilas 'that he had at first leaned towards participation, but that the Politburo had disavowed the Marshall Plan and directed him to oppose it'.[75] This was a major blunder. The proper course would have been to cooperate, thus returning the ball to the American court. For the unspecific inclusion of all Europe in the American initiative had been 'a calculated risk both as regards the Russians and Congress' taken to prevent the USA incurring the blame for dividing the continent. The risk was that 'If the Russians came in the whole project would probably be unworkable because the amount of money involved in restoring both Eastern and Western Europe would be so colossal it could never be got from Congress, especially in view of the strong and growing reaction against the Soviet Union'.[76]

The British and French governments were, for similar reasons, equally relieved by Molotov's intransigence and proceeded without him, inviting all European countries except the USSR and Franco's Spain to meet in July. This posed the threat to Soviet control in Eastern Europe that, if countries there were to participate in a planned continental recovery programme, they would have to reorient their economies to the West and open them to a measure of external supervision, with possible political consequences.

72. See e.g. Eugenio Reale, *Avec Jaques Duclos au Banc des Accusés à la réunion Constitutive du Kominform*, tr. P. Bonuzzi (Paris, 1960), pp. 81–2 (France), p. 134 (Italy)

73. A year earlier Léon Blum had already reinforced his plea for a US loan by emphasising the imminence of elections and stressing that, without help, France 'would enter into one of those states of evolution whose end could not be predicted'

74. A. Platt and R. Leonardi, 'American Foreign Policy and the Postwar Italian Left', *Political Science Quarterly*, xciii (1978–9) esp. pp. 198–9; *FRUS*, 1947 iii esp. pp. 893–5, 904–13

75. M. Djilas, *Rise and Fall* (1985) p. 127

76. Acheson's recollections, as recorded in Jones, *The Fifteen Weeks* pp. 252–3

Perhaps through an oversight, Czechoslovakia was not initially instructed to refuse the invitation and (like Poland) decided to attend. At which point its (communist) Prime Minister was summoned to Moscow and abruptly ordered to stay away.[77] Accordingly the six East European states under communist control, plus Czechoslovakia and Finland, all refused to come, and the (difficult) process of drawing up a recovery programme proceeded without them.

Stalin then added a second blunder by seeking to use the Western communist parties to sabotage the programme. On their exclusion from office the Italian and French parties had remained fairly moderate, hoping to return to the government coalition and looking for alliances with left-wing elements of the governing parties. The PCI at least also favoured accepting Marshall Aid. In September 1947 both were summoned to a conference in Poland, stage-managed by Zhdanov and Malenkov. They were roughly harangued and forced to practise self-criticism: Duclos confessed to 'opportunism, legalitarianism, parliamentary illusions' and promised to 'mobilise the people of France against American imperialism'. Zhdanov concluded by ruling out an armed uprising as hopeless, but instructing the PCF to view itself as a party of opposition and demanding violent attacks on the socialists.[78]

Why Stalin reacted so strongly to the Marshall Plan we can only speculate. But he had probably pinned his hopes for communist expansion on to an economic collapse of Western Europe. He had, Khrushchev recalls, been

> convinced that after the war Germany would stage a revolution and follow the path of creating a proletarian state. Stalin wasn't the only one who incorrectly predicted this. All of us thought it would happen, because we wanted it so much . . .
>
> We had the same hopes for France and Italy. . . . Just as Russia came out of World War I, made the revolution, and established Soviet power, so after the catastrophe of World War II, Europe too might become Soviet. Everyone would take the path from capitalism to socialism.
>
> However, after Potsdam, events did not develop in our favor. The powerful economy of the United States prevented the devastated economies of the European countries from reaching the point of a revolutionary explosion. Things did not happen the way we wanted and

---

77. *FRUS*, 1947 iii pp. 319–20

78. Reale, *Avec Jacques Duclos* esp. pp. 23, 34, 81–2, 131, 134, 138–9, 153–4, 163, 175–7. Kardelj asserted that 'Peaceful development of socialism by parliamentary manoeuvres' was only possible in 'eastern countries like Poland and Bulgaria, where the directing role belongs to Communist Parties with solid positions acquired during the armed struggle'

predicted in accordance with Marxist-Leninist theory. Unfortunately, all these countries stayed capitalist, and we were disappointed.[79]

The order that communist parties should go into outright opposition in a last-ditch attempt to block the Marshall Plan had the effect of internalising the Cold War into the politics of (at least) France and Italy, in both of which, for over two decades, a substantial minority identified with Moscow rather than with their own government. (In Italy indeed the cleavage between Moscow and Washington was for many years the principal one in politics.) In November 1947 the communist-led French trades union federation called for general strikes. These soon had 3 million workers out and many factories occupied, and led later to explosions and train derailments. They brought down the government and created an atmosphere of crisis. But a new government mobilised army reservists, disbanded communist units of the riot police and deployed the remainder, and passed fierce anti-picketing legislation. With British encouragement, the USA helped by extending interim financial aid, but it also provided more covert assistance. Thus, responding inter alia to an appeal from Léon Blum, it financed a breakaway anti-communist trades union movement (the *Force Ouvrière*); the money came initially from the American unions,[80] but the cost ($1 million per year by the early 1950s) was later assumed by the CIA. Italy, which was not evacuated by Anglo-American troops till December 1947, was quieter. But all manner of dangers were anticipated in connection with the 1948 elections, which the communists and majority socialists contested as a Popular Front – helped, it was believed, by both Soviet subventions and captured fascist gold. A major operation was launched to influence the result, ranging from public promises over Trieste and threats that US aid would be cut in the event of a communist victory, to coordinated lobbying by Italian-Americans and the expenditure of some $10 million on electoral organisation, bribes and propaganda. This involvement had its limits: military intervention was excluded except in response to a Communist rising *after* electoral defeat.[81] But the question did not arise, the DC

79. *Khrushchev Remembers* iii pp. 99–100; see also Taubman, *Stalin's American Policy* pp. 135–9

80. These had worried as early as 1945 about a communist take-over of Europe, and so had assisted non-communist unions

81. Although if the communists obtained *domination* of the Italian government by legal means, the National Security Council recommended US support for 'the anti-Communist Italian underground'

(helped also by the Church, and by indigenous anti-communist sentiment) unexpectedly gained 49 per cent to the Popular Front's 31 per cent. This was deemed to prove the efficacy of covert action, which, from having previously been very small beer,[82] now grew fast both geographically and financially (the budget of the 'Office of Policy Coordination' increasing from $4.7 million in early 1949 to $200 million in 1953).[83]

WEST GERMAN CURRENCY REFORM 1948

Contemporaneous with the French strikes was the London Foreign Ministers' meeting in November–December 1947, held to resume discussion of Germany after the spring failure of the Moscow conference. As at Paris over the economic recovery programme, so now the Western Powers were determined to proceed whatever the Soviet attitude. Such determination, Bevin felt, might just produce a last-minute Soviet U-turn and agreement; but the worst possible outcome, and the one the Russians were thought to favour, was endless indecision that would prevent German, hence West European, economic and political revival. Unsurprisingly the London conference failed, the sticking point being Soviet refusal to agree, in advance of a general reparations settlement, that the Powers should account for the reparations they had so far removed. One last initiative was then made within a Four Power framework, an Anglo-American attempt to secure Allied Control Council agreement on an all-German currency reform. But relationships within the Council cooled rapidly in March (partly no doubt in response to the meeting of another, purely Western, London conference on Germany) and the Russians walked out for good on 20 March 1948. Thereafter both Western and Eastern currency reforms went ahead in parallel.

Even gaining Western agreement was not easy, and the extension of currency reform to the French zone needed eleventh-hour crisis

82. The Church Committee dated the first covert action to 1947; Barnes (articles cited in n. 83) suspects 1946, and mentions that subsidies for the centrist French press date from an approach by a Resistance hero in 1945

83. R.W. Johnson, *The Long March of the French Left* (1981) chap. 2; P.M. Williams, *Crisis and Compromise: Politics in the Fourth Republic* (1964) p. 347; Platt and Leonardi, pp. 201–2; Trevor Barnes, 'The Secret Cold War: The C.I.A. and American Foreign Policy in Europe, 1946–56' (2 parts), *Historical Journal* xxiv and xxv (1981, 1982)

negotiations. French consent stemmed mainly from the changed international situation (especially after the February–March Prague 'coup'), and from limited British concessions over control of the Ruhr – but also from the manifest Anglo-American readiness to go it alone in Bizonia, and from US hints that they would enter no commitments against either German or Soviet aggression unless agreement was reached.[84] In the end, though, 20 June 1948 saw the implementation in all three zones of what turned out to be a spectacularly successful package of currency reform and economic liberalisation. The London conference also called for an assembly to draft a constitution for what would presumably become a new West German state.

Stalin must have expected this: in January and February he had told Yugoslav and Bulgarian delegations that 'The West will make Western Germany their own, and we shall turn Eastern Germany into our own state'.[85] But such an outcome entailed risks since, if only for reasons of size, Western Germany was the more likely of the two to become the embodiment of German national sentiment. (Bevin had in fact written in January that, though the division of Germany was likely to deepen, it would not last indefinitely: 'The problem for us is to bring unity about as soon as possible but in such a way as to ensure that the forces of attraction operate from the West upon the East and not vice versa'.)[86] So Stalin tried exerting pressure by squeezing Berlin, a city under Four Power occupation but deep within the Soviet zone.

THE BERLIN BLOCKADE 1948–9

The first half of 1948 saw a number of interferences with Western overland access;[87] they hardened convictions that to abandon Berlin would be a great blow to Western prestige and thus to the growing Western alignment of the rest of Europe. In June the USSR shut off both electricity supplies and overland communication to the Western sectors. The immediate occasion was a dispute over

84. *FRUS*, 1948 ii pp. 275–7
85. Djilas, *Conversations with Stalin* p. 119
86. Alan Bullock, *Ernest Bevin: Foreign Secretary 1945–51* (1983) p. 515
87. Arrangements for overland access to Berlin's Western sectors had been agreed orally between the Americans and Russians in June 1945, a supplementary agreement about air corridors being committed to writing that September

which currency (the Soviet zone mark *tout court*, the Soviet mark but issued under Four Power supervision, or both the Soviet and Western marks)[88] should be used in Berlin. But the USSR made it clear that its real concern was to stop the convocation of a West German constituent assembly and return the German question to a Four Power basis, though a hint was also dropped that friction could be avoided if the West would swap its sectors of Berlin for a slice of the Soviet zone (an interesting idea that was never followed up).

A blockade of Berlin had been forecast, but no agreement sought as to how to counter it. General Clay believed that the Russians were only bluffing, and that they would not in fact interfere with an army-escorted land convoy. But he could not convince anybody else. Instead Britain and the USA tried an airlift. This was a fairly desperate expedient to buy time, since West Berlin had stockpiles for only between one and two months and nobody in mid-1948 believed that 2.5 million civilians could be indefinitely supplied by air: on 27 June Marshall talked of zero hour not being reached for two to three weeks, and as late as 19 July it was thought the airlift would be viable only till October. But the hope that, within this time, diplomatic discussions could be opened was well founded. Indeed on 2 August Stalin suddenly suggested to the Western ambassadors in Moscow a lifting of the blockade on conditions that they personally regarded as acceptable.[89] But when it came to working out the details both sides hardened their positions, and though things again looked promising in late August, they stalled in September, then again at the UN in October–November. By which time, having failed to paralyse the elected Berlin government by mob violence, the Soviets established a breakaway government for their sector and settled down to wait for

---

88. Britain and France induced the USA to accept the Soviet mark. But all insisted that its printing would have to be under Four Power supervision, since the USA had long suspected – perhaps unjustly (J H Backer, *The Decision to Divide Germany* (Durham, NC, 1978) pp. 123 ff) – the Russians of lavishly printing occupation currency that then had to be supported with dollars. (The suspicion, and insistence on supervision, had earlier blocked all ideas of a joint currency reform for Germany as a whole.) The Russians rejected supervision and unilaterally introduced their currency to the whole of Berlin; on US insistence the West mark was introduced as of equal legal status with the Soviet in the Western sectors. The Soviets replied with the blockade and a proclamation declaring the end of Four Power government of the city

89. Berlin should use the Soviet mark, and there should be a Four Power meeting on Germany. Suspension of the London Conference decisions was not a precondition, though it should be recorded as the Soviets' 'insistent wish'

the winter. With the advent of fog in late December supplies fell very low, but recovered with the return of fine weather in January 1949. Stalin first hinted at the lifting of the blockade late that month – a counter-embargo on deliveries from western Germany had hit hard[90] – and, after leisurely back-channel negotiations, the blockade ended in May 1949 against an agreement to hold a Four Power meeting on Germany later that month. By now, though, new constitutions had been adopted in both Eastern and Western Germany; unsurprisingly the Four Power meeting brought no agreement.

In negotiations during the blockade France and Britain had sometimes favoured a softer line than the USA, which could have led to trouble had conditions become critical. Both, however, contributed energetically to the airlift. It succeeded, but only as a result of the concentration on Berlin of much of the Anglo-American transport capacity – over the protests of the ever-timorous US Chiefs of Staff. The decision to do so had been made possible by Western confidence (slightly dented in September–October 1948) that the Russians did not intend war and would therefore not allow things to escalate further, a confidence reinforced by the US stockpile of fifty atom bombs. Truman still withheld these bombs from military control, but June–July 1948 saw British requests for the basing of nuclear bombers in the UK as a deterrent. The USA *appeared* to comply.[91] Some at least of the Americans supporting these requests reckoned, correctly, that, once deployed, the planes would become an accepted fixture. One result of the Berlin Blockade, therefore, was to provide the USA with forward bases. Still more important was its effect on relations between Berliners, and to a lesser extent West Germans, and the occupying Powers. For the latter Berlin was transmogrified into a symbol of freedom, while in December 1948 elections West Berliners overwhelmingly endorsed their occupiers as partners and protectors. In West Germany itself the effect was less marked: when (in late 1949) the Opposition called Adenauer 'the Chancellor of the Allies' it was not a compliment. But the Western refusal to abandon Berlin and the generally (though not universally) perceived need for protection against further communist expansion was one reason why relations

90. Also on deliveries through the US zone; more forceful measures, like closing the exits to the Black and Baltic Seas, were never risked

91. Actually the aircraft dispatched, though of the appropriate configuration, had not been converted to deliver atom bombs. Converted bombers did not come until 1949

in the 1950s ran more smoothly than they had done in the 1920s. The blockade had been another of Stalin's mistakes.[92]

THE NORTH ATLANTIC TREATY 1949

In June 1947 the US administration had proposed, and almost a year later Congress had legislated for, economic assistance to promote an Atlantic-oriented West European recovery. Security was the other side of the coin. It is arguable that the first country to seek a multilateral security system outside the UN was Canada.[93] Be that as it may, in early December 1947 one Canadian reported his impression that the US authorities 'were casting about to see if proposals for a Mutual Defence Treaty could not be brought forward from some other source than themselves'.[94] If so, Bevin soon obliged them, floating rather vague ideas of a 'Western democratic system' 'with the backing of the Americas and the Dominions' between December 1947 and January 1948. The US State Department made encouraging noises and urged both on Bevin and on Spaak of Belgium the example of the September 1947 Rio Inter-American Treaty of Reciprocal Assistance. Bevin then made a public call for a Western Union based on treaties between the UK, France and the Benelux powers. Within a couple of months he had secured both the multilateral Brussels Treaty between these countries (directed against any revival of German aggression but also providing for mutual assistance in the event of 'an armed attack in Europe') and the inauguration of secret Anglo-Canadian-US discussions in Washington 'on the establishment of an Atlantic security system'. The pace had undoubtedly been increased by the Prague 'coup' in February 1948 which, though discounted in advance, nevertheless horrified the West when it actually happened, and by simultaneous Soviet pressure on Norway and Finland. Subsequent negotiations were

92. The best study of the blockade is A. Shlaim, *The United States and the Berlin Blockade 1948–1949* (Berkeley, Calif., 1983)

93. East–West considerations apart, Canada sought in an alliance what it had failed to find in the UN, an effective multilateral context that would afford it more scope than would bilateral dealings with the overwhelmingly larger USA

94. J.W. Holmes, *Canada and the Search for World Order 1943–1957*, ii (Toronto, 1983) p. 105

slower and more difficult. There were differences as to which countries should be included in a North Atlantic Treaty, whether it should cover what was then the Algerian portion of metropolitan France, and above all as to how it could be made acceptable to Congress in view of the traditional US suspicion of entangling alliances. But a fillip was given to proceedings by the unexpected Democrat victory in the 1948 elections, and a treaty finally signed in April 1949.

Obviously the treaty was meant to deter: in Bevin's words, 'to inspire the Soviet Government with enough respect for the West to remove temptation from them and so ensure a long period of peace'. But on both sides of the Atlantic people looked quite as much to its psychological effects *within* Western Europe: in Bevin's words,

> Another essential thing . . . is to give confidence. That confidence would have very great repercussions and make the economic steps that have been taken more effective. Therefore the construction of a North Atlantic defence system would put heart into the whole of western Europe and would encourage them in their resistance to the infiltration tactics which they have had to face hitherto.

Kennan was more forthright: the basic Russian intent was 'the conquest of western Europe by political means', military force playing 'a major role only as a means of intimidation'; 'A North Atlantic Security Pact will affect the political war only insofar as it operates to stiffen the self-confidence of the western Europeans in the face of Soviet pressure'; indeed 'the need for military alliances and rearmament on the part of the western Europeans is primarily a *subjective* one . . .'. Beyond this, both Bevin and Kennan had their eye on the treaty's broader implications for the German question, Kennan arguing that only a Western union 'holds out any hope of restoring the balance of power in Europe without permitting Germany to become again the dominant power', Bevin that 'if the new defence system is so framed that it relates to any aggressor [i.e. to Germany as well as the USSR] it would give all the European states such confidence that it might well be that the age-long trouble between Germany and France might tend to disappear'.[95]

95. *FRUS*, 1948 iii esp. pp. 48, 78–9 (Bevin), pp. 7, 285 (Kennan); on this occasion Kennan's views appear to have been generally accepted in the US State Department

SHIFTS IN US POLICY; THE EXTENSION OF 'CONTAINMENT' TO EAST ASIA

I have stressed non-military aspects of the North Atlantic Treaty because I see the United States, in the late 1940s, operating rather as it had done in 1940–1, that is keeping what it perceived as indirect security threats at a distance by buttressing, with economic aid and off-shore military support, friendly Powers that were geographically nearer the front line. In 1941 this policy had been finally destroyed by its response to Japan's occupation of southern Indo-China. In 1950 events in Korea were to play a similar role. But the policy's foundations had already been called into question by the Soviet explosion of an atomic device in September 1949.

Postwar American military expenditure had been kept low – a ceiling of $15 billion per year was imposed in 1948 – partly in the belief that the USSR was not seeking a hot war, but also through confidence stemming from the US nuclear monopoly. In theory people accepted that this monopoly would not last, but in practice they behaved as if it would, and were correspondingly jolted by the Russian test. One response was Truman's rapid authorisation of the development of a hydrogen bomb, but another was a general survey of the US strategic position and needs. This survey (NSC-68), drafted in February–March 1950, has become famous, perhaps too much so.[96] Its purpose, one of its chief sponsors (Acheson) has recalled, 'was to so bludgeon the mass mind of "top government" that not only could the President make a decision [for rearmament] but that the decision could be carried out'. Accordingly it did not understate the drive of Soviet military spending, and, while admitting that the USSR 'followed the sound principle of seeking maximum results with minimum risks and commitments', stressed that there was no ground 'for predicting that, should the Kremlin become convinced that it could cause our downfall by one conclusive blow, it would not seek that solution'; it guessed that the USSR might have sufficient bombs for a surprise attack on the USA by mid-1954. The recommendation was a rapid American build-up, both to limit this danger and to acquire non-nuclear options to preclude the risk of having no better choice than to capitulate or precipitate a global war 'at any of a number of pressure points'.

96. Text in *FRUS*, 1950 i pp. 237 ff. Its bureaucratic fortunes and significance are discussed by Paul Hammond in W.R. Schilling, P.Y. Hammond and G.H. Snyder, *Strategy, Politics and Defense Budgets* (New York, 1962), chap. 2. See also Dean Acheson, *Present at the Creation* (1970) pp. 343, 347–9, 373–5

The nature and cost of this build-up was deliberately left unspecified – the State Department was thinking in terms of a $35 billion or even $50 billion defence budget, service planners of perhaps $18 billion[97] – but NSC-68 did challenge the conventional economics then dominant, observing that the programme might even boost the US economy and increase personal consumption (as had occurred between 1939 and 1944). Truman promptly referred the document for further detail and costing. There is no evidence that it affected his response to the outbreak of fighting in Korea in June. Accordingly it was not, in itself, a cause of the 'globalisation' of containment as is sometimes suggested. Indeed it is far from clear that, but for the Korean War, NSC–68 would even have produced a great change in defence spending. Truman continued to talk of the possibility of a *reduced* defence budget, the Chairman of the Senate Finance Committee seems to have regarded NSC-68's arguments as sound but politically unrealistic,[98] and its military sponsors would have been satisfied with comparatively small increases. However the Korean War appeared to validate NSC–68's forebodings. The war would in any case have led to significant rearmament. The existence of NSC–68 further eased the way, stilling doubts as to the economic consequences and providing a framework in which rearmament appeared not as a panic reaction but as the response to a considered appraisal of need.

That said, the Korean War remains the primary cause of the shift in the US stance. To understand it we must go back a little. In the immediately postwar period continental East Asia had not been a primary concern of either the Soviet Union or the United States. At Yalta Stalin's readiness to enter the war against Japan had secured Russia promises, roughly, of a return to the position it had enjoyed before its defeat by Japan forty years earlier. In August 1945 he made sure of them on the ground, and also secured the acquiescence of the Chinese Nationalist government under Chiang Kai-Shek. This acquiescence must have seemed to Stalin a positive feature, not lightly to be cast away, and may have explained his recognition of (and continued negotiation with) that government well into 1949. But to keep it weak the USSR continued its long-standing assistance to the Chinese communists, albeit fairly tepidly, and also its desultory penetration of the lightly settled central Asian borderlands. It also gave a high priority to looting

97. Schilling, Hammond and Snyder, *Strategy, Politics and Defense Budgets* p. 319
98. ibid, pp. 329, 331

Manchurian industry, but then withdrew in such a way as to leave the Nationalists in control in most of the south, the communists in the north and east. The Russians also enabled the communists to capture Japanese arms, and, when some were pushed over the border into Korea in 1946, regrouped and returned them next year with an added Korean contingent. Stalin clearly wished to keep the communist armies in being. But in January 1948 he privately offered the Nationalist government his mediation in the Civil War, and also confessed to the Yugoslavs that he had discouraged communist offensives and been surprised by their success. An early communist take-over of the whole of China can have formed no part of his postwar plans.[99]

US policy was also mixed. There was a long-standing sentimental attachment to China. Roosevelt, who had a better recognition of China's long-term potential than any other world statesman, pushed the country prematurely as one of the 'Four Policemen' with a permanent seat on the UN Security Council. The USA airlifted Kuomintang (KMT) troops, and even deployed its own, to limit communist gains in the scramble for territory that followed the Japanese surrender. On the other hand it pressed for the re-constitution of the KMT–communist coalition ostensibly concluded in 1937, its special ambassador General Marshall appearing to achieve considerable success in the first half of 1946. But Chiang then decided to drive for victory. For almost a year he appeared to be achieving it, but by mid-1947 his Nationalist forces were over-extended, and, although still numerically superior, were tied up in garrison duty, to be cut off by communist guerrillas and harassed by counter-offensives. In 1948 they were catastrophically defeated in both Manchuria and north-eastern China. In 1949 Nationalist resistance collapsed, the Kuomintang fled to the island of Taiwan, and the communists formally proclaimed the People's Republic. So the largest country in the world went communist at just the time that the United States was building up Western Europe in the name of containment.

On the other hand the communists were not conciliated. The USA had supported Chiang's government (which was, admittedly, generally recognised as the legitimate government of all China) in

99. Immanuel C.Y. Hsu, *The Rise of Modern China* (New York, 1990 edn) chaps. 24, 25; Garthoff, *Sino–Soviet Military Relations* pp. 40–3 and chap. 4; R.R. Simmons, *The Strained Alliance: Peking, Pyongyang, Moscow and the Politics of the Korean War* (New York, 1975) chap. 3. The Chinese civil war is further discussed in *The Post-Imperial Age* chap.5

the rush for arms and territory that followed Japan's surrender. From September 1945 to March 1949 US aid amounted, in all, to some $3 billion; and it continued to trickle on long after the Nationalists had clearly lost. In the light of the subsequent Sino–Soviet split a number of missed opportunities have been discerned in US–Chinese communist relations. Whether they were real it is impossible to tell. But nothing came of them. In mid-1949 Mao proclaimed the need to 'lean to one side', a process apparently consolidated by the February 1950 Sino–Soviet treaty.

The USA's comparative unconcern at the Kuomintang débâcle was partly due to despair over its leadership (described by Truman as 'grafters and crooks'). But it is significant that, when asked in mid-1947 to list areas of strategic importance to the USA, the Joint Chiefs of Staff put Europe (including Greece) top and China only thirteenth. In 1949 this perception was modified by recognition that the communist surge might well not remain confined to China. The British were in fact already worried in 1948 about South-East Asia (where there were communist insurgencies in French Indo-China and in Malaya plus an attempted rising in Java), and had been trying to orchestrate a response by local states backed (as in Western Europe) by US assistance. Initially the Americans had not been interested. But in February 1949 the US State Department's Policy Planning Staff (still headed by Kennan) declared the area to be 'the target of a coordinated offensive plainly directed by the Kremlin', whose loss would affect Japanese, Indian and Australian security; the region was, therefore, 'a vital sector on the line of containment'. In June the National Security Council found that the fall of China threatened all of South-East Asia; Secretary of State Acheson wrote that the USA would not allow another Asian nation to fall to the communists. Nor did he accept the idea that Asian communism was different from European and more properly viewed as just another manifestation of local nationalism: 'Question whether Ho . . . nationalist or Commie', he had cabled, 'is irrelevant. All Stalinists in colonial areas are nationalists. With achievement of national aims (i.e. independence) their objective necessarily becomes subordination state to Commie purposes and ruthless extermination [of] not only opposition groups but all elements suspected [of] even slightest deviation'. Accordingly he favoured strengthening China's neighbours by building up their internal stability and living standards, and, above all, getting 'on the side of Nationalist movements'. So, when the British again raised the question in December, he was able to tell them he had 'scratched together' the symbolic sum of $75 million for the purpose and would provide some military assistance to France in Indo-China, while pressing them to remove 'barriers to the obtaining by Bao Dai or other non-communist nationalist leaders of the support of a substantial proportion of the Vietnamese'.

Actual disbursements were slow – a mere $48.5 million for South-East Asia by June 1950[100] – and we cannot say how far things would have gone but for the Korean War. US strategy rested on a 'defensive perimeter' of islands in the West Pacific, running from Japan to the Philippines. The chief break in this chain was Taiwan. It had been readily recognised that it was not in the US interest that this should fall to the communists. Despite official statements to the contrary, minor military and civil aid continued to reach the Nationalists there. However, Americans had no confidence in their determination seriously to defend themselves, and most were prepared to write Taiwan off. By June 1950, there were signs of a change: Dean Rusk and, more significantly, General MacArthur urged its defence or neutralisation. MacArthur's memorandum was discussed in the immediate aftermath of the North Korean invasion, and on 27 June 1950 Truman announced the interposition of his fleet between Taiwan and the mainland. It cannot be certain that the communists would otherwise have conquered Taiwan (which is over 100 miles offshore). But the USA had now intervened directly to prevent the termination of the Chinese Civil War; and although this did not prove a permanent barrier to improved Sino-American relations, it was (and remains) a considerable obstacle.[101]

100. Douglas Macdonald in Jervis and Snyder, *Dominoes and Bandwagons* pp. 120, 126–30; *FRUS,* 1949 ix p. 465; Ritchie Ovendale, 'Britain, the United States and the Cold War in South-East Asia 1949–50', *International Affairs* lviii (1982)
    101. *FRUS,* 1950 vi pp. 349–51, 366–7; 1950 vii pp. 157–8, 161–5

CHAPTER FOUR

The Korean War and its International Consequences

Although US shifts towards greater defence spending and a geographical extension of containment can be discerned before the Korean War,[1] the war was at least the catalyst, probably the necessary condition, for their consolidation. Its background can be briefly stated.

THE PARTITION OF KOREA 1945

There had been agreement at the Yalta conference that Korea, then a Japanese colony, should proceed to independence 'in due course'; but for the purpose of receiving the surrender of Japanese troops, it was divided between the US and Soviet armies. In mid-1945 the USA was anxious to check the spread of Soviet influence in the Far East, and US Secretary of State Byrnes had sought a dividing line 'as far north as possible'. Accordingly the USA had, without any very deep thought, suggested the 28th Parallel, which Stalin accepted without demur: it left two-thirds of the population in the South, but the more industrialised area in the North. The Soviets, who seem to have had a prior interest in the country,[2] moved rapidly to create, and install in government, a Communist Party, suppressing a number of anti-communist riots and risings. In the South the Americans refused to recognise the broadly leftist 'People's Republic' that had been proclaimed between the Japanese decision to surrender and their own arrival.

1. Rusk had urged the neutralisation of Taiwan partly to counter the view that the USA would let anything slip except the Americas and Western Europe
2. Leonhard recalls the training of Koreans in an exceptionally secret Comintern school near Ufa in 1942: *Child of the Revolution* pp.178–9

Instead they operated first through the Japanese authorities and then through their own military government. Fear of communism led them, in conditions of sporadic risings and considerable social disturbance, to a tough maintenance of order that some historians see as a counter-revolution. This policy may have made possible a revival of conservative forces; these certainly dominated the indirect elections to a consultative legislature in October 1946 (though the Americans then sought to redress the balance by coopting moderates). During 1946–7 there were inconclusive US–Soviet negotiations as to how to create a single Provisional Government for the whole country. These broke down after Molotov quit the Paris conference on Marshall Aid in July 1947.

At the time the USA considered that Korea was of negligible strategic significance, so it decided to install an indigenous government in the south and withdraw with the minimum of bad effects. The United States' chosen medium was the United Nations, which agreed to observe elections and advise on the installation of a government for the whole peninsula. The Soviet Union firmly excluded the UN's monitoring commission from the north; but, despite Australian, Canadian and Indian fears that to hold elections in the south only would perpetuate partition, the UN decided to go ahead. Elections were held in May 1948, and broadly endorsed by the UN commission (though the number of its observers had in fact been very limited). July saw the constitution of a Republic of Korea under the presidency of the temperamentally authoritarian Syngman Rhee, and in December it was recognised by the UN as 'the only such [lawful] Government in Korea'. Meanwhile in the North the Russians had countered by establishing a Democratic People's Republic that also claimed authority throughout the peninsula; in December they withdrew their troops. In 1949 the USA did likewise, being determined not to be sucked into hostilities by a Northern invasion (which it thought quite likely). However, it did not want to see South Korea collapse, and provided enough economic and military aid to enable it to handle internal challenges and guerrilla infiltration. So by 1950 South Korea had consolidated its domestic security position. But Rhee still faced problems since his party received a set-back in elections in May, while in June the price of rice rose by one-third.[3]

---

3. *The Post-Imperial Age* chap.8; Peter Lowe, *The Origins of the Korean War* (1986) chaps 2, 3; Callum MacDonald, *Korea: The War before Vietnam* (1986) chap. 1; Simmons, *The Strained Alliance* p. 115; Kathryn Weathersby, *Soviet Aims in Korea and the Origins of the Korean War, 1945–50: New Evidence from Russian Archives* Cold War International History Project (CWIHP) Working Paper 8, Washington, DC (1993) pp. 8–23

KIM IL SUNG'S PLAN FOR FORCEFUL REUNIFICATION 1949–50

The origins of the Korean War became a happy hunting ground for conspiracy theorists, perhaps because of its impact on events outside the peninsula. Evidence is now emerging to confirm Khrushchev's account: 'it was the initiative of Comrade Kim Il Sung,[4] and it was supported by Stalin and many others – in fact, by everybody'. The North Korean leader first proposed an invasion to Stalin in 1949, claiming 'that South Korea was blanketed with Party organisations and that the people would rise up in revolt when the Party gave the signal'.[5] Stalin consulted Mao, who approved, arguing 'that the USA would not intervene since the war would be an internal [Korean] matter'.[6] Stalin was less sure, but 'inclined to think that if the war were fought swiftly – and Kim Il Sung was sure it could be won swiftly – then intervention by the USA could be avoided'. Cautiously, though, after massively equipping the North Korean Army, he pulled back military advisers so that there should be no provable link with the USSR (for which Khrushchev blamed him, feeling that the commitment of one or two Soviet tank corps would have settled the issue).[7]

The invasion on 25 June 1950 caught Truman on holiday. He later wrote that, as he flew back to Washington, he recalled Manchuria (1931), Ethiopia (1935–6) and Austria (1938) where the democracies' inaction had simply encouraged further aggression:

> If this was allowed to go unchallenged it would mean a third World War, just as similar incidents had brought on the Second. . . . It was also clear to me that the foundations and the principles of the United Nations were at stake unless this unprovoked attack on Korea could be stopped.

Such perceptions were not confined to the USA; a leading French

4. Rhee was just as keen to liberate the North (Simmons, *The Strained Alliance* pp. 115–16); but the USA did not give him the go-ahead

5. It was apparently believed in the North that there were 77,000 guerrillas (and 500,000 members of the communist underground) in the South: Simmons, *The Strained Alliance* pp. 109, 115. In fact the Northern invasion did not touch off a mass rising

6. China had apparently revised its view of the USA, holding (by Jan. 1950) that it could not mount major operations in the Far East for at least five years: Chen, Jian, *The Sino-Soviet Alliance and China's Entry into the Korean War*, CWIHP Working Paper 1, Washington, DC (1992) p. 19

7. *Khrushchev Remembers* i chap. 11, iii pp. 144–6; Cold War International History Project *Bulletin* 8 (1993) pp. 14–18, 34; see also *The Post-Imperial Age* chap.8

official thought that the loss of Korea would 'irretrievably impair' Western prestige and drew parallels with 1938.

THE WESTERN RESPONSE

According to Acheson, 'the governments of many Western European nations appeared to be in a state of near panic, as they watched to see whether the United States would act or not'; there were US fears that, if it did not, Europe would go neutralist.[8] The US decision to respond, therefore, was taken in the light not of feelings about Korea itself, or even about its strategic significance (which, in Japan at least, is regarded as considerable), but of a general view of the international system. The USA instantly referred the question to the UN Security Council, which (as a result of the then Soviet boycott) was able to condemn the invasion and call on North Korea to withdraw.[9] To nobody's surprise nothing happened. The USA then extended air and naval support to South Korea in the knowledge that the UN would endorse the action, but before it had actually called on its members to help repel the attack.[10] The USA would presumably have acted as it did even had the Soviet delegate been present to cast a veto. But the view that the UN should be able, and that the League of Nations should have attempted, to provide collective security in such situations was an important component of the Truman administration's outlook. Equally UN support did much to legitimise, at home and abroad, a war in which the command, and all the crucial decisions, were taken by Americans; eventually (and after some US pressure) fifteen other countries (besides South Korea itself) contributed troops, though only those from the British Commonwealth and Turkey had much military value.[11]

The initial US (and British) contribution was of naval and air support, in line with the offshore nature of its then defence posture. Originally it was hoped (despite US Army scepticism) that

---

8. Harry S. Truman, *Years of Trial and Hope, 1946–1953* (1956) p. 351; Deborah Larson, in Jervis and Snyder, *Dominoes and Bandwagons* pp. 96–8
9. Stalin was warned that this would happen, but persisted in continuing the Soviet boycott of the Security Council: Andrei Gromyko, *Memories* (London, 1990) pp. 131–2
10. *History of the JCS*, iii pp.94–5
11. ibid, pp. 1103–4

this would suffice. By the end of June it was clear that it would not; and Truman authorised the commitment of combat troops. Assessments of the forces needed steadily escalated, but by mid-July General MacArthur was confident: 'I intend to destroy and not to drive back the North Korean forces. . . . I may need to occupy all of North Korea. In the aftermath of operations, the problem is to compose and unite Korea'.[12] MacArthur's strategy, an amphibious landing at Inchon hundreds of miles behind the current front, had technical flaws, but he staked his reputation on it. When executed on 15 September 1950, it succeeded brilliantly – a fortnight later North Korean forces south of the 38th Parallel had been destroyed. This must have enhanced yet further Washington's disposition to defer to MacArthur.

THE UN INVASION OF NORTH KOREA, CHINA'S INTERVENTION AND US RESPONSES 1950–1

Victory raised the question of what to do next. Initially the US administration had proclaimed, publicly and privately, that its intervention was intended only to restore the prewar position. But opinion had been hardening during the summer in favour of overrunning the North; on 27 September MacArthur was directed to do so provided there was no likelihood of major Soviet or Chinese intervention. In retrospect this was a disastrous mistake. At the time it was seen as a natural punishment for aggression (the Allies had not halted in 1944–5 on reaching Germany's frontiers), as the simplest way of preventing the regrouping of North Korean forces and another round of fighting, and, above all, as the implementation of the 1947 UN policy of re-uniting Korea through free elections. On 7 October 1950 a British Resolution was carried overwhelmingly in the General Assembly calling on UN forces to cross the Parallel, restore 'stability throughout Korea' and hold elections.[13] They then followed the South Koreans over. No restrictions were placed on MacArthur's deployments. In late September he had envisaged halting foreign troops at the narrowest point (the 'neck') of the peninsula and using only Koreans beyond

12. *History of the JCS*, iii p. 222
13. With this in mind, the UN Command itself administered, until the 1953 armistice, occupied territory north of the parallel, rather than simply turning it over to South Korea

it. Such a deployment might well have enabled him to withstand even Chinese intervention, and again has much to commend it in retrospect.[14] But on 17 October MacArthur ordered a further bound, and thereafter he headed hard for the international frontier with China along the Yalu river. There is evidence of increasing concern (retrospectively magnified) in Washington; but MacArthur commanded enormous prestige, and his actions were always endorsed.

The orders given him on 27 September to proceed north had been conditional on the absence of any entry, or threatened entry, into North Korea of either Soviet or Chinese forces, though on 9 October he was authorised to disregard minor Chinese involvement. On 3 October Zhou En-lai warned the Indian ambassador (and declared on the radio) that China would intervene if UN, as opposed to South Korean, troops crossed the parallel. But this was never formally repeated, and was written off as a bluff – as was a sharp but brief attack by Chinese forces four weeks later. In fact China had already decided on involvement. In July 1950, after the USA had committed forces in *South* Korea and the Taiwan straits, China had postponed its projected invasion of Taiwan and started to ready itself for 'an intervention in the Korean War if necessary'; for, Mao remarked nex month, 'If the U.S. imperialists won the war, they would become more arrogant and would threaten us'. Preparations were to be completed by the end of September. Before then the Inchon landing had added to their urgency. Khrushchev tells us that Stalin would have let North Korea go under, but that he accepted a Chinese offer to intervene. The Chinese add that he even promised to provide air cover. Thus reassured, China decided, two days after South Korean forces had crossed the 38th Parallel to enter the war in mid-October. Stalin then got cold feet, went back on his promise of Soviet air support, and thus forced the Chinese Politburo to reconsider. But Mao still pressed for intervention, and Chinese troops started to move into North Korea in strength on 19 October 1950. They had been warned to prepare for a long and difficult war, but their aim was victory: 'we are going' Mao had told Stalin on 2 October, 'to

---

14. It was to be urged by the UK, but unfortunately not till after UN forces had passed the neck. They would therefore have had to withdraw, and, for this and other reasons, the proposal was unacceptable in Washington: P.N. Farrar, 'Britain's Proposal for a Buffer Zone South of the Yalu in November 1950', *Journal of Contemporary History* xviii (1983)

annihilate the aggression troops of America and other countries, and drive them out'.[15]

In late November MacArthur launched a final offensive to reach the Yalu river, but he coincided with China's counter-offensive. This initially went very well, and the Chinese military was consistently over-confident: 'The American troops were crushed', Khrushchev says, 'and the war ended many times in these battle reports'.[16] Like the UN forces they pushed their luck too far.

In December 1950 Washington was in a flat spin, without a policy but revolving ideas of evacuating Korea and/or expanding the war beyond the peninsula. It would have jumped at a cease-fire, and endorsed Arab–Asian attempts to secure one through the UN. Zhou En-lai refused, declaring that the 38th Parallel had been 'obliterated forever' by the invasion of North Korea, and demanding the evacuation of all foreign troops plus American departure from Taiwan and the seating of Communist China in the UN. A further offensive (31 December–10 January) took the Chinese south of the South Korean capital of Seoul. On 11 January 1951 another cease-fire plan was put to the General Assembly, in many ways rather nebulous but involving withdrawal of foreign troops and a conference to settle the status of Taiwan and Chinese representation at the UN. The US administration accepted, preferring domestic political trouble to the risk of alienating its allies, and hoping that the Chinese would decline – which on 17 January they did, substantially maintaining their previous position. By then the USA had become more confident as to the military situation; at the end of the month it proceeded to have China declared an 'aggressor' under the new UN 'uniting for peace' procedure (see p. 115),[17] despite Chinese warnings that this would 'close the door' on any possibility of peace.

Counter-offensives from late January to April took UN forces just past the Parallel. The USA now determined to seek a cease-fire, though the chances of obtaining one were not enhanced by MacArthur's unauthorised demand on 24 March 1951 that the enemy commander meet him in the field to arrange the bloodless

15. Chen, *The Sino-Soviet Alliance and China's Entry into the Korean War* pp. 22–30; *Khrushchev Remembers* iii p. 147; Weathersby, 'New Findings on the Korean War' (CWIHP *Bulletin* 3, 1993) pp. 14–15, 16 and *Soviet Aims in Korea and the Origins of the Korean War* pp. 27–8. After March 1951 Stalin did at length commit Soviet planes to combat, but (to preserve deniability) only over communist-held territory

16. *Khrushchev Remembers* i pp. 336–7

17. This could have led to the imposition of serious sanctions, but in practice the USA's allies declined to go so far. *History of the JCS*, iii pp. 385, 428–30; Acheson, *Present at the Creation* p. 513; Simmons, *The Strained Alliance* pp. 188–90

realisation of UN 'political objectives', plus his implicit threat of expanding the war into China. This demand was one of the reasons for his dismissal, but it is unlikely that it had much effect on Chinese behaviour. Late April saw a well-prepared Chinese offensive, which at one point came within five miles of Seoul; at the end of May this was driven back with such heavy losses that the new UN commander could report that for the next two months the military situation would offer 'optimum advantages in support of . . . diplomatic negotiations'. Various soundings of the Soviet Union and China had already been made in mid-May, but to no purpose. So Kennan was asked to speak ominously but unofficially to the Soviet UN ambassador:

> Our two countries seemed to be headed for what could be a most dangerous collision. . . . This was definitely not the purpose of American actions or policy. It was hard for us to believe that it was desired by the Soviet Union. Whether or not it was desired by Peking, it seemed the inevitable result of the course the Chinese were steering. If the drift to serious trouble was to be stopped, the method would seem to be an armistice and cease-fire in Korea at about where the forces stood.[18]

Whether through fear, or through a concern not to lose further territory in Korea, the Russians proposed talks; these began in early July 1951.

CEASE-FIRE TALKS 1951–3 AND THE 1953 ARMISTICE

Fighting eased off but did not end, owing to an American concern that, if it did, public opinion would insist on bringing the boys home as in 1945, leaving the UN Command helpless if the communists chose to break off talks. In fact the talks dragged on for two years – which greatly soured the US domestic response to 'Truman's War' – and almost half of all US casualties were incurred after they had started, many (admittedly) at the very end when the talks were at last making progress. Negotiations were always difficult, but in November 1951 agreement was reached on an armistice line along the current front (a position slightly more favourable to South Korea than the 38th Parallel). Thereafter the chief, and from May 1952 the only, issue was that of the repatriation of prisoners

18. *History of the JCS*, iii pp. 502, 527, 564; Acheson, *Present at the Creation* p. 532

against their will. About half of all communist (two-thirds of all Chinese) prisoners refused to return; the UN Command would not compel them to do so, not only for propaganda reasons but also because it did not want to expose them to the fate of the Russians returned after Yalta; and though the Chinese often seemed prepared to overlook Korean prisoners, they insisted on getting all theirs back.

By October 1952 the UN Command had made a final offer, and, as it was not accepted, recessed the armistice talks indefinitely. Thoughts then turned to the possibilities of coercive action, but most US generals doubted the chances of any significant victory on the ground without major reinforcements; renewed heavy fighting in October–November 1952 confirmed this judgement. The new UN Commander favoured a large troop build-up and a drive for either the neck of the peninsula or the Yalu river, backed by strikes against supply centres and airfields in China. But, given the calls on US troops elsewhere, the Chiefs of Staff were unenthusiastic. During his visit to Korea in December 1952, President-elect Eisenhower made it clear that he favoured a cease-fire in place. Once in office he made no definite plans for major operations, but hinted discreetly in a number of quarters 'that, in the absence of satisfactory [negotiating] progress, we intended to move decisively without inhibition in our choice of weapons, and would no longer be responsible for confining hostilities to the Korean peninsula'. More important, probably, was Stalin's death on 5 March 1953; Zhou Enlai raised the question when in Moscow for his funeral, and there was ready agreement on the desirability of resuming negotiations.[19] Once more these were slow; they were further complicated by the determined resistance of Syngman Rhee to any armistice that left Korea divided; and they were marred by the escalation of US bombing and by heavy final communist offensives. Ultimately the communists dropped their demand for the forcible repatriation of prisoners,[20] and a cease-fire took effect that has lasted (uneasily) to this day.

The cost of the war had been horrific: perhaps 0.9 million Chinese, 1.5 million North Korean, and 1.3 million South Korean

19. Dwight D. Eisenhower, *Mandate for Change* (1963) p. 181; in May he told the NSC that, if talks failed, he favoured decisive atomic strikes against China: 'the quicker the operation was mounted, the less the danger of Soviet intervention' (*The [London] Times*, 9 June 1984, p. 3). Weathersby, 'New Findings on the Korean War' (CWIHP *Bulletin* 3, 1993) pp. 15, 17

20. Face-saving arrangements were made for each power to interview those of its prisoners who did not wish to return, under the supervision of neutral Indian troops. Very few changed their minds as a result

(mostly civilian) casualties, plus 34,000 US dead (and over 100,000 wounded).[21] The peninsula ended, as it had begun, far more harshly partitioned than Germany. The possibility of another Northern invasion remained; partly for this reason, partly to induce Rhee to accept the armistice, the USA concluded a defence agreement with South Korea and has retained troops there. Nevertheless the Northern threat provided a rationale for continued authoritarian rule in the South, though this may also have been a necessary condition for the spectacular economic growth that began in the 1960s.

IMPLICATIONS OF THE WAR

The war had, in part, been fought to demonstrate the UN's ability to provide collective security. Indeed in 1950 the USA secured the (legally dubious) 'Uniting for Peace' resolution that enabled the UN General Assembly to act by a two-thirds majority when the Security Council was deadlocked by a veto. But the 'Uniting for Peace' procedure has never led to anything concrete. And after Korea, the UN showed no further disposition to embark on coercive military action until Iraq's 1990 annexation of Kuwait, after the 'end of the Cold War'. But if the Korean War did not constitute the hoped-for precedent for the successful operation of collective security, it did set others. Crossing the 38th Parallel had brought China into the war. The Americans were not going to make that mistake again; so, though they bombed North Vietnam in the 1960s and 1970s, they never invaded it. More generally, Korea was, for most of its course, a 'limited war' in the sense that the UN fought not for outright victory but only to induce the enemy to conclude an armistice broadly along the prewar border. This is in fact the response prescribed by the international law doctrine of the right to self-defence. But much American public opinion, prone to viewing international relations in more black and white terms, found fighting for such restricted objectives uncongenial, even immoral. Nor did it relish according immunity to communist supply and air bases just over the Chinese border, which appeared to expose UN forces to unnecessary risks in deference to half-hearted European allies. Nevertheless both North Korean immunity from invasion and

21. Simmons, *The Strained Alliance* pp. 213, 242. War and refugee movements left the North Korean population 1 million lower in 1953 than it had been in 1949

the existence of 'sanctuary' areas outside the combat zone came to constitute precedents. These have certainly not always been followed, but they have often affected military operations, and world opinion tends to regard it as illegitimate when they are breached.

Initially the Korean War strengthened the Sino-Soviet alliance. But in the longer run the fact that China had to *buy* the necessary military supplies from the USSR clearly rankled. Although China's self-esteem was boosted by its early military successes, China's losses were such that in 1954, Zhou Enlai told Khrushchev, it was in no condition to intervene in Indo-China to rescue the Vietminh if the French got the upper hand.[22] More intangible were the consequences for relations with the USA and Taiwan. Intervention sealed 'Red China's' hostility with the USA and elevated it, for two decades, into prime position in American demonology. This rift was admittedly overcome in the 1970s. That between China and Taiwan ran deeper. It may be that the communists could never have conquered Taiwan anyway. But the Korean War effectively incorporated the island into the United States' defence perimeter, and led to the resumption of US aid on a large scale. This time the Nationalists used it well.

Still more important, perhaps, was the effect of the Korean War on two ex-enemy states, Japan and West Germany. Truman had already decided before the outbreak of the Korean War to push for a peace treaty with Japan that would preserve US bases there, even if it meant (as in the event it did) that the USSR would not sign. But the war both added urgency and provided a propitious environment for such a policy. It also hardened US determination that Japan should not risk becoming dependent on trade with mainland China, and that it should make peace with Chiang Kai-shek, not Mao Zedong. All this ensured that, even after independence, Japan was locked firmly into the American sphere.[23]

GERMAN REARMAMENT

More complicated, but (as people then thought) more important, were moves towards West German rearmament. There can be no

22. *Khrushchev Remembers* i p. 443
23. US–Japanese relations are discussed more fully in *The Post-Imperial Age* chap.7

doubt that Soviet military strength in Central Europe was vastly greater than NATO's: at the time 175 Soviet divisions were believed to be ready for use. Although this estimate has since been cut to about sixty, they still out-classed the (at best) six Western divisions on the German front.[24] US war plans called for the evacuation of Europe to the north of the Pyrenees and the establishment of offshore bases in the UK and North Africa. So it is not surprising that the earliest advocates of German rearmament were to be found among the US, British and indeed French military. Both the USA and Britain had begun to contemplate some *eventual* West German rearmament within a NATO framework. But the idea was generally unpalatable, and Acheson concluded from the May 1950 NATO council that moves towards it could destroy the welcome new French plan for a European Coal and Steel Community (ECSC). Nor did there seem any urgency; none of the NATO Foreign Ministers had seen any immediate threat of war.[25]

Korea changed things. There were uncomfortable (though not exact) parallels with a divided Germany. 'One thing is certain, they [the North Koreans] did not do this purely on their own but as part of the world strategy of international communism',[26] which could, presumably, no longer be counted on not to exploit conventional force superiority. The United States, which had already been cogitating major rearmament (NSC-68), at once decided on it, and remained very apprehensive of Soviet intentions for the next two and a half years. So initially were Western Europeans.[27] In July 1950 reports from US missions in Europe converted Acheson to the view that West Germany would have to be rearmed and that the USA would have to give an immediate lead.

At first it tried to insist on a 'single package', US troop reinforcements for Europe, the redesign of the NATO command structure to secure strategic integration, and German rearmament. In response to strong French criticism a less rigid posture was adopted, but it was always clear that refusing German rearmament would jeopardise US protection. Equally the American decision to commit troops to Europe was not easily made. For in the aftermath

24. R. McGeehan, *The German Rearmament Question. American Diplomacy and European Defense after World War II* (Urbana, Ill., 1971) pp. 6–7, 102

25. *History of the JCS*, iv p. 193; McGeehan, *German Rearmament* p.3; Deighton, *Britain and the Cold War* pp. 276–8

26. Dulles, July 1950 (McGeehan, *German Rearmament* p. 21)

27. Acheson recalls both French and Belgian queries in December 1950 as to whether there would be war in three months (*Present at the Creation* p. 487), though such feelings subsided faster than in the USA

of Republican victories in the November 1950 elections and of Chinese intervention in Korea, some Republicans sought a 're-examination' of foreign policy – concentration on air and sea power to 'preserve this Western Hemisphere Gibraltar of Western Civilization', holding the offshore islands of Britain and Japan but largely leaving Europe to defend itself. Hearings on these ideas took up the first quarter of 1951, the most persuasive testimony to the contrary being given by the newly designated Supreme Allied Commander Europe (SACEUR), General Eisenhower, who maintained that six US and thirty-four other NATO divisions would suffice to protect 'rather significant portions' of Western Europe. Eventually the US Senate grudgingly approved both Eisenhower's new post and the dispatch of four divisions (taking the US total in Europe to six).[28] By the end of 1951 they had arrived. Eisenhower viewed them as a temporary expedient to cover European rearmament, but US troops are still (1993) there – a symbol of determination to defend Western Europe, or, as many strategic commentators had it, 'hostages' to ensure the commitment of US nuclear deterrence. It took until 1952 to negotiate a satisfactory NATO command structure. How much it amounted to could have been shown only in war – certainly not to the standardisation of equipment or even the effective control of force levels, but equally clearly to far more than say the prewar Franco-Czech alliance or Franco-British partnership. De Gaulle was to see it as a vehicle of American 'hegemony' incompatible with French national sovereignty.

German rearmament proved more thorny. East–West relations apart, there was no urgency. Probably most West Germans were opposed: their ideal would have been the deployment of more Anglo-American troops. But since much of the Christian Democrat leadership favoured a German military contribution, the issue would presumably have come up some time. Adenauer apparently said privately in 1949 that within four years there would again be Germans in uniform, and in December he made several pronouncements about the possibility of a German contribution to a European army. He says he saw that 'Rearmament might be the way of gaining full sovereignty for the Federal Republic'.[29] In August 1950 he first proposed a West German paramilitary police

---

28. Acheson, *Present at the Creation* pp. 488–96; S.E. Ambrose, *Eisenhower 1890–1952* (1984) pp. 496–510

29. T. Prittie, *The Velvet Chancellors* (1979) p. 80 and *Konrad Adenauer* (1972) pp. 157–8; K. Adenauer, *Memoirs 1945–53* (English translation, 1966) p. 270

force of 150,000 (to counter the 50,000 already raised in East Germany), then urged a German military contribution to a European army linked with a drastic modification of the occupation regime. The chief obstacle was France's continuing fear of a country that, even partitioned, was more populous and industrialised than itself. Adenauer's bids might have been disregarded; US proposals, made formally in September, could not. Things might, as Bevin suggested, have gone more smoothly had the USA simply pushed the paramilitary police proposal. Instead it conditioned its enhanced support for NATO on acceptance of a force containing German units. France's counter in October was the 'Pleven Plan', a European army (linked to the ECSC but at the disposal of SACEUR) that would include, within an integrated structure, German 'combat teams' 800–1,200 strong, that is too small to be dangerous. The plan prompted jibes about creating German forces that should be stronger than Russia but weaker than France; it certainly served the purpose of delaying things.

Intensive negotiation gradually modified both the French and the American stances – France eventually accepting division-sized (12,000) German units and eliminating many obviously discriminatory provisions, the United States recognising in July 1951 that progress could come only through a European army and European Defence Community (EDC).[30] Meanwhile West Germany bargained (hard) its readiness to make a defence contribution against successive relaxations of occupation controls. The Americans had originally hoped to start recruiting German units in 1951, and France came under pressure to reach a conclusion by the end of the year. Inevitably things took a little longer. But after further negotiations (especially in London and Lisbon in February 1952) and Anglo-American reassurances to France of assistance were West Germany to break from the EDC, the treaty was signed in May 1952, as part of a package providing for the restoration of sovereignty to West Germany when it was ratified.

Thereafter US diplomatic pressure eased, and ratification, as we shall see in the next chapter, stalled. The first West German conscripts were not called up until 1957. If 1954 had really been, as the Americans feared, the 'year of maximum danger', they would

30. As agreed in November 1951, this was to have fourteen French, twelve German and twelve Italian, and five Benelux divisions, all with a common logistics system but with integrated international command only at corps and army level. France would have six extra, purely national, divisions: McGeehan, *German Rearmament* pp. 155–6

have come too late. The decision for rearmament remains controversial. Did it, as the SPD maintained at the time, seal the partition of Germany (at least until 1990)? Or was it essential for the credibility of NATO's conventional defence, and indeed for NATO's survival after de Gaulle's withdrawal in 1965? Finally, was it important for Germany's smooth reintegration into Western Europe that the traumatic issue of rearmament was pushed not, as after the First World War, by the Germans themselves but by the Americans?

CHAPTER FIVE

Stalin's Death and the First Détente

INTERPRETATIONS OF STALIN'S LATER FOREIGN POLICY

In 1951 Stalin was overheard to soliloquise, 'I'm finished. I trust no one, not even myself'. Distrust was a feature of his closing years: was Voroshilov an English spy, had Molotov travelled by train in the United States and did that mean that he had his own private railway car bought with American money, etc. etc.? Stalin kept his cards so close to his chest that there is much disagreement as to what his foreign policy really was. Nor need one assume that he was necessarily consistent: in an earlier period his 1937 purge of the officer corps had very seriously undercut Soviet foreign policies in other directions. One interpretation might be that he saw the West as hostile and dangerous – 'You'll see, when I am gone the imperialist powers will wring your neck like chickens' – and 'lived in terror of enemy attack. For him foreign policy meant keeping the anti-aircraft units around Moscow on a twenty-four-hour alert'. There were periodic panics, for example that the United States would send in troops to contest the communist take-over in Czecho-slovakia in 1948 or that (at US instigation) Turkey was about to attack Bulgaria. Khrushchev further maintains that, 'In the days leading up to Stalin's death, we believed that America would invade the Soviet Union and we would go to war. Stalin trembled at this prospect [having never got over the ghastly experience of the German attack in 1941]. . . . He knew that we were weaker than the United States [in nuclear, if not conventional, weapons] . . . [and] never did anything that might provoke a war with the United

States'.[1] But political countermeasures did not go beyond a barrage of propaganda, designed to appeal to West European peoples and 'peace movements' over the heads of their governments, perhaps also to drive wedges between these governments and the United States. Such initiatives were commonly launched shortly before major measures of Western consolidation, like the signing of NATO in early 1949, the establishment of West Germany that summer, or the 1952 treaties to end its occupation and create the European Defence Community (EDC). These initiatives were handled badly, perhaps because Stalin had discarded diplomatic advisers with experience of foreign countries, perhaps because he himself now lacked energy. Certainly Americans counted themselves lucky that 'the Soviets played their cards all the wrong way'. Friendly gestures were cancelled out by automatic reversions to a strident and hostile tone; important overtures (like the apparent offer of German reunification in 1952) were simply dropped when they met no immediate response, instead of being so pressed as to force Western governments either to address them or at least to pay a political price for not doing so.

Alternatively it is contended that, whatever his behaviour within the socialist camp, Stalin had by the end of his life come round to seeking rather warmer relations with the West. This view rests not only on hints of readiness to bring the Korean War to an end,[2] and on his expression of readiness to meet the incoming US President (Eisenhower), but also on his last important book, *Economic Problems of Socialism in the U.S.S.R.* (September 1952), which is held to have anticipated later doctrines of peaceful coexistence. Here Stalin claimed that capitalist countries would find their industries operating 'more and more below capacity' as a result of the breakaway of, and competition from, the socialist camp. Attempts to offset this (like 'the "Marshall Plan", the war in Korea, frantic rearmament') were merely clutching at straws. In this 'general crisis of the world capitalist system', the other capitalist countries would not 'tolerate the domination and oppression of the United States endlessly' but would 'endeavour to tear loose from American bondage and take the path of independent development'. *Intra-imperialist* wars were therefore inevitable. But capitalist–socialist contradictions were in practice less urgent. For war with the USSR might destroy capitalism itself, whereas 'war between capitalist

1. *Khrushchev Remembers* i pp. 273–5, 356–7, ii pp. 188–9, iii pp. 100–1
2. Schweitzer, *The Changing Western Analysis of the Soviet Threat* p. 292

countries puts in question only the supremacy of certain capitalist countries over others'. Besides 'the capitalists, although they clamour, for "propaganda" purposes, about the aggressiveness of the Soviet Union, . . . are aware of the Soviet Union's peaceful policy and know that it will not itself attack capitalist countries'.

The only tangible expression of this new Soviet approach was the 10 March 1952 offer of a reunited, neutral but armed Germany.[3] Western governments were undecided: was this simply a manoeuvre, to preclude the incorporation of the Federal Republic into the EDC, that would evaporate as soon as it had served its purpose; or was it a genuine offer? The British Foreign Secretary, Eden, at least, seems to have thought the latter: on a report that the French Foreign Office was inclining to believe it 'a serious but very dangerous attempt to settle the German question', he noted 'Which has been my view all along, i.e. that the Soviets are sincere in these proposals because, though there is danger in them, they would on balance . . . suit them well'.[4] Stalin's overture was unwelcome to the West as tending, whether or not it was genuine, to undercut Adenauer and his policy of Westwards integration. Nor did the prospect of a reunited Germany evoke much enthusiasm.[5] Accordingly the chief (and successful) thrust of Western diplomacy was so to reply to Soviet notes as not to disturb either the completion of the EDC or political support in West Germany for this cause and its embodiment, Chancellor Adenauer. Nevertheless Acheson came by late April to favour talks with the Russians: 'it is in our interest to expose Soviet insincerity at the earliest possible date and in any event before [West German] legislation debates are concluded'; but 'If Soviets are really prepared to open [the] Eastern Zone, we should force their hand. We can *not* allow our plans to be thwarted merely by *speculation* that Soviets may be ready actually to pay a high price'. London and Paris were cool, but the decisive

3. RIIA *Documents* . . . *1952* pp.85 ff (Soviet notes of 10 March, 9 April and 24 May, US notes of 25 March and 13 May)

4. Rolf Steininger, *Eine Chance zur Wiedervereinigung? Die Stalin–Note von 10 März 1952, Archiv für Sozialgeschichte* (Beiheft 12, 1985) translated, with fewer documents, as *The German Question: The Stalin Note of 1952 and the Problem of Reunification* (New York, 1990) pp.136, 167

5. Some feared it per se. Others felt that it might be vulnerable to Soviet attraction through trade and (at the crucial moment) an offer to restore Eastern territory, especially were economic adversity to displace the likely initial SPD government by a more adventurist and Rapallo-minded right-authoritarian one. A few felt that any unattached Germany would be vulnerable to minority communist take-over, East European style. Lastly the appearance of détente with the USSR might inhibit consolidation and rearmament of the rest of Western Europe

opposition was probably that coming from Adenauer after he had considered the question all day and 'through half the night'.[6]

Since the talks were not pursued, we shall never know for certain what lay behind Stalin's offer. He did tell the Italian fellow-traveller Nenni in July 1952 that, though he had just come to think unification impossible, he would earlier

> have sacrificed the East German Communists so as to bring about a Germany ruled by a government friendly to the West but containing a strong leftist opposition as in Italy today. Stalin felt a weak Germany containing strong political forces looking both to the West and to the Soviet Union would bring about a political equilibrium sufficient to stop any drift to war.[7]

But, if so, it is odd that he had not made a greater effort to get this across, by, for instance, talking directly to Western ambassadors or (as on earlier occasions) using intermediaries to contact the US administration. Moreover there are no signs that the offer worried the East German leaders. When they visited Moscow to seek his advice on the 'consolidation of democratic [i.e. their own] legitimacy', Stalin told them on 1 April to 'create a People's Army – quietly', and to fill themselves with a 'fighting spirit – we will help you'. He later added that the West had hitherto turned down all initiatives, so there could be 'no compromises': the 'demarcation line' with West Germany was a 'dangerous frontier' behind which should stand 'in the first line German-Stasi' and then Soviet troops.[8] These observations followed the Western response of 25 March, which had certainly not jumped at the Soviet offer of the 10th but had (at least ostensibly) sought discussion of other ways of achieving monitored free elections and reunification. They preceded Stalin's own further note of 9 April, asking 'whether Germany will be re-established as a united independent peace-loving state . . . or whether the division of Germany, and . . . with it the threat of war in Europe, will remain'. As we have seen, Acheson (though suspecting insincerity) came to feel at the end of

---

6. Steininger, *Eine Chance?* esp. pp.233, 241

7. Canadian report of what the Italian ambassador in Moscow said Nenni told him: Steininger, *Eine Chance?* p.282. On the other hand, some ten lines of a March 1952 US report from Berlin, supposedly evidence for believing a major concern of Stalin's note was to legitimise further unilateral development of East Germany, was still classified in 1985: ibid, p.153

8. Gerhard Wettig, 'Die Stalin-Note vom 10 März 1952 als geschichtswissen-schaftliches Problem', *Deutschland Archiv* Feb. 1992 esp. pp.161–3, citing Pieck's notes of the meetings. (The Stasi were the East German security police.)

the month that this should be followed up. Admittedly Adenauer vetoed such a response. But Stalin's exchanges with the East Germans suggest that by early April he was no longer looking for one, and probably never had been. This seems to have been Molotov's later judgement – that Stalin would never have forsaken the socialist regime in Berlin.[9]

A much harsher picture comes from the Czech historian, Karel Kaplan. In 1946 Stalin was talking about another war with *Germany*; in September 1948 he told Gottwald that sooner or later the USSR would have to fight America. In 1949 there was massive rearmament (defence accounted for one-third of all expenditure under the Czech 1949–53 Five Year Plan); in January 1951 East European Party Secretaries and Defence Ministers were summoned to Moscow, where Stalin portrayed a window of opportunity. By 1955 at latest the USA would have completed the ring of bases needed for an atomic assault on the USSR and acquired the means for the rapid reinforcement of Western Europe; in the mean time there was a heavy Soviet military predominance. No European army could resist effectively, and there might well be no attempt to do so; the existing US forces were not great, and, despite their advanced technology, had been shown up in Korea (this was at the time of maximum Chinese success there). Accordingly there should be a complete mobilisation of resources to permit the military occupation of Western Europe – before it was too late. Tasks were then assigned to each East European state. This knowledge, Kaplan states, was very closely held, but it remained policy up to Stalin's death. Shortly thereafter disturbances erupted in East Germany and Czechoslovakia, partly as a result of the pressure of rearmament on living standards, and Stalin's successors dropped the policy. Kaplan quotes the Czech leader Novotny as saying in March 1956 that the socialist camp now had to struggle for peace; there was no question of an 'opportunistic' policy:

> Here is the new and revolutionary change in the policy followed until recently by the C.P.S.U. and other Communist parties, a change that reversed the line followed by Stalin up to his death. Had we continued in that direction there would certainly not be today a certain relaxation

9. James Richter, *Reexamining Soviet Policy towards Germany during the Beria Interregnum (Cold War International History Project*, Working Paper 3, Washington, DC, 1992) p.8, citing *One Hundred Forty Conversations with Molotov: From the Diary of F. Chuyev* (Moscow, 1991, in Russian) p.335

of international tension. We should today find ourselves in the situation that the capitalists had anticipated – on the eve of war.[10]

WESTERN APPROACHES

Whatever had been Stalin's real intentions, on his death in March 1953 his successors embarked on measures of conciliation – agreeing a new UN Secretary-General, dropping Soviet demands on Turkey and proposing border negotiations with Iran, and encouraging a Korean armistice. That summer Malenkov listed Soviet efforts to lessen international tensions, and declared that 'We stand, as we have always stood, for the peaceful coexistence of the two systems. We hold that there are no objective reasons for clashes between the United States of America and the Soviet Union.' This new approach, though characterised by the British Foreign Office only as 'leaving off doing things which we have not been doing to them', forced the West to consider how it should respond.

Hitherto the leading Western policy had been that of creating facts. People who had had the experience of negotiating with the Russians in the later 1940s were in no hurry to resume. Acheson, admittedly, was prepared for talks on Stalin's 1952 German reunification proposals. But his usual feelings were represented by his claims that 'all important outstanding issues' had been repeatedly discussed, and that the Russians clearly did not want to settle 'as long as they feel there is any possibility they can exploit them for their own objectives of world domination. It is only when they come to the conclusion that they cannot . . . that they will make agreements, and they will let it be known when they have reached that decision.' For

10. Kaplan says that his attention was first directed to this episode by the April 1956 contention of the Czech Minister of Defence, Cepicka, that any judgement on his earlier conduct should take into account the climate of preparation for war with the West – 'consultations in Moscow in 1951 – S[talin] assessed the situation – 3 or 4 years of time'. Much of Kaplan's account is derived from interviews in the 1960s with Cepicka, who regretted that the plan had been abandoned: 'Il piano di Stalin', *Panorama* 26 April 1977 pp.169–89, and his *Dans les Archives du Comité Central* (Paris, 1978) pp.164–6. (It should perhaps be noted that, in recounting the January 1951 conference, Kaplan incorrectly describes Molotov as Foreign Minister.) Boris Nicolaevsky also believed Stalin to have switched in 1951 to a policy of early war, but picked up a story to the effect that the technical military plans were shatteringly criticised in 1952 by Marshal Zhukov, *Power and the Soviet Elite* (1966) pp. 170, 248–9

the Soviet Government is highly realistic and we have seen time after time that it can adjust itself to facts when facts exist. . . . So it has been our basic policy to build situations which will extend the area of possible agreement, that is to create strength instead of the weakness which exists in many quarters. (He cited the rebuilding of Germany, E[uropean] R[ecovery] P[rogam], the arms programme and Point 4 aid as ways in which this was being done.)[11]

Western documents are replete with references to such views, and to their corollary that if Western unity and power continued to build, the Russians would become too overstretched to maintain all their postwar gains, and so be forced to offer major concessions. But these arguments may *sometimes* have been no more than tactics to justify a fundamental unwillingness to jeopardise the status quo by negotiation. Both Eden and Adenauer feared Stalin's 1952 apparent offer of German reunion. Both therefore successfully put it to their countries' Cabinets that, in Eden's words, the proposals

> had doubtless been prompted by the progress achieved at the Lisbon meeting of the North Atlantic Treaty Council towards the establishment of a European Defence Community . . . the wise course was for the Western Powers to go forward . . . with a view to bringing Western Germany into the European Defence Community. . . . When these negotiations were even nearer to completion, the Soviet Government might come forward with a more satisfactory offer. The test of their sincerity would be their willingness to agree to the holding of *free* elections under independent supervision throughout Germany.

Privately, however, Eden was wondering whether, even if the Soviet Union met all Western requirements about free German elections, it might not, by the introduction of 'other conditions . . . e.g. Austria' still be possible to block the dangerous prospect of an agreement that would probably bring to power a neutralist SPD government.[12]

Adenauer's position is more controversial. German reunification was certainly not his top priority. He had told the Allied High Commissioners that

> The Federal Government wants a German unity whereby the whole of Germany is integrated into the West. The Soviets want Germany's unity but without integration into the western community. They do not want this because it is clear that an integration of Europe is impossible

---

11. Coral Bell, *Negotiation from Strength* (1962) pp.13–14 (citing the *Department of State Bulletin*, 20 Feb. and 20 March 1950)

12. Cabinet Conclusions, 12 March 1952, and Eden's marginal notes on a 15 March internal FO minute: Steininger, *Eine Chance?* pp. 120, 142

without a simultaneous integration of Germany. . . . To stop Germany's integration into Europe would be a great success for which it would be worth paying a price. If one believed – and he, the Chancellor, was of this opinion – that such integration was in the long term imperative, then one must set out on this route regardless of what Russia did or did not do. Soviet Russia had met a decisive defeat [over the Japanese peace treaty] at San Francisco. It would meet further defeats when it failed to prevent the integration of West Germany into the West.

Similarly in late 1955 he told the British that 'when he disappeared from the scene a future German government might do a deal with Russia at German expense. Consequently, he felt that the integration of West Germany into the West was more important than the reunification of Germany'.[13]

Adenauer saw Stalin's 1952 note as a propaganda move against the EDC; in any case he held that even a united Germany could not stand alone, neutral between East and West, without eventually succumbing to the Soviet Union. So he discouraged all attempts to probe the 'offer', treating it merely as confirmation of the correctness of existing policy 'to help make the West strong enough to induce the Russians to want to compromise. . . . I believe the latest Russian proposals are a proof that if we continue to do this the point will soon be reached when the Russians are ready to negotiate sensibly'. 'When these talks come, they will have to deal not only with the German Soviet–zone but with the whole of Eastern Europe. That is why talks . . . should not come too soon as things are not yet that far advanced. We must get into talks with the Soviets at exactly the right moment'. Adenauer's perception of 'overwhelming [Soviet] problems at home' ('even an asiatic-style dictatorship must feed its people'),[14] as much as his confidence in Western consolidation, led him to claim that this moment would come surprisingly soon – to British journalists' questions as to whether it 'would be twenty-five or 100 years from now, the Chancellor replied that it would be in five or ten years' time. By 1955 America would be strong and Europe relatively so . . . what

---

13. 24 Sept. 1951 (in response to an East German overture on reunification) – Hans-Peter Schwarz (ed.) *Akten zur Auswärtigen Politik der Bundesrepublik Deutschland*, i *Adenauer und die Hohen Kommissare 1949–1951* (Munich, 1989) p. 381 – cf. also p. 307; Steininger, in Richard H. Immerman (ed.) *John Foster Dulles and the Diplomacy of the Cold War* (Princeton, NJ, 1990) pp. 107–8

14. After 1955 Adenauer added to his list of anticipated Soviet problems a major clash with China

matters is to choose the right moment, not too soon and not too late'.[15]

Clearly many people genuinely believed this; for Adenauer retained the support of his Cabinet, coalition, and electorate. In the long run, the events of 1989–90 proved him right. But from the mid-1950s to the late 1980s such a development looked highly unlikely; much controversy was devoted to the question of whether (as the SPD maintained at the time) Adenauer had thrown away the last chance for reunification by his rejection of German neutrality and holding out for the whole loaf of full integration into the West.

CHURCHILL, BERIA AND GERMAN REUNIFICATION

The leading proponent of *early* negotiations with the Russians was Winston Churchill. He had first urged 'a parley at the summit' in 1950 (probably in reaction to the Soviet acquisition of the atom bomb), but had since abandoned hopes of dealing with Stalin and had in 1952 endorsed Eden's cautious handling of the German reunification issue. Stalin's death changed things. Malenkov declared that there was no dispute with the USA that 'cannot be decided by peaceful means on the basis of mutual understanding'. Eisenhower responded by calling for deeds not words, but in a speech made memorable by its title, 'The Chance for Peace', and by its emphasis on the appalling waste of resources inherent in the arms race. Such exchanges evoked a sense of expectation in the West. American public opinion had, somewhat surprisingly, always favoured a summit, but this was offset by the strength of anti-communists in Congress and by Eisenhower's fears that a summit involving Britain and France as well as the USA and USSR might erode Western unity.[16] In Britain, Churchill was able, and indeed under a certain amount of pressure, to seek a renewal of

15. Karl-Günther von Hase, Hans-Peter Schwarz, Christian Watrin, *Adenauer at Oxford* (Oxford, 1983) pp.34–5; Steininger, *Eine Chance?* pp.28–36; Bell, *Negotiation from Strength* p. 98n.
16. That autumn the US administration considered proposing (in a speech, not a summit) a 'broad zone of restricted armaments in Europe, with Soviets withdrawn from satellites and U.S. from Europe'. But there were fears as to the signals this would send to American allies and of the implications for US nuclear capabilities. Dulles decided not to press the idea, at least until after the firm establishment of the EDC: Gaddis, in Immerman, *Dulles and the Diplomacy of the Cold War* pp. 67–9

East–West dialogue: 'jaw-jaw is better than war-war', he declared in 1954. Promoting it was perhaps his chief concern during the closing period of his political career; the next two Prime Ministers both followed in his footsteps, partly no doubt because of the attractions, international and domestic, of acting as broker between the new giants.

Churchill's hand was further strengthened in April 1953 by Eden's temporary absence from the political scene as the result of an unsuccessful operation. Churchill started by pressing privately for a summit, then in May went public with a call for an informal conference

> confined to the smallest number of Powers and persons possible . . . It might well be that no hard-faced agreements would be reached, but there might be a general feeling among those gathered together that they might do something better than tear the human race, including themselves, to bits.

Elsewhere in the speech he held out hopes for limited settlements ('peace in Korea, the conclusion of an Austrian Treaty' that 'might lead to an easement in our relations for the next few years, which might in itself open new prospects . . .'); more ambitiously he floated the idea of an externally guaranteed Locarno-type pact[17] between Germany and the USSR.[18] Privately Churchill was working on ideas, bitterly contested by the Foreign Office, for an agreement with the USSR on the basis of its own ostensible policy – a reunited and (in the Western sense) free, but neutral, Germany – with some kind of provision (whether a strengthened UN or a new Locarno) for Soviet security.[19]

There are those who believe that a historic chance was missed by

17. The Locarno Treaties of 1925, involving mutual Franco-German acceptance of their postwar frontiers and an Anglo-Italian guarantee of military assistance to whichever country suffered aggression, enormously improved Western European relations at the time – but did not last

18. *Parl. Deb.* (Hansard), 5th series, vol. 515, 895–7. Soviet analysts working to the Praesidium were initially suspicious of Churchill's speech; in October 1953 they concluded that he was sincere in advocating a guaranteed non-aggression treaty between the EDC (including a reunified Germany) and the USSR plus the People's Democracies – Vladislav Zubok, *Soviet Intelligence and the Cold War: The "Small" Committee of Information, 1952–53* Cold War International History Project, Working Paper 4, Washington, DC (1992) pp.22–3 – but by then there was no Soviet readiness to abandon East Germany

19. See e.g. J. Foschepoth, 'Churchill, Adenauer und die Neutralisierung Deutschlands', *Europa Archiv*, xvii (1984) pp.1286–301; also A. Glees, 'Churchill's Last Gambit', *Encounter* lxiv (April 1985)

not following Churchill's advice.[20] This cannot be conclusively disproved, but it is coming to seem unlikely. We now know that the the Soviet Praesidium was deeply divided. On 27 May 1953 Beria declared that East Germany was 'not even a real state. It's only kept in being by Soviet troops, even if we do call it the "German Democratic Republic" '; he suggested that socialism there could be abandoned so long as a reunified Germany remained 'peace-loving'. But he was opposed by Molotov, Khrushchev and probably also Malenkov. The question was then referred to a committee. After further argument a compromise was accepted, and embodied in early June in instructions to the East Germans. These contained concessions to Beria, notably partial agricultural de-collectivisation; and they left the door open for a change of mind, by subordinating the implementation of measures 'strengthening the GDR' to consideration of 'the real conditions within the GDR as well as the situation of Germany as a whole and the international situation'. But though Moscow called off the 'accelerated construction of socialism' (which had landed the DDR in economic difficulties and prompted an exodus to the West), it aimed at 'the recovery of the political situation in the GDR' and placed the 'widening of the base for a mass movement for the creation of a unified, democratic, peace-loving, independent Germany' largely in the context of 'the exploitation of every oppositional current against the tactics of the mercenary Adenauer regime'[21] On the ground in East Germany, the instructions proved a disaster. For the discontinuance of the 'accelerated construction of socialism' shook the regime's prestige. But its recent enhancement of work norms was – perhaps inadvertently – allowed to stand. The result, on 16–17 June, was massive strikes, developing into calls for free elections and German reunification, that had to be suppressed by Soviet troops. At first Ulbricht's Politburo opponents sought to pin the blame on him and squeeze him out of his position as General Secretary. But on 26 June Beria was arrested, the tune of Soviet representatives in Berlin changed, and Ulbricht turned the tables on his opponents, accusing them next month of aligning themselves with Beria and planning to 'restore capitalism' in the DDR. Meanwhile Beria's German policy

20. Brandt's retrospective view was that 'there was real crisis in the Soviet leadership . . .; [they] . . . might have agreed to German reunification, with the Communist . . . Party in the minority': Terence Prittie, *The Velvet Chancellors, A History of Post-War Germany* (1979) p.73

21. Richter, *Reexamining Soviet Policy towards Germany* pp.14–22; Zubok, *Soviet Intelligence and the Cold War* p.16; Andrei Gromyko, *Memories* (paperback edn, 1989) pp.407–8

had been much denounced in the Central Committee Plenum held in July to approve his arrest, Khrushchev observing that it would have placed '18 million Germans under the mastery of American imperialism', and that no treaty could really guarantee Germany's neutrality since 'if a treaty is not reinforced by strength, then it is nothing, and others will laugh at us and consider us naive'.[22]

Whatever the prospect of an initiative on Churchill's lines, the British Prime Minister (partially disabled by a stroke in late June) was unable to sell, even to his own Cabinet, his German policy of *insisting* on immediate French ratification of the European Defence Community, armed with which the West could then urge on the USSR German reunification as the only alternative. The prevailing view was still fear of jeopardising the linked goals of West German integration in the EDC and of Adenauer's victory in the 1953 elections, and instead reaching a situation where the Soviets could endlessly string out negotiations on Germany as they had on Austrian independence. They would probably not gamble on free elections, which might merely 'add another 18 million anti-Communist Germans to the Federal Republic . . . [and] set a dangerous precedent for retreat in Eastern Europe'. But if they did, the result could

> be highly dangerous for the West. A neutralised Germany with no ties with the West would, if disarmed, soon fall a prey to Russia. If armed, as proposed last year by the Russians, it would soon fall back on the traditional German policy of balancing East against West, or, still worse, into a modern version of Rapallo under which the Germans would attempt to regain their lost Eastern territories by aligning themselves with the Soviet Union. Before long such a Germany might be little better than a Soviet satellite and the balance of power within Europe would have been fatally shifted to our disadvantage.[23]

Further, as Selwyn Lloyd contended in less official language,

> Germany is the key to the peace of Europe. A divided Europe has meant a divided Germany. To unite Germany while Europe is divided even if practicable is fraught with danger for all. Therefore, everyone – Dr. Adenauer, the Russians, the Americans, the French and ourselves – feel in our hearts that a divided Germany is safer for the time being. But none of us dare say so openly because of the effect on German public opinion. Therefore we all publicly support a united Germany, each on his own terms.[24]

22. Richter, *Reexamining Soviet Policy towards Germany* esp. pp.11–13, 18–20
23. Cabinet Memoranda, 3 July 1953 (PRO Cab 129/161)
24. To Churchill, 22 June 1953 (PRO, PREM 11/449) – quoted by Foschepoth, *Journal of Contemporary History*, xxi (1986) p.411

In these circumstances the issue of German reunification was bound to be aired, albeit with great caution. Churchill would have liked to raise it at a resumed Potsdam summit meeting, and periodically threatened himself to hold conversations with Malenkov if the Americans would not accept an East–West summit. Eisenhower restrained him, but agreed to a Western (US-British-French) summit. Churchill's stroke, however, forced its post-ponement (to Bermuda in December) and the substitution of more workmanlike Tripartite talks in Washington in July at Foreign Secretary level. This meeting invited the USSR to a Foreign Ministers' conference to discuss the holding of free elections and the constitution of an all-German government. In August the Soviet Union accepted a conference in principle, but urged a Five Power conference (including the Chinese People's Republic) and a wider agenda, and continued (as it had in August 1952) to resist external supervision of the elections. The omens for agreement were not promising. But a Four Power Foreign Ministers' conference in Berlin was eventually settled on for January 1954, the first such meeting since 1949. Its discussion of Germany went nowhere fast: the West insisted that a reunited Germany be free to adhere to the European Defence Community, Molotov that the East and West German parliaments should begin by establishing an all-German government that would then conduct elections without external supervision.

THE GENEVA CONFERENCE ON KOREA AND INDO–CHINA 1954

Complete deadlock was thus reached in Europe. But the Russians did secure agreement on a further conference to meet in Geneva in April 1954 and discuss, with Chinese communist participation, both Korea and Indo-China. They owed this success partly to common sense. The Korean armistice agreement of July 1953 had called for a peace conference, but all attempts to agree its composition had failed, so it was natural to hitch it on to the Foreign Ministers' meeting with the addition of all countries whose armed forces had participated in the war. That the Geneva conference was also to discuss Indo-China was chiefly due to the French. By 1953 France had tired of the fighting there,[25] and Bidault suggested at the

25. Indo-China is discussed more fully in *The Post-Imperial Age* chap. 2

Tripartite talks in Washington that the anticipated Korean conference should also discuss Indo-China. The idea met with initial British, and more durable American, reluctance (both countries hoped to keep the French fighting). France returned at intervals thereafter to the idea of a *Five* Power Conference: its hope was that the inclusion of communist China for the first time in a major international gathering would lead it in exchange to press restraint on the insurgent Vietminh. The Americans, of course, disliked thus conferring status on China, but at Berlin they had to give way for fear of undermining the only French government that seemed likely at least to continue fighting in Indo-China meanwhile, and also to ratify the EDC that was so central to US policy on Germany. Dulles privately doubted whether this Geneva conference would have important consequences.[26] As far as Korea was concerned he was quite right – disagreement on Korean reunification closely paralleled that at Berlin on Germany – but Indo-China was another matter.

The approach to the conference had been ominous. France had sought to entice the Vietminh into a set-piece battle in which they would be destroyed by superior fire power. So in November 1953 French and Vietnamese forces were airlifted to Dien Bien Phu, deep in the interior, where from March to May 1954 they were attacked by a combination of remarkably effective close quarters fighting and long-range shelling by artillery (probably recently brought in from China) that the French simply had not anticipated.

On 22 March 1954 the French Chief of Staff General Ely visited Washington to seek help, thereby inaugurating a period of intense and bad-tempered triangular diplomacy between Paris, Washington and London. Ely's counterpart Admiral Radford, who was in any case a partisan of US intervention, was told by Eisenhower (in Ely's presence) to respond quickly to his requests on Dien Bien Phu. The upshot was the drafting of a plan (Operation Vulture) for non-nuclear US air strikes to seek to lift the siege; there was no US commitment, but Radford's manner may have given France cause to expect its implementation.

Eisenhower was only briefly tempted by the idea of air strikes to save Dien Bien Phu. But he was concerned over Indo-China in general: when his Defense Secretary suggested forgetting about it

26. Sir James Cable, *The Geneva Conference of 1954 on Indochina* (1986) pp.22–4, 35–8, 43–4, 50; Historical Division Joint Chiefs of Staff, *The Joint Chiefs of Staff and the War in Vietnam: History of the Indo-China Incident 1940–54* (Washington, DC, National Archives) pp. 362–3

and concentrating on the defence of the rest of South-East Asia, Eisenhower replied that 'the collapse of Indochina would result in the fall of all Southeast Asia to the Communists'. He was not, however, prepared for sustained unilateral US action; and congressional leaders were to insist (on 4 April) that there be 'no more Koreas with the United States furnishing 90 percent of the manpower'. Instead Eisenhower's solution was 'United Action'. He had come, he told Churchill that evening in a personal letter,

> to the conclusion that there is no negotiated solution to the Indochina problem which in its essence would not be either a face-saving device to cover a French surrender or [one] to cover a Communist retirement . . .

He therefore proposed a coalition of the US, UK, France, Australia, New Zealand, Thailand and the Philippines. He clearly hoped that the mere existence of such an alliance would suffice – as he later put it, 'The general security and peaceful purposes . . . of such a concert of nations should be announced publicly – as in NATO. Then we possibly wouldn't *have* to fight'. But, his letter to Churchill continued, it

> must be willing to fight if necessary . . . If the members of the alliance are sufficiently resolute it should be able to make it clear to the Chinese Communists that the continuation of their material support for the Viet Minh will inevitably lead to the growing power of the forces arrayed against them.
>   . . . If we grasp this . . . [nettle] together I believe that we will enormously increase our chances of bringing the Chinese to believe that their interests lie in the direction of a discreet disengagement. In such a contingency we could approach the Geneva conference with the position of the free world not only unimpaired but strengthened.[27]

One historian speculates that Eisenhower may have been right – 'In the light of what we now know from Communist sources' of Vietminh weakness and Chinese unwillingness to rescue them, 'it seems unlikely that either the Russians or the Chinese would have risked a world war for the sake of the Vietminh'[28] At the time Eden

27. These paragraphs derive chiefly from Lawrence S. Kaplan, Denise Artaud, Mark R. Rubin (eds), *Dien Bien Phu and the Crisis of Franco-American Relations, 1954–5* (Wilmington, Delaware, 1990) chaps. 3–5 and Geoffrey Warner, 'The United States and Vietnam: two episodes', *International Affairs* lxv (1989) pp.516–8: Eisenhower's 4 April 1954 letter to Churchill is printed in *FRUS*, 1952–4 xiii pp.1239–41
28. Geoffrey Warner in Kaplan, Artaud, Rubin, *Dien Bien Phu* p.74, referring implicitly to *Khrushchev Remembers* i pp.442–3 and J. Radvanyi, *Delusion and Reality* (South Bend, Indiana, 1978) pp.8–10

thought otherwise: warnings might deter China from 'some unspecified future action' but not 'from action in which she is already engaged. It is hard to see that threat would be sufficiently potent to make China swallow so humiliating a rebuff as the abandonment of the Vietminh without any face-saving concession in return'. So 'the coalition would have to withdraw ignominiously or else embark on warlike action against China' that would probably be ineffective but that would give China 'every excuse for invoking the Sino-Soviet treaty and thus might lead to a world war'. A visit from Dulles produced only agreement on negotiations to establish a coalition, with the proviso that no announcement be made until after it was clear how the Geneva conference was going; even these fell through with considerable mutual acrimony.

Meanwhile the French position in Dien Bien Phu was weakening, and France had begun to beg for the implementation of Operation Vulture. At the same time feeling was growing in Paris in favour of a pull-out, especially as the condition of US aid appeared to be the internationalisation of the war and the displacement of French control. During a second visit to Europe, Dulles seems to have been desperate to stimulate French resistance. On 22 April the French understood him to have offered them two atom bombs for use in Vietnam. On 24–5 April Britain was placed under considerable pressure to join, Dulles indicating that the US would give the French immediate military help providing the UK did so too. Eden, however, persuaded his colleagues that 'large parts of Indo-China' would inevitably

> fall under Communist control, and the best hope of a lasting settlement lay in some form of partition. Our object should therefore be to strengthen the negotiating position of the French at the Geneva Conference. Their position would not be strengthened by a premature military intervention which would soon be seen to have been ineffective . . . France's Allies could at the moment make a better impression on the Chinese if they left them to guess what action they might subsequently take to help the French . . .

The ministerial meeting was, however, prepared to join a collective defence of South-East Asia *after* the Geneva conference, hopefully by way of guaranteeing the resultant settlement.

The British refusal was decisive. Both Dulles and Eisenhower told the French there could be no US intervention without a pre-liminary multi-lateral treaty. On 29 April the National Security Council decided to 'hold up for the time being any military action on Indo-China' pending developments at Geneva, while exploring the possibility of a coalition without Britain. There were US–French talks on this. But the US insisted on the internationalisation of the conflict and stressed that the French Associated States (Vietnam, Laos and Cambodia) would only fight if accorded full independence. France had never been attracted by the idea of thus fighting somebody else's war. It just might have accepted in late April to save Dien Bien Phu, but this fell on 7 May. So France would only 'discuss' US conditions, while itself insisting on a promise Eisenhower would not give of the commitment of American ground troops. The talks, therefore, achieved little; they stopped when Mendès–France became prime minister in mid-June.

After all this, and a slow and sticky start, the Geneva conference went quite well. Arguably most of the participants were resigned to the partition of Vietnam. Eden had clearly accepted the idea, while Eisenhower suggested at the end of April that something along the lines of Germany 'was the most you could ask' in existing circumstances. At a preparatory meeting in Moscow China showed itself very concerned at the possibility of being drawn in by an expansion of the fighting; quite apart from its losses in Korea, 'this would oppose China to the other peoples of South-East Asia and allow the USA the possibility of creating a bloc extending from India to Indonesia'. At the conference Zhou Enlai spoke positively to Bidault and Eden of Laos and Cambodia as neutral countries under their existing monarchies, and left Mendès-France with the impression that he preferred even the prolonged existence of two separate states in Vietnam provided the South did not fall under a foreign power.[29] The French attitude was mercurial, unnerved by the fall of Dien Bien Phu but finding it difficult to make concessions and continuing to explore the option of American intervention. But on 13 June 1954 the new Prime Minister, Pierre Mendès-France, publicly determined to secure a ccase-fire by 20 July and shortly afterwards began direct talks with the Vietminh. The Vietminh themselves did *not* want partition, but they had been much harder pressed early in the year than Westerners had realised, and had, before the start of the conference, been looking for no more than a cease-fire in place.[30] On 10 June they first indicated a readiness to settle for French evacuation of the North; and over the next month concessions appear to have been

---

29. F. Joyeaux, *La Chine et le règlement du premier conflit d'Indochine (Genève 1954)* (Paris, 1979) pp. 70–1, 322–3, 346; Cable, *Geneva Conference* pp.97–8
30. *Khrushchev Remembers* i pp.442–3

extracted from them by China, their chief source of weapons. By Mendès-France's deadline it had been agreed that Vietnam should be temporarily divided near the 17th Parallel, subject (on paper) to reunification by free elections two years later; neither zone should form part of any military alliance. Cambodia and Laos were to be independent and to abstain from seeking any military aid bar a small French training mission in Laos.

These terms were in fact not far short of the seven points agreed in June between Dulles and Eden, which (Dulles told Mendès-France) 'constitute a minimum as far as the U.S. is concerned' though, he feared, 'merely an optimum solution as far as your Government and perhaps the U.K. are concerned'. However, the United States was not enamoured of the neutralisation provisions. Since it was not prepared to intervene militarily, there was little it could do at Geneva to prevent France settling for whatever was obtainable. But it would not itself sign, merely undertake to note the agreements and not to use force to upset them.[31] The other unreconciled party was the new government of French (after the armistice, of South) Vietnam, headed by Ngo Dinh Diem, which had been kept apart from the Franco-Vietminh negotiations. The two rapidly drew together, and by November Eisenhower had agreed on a military mission and a $400 million aid package 'to maintain and support a friendly and independent non-Communist government in Vietnam and to assist it in diminishing and ultimately eradicating Communist subversion and influence'.

The other half of US policy to limit the spread of communism was 'the rapid organization of a collective defense in South-east Asia'. This had been one purpose of the administration's earlier pursuit of 'United Action' in Vietnam; while the British had then refused to commit themselves to anything that would pre-empt the holding of the Geneva conference, they were now agreeable to the collective guarantee of its outcome. Such a guarantee might have taken a 'Locarno' form, that is a guarantee of all the parties by both China (and allies) and the USA (and allies) and, possibly, by Asian states like India. This might have been acceptable to the People's Republic (which would, *inter alia*, have gained further recognition thereby); but it was rejected by the USA as expressing a moral approval of a communist success. So instead there was to be a defensive South-East Asia Treaty Organisation (SEATO), modelled

31. Even this pledge was somewhat stretched by the dispatch of a CIA sabotage team to disrupt the Vietminh's take-over of Hanoi

on NATO. Few newly independent states were keen to join, so it came into existence in September 1954 with only three Asian members, the heavily aligned Philippines, Thailand and Pakistan, plus the USA, UK, France, Australia and New Zealand. Although the Geneva conference had precluded Laos, Cambodia, and (South) Vietnam from membership, the area covered by the pact's obligations was so defined as to include them.

THE CHINESE OFFSHORE ISLANDS CRISIS 1954–5

SEATO never amounted to much; it has been described as a whole 'zoo of paper tigers'. But, together with South Vietnam's rapid shift from French to US tutelage, it destroyed one of the chief gains China thought it had secured from the Geneva conference: the exclusion of US influence from South-East Asia, which would be divided between weak neutral states accepting a loose Chinese hegemony. This disappointment may have underlain the next crisis, that over the 'offshore islands' which was to prove one of the most alarming in the entire postwar period.[32] These islands, Quemoy, Matsu and the Tachens, were very close to the Chinese mainland but still held by the Nationalists on Taiwan. The communists started shelling them in September 1954, and were apparently building up towards an invasion. The islands themselves were of little military value, and European statesmen (in Eisenhower's words) considered 'America reckless, impulsive and immature' in not letting them go. Chiang Kai-shek had stationed 70,000 troops there, however, and Eisenhower worried that, if he lost them, his regime might again unravel (as it had done only a few years earlier on the mainland). Eisenhower recognised the dangers if the USA got deeply involved in defending them: 'When we talk of general war with Communist China, what we mean is general war with the USSR also'. For 'If the Soviets did not abide by their treaty . . . and go to war in support of their Chinese ally, the Soviet empire would quickly go to pieces'. But initially he felt fairly confident that he could prevent matters

---

32. It is correspondingly controversial. My account derives from Gordon Chang, 'To the Nuclear Brink: Eisenhower, Dulles, and the Quemoy-Matsu Crisis' (which has a map) and H.W. Brands, 'Testing Massive Retaliation: Credibility and Crisis Management in the Taiwan Strait' – both in *International Security* xii (1988); cf. also Ambrose, *Eisenhower the President*, chaps 9,10

coming to such a pass. One tactic was to get New Zealand to refer the question to the UN Security Council with a view to securing the islands' demilitarisation. This might split the Soviet Union from China should it decide not to use its veto and so spoil its new peace-loving image. However, Chiang's 'Republic of China' also had a veto. To prevent Chiang using it, he was offered a defence treaty that committed the USA to defending Taiwan and the Pescadores and left deliberately vague whether it would also protect the offshore islands. But Beijing then jailed thirteen US airmen shot down over its territory during the Korean War; this created such a domestic storm in the USA that it was thought best to postpone the UN initiative until the dust had settled.

In January 1955 China overran one of the Tachen islands. The others (which were too distant for air cover from Taiwan) were thought to be indefensible; so the Americans bribed Chiang into permitting their evacuation by promising to protect Quemoy and Matsu. The administration had originally decided to make this promise public for its deterrent effect, but it eventually decided not to – perhaps to ease the passage through Congress of a resolution giving Eisenhower the authority, if he judged it necessary, to commit US forces to action in defence of Taiwan and 'closely related localities'. Chiang felt betrayed.

By March things were worse, and Dulles returned from a Far Eastern visit convinced there was 'at least an even chance' that China would attack Quemoy and Matsu and that the USA would have to fight. He and Eisenhower started to prepare American – and Chinese – opinion for the use of nuclear weapons: 'Yes, of course they would be used. In any combat where these things can be used on strictly military targets and for strictly military purposes, I see no reason why they shouldn't be used just exactly as you would use a bullet or anything else'. Privately, though, Eisenhower sought to bolster Chiang's own forces to avoid the need for direct intervention, and said that if the USA had to join in it would do so first with conventional weapons; atomic ones 'should only come at the end'. Tension was further raised when the Chief of Naval Operations told the press that the USA had plans for all-out nuclear attack on China and that he personally expected hostilities by 15 April.[33]

---

33. Though furious about this indiscretion, Eisenhower felt the Admiral might just be right as 'the Red Chinese appear to be completely reckless . . . possibly overconfident, and completely indifferent as to human losses'. But he doubted it: 'most of the calamities that we anticipate never really occur'

On 5 April 1955 Eisenhower wrote that they could no longer inertly await the moment of decision 'between two unacceptable choices', war or a retreat in the face of Chinese attack that could lead to the disintegration of 'all Asian opposition' to communism, and asked for ideas. This led to a mission being sent to Chiang, offering, if he agreed to evacuate the remaining islands, to institute a naval blockade of the Chinese coast opposite Taiwan – which would have proved both provocative and dangerous – and threatening, if he did not, to drop the US promise to protect Quemoy and Matsu. Chiang still refused, citing his betrayal over the Tachen Islands.

In the meantime China had changed course. The USA later heard, and credited, a rumour that Zhou Enlai had secretly flown to Moscow and been told that the Soviet Union would not support China in a war over the islands. Another view is that China had never meant to expel the Nationalists from *all* the offshore islands. For these were indubitably Chinese, whereas links between the island of Taiwan and China had been surprisingly tenuous before 1895; Taiwan had then for fifty years been ceded to Japan; and the majority of Taiwan's inhabitants were in the 1950s probably quite prepared to embrace a specifically Taiwanese, as opposed to Chinese, political identity. From this perspective Chiang's retention of Quemoy and Matsu, and claim to be the ruler of all China, may also have been a *Communist* Chinese interest: it would anchor Taiwan/Nationalist China to China proper in a situation of 'one country/two systems' that still afforded some hope of future reunion.[34] Anyway at the Bandung conference, Zhou made friendly noises towards the USA and offered negotiations. Eisenhower responded; Zhou went halfway towards giving the assurance that the USA had been appealing for via friendly Asian states, declaring that China was 'willing to strive for the liberation of Formosa by friendly means as far as this is possible'. Tension was gradually wound down, the imprisoned US airmen were released, and talks started in August 1955 – though apart from bestowing a modicum of US recognition on communist China, they achieved nothing.

34. It is interesting that in late 1955 China was charging that the USA wanted to 'hoodwink world public opinion by arranging for the traitorous Chiang Kai-shek group to "quit" the coastal islands', while after the 1958 crisis Mao praised the Taiwanese public for its loyalty to the concept of a single China and claimed the Americans were trying 'to force on us [both] a Two China policy': Nancy Bernkopf Tucker, in Immerman, *Dulles and the Diplomacy of the Cold War* pp. 259–60

FRENCH OPPOSITION TO THE EUROPEAN DEFENCE COMMUNITY

By this time events in Europe were moving rapidly towards détente. In 1954 the chief Anglo-American concern had been to secure, and Soviet to prevent, the achievement of the linked goals of West German independence and incorporation into the Western defensive structure. To this end the Soviets constantly floated alternative schemes for European security; in March 1954 they even suggested that they too should join NATO; but more usually they proposed some form of pan-European pact ideally without, but probably including, the United States. The West was not prepared to consider anything of the kind until after a West German settlement.

In the first half of 1954 such a settlement was looked for from the European Defence Community, which still needed French ratification. As we have seen the EDC had originally been a French idea to delay and water down German rearmament. Now things had come to the point, it no longer looked attractive; the French still feared German rearmament and were not prepared to relinquish (to the EDC) control over their own army. Knowing that the chances of ratification were slim, French governments (to the fury of their partners) kept putting off submitting the EDC to Parliament. Mendès-France was more decisive: after a vain plea to renegotiate its terms, he put the EDC to a free vote of the National Assembly, which buried it on 30 August 1954.[35] This was, potentially, a disaster, and both the USA and Britain moved rapidly to counter it. The United States leaned towards a NATO conference that (faced with a US ultimatum) would simply admit West Germany as an equal partner.[36] Eden proceeded with a round of diplomatic visits, securing the support of both Dulles and Mendès-France for a more elaborate approach via German membership not only of NATO but also of the 1948 'Western European Union' (WEU). This had the effect of making possible the imposition of limits (some, but not all, apparently multilateral)

35. There is a view that Mendès-France's dispatch of the EDC was a quid pro quo for Soviet helpfulness over Indo-China at the Geneva conference, but this is apparently a myth: Denise Artaud in Kaplan, Artaud, Rubin, *Dien Bien Phu* pp.263–4. Mendès-France himself told Churchill on 23 August that France would reject the EDC, but would 'never dare to reject an alternative, even that of German entry into NATO': Immerman, *Dulles and the Diplomacy of the Cold War* p. 100

36. Ambrose, *Eisenhower the President* pp. 210–11

on German rearmament.[37] The way was further smoothed by a West German pledge never to use force to achieve reunion or territorial revision, and by a British promise, not unbreakable but firmer than ever before, as to the continued maintenance of substantial forces on the continent. The result was the conclusion in October of the Paris agreements, which, if ratified, would incorporate a sovereign West Germany into the NATO alliance.

Though it is hard to square with their ostensible proposal of a neutral, united, and armed Germany, the Russians appear to have been genuinely worried at the prospect of a rearmed and revisionist West Germany. Mikoyan once said they had considered a range of responses, including the absorption of their zone of Austria into the Eastern bloc.[38] Probably the chief purpose of the more relaxed tone of Soviet diplomacy in the first half of 1954 had been to convince Western opinion that West German rearmament was no longer necessary. When the French National Assembly rejected the EDC it appeared to have been achieved; the Paris agreements therefore came as a disappointment. This may be sufficient explanation of the subsequent sharpening of the Soviet tone: 'The carrying out of the . . . Paris Agreements would mean that the unification of Germany through the holding of free all-German elections would be sacrificed for the present plans to restore German militarism – that mortal enemy of all the peoples of Europe, including the German people themselves'.[39] Or it may be that the harshness resulted from a Molotov–Khrushchev alignment in a Kremlin power struggle against Malenkov. In any case it failed. The French National Assembly nearly rejected the Paris Agreements on 24 December 1954, but finally accepted them after Christmas when Mendès-France made them a question of confidence.

37. All WEU members accepted maximum levels for their forces *on the continent* and agreed not to deploy these without the consent of the Supreme Allied Commander Europe (an American); Germany, unlike e.g. France, had no other forces. Germany undertook not to manufacture atomic, biological or chemical weapons, nor, without the consent of a two-thirds majority in the WEU, to build long-range missiles, heavy bombers, or war ships/submarines of any appreciable size. The WEU was to monitor compliance with these conditions: Ruhm von Oppen, *Documents on Germany under Occupation* esp. pp. 642–4. These constraints were to some extent paper ones: in the 1960s France withdrew all its troops from SACEUR's control, while limitations on German submarines have been relaxed. But they served their purpose of producing a feeling of security; in fact no states have wished to exceed their maximum force levels, and concern has more usually arisen from their reluctance to spend enough on conventional defence

38. Sven Allard, *Russia and the Austrian State Treaty: A Case Study of Soviet Policy in Europe* (Pennsylvania State University, 1970) p. 141

39. 13 November: RIIA, *Documents . . . 1954* pp. 58–9

AUSTRIAN INDEPENDENCE 1955

There still remained a possibility of rejection by the French Senate; this may have led the Russians to seek yet another conference, with the bait of discussing internationally supervised elections for Germany and also that of ending the occupation of Austria (on which they had been distinctly unforthcoming of late). Accordingly in February 1955 (despite the Offshore Islands crisis) Molotov started pressing, both publicly and through the Austrian ambassador in Moscow, for an Austrian settlement on the basis of neutrality and guarantees against future union with Germany. These overtures gained momentum despite both Western disinterest in any conference on Germany and the increasing likelihood that the Senate would ratify the Paris Agreements (as it did on 27 March). By April 1955 the Russians were negotiating in Moscow with the Austrians the outlines of a settlement (providing for the withdrawal of all occupation forces, Austrian adoption of 'Neutrality after the Swiss model', and delivery of petroleum and other products to the USSR). As Bulganin explained, the Russians had for five years stalled on Austria so as to be able to link its fate to progress on the German question. 'Now a solution to the German problem has been found that is unfortunate. We had to take this into account and draw the consequences for ourselves'.[40] Hence the emergence of a 'new general line', and of so great a Soviet eagerness at the final negotiations with the other occupying Powers that the latter were able to secure several minor concessions they had been quite prepared to forego in earlier discussions. The Austrian State Treaty was signed on 15 May 1955; on the 14th Molotov had informally agreed to a summit meeting in Geneva in July.

THE GENEVA SUMMIT 1955

The neutralisation of Austria came during a period of considerable activity and important new initiatives in Soviet diplomacy. The details are not entirely clear. But Malenkov's forced resignation in February 1955 as Chairman of the Council of Ministers was followed

---

40. Allard, *Russia and the Austrian State Treaty* p. 107; V. Mastny, 'Kremlin Politics and the Austrian Settlement', *Problems of Communism* xxxi (July–Aug. 1982) p.46

by a struggle between Khrushchev and Molotov (notably at a Central Committee plenum in July) that led to the latter's public self-criticism in the autumn. Points of conflict may have included Austria, and certainly covered the formation in May 1955 of a military pact (the Warsaw Pact) for the whole of Eastern Europe (bar Yugoslavia) and Khrushchev's visit to Yugoslavia at the end of the month in an attempt to heal the rift of 1948 and to draw Yugoslavia back into 'the camp'. More generally Khrushchev seems to have favoured a combination of the consolidation of the socialist camp and, outside it, of a more flexible policy that might include selective concessions (for instance the evacuation of Austria and, later that year, of the Soviet military base in Finland) to facilitate advances elsewhere. Western Europe Khrushchev regarded as broadly stabilised; the weak points of the capitalist world were chiefly in the former colonies which, though not yet ready for a social revolution, might be ready for an 'anti-imperialist' one. The principal consequences (in 1955) of this approach were an arms deal with Egypt and a visit by Khrushchev and Bulganin to India, Burma and Afghanistan. But readiness for a summit meeting with Western leaders also fitted into this pattern, and gave the Russians the opportunity of overcoming feelings (instilled into them by Stalin) of their own inferiority and incapacity to handle their Western counterparts.[41]

On the Western side the United States had always been the country most reluctant to contemplate a summit, but Eisenhower had in November 1954 reduced his preconditions to one – agreement on an Austrian Treaty 'would indicate real sincerity on the part of the Communist world to go into further negotiations'. In April 1955 the new British Prime Minister, Eden, in his run-up to elections, resumed pressure for a summit. Eisenhower was attracted by the light that such a meeting might shed on the real distribution of power within the post-Malenkov Soviet leadership. He may also have hoped to secure Soviet acceptance of his 'open skies' proposal (of mutual aerial inspection by the two sides as a security for disarmament), which he sprang on the conference in a dramatic speech. The proposal did at least pinpoint the true location of

41. Minutes of the Central Committee meeting were seen by a Polish official, Seweryn Bialer, who subsequently defected. His account has been used by Allard, *Russia and the Austrian State Treaty* pp.216–19, Wolfgang Leonhard, *The Kremlin since Stalin* (1962) pp. 106–10, and Mastny, 'Kremlin Politics and the Austrian Settlement' – which, however, doubts Molotov's opposition to the evacuation of Austria. See also *Khrushchev Remembers* i chaps 12, 13, ii pp.194, 223–5, iii pp. 68–9, 74–80, 85–7

power on the Soviet side; the reply of the delegation's ostensible leader, Bulganin, was not unsympathetic, but after the session Khrushchev came up to Eisenhower and turned the idea down flat.

However, the Geneva summit had been billed not as one at which agreements would be reached (like the wartime Teheran, Yalta and Potsdam meetings) but as a device to improve the atmosphere and encourage more detailed discussions at Foreign Secretary and diplomatic levels. As far as atmosphere went the effect was, for a time, remarkable. Eisenhower's final words at the conference were 'the prospects of lasting peace with justice, well-being and broader freedom, are brighter. The dangers of the overwhelming tragedy of modern war are less'. Unsurprisingly there was much talk of the 'spirit of Geneva', which was also encouraged by the new and less barbaric face the Soviet Union now presented to the world. Even Dulles, who had been acutely conscious both of the dangers this might pose to the Western alliance and of those that might result from a sudden puncturing of unrealistically high expectations, is reported as saying privately in 1956:

> So long as the Soviets under Stalin continued to behave so badly . . ., it was relatively easy for our side to maintain a certain social ostracism toward them. . . . The man who spits in your eye, puts poison in your soup . . ., is the kind of person you just don't want around. . . . And what is more important, everybody else understands.
>
> Now. . . . Frowns have given way to smiles. Guns have given way to offers of economic aid . . . – with the repudiation of Stalin, with the rehabilitation of scores of officials, scientists, soldiers . . . , with the apparent acceptance of Tito, and therefore of Titoism – with all these things going on, it is very difficult for the U.S. to say to its allies that all of this means nothing, that it is a trick, that the ostracism must be maintained.
>
> I don't think anyone wants to turn the clock back . . ., and furthermore I doubt if anyone could if he tried. We may be in very grave long-term danger because of the Soviets' new economic competition, but I would rather be trying to work out the answers to that one instead of trying to find an answer to H-bomb competition.
>
> Back in 1950 or '51, I spent $1,000 to build a bomb-proof cellar in my New York house . . . today I just would not spend that thousand dollars . . ., because I don't think that is the way the struggle is shaping up any more.[42]

But if the Geneva summit improved the atmosphere, it also showed further agreements on high politics to be unlikely (whereas the previous two years had seen such agreements on Korea, Indo-China

42. April 1956: Cook, *The Declassified Eisenhower* p. 200

and Austria). We have noted the failure of proposals for inspection, without which there would clearly be no nuclear disarmament. A fortnight after the conference the Russians staged a series of hydrogen bomb tests that demonstrated their ability to drop such bombs from aircraft (as opposed to simply exploding them on the ground) and led to fears that they had acquired a technological lead. Meanwhile on Germany Bulganin had declared at Geneva that the inclusion of the Federal Republic in NATO had made reunification impossible. Admittedly the conference communiqué (perhaps reflecting Bulganin's diplomatic inexperience) appeared to suggest otherwise.[43] But Khrushchev's speech in East Berlin on his way home cast doubt on this; in September 1955 the Soviets accorded East Germany full independence. So discussion of German reunion at the Foreign Ministers' conference (also at Geneva) in October 1955 was not a success.

EAST–WEST SUMMITS AND THEIR LIMITATIONS

This dented, but did not wholly destroy, the 'spirit of Geneva'. The summit had established the principle that East and West should both talk and be seen to talk. Adenauer went to Moscow in September 1955, and, after extremely tense negotiations (in which, if Khrushchev is to be believed, Adenauer offered loans and reparations payments in exchange for unification),[44] established diplomatic relations between West Germany and the USSR, securing in exchange the release of some 30,000 prisoners of war/civilian deportees.[45] In 1956 (as arranged at Geneva) the Soviet leaders made what seemed a highly successful visit to Britain – though in retrospect its most significant aspect was the warnings each side gave about the other's policies in the Middle East.[46] There was meant to follow a return visit by Eden to Moscow, also a

43. 'the settlement of the German question and the reunification of Germany by means of free elections shall be carried out in conformity with the national interests of the German people and the interests of European security.'

44. *Khrushchev Remembers* ii p. 358

45. Distinctly more than the 10,000 'war criminals' who were all the Soviets had previously admitted holding, though markedly fewer than the 130,000 the West Germans attributed to them. For years West German public opinion regarded the prisoners' release as Adenauer's principal achievement

46. See e.g. Harold Macmillan, *Memoirs* iv 'Riding the Storm' (1971) pp. 95–6; *Khrushchev Remembers* i p. 367

Soviet visit to the United States. Hungary and Suez interrupted the process, but the idea of summit meetings remained. Khrushchev suggested one in connection with the 1958 Middle East crisis. In 1959 Macmillan resurrected the invitation to Moscow in response to an apparent ultimatum over Berlin; later that year the same problem led Eisenhower to invite Khrushchev to the USA; and a Four Power summit was arranged for Paris for 1960, its collapse being followed in 1961 by a Kennedy–Khrushchev meeting in Vienna.

It was less clear what should be the content of these meetings and, more generally, of the East–West relationship. Certainly not negotiation from Western strength. Khrushchev ends his account of the Geneva summit with the claim that it had been 'an important breakthrough': he concluded that

> our enemies probably feared us as much as we feared them . . . [they] now realized that we were able to resist their pressure and see through their tricks . . . that they had to respect our borders and our rights, and that they couldn't get what they wanted by force or blackmail . . . they would have to build their relations with us on new assumptions and new expectations if they really wanted peace.

If not negotiation from strength, then there might be a limited scope for crisis management. The idea was around in 1958–9, but in general there has been a marked, and laudable, preference for crisis avoidance rather than crisis management: Khrushchev never did act on his threat to transfer to East Germany control over access to West Berlin. The few direct East–West crises, notably the Cuban missile crisis of 1962, were not in fact handled at the summit. Nor, finally, were East–West relations good enough (at least until the later 1980s) to permit attempts to manage other people's crises by a superpower condominium.

What remained was mostly more humdrum. Participants naturally claimed that they gained a better understanding of each other's positions, and this may sometimes have been useful in avoiding trouble.[47] High-level meetings will also have given a certain stimulus to contacts and consultations at lower levels; Khrushchev and Bulganin took an eminent scientist with them on their British visit 'because we wanted to establish contacts with the British scientific community'. In the long run such contacts can significantly alter countries' perceptions of each other; they may

47. Equally both Khrushchev's 1958 summit call and his 1959 visit to the USA strained Sino-Soviet relations

indeed have proved a factor in changing the image that many Soviet citizens had of the West.[48] But this process, necessarily slow, was even slower in the East–West case since it has often been so obviously subject to politics and official management. In the 1950s even National Exhibitions were rather the subject of competition and controversy, leading to a heated set-to between Khrushchev and Vice-President Nixon in 1959 over the usefulness or otherwise of American household gadgets (the 'kitchen debate').

One subject, however, is far more eye-catching – nuclear weapons. These have been peculiarly the province of the Great Powers, and to a very considerable extent of the two superpowers. Arms negotiations have been so important a theme in the East–West relationship that it will be convenient to discuss them in a separate chapter.

48. Of course we do not know how widespread favourable images were even in the USSR of the 1950s

CHAPTER SIX

The Strategic Dimension of East–West Competition

Military competition represented an important dimension of East–West rivalry, and, especially in the 1970s and 1980s, it came to form the staple of US–Soviet negotiations. In part this was because there were few other subjects in high politics that could profitably be discussed. It came too from the fact that leaders on both sides were not only sobered by the knowledge that they had the capacity to bring unimaginable catastrophe on the world, but also imbued by the feeling that this set them apart from other statesmen. As Kissinger's aide, Helmut Sonnenfeldt, put it

> Americans and Soviets do have certain concerns not shared by other nations. Control of the vast machinery of destruction, the fear of war, and concern about the responsibility of preventing horrible wars perhaps unite us with the Soviets even more than with our closest friends because we have looked into the abyss together.[1]

Given these perspectives, and since the subject is highly technical, it will be convenient to abstract the strategic dimension (as far as possible) from our general account of East–West relations and attempt to survey it in this chapter.

The likely consequences of war probably go far towards explaining why both the Soviet Union and the United States were far more cautious than earlier Great Powers had been. They avoided mutual hostilities; except perhaps around 1950–1 and conceivably during the 1961–2 Berlin and Cuba crises and the 1981–4 Andropov era in the USSR, nobody had any real fear of

---

1. L. Sloss and M. Scott Davies (eds), *A Game for High Stakes* (Cambridge, Mass., 1986) p. 26

these breaking out.[2] Certainly when US and British troops were really preparing to fight Iraq in 1990, they were given a level of training, spare parts and ammunition far higher than that which had been thought adequate when they were only passively confronting the forces of the Warsaw Pact in Germany. But if hostilities were not expected, East–West relations were antagonistic; both sides felt that, if they let their guard really drop, they would certainly suffer politically and might encourage their opponent to take cruder advantage of the changed military position. This meant that considerable military and intellectual interests were professionally devoted to the maintenance of a credible defence posture. So much thought was devoted to developing, and securing political backing for, strategies for conflicts that fortunately never occurred.

Writing about them is necessarily a rather theoretical exercise, and it is the more so since we are not comparing like with like. This is the case even in the nuclear field, and it is even more true of the conventional balance in Europe. As one scholar remarked, the NATO and Warsaw Pact

> military doctrines, which determine how each alliance builds and organizes its military forces, are quite different . . . the Pact prefers large numbers of major weapons and formations (. . . 'tooth') over training . . . , logistics, and the command and control functions . . . (. . . often referred to as 'tail') . . .
>
> In terms of military operations, Pact doctrine tends to extol the advantages of the offense. This is fairly explicit in Soviet military writings. On the other hand, . . . NATO tends to a more balanced view of the relative advantages of defensive and offensive tactics . . .
>
> The net result . . . is that the Warsaw Pact generates military forces that, at first glance, look substantially more formidable than those of NATO. Although official comparisons of . . . defense spending have consistently shown NATO outspending the Pact . . . ($360 billion vs. $320 billion in 1982 according to a recent Department of Defense estimate), the tendency in both official and unofficial balance assessments has been to highlight Pact advantages in tanks, guns, planes or divisions. The possibility that NATO's higher spending might be generating less visible, but equally important, . . . military capability seldom receives much consideration.[3]

2. For Andropov's fears, see pp. 10, 334; for more general official attitudes in the 1950s and 1980s, Schweitzer, *The Changing Western Analysis of the Soviet Threat passim*

3. Barry Posen, 'Measuring the European Conventional Balance', *International Security* ix (1984–5) pp. 51–2. Another reason for NATO's apparently poor showing is its refusal to standardise on US (as the Pact did on Soviet) equipment; this increases costs and also hampers cooperation between units of different nationalities

THE DEFENCE OF WESTERN EUROPE

Stalin's Soviet Union was a formidable military force, but its capacity to project power to distant parts of the globe was much inferior to Britain's, let alone the USA's. So any military interaction with the West would be primarily in Europe. After Stalin's death, the USSR acquired a 'strategic' capability to hit the USA with rocket-borne nuclear weapons, and by the 1970s was thus broadly on a par with the United States. In the 'conventional' field it developed ocean-going navies and an airlift capable of ferrying significant numbers of Cuban troops to Angola and Ethiopia. But outside Europe its presence (and in most areas its potential power)[4] remained inferior to that of the West. So the most important conventional military confrontation was that in Central Europe.

After the destruction of Germany potential Soviet preponderance in Europe was arguably as much a function of geography as the even more marked US preponderance in the Pacific that followed the defeat of Japan. It seemed more important since Europe had been, until recently, the centre of the world; and Western European resources were such that a state dominating Europe from the Atlantic to the Urals might well come to dominate the world. In 1917 and 1941 the USA had intervened to prevent this, and during the Cold War it did so again. Initially the perceived threat was one of economic collapse, subversion, intimidation and political take-over rather than of open conventional invasion. But in 1950 NATO came, not necessarily wrongly, to fear the latter. The response was, as we have seen, the dispatch of US troops to Germany and the decision to build up the conventional forces of the alliance. In February 1952 the Lisbon NATO Council meeting set a target of 96 divisions (including reserves) in Western Europe – to counter what was then estimated at 175 rather smaller Soviet divisions that could be considerably increased on mobilisation. The initial Western rearmament was considerable – US defence expenditure in 1953 was nearly four times, British nearly double, that of 1950.[5] But neither country was prepared to continue at these levels. Even at the 1952 Lisbon NATO Council meeting in

---

4. The USSR perhaps possessed, but did not exercise, the capacity to intervene massively in the Persian Gulf

5. Such spending accounted, on one calculation, for nearly 14% of GNP in the USA, over 10.5% in Britain (nearly 2% more than in the rearmament year of 1938): J.L. Gaddis, *Strategies of Containment* (paperback edn, 1982) p. 359; A. Seldon, *Churchill's Indian Summer* (1981) pp. 499–500

1952 Eden was also grappling with a British Cabinet crisis over economic policy, which led him to favour substantial cuts in the rearmament programme. In a defence review that summer the British Chiefs of Staff were no longer, as in 1950, apprehensive of an imminent Russian attack but instead expected a prolonged Cold War. In December 1952 British lobbying contributed to a modification of NATO's Lisbon targets.[6]

The USA's conversion came with the change of President in 1953. Eisenhower rejected the idea of preparing for a year of 'maximum danger' (1954), and held that 'If you are going on the defensive, you have got to get a level of preparation you can sustain over the years'. So he aimed at a 25 per cent reduction in military personnel, rather more in costs, by 1957–8. This would involve bringing home substantial numbers of foreign-based troops; the United States could not afford to maintain 'a sort of Roman wall to protect the world'. But this 'New Look' did not involve any abandonment of commitments. Instead primary (though not exclusive) responsibility for local ground defence should rest on the USA allies. They would be backed as necessary by US nuclear power: 'In the event of hostilities', declared the new policy directive NSC 162/2, 'the United States will consider nuclear weapons to be as available for use as any other munitions'. These weapons would be not only strategic but also, especially in Europe, 'tactical', that is intended for battlefield use. Deployment of tactical nuclear weapons began in 1954, and they seemed admirably suited to remedy NATO's shortfall in conventional troops. As General Gruenther, the Supreme Allied Commander Europe (SACEUR) explained, NATO forces constituted a 'shield' that would compel 'an enemy to concentrate prior to attacking. In doing so, the concentrating force would be extremely vulnerable to losses from atomic weapon attacks'.[7] In line with this thinking NATO authorised its commanders, in December 1954, to base their planning on the use of nuclear weapons. But strangely little effort was devoted to reducing the radioactive contamination that would flow from the tactical use of such weapons.

The strategy of the shield did not, in theory, involve any reduction of NATO forces in being, though it did restrict the

---

6. Other countries too cut defence spending for financial reasons: Seldon, *Churchill's Indian Summer* p. 332; M. Gowing, *Independence and Deterrence: Britain and Atomic Energy, 1945–1952*, i (1974) pp. 440–1; Lord [H.L.] Ismay, *NATO: The First Five Years* (no pl., 1955) pp. 47, 104, 106, 107, 111

7. Ismay, *NATO: The First Five Years* p. 108

length of time for which they might be expected to have to fight (and hence the importance of reserves). Thus in 1957 NATO adopted a target of 30 combat-ready divisions for the central front (as against the 25 envisaged at Lisbon), while reducing the alliance grand total (including reserves) from 96 to some 70–75. But countries that no longer feared an imminent Soviet attack found appealing the idea that, with tactical nuclear weapons, troop numbers were less important. In 1954 France began withdrawing divisions (ultimately four) for use in Algeria; in 1956 West Germany responded to the domestic unpopularity of conscription by reducing its target force from 500,000 to 350,000; in 1957 Britain withdrew two divisions, and in 1959 it abandoned conscription; thus considerably reducing its trained reserves. Eisenhower also withdrew some troops as he had always intended; but his options were severely restricted by the outcry that – especially in Germany – followed the leaking in 1956 of the 'Radford memorandum' that proposed reducing US forces in Europe to token levels. The corollary of all this was that there came to be available for the central front not 30 but only some 16–18 combat-ready divisions, and that these relied on the early use of nuclear weapons: their adoption by the *Bundeswehr* in 1958 (albeit with continued US control over the warheads) was wildly unpopular in West Germany, though the political storm soon subsided (perhaps because of renewed Soviet pressure on Berlin).[8]

By the end of the 1950s, therefore, NATO's more ambitious targets were clearly not going to be met. Its conventional forces constituted something between a 'shield' – capable, if not of indefinite resistance, at least of compelling (in the event of any invasion) a major and deliberate concentration of Soviet forces that would be vulnerable to nuclear attack – and a 'trip-wire' that would set off nuclear weapons in the event of any sizeable incursion. In either case strategy depended on a readiness to use nuclear weapons first. The 1960s saw attempts to modify this stance, for the Kennedy administration distrusted over-reliance on nuclear weapons and sought additional options, both globally and in the European context. This occasioned European worries that the USA was in fact withdrawing its nuclear protection. But NATO formally adopted the policy of conventional resistance designed to impose

---

8. R.E. Osgood, *NATO. The Entangling Alliance* (Chicago, Ill., 1962) esp. pp. 117–21; R. Hilsman in K. Knorr (ed.) *NATO and American Security* (Princeton, NJ, 1959) pp. 30–1

on aggression a 'pause', during which reflection and diplomacy might avoid a renewed assault that would lead to nuclear war. A further development was the 1967 strategy of 'flexible response', that is of retaining for as long as possible the option of meeting aggression without automatically resorting to nuclear reprisals. At a more concrete level, the 1961 Berlin crisis had led to German readoption of a 500,000-strong *Bundeswehr*, to the demonstrative dispatch of 40,000 US troops to Germany, and to the return of two French divisions from Algeria.

But important forces were working in the opposite directions. The Kennedy approach to nuclear weapons notwithstanding, the number of tactical warheads in Western Europe doubled in 1961–3. Although the Berlin crisis led to a conventional build-up, this was untypical. In 1966 France withdrew from NATO's supranational command structure, which both complicated logistics and made French military aid in war theoretically uncertain and in any case more difficult to plan. Later in the decade the USA itself resumed withdrawing troops, partly for use in Vietnam and partly for economic reasons; total US forces in Europe fell from 434,000 in 1962 to 300,000 in 1979, despite an increase in Soviet strength in the 1970s. Over the same period most NATO countries allowed their defence spending (as a proportion of GNP) to fall gradually.[9] Much of the explanation must be that there seemed no great need for such spending and that the political constituencies for domestic expenditure were stronger. But the trend also reflected a definite strategic outlook on the part of most European governments – a distaste for any policy that by forswearing nuclear retaliation against a major incursion, or even (through massive conventional arma-

9. Defence spending as a proportion of GNP (1962 of National Income, 1984 of GDP) – selected NATO countries:

	1962	1965	1970	1975	1980	1984
Belgium	3.8	2.9	2.8	3.0	3.3	3.2
Canada	5.6	3.2	2.5	2.2	2.4	2.3
Denmark	3.2	2.6	2.3	2.2	2.4	2.3
France	7.2	5.6	4.0	3.9	3.9	4.1
Germany	5.9	4.9	3.0	3.9[*]	3.2[*]	3.3
Italy	4.4	2.9	2.8	2.6	2.4	2.7
Netherlands	5.0	4.3	3.5	3.6	3.4	3.2
UK	6.7	6.3	4.9	4.9	5.1	5.5
USA	11.3	8.0	7.8	5.8	5.5	6.4

[*] includes financial aid to West Berlin.

Source: International Institute for Strategic Studies (IISS) *The Military Balance 1986–7*

ment) rendering it less likely, would risk making conventional war seem a possible option. Such war had been destructive enough in 1939–45 and would be far worse now. So though European *peoples* periodically showed alarm at the prospect of being defended by American nuclear weapons,[10] the nightmare of most *governments* was that Europe might become 'uncoupled' from American strategic power and so fearful of Soviet 'nuclear blackmail' or even conventional invasion.

SOVIET POLICY TOWARDS WESTERN EUROPE

Soviet policy appears more straightforward. Stalin had no direct defence against a US nuclear monopoly. One response was to give maximum priority to the development of nuclear weapons. Although they were tested in his lifetime (an 'atomic' explosion in 1949 and a small 'hydrogen'-type explosion in the summer of 1953), the USSR is believed to have had no bomb operationally deployed in January 1953, at which time the USA had 1,600.[11] As a (poor) substitute Stalin posed the threat of overrunning a largely undefended Western Europe with his conventional forces: Khrushchev tells us these were raised from a low of 2.9 million in 1948 to a peak of 5.7 million in 1955 (a figure that, if true, was above Western estimates); the period also saw the build-up of East European armies to about 1.5 million (half, apparently, of some combat value) in 1953. Khrushchev (like Eisenhower) believed in cutting conventional defence spending, to the benefit of rockets and nuclear bombs. He claimed to have reduced Soviet forces to 3.6 million in 1960, then set a target of 2.4 million. His cuts, however, encountered intense military opposition and were reversed with the 1961 Berlin crisis. Since Khrushchev's fall (or perhaps since the 1962 Cuban missile crisis) defence expenditure again built up – perhaps by 4–5 per cent per year before 1976, 2 per cent per year in 1976–82 and 3–5 per cent per year in 1982–5;[12] these rates were initially in line with the growth of the Soviet

10. The famous 1955 'Carte Blanche' exercise with tactical weapons was deemed to have 'killed' 1.7 million Germans and 'incapacitated' a further 3.5 million

11. Ambrose, *Eisenhower the President* p. 93

12. T. Wolfe, *Soviet Power and Europe, 1945–70* (Baltimore, Md, 1970) esp. pp. 10n, 42–3, 165; IISS, *The Military Balance 1986–7* pp. 32, 34–5; D. Holloway, *The Soviet Union and the Arms Race* (1984 edn) pp. 114–17

economy as a whole, but by the 1980s defence was probably outpacing such growth and its increasing costs becoming a significant burden.

Of course not all Soviet power was targeted on Western Europe: Khrushchev records participating, sceptically, in a map exercise in which the Black Sea fleet broke through into the Mediterranean and landed in the Middle East;[13] and in later years extra-European missions certainly grew. But the great bulk of Soviet forces were stationed in the west of the USSR and in Eastern Europe, whence they could simultaneously deter trouble in the 'satellites' and pose an invasion threat to the West. The military thinking of the Red Army was offensive: according to General Shtemenko, 'orienting oneself on the strategic defense . . . means dooming oneself beforehand to irreparable losses and defeat'.[14] So training concentrated on the development of the offensive.

Initially it was felt that this would inevitably encounter nuclear resistance, but by the end of the 1960s the Soviets came to feel they were achieving nuclear parity, both strategic and tactical, and saw NATO's abandonment of 'massive retaliation' for 'flexible response' as a consequence. This opened up, at least in theory, the possibility of a purely conventional war, especially if the USSR preserved what the Americans term 'escalation dominance'.[15] It has been argued that the Soviet arms build-up of the 1970s was largely designed to provide such a conventional option.[16] How much progress the Soviets actually made to this end (which would include the destruction by conventional means of NATO theatre and tactical nuclear weapons) it is impossible to say. But some German analysts have concluded (on the basis of East German documents) that Warsaw Pact goals – a drive to the borders of France in a fortnight,

13. *Khrushchev Remembers* ii p. 29
14. Wolfe, *Soviet Power and Europe* p. 200
15. The ability to prevail at any given level of weaponry, imposing on the adversary the responsibility of deciding whether or not to escalate to (or within) the nuclear field and/or to extend the types of target chosen – in the knowledge that at each level he faced at least proportionate retaliation
16. P. A. Petersen and J.G. Hines, 'The Conventional Offensive in Soviet Theater Strategy', *Orbis* Fall 1983, esp. pp. 698–701, 708, 731–3. Among the defectors to mention such plans was the Hungarian diplomat Radvanyi. His 1967 defection was prompted by fears (voiced by the Soviet military attaché in Washington) of a military-backed take-over in Moscow, and reports of plans for 'a thundering attack in Western Europe . . . . According to Meshcheryakov, the Russian armed forces are so powerful and mobile that when the Western world woke up it would be too late – the Red Army would already be at the English Channel. The United States and its NATO allies would not have enough power to resist with conventional weapons and would not dare to use the atomic bomb: *Delusion and Reality* pp. 232 ff

to those of Spain in a month – were so ambitious that the employment of tactical nuclear and chemical weapons would have been 'almost obligatory' while many training exercises assumed their extensive use to break through Western defences.[17]

NATO, for its part, did not believe it could handle a sustained attack without resort to the first use of nuclear weapons. Concern as to Soviet capabilities led it in 1977–9 to adopt countermeasures, including a resolution to increase defence expenditure by 3 per cent per year in real terms; by no means all member states lived up to this, but some of the effects are visible in the figures recorded in note 9 (p. 155).

Conventional strength in Europe was one aspect of Soviet defence policy, nuclear weaponry another. Initially this too was directed against Western Europe for the simple reason that the US could not be reached, a position that lasted in essence into the 1960s. So, in 1961, West European vulnerability was pointedly stressed; *Izvestia* declared

> Khrushchev believes absolutely that when it comes to a showdown, Britain, France and Italy would refuse to join the United States in a war over Berlin for fear of their absolute destruction. Quite blandly he asserts that these countries are, figuratively speaking, hostages to the USSR and a guarantee against war.[18]

In the 1960s, as we shall see, the USSR did acquire an inter-continental (ICBM) capability against the USA. But it did not scrap its intermediate range ballistic missiles (IRBMs) targeted on Western Europe (unlike the USA, which for various reasons did dismantle the IRBMs it had from 1957 onwards deployed in Europe). Instead in the 1970s the USSR modernised them, substituting mobile SS-20s for the fixed base SS-4s and SS-5s (and highly advanced 'Backfire' bombers for the older 'Badgers' and 'Blinders'). The overall number of delivery systems was in fact reduced, but their capacity greatly increased since the SS-20 had three independently targetable warheads. Neither the arms control

---

17. 'Except for a few exercises in the late 1980s,' the Federal German Ministry of Defence notes, 'defense against a NATO attack was not practiced'; it was also struck both by the high degree of readiness at which East German bases were always kept and by the discovery of already minted victory medals: 'Warsaw Pact Military Planning in Central Europe: Revelations from the East German Archives', *Cold War International History Project Bulletin* 2 (1992) pp. 1, 13–19; *Sunday Times*, 28 March 1993, p. I.24

18. Holloway, *The Soviet Union and the Arms Race* pp.66–7; *Khrushchev Remembers* ii pp.47–8. Another purpose of targeting Western Europe will have been to catch US bombers/missiles on the ground and so reduce damage to the USSR

discussions of the 1970s – which touched only on weapons capable of striking the two superpowers (a Soviet definition of 'strategic') – nor the resulting treaties – which side-stepped the small British and French deterrents and dealt only with inter-continental weapons – impeded this Soviet 'theatre' modernisation. But, from the West European perspective, Soviet IRBMs were quite as 'strategic' as British or French missiles and far more numerous.[19]

REACTIONS TO SOVIET BUILD-UP; NATO'S 1979 RESPONSE

In conjunction with the build-up of Soviet conventional forces and ICBMs, the SS-20 deployment gave rise to much Western concern. For it seemed to presage Soviet escalation dominance: an offensive conventional superiority; nuclear superiority within Europe; at least 'strategic' parity with the USA, which might inhibit the covering of Western Europe with the American 'strategic umbrella'. Questions had been raised for some time as to this umbrella. As early as 1959 US Secretary of State Herter had doubted whether any President would engage 'in all-out war unless we were in danger of all-out devastation ourselves'. Such doubts, fed by the 1960s American stress on conventional options, served as an explicit rationale for the development of the French nuclear deterrent. But they were consistently and forcefully disavowed by US leaders confident of a continued marked nuclear advantage over the Soviet Union. From the mid-1970s the unexpectedly rapid Soviet development of multiple warheads shrank this lead and opened up the possibility that the US ICBM force might itself become vulnerable. These changes were among the factors that led Defense Secretary Schlesinger in 1974 to recast US doctrine to enhance 'limited nuclear options' for the support of 'extended deterrence'.

Nevertheless the advent of strategic parity led, as Kissinger subsequently put it, to repeated European demands for 'additional reassurances of an undiminished American commitment', and later to tactful pressure, notably by Chancellor Schmidt, for an improvement in the European theatre nuclear balance. The need for some such reassurance was enhanced by President Carter's apparent indecision, evident in (for instance) his 1978 abandonment of his

19. Holloway, *The Soviet Union and the Arms Race* pp. 74–5

own proposal for the deployment of 'neutron' anti-personnel bombs, *after* European governments had incurred political costs by accepting it.[20] Hence the 1979 NATO decision to deploy 576 US 'cruise' and Pershing intermediate-range missiles. These would, it was claimed, both reduce the risk of attack or blackmail by Soviet SS-20s and 'strengthen the linkage between NATO's conventional forces and US intercontinental strategic systems'. (Presumably, though this was *not* explicitly stated, decisions on the use of those missiles deployed in Germany and the Low Countries in the path of a Soviet invasion could not long be postponed; since the missiles could strike targets in the Soviet Union, their impact could be 'strategic'.) This NATO decision was to prove central to the politics of the 1980s.

US NUCLEAR SUPERIORITY IN THE 1950s AND 1960s

The most important dimension of Soviet nuclear policy was, however, that targeted directly against the United States. In the 1950s Soviet capacities were, as we have seen, very limited. The decision to concentrate on rockets rather than aircraft as delivery systems prolonged the period of this weakness. The USSR covered this with bluff. In 1955 US observers were misled by repeated bomber overflights at parades into a gross overestimate of their numbers. Then in 1957 the Soviet Union put the world's first satellite into space. Khrushchev played this success for all it was worth, boasting that he could send rockets anywhere on earth with such accuracy as to hit a fly. This led many Americans to fear that a 'missile gap' had opened up. But Eisenhower knew – in part from U2 reconnaissance overflights conducted since 1956 – that it had not, and was thus emboldened to resist congressional pressure for a massive increase in the US missile programme.

Khrushchev's expectations were the opposite – that given American superiority, overflights and other intelligence would make it 'easier for them to determine the most expedient moment to

20. Cf. the Herblock cartoon on 'Carter Policy Turns' captioned 'It's the Cartron bomb – it knocks down supporters without damaging opponents'. Z. Brzezinski, while not clearing Carter of indecision, does contend that Schmidt's acceptance of the bomb was ambivalent and that he 'maneuvered to make the decision appear a purely American one': *Power and Principle* (New York, 1983) pp.301–6

start a war'.[21] The cure, of course, was the acquisition of equality. An opportunity to achieve this through a quick fix came when Cuba turned to the Soviet Union in 1961 for protection after a CIA attempt to topple Castro's leadership through an émigré invasion. Agreement was secured for the installation of forty-two medium-range missile launchers, a great adjunct to Soviet strength given that the USSR then had only about twenty ICBMs, which (Kissinger says) took longer to fuel than it would have taken US forward-based bombers to reach them.[22] The deployment was, however, detected while still incomplete, and Kennedy forced the missiles' withdrawal (see pp. 227–31). A Soviet diplomat negotiating this withdrawal remarked, 'You Americans will never be able to do this to us again';[23] and some historians claim (though others deny) that, while humiliation over Cuba certainly improved the climate of East–West relations in the short run, it also spurred the subsequent Soviet defence build-up.

In the early 1960s, however, it was the American build-up that was more in evidence. During his 1960 election campaign Kennedy had promised to close the 'missile gap'; by the time he discovered it was really an inverse gap in the USA's favour, it was too late to alter course. Eisenhower had developed high quality missiles: 'Minuteman' ICBMs, which appeared to be invulnerable in their hardened underground silos, and Polaris submarine-launched ballistic missiles (SLBMs) that were also invulnerable though less accurate. These programmes were rapidly carried forward, until in 1967 the USA had 1,054 ICBMs and 656 SLBMs. That, Defense Secretary McNamara decided, was enough; in future the USA would rely not on more rockets but on multiplying the number of warheads carried.

'HEALEY'S THEOREM'

The question 'Enough for what?' raises the whole area of atomic strategy. This has generated a vast literature, necessarily theoretical. One reaction is that of Kennedy's National Security Adviser, McGeorge Bundy:

21. *Khrushchev Remembers* ii pp.410–11
22. *New York Times*, 29 Jan. 1989 pp. 1, 10; H.A. Kissinger, 'NATO: The Next Thirty Years', *Survival* xxi (1979) p. 265
23. Kissinger, *Memoirs* i p. 197

> There is an enormous gulf between what political leaders really think about nuclear weapons and what is assumed . . . in simulated strategic warfare. Think Tank analysts can set levels of 'acceptable' damage well up in the tens of millions of lives. They can assume that the loss of dozens of great cities is somehow a real choice. . . . In the real world of real political leaders – whether here or in the Soviet Union – a decision that would bring even one hydrogen bomb on one city of one's own country would be recognized in advance as a catastrophic blunder; ten bombs on ten cities would be a disaster beyond history; and a hundred bombs on a hundred cities are unthinkable.[24]

It is likely that most Western, and especially West European, governments worked chiefly on this basis. What they saw as important was the preservation of ambiguity. Any serious conventional invasion might meet a nuclear response; once the fire-break between conventional and nuclear (even tactical nuclear) weapons was crossed, there might well be escalation to major nuclear war. But, according to what has been termed 'Healey's Theorem',[25] 'if there is one chance in a hundred of nuclear weapons being used, the odds would be enough to deter an aggressor'. The Gaullist advocates of the French deterrent in the 1960s added that the existence of a number of independent centres of nuclear decision-making must complicate the potential aggressor's calculations of the likelihood of nuclear response and hence add to deterrence. This doctrine cannot be regarded as intellectually rigorous. But it must derive some support from the fact that neither the Cold War nor the possibly even more acute Sino-Soviet antagonism led to serious hostilities between the major powers – unlike many earlier Great Power rivalries and a number of contemporary confrontations between non-nuclear powers in the Middle East and South Asia.

EVOLUTION OF US STRATEGIC DOCTRINE; 'MUTUAL ASSURED DESTRUCTION'

'Healey's Theorem' also had much support in the United States, but it does not explain the evolution of the American nuclear

24. Quoted by L. Freedman, 'The First Two Generations of Nuclear Strategists', in P. Paret (ed.) *Makers of Modern Strategy from Machiavelli to the Nuclear Age* (Oxford, 1968) p. 769. It has, however, been observed that Stalin did inflict comparable casualties on his people in the 1930s in the general pursuit of Soviet power

25. Named after the British Defence Minister, 1964–70. Bundy professed belief in this theorem in his defence of conventional strategic doctrine against Kissinger's recantation and criticisms: 'The Future of Strategic Deterrence', *Survival* xxi (1979) pp.271–2

arsenal into what is very much more than a minimum deterrent. Initially things were fairly simple. The 1940s, and still more the 1950s, saw an enormous build-up in the manned bomber force under Strategic Air Command (SAC). This would initially have dropped such few atom bombs as were available on industrial complexes in Soviet cities, the only targets it could be confident of finding. Even if all 133 bombs went off perfectly, it was reported in 1949 that this would not 'bring about capitulation' or even halt an invasion of Western Europe. As more bombs became available, as intelligence improved, and as the USSR itself started to acquire nuclear weapons, SAC added more targets (reaching 3,261 by early 1957) – to retard the Red Army's conventional advance and to destroy Soviet command, air and nuclear bases. SAC's priorities were challenged in the later 1950s by the US Navy, which advocated limiting deterrence to an invulnerable force (presumably its own Polaris SLBMs then under development) capable of destroying 200 Soviet cities. The result was a study that predictably came out for an 'optimum mix' of 'high priority military, industrial and governmental control targets', and the construction of a Single Integrated Operations Plan (SIOP) to eliminate inter-service targeting duplication in achieving this. Were the Plan ever to have been implemented, all these targets would have been struck at the outset, leaving nothing in reserve. The incoming Kennedy administration was shocked by this all-or-nothing approach; McNamara soon had the SIOP reworked to concentrate initial attacks on Soviet forces and their infrastructure/communications, while 'holding in protected reserve forces capable of destroying urban society'.

At the operational level the new SIOP lasted little altered into the 1970s.[26] Although McNamara began by publicising the new idea of sparing Soviet cities (while retaining the capacity to destroy them) in the hope that this would lead the enemy to reciprocate,[27] his *speeches* soon changed – to stress the importance of being seen to possess the capacity to absorb any conceivable Russian strike and still be able to destroy Soviet society. This had admittedly always

26. The previous section derives chiefly from: A.L. Friedberg, 'The Evolution of U.S. Strategic Doctrine, 1945–1980', in S.P. Huntington (ed.) *The Strategic Imperative: New Policies for American Security* (Cambridge, Mass., 1982); and D.A. Rosenberg, 'The Origins of Overkill: Nuclear Weapons and American Security, 1945–1960', *International Security* vii (1963)

27. Eisenhower had regarded counter-force second strikes as unfeasible. If the worst came to the worst, 'We are not going to be searching out mobile bases for ICBMs, we are going to be hitting the big industrial and control complexes': Rosenberg, 'The Origins of Overkill' p. 62

been McNamara's bottom line. But he came to focus almost entirely on 'Assured Destruction', having discovered that the more he emphasised 'options' and 'counter-force targeting', the more weapons the military demanded to make this possible.

However, 'Assured Destruction' was more than just a device for bureaucratic in-fighting; it was also central to the doctrine of 'arms control' as it emerged in the 1960s.

As long as the United States possessed under all circumstances the capability of destroying about a quarter of Soviet population and half Soviet industry, it was held, 'deterrence' was assured, since there could be no conceivable Soviet incentive to push the USA to such retaliation. From this perspective, all that mattered was the survivability of the US deterrent, which seemed assured by its continued development as a 'triad' along lines that were probably in any case inescapably determined by service interests: ICBMs in their 'hardened' silos; SLBMs fired from submarines that an enemy would find very hard to locate; and manned bombers that could escape attack by leaving the ground in an emergency.[28]

Logically, what went for the United States went also for the Soviet Union. McNamara accepted this; as early as 1961 he had told the President that a capability to destroy all Soviet nuclear weapons was not only 'almost certainly unfeasible' but also undesirable since it 'would put the Soviets in a position which they would be likely to consider intolerable'.[29] He came to see Soviet acquisition of an 'Assured Destruction' capability as not only inevitable but also stabilising, since once they had attained it (by the later 1960s) they would no longer feel any need to get their blow in first.

Accordingly 'Mutual Assured Destruction' (MAD) became widely valued in Washington. It was thought that there was an objective mutual US–Soviet interest in preserving this condition, by negotiated arms control, in as stable and cheap a form as possible. Perhaps the Soviets did not yet fully recognise this. But, if so, educating them would be a subsidiary function of Strategic Arms Limitation Talks (SALT).

---

28. Democratic administrations would happily not have replaced manned bombers when they became obsolete. But, at least in the 1960s, they had massive congressional support, and simply scrapping them was never an option. Besides they had non-nuclear uses (in Vietnam); in the 1980s their strategic significance was revived by the advent of air-launched cruise missiles

29. Rosenberg, 'The Origins of Overkill' p. 68

NUCLEAR TEST BAN TREATY 1963

Arms control theory was not the only source of the SALT process. Others were the long-established habit of nuclear conversations, Soviet needs, and the defence problems of the Nixon administration. Nuclear conversations had begun as a result of the growing concern in the 1950s as to the consequences of atomic testing in the atmosphere, a subject initially brought to international notice in 1954 when unexpected winds carried fall-out from a US test to contaminate some Pacific islanders and, more deeply, the crew of a Japanese fishing boat, the *Lucky Dragon*. The Indian Prime Minister, Nehru, invoked Asian sentiment and called for immediate test suspension and the working out of a comprehensive disarmament agreement. This soon led to the appointment of a UN disarmament subcommittee and the tabling of proposals by both East and West. At least initially these should be seen as propaganda, but it is significant that it was felt necessary to appeal to, and reassure, public opinion both internationally and in the USA and Britain. Still tests continued to multiply.

A breakthrough came in 1958, when, on the completion of a major Soviet series, Khrushchev announced a moratorium. Eisenhower (who had for some time been worried by fall-out) responded by suggesting a technical meeting of Soviet and American scientists to examine the possibility of monitoring a test ban. This Geneva meeting went well, and the world was impressed by the apparent ability of the scientific community to talk across the East–West divide.[30] Eisenhower, having completed his series, then proposed negotiations for a general test-ban treaty and announced a suspension of explosions as from 31 October 1958 to facilitate these. There followed a positive orgy as the USA, UK and USSR sought to squeeze in last-minute tests, then a lull until the first French test in 1960. The negotiations for a complete ban failed: Eisenhower's scientific advisers had been too sanguine, and had to concede (to their pro-testing compatriots) the possibility of concealing underground tests of up to 20 kilotons, barring an inspection system far more elaborate than that envisaged by the 1958 Geneva meeting and quite unacceptable to the USSR. Still the three nuclear powers continued to observe the moratorium. We know, though, that there were strong lobbies within Washington for

---

30. Similar instances were the 1957 Pugwash conference, and the 1958 Geneva conference on the prevention of surprise attack

the resumption of testing, and may presume that the same was true in Moscow: in September 1961, coincident with Khrushchev's general challenge to the West, the Soviet Union resumed massive tests in the atmosphere. The USA promptly followed, initially underground but in 1962 also in the atmosphere. However, when tensions again subsided after the Cuban missile crisis, agreement was fairly readily reached: the vexed issue of inspection was bypassed by permitting underground tests, but the USA, USSR, UK, and (by adhesion to the 1963 Test Ban Treaty) most other countries foreswore atmospheric testing.[31]

This was arguably the most significant postwar arms agreement reached (at least until 1990) in that it removed a source of radioactive fall-out that was killing people and that threatened, if tests continued to multiply, to cause appreciable contamination. (It also greatly worsened Sino–Soviet relations – see pp. 283–4, 439.) But the treaty certainly did not halt the arms race. Some say the United States, by not moving decisively to end testing in the early 1950s, missed a great opportunity to halt the nuclear race while it was ahead. This seems unlikely. Both France and China went forward with atmospheric testing despite the 1963 treaty (to which they did not adhere), until they felt that their weapons technology was sufficiently developed. Had there been earlier attempts at a ban, the USSR and Britain would presumably have done the same. Just possibly, though, the conclusion in the later 1950s of a complete Test Ban Treaty, even if inadequately monitored, might have inhibited the subsequent arms build-up by preventing the testing of small warheads for multiple-tipped missiles. The chief immediate obstacle to such a treaty was the USSR's unreadiness to permit more than a very limited number of inspections on its territory of doubtful occurrences (like earthquakes) that resembled tests. Other countries, too, were probably less tolerant of inspection than they portrayed themselves; but Soviet hostility to the idea from Stalin to Chernenko, though it had some reasonable basis,[32] verged on

31. R.A. Divine, *Blowing in the Wind: The Nuclear Test Ban Debate 1956–60* (New York, 1978). A US–USSR Treaty banning underground tests of over 150 kilotons was signed in 1974, but not ratified until 1990 (owing to concern over verification). Negotiations for a complete test ban have never made much progress, but the end of the Cold War brought unilateral moves towards suspension, in which the USA eventually joined with legislation to end tests after 1996

32. Since Western society was more open, the USSR had in its ability to exclude foreigners, a comparative espionage advantage that it did not want to jeopardise. Khrushchev also feared that the USA would be dangerously encouraged were it to discover just how weak the Soviet Union was

paranoia. Without inspection a ban looked uninviting. Admittedly most (perhaps even all) underground tests have been detected by foreign seismic stations. However the possibility of cheating did not seem negligible (especially given the recent bypassing of the Korean armistice provisions for monitoring communist troop movements); and there have in fact been some unexplained occurrences.[33]

NUCLEAR NON-PROLIFERATION TREATY 1968

Be that as it may, one of the features of the Test Ban Treaty was that it gave status to the three chief nuclear powers, a status they had a common interest in maintaining. This distaste for further nuclear proliferation severely strained US–French relations in the 1960s and had far graver consequences for the Soviet-Chinese alliance. But it also led on naturally to the next stage in the US–Soviet nuclear relationship, the pursuit of a Non-Proliferation Treaty to keep these terrible weapons in safe (i.e. existing) hands. Negotiating this was more complicated since it involved the attempt to ensure that other countries did not divert nuclear fuel and turn it into bombs. As atomic electricity-generation then looked economically very promising, these countries (even if willing to forgo nuclear weapons) did not wish to be disadvantaged by constraints on their peaceful use of nuclear technology that did not apply to the atomic weapons powers. But by 1968 a treaty was concluded providing for such inspection by an International Atomic Energy Agency (IAEA) based in Vienna. Some see this, and the treaty's ratification (by 1985) by 131 states, as a considerable achievement. I do not. The treaty may well have prevented Sweden's development of nuclear weapons and provided further reassurances against their acquisition by West Germany. It also erected some controls to deter the diversion of fissile material; these were reinforced both by collective agreements of the 'Nuclear Suppliers Group' (comprising industrialised countries of both West and East), and by the unilateral requirements of individual supplying countries. But of the

33. Apparently the CIA did pick up the disastrous underground nuclear waste explosion in the South Urals of 1957–8, but it was not generally known in the West; when it came to light in the mid–1970s many Western experts (including the UK Atomic Energy Authority) at first refused to believe it possible: Z.A. Medvedev, *Soviet Science* (Oxford, 1979) Appendix 2. Experts were also divided as to whether a 1979 occurrence off South Africa was purely natural or an Israeli/South African test

Non-Proliferation Treaty's signatories, Libya has sought (albeit unsuccessfully) to buy a bomb; North Korea refused to allow IAEA inspection and is currently thought to be on the verge of making a bomb. Iraq did allow inspections, which satisfied the IAEA, but Israel had better information, and in 1981 bombed Iraq's research reactor. Iraq had in fact been actively seeking to develop a bomb since 1974. It was not deterred by Israel's action, and appears to have been within twelve to eighteen months of producing its first weapon when it was defeated in 1991 by UN forces. The cease-fire agreement provided for IAEA inspectors to track down and destroy all Iraqi nuclear facilities; despite receiving numerous leads from dissidents, they are (in 1993) still not sure they have found everything.[34] Moreover, several significant countries refused to sign the treaty. Of these Israel, though it has never publicly claimed the status, is definitely a nuclear power; a dissident disclosed in 1986 that it had built between 100 and 200 atom bombs and was developing thermonuclear weapons. South Africa recently surprised the world by admitting that, in the 1980s, it built six atom bombs. India detonated a 'peaceful nuclear explosion' in 1974, though it has since adopted a low profile. Pakistan has pursued a counter-vailing bomb, though whether it has quite achieved one is in 1993 still not entirely clear.[35]

However, if the Non-Proliferation Treaty had only limited success, it did continue the habit of East–West nuclear negotiation that had begun in the 1950s. It was reinforced by other treaties, also negotiated in the United Nations forum: 'on the Principles of the . . . Exploration and Use of Outer Space' (which banned the positioning of nuclear weapons in orbit around the earth) and on the 'Rescue and Return of Astronauts and Space Objects' (both of 1966–7), on the prohibition of the emplacement of nuclear weapons on the seabed (1970–1), and the 1972 'Convention on the Prohibition . . . of Bacteriological (Biological) and Toxin Weapons' (though, it is now admitted, this last was never observed by the USSR).[36] Some of these treaties were unimportant: there

---

34. There are also claims that it passed both uranium and scientists on to Algeria, and that this may be able to build bombs by 1995. M. Heikal, *The Road to Ramadan* (paperback edn, 1976) pp. 74–5; *Keesing's*, 30435, 31909, 34268; *Sunday Times*, 11 Oct. 1981, 2 Jan. 1992 pp. 1–2; *International Herald Tribune*, 14 Oct. 1991 pp. 1, 5

35. *Keesing's*, 34773 (Israel), 26585 (India), 34996, 35511, 37761 (Pakistan), 33092 (Argentine), 37496 (Brazil), 39350 (South Africa); *Observer*, 27 March 1988 p. 25; *Sunday Times*, 15 April 1984 p. 34, 14 Aug. 1988 p. 1.

36. *Keesing's*, 39121

were better places to put nuclear weapons than on the seabed. But they, and more narrowly US–Soviet arrangements like the 1968 start of a Moscow–New York air service, were deliberately played up to stress the partnership side of the superpower relationship. They may have helped the opening of Strategic Arms Limitation Talks (SALT) on far more central, hence sensitive, aspects of the power position.

STRATEGIC ARMS LIMITATION TALKS; ABM AND SALT I TREATIES 1972

The chief reason for these talks must have been that both sides hoped to gain from them. Many of these anticipated gains, of course, lay outside the nuclear-strategic field and will be considered in our more general discussion on détente (see chaps 11, 9). But a major catalyst was the – leisurely – Soviet deployment, from 1963, of the 'Galosh' anti-ballistic missile (ABM) system to protect Moscow, and the inauguration of anti-aircraft defences that the Americans initially saw as another ABM line from the Baltic to Archangel. These deployments led to considerable concern in Congress, hence to a 1967 decision to deploy US ABMs. The Johnson administration dragged its feet, preferring on the one hand to improve its missiles' penetrating power by developing multiple warheads (MIRVs) and, on the other, to seek negotiations with the USSR that would ban ABMs and so conserve Mutual Assured Destruction.[37] Nixon, too, wished to negotiate, but he also decided in 1969 to go ahead with a modified ABM system, 'Safeguard'. Sentiment in Congress had by now swung round; in August 1969 Safeguard was kept alive only by the Vice-President's casting vote, and the administration was eventually reduced to lobbying for it as a bargaining chip in arms control negotiations. It is, however, unlikely that the Soviet Politburo, which lacked experience of independent parliaments, appreciated this major weakness in the US negotiating position.

Kosygin showed no receptiveness to ideas about the desirability of a Mutual Assured Destruction posture. Defensive systems, he

37. The USA started developing MIRVs to make possible the coverage of a greatly expanded Soviet target list: Seymour Hersh, *The Price of Power: Kissinger in the White House* (New York, 1983) p. 150. But the advent of an ABM threat to the US deterrent soon provided an extra rationale. They were flight-tested in 1968, deployed in 1969

observed, were not 'a cause of the arms race but designed instead to prevent the death of people'; nor, at the June 1967 Glassboro summit, would he contemplate negotiations to ban ABMs. But in 1968 the USSR decided (possibly over military opposition) to open talks, perhaps to encourage other countries to accede to the Nuclear Non-Proliferation Treaty, but probably chiefly from fear that an effective US ABM system would shut off the recently acquired Soviet capability to inflict major damage on the continental United States. Galosh, after all, did not work very well, and its US counterpart would probably be more sophisticated. Before talks actually opened, the Warsaw Pact invasion of Czechoslovakia supervened, but this only made the USSR the more anxious to hold them to divert attention; nor did the Johnson administration want more than a symbolic delay. This delay was stretched by the change of US administration, but SALT talks formally began in November 1969.

Nixon certainly hoped that they would encourage the Soviet Union to help end the Vietnam War. He also needed to cash the bargaining chip of his Safeguard ABM system before Congress axed it. But his chief strategic worry was the unexpectedly rapid growth in the numbers of Soviet ICBMs which the USA was then ill-placed to match – partly because it had stopped deploying additional missile launchers in 1967 and partly because of the extensive hostility to new defence programmes. So, despite occasional wavering, the White House made an ABM agreement conditional on one restricting ICBM numbers. As Kissinger later put it, 'We traded the defensive for the offensive limitations'.[38] The actual negotiations had their ridiculous side. Soviet military men were furious when Americans discussed the performance of Soviet weapons in the hearing of representatives of the Soviet Foreign Office, who had no clearance for such secret information. On the American side, Kissinger insulated himself from Washington pressures and leaks by confining serious negotiation to the 'back-channel' between himself and Soviet ambassador Dobrynin; the official US SALT delegation sometimes only learned what was going on by courtesy of their better briefed Soviet counterparts. Still, 1972 saw the conclusion and signature at the Moscow summit

---

38. Kissinger, *Memoirs* i p. 1,245; cf. also Nixon's June 1972 statement that the absence of arms limitation would have been disadvantageous 'since we have no current building programmes for the categories of weapons which have been frozen, and since no new building programme could have produced any new weapons in those categories during the period of the freeze' (*Keesing's*, 25136)

of an ABM Treaty and an 'Interim Agreement on . . . the Limitation of Strategic Offensive Arms'.[39]

MIRVS; VULNERABILITY OF US ICBMs, AND IMPLICATIONS FOR 'EXTENDED DETERRENCE'

The ABM Treaty sought to prevent 'defensive' technologies upsetting 'strategic stability', but offensive innovation might have the same effect. The first SALT negotiations may have missed an important chance to foreclose this by banning multiple warheads. Instead they concentrated on reaching an Interim Agreement, to which we shall return, limiting the numbers of nuclear missiles. Yet, in conditions of approximate parity, single-headed missiles do not offer much scope for a disarming first strike: given the certainty of errors and malfunctions, it will need more than one of your own missiles to kill one of your opponent's. However, if each of your missiles carries several (preferably independently targetable) warheads, at least a theoretical possibility opens up of a disarming strike that still leaves you plenty of rockets in reserve. Recognising this, the Johnson and Nixon administrations did make some moves to limit the threat to Soviet silos.[40] However, neither was prepared to forgo MIRVs, which were tested in 1968–9 and deployed from 1969. Kissinger was warned that, if MIRVs were not banned and the Soviets also acquired them, the US land-based ICBMs would become vulnerable. He nevertheless went ahead, regarding much of the opposition as the standard (and sometimes contradictory) resistance to all new US programmes, and advising Nixon that a freeze on MIRVs 'might create pressures to halt the Minuteman III and Poseidon programs [that were to carry them] . . . thus further unravelling the U.S. strategic program'. An additional consideration was the then widespread underestimate of the time it would take the USSR to acquire workable MIRVs.[41]

Given that the USA already had a deployable MIRV system by the time SALT talks started (which would not have been the case had they opened, as originally intended, in 1968), it would have been

39. For texts, see *Keesing's*, 25310 ff and W. Stützle, B. Jasani and R. Cowen (eds) *The ABM Treaty* (Oxford, 1987) Appendix

40. T. Greenwood, *Making the MIRV: A Study of Defense Decision Making* (Cambridge, Mass., 1975) pp. 70–1

41. Kissinger, *Memoirs* i pp. 210–12; Hersh, *The Price of Power* chaps 12, 13

hard to negotiate an arrangement that did not *either* freeze Soviet inferiority (by banning tests) *or* neutralise the current US advantage by banning deployment while leaving Soviet development free to catch up.[42] Proposals along these lines were made in 1970, but there was no serious negotiation and probably neither side wished it.[43] According to his retrospective account, Kissinger had always doubted whether a MIRV ban was acceptable either to the Pentagon or to the Soviets and manoeuvred accordingly. But by 1974 he was already openly wishing that he had in 1969–70 thought through the implications of a MIRVed world more thoroughly.[44]

Their importance was magnified by the fact that the USA came in the 1970s to place more reliance than ever before on its now potentially vulnerable ICBMs.[45] This arose partly out of a concern for the continuing deficiencies in SIOP (even as reworked by McNamara), and partly from a need to be able to reassure Western Europe that it was still effectively covered by extended American deterrence even in an era of approximate US–Soviet strategic parity. The reworked SIOP had given a US President a choice between options; but as late as 1974 the smallest apparently involved the use of 2,500 strategic weapons plus, probably, 1,000 NATO strikes from Europe.[46] So there was more point than is sometimes allowed to Nixon's 1970 rhetorical question, 'Should a President, in the event of a nuclear attack, be left with the single option of ordering the mass destruction of enemy civilians, in the face of the certainty that it would be followed by the mass slaughter of Americans?' Accordingly SIOP was reworked 'to provide the President with a wider set of much more selective targeting options',[47] and the result

42. The US advantage came to seem increasingly important as the USSR overhauled the USA in numbers of missiles and explosive megatonnage

43. Garthoff's contacts on the Soviet delegation encouraged him to believe that it might have been receptive to further exploration; but that delegation's head, Semenov, suggested that the MIRV issue would only impede agreement on other matters

44. Kissinger, *Memoirs* i pp. 541–8; R.L. Garthoff, *Détente and Confrontation. American-Soviet Relations from Nixon to Reagan* (Washington, DC, 1985) pp. 133–41; Gerard Smith, *Doubletalk* (Garden City, NY, 1980) chap. 4 and pp. 471–2

45. The first Soviet tests of true MIRVs came in 1973, with significant deployment from 1975. The USSR may not have achieved a reliable capacity to destroy the bulk of US silos until 1983–4 – W.T. Lee and R.F. Staar, *Soviet Military Policy since World War II* (Stanford, Calif., 1986) pp. 160–1 – but the perception that this would come was already influential by the mid-1970s

46. A.H. Cordesman, *Deterrence in the 1980s: Part 1. American Forces and Extended Deterrence* (IISS, Adelphi Paper no. 175) p. 13

47. Friedberg, 'Evolution of U.S. Strategic Doctrine 1945–80' pp. 61, 75 – Nixon was questioning the doctrine of 'assured destruction'

was announced in 1974 as the Schlesinger Doctrine. Asked to suggest a 'real' example when a limited number of nuclear weapons might be used, Defense Secretary Schlesinger replied:

> the overrunning of Western Europe. This would be a major defeat for the NATO alliance and for the United States. I don't know what we would do under these circumstances in terms of the strategic forces, but I believe that it is necessary for our strategic forces to continue to be locked into the defence of Europe in the minds of Europeans and of the Soviet Union. That would be one of the circumstances. It is very hard for me . . . to think of other circumstances in which the advantages involved in the use of nuclear weapons could in any way be commensurate with the risks.[48]

Parallel to SIOP, NATO also had a less destructive 'nuclear operations plan' (NOP) for 'graduated strikes at strictly military targets in the hope of ending any major war before it develops into a holocaust'. This would have used SACEUR's 4,000 US warheads plus (probably) part of the British and French deterrents.[49] It is therefore not clear why so much stress was laid in the 1970s and 1980s – at least at the declaratory level – on the need to be able to perform the same functions with US 'strategic' weapons. But this capacity was portrayed as essential for the credibility of both 'extended deterrence' and NATO's 'flexible response' strategy. For several reasons it was the land-based ICBMs that were best suited to this mission.[50] Unfortunately this was the most vulnerable part of the US strategic triad.

> During 1975–8 it steadily became clear that the U.S.S.R. would create a major counterforce capability against the *Minuteman* force by the early 1980s. Virtually every three months . . . the US discovered yet another significant improvement in Soviet ICBM design . . . accuracy . . . reliability and fractionation capability.[51]

Fear of ICBM vulnerability led in three directions: a vain search for an invulnerable basing mode for US ICBMs; acquisition of some countervailing capability against Soviet ICBMs; and criticism of an allegedly complacent liberal establishment that had exposed the USA to such vulnerability. The Ford administration bequeathed to

48. Lynn Etheridge Davis, *Limited Nuclear Options: Deterrence and the New American Doctrine*, 1975–6 (IISS, Adelphi Paper no. 121, p. 5)
49. Richard Ullman, 'The Covert French Connection', *Foreign Policy* lxxv (1989) pp. 24–7
50. Bombers might not get through. Communications difficulties with submarines inhibit continuous, hence detailed, command and control; and their missiles are both less easily retargetable and less accurate
51. Cordesman, *Deterrence in the 1980s* p. 19

its successor the decision to deploy a far more accurate, hence powerful, warhead (Mark 12A) cum guidance system on *some* of the Minuteman III missiles, and this was promptly endorsed. Official estimates of the implications vary considerably. But an Arms Control Impact Statement of March 1979 suggested that, were Mark 12A to be fitted to *all* 550 Minuteman IIIs (in fact it was fitted only to 300), Soviet ICBMs would by 1982 become distinctly vulnerable.[52] The Russians will have found such vulnerability the more alarming since ICBMs account for a far greater proportion of Soviet than of US warheads. As early as the 1974 summit, Brezhnev had briefed Nixon on what he claimed was the US first strike potential; as we have seen (pp. 10, 334), in 1981–4 Andropov apparently feared that the West was planning for offensive nuclear war.

US INTERPRETATIONS OF SOVIET INTENTIONS

The Americans too were wondering precisely what the Russians were up to. Originally it had been assumed that the ABM Treaty and SALT dialogue indicated their acceptance of US ideas of strategic stability through Mutually Assured Destruction;[53] it was easy to quote Soviet leaders to the effect that nuclear war would be a disaster for all concerned. Now a rival school came to feel that the USSR was seeking a superiority in both offensive and defensive weapons that would enable it to fight and win a nuclear war. As is often the case, the parties to the debate directed their gaze in different directions. Optimists ('doves') focused on the statements of the Soviet political leadership (which from 1977 onwards explicitly denied that Russia sought military superiority); pessimists ('hawks') regarded these as soft soap, emphasising aspirations to just such superiority and claims of 'the objective possibility of achieving victory' in Soviet military writing (notably the classified internal journal, *Military Thought*). Doves noted that the USSR was well behind in overall numbers of warheads: they held that part of

52. Garthoff, *Détente and Confrontation* pp. 791, 798; John Prados, *The Soviet Estimate. U.S: Intelligence Analysis & Russian Military Strength* (New York, 1982) pp. 289–90. The deployment in Europe of Pershing II (and cruise) missiles would worsen this vulnerability

53. Both adherents and assailants of MAD often underestimated the extent to which US nuclear targeting diverged from it

the trouble lay in the lag between the formal concession in the first SALT negotiations of Soviet strategic equality and its real acquisition; so what hawks saw as a bid for superiority was really just the actualisation of this parity. Hawks looked rather at Soviet conventional build-up (at a time when US defence spending was falling), at the emphasis on chemical weapons (whose production the US unilaterally suspended in 1969), and at the numbers and power of Soviet ICBMs rather than the comparison with the US triad as a whole.[54]

Within the USA, the hawks gained the upper hand in the later 1970s. To some extent this simply reflected the souring of détente. But an important development was the 1976 competition (over the National Intelligence Estimate) between the CIA – which had overreacted to its earlier mistaken apprehensions of a bomber and missile gap, and was in any case suspect of tailoring estimates to meet political pressures – and a 'B team' chosen to oppose its 'arms control bias'. The B team claimed victory. It also played some role in turning the CIA around; in 1976 the latter doubled its estimate of the cost of defence to the Soviet economy, and subsequently acquiesced in worried estimates of Soviet arms levels. All this was probably not without effect on the Carter administration, in which hawks like National Security Adviser Brzezinski became increasingly influential. It came to take note of Soviet military literature and to sponsor significant rearmament.[55] Moreover the B team, and a distinguished array of sympathetic past and present political figures, went public after the 1976 election under the guise of the 'Committee on the Present Danger'. Its propaganda contributed to growing congressional qualms about SALT, but its real importance came in 1980. Just as the Democrats had used feelings of a 'missile gap' in 1960, so Reagan now rode the new mood; after the election his transition team cited twelve 'intelligence failures', notably 'the general and continuing failure to predict the actual size and scope of the Soviet military effort' and 'the consistent gross misstatement

54. See e.g. J. Baylis and G. Segal (eds) *Soviet Strategy* (1981) esp. chap. 1, and J. Van Oudenaren, *Deterrence, War Fighting and Soviet Military Doctrine* (1986 – Adelphi Paper no. 210); also the tables in Cordesman, *Deterrence in the 1980s* pp. 47–9

55. In 1980 Defense Secretary Brown told the Senate that, while the new Presidential Directive 'does *not* assume that a nuclear war will necessarily be prolonged . . . [it] *does* take into account Soviet literature which considers such a scenario to be a real possibility': Friedberg, 'Evolution of U.S. Strategic Doctrine 1945–80' p. 83. This represented a certain East–West convergence, but on the basis of Soviet military doctrine, not American MAD

of Soviet global objectives'.[56] Much of Reagan's first term has to be seen against this background.

SALT II NEGOTIATIONS 1972–9

All this was what 'arms controllers' aim to prevent. They seek a stable balance that cannot easily be upset, confidence that neither side wishes to upset it, and some system of verification to show that neither is upsetting it. From this perspective the Strategic Arms Limitation Treaties of the 1970s left much to be desired. SALT I (in 1972) represented an exchange of defensive for offensive limitations. The USSR may have felt itself the chief defensive gainer; it accepted limits on offensive missile numbers that impinged slightly on its own building programmes and not at all on those of the United States (which had no immediate deployment plans anyway).[57] But the USA made no bones about its intention to continue developing new strategic systems, while Brezhnev was overheard to confirm that the agreement on silo dimensions would not impede the USSR's new rockets.[58] So much hung on the extent to which subsequent negotiations could convert the 1972 'Interim Agreement' into a more comprehensive settlement.

The problem was largely one of asymmetries. To offset apparent Soviet conventional force supremacy in Europe, the USA 'needed' to 'extend' deterrence (which made demands on its nuclear forces beyond the requirements of an insular Power). 'Forward-based' systems in Europe could hit the Soviet Union,[59] whereas their Soviet counterparts (though, to West European eyes, more considerable) could not reach the United States. Even within the 'strategic' systems to which the talks were confined, after 1972 the

56. Prados, *The Soviet Estimate* pp. 248–57, 279; John Ranelagh, *The Agency. The Rise and Decline of the CIA* (1986) pp. 663–4; IISS, *The Military Balance, 1987–8* p. 31

57.   USA: 1,054 ICBMs + 656 SLBMs = 1,710
      USSR: 1,618–1,408 ICBMs + 740–950 SLBMs = 2,358
(IISS, *The Military Balance, 1972–3*, pp. 3, 83–5)

58. For Brezhnev, Hersh, *The Price of Power* p. 547; Defense Secretary Laird told the House that 'Just as the Moscow agreements were made possible by our successful action in such programs as Safeguard, Poseidon and Minuteman III, these future negotiations in which we are pledged can only succeed if we are equally successful in implementing such programs as the Trident system, the B-1 bomber' etc. etc. (Smith, *Doubletalk* p. 340)

59. As could the Chinese, French and British deterrents (though arguably the complex 1972 deal on Soviet SLBMs made informal allowance for the latter two)

USSR led in overall rocket numbers, throw-weight, etc., the USA in numbers of warheads and so on.

One of the greatest contributions to stability would have been for the Warsaw Pact to switch to a *defensive* conventional military posture and strategy. Negotiations did not directly address such topics. In the 1950s there had been proposals (chiefly Polish) for a degree of military disengagement in Central Europe. Eden was quite interested. But the West saw them (not necessarily wrongly) as tending to freeze Germany into a special status, impede West German rearmament, and remove US troops from Europe.[60] Discussion flagged in the 1960s, but détente led to new negotiations. NATO was, in fact, fortunate that it did so, for in May 1971 the US Administration was shaken by Senator Mansfield's amendment seeking a mandatory unilateral 50 per cent cut in US forces in Europe. This was eventually defeated, but only after Acheson's mobilisation against it of virtually the entire former foreign and defence policy establishment – and by a helpful speech of Brezhnev's offering negotiations on mutual reductions.[61]

Brezhnev's motives can only be guessed. Presumably he did not wish the controversy to endanger the current negotiations over Berlin or SALT; he also insisted on conditioning the force reduction negotiations on his pet plan for a European Security Conference that he saw as ratifying the Soviet Union's major gain from the Second World War, the post-1945 East European order. This conference, and those that followed it up, did agree on 'confidence building measures' like the notification, and observation by representatives of the opposing alliance, of significant military manoeuvres. But the Vienna conference on the Mutual Reduction of Forces (MBFR) in Central Europe, which opened in 1973, dragged on without any outcome. Kissinger says, 'We succeeded in keeping the issue of mutual force reductions alive to block unilateral American withdrawals by the Congress; at the same time we succeeded in prolonging the negotiation without disadvantageous result'. This assessment may do the USA a certain injustice: in December 1975 it did suggest trading off some of its 'forward-based' nuclear systems (on which the USSR always focused attention) against Soviet tanks (the chief Western bugbear).[62]

---

60. Had both US and Soviet troops gone home, the Americans would, for geographical reasons, have found it harder to return in a crisis

61. Kissinger, *Memoirs* i pp. 938–47; Garthoff, *Détente and Confrontation* pp. 115–16

62. Kissinger, *Memoirs* i pp. 947–9; R.F. Staar, *USSR Foreign Policies after Detente* (Stanford, Calif., 1987 edn.) p. 185

Negotiations were always being left in Vienna, not taken up on a direct back-channel basis between the superpowers, however, and they got thoroughly bogged down over an inability to agree the size of the forces at issue.

So the burden of ensuring military stability rested on negotiations over nuclear rather than conventional arms. 1972 saw the limitation of strategic missile numbers. The parties then proceeded to discuss a more comprehensive settlement, but as they were both deploying improved weapons, the longer they took the worse the problem of ICBM 'vulnerability' would become. 1973 was largely taken up with advancing maximum negotiating positions on both sides, and by internal fighting in Washington. Part of the problem here was Senator Jackson, a liberal, Cold Warrior, and would-be Democratic presidential candidate in 1976. He had accepted SALT I even though it allowed the USSR more missiles than the USA; but he carried against the administration a call for a future treaty 'which would not limit the United States to levels of intercontinental strategic forces inferior to the limits provided for the Soviet Union'.[63] The language was vague; but it strengthened reluctance in Washington to accept any formal deal involving a visible US inferiority, that is, any deal not based on (at least) 'equal aggregates'. Kissinger, on the other hand, conscious that Congress would not support extra defence spending, preferred to trade acceptance of the existing Soviet numerical superiority against limits on its MIRVed rockets that would lessen the prospective threat to US ICBMs. In March 1974, after some difficult meetings, Kissinger did secure Brezhnev's acceptance of the idea of such an exchange. But Kissinger proved constrained by disputes in Washington that Nixon (now engulfed in Watergate) lacked the authority to settle. At the ensuing summit Brezhnev seemed ready to bargain, but not on the basis of what Kissinger felt able to offer. So it was agreed merely to pursue the matter further, either on the basis of 'counterbalancing asymmetries' or on that of 'equal aggregates.'[64]

Nixon resigned in August 1974. Gromyko made encouraging noises to his successor, President Ford, and Kissinger was soon back in Moscow, where the outlines of a deal on either basis were struck and a summit arranged for Vladivostok in November. To avoid trouble with Defense Secretary Schlesinger, Ford chose to go for

63. *Keesing's*, 25585
64. Kissinger, *Memoirs* ii pp. 1006–28, 1153–72; Garthoff, *Détente and Confrontation* pp. 418–30

equal aggregates. So at Vladivostok he and Brezhnev settled that, by 1985, the two countries would converge on the basis of 2,400 inter-continental launchers (including heavy bombers as well as missiles), of which no more than 1,320 should be MIRVed. This achieved formal equality, though the Soviets saw the disregarding of US 'forward-based systems' as a considerable concession. But the levels of MIRVed launchers were higher than those talked of earlier in the year; warhead numbers were free to grow; and the prospect of ICBM vulnerability was not reduced.[65]

It was hoped that the various points left open at Vladivostok would soon be tidied up and a treaty signed, but again the early stages of negotiation dragged, and 1975 saw little movement. Kissinger's January 1976 Moscow visit achieved, if not complete agreement, at least substantial progress. The Pentagon, however, was hostile. So, after trying unsuccessfully for a three-year interim agreement, President Ford decided that further SALT negotiations would have to wait till after the 1976 election (which he lost).[66] The new Carter administration did not want simply to pick up where the Republicans had stopped. It hoped to unite Kissinger's critics, both conservative and liberal, behind a search for much deeper cuts. There was also a feeling, probably correct, that the President could best sell a comprehensive settlement within Washington during his first year in office. So Carter disregarded clear Soviet warnings that any deal would have to be based on both Vladivostok and the formula agreed with Kissinger in January 1976. The new US proposals were turned down flat; and the inexperienced Secretary of State, Cyrus Vance, then gave details in a press conference, thus breaching the convention that negotiating positions were confidential. This angered the Russians. It also provided a benchmark against which SALT critics could test later agreements and find them wanting. However, the negotiating climate improved surprisingly quickly, and by September 1977 the numerical limits under consideration were very close to those ultimately agreed.

That further negotiations took so long was due not only to the worsening international climate, but also to the introduction of important new issues over verification, maximum numbers of warheads per missile, and the testing and deployment of new missile types. In these respects the SALT II treaty, finally signed at the June 1979 Vienna summit, represented a distinct improvement on either

65. Garthoff, *Détente and Confrontation* pp. 442–6; *Keesing's*, 26869
66. Garthoff, *Détente and Confrontation* pp. 446–52, 540–4

Vladivostok or the tentative January 1976 agreement. Furthermore there were to be new negotiations for 'significant and substantial reductions', which might also address the question of forward-based systems. But the deployment of ground-launched cruise missiles, and of mobile ICBMs, was delayed only until 1982. The Carter administration was now lobbying for the NATO decision, finally reached in December 1979 (see pp. 160, 181), to deploy mobile cruise and Pershing II missiles, albeit subject to the offer of prior negotiations. It also decided to shuttle the new mobile MX missile between multiple-protective shelters, although at Vienna the Soviet Defence Minister had (with some justice) declared this mode of deployment to be unverifiable and so incompatible with the treaty.[67]

SALT II can, therefore, be seen only as a limited arms control success. It immediately ran into trouble in the US Senate – after lengthy hearings the Foreign Relations Committee commended it only by 9 votes to 6, while the Armed Services Committee called nem. con. for 'major changes'. So its chances did not look good in January 1980, when Carter temp- orarily withdrew it in response to the Soviet invasion of Afghanistan. Thereafter it remained in limbo. Ostensibly both countries con- tinued to observe it. But, in the US perspective, the Soviet Union did not reduce its missile launchers from its current 2,500,[68] deployed more than the one permitted new type of missile, and impeded verification by encryption and jamming. In May 1986 Reagan warned that, failing action to remedy 'direct Soviet non- compliance', the USA would no longer adhere to treaty limits – by suppressing old submarines to leave room for bombers carrying air-launched cruise missiles (ALCMs) – and in November (after the failed Reykjavik summit) he deliberately exceeded them, though not by much.[69]

67. *Keesing's*, 30119 ff; Garthoff, *Détente and Confrontation* pp.732–5, 741–5, chap. 23; Brzezinski, *Power and Principle* pp. 156–7, chap. 9

68. The treaty had limited launchers to 2,400 (reducing to 2,250 in 1981) – with a sub-ceiling of 1,320 MIRVed 'strategic' missiles/ALCM-carrying heavy bombers (within which there could be no more than 820 ICBMs, or 1,200 ICBMs and SLBMs combined)

69. *The Economist*, 18 May 1985 pp.16–17, 15 June 1985 p.18; Staar, *USSR Foreign Policies after Detente* pp.267, 269; *Keesing's*, 34972–4

CRUISE AND PERSHING MISSILES IN EUROPE 1983

Arms control was thus at a discount when Reagan took office, but it was nevertheless to occupy a central place in East–West relations for most of the 1980s. Initially the limelight was taken by intermediate range (INF) missiles. The 1979 NATO decision to deploy ground-launched cruise (GLCMs) and Pershing missiles in 1983 had reflected differing and to some extent incompatible concerns. The military wanted actual deployment to enhance its capacity for 'flexible response' to Soviet conventional aggression. But deployment was generally represented as a small counter to the steady build-up of Soviet SS-20 missiles; many governments hoped that if these could be bargained away it would not prove necessary. So NATO also called for Soviet–American negotiations on INF missiles. Brezhnev professed a readiness to talk. Washington was in no great hurry, and both the Carter and Reagan administrations came under pressure from West Germany to move faster.[70] Talks formally began in November 1981, but the omens were not good. The international climate was promptly soured by the suppression of Solidarity in Poland; in any case the US and Soviet negotiating positions were poles apart. The USA sought the 'zero option' of complete abolition of INF missiles; but some in the administration (though perhaps not Reagan himself) saw this as good propaganda but quite unrealisable, and as a way to prevent the negotiations blocking deployment. The Soviets, for their part, said there was already a rough East–West INF parity that NATO deployment would upset. From this basis they too made propaganda offers to halt further SS-20 deployment (or even cut existing numbers) provided the USA did not deploy, which the USA always rejected as tending only to perpetuate the existing Soviet INF superiority. In July 1982 the negotiators at Geneva jointly formulated a solution, the reduction of SS-20s to 75, to be counterbalanced by 75 US GLCMs but by none of the more feared Pershings. But neither Moscow nor Washington wished to pursue this.[71]

Moscow indeed had very little incentive to do so as long as there was a chance that the huge protest movements would make deployment in Western Europe impossible. There was the encouraging precedent of the neutron bomb. The early 1980s saw in Britain the revival of the Campaign for Nuclear Disarmament (CND, last

70. *Keesing's*, 30159–60, 31099–100
71. *Keesing's*, 31979–85, 32461; Garthoff, *Détente and Confrontation* pp.1024–5

significant twenty years before) and the Opposition Labour Party's conversion to full unilateralism.[72] In 1979 one House of the Dutch Parliament had voted against deployment, and in 1980 Belgian political divisions led to the postponement of any decision as to whether to allow it. Anti-nuclear sentiment also grew steadily in the German SPD, though it did not capture the party until 1973 after this had lost office.[73] This upsurge of feeling stemmed chiefly from fear that the NATO deployment might be followed by an arms race spiralling into nuclear war. It also reflected distrust of Reagan, who was believed to take 'cowboy' attitudes and to be ready to countenance a nuclear war that the advent of INF missiles would enable him to confine to Europe.[74] Some observers thought that, in rearming to counter swelling Soviet military power, NATO might have undercut the domestic consensus that sustained Western Europe's Atlantic orientation. Against this background the Soviet and US governments turned increasingly to abuse, and to appealing to Western public opinion with lurid pictures of their opponent's defence programmes and capabilities.

Negotiations deadlocked, the chief new development being the Soviet attempt (from late 1982) to draw the British and French deterrents into the INF talks, which Britain, France and the USA all rejected out of hand. But the course of their domestic politics in 1982–3 made it clear that both Britain and West Germany would continue to be led by governments committed to INF deployment; the installation of missiles began there (and in Italy) in November 1983. The immediate Soviet response was to break off both the INF negotiations and those for a 'Strategic Arms Reduction Treaty' (START), which had begun in mid-1982. But if the USSR really did feel threatened by the Pershing missiles, it now had an incentive to

72. The salience of nuclear issues was further enhanced by the British government's decision to start replacing its elderly Polaris SLBMs by the more powerful Tridents

73. Anti-nuclear sentiment was even stronger in Denmark (though this was not scheduled to accept GLCMs), less marked in Italy (which was), and only slight in France (which was not directly involved but which strongly supported the decision to deploy)

74. People were alarmed by the new Pentagon policy, formulated in 1980 and 1983, of seeking (as a deterrent) the capability to 'prevail' in a limited but protracted nuclear war. They fastened on to Reagan's 1981 answer to the question of whether a nuclear exchange could be limited, 'I don't honestly know . . . [but] the only defence is, well, you shoot yours and we'll shoot ours . . . . And if you had that kind of stalemate, I could see where you could have the exchange of weapons against troops in the field without it bringing either one of the powers to pushing the button': *Keesing's*, 31430, 31977, 31983

talk. Early 1984 saw both the death of Andropov and the softening of American rhetoric; also it was clear that Reagan would be re-elected. So in September Gromyko returned to Washington. Once the election was over it was announced that he and Secretary Shultz would discuss resuming arms control negotiations that should now also extend to space weapons.[75] 'Nuclear and Space' talks restarted in Geneva in March 1985.

'STAR WARS', THE 1986 REYKJAVIK SUMMIT AND 1987 INF TREATY

Soviet insistence on including space reflected a new perceived vulnerability. Unlike the USA, the USSR had deployed, and in the early 1980s expanded, the ABM system permitted it by the ABM Treaty.[76] It also conducted an extensive research programme, though it would not admit as much until 1987.[77] In due course some Americans became worried, and from 1977–8 the White House apparently started funding investigation of a possible anti-missile screen using lasers and particle beams. The programme continued to grow under the Reagan presidency; in 1983 Reagan finally went public with a call for a 'Strategic Defense Initiative' (SDI) – research to determine the feasibility of 'rendering the ballistic missile threat impotent and obsolete'.[78] Many scientists (especially in Western Europe) saw this as quite impossible. But the Soviet Union had a healthy respect for US technological capability, and by 1985 it was worried: its London embassy was told that SDI systems would eventually be able to intercept 90 per cent of Soviet strategic missiles, and that there was little chance of Soviet research keeping pace with American. In any case the USSR might not be able to afford it; in a 1986 broadcast Gorbachev focused on SDI and accused Washington of using the arms race to 'exhaust the Soviet

---

75. *Keesing's*, 33347–50

76. The treaty allowed each country two ABM sites (reduced to one by agreement in 1974). But no sooner had the US system become fully operational in 1975 than it was dismantled as an economy – a foolish one given the growing concern about the vulnerability of American ICBMs

77. *Keesing's*, 35553; cf. also *The ABM Treaty*, Paper 4 and pp.192, 198–9, and US administration estimates that the USSR would spend $26 billion on *its* SDI in 1985–9: *Keesing's*, 33915

78. David Baker, 'The Making of Star Wars', *New Scientist*, 9 July 1987 pp.36–40; Prados, *The Soviet Estimate* pp. 286–8

Union economically'.[79] Accordingly he gave a very high priority in 1985–7 to propagandising against, and trying to negotiate away, the American SDI programme.

Gorbachev was also moved by a simple wish to reduce dangerous international tensions and by a general belief that the USSR would be internationally more influential if it emerged from isolation. He began in July 1985 by announcing a temporary moratorium on nuclear tests and challenging the USA to respond.[80] Then in November he and Reagan met with remarkable success. Both men (though *not* their wives) got on well together; they found common ground in deploring the dangers of a nuclear arms race, and they agreed on further meetings. The resumed Geneva negotiations had made no progress. So in 1986 Gorbachev started making concessions, soft-pedalling the link that the USSR had sought to establish between SS-20s and the British and French deterrents and proposing the elimination from Europe of longer (over 1,000 km) range missiles. But the talks still dragged, US–Soviet relations were soured by several extraneous episodes, and the next summit had to be postponed. It was finally arranged, at short notice, for October 1986 in Reykjavik. There Gorbachev tried to bounce Reagan into dropping SDI. He began by making tantalising offers in other areas. On INF, the link with the British and French deterrents was dropped altogether; the 'zero option' was accepted for Europe, while SS-20s in the Soviet Far East (about which Japan was becoming worried) would be reduced to 100 (counterbalanced by 100 US missiles in Alaska). Furthermore, the two leaders apparently agreed in principle to a 50 per cent cut in strategic nuclear weapons over five years and their total abolition in ten. But Gorbachev then insisted that all this be conditional on the halting of all non-laboratory SDI testing and development. Reagan refused, the conference broke up with much acrimony, and in its aftermath the USA decided (in the light of what it proclaimed to be a long list of Soviet violations) on a token departure from the limits set by SALT II.[81]

Reagan's apparent readiness to abolish nuclear weapons had alarmed many people, notably Mrs Thatcher, who believed that it was these that had kept the peace in the postwar era. She seems to have pressed Washington strongly to go back to seeking an INF

---

79. Andrew and Gordievsky, *KGB* pp.508–9; Sheehy, *Gorbachev* pp.228–9
80. It refused; questions of verification apart, the ending of tests would have had implications for SDI
81. Sheehy, *Gorbachev* pp.224–31; *Keesing's*, 34791 ff, 35603 ff

treaty, a 50 per cent reduction in (but not the abolition of) strategic weapons, and a ban on chemical weapons;[82] in her March 1987 visit to Moscow she helped broker discussions along these lines.[83] In September the US and Soviet Foreign Ministers announced agreement in principle on the INF 'zero option' and on seeking a 50 per cent cut in strategic weapons. Gorbachev still tried to bring in SDI, but proved ready to leave it on one side when the USA refused. Details were tied up at a summit in Washington, and an INF treaty signed that provided for the verified destruction of all ground-launched missiles with a range of 500–5,500 km (including those in the Far East).[84]

The world hailed it as the most important disarmament treaty ever signed, and it was indeed the first since the Washington and London Naval Treaties of 1922 and 1930 to provide for any significant destruction of weapons systems. But it did pose problems for NATO: SACEUR was distinctly unhappy, and both the Pentagon and the West German government had, at various stages, been worried by the disappearance of shorter range missiles.[85] For this might lead on to a denuclearised Western Europe vulnerable to political pressure stemming from Soviet conventional superiority. The need to replace NATO's ageing short-range Lance missiles brought up the question in a concrete form, and led in 1989 to sharp exchanges between the British and West German governments – the former seeing it as essential for the preservation of flexible response (as opposed to the less credible automatic massive retaliation), whereas the latter had been brought by public opinion to resist it as likely to concentrate the danger of nuclear explosions exclusively on German territory (East and West).

82. Though the USSR did not until 1987 officially admit to possessing chemical weapons, its military training clearly envisaged their use. Thereafter mutual inspection of chemical facilities was agreed (though the UK was unhappy with Soviet obstruction on the ground). Talks proceeded within the UN for a general ban, and in 1989 the US delegate said that the difficulties that had arisen were not with the USSR. A draft treaty was agreed in 1992, but a number of countries had serious reservations

83. Sir Julian Bullard in Schweitzer, *Changing Western Analysis of the Soviet Threat* p.144; Sheehy, *Gorbachev* pp.235 ff., 245

84. *Keesing's*, 35485, 35601 ff

85. One of the few concessions that the USSR managed to insist on was that West Germany should destroy its short-range (Pershing I) missiles (which carried US warheads)

GORBACHEV'S DEFENCE CUTS, AND THE PARIS CHARTER 1990

Events soon made such disputes obsolete by reducing Soviet conventional superiority. Until 1987 Gorbachev had let defence spending go on rising; he then froze it, and turned actively towards shifting the military away from its traditional offensive orientation towards his new concept of 'reasonable sufficiency'. In 1988 he proposed a pan-European disarmament summit, and in December announced significant unilateral cuts. NATO responded by suggesting East–West reductions to a common ceiling (thus eliminating the Warsaw Pact superiority that it put at three to one in tanks). In early 1989 the useless MBFR talks were replaced by geographically less restricted ones, and in May the Warsaw Pact agreed to common ceilings in central Europe. Later that year communist rule in Eastern Europe collapsed. Czechoslovakia and Hungary then started pressing strongly for the withdrawal of Soviet forces, while the utility of those stationed in East Germany became questionable. The USSR chose to make a graceful exit, agreeing to leave Czechoslovakia and Hungary in a little over a year. Nor did it stand in the way of German reunion or seek to prevent reunited Germany remaining in NATO. Instead it struck a deal that its forces could stay in eastern Germany until 1994 (see pp. 458–9). In return all NATO forces would be banned from eastern Germany until then, with only German NATO units being allowed there subsequently. Moreover so far from increasing its armed forces as a result of taking over the DDR, Germany undertook to cut them from half a million to 370,000 – a level that the USSR could have no cause to fear. Against this background of general thaw US–Soviet negotiations proceeded to set limits for the conventional forces NATO and the Warsaw Pact could deploy in Europe, with sub-limits for the maximum number of tanks allowed to any one country (i.e. the USSR), though with the safety valve that Soviet forces in Asia were not covered and that the USSR was known to be relocating equipment east of the Urals. The settlement – incorporated in the November 1990 Charter of Paris – presumed the continued existence of the two alliance systems (albeit 'no longer adversaries'), but there were signs that the Warsaw Pact was falling apart. Most of its members feared their recent Soviet overlords and hoped for, at least, Western diplomatic protection; the final negotiating hurdle had been a dispute between the USSR and other Pact members. After the signature of the Paris Charter, the Pact promptly fell apart, agreeing to dissolve by 1992 and in fact doing so on 1 April 1991.[86]

START I AND II

The Paris Charter had sought to draw a line under the Cold War. But in early 1991 the USSR's lurch towards a harder political line, together with such patent evasions as the labelling of three armoured divisions as 'naval' and so exempt from the Charter, raised fears that this would not be ratified. By June, however, the clouds had cleared;[87] at a Moscow summit in July, Gorbachev and Bush signed a Strategic Arms Reduction Treaty (START I) cutting such weapons by about one-third.[88] But such was the then turmoil in the USSR that the media now saw the Bush–Gorbachev summit and START rather as a relic from a bygone era of bipolar US–Soviet power parity. Then in August Moscow hardliners staged a coup, whose failure led to the progressive disintegration of the USSR. This further reduced any danger of Soviet invasion, but it led to a new concern that the Soviet nuclear weapons deployed outside Russia might come under the control of peripheral feuding Republics. Yeltsin promptly sought to return them to Russian soil, and also declared a wish for deep further cuts in nuclear weapons. Bush responded by himself making far-reaching proposals. 1992 proved something of an *annus mirabilis* for arms control;[89] and January 1993 saw the signature of the START II treaty under which the US and Russia would, over the next decade, cut their nuclear warheads to between 3,000 and 3,500. Implementation, however, depended on the ratification of both START and the Nuclear Non-proliferation Treaty by the other successor states (Belarus, Kazakhstan and Ukraine) with ex-Soviet nuclear weapons on their territory.[90] In principle, all had agreed to return these weapons to

---

86. *Keesing's*, 37267, 37552, 37796–7, 37838, 38026
87. *The Independent*, 15 June 1991 p.10
88. To 1,600 launchers and 6,000 warheads apiece; there was also tacit agreement to limit to 880 missiles launched from surface ships: *The Independent*, 8 June 1991 p.10; *The Times*, 30 July 1991 p.8
89. Ceilings were agreed in the CSCE for national land forces in Europe. A system of inspections was set in place to verify observance of the 1972 treaty banning biological weapons. And there were to be talks on US-Russian cooperation over a joint anti-missile 'Global Defence System': *Keesing's* 39121; *The Independent*, 30 Dec. 1992 pp. 1, 7
90. *Keesing's*, 38792, 39296-7

Russia or destroy them by the end of the decade; but in 1993 nuclear control and dismantlement got caught up in the general complex of disputes between the Ukraine and Russia.

CHAPTER SEVEN

The Khrushchev Years

The summer of 1955 had seen 'the spirit of Geneva'. By November 1956 East–West relations appeared to have collapsed, with Soviet troops repressing a revolution in Hungary to Western denunciations, while Khrushchev responded to the Anglo-French assault on Suez with at least verbal threats of rocket attacks. Both crises had local origins, but both had implications for the world 'correlation of forces' and were accordingly assimilated into East–West rivalry.

Khrushchev, as we shall see, had embarked on a policy of competitive coexistence. But a precondition was that Soviet hegemony in Eastern Europe remain sacrosanct: 'Khrushchev said that recognition of the present status quo in Europe was the essential condition for any talks and that this must be made quite clear to the West'. In 1956 this hegemony had seemed threatened; this was chiefly Khrushchev's own fault. As a number of his domestic opponents pointed out, he had upset things by his 1955 overtures to Tito – previously regarded as a schismatic – and by his 1956 denunciation of Stalin. Khrushchev naturally preferred to lay the blame elsewhere: 'This time the West had dared to provoke a revolt in Poland, tomorrow it would be somewhere else; they thought the time had come to change the results of World War II. "We must give them a rap over the knuckles".'[1]

1. V. Micunovic, *Moscow Diary* (1980) pp.87, 337–8

WESTERN ATTEMPTS TO DESTABILISE ALBANIA 1949–53

There really had been Western subversion in Eastern Europe, but chiefly several years earlier. The most vulnerable target was Albania, which was (after 1948) geographically isolated from the rest of the 'camp'. Britain had been at odds with it since 1946 when 44 British sailors had been killed by mines in the (international) Corfu straits. Albania was, moreover, supplying considerable assistance to the communist rebellion in Greece. Early in 1949 Bevin approved a plan 'to detach Albania from the [Soviet] orbit' by reactivating war-time Resistance networks there. The Americans agreed to join in; in October twenty émigré Albanians were landed by boat to link up with anti-communists and recruit sympathisers in their home areas. During 1950 and 1951 there were similar small-scale overland infiltration and US-managed parachute drops. The latter had clearly been betrayed to the Albanian authorities, who staged a broadcast trial of captured infiltrators in late 1951. The British then abandoned the operation in despair. But the Americans persisted, having discovered a more effective leader, Matjani, and receiving apparently encouraging radio reports in 1952–3. These turned out to be Albanian government hoaxes that lured Matjani to his doom in May 1953, and the whole episode was broadcast in December. In the words of a CIA officer of the time: 'The Albanian was the first and only attempt by Washington to unseat a communist regime within the Soviet orbit. It taught a clear lesson. . . . Even a weak regime could not be overthrown by covert military action alone'. Actually the lesson is not clear: covert action did prove successful in Iran and Guatemala, and Hungary was to show in 1956 that communist regimes can simply disintegrate. But the wartime Resistance movements, on the experience of which Britain had been drawing, had not by themselves liberated any state.[2] Moreover, the Albanian intervention was limited by Anglo-American deter-mination to provide 'capacity for plausible denial'; sympathisers within Albania noted the contrast with Second World War operations, and indicated that they would rebel only when there were substantial drops of men and supplies. In any case the British official jointly controlling operations from Washington was Kim

2. Both Yugoslavia and Albania claim to have liberated themselves. But the German withdrawal was due not to local partisans but to the need to pull troops back to defend Germany itself from direct invasion. Also, as the USSR often insisted, the Red Army played a considerable role in the liberation of northern Yugoslavia

Philby, a KGB agent, which may be one explanation of the Albanian government's excellent preparedness.[3]

Nothing as ambitious as the Albanian operation was ever attempted elsewhere. But agents were similarly infiltrated and occasional supplies dropped into the Baltic states and the Ukraine (1949–56) to establish contact with the nationalist resistance, though more to gather intelligence than to sustain fighting. From 1950 equipment and money were dropped to a Polish organisation, WIN, to create an underground that could, by sabotage, delay any Soviet invasion of Western Europe; in December 1952 the Polish authorities revealed that WIN had been a hoax, operating entirely under their control.[4] Such fiascos led to gradual disillusion; and in 1953 the new Director of Central Intelligence, Allen Dulles, reluctantly suspended the construction of East European networks,[5] though paramilitary training of émigrés continued.

THE 1953 DECISION AGAINST 'ROLL-BACK'; US QUIESCENCE DURING THE 1953 BERLIN RISING AND 1956 POLISH DISTURBANCES

To judge by political rhetoric, one would have expected a rather different pattern. The Truman administration had favoured 'containment', a policy that, whatever its hopes for an ultimate internal collapse of Soviet power, implied leaving Eastern Europe to its fate. In 1952 the Republican platform described it as a 'negative, futile and immoral policy . . . which abandons countless human beings to a despotism and godless terrorism which in turn enables the rulers to forge the captives into a weapon for our destruction'; John Foster Dulles promised 'to shift from a purely defensive policy to a psychological offensive, a liberation policy, which will try to give hope and a resistance mood inside the Soviet empire'.[6] This declaratory policy (now commonly called 'roll-back') seemed to go well beyond 'containment', but was in fact very similar. For privately

---

3. Information also leaked through the émigré community: N. Bethell, *The Great Betrayal: The Untold Story of Kim Philby's Biggest Coup* (1984); Harry Rositzke, *The CIA's Secret Operations* (New York, 1977) p.173
4. John Prados, *Presidents' Secret Wars* (New York, 1986) esp. pp.40–4, 52–9; Ranelagh, *The Agency* p.227; Thomas Powers, *The Man who Kept the Secrets. Richard Helms and the CIA* (paperback edn, 1979) pp.46 ff.
5. Powers, *The Man who Kept the Secrets* pp.54–5; Prados, *Presidents' Secret Wars* p.59
6. Townsend Hoopes, *The Devil and John Foster Dulles* (1974) pp.130–1

Dulles saw 'total war' as 'an incalculable disaster', and felt that any overt attempt to detach Eastern Europe from Soviet control might set it off. So it was better to wait for time and local nationalisms to bring changes, albeit with the assistance of as much pressure as could safely be applied. At least to begin with, he hoped this would not take too long.[7] Stalin's death, he had told the National Security Council, was likely to reveal the 'rottenness' in the communist system: Soviet power was 'already overstretched and represents tyrannical rule over unwilling peoples. If we keep the pressures on, psychological and otherwise, we may either force the collapse of the Kremlin regime or else transform the Soviet orbit from a union of satellites dedicated to oppression, into a coalition for defense only'.[8]

A similar conclusion emerged from the mid-1953 'Solarium' study, in which White House task forces considered options ranging from the continuation of containment to much increased 'efforts to disturb and weaken the Soviet bloc'. Eisenhower's preference was for a course closer to the first alternative, but not excluding some 'Actions to Exploit the Unrest in the Satellite States'.[9] Most of these actions were probably rather minor, a further enhancement of Radios Free Europe and Liberation (started in 1950–1) and of the eastwards dispatch of propaganda leaflets (ultimately 300 million) by balloon. Some represented conventional intelligence coups, and perhaps the spreading of important disinformation, via Eastern informants and defectors. The most visible success was the acquisition and publishing of Khrushchev's Secret Speech denouncing Stalin to the 20th Party Congress.[10] Khrushchev had intended this to be released only within Party circles and under heavy explanatory guidance; its broadcasting by the West must have put the Stalinist leaders of Eastern Europe even more on the defensive and added

7. Dulles never professed to know when the break-up would come. In 1955 he told the KMT Foreign Minister it could be within a year or 'some years away', but in August 1954 he talked of 25 years (and wondered whether the West would be able to wait that long), in January 1956 of 100 years. By late 1958 he was prepared to say publicly that he was not sure 'that Communism as a social and economic structure will wither away', but that he did expect 'an evolution, away from what I call international communism . . . which tries to spread its creed all over the world . . . to a system which puts more emphasis upon national welfare . . . and [which] will give up this fantastic dream of world conquest'

8. J.L. Gaddis in Immerman, *Dulles and the Diplomacy of the Cold War* pp.53–4, 59–68 – a revisionist work

9. Prados, *Presidents' Secret Wars* pp.120–1

10. Ranelagh, *The Agency* pp.255–6, 185–8; Powers, *The Man who Kept the Secrets* pp.405–6

to Mao Zedong's irritation that he had not been consulted about it beforehand.

When things came to the test of a real rising in Eastern Europe, however, the USA drew back. In June 1953 news of the Berlin riots and their demands was beamed to East Germany by the American Sector Radio, but the CIA's Berlin station chief was refused permission to arm the rioters; the USA tacitly acquiesced in their suppression by Soviet troops and then offered the USSR food aid for East Germany. The CIA was later asked to study possible countermeasures and sanctions in the event of renewed East European unrest, but concluded that little could be done.[11] This conclusion was to be more seriously tested in 1956. The then developments in Poland (see pp. 422–3) seem to have owed nothing to the West, nor, in the event, did they demand any Western reaction. But John Foster Dulles declared publicly that, in what he regarded as the unlikely event of Soviet coercion, the USA would not intervene militarily.[12]

THE WEST AND THE 1956 HUNGARIAN RISING

Poland's crisis in October 1956 touched off public meetings in Hungary, and these served as a catalyst for a revolution there. The revolution's roots were again domestic, but its outbreak set off a good deal of fighting and the apparent defeat of the first Soviet military intervention. So there was plenty for Radio Free Europe to report. A post-mortem study found that the radio had not deliberately sought to inspire revolution; but it had sometimes passed from simply reporting revolutionary demands to identifying with them, and had occasionally even offered tactical advice. Its audiences no doubt exaggerated the degree of US support that this implied, and refugees later told Vice-President Nixon that the radio had played a part in encouraging the revolution.[13] But the United States never went beyond broadcasts. There were those in the CIA who wished to do so, but Allen Dulles was hostile and Eisenhower

11. Prados, *Presidents' Secret Wars* p.120; Ranelagh, *The Agency* pp.258–9, 287; Powers, *The Man who Kept the Secrets* pp.55–7

12. Brian McCauley, 'Hungary and Suez, 1956: The Limits of Soviet and American Power', *Journal of Contemporary History* xvi (1981) p.781

13. Prados, *Presidents' Secret Wars* pp.125–6; Ranelagh, *The Agency* pp.308–9; Richard Nixon, *Memoirs* (paperback edn, 1979) p.183

adamant – twice vetoing proposals to drop arms. (Instead the United States again offered food aid.)

26 October had in fact seen a decision taken to try to reassure the Soviet Union. Eisenhower doubted whether Soviet leaders genuinely anticipated a Western invasion, but Khrushchev appeared insecure; faced with the weakening of its hold over its satellites, 'might not the Soviet Union be tempted to resort to extreme measures, even to start a world war?' Also (as Eisenhower was later to emphasise to critics) since NATO had no common frontier with Hungary and no way of intervening on the ground, his only available option was to use (or, presumably, threaten to use) nuclear weapons.[14] So it was decided to tell the USSR that 'We do not look upon these nations as potential military allies'. But the message may have seemed to the Kremlin less than reassuring, since it also said they 'should have sovereignty restored to them, and that they should have governments of their own free choosing. . . . We see them as friends and as part of a new and friendly and no longer divided Europe'. Dulles had earlier spoken of according aid to East European nations during their 'economic adjustment' away from exclusive dependence on the USSR, albeit without any pre-conditions that they renounce Communism. The State Department was looking, as an internal circular of 2 November shows, to a transformation of Eastern Europe into a collection of 'national Communist regimes' presumably on the Yugoslav model.[15] This accorded with a Soviet Declaration on 31 October that the socialist states could build their relations 'only on the principles of complete equality . . . and of non-interference in one another's internal affairs'. But it had very little in common with the real Soviet view of the 'camp'. Nor did it address what Khrushchev saw as the problem of the likely restoration of capitalism in Hungary:

> If we let things take their course the West would say we are either stupid or weak, and that's one and the same thing. We cannot possibly permit it, either as Communists and internationalists or as the Soviet state. We would have capitalists on the frontiers of the Soviet Union.[16]

14. Ambrose, *Eisenhower, The President* p.372; some people in the CIA deployed the case for a nuclear ultimatum to the USSR: Ranelagh, *The Agency* p.306

15. McCauley, 'Hungary and Suez' pp.782–4, 791; Dwight D. Eisenhower, *White House Years, ii (Waging Peace, 1956–1961)* (1966) p.70 (hereafter cited as Eisenhower, *Memoirs* ii)

16. For Khrushchev's explanation to the Yugoslavs of his decision to use force, see Micunovic, *Moscow Diary* pp.132–40 (esp. 133)

Eisenhower says that (unlike Allen Dulles) he always suspected the 31 October Declaration; and in the first days of November there was much evidence that Soviet troops were not really withdrawing but regrouping for a new offensive. An opportunity for further diplomatic involvement was presented by the Hungarian Prime Minister's appeals of 1 and 2 November to the United Nations and the 'four great Powers' to guarantee Hungarian neutrality. But in fact US action, even within the UN, was dilatory and at points obstructive. So no steps were taken to challenge the Soviet invasion before it was implemented on 4 November; there are, indeed, allegations that Khrushchev was sent a message confirming US disinterest.[17]

US inaction is sometimes blamed on the simultaneous Suez crisis;[18] certainly this (plus the American elections) consumed much time and nervous energy. However, both the public decision not to intervene in the event of Soviet coercion of Poland and that of 26 October to try to reassure the Soviet Union over Hungary antedate the start of Middle Eastern hostilities. Equally Khrushchev was claiming as early as 24 October that the Soviet leadership was unanimously prepared (if necessary) to use force in Hungary. The actual decision to do so now appears to have been taken, with some wavering (perhaps because of the difficulty of securing Chinese approval), in lengthy sessions spread over 30–31 October. By 31 October the Anglo-French ultimatum to Egypt, and the USA's condemnation of it in the UN, would have been known in Moscow; so it could, chronologically, have been a factor in the Soviet decision to intervene. But in justifying this, it was rather the consequences for Eastern Europe if Hungary stopped being communist that Khrushchev (and others) always stressed. The most that can be said of Suez (in this context) is that, in Khrushchev's words, Anglo-French actions would provide 'a favourable moment. . . . There would be confusion and uproar in the West and the United

17. Eisenhower, *Memoirs* ii chap. 3; RIIA, *Documents on International Affairs 1956* pp.475, 480; McCauley, 'Hungary and Suez' esp. pp.792–4. McCauley notes that both memoir-writers and the subsequent declassifiers of US documents are very quiet on the period 1–3 November as it affected Hungary

18. Csaba Békés notes that Britain and France wished to transfer the Hungarian question from the UN Security Council to the General Assembly, which had been seized of the 'Suez' war since 31 October; the USA did not wish the General Assembly to be thus sidetracked, and so delayed UN proceedings on Hungary until after the actual 4 November Soviet invasion: 'New Findings on the 1956 Hungarian Revolution', *Cold War International History project Bulletin* 2 (1992) p.3

Nations, but it would be less at a time when Britain, France and Israel were waging a war against Egypt'.[19]

KHRUSHCHEV AND THE POLICY OF 'PEACEFUL COEXISTENCE'

If Eastern Europe constituted the Soviet sphere, much of the rest of the world was under, or just emerging from, colonial rule. Stalin had in fact conducted some postwar probes, by supporting the emergence of Israel in 1947–8 and probably also by encouraging insurgency in South-East Asia in 1948. Khrushchev tells us that his expectations were very limited: he had qualms about having recognised Ho Chi Minh's revolutionary government as he 'did not believe in the possibility of victory for Vietnam'; and he refused to send arms to King Farouk of Egypt, declaring 'in my presence that the Near East was part of Britain's sphere of influence and that therefore we couldn't go sticking our noses into Egypt's affairs'.[20] After Stalin's death Molotov continued to defend and advocate Stalin's policies. Khrushchev used his support to topple Malenkov from the premiership, but then turned on him in 1955. Despite Khrushchev's initial success, the antagonism rumbled on until 1957, when it flared up again in the so-called 'Anti-Party Group' attempt to depose Khrushchev. As Khrushchev described this to Nasser in 1958, Molotov 'thought we should go back to traditional policies':

> first . . . we should draw a line in Europe beyond which we should allow no retreat. Second, we should refuse to discuss anything affecting countries on our side of that line. Third, we should stop what he called 'adventurism', in which he included our interest in your part of the world. . . . I told Molotov that to adopt a purely defensive position in Europe would be a mistake, because there are so many currents flowing over Europe, and the socialist movement in western Europe is becoming very important. Offence is the best form of defence. I said that we needed a new, active diplomacy because the impossibility of a nuclear war meant that the struggle between us and the capitalists was taking on new forms. I told them: 'I'm not an adventurer, but we must aid national liberation movements, and if imperialism controls somewhere

19. ibid, p.2; *Khrushchev Remembers* i pp.380–2; Micunovic, *Moscow Diary* pp. 132–40; John C. Campbell, in W. Roger Louis and Roger Owen (eds) *Suez 1956: The Crisis and its Consequences* (Oxford, 1989) pp. 242–3; M. Tatu in S.S. Kaplan (ed.) *Diplomacy of Power* (Washington, DC, 1981) p. 21
  20. *Khrushchev Remembers* iii pp.155–6, i p.394

like the Middle East it could liquidate the national liberation movements there and bring to power reactionary forces which would be ready to play their part in a policy of encirclement of the Soviet Union.'[21]

Khrushchev was no doubt putting special stress on those aspects of the dispute that most concerned Nasser,[22] but they did go to the heart of his foreign policy. This he set out at length in the Central Committee report to the 1956 Twentieth Party Congress.[23] A 'vast zone of peace has emerged in the world, including the peace-loving States, both Socialist and non-Socialist, of Europe and Asia, . . . inhabited by . . . the majority of the population of our planet'. This meant that, despite the earlier Marxist-Leninist thesis, war with imperialism was no longer 'fatalistically inevitable', which was just as well, 'for in present-day conditions . . . there are only two ways: either peaceful co-existence or the most destructive war in history'. So 'when we say that the Socialist system will win in the competition' with capitalism, 'this by no means signifies that its victory will be achieved through armed interference'.

One ground for Khrushchev's confidence was economic: 'Our certainty of the victory of Communism is based on the fact that the Socialist mode of production possesses decisive advantages over the capitalist mode'. He had begun his report by claiming a 1,949 per cent increase in Soviet industrial production since 1929, as against one of 134 per cent for the USA and 93 per cent for capitalist states in general. He seems to have looked for the sort of phenomenon that did actually occur in 1989–91, only in the opposite direction: the internal disintegration of a system that had, comparatively speaking, failed to deliver the goods. He often rubbed this in to foreigners; thus he told Adenauer in 1955 that ' "You are condemned to go under and we will be master of the world!" I

21. M. Heikal, *Sphinx and Commissar: The Rise and Fall of Soviet Influence in the Arab World* (1978) pp.91–2
22. The chief issue had been the handling of Yugoslavia, which had major implications for the rest of Eastern Europe. Khrushchev also claims that Molotov had opposed Austrian independence, Soviet troop withdrawals from Finland, and the opening of negotiations with Japan, and more surprisingly that he had also had initial reservations about including Albania and East Germany in the Warsaw Pact – see the Polish defector Seweryn Bialer's account of the minutes of the secret July 1955 Central Committee Plenum: 'I chose Truth', *News from behind the Iron Curtain* (New York) v (Oct. 1956) esp. pp.10–11; *Khrushchev Remembers* ii pp.222–5, iii pp.69–70, 75–80, 86–8. Molotov had to confess to the Twentieth Party Congress that the Foreign Ministry had failed to appreciate the importance of the 'colonial liberation movements': *Keesing's*, 14748
23. *Keesing's*, 14745–6

think it was really important to him.' Similarly Khrushchev explained to the London *Times* that he did not need to teach the British

> to effect a revolution and establish a socialist system in their country. They will do it themselves when they come to realise that the system which we have here . . . presents greater advantages to the peoples than the capitalist system, that the socialist system offers unlimited possibilities.[24]

The other basis for Khrushchev's confidence lay in 'the disintegration of the imperialist colonial system', which he described to the Twentieth Party Congress as a 'development of world historical significance' and which the 1960 Moscow Conference of eighty-one Communist parties was to rate as 'second only to the formation of the world socialist system'. Khrushchev implied in 1956 that the newly emancipated states were natural allies of the 'world camp of Socialism'; in 1959 he spelt things out more fully to the next Congress:

> if we take the countries forming the world socialist system and the countries waging a courageous struggle against imperialism . . . for their freedom and independence, we shall find that the scales have already turned in favour of these peace-loving countries. . . .
> One of the cardinal conclusions to be drawn from an analysis of the present balance of forces in the world is that most colonial and semi-colonial countries, which have only recently been the reserve and the rear of imperialism, are no longer that.[25]

To Khrushchev this was an inevitable process: Iran, he told Kennedy at the 1962 Vienna summit, was a typical unstable pro-Western country about to experience political upheaval; the USSR would no doubt be blamed, but it would not in fact have been involved.[26] But the process was also desirable and to be forwarded. Many of his early 1960s polemics with the Chinese revolved around their refusal to accept his contention that peaceful coexistence provided a more favourable context than hardline confrontation for the development of the 'national liberation movement'.[27] His 1961 Party Programme declared it the CPSU's duty 'to support the

24. K. Adenauer, *Erinnerungen* ii 1953–5 (Stuttgart, 1966) pp.520, 554; N.S. Khrushchev, *For Victory in Peaceful Competition with Capitalism* (1960) p.88
25. *Keesing's*, 14745; RIIA, *Documents 1960* p.230; N.S. Khrushchov [*sic*], *World Without Arms World Without Wars* i (Moscow, 1959) p.65
26. Barry Rubin, *Paved with Good Intentions: The American Experience and Iran* (New York, 1980) p.107
27. RIIA, *Documents 1963* pp.231 ff (Chinese polemic), and 250 ff – esp. pp.267, 275 – (Soviet reply)

sacred struggle of the oppressed peoples and their just anti-imperialist wars of national liberation'. When, at the Vienna summit, Kennedy sought to dissuade him from eliminating free systems in areas hitherto associated with the West, Khrushchev categorically rejected any such attempt to 'freeze' existing conditions. As he later told a visiting US Senator,

> We in the U.S.S.R. feel that the revolutionary process should have the right to exist . . . the right to rebel, and the Soviet right to help combat reactionary governments . . . is the question of questions. This question is at the heart of our relations with you. . . . Kennedy could not understand this.[28]

IMPLICATIONS OF SOVIET AID TO, AND TRADE WITH, THE THIRD WORLD

Khrushchev began his new policy in 1955 by visiting, and offering aid to, India, Burma and Afghanistan. This offer of economic assistance introduced a new dimension into East–West competition. It led, at the time, to a good deal of Western concern. For the socialist planned economies appeared to have the advantage that they could easily direct the giving of aid or the purchase of products that might not be in demand on the open market. Such barter deals had been practised in the 1930s by Nazi Germany; they had gone far to bind Eastern Europe to it economically, and in the 1950s there was a tendency to overestimate their political consequences. The 1950s also tended to exaggerate the economic achievements of the planned Stalinist economic system with its accent on heavy industry; for the Soviet growth-rate was high and Khrushchev was continually looking forward to overtaking the USA. So it was natural for countries like Egypt and India to wish to move in this direction, and for the USSR to encourage them. But in the longer run this economic approach has come to look less

28. *Keesing's*, 18468; *Khrushchev Remembers*, ii pp.495–7; Arthur M. Schlesinger, *A Thousand Days: John F. Kennedy in the White House* (London edn, 1965) pp.325–33. Khrushchev's chief concern was to wean countries from their Western orientation: he had little use for 'temporary people' like Sir Abubakar Tafawa Balewa of Nigeria, who was 'building a new independent state' but who 'went out of his way to be accommodating to Great Britain'. The question of whether they persecuted their own communists was distinctly secondary. But where occasion arose, he encouraged development along socialist lines (cf. his advice to Nasser on agriculture). He was also prepared to deal with communist generals behind the back of the friendly Indonesian leader Sukarno: *Khrushchev Remembers* i pp.410–12, ii pp.323, 480

impressive, leading some politicians (for instance Sadat) to seek to break with it and try other systems. Soviet aid, too, had certain limitations: Mohamed Heikal's instruction manual for Third World leaders (derived largely from Nasser) recalls that 'agriculture is the Soviets' Achilles heel. You can ask them for arms, or factories, but, unless you are in a real crisis, never ask for wheat. They will almost certainly be unable to provide it'. Heikal also mentions that, in the late 1960s, Soviet teams (in contrast to American) could not drill deep enough to find oil.[29] Even setting such considerations aside, the socialist economies were always both smaller and more self-sufficient than the 'advanced capitalist' OECD (Organisation for Economic Co-operation and Development) ones; so their inter-national economic weight was inevitably less.

But if Soviet economic competition was less serious than originally feared, it was still significant. At the least it enabled Third World states to play East off against West. Nasser wanted the West to build him the Aswan Dam, and used the possibility of turning to the Soviet Union to secure Western credits. Admittedly these were later withdrawn, but the USSR then stepped in to undertake the project. Although Soviet economic aid was not extensive,[30] the Russians (and occasionally also the Chinese)[31] were capable of replacing the West in an emergency. Thus in 1969 the USSR offered Iraq technical assistance and loans to develop the North Rumaila oilfield, whose nationalisation the Western-owned Iraq Petroleum Company (IPC) was contesting; the USSR was also among the countries prepared to take oil from the Kirkuk field when this was nationalised in 1972 and the IPC sought to have it boycotted.[32] Similarly as the USA imposed sanctions on Castro's Cuba, the USSR stepped in to counteract them. In *this* instance it was rewarded by the acquisition of a new member of the socialist camp, but at a cost that had risen to some $4.6 billion per year by 1984 (and that some say made the USSR think twice in the 1960s about picking up more such clients).[33]

29. Heikal, *Sphinx and Commissar* pp.30, 212

30. The CIA calculates 'Gross Official Bilateral Capital Flows to the Less Developed Countries' during 1954–78 as $193 billion from OECD countries, $21 billion from OPEC countries, and $14 billion from communist countries *Handbook of Economic Statistics, 1980*, Tables 70, 74

31. When Western Powers declined to finance a Tanzania–Zambia railway (regarding it, correctly, as a waste of money), the two countries reluctantly turned to China, who built it between 1970 and 1976 on very easy terms: *Keesing's,* 27900

32. *Keesing's,* 24648, 25201, 25455

33. Staar, *USSR Foreign Policies after Detente* p.145

Khrushchev's other major Third World initiative in 1955 was the sale of (ostensibly Czech) arms to Egypt. Supplying arms has its problems, for the recipients are likely to seek modern weapons, but may well lose them to your enemies (over the years Israel deliberately captured from Egypt a range of Soviet weaponry for transfer to the USA). Refusal to supply up-to-date equipment can give offence, however, and a country's prestige can (and in the Middle East has) become tied in with the military success of the purchasers of its arms. But, when all is said, arms sales are profitable, and they constituted a field in which the USSR was well equipped to compete. From at least the early 1960s, therefore, it was almost always the leading weapons exporter to the Third World.[34] Both buyers and sellers perceive arms sales as not merely financial but also political transactions, and they also provide a constituency within the recipient military that should be favourably inclined towards the supplier. This can only be a slippery source of influence, but then today most sources of influence are slippery. It was to its readiness to supply arms that the Soviet Union owed much of its position in the Middle East.

THE USSR AND EGYPT 1955–6

In 1955 the Middle East still seemed to be a largely British sphere, but it was in considerable turmoil.[35] It had been rent by the establishment of Israel and the humiliating 1948–9 defeat of the Arabs; thereafter Arab–Israeli frontiers had stayed closed, save only for frequent and bloody border incidents. Also Egypt had only just managed (after a long struggle) to force Britain to give up its Suez Canal bases, and Anglo-Egyptian relations were still fragile – especially as Nasser hoped to use his enormous charisma and appeal to Arab nationalism to destroy the traditional (and mostly pro British) regimes in other countries in an extension of his own Egyptian revolution. Nasser had originally sought arms from the United States, but he ran up against the 1950 Tripartite Declaration in which the major Western suppliers, Britain, France and the USA, had undertaken to maintain a rough arms balance between Israel

---

34. *SIPRI [Stockholm International Peace Research Institute] Yearbook, World Armaments and Disarmament* (Oxford), *1983* p.272, *1987* p.184 – the exception is the period 1973–7

35. For a fuller discussion, see *The Post-Imperial Age* chaps 10, 11

and the Arabs. By approaching the USSR, Nasser introduced a new player and broke out of the Western strait-jacket.

The approach was made via Zhou Enlai, who recommended it to Moscow with the advice

> that we must expect a major collision in the Middle East between what . . . [Nasser] calls the new forces of Arab nationalism and the colonialists and reactionaries who oppose it.
>
> . . . It is impossible for the socialist camp to adopt the role of a spectator. . . . As I see it, our position obliges us to assist the nationalist forces in this battle for two reasons – because their victory would be in the interest of the socialist camp and because it would thwart all attempts of the western imperialists to complete the encirclement of the eastern camp. My conclusion is that the logic of history points to the nationalist movement as the coming force in the Middle East, and that we should make our approach to it [as early and] as friendly as we can.

Acting on this advice, the Russians initiated military discussions, and sent the editor of *Pravda* to check Nasser out. Nasser made it clear that he was *not* a communist, but Shepilov was able to report that he seemed both determined and reliable. The deal went ahead, and was hurriedly announced by Nasser in September to forestall US pressure to cancel it.[36]

The Egyptians maintain that, at this stage, Soviet commitment was still distinctly conditional, and that Khrushchev and Bulganin were tempted (during their 1956 visit to London) by Eden's invitation to subscribe to the Tripartite Declaration, which would have accorded them a new standing in Middle Eastern affairs. It was partly to circumvent this possibility and gain access to another arms supplier that Nasser recognised communist China in May.[37] This in turn infuriated Dulles and contributed to the brusque way in which he withdrew the offer of aid for the Aswan Dam. Nasser's response was to nationalise the Suez Canal. A surprised but delighted Khrushchev accelerated military deliveries to Egypt, while threatening the British and French ambassadors 'that Egypt would not be left alone in an armed battle if the West launched it'. But, despite Eden's April 1956 warnings that Britain would if necessary fight for its vital Middle Eastern interests, it does not look as if Khrushchev anticipated having to make his threat good.[38]

36. Heikal, *Sphinx and Commissar* pp.58–63

37. ibid, pp.66–7; Heikal, *Cutting the Lion's Tale: Suez through Egyptian Eyes* (1986) pp.102–3

38. Micunovic, *Moscow Diary* pp.103–4, 117. For a fuller treatment of the Suez crisis, see *The Post-Imperial Age* chap.11

When war actually broke out, Khrushchev and Zhukov were profuse in their explanations that it was geographically impossible for them to intervene. Eisenhower had felt much the same about Hungary. But whereas this had led the USA to eschew threats, the fact that the Anglo-French invasion of Egypt was opposed also by the United States gave the USSR an opening. So late on 5 November 1956 it approached the UN and USA to suggest a joint Soviet–US military force to end the invasion, and sent ferocious letters to Britain, France and Israel apprising them of this; Eden was also told that, 'Were rocket weapons used against Britain and France, you would, most probably, call this a barbarous action. But how does the inhuman attack launched . . . against a practically defenceless Egypt differ . . .?' All this committed the USSR to very little. Khrushchev was later to say that the USSR had never contemplated unilateral action in the Middle East and that the proposal for joint action with the USA was advanced for propaganda purposes;[39] and although the reference to rocket attacks was obviously meant to be alarming, it was not a direct threat. The White House promptly termed the suggestion of joint US–Soviet action 'unthinkable' and observed that it would 'oppose' the introduction of any new forces into the Middle East other than that already authorised by the UN. Eisenhower's private language was distinctly stronger, and he prepared to place US forces on the alert as a warning to Khrushchev.[40] He continued his financial pressure on London, however, and it was this that induced Eden to call a cease-fire on 6 November while he still controlled only half the Suez Canal, too little to give him any leverage over the subsequent settlement.

THE EISENHOWER DOCTRINE 1957

It was, then, not the Soviet Union that had saved Egypt. Privately Nasser recognised this.[41] But he had no interest in contesting the enormous popularity the Soviet démarche earned in the Arab world, especially as the USSR soon promised to make good

39. McCauley, 'Hungary and Suez' pp.786–8; Charles Bohlen, *Witness to History* (1973) p.434; *Khrushchev Remembers*, i pp.397–8

40. Eisenhower, *Memoirs* ii p.91; Ambrose, *Eisenhower: The President* pp.368–9

41. M. Heikal, *Nasser: The Cairo Documents* (1972) pp.139, 142; O. Smolyansky, 'Moscow and the Suez Crisis: A Reappraisal', *Political Science Quarterly* xxx (1965) p.602; McCauley, 'Hungary and Suez' pp.786, 797

Egyptian arms losses in the war, whereas the United States combined its legalistic determination to secure Britain, France and Israel's total withdrawal with a continued hostility to Nasserism. The 1955 arms deal had brought the Soviet Union into the Middle East in alliance with radical Arab nationalism. The Suez invasion had failed to check this process; by forcing withdrawal the USA had finally destroyed British pre-eminence in the area. Eisenhower perceived the result as a 'vacuum', and in January 1957 told congressional leaders that it 'must be filled by the United States before it is filled by Russia'. This led to congressional approval of what came to be known as the Eisenhower Doctrine, which sought (as Dulles explained) 'to deal with the possibility of Communist aggression, direct and indirect'.[42] Both Eisenhower and Dulles conceded that the Middle East also had 'Problems other than of Communist Source', but they clearly saw it as having become a key arena of East–West rivalry. So did the Russians. Admittedly they were attracted, then and later, by the idea of entering into a partnership to control the region. But the West did not respond, and probably Khrushchev did not expect it to.[43] Failing such a development, Mikoyan told the US ambassador in 1957: 'We are going to do everything we can to oppose the establishment of Western military strength in that area, and particularly yours'.[44] The stage was therefore set for a US–Soviet clash.

JORDAN, SYRIA AND THE LEBANON 1957–8

For this the condition of the Middle East in 1957 afforded many opportunities. The sense that there existed a single Arab nation legitimated, and similarities of language and culture facilitated, intervention by one Arab state in the internal politics of another, generally through a mixture of propaganda and subversion. Such an environment also encouraged the intervention of external 'intelligence' agencies (of which we know most about the American). In 1957 the future of the apparently shaky regimes in

42. Eisenhower, *Memoirs* ii p.178; RIIA, *Documents 1957* pp.233 ff, 267–9
43. He told a worried Egyptian delegation in 1957, 'We are quite aware that they have no intention of allowing us any role in the Middle East – or anywhere else for that matter – unless we completely change our skins; and that is a day which they will no more see than a man can see his ears': *Sphinx and Commissar*, p.83
44. Bohlen, *Witness to History* p.450

Jordan, Syria and the Lebanon seemed to be at stake. King Hussein managed to stabilise Jordan, dismissing his Cabinet after it had decided to open relations with the USSR. He was assisted by a reconciliation with King Saud of Saudi Arabia (who had himself been assiduously courted by Eisenhower but subjected to assassination plots from elsewhere), and also by a $10 million US loan and protective movements on the part of the US Sixth Fleet. Then in June 1957 status quo parties did well in the Lebanese elections despite Egypt's alleged commitment of £0.7 million on the other side.[45]

There remained Syria. The USA had sponsored a coup in 1956, but the outbreak of the Suez hostilities had pre-empted it. The enterprise apparently resumed in 1957, but the Syrian authorities discovered and denounced it in August. By now Syria appeared to be moving towards the Russians, having secured massive aid and arms promises in July, and installed a new (and in conservative eyes suspect) Chief of Staff. So, as Eisenhower puts it:

> Syria's neighbors, including her fellow Arab nations, had come to the conclusion that the present regime in Syria had to go: otherwise the takeover by the Communists would soon be complete.
>
> In these circumstances most Middle East countries seemed to believe that direct military action would be necessary.

Syria's neighbours accordingly agreed to mobilise to induce it to disperse its forces, after which Iraq would attack. The United States' part was to 'see that no outside countries – for example, Israel or the USSR – would interfere', and it staged demonstrative fleet and air movements. At this stage the Arab countries involved got cold feet. Turkey would have been prepared to go ahead on its own with the 50,000 troops concentrated for 'manoeuvres' on its Syrian border; but Eisenhower claims that, in the absence of any Arab support for intervention, the USA shifted in September to restraining Turkey. So, more openly, did the USSR, warning Turkey that it would 'suffer' if it attacked Syria, and sending token warships to Syria. Later, in October, buoyed by the prestige of the first ever successful launch of a satellite ('sputnik'), Khrushchev renewed the threats, and was in turn reminded by Dulles that the United States would respond by hitting the USSR.[46] But by then the crisis was subsiding, and many of these statements were being made for the

45. Eisenhower, *Memoirs* ii esp. pp.190–1, 194; R. Lacey, *The Kingdom* (New York, 1981) pp.315–17; RIIA, *Survey of International Affairs 1956–1958* pp.171–5
46. Prados, *Presidents' Secret Wars* pp.128–30; Eisenhower, *Memoirs* ii pp.196–203

record. Nasser's contribution to this phase was to airlift troops into Syria in October; he came to appear to the mutually suspicious Syrians as a possible saviour. In November a meeting of Syrian and Egyptian parliamentarians advocated a union of the two countries. They were strongly supported by the Syrian military. Nasser was persuaded; and the 'United Arab Republic' (UAR) was finally proclaimed in Damascus amid great enthusiasm in February 1958.

Trouble next struck in the Lebanon, whose President Chamoun had sought to amend the Constitution to gain himself a second term of office. Chamoun saw the resulting disturbances in (over-simplified) terms of a cleavage between conservatism and Nasserite Arabism, sounded out American willingness to intervene, and also appealed to the UN claiming UAR subversion. But by early July the crisis appeared to have passed, with Chamoun declaring his readiness to retire at the end of his constitutional term.

THE IRAQI REVOLUTION 1958

On 14 July 1958 some Iraqi units that had been ordered into Jordan (whether to stabilise it or, as the Egyptians claim, as a pre-liminary to an attack on Syria) staged a coup as they passed through Baghdad, the capital of Iraq. The King, the Crown Prince, and political strongman Nuri es Said were killed, and a Republic was proclaimed under Brigadier Kassem. Iraq had long been one of the pillars of the pro-British and pro-Western configuration of the Middle East; its sudden revolution seemed to sweep all this away, leaving Nasserism triumphant. The obvious question was whether the West would take it lying down. Saud (whose family had admittedly now forced him to relinquish much of his power) secretly demanded 'that the Baghdad Pact powers intervene in Iraq, on pain of Saudi Arabia's having to "go along" with the United Arab Republic'. Turkey was very anxious to oblige, and countries that felt themselves more directly at risk sought stabilisation by US or British troops. The now neurotic Chamoun appealed to Eisenhower on the 14th, Hussein to Britain on the 16th.[47] On 15 July 1958 US troops landed on the crowded Beirut bathing beaches (supposedly much to the profit of local ice-cream vendors), in what

47. Eisenhower, *Memoirs* ii pp.265–72; Harold Macmillan, *Memoirs* iv (*Riding the Storm 1956–1959*) esp. pp.513, 516, 522

was intended chiefly as a demonstration of strength; by early August they totalled 14,000, including tanks and atomic-capable artillery.[48] The British drop of 2,200 paratroops on 17 July was a more risky affair, large enough to secure Amman airport and if necessary to take on the mob, but not enough to handle Jordanian armour had the army mutinied. Both forces in fact achieved their goals, but given the logistic difficulties of putting them in place,[49] neither the USA nor Britain would have had any spare capacity to invade Iraq. Nor were they anxious to give the go-ahead for a Turkish invasion or risk in any way provoking an Iraqi attack on Jordan or Kuwait.

Khrushchev, however, was highly concerned. He had been delighted by the Iraqi revolution, and was anxious not in any way to jeopardise it. He pressed Nasser (who happened to be in Yugoslavia) to fly to Moscow, and, after some bravado, told him of Eden's 1956 threat to fight if his oil was endangered. Khrushchev therefore counselled prudence and reassurances to the West that oil supplies would be maintained: 'Remember, this is a game of nerves. . . . The possibility of nuclear war is always there, but the moments of greatest risk are in the first shock of new events. If you can get through this period all right, you will be safe'. Khrushchev's own contribution to this process was, on the one hand, to stage manoeuvres (but, as he emphatically reminded Nasser, 'nothing more than manoeuvres'),[50] and, on the other, to call on 19 July for an urgent summit meeting. Both France and Britain would have been happy to hold one, but the United States was not – and succeeded in stalling. As far as the Middle East was concerned, this did not matter, for things settled down very quickly. A US envoy managed to negotiate a political settlement in the Lebanon, and the army commander, General Chehab, was elected to succeed

48. Eisenhower, *Memoirs* ii p.286. Though chiefly demonstrative, US strength may also have reinforced diplomacy in dissuading elements of the Lebanese army from resisting

49. The original contingency plan (drafted in Nov. 1957) had called for joint Anglo-American action in the Lebanon. When Eisenhower determined that it should be all-American (to leave British troops for use elsewhere), the intervention force could be assembled in time only by overflying neutral Austria (which protested): *The Joint Chiefs of Staff and National Policy 1957–60*, (National Archives, Washington) esp. pp.426–7, 445, 454. British forces for Amman had to overfly Israel, which later made difficulties about their resupply (as did Saudi Arabia); to avoid using the Suez Canal, the further battalion that reached Akaba in early August had to be drawn from Aden, which reduced reserves that might be needed to hold Kuwait: Macmillan, *Memoirs* iv pp.519–25. US Marines were sent to the Gulf as a possible reinforcement: Barry M. Blechman and Stephen Kaplan (eds), *Force without War: U.S. Armed Forces as a Political Instrument* (Washington, DC, 1978) p.238

50. Heikal, *Sphinx and Commissar* esp. p.98; *Nasser: The Cairo Documents* pp.131–2

President Chamoun when he retired in September. Meanwhile the new regime in Iraq had proved conciliatory. On 28 July 1958 a Baghdad Pact meeting in London decided that it should be recognised. At a special session of the UN General Assembly the Arab states all agreed on 21 August to propose a moderate resolution inviting Secretary-General Hammarskjöld to make practical arrangements to consolidate Jordan and the Lebanon. Accordingly he toured the Middle East, and the autumn saw US and British withdrawals.[51]

SOVIET–EGYPTIAN COOLNESS 1959

This proved to inaugurate something of a lull in the Arab world. For the remaining conservative regimes proved far more stable than most people had expected, while events in 1959 led to a temporary Soviet–Egyptian estrangement. The chief cause was probably Egypt's backing of an unsuccessful coup against the independent-minded and increasingly communist-inclined regime in Iraq. This naturally drew the USSR even closer to Brigadier Kassem, who seemed a still more promising leader than Nasser, but who was in his turn to be killed in a 1963 rising. Khrushchev also began to criticise Nasser for talking about socialism but attacking communists. Nasser saw this as dictation and replied in kind, which led to a vitriolic exchange of letters raking up past incidents. As a result Nasser moved some way back towards the United States, transferring thither in October 1959 all the 250 Egyptian students who had gone to Soviet universities. The resultant coolness was only gradually cleared up; and, for the time being, the Middle East ceased to be the major arena of East–West competition.[52]

THE CHINESE OFFSHORE ISLANDS CRISIS 1958

The events of July 1958 had a sequel in the Far East. In calling for a summit, Khrushchev had insisted that it consist of the USA, USSR, Britain, France and India – India being close to Nasser and more acceptable to the USA than communist China. China did not like

51. RIIA, *Survey 1956–8* pp.374–92
52. Heikal, *Nasser: The Cairo Documents* chap. 4, *Sphinx and Commissar* pp.101–14

East–West cooperation anyway, and particularly did not care for its proposed displacement by its rival India. Presumably as a result of Chinese displeasure, Khrushchev made a hurried visit to Beijing on 31 July 1958 and thereafter abandoned the idea. During the visit Mao alarmed Khrushchev by suggesting that, on the basis of their total population, the socialist countries were well placed to fight the capitalists. Later he told the Soviet Foreign Minister, Gromyko, that if the renewed tension over Quemoy and Matsu escalated into war, Chinese forces should flee precipitately, luring US troops into the interior where the Soviet Union should 'give them everything you've got'.[53]

Gromyko was unenthusiastic. But on 23 August heavy artillery bombardment of Quemoy began, soon accompanied by broadcasts about its imminent invasion and Chinese determination to liberate Taiwan. Chiang Kai-shek had again concentrated on the offshore islands far more men than were optimal for defence, and their resupply was not easy. As in 1955 Eisenhower supported Chiang, convoying Nationalist supplies in international waters but reserving to himself the decision as to further military action. This time he was rather more confident that he would not be pushed to extremes, but the apparent prospect of a major war for the offshore islands was even more unpopular: at one point Eisenhower told the more belligerent Dulles that 'as much as two-thirds of the world, and 50% of U.S. opinion, opposes the course which we have been following', and he was worried that NATO might be 'beginning to fall apart'. Nevertheless he was succesful. One explanation is simply that the Nationalists established air supremacy (with the aid of US Sidewinder missiles) and (using US-supplied landing craft) succeeded in fighting supplies through to Quemoy. Another view is that the Chinese communists were worried by the flexibility that the USA showed in secret negotiations in Warsaw: this might have led to the abandonment of the islands and the establishment of a UN trusteeship over Taiwan, hence to Taiwan's definitive separation from China. In any case the bombardment was relaxed in October. In a flying visit to Taiwan, Dulles read the riot act, emphasising Chiang's political isolation and the suspicion that he positively 'wants to endanger the peace and involve the US, as the only means of returning to the mainland'. The Korean and Indo-Chinese 'civil wars' had been 'ended by armistice', and Chiang should in future

53. *Khrushchev Remembers* ii p.260; RIIA, *Survey 1956–8* p.538; Andrei Gromyko, *Memories* (paperback edn, 1989) pp.321–3

behave as if an armistice were in effect. On 23 October Chiang renounced the use of force to return to the mainland; two days later the communists declared that they would bombard Quemoy only on odd days of the month.[54]

KHRUSHCHEV'S VIEW OF THE INTERNATIONAL SCENE 1957–8

In 1957 and 1958 there were not only very serious international crises but also a number of more hopeful signs (notably the moratorium on nuclear tests), a mixture that was to persist for some years. At a party on New Year's Eve 1957 Khrushchev toasted Eisenhower and declared that a US–Soviet understanding could only be to everybody's advantage. This was followed up by proposals in January 1958 for an East–West conference, in June for talks on economic cooperation (and US credits), and in July for a Five Power summit on the Middle East. Khrushchev seemed to wish to establish the USSR as the second 'superpower', with the same sort of standing as the United States; he was to be delighted when Macmillan and de Gaulle later admitted that they were no longer in the same league.[55] He probably also hoped to exploit contradictions between the United States and its allies; and he was prepared to offend China in the pursuit of these goals. But Khrushchev always saw East–West relations as adversarial; his expectations of possible accommodations were not high. Thus he told the Yugoslav ambassador in February 1958 that 'talks would probably take place this year, but that the prospects were not very good for agreement on major issues', in October that

> he did not count on a worsening of East–West relations, and certainly did not believe there was a danger of serious conflict breaking out. He said that capitalism was getting steadily weaker. Africa was the centre of the struggle between socialism and imperialism.
>
> 'If we weren't strong . . . would it really be possible for Nasser, Sukarno, or the new government in Iraq . . . to hold on to power? The United States would send troops in. . . . The Soviet Union will continue to fight stubbornly for peace, which we have especial need of

54. P.P.P.C. Cheng, *Truce Negotiations over Korea and Quemoy* (Washington, DC, 1977) chap. 3; Ambrose, *Eisenhower: The President* pp.482–5; Hoopes, *The Devil and John Foster Dulles* chap. 17; R.L. Garthoff (ed.), *Sino-Soviet Military Relations* pp.109–11, chap. 7

55. *Khrushchev Remembers* ii pp.439, 460

for the next fifteen or twenty years. After that no one will be able to go to war even if he wants to. The United States doesn't yet want any relaxation in Europe because that would lead to a general relaxation, would weaken the system of American domination [and military alliances/bases] in vast areas around the world, . . . and that would in turn produce political problems at home.'

. . . He mentioned certain [recent] events [Suez, the Iraqi revolution, etc.] which were of special importance for the relation of forces on the world scene and said all of them had been bad for imperialism and the Americans.[56]

THE BERLIN QUESTION 1958–9

Khrushchev's next move came over Berlin. Since the blockade the city had been administratively divided, with the Soviet sector under communist local government while the three Western sectors formed a unit with an elected mayor and senate. Each side was assimilated for most purposes into its own Germany, but the city remained open, with people able to pass readily from one side to the other, and was in law still subject to Four Power military occupation. Access from West Germany was governed by a complex of arrangements, written and unwritten. Land access was subject to periodic interference that could be alarming but that never in fact proved damaging; it continued, even after the USSR had in 1955 conceded independence to East Germany (the DDR), to be run or supervised on a Four Power basis. Since the blockade West German subsidies had built West Berlin into a show-case far richer than the East, but it could not have been maintained at this level by an airlift alone. Nor, despite a good deal of contingency planning, was there ever much likelihood of NATO forces being able to open the motorways across East Germany if the USSR really decided to close them. So, in the last analysis, the Western position in Berlin rested on Soviet restraint and/or on the ability of Western nuclear power to deter the USSR from taking (or allowing East Germany to take) any sustained disruptive action. To add to the difficulties, the West did not officially accept either the partition of Germany or the (undoubtedly unrepresentative) East German regime. West Germany, which had now emerged as a key component of NATO, was adamant that this state of affairs should continue (even though it itself concluded de facto trade agreements with the DDR). Yet

56. Micunovic, *Moscow Diary* pp.335–8, 342, 391, 431–2

from 1958 onwards the USSR threatened to transfer all control over Berlin access to the DDR, which could then compel the West either to recognise it or to precipitate a blockade by refusing to accept DDR management of the access routes. 'When I go to sleep at night', Secretary of State Dean Rusk was to say, 'I try not to think about Berlin'. Khrushchev, admittedly, was usually more relaxed: 'They will not start a war. Of course, in signing a [separate] peace treaty [with the DDR], we will have to put our rockets on military alert. But, luckily, our adversaries still haven't gone crazy; they still think and their nerves still aren't bad'.[57]

It is not entirely clear why Khrushchev decided to re-open the question in 1958. One factor was the West German army's equipment with nuclear weapons (albeit subject to continued US custody of their warheads, a safeguard that the East tended to neglect or regard as unreal). As a result of its war-time experience, the USSR was probably genuinely alarmed. But in view of the wave of anti-nuclear West German opposition, it also saw an opportunity of putting a spanner in the works: 'our general goal', a Soviet ambassador explained, 'is to continue to exert a braking influence . . . If all countries of the socialist camp unite their forces in this direction, then the arming of the *Bundeswehr* could be delayed for 2–3 years, which would be a serious victory for our general cause'.[58] More generally, Moscow had for some time been worried about the vulnerability of its Central European position to a revival of West German power. In the autumn of 1958 its ambassadors and the East German leadership were convincing each other that a Western campaign of destabilisation was imminent.[59] In October Khrushchev himself told Walter Lippmann that the situation resembled that on the eve of the Second World War, with America again pushing Germany against the East: 'Americans seem not to realize the

57. Hope M. Harrison, *Ulbricht and the concrete 'Rose': new archival evidence on the dynamics of Soviet-East German relations and the Berlin crisis, 1958–1961* Cold War International History Project, Working Paper no. 5, Washington, DC (1993) Appendix A (Nov. 1960). In 1961 de Gaulle was similarly confident that if Khrushchev had really meant to go to war over Berlin, ' he would have done so already' (ibid. p.37)

58. Harrison, *Ulbricht and the concrete 'Rose'* pp.12–13

59. 'according to the data we have, the West is preparing to carry out a series of significant economic and political measures against the' DDR [Pervukhin]; as part of a NATO plan, 'West German ruling circles were preparing a broad plan of subversive activity against the . . . [DDR] and the countries of the socialist camp' [Ulbricht]; 'It is possible that the West will not stop at limited local provocations on . . . [DDR] territory. It might be enough for the West to organize a provocation in one or several villages, so that then the whole world would shout about it' [Smirnov] – Harrison, *Ulbricht and the concrete 'Rose'* p.14

dangers which their present policies may well bring them', and the USA 'may someday pay in blood for having encouraged such people'.[60] The raising of the Berlin question in late 1958 was, therefore, in a sense pre-emptive.

Whatever Khrushchev's original intentions, the Berlin problem built up a momentum that made it increasingly difficult for him to back off. By 1961 his prestige was engaged in its resolution. Also there was a sharp increase in the number of East German refugees, who were disproportionately young, male, educated, and therefore economically valuable. Almost all came through Berlin, since the DDR's other borders were controlled; the more Khrushchev pressed the Berlin issue, the greater the rush to get out while there was still time – *Torschlusspanik*.[61] By 1961 this exodus may have come to threaten the viability of the DDR; by July 1961 Ulbricht was sending messages to the effect that 'if the present system of open borders remains, collapse is inevitable' and that 'he refuses all responsibility for what would then happen'.[62]

The crisis may be said to have begun in November 1958 when the Soviet ambassador told Adenauer that the USSR intended 'to liquidate the occupation statutes concerning Berlin'. The message was then spelt out in a long note: there should be general negotiations on a German peace treaty, and on the reconstitution of West Berlin as a Free City that would arrange 'guarantees of unhindered communications' with East Germany and in return 'commit itself not to tolerate on its territory hostile subversive activity' against that state; six months should be adequate for these negotiations; but if the time was not used to reach 'an appropriate agreement' the Soviet Union would sign a peace treaty with East Germany that would leave the latter in full control of all movement across its territory; the entire Warsaw Pact would support it in the event of any 'aggressive action' (i.e. Western attempt to enforce

60. Vladislav M. Zubok, *Khrushchev and the Berlin Crisis (1958–1962)* Cold War International History Project, Working Paper no. 6, Washington, DC (1993) p.8; Khrushchev also compared Adenauer to Hindenburg

61. Refugee numbers went from 10,000 a month in September 1958 (before the crisis) to: 140,000 in 1959; 200,000 in 1960; 80,000 (Jan.–May 1961); 20,000 (June); over 30,000 (July), and 20,000 (1–12 August): H.M. Catudal, *Kennedy and the Berlin Wall Crisis* (Berlin, 1980) pp.23, 29, 48, 164; Jack M. Schick, *The Berlin Crisis 1958–62* (Philadelphia, Pa., 1971) p. 159; R.M. Slusser in Blechman and Kaplan, *Force without War* p.347

62. Harrison, *Ulbricht and the concrete 'Rose'* p.47; Western intelligence, though, suspected that the East Germans might actually be encouraging the flight so as to build up their case for immediate Soviet action (ibid. p.35)

previous rights).[63] What really caused alarm was the fear that, by specifying a six months' time limit, Khrushchev might have left himself no option but to take some drastic action if his wishes were not met. The Western reply (on 31 December) professed readiness for Four Power negotiations provided they were not conducted under time limits and threats of unilateral action. In January 1959 Mikoyan made soothing noises; but a Russian note reiterated that Western refusal to negotiate 'with a view to normalising the situation in Berlin' would lead to a direct Soviet settlement with the DDR. Macmillan, the Western leader most alarmed by the crisis's potential for war and most anxious to revive summit diplomacy, then invited himself to Moscow for a personal exploratory visit (a move de Gaulle regarded as unwise, and Adenauer as an electoral gimmick). During his visit Macmillan was accorded the classic friendly–hostile–friendly treatment; at its end Khrushchev agreed to shelve the time limit and accept negotiations initially at Foreign Minister level, while Macmillan appears to have promised to work for a summit.[64]

Foreign Ministers accordingly met in May 1959 in Geneva, where they continued (with intermissions) until August. Despite Eisenhower's threat to put them in a plane and keep them airborne until they settled, they failed to make progress – on Berlin, the broader German question, European military security, or an atomic test ban. On Berlin the Russians insisted on their 'free city' proposal, and went no further than offering the West the choice between withdrawing their garrisons altogether, replacing them with UN troops, or keeping them but adding a Soviet contingent; the Soviet Union was also prepared to permit the current Western occupation to continue for a further eighteen months while the two Germanies worked out a peace treaty. The West rejected all these proposals. Instead it was prepared to offer minor reductions in the size of its garrison, and to discuss the prohibition of intelligence and propaganda activities in West Berlin;[65] and it floated the idea of a Four Power Commission, advised by East and West Germany, to manage access to the city. Faced with this deadlock Eisenhower sent Khrushchev an invitation to visit the USA. The invitation was meant

---

63. RIIA, *Documents 1958* pp.146–64
64. For Macmillan's promise, Eisenhower, *Memoirs* ii p.401
65. Schick, *The Berlin Crisis* esp. pp.72–85. The renunciation of intelligence gathering (e.g. by radio monitoring) would have been a real loss to the West; that of 'propaganda activities' could conceivably have given the East some standing in West Berlin to determine what constituted 'propaganda'

to be accompanied by an oral message making it conditional on progress at Geneva, but this was never delivered, so Khrushchev could accept the invitation (for which he had been angling since January) without making any concessions. Still the fact that he was looking forward to touring the USA made any dangerous Soviet move unlikely in the mean time.

KHRUSHCHEV'S VISIT TO THE USA 1959

Khrushchev's US tour was not without upsets – over the refusal to let him visit Disneyland for fear of asassination, and, more revealingly, a row with organised labour[66] – but in general it went well and his extrovert ebullience made a good impression. Public relations apart, by admiring the helicopter in which Eisenhower took him for a ride Khrushchev managed to purchase (and then copy) two such machines, whose export would otherwise have been embargoed; Eisenhower also gave him a couple of his own prize cattle. But Khrushchev was less impressed than Eisenhower had hoped with the American way of life: individual houses and cars were simply wasteful, while as for leisure motoring, 'Your people do not seem to like the place where they live and always want to be on the move going some place else'. Nor did they agree in discussions of disarmament or of ways to police a nuclear test ban. But on Berlin Eisenhower's insistence that he would never negotiate under the duress of a time limit ultimately induced Khrushchev to withdraw his deadline. In return Eisenhower agreed to a summit, after which he would pay a return visit to the Soviet Union.[67] So Khrushchev's visit seemed a great success; there was much talk of the 'spirit of Camp David' (the venue for the final discussions), and the stage seemed set (in Eisenhower's words) for negotiations

> to get a solution that will protect the legitimate interests of the Soviets, the East Germans, the West Germans, and above all, the people of West Berlin . . . these negotiations should not be prolonged indefinitely but there could be no fixed time limit on them.

That a US President should mention 'the East Germans' in this way

66. The mainstream deliberately ignored him. He had a meeting with liberals like Walter Reuther, but it degenerated into a row over trade union and other civil liberties in the East – Khrushchev later remarked that 'We hanged the likes of Reuther in Russia in 1917'
67. *Khrushchev Remembers* ii p.37; Eisenhower, *Memoirs* ii pp.446–7

was unusual; Eisenhower seemed to indicate further flexibility when he volunteered at a press conference that 'I don't know what kind of solution may finally prove acceptable . . ., but you must start off from this. The situation is abnormal.'[68]

THE PARIS SUMMIT AND THE U2 INCIDENT 1960

Arranging a summit took a long time, partly due to the wanderlust that seems to have seized all the principals; but, as Macmillan says, 'If all the Heads of State were swanning around each others' territories, one could hardly believe that there would be a sudden and painful explosion'. Another apparently hopeful sign was the growing agreement that the summit, when it came, would be merely the first of a series that would rotate around the capitals of the Big Four. Macmillan was the principal proponent of such a system, hoping, rather unrealistically, that such meetings might eventually succeed, where the UN Security Council had failed, in regulating the major problems of the world. (He told Khrushchev he hoped to reach a position 'in which the four Heads of Government could sit down together . . . to make a start in solving those questions on which unhappily there are still differences of view between us. Such discussions are the only hope which I can see for progress for our peoples and for the world'.)[69]

What the statesmen were actually going to say at these summits is less clear. Public Soviet and American speeches on Berlin reverted to a hardline in 1960. Privately de Gaulle appealed to Khrushchev, during his state visit to France, to let sleeping dogs lie; the current situation in Germany really did not threaten anybody.[70] Macmillan maintains that de Gaulle expected Khrushchev eventually to accept something along the lines the Western Foreign Ministers had proposed at the 1959 Geneva conference, while Eisenhower hoped to get a Berlin settlement in exchange for promising to accept the Oder-Neisse line for ever.[71] De Gaulle paints a more lurid picture:

68. *Keesing's*, 17085; Schick, *The Berlin Crisis* pp.100–1; J.L. Richardson, *Germany and the Atlantic Alliance* (Cambridge, Mass., 1966) p.272

69. Macmillan, *Memoirs* v pp.105, 107, 114, 188, 199

70. *Khrushchev Remembers* ii pp.441–2; Charles de Gaulle, *Memoirs of Hope* (1971) pp.226–9

71. Macmillan, *Memoirs* v pp.191, 193. To oblige the Federal Republic, the West had hitherto withheld recognition of Poland's 1945 acquisition of the lands east of the Oder–Neisse line

on the eve of the summit he found the Anglo-Saxons inclined to compensate for Eisenhower's U2 gaffe by making concessions, with Macmillan leaning towards troop withdrawals and the reconstitution of West Berlin as a free city under UN guarantee. However, he persuaded them that abandoning Berlin in the current state of tension would have disastrous consequences, and that attempts to resolve the German question could be fruitful only after détente and cooperation had been restored.[72]

In the event the U2 incident shipwrecked the summit before it had really started. Ever since the onset of the Cold War the Pentagon had been alarmed by its ignorance of what was going on inside the Soviet Union and had sought both general intelligence and the ability to monitor the rise of day-to-day military activity that would presage a sudden attack. This concern had led, between 1949 and 1954, to the overflights and parachuting in of agents that we have already noted. After their discontinuance, planning turned instead to the development of a spy plane that could fly so high as to be invulnerable; from 1956 to 1960 the CIA conducted some twenty such U2 overflights, which the Soviets could detect but not shoot down. All were personally authorised by the President, who valued them as reassurance that the much-vaunted Soviet lead in missiles did not exist, and who also saw such a capability as essential to monitor any nuclear test ban that might be negotiated. Eisenhower was, however, cautious, the CIA thought too cautious,[73] in authorising such flights, and aware that they could have disastrous diplomatic consequences; in February 1960 'The President said that he has one tremendous asset in a summit meeting, . . . his reputation for honesty. If one of these aircraft were lost when we are engaged in apparently sincere deliberations, it could be put on display in Moscow and ruin the President's effectiveness'.[74] This is exactly what happened.

A flight on the last permitted day before the summit, 1 May 1960, was shot down, and the plane and pilot recovered more or less intact. Khrushchev trapped the Americans, by announcing the shooting but displaying a photograph of the wrong type of plane. Believing the U2 would have autodestructed, the USA made

72. de Gaulle, *Memoirs of Hope* p.249 (cf. also pp.222–4); Eisenhower recalled 'no major disagreements' on Berlin, Macmillan that 'no one got down to brass tacks'
73. Ranelagh, *The Agency* pp.31–48. To circumvent Eisenhower's caution the CIA transferred some U2s to Britain to operate independently. U2s were also flown over China by the Nationalists
74. Ambrose, *Eisenhower: The President* p.568

disingenuous statements about weather research and accidental violation of Soviet territory, whereupon Khrushchev put on show both plane and pilot. After some further covering up, Eisenhower admitted on 11 May that he had personally authorised the overflights, which, while 'distasteful', were (given Soviet secretiveness) needed to ensure against another Pearl Harbor.[75] The Russians nevertheless decided not to abort the summit; but Khrushchev says he changed his mind on the flight to Paris,[76] and on arrival he demanded a personal apology from Eisenhower as a prerequisite for further discussions. Although it now belatedly emerged that Eisenhower had called the U2 programme off, neither Macmillan nor de Gaulle could dissuade Khrushchev; and that was the end of the Paris summit. There was, however, one side-effect. De Gaulle asked Khrushchev how he distinguished between the U2 overflight and the much vaunted transiting of France eighteen times a day by Soviet satellites that probably also contained cameras; Khrushchev could only protest that the two cases were quite different, adding (according to Eisenhower) that any country was welcome to photograph the Soviet Union from satellites.[77] Satellite photography would, of course, have come anyway: there was then no way of shooting satellites down, and the US programme was well advanced, becoming fully operational in 1961. But it was from the outset regarded as internationally acceptable. The superpower arms limitation agreements of the 1970s were to be explicitly postulated on such 'national technical means of verification'. The Soviet Union still rejected on-site inspection, but it was sometimes at pains to facilitate satellite photography that would reassure the USA it was not cheating.

Nobody knows why Khrushchev behaved as he did at Paris. Some have suggested power rivalries in the Kremlin, others that he broke off the summit because he did not expect to achieve much on Berlin. The simplest explanation is that he worked himself into a rage over Eisenhower's 11 May statement and thereafter would have nothing to do with him; instead he suggested postponing the summit until next year, that is to the next US administration. The summit's collapse naturally occasioned alarm and gloom at the time, and it proved fatal to the kind of Four Power diplomacy

75. It seems Khrushchev would rather Eisenhower had disclaimed responsibility and professed to have been unable to control his subordinates; but this too would have destroyed his credibility

76. *Khrushchev Remembers* ii pp.450–2

77. Eisenhower, *Memoirs* ii p.556

Macmillan had been seeking. But Gromyko was promising Western foreign ministers there would be no unilateral action against West Berlin. While on his way home Khrushchev declared it 'worthwhile to wait a little longer and try to find a solution'.

The East Germans, however, were becoming impatient. In October their talk about closing the border between East and West Berlin alarmed the Soviet embassy. But their position was weakened by their vulnerability to the cut-off of West German trade that they expected would follow the signature of a Soviet-East German treaty; to counter this they asked for massive Soviet aid (including a quite unacceptable 68 tons of gold). The upshot was a meeting between Khrushchev and Ulbricht on 30 November, at which it was agreed that the DDR's economy should be disengaged from West Germany's and integrated instead in to that of the 'socialist camp'. East Germany would take no precipitate action on Berlin. But Khrushchev undertook to settle the question in 1961. His preferred outcome would be a two-year interim agreement on a temporary status for Berlin, at the end of which (failing an unlikely deal between the two Germanies) Western rights there would lapse and the USSR would sign a peace treaty with East Germany. (This would, of course, provide more time for the reorientation of the DDR's economy.) If, however, the West refused such an interim agreement, the USSR would proceed directly to an East German peace treaty, and would 'work out with you a tactic of gradual ousting of the Western powers from West Berlin, but without war'.[78]

THE VIENNA SUMMIT 1961

Despite what now seem minor border pinpricks, intense Eastern pressure did not resume until February 1961, when the Russians declared that the question could not wait till after the West German elections in September. In March the Kennedy administration indicated that it was approaching Berlin *de novo*, so was not bound by the concessions offered at Geneva in 1959 (or contemplated for Paris in 1960).[79] There ensued a round of intense American and Western planning. Kennedy had already suggested a summit to Khrushchev; and in May, after the disastrous American Bay of Pigs

78. Harrison, *Ulbricht and the concrete 'Rose'* pp.27–31 and Appendices A to C
79. Blechman and Kaplan, *Force without War* pp.348, 409.

bungle over a guerilla invasion of Cuba (see pp. 226–7), the Russians took him up on this and it was agreed to meet in June in Vienna. Both leaders appear to have approached the summit with some optimism. Kennedy was briefed that there would 'probably be considerable flexibility' in Khrushchev's position. Khrushchev had reason to believe that people in Kennedy's entourage were ready for a change in Berlin, and the Soviet ambassador in Washington may have told him that Kennedy was only pretending to be strong and that he would retreat when placed under pressure.[80]

The Vienna summit went badly. Khrushchev admittedly showed himself relatively uninterested in Laos and agreeable to the Soviet–US–British diplomatic coordination that was temporarily to resolve that country's crisis (see p. 245). But what he really wanted to talk about was Berlin, and here there was deadlock. Unless the West accepted his ideas for a peace treaty, Khrushchev would sign a treaty with the DDR by December; he confirmed that this would have the effect of blocking access to West Berlin, and that he would respond with force to any violation of East German borders. Kennedy conceded that Khrushchev could do what he liked about East Germany, but he would not tolerate interference with West Berlin or its access routes. The exchange ended with Khrushchev declaring, 'I want peace, but if you want war, then that is your problem . . .', and Kennedy responding, 'If that is true, then it is going to be a cold winter'.[81]

Kennedy took all this very much to heart, believing that Khrushchev regarded him as weak (especially after the Bay of Pigs fiasco) and was challenging him accordingly – though ex-ambassador Bohlen thought that was how Khrushchev always talked. There followed an intensification of contingency planning, a demonstrative US military build-up, and Khrushchev's cancellation of his proposed defence cuts and further alarming conversations with Western visitors and diplomats. Meanwhile the exodus from the DDR mounted, leaving people to speculate on the possibility of another East German rising or of the installation of controls on movement between the DDR and East Berlin.

80. Harrison, *Ulbricht and the concrete 'Rose'* p.37; Zubok, *Khrushchev and the Berlin Crisis* pp.17–19

81. Catudal, *Kennedy and the Berlin Wall Crisis* pp.114–18

THE BERLIN WALL AND ITS SEQUEL 1961-2

With hindsight it would seem that Khrushchev concluded from a careful reading of Kennedy's speeches, and perhaps from KGB informants, that the United States really would go nuclear to defend West Berlin but *not* the undivided status of the city as a whole; Kennedy had indeed directed military reaction only if 'our presence in' or 'our access' to West Berlin were threatened.[82] The DDR had long been pressing for the control of movement between East and West Berlin, and Khrushchev suddenly had his ambassador tell Ulbricht to work out (with the Soviet military commander and diplomats) ways of effecting this. Ulbricht then brought the plans to Moscow, where (by one account) Khrushchev vetoed the idea of closing the air corridors out of West Berlin. The general situation was discussed at a Warsaw Pact meeting of 3–5 August 1961. Here, in response to another desperate plea by Ulbricht for the refugee flood to be curbed, Khrushchev is reported (by the same source) as having authorised him to erect barriers within Berlin at the sectoral border, 'but not one millimeter further'.[83] In the early hours of Sunday 13 August the East Germans suddenly strung barbed wire along the border, catching the West completely by surprise (as the crisis had not been expected to break until September). Kennedy was not reached for a good eight hours; he then instructed Secretary of State Rusk to make a statement but do nothing to aggravate the situation further: 'Go to the ball game as you had planned, I am going sailing'.[84]

West Berlin politicians felt let down by the sluggish and low-key Western response. Intellectually they knew there was no deep commitment to the undivided nature of the city: Brandt's Press Secretary, Egon Bahr, is said to have exclaimed over NATO's May 1961 reaffirmation of rights in West Berlin, 'That is almost an invitation to the Soviets to do what they want with the Eastern

---

82. Andrew and Gordievsky, *KGB* p 368; Catudal, *Kennedy and the Berlin Wall Crisis* pp.175, 244–5. It has been alleged that an arrangement was secretly worked out with Khrushchev in late July (through a private visit by John McCloy, the former US High Commissioner in Germany); but the claim is backed by no evidence and does not fit McCloy's cabled report of the meeting (ibid., pp.189–200)

83. Zubok, *Khrushchev and the Berlin Crisis* pp.22–4; Harrison, *Ulbricht and the concrete 'Rose'* pp.47–50, Appendices G, H, I; Catudal, *Kennedy and the Berlin Wall Crisis* pp.208–12. Excerpts from Khrushchev's rambling but interesting speech on 4 August are printed in the Cold War International History Project *Bulletin* 3 (1993) pp. 59–61; they make it clear that he feared not only war (in view of what he saw as Kennedy's weakness), but also Western economic sanctions

84. Catudal, *Kennedy and the Berlin Wall Crisis* p. 38

sector'.[85] Nor did they have any constructive suggestions beyond measures to boost West Berliners' confidence. But they had never really expected the 'West' to allow itself to be so pushed around. As the then Mayor of West Berlin, Willy Brandt, later put it:

> We lost illusions . . . illusions that had clung to something that no longer existed in fact. Ulbricht had been allowed to take a swipe at the Western super-power, and the United States merely winced with annoyance. My political deliberatons in the years that followed were substantially influenced by this day's experience, and it was against this background that my so-called Ostpolitik – the beginning of détente – took shape. . . . My new and inescapable realization was that traditional patterns of Western policy had proved ineffective, if not downright unrealistic.[86]

Inevitably there have been suggestions that the West should have reacted more strongly, that if its troops had simply torn down the barbed wire they would not have been resisted. One cannot know for certain, but I doubt it.[87] Anyway no interference was attempted. The barbed wire progressively hardened into a Wall, the concrete embodiment of the division of Europe, guarded by troops who, right up to the spring of 1989, shot would-be escapers, and shown off to Western visitors and (surprisingly) also by Ulbricht to Eastern delegations.

Tension did not subside after the erection of the Wall. And Khrushchev decided to push things further by resuming nuclear tests in the atmosphere after a three-year break. When the scientist Sakharov objected, he explained his approach: 'Only force – only the disorientation of the enemy. We can't say aloud that we are carrying out our policy from a position of strength, but that's the way it must be'. In early September 1961 he conducted fifteen tests, one of an unprecedented 57 megatons, and boasted of the ability to construct a 100 megaton warhead.[88] September also saw – as a gesture to reassure the West Berliners – the appointment as US Commander of General Clay, the hero of the blockade. His

85. ibid, p.145
86. W. Brandt, *People and Politics: The Years 1960–1975* p.20
87. Apparently the East German troops actually erecting the wire had no ammunition. Beyond that there are different stories. Séjna says Khrushchev gave instructions that, if interfered with, they should drop back up to 300 metres, trying again each 100 metres; at 300 metres they should await the arrival of Soviet troops. The *Penkovskiy Papers* (another problematic source) claims that there was fear of an East German rising, but also preparations to fight over Berlin if necessary, initially with DDR troops but, if they failed, also with Soviet ones
88. A.D. Sakharov, *Sakharov Speaks* (1974) p.33; *Khrushchev Remembers* ii pp.69–71; *Keesing's*, 18326

determination to maintain the vestigial rights of Western military personnel freely to enter and drive around East Berlin occasioned the most dramatic moment of the crisis, the confrontation in October of US and Soviet tanks at Checkpoint Charlie. Earlier, in late August 1961, Moscow had threatened to interrupt air access to the city and drawn an immediate warning from the White House. The air corridors were accordingly never closed, but there was a good deal of harassment of Western airliners, declining in late 1961 but resuming in February–March 1962 with Soviet military flights in the corridor (partly to influence the negotiations then in progress).

Discussions of the Berlin problem were quietly resumed in the autumn, though Kennedy rejected a Soviet offer to guarantee access to West Berlin if the USA signed a treaty recognising the DDR; in October Khrushchev withdrew his December deadline for concluding a unilateral treaty with the DDR. In December NATO formally agreed, over French opposition, on active negotiations, which were pursued at various forums – notably the fringes of the perennial Geneva disarmament conference in March 1962. But West Germany became increasingly stubborn, and the Soviet position also hardened. As one official remarked of the final meeting, 'They really just keep going round in circles'. Tension accordingly rose in the summer with further incidents. In September 1962 a Soviet note again stressed the necessity, 'at long last, to liquidate the occupation regime in West Berlin on the basis of signing a German peace treaty' and withdrawing Western troops. Kennedy responded by seeking congressional authority to mobilise 150,000 reserve soldiers. But the Russians then indicated that they would not propose new Berlin negotiations till after the November congressional elections.

By then they expected to have in place in Cuba missiles that could, for the first time, provide a credible capability to mount nuclear strikes on the United States. Khrushchev let it be known that he proposed to address the UN, and the assumption is that he meant to reveal the changed balance of power and make new demands on the subjects currently in contention.[89] In fact the United States discovered the missiles while they were still being secretly installed, and forced their withdrawal. In so doing the USA had the advantage of overwhelming local military supremacy, and the ability to impose a naval blockade on Cuba. The Soviet Union

89. Berlin; Germany; a nuclear-free zone in the two Germanies that would eliminate the tactical nuclear weapons on which NATO relied; troop disengagement; nuclear testing and inspection; probably also Cuba, the Congo, and the structure of the UN

could obviously have retaliated by interfering with access to Berlin, where it enjoyed a comparable superiority. Kennedy's speech announcing the blockade sought to head this off: 'Any hostile move anywhere in the world against the safety and freedom of peoples to whom we are committed – including in particular the brave people of West Berlin – will be met by whatever action is needed'. A Soviet official did in fact suggest action against West Berlin but Khrushchev abruptly rejected the idea.[90] The resolution of the crisis then ushered in a period of détente, during which the Berlin issue gradually receded from the centre-stage of world politics. Minor incidents continued, as did interferences with access (particularly when official West German functions were staged in West Berlin). But the city's situation came increasingly to be accepted by all parties as routine – artificial and undesirable no doubt, but not something that could readily be changed. Moreover once the Wall had ended the East German exodus, the Ulbricht regime recovered confidence and managed to restore and develop the economy, if not to anything like West German standards, at least as the wealthiest per capita in Eastern Europe. The DDR had come to stay, and the next phase in the unfolding of the German question (see pp.273–9) was to be West Germany's gradual accommodation to that fact.

LATIN AMERICA IN THE 1950s; THE CUBAN REVOLUTION

I have argued that the Cuban missile crisis was, with the erection of the Wall, the chief factor in the resolution of the Berlin crisis. It was also probably the most dramatic postwar crisis, and arguably the only one where one superpower was seeking not simply to deter the other from taking action but rather to compel the retraction of action already taken. To understand the background, we need to glance briefly at earlier history. Since the 1820s it had been a fixed aim of United States policy (enshrined in the Monroe Doctrine) to exclude from the Americas external rule or military involvement. The USA had taken advantage of both world wars to acquire insular possessions and military bases that would keep hostile forces at a

90. Schick, *The Berlin Crisis* p.219; Zubok, *Khrushchev and the Berlin Crisis* p. 26. Western forces were readied for a probe down the Berlin autobahn in the event that traffic was blocked

distance. Early in the Second World War it had successfully organised most of Latin America to extrude fascist influence and penetration. After 1945 it was equally anxious to keep out 'international communism'. This was, at first, even easier, since communism had few governmental sympathisers. The isolation of Latin American politics from East–West rivalry is very striking: Colombia was devastated, between 1948 and 1958 (or 1962), by the *violencia*, civil disorder that cost some 200,000 lives; but though local communists were accused of having exacerbated it, there is general agreement that it was basically a struggle between the Liberals and the Conservatives, leading eventually to agreement that they should alternate in office for sixteen years from 1958.[91] To Washington the *violencia* appeared less threatening than the leftwards trend in Guatemala, which Eisenhower's brother reported as having 'succumbed to Communist infiltration'; if the Russians ever obtained a base there, they could export subversion and revolution to neighbouring countries. 'My God', Eisenhower remarked, 'just think what it would mean to us if Mexico went Communist'.[92] To foreclose such a possibility, he covertly helped install a new military regime in Guatemala.[93]

Washington may well have been too prone to see reds under the bed in Guatemala. Surprisingly it was not quite ready enough to see them in Cuba. At the start of 1958 the authoritarian Batista regime had seemed reasonably in control. It was faced with urban terrorism (which it handled brutally) and a diaspora of small guerrilla groups in the mountains, mostly traditional bandits but including a few hundred men under Fidel Castro who had emerged (through skilful publicity and the division and discrediting of more orthodox politicians) as the leading opposition figure. Batista had enjoyed widespread sympathy after the assault on his palace in 1957, and as late as April 1958 the opposition's call for a general strike was a complete failure. But when Batista followed this up with a major assault on Castro's Sierra Maestra stronghold, first his army and then his regime disintegrated without any very serious fighting. Parts of the US administration had for some time been anxious to edge Batista out. But the exercise was badly handled, probably because it was not accorded priority or high level political attention;

91. *Encyclopaedia Britannica*; Richard Gott, *Rural Guerillas in Latin America* (Harmondsworth, 1973) Part 3.

92. Ambrose, *Eisenhower: The President* pp.192, 197

93. Post-1945 Latin America is more fully discussed in *The Post-Imperial Age* chap.16

in December 1958 Eisenhower was obviously not au fait with the Cuban situation.[94] When Batista was finally induced, by direct pressure, to leave, which he did on 1 January 1959, there had still been no clear US planning for the succession. This therefore fell into Castro's lap.

Historians are still divided as to when and why Castro became communist. The usual view is that, during his rebellion against Batista, he had had no distinctive views on government beyond a general liberal nationalism. Between January 1959 and early 1961 he decided, probably by stages, that, in the face of internal opposition and US economic pressure, he could best conduct his revolution by taking over, and then working through, the Communist Party. From December 1961 onwards, however, Castro was to proclaim that he had always been at least loosely Marxist-Leninist but had disguised these views in order to seize power. Partly, though not entirely, on the basis of such retrospective information, Tad Szulc argues that at the January 1959 take-over Castro paralleled the new official administration with a 'hidden government', the Office of Revolutionary Plans and Coordination.[95] Whatever the truth, by November 1959 Castro's domestic nationalisations, stridently anti-USA tone at the United Nations, and subversion elsewhere in Latin America had alarmed Washington. In March 1960 Eisenhower approved the creation of 'a paramilitary force outside of Cuba for future guerrilla action', while planning also started (later that year) for Castro's assassination.[96]

THE BAY OF PIGS 1961

Little had come of all this by the time Kennedy succeeded Eisenhower in January 1961. Cuban émigrés were receiving military training in Guatemala, however, and it was clear that their morale would suffer were they not used soon. Kennedy thus inherited a bad situation, and soon made it worse. He decided to go ahead with the invasion of Cuba (in April); but he tinkered with the plan's

---

94. Ambrose, *Eisenhower: The President* p.505
95. Hugh Thomas, *Cuba or the Pursuit of Freedom* (1971) *passim*; Tad Szulc, *Fidel: A Critical Portrait* (New York, 1986) esp. pp.472–80
96. Stephen Rabe, *Eisenhower and Latin America: The Foreign Policy of Anticommunism* (Chapel Hill, NC, 1988) chaps 7, 9; Ranelagh, *The Agency* p.357; Szulc, *Fidel* p.672; Ambrose, *Eisenhower: The President* p.557; Powers, *The Man who Kept the Secrets* pp.186–92

details, moving the proposed landing site to the Bay of Pigs (an unsuitable choice). Worse still, when the cover story for the preliminary CIA bombing of the Cuban air force fell apart, Kennedy refused to authorise the second strike that would have completed the job. The landing was accordingly shot up by the surviving Cuban planes, and the forces that came ashore were destroyed by the unexpectedly rapid deployment of the Cuban army. Kennedy's refusal to provide proper air cover stemmed, as he later explained to Eisenhower, from a fear that 'if it was learned that we [the United States] were really doing this rather than these rebels, the Soviets would be very apt to cause trouble in Berlin'. Eisenhower regarded this as ridiculous: US involvement in so large an invasion could never have been hidden; the Soviets would have respected such a show of strength, but would now probably be emboldened 'to do something that they would otherwise not do'.[97]

THE CUBAN MISSILE CRISIS 1962

That the Bay of Pigs had any such consequences is doubtful. Kennedy certainly feared that it would encourage Khrushchev to test him; but, as we have seen, Khrushchev's Berlin policy in 1961 was quite cautious.[98] Equally the Russians subsequently justified their introduction of offensive missiles into Cuba as an attempt to prevent any further attempts at invasion.[99] Cuba could have been more easily, and safely, protected by the less provocative stationing only of conventional Soviet troops. Although accounts of the decision to deploy missiles differ – Castro has at various times given four different ones –, it seems most likely that Khrushchev found the opportunity to improve his strategic position *vis-à-vis* the USA irresistibly attractive.

97. Thomas Patterson, *Kennedy's Quest for Victory: American Foreign Policy, 1961–1963* (New York, 1989) chap. 5; Prados, *Presidents' Secret Wars* chaps 10–11; Thomas, *Cuba* chap. 106; Ambrose, *Eisenhower: The President* pp.608–10, 638–9. Eisenhower told Kennedy that 'when you go into this kind of thing' 'It must be a success'; but, unlike Nixon, he warned that only in exceptional circumstances would the American people approve direct military invasion of Cuba by their own forces

98. Zubok indeed argues that, in later July, it was his perception of Kennedy's *weakness* that made Khrushchev cautious. 'When our "friend" Dulles was alive, there was more stability.' But Kennedy 'will be called a coward' if he pulls back from the brink; and he was 'too much of a light-weight', no match for the US military–industrial complex (*Khrushchev and the Berlin Crisis* pp.21–2)

99. They also say they feared the CIA's 1962 'Operation Mongoose' (large contra-type raids on Cuba) would develop into a repetition of the 1961 invasion

Had he proceeded openly, his actions would have been broadly comparable with the earlier American location of Jupiter IRBMs in Turkey just next to the USSR.[100] But Khrushchev insisted on doing so secretly, intending to reveal their deployment only after the November US congressional elections: 'Confront them with an established fact. The Americans are a pragmatic people. They'll accept it, like we had to in Turkey. Then we'll be able to negotiate with America on a basis of parity.' Meanwhile he gave copious assurances that 'no missile capable of reaching the United States will be placed in Cuba'.[101] The revelation of these lies gravely damaged the Soviet position in the subsequent crisis, and helped persuade otherwise left-leaning African states to deny Soviet aircraft landing rights, which meant that all supplies for Cuba would have to be brought in by sea. The attempt to proceed secretly was very nearly successful, however, for most Americans were convinced that the USSR would never embark on anything so foolhardy. One exception was the new head of the CIA, McCone, who was primed by French intelligence. From his honeymoon in Paris he badgered Washington with telegrams, but it was reluctant to risk the loss of another U2 – one was shot down over China in September – and western Cuba was left unsurveyed from 5 September to 14 October 1962. Ultimately McCone got his flight; and early on 16 October Kennedy was presented with clear evidence of the presence of Soviet ballistic missiles.[102]

The next few days were spent deciding what to do, in the knowledge that little time remained before the missiles became operational. Acquiescence was ruled out by Kennedy's earlier statements,[103] and would not anyway have been tolerated by American public opinion. The idea of taking the question up privately with Khrushchev was considered, but it seemed impossible to draft a

100. Fifteen *Jupiters* became operational there in October 1962; thirty were based in Italy the previous year. There had also been sixty *Thors* in the UK following a 1957 agreement; but they were removed in the second half of 1962: R.L. Garthoff, *Reflections on the Cuban Missile Crisis* (Washington, DC, 1987) p.43n.

101. ibid, p.27; Philip Knightley and Peter Pringle, 'The Cuban Missile Crisis 1962', *The Independent* 5 and 6 Oct. 1992 p.19. Khrushchev (*Khrushchev Remembers*, iii pp.170, 173) says that forty-two missiles were to be installed, four or five of them capable of covering virtually all North America

102. Knightley and Pringle, *The Independent* 5 Oct. 1992; G.T. Allison, *Essence of Decision: Explaining the Cuban Missile Crisis*, (Boston, Mass., 1971) pp. 190–2, 317n

103. To head off congressional claims that he was covering up the existence of missiles there, he had twice warned that he would not permit Cuba to 'become an offensive military base of significant capacity'. The warnings were reinforced by Congressional resolutions and by a statement by twenty Latin American Foreign Ministers: Garthoff, *The Cuban Missile Crisis* pp.14–19

letter that would be forceful enough to be effective without at the same time provoking a crisis.[104] There remained only the options of direct or indirect action. Many were attracted to the idea of simply bombing the missile sites. But it became clear that this would not be easy: it would kill appreciable numbers of the Russians working on them; some missiles might be missed; and if any were already armed, it might provide an incentive to fire them. In any case it might lead to a Soviet response, and thence escalate via US reprisals into a full-scale war that neither side originally wanted – in Kennedy's view the First World War had begun like this.[105] An alternative to bombing would be a US invasion of Cuba, which would encounter the same difficulties on a larger scale, but would (if resolutely proceeded with) eliminate the Castro problem once and for all. Inevitably there were inconsistent shifts of position, but the general tendency was for attitudes to soften as discussion proceeded; most importantly this was true of Kennedy himself. The final decision was to prepare to stage an invasion and to place Strategic Air Command on high alert (DEFCON 2) to deter the Russians, but first to try the effect of indirect action in the form of a blockade.

So on 22 October 1962 Kennedy announced the imposition of a 'quarantine' under which the US Navy would check all cargoes for Cuba.[106] He also embarked on a public relations campaign and the briefing of allies and neutrals. Partly because the Soviet Union persisted (at the UN and elsewhere) in denying the missiles' existence, this proved a great success; on 23 October the Organisation of American States endorsed the 'quarantine' *nem.con.* On the 24th sixteen Soviet freighters stopped just before meeting the quarantine line, and five (thought to be those carrying nuclear warheads) soon turned back. This was taken to be encouraging, though in fact warheads had already reached Cuba.[107] Anyway the completion of the launching sites proceeded apace. Since the United States could not be sure that the missiles there were not armed, it still felt the need to insist on their dismantling and to prepare to take direct action on the 30th to effect this.[108]

104. ibid, pp.28–9
105. He had been reading Barbara Tuchman's *The Guns of August*. The other influential analogy was 1941 – for opponents of a sudden air strike labelled it 'a Pearl Harbor in reverse', a course alien to all America's traditions and history – Allison, *Essence of Decision* pp.217–18, 197
106. Technically this was a breach of international law, as war had not actually been declared on Cuba; but the USA had already thus proceeded against Guatemala in 1954
107. Knightley and Pringle, *The Independent* 5 Oct. 1992
108. Garthoff, *The Cuban Missile Crisis* p.54

On 26 October the Soviets informally suggested that they would withdraw the missiles in exchange for an American assurance that Cuba would not be invaded. That evening Khrushchev implied as much in a letter to Kennedy; it has been claimed that Kennedy had his brother Bobby call on the Soviet ambassador to press for a settlement and indicate that he might be prepared for this also to include the US missiles in Turkey. On the morning of the 27th (Washington time), however, another letter arrived from Moscow that formally linked the US missiles in Turkey with the Soviet ones in Cuba. Kennedy had not prepared his advisers for this linkage. Especially given the simultaneous downing of a U2 over Cuba and the organisation of anti-USA demonstrations in Moscow, the new letter suggested to Washington a hardening of the Soviet stance, perhaps even the disavowal of Khrushchev by his colleagues. Kennedy decided to answer the earlier letter, but he added an assurance that, though there could be no formal deal over the Turkish missiles, they would in fact be removed when the crisis was over. He further gave Ambassador Dobrynin (via his brother) two important oral messages: if the Soviets did not promptly agree to withdraw the Cuban missiles, the USA 'would remove them' soon; although the Turkish and Italian missiles could not formally be included in a bargain, they would be gone in a few months. Khrushchev accepted that an attack on Cuba was imminent:[109] he was not reassured by Castro's suggestion that he pre-empt with a nuclear attack on the United States and he knew that the local Soviet commander might use tactical nuclear weapons to ward off a US invasion.[110] So he hastily accepted Kennedy's letter of the 27th and began dismantling the missiles at once. He later justified this decision as having prevented general war or alternatively a US conquest of Cuba.[111]

The acute phase of the crisis accordingly ended on 28 October. Tidying up the details took another month, and loose ends were left that were later to be of some importance. (Thus the USSR undertook to withdraw its Ilyushin bombers from Cuba, but was

109. Garthoff argues that Kennedy would in fact have tried to avoid immediate action by having the UN Secretary-General propose the removal of missiles from both Cuba and Turkey: *The Cuban Missile Crisis* pp.59–60

110. Knightley and Pringle, *The Independent* 5 Oct. 1992; cf. also *Khrushchev Remembers* iii p.178; Cold War International History Project *Bulletin* 3 (1993) pp. 40–50

111. Garthoff, *The Cuban Missile Crisis* pp.48–60; Knightley and Pringle, *The Independent* 6 Oct. 1992; *Khrushchev Remembers* iii pp.176–7

vaguer on the Soviet combat troops originally introduced to defend the missiles. The legitimacy of any Soviet submarine base was left unsettled once it was clear that none was under construction.)[112] The chief difficulty proved to be Castro: he was so angry at what he saw as Russian betrayal that he agreed to talk to the Soviet emissary Mikoyan only when the latter threatened to cut off his oil supplies; even so he adamantly refused to allow UN verification of the missiles' departure. Other ways of satisfying the USA on this were eventually found. But, in the absence of UN inspection, Kennedy would not officially promise not to invade Cuba, so the 1962 understanding with Khrushchev remained informal until 1970. The Soviets then secured its written reaffirmation in August, the month before they were discovered to be rapidly constructing an SLBM base at Cienfuegos.[113]

KHRUSHCHEV'S POSITION AFTER THE CRISIS

Kennedy's prestige gained enormously from the outcome of the Cuban missile crisis. Khrushchev's did not, for Kennedy had insisted that his personal undertaking to trade the missiles in Turkey and Italy for those in Cuba be kept secret,[114] and Soviet action had appeared either adventurist, or capitulationist, or (the Chinese said) both. But Khrushchev was not as much weakened as is sometimes suggested: in November 1962 he was able to push through his most disruptive organisational reform ever, the division into two of most levels of the Soviet Communist Party. What did change was the confrontational approach to the West of 1961-2 (Berlin, the resumption of massive and demonstrative nuclear testing, Cuba). At one stage in the crisis Khrushchev had sought reassurance from his military that calling Kennedy's bluff would not lead to a nuclear holocaust, and been appalled at their response.[115] Now, he told the

112. Garthoff, *The Cuban Missile Crisis* pp.65–78, 99–101; Kissinger, *Memoirs* i p.633; J Radvanyi, *Hungary and the Superpowers*, (Stanford, Calif., 1972) pp.137–8

113. Nixon insisted, in secret, that it be scrapped: Radvanyi, *Hungary and the Superpowers* pp.135–6; Garthoff, *The Cuban Missile Crisis* pp.95–101; Kissinger, *Memoirs* i chap. 16

114. When on 29 Oct. he tried to tie Kennedy down in writing, he was told that the deal would be off if the USSR ever publicly alluded to it: Garthoff, *The Cuban Missile Crisis* p.55

115. 'They looked at me as if I was out of my mind, or what was worse, a traitor. The biggest tragedy as they saw it was not that our country might be devastated and everything lost, but that the Chinese or Albanians might accuse us of appeasement or weakness': Knightley and Pringle, *The Independent* 6 Oct. 1992

Hungarian Kadar, 'the Soviet leadership felt it was in the interest of the socialist "commonwealth" to work for a temporary reduction of international tensions . . . to achieve this goal the Soviet Union would adopt a more flexible position in the on-going nuclear test-ban talks'.[116] Indeed it is possible that Khrushchev was preparing an initiative towards (as the communiqués of his 1964 Scandinavian visit put it) 'a peaceful and enduring settlement of the European security problem'; in particular he sent his son-in-law to Bonn in July 1964, and in September himself proposed a working visit there. This upset his colleagues and featured in the explanation of his 'resignation' in October 1964, though their stated objections were to the style not the content of his policy.

116. Radvanyi, *Hungary and the Superpowers* pp. 140–1

CHAPTER EIGHT

The Vietnam War and Other Proxy Conflicts of the 1960s and 1970s

Since the Cuban missile crisis of 1962 (see pp. 227–32), East–West crises involving any prospect of superpower collision have been very rare; examples include the Cienfuegos affair, the 1967 and 1973 Arab-Israeli wars (at the end of both of which the Soviet Union threatened direct action if Israel pushed its victory any further), and perhaps the 1971 Indo-Pakistani war (which, the USA feared, might expand to involve China, the USSR and the USA itself if India did not stop). Instead the chief theme now becomes that of attempts to construct East–West relationships involving cooperation as well as competition, notably Brandt's *Ostpolitik* and the détente policies of the Brezhnev and Nixon administrations. The shift was both gratifying and important, but it must not lead us to overlook the extent to which rivalry proceeded through struggles – often, but not always, clandestine or by proxy – outside Europe. These were closely entwined in local circumstance and are often best viewed outside the Cold War context. But the East–West tensions of the 1960s and early 1970s cannot be understood without at least a brief general *tour d'horizon* and a slightly longer look at the greatest of these struggles, the Vietnam War.

CUBA AND LATIN AMERICA IN THE 1960s

Kennedy had more or less promised not to *invade* Cuba, but attempts to assassinate Castro did not stop until the succession of President Johnson. Castro, for his part, had been interfering abroad ever since 1959, when he sponsored an exile invasion of the

Dominican Republic;[1] he continued to do so with gusto. Much of Cuba's destabilising effect was simply that of example and propaganda; it must be remembered that insurgencies were common in Central America, as was cross-border involvement. But the Cuban revolution had been deceptively easy, and there were hopes that it could be generally replicated: 'Given suitable operating country, land hunger, and injustices', Che Guevara wrote in 1960,[2] 'a hard core of 30 to 50 men [Castro had originally had about 20 in the Sierra Maestra] is enough to set off armed revolutions in any Latin American country'. Not so. In the mid-1960s there appears to have been Cuban involvement in insurrections in Venezuela, Guatemala, Peru, Bolivia, and perhaps Colombia. None succeeded; Guevara's failure and death in an ambitious 1966–7 attempt to establish 'the continental command' in Bolivia became well chronicled when Castro published his diary.[3] Among the reasons for these failures were a disappointing lack of peasant support, greater strength on the part of most governments than had been anticipated, and the readiness of weaker ones (like Peru and Bolivia) to turn to the CIA for help. Cooperation with local communists was at best limited: they often did not relish submitting to Cuban command. Also guerrilla insurgency appeared closer to the Chinese than to the Soviet approach; so, as Sino-Soviet rivalry deepened, Moscow-oriented parties might condemn such rebellion as 'an erroneous form of revolution'. Nevertheless they too practised it, while the KGB appears sometimes to have funded insurrection, and indeed itself to have planted North Korean trained guerrillas in Mexico.[4]

ZAÏRE

The other great venue for clandestine operations was newly decolonised Africa. The biggest prize was the former Belgian Congo

1. Thomas, *Cuba* p.1,228
2. *Keesing's*, 23108. For a slightly different version see Guevara's very influential *Guerilla Warfare* (paperback edn, 1969) p.123
3. *Keesing's*, 23108 ff, 23235, 23855 (Bolivia – and Peru, for which cf. also 23101), 20071, 22119 (Venezuela), 24828 (Colombia); Gott, *Rural Guerillas in Latin America* esp. pp.52–6, 295–6; Ranelagh, *The Agency* p.424; V. Marchetti and J.D. Marks, *The CIA and the Cult of Intelligence* (1974) pp.123 ff
4. Money from the Italian communists (very probably a conduit) for Venezuela, *Keesing's*, 20875; from the KGB for Colombia, John Barron, *KGB* (1974) p.256; the destabilisation of Mexico, ibid. chap. 11, *Keesing's*. 24899–90

(now Zaïre),[5] which disintegrated into military mutinies and governmental fragmentation after its sudden decolonisation in July 1960. Ostensibly it was then stabilised by UN troops, not only for humanitarian reasons, but also to preserve it from external intervention. In practice such intervention continued, albeit mostly unofficially. Both the USSR and China involved themselves; Belgium was accused of backing the secession of the copper-rich province of Katanga. But it was the United States that largely managed to control events, both through its influence in the UN and through the Congolese Army Chief of Staff, Joseph Mobutu. Some developments, notably the eventual UN subjugation of Katanga in December 1962, were approved by 'progressive' opinion. Others were not. In August 1960 Prime Minister Lumumba turned against the United Nations, which he saw as insufficiently supportive of his central government, and sought Soviet aid; he seemed to the Americans to have been bought, and to be on the point of inviting direct Soviet intervention. He was dismissed by the Congolese President in September, and murdered in January.[6] UN forces were finally withdrawn in mid-1964. But by then former Lumumbists had again mounted a rebellion in the north-east,[7] which had by September proclaimed the 'People's Republic of the Congo'. This attracted 'progressive' support: by February 1965 twenty-nine aircraft loads of supplies had reached the southern Sudan for onwards transit, while Chinese and other equipment arrived via Tanzania/Uganda. Egypt claimed to have trained over 2,000 Congolese fighters; Che Guevara also visited the rebellion but decided its prospects were hopeless. On the other side, Congolese government troops drove north, much aided by a CIA-supplied air force, white mercenaries, and a Belgian paratroop drop (largely, but one suspects not entirely, to rescue European hostages) on the principal city, Stanleyville, in November. By mid-1965 fighting was substantially over; in November Mobutu staged a coup and declared himself President.[8]

5. Mao was quoted as saying in 1964 to a Chinese diplomat (who subsequently defected), 'If we can take the Congo, we can have all of Africa': Bruce D. Larkin, *China and Africa 1949–1970* (Berkeley, Calif., 1971) p.72

6. The CIA did make plans for his assassination; but the January murder was a Congolese/Katangan affair, and no foreign encouragement seems to have been needed

7. From late 1960 to January 1963 there had been a breakaway Lumumbist regime which was extinguished by the UN in parallel with its action against Tshombe's Katanga

8. Keesing's Research Report, *Africa Independent: A Survey of Political Developments* (New York, 1972) pp.252–67; *Keesing's*, 20561–4, 20803; Ambrose, *Eisenhower. The*

AFRICA IN THE 1960s: THE OAU; THE NIGERIAN CIVIL WAR; KENYA; GHANA.

Over much of the rest of Africa decolonisation had proceeded more smoothly. The newly independent states were at first assiduously wooed; left-leaning Guinea, in particular, was showered with attention by a Kennedy administration anxious to prove that (unlike its predecessor) it could befriend progressive and neutralist countries. Many of the early diplomatic alignments reflected personal, local, or Pan-African issues and rivalries. But from 1960 to 1963 there appeared to be a broad division between a moderate Brazzaville and a more radical Casablanca group of states. In 1963 they came together to form a single Organisation of African Unity (OAU), whose Charter affirmed 'a policy of non-alignment with regard to all blocs'. This dampened, though it certainly did not end, the extension into Africa of East–West rivalries. For a time it seemed that these would be supplemented by Sino-Soviet competition, since China was anxious to round up Third World support against the USSR and secure its exclusion from the projected June 1964 Afro-Asian Conference in Algiers. To this end Zhou Enlai toured ten Arab/African countries in the 1963–4 winter with an enormous and conspicuous entourage. Unfortunately China also wished to appear the patron of real revolution, as opposed to the USSR's moderate revisionism; and Zhou's ritual remarks to the effect that 'an excellent revolutionary situation exists in Africa' seemed a threat to many of the newly established governments.[9]

Nor were their fears unreasonable. For most governments were insecure, subversion was rife, and plotters naturally sought external aid. Ruth First lists thirty-six military coups (successful and attempted) in the 1960s.[10] These obviously all had a local context, and it should be stressed that the issues could be quite other than those of East–West rivalry. Thus the largest African state, Nigeria, fell victim to tribally motivated coups, leading to massacres of Ibos, then to the attempted secession of the predominantly Ibo 'Biafra'. Biafra was reconquered in the 1967–70 civil war; during this,

---

President pp.586–9; Prados, *President's Secret Wars* pp.232–7; Ranelagh, *The Agency* pp.338–44; Marchetti and Marks, *The CIA and the Cult of Intelligence* pp.125–6; Barron, *KGB* p. 256; Larkin, *China and Africa* pp.73–4, 181. The Congo is further discussed in *The Post-Imperial Age* chap.19

9. James Mayall, *Africa: The Cold War and After* (1971) pp.29, 122, 148; Keesing's Research Report, *Africa Independent* p.3; Larkin, *China and Africa* esp. pp.69–70, 80–1

10. Ruth First, *The Barrel of a Gun* (1970) pp.xii–xiv

Nigeria drew arms from Britain, the USSR and Egypt, while Biafra enjoyed Tanzanian and Chinese endorsement, Roman Catholic publicity assistance and humanitarian aid, and initially more clandestine support from France and Portugal.[11]

Many internal convulsions were accompanied by allegations of communist subversion and by expulsions of Soviet or Chinese personnel. To take only two examples, during 1965 the Vice-President of Kenya, Oginga Odinga, attacked government policy as too pro-Western and so was gradually stripped of his offices. During this process it was announced that China, the USSR and other countries had been training prospective rebels and that in 1964–5 £400,000 had been spent on undermining the Kenyan government; in March 1966 communist diplomats and journalists were expelled, and further expulsions followed in 1967, 1968 and 1969.

In Ghana, the first President, Kwame Nkrumah, succumbed to megalomania. This led him to recruit 'freedom fighters' to promote 'Nkrumaism' ('African in context, but Marxist in form') not only in reactionary states but also in countries like Tanzania. For their training he turned first to Russian and then to Chinese instructors (his successors accused him of cribbing their lecture notes to prepare a book on the *Strategy and Tactics of Revolutionary Warfare with Particular Reference to the African Revolution*). He also sought East German assistance with the creation of an All-African Intelligence Service and the development of Ghanaian security, while Russians trained a rapidly expanding presidential guard. He was, however, overthrown by what he regarded as a Western-promoted military coup in 1966, following which 1100 Russians, 430 Chinese, and 'scores' of other communists were expelled.[12]

THE MIDDLE EAST

We have already noted the 1955–8 struggle for influence in the Middle East (pp. 201–8); we shall return in due course to the crises

11. A.H.M. Kirk Greene, *Crisis and Conflict in Nigeria: A Documentary Sourcebook* ii (1971) pp.46–9, 56, 76, 79, 85, 88, 111, 140, 245–6, 329

12. Admittedly some of those expelled were bona fide development technicians. Larkin, *China and Africa* p.136; Keesing's Research Report, *Africa Independent* pp.131–4; *Keesing's*, 21345, 22277, 23423 (Kenya), 21273–4 (Ghana); Ghana Ministry of Information, *Nkrumah's Subversion in Africa* (Accra, 1966); Prados, *Presidents' Secret Wars* p.237

connected with the 1967–73 wars (see pp. 304, 315–19). Here we need only note that, in April 1967, a somewhat bibulous Brezhnev assured Gomulka and Ulbricht that 'Even our opponents cannot deny that we have achieved major successes in the Near East. We have already partially succeeded in driving the Americans out of this part of the world and we shall soon be in a position to deal them a decisive blow'. He was in fact over-sanguine, but Eugene Rostow, then responsible for the Middle East within the US State Department, saw things in much the same light:

> The Middle Eastern crisis is not a regional quarrel about Israel's right to exist. It is, on the contrary, a fissure in the foundation of world politics – a Soviet challenge. . . . The first purpose of the Soviet effort is to achieve . . . control of the Mediterranean, the Middle East and the Persian Gulf area. On that footing, the next step would be to drive the United States out of Europe, and to have NATO dismantled.[13]

INDIA AND PAKISTAN

In the Indian sub-continent East–West rivalry was more subdued, but still evident. The basic fact of politics was Indo-Pakistani enmity, particularly over the disposition of Kashmir. In the 1950s Pakistan had turned for arms and sympathy to the Western alliance, and in the 1960s it had added the friendship of China (whose border disputes with India had led to two small frontier wars). India, despite some US attempts to woo it (especially after its 1962 defeat by China), looked most readily in geopolitical (though not domestic) terms to the Soviet Union, Pakistan's enemy and by the 1960s also China's. The 1965 Indo-Pakistani war had no direct East–West repercussions. But it was something of a blow to Pakistan's oddly assorted patrons, China and the USA, that in January 1966 it allowed the USSR to mediate its dispute with India (at Tashkent). However Pakistan's relations with both China and the USA improved later in the decade, and it arranged the secret Kissinger visits that brought détente between the two. So when Pakistan ran into trouble its President, Yahya Khan, was confident that 'both Chinese and Americans will help us, how could they forget our

---

13. Erwin Weit, *Eyewitness: The Autobiography of Gomulka's Interpreter* (1973), p.139; E. Rostow, 'The Middle Eastern Crisis in the Perspective of World Politics', *International Affairs* xlvii (1971) pp.275–6. The Middle East is further discussed in *The Post-Imperial Age* chaps 12, 15

services over the last two years?'[14] Trouble had come in 1971, when Yahya Khan responded to the overwhelming electoral success of the East Pakistan autonomist party with extremely bloody repression. India did not intend either to saddle itself indefinitely with the millions of refugees this precipitated or to pass up a golden opportunity to break up Pakistan and achieve indisputable primacy on the sub-continent.

In July 1971 Kissinger warned the Indian ambassador that China, which had apparently cautioned India against invading East Pakistan during the 1965 war, might intervene in the event of another conflict. In August India countered by concluding with the Soviet Union a treaty whose literal terms were anodyne, but which in effect assured it Soviet protection against third-party intervention. The resulting crisis has been very differently interpreted. Nixon and Kissinger suggest that the problem of East Pakistan might have been sorted out by secret negotiations, had India been prepared to give these time. They also had intelligence from within the Indian Cabinet that the Prime Minister, Mrs Gandhi, was really seeking not only the liberation of East, but also the break-up of West, Pakistan. Their critics doubt both the prospects of the negotiations and the trustworthiness of the intelligence reports from Mrs Gandhi's rival, Moraji Desai; they also depict the US administration as so obsessed by global politics that it could see South Asia only in this light. 'The Indo-Pakistani conflict', two of Kissinger's aides wrote after the Soviet–Indian treaty, 'becomes a sort of Sino-Soviet clash by proxy'. So, Kissinger remarked, 'We don't really have any choice. We can't allow a friend of ours and China's to get screwed in a conflict with a friend of Russia's'. Or, as another Kissinger aide explained in a more formal context, 'We had to show China that we respect a mutual friend and opposed the crossing of international borders. So it was not so much a "thanks, Yahya, for helping us with China" as demonstrating to China we were a reliable country to deal with'.

Indian troops started to penetrate East Pakistan in late November 1971, making excellent progress with the aid of local guerrillas. The crisis heightened when on 3 December President Yahya launched air strikes from, and so extended the fighting to, West Pakistan. There was, clearly, some potential for even wider trouble: China alerted troops on the Indian border; the USSR blocked UN calls for a cease-fire and moved troops to the Chinese border; and the USA ordered an aircraft carrier into the Bay of

14. D.K. Hall in Blechman and Kaplan, *Force without War* p.208

Bengal. The chief American worry was probably of some definite Chinese intervention that the USA would either have to support, which might be risky, or back away from and so halt the current Chinese realignment towards the American side in the Cold War. To pre-empt this the US administration pressed the Soviet Union[15] (which it saw as trying to drag things out and so allow time for an Indian victory) to restrain India and, more specifically, to guarantee that there would be no territorial annexations in the West. Opinion differs as to whether these had ever been intended.[16] But by 16 December 1971 the USSR was able to offer private assurances. On the 17th Pakistan's forces in the East surrendered, leaving India free to reconstitute it as the independent country of Bangladesh. The crisis subsided, without, as it turned out, any major geopolitical consequences outside the subcontinent.[17]

INDONESIA

South-East Asia's troubles were more protracted. They are most often seen in connection with Vietnam (to which we must turn shortly), but the largest country in the region is Indonesia. The United States had long been conscious of its potential. After 1945 it had leant on the colonial power, the Netherlands, to leave. In the mid-1950s the Indonesian President, Sukarno, turned increasingly to a flamboyant neutralism in foreign relations – he was, with Nehru, Nasser and Tito, one of the leaders of the non-aligned movement – while domestically he improved the position of the Communist Party and distanced himself from the largely pro-Western forces that had previously been dominant. This led to military dissatisfaction, and regional commanders gradually drifted into revolt in 1956–7; they approached the USA, and, on being accorded arms and CIA aeroplanes, declared their independence in 1958. Dulles privately explained that 'as between a territorially

15. By using the hot line, and by implying that the planned 1972 Nixon–Brezhnev summit was at risk
16. Guarantees were forthcoming that there would be no annexations from West Pakistan proper, but in India's eyes this did not include Azad Kashmir, and there were fears that its loss would be enough to trigger West Pakistan's disintegration
17. Nixon, *Memoirs* pp.525–30; Kissinger, *Memoirs* i chap. 21; Hersh, *The Price of Power* chap. 32; Blechman and Kaplan, *Force without War* pp.176–210; Y.Y.I. Vertzberger, *China's Southwestern Strategy* (New York, 1985) pp.40, 58

united Indonesia which is leaning toward Communism and a break-up of that country into geographical units, I prefer the latter'. The revolt was soon suppressed,[18] and the episode produced an understandable coolness.

However, Sukarno needed outside support for territorial expansion. The Dutch had continued to occupy Western New Guinea (West Irian), which was contiguous to Indonesia but ethnically very different; from 1960 Sukarno brought the question to a head. In 1961 he secured from the Soviet Union warships, aircraft, and military technicians, then used this support to put pressure on the USA. He further raised tension in 1962 by seeking, albeit with total lack of success, to infiltrate small bodies of troops into West Irian; and he rejected the Dutch offer of a UN-conducted plebiscite, which would almost certainly have gone against him. Kennedy 'regarded Indonesia, this country of a hundred million people, so rich in oil, tin and rubber, as one of the potentially significant nations of Asia'; he also sought to avoid both war and driving Indonesia into Moscow's arms. So he conducted an exercise in appeasement, pressing the Dutch into agreeing in August 1962 to turn West Irian over (via the UN).[19]

Sukarno's next target was the British colonies in North Borneo (Sabah, Sarawak, and the protectorate of Brunei). Their destiny had become linked to the decolonisation of Singapore. For Singapore's Prime Minister, Lee Kuan Yew, agreed with his Malayan counterpart, Tunku Abdul Rahman, that, while Singapore could not remain a British dependency, it would be dangerously exposed (in terms of both security and economics) if it proceeded to independence on its own: it should therefore join Malaya. But the adhesion of so many ethnic Chinese might upset Malaya's political equilibrium, and the Tunku insisted that it be balanced by the simultaneous accession of the north Borneo colonies to what would then be known as Malaysia. The British were agreeable, provided they could retain the military basing rights they currently enjoyed. But this made the whole scheme all the more obnoxious to Sukarno; it smelt of 'neocolonialism', and it would constitute a barrier to future Indonesian expansion.

Preparations were pushed forward over-rapidly in 1962, partly in response to Lee's domestic difficulties. In December there followed

---

18. Prados, *Presidents' Secret Wars* chap. 8
19. Schlesinger, *A Thousand Days* pp.464–6; *Keesing's,* 18845 ff. West Irian is now known as Irian Jaya

a small revolt in Brunei; although this was rapidly suppressed, it must have encouraged Sukarno to stage a repeat of the West Irian affair. So from 1963 onwards, he started raids into, and guerrilla infiltration of, the north Borneo territories (and on one occasion Malaya proper) – initially interspersed with negotiations for an Indonesian-led federation of itself, Malaya and the Philippines (Maphilindo). Once again the Indonesian incursions were militarily ineffective, but the United States leant on Macmillan and the Tunku to appease Sukarno. Neither were forthcoming. Since Malaysia was an indigenous state and the UN had certified that Sabah and Sarawak's adhesion to it had popular support,[20] Malaysia's diplomatic position was a good deal stronger than had been the Dutch one over West Irian. In 1964 Indonesia gained little sympathy either from Moscow or from the conference of non-aligned countries in Cairo; in January 1965 Malaysia was elected to the UN Security Council, and Indonesia withdrew from the UN in disgust.[21] So from late 1964 onwards Sukarno threw himself into the arms of China. The two countries talked of the emergence of 'one Asian bloc of more than 700 million people', of the creation to replace the UN of a 'Conference of New Emerging Forces' based on opposition to imperialism and neocolonialism, and, of course, of the need to crush Malaysia. China also seems to have been prepared to play up to Sukarno's vanity by staging its next nuclear test on his territory and allowing him to claim it as Indonesian. It also pressed on him small arms for the formation of a militia that would serve to counterbalance the largely anti-communist Indonesian army.

Internally, too, Sukarno was becoming increasingly radical, and tolerant of the large Indonesian Communist Party (PKI). This in turn supported him, made further demands, and seized every opportunity of enhancing its position. The army's unhappiness mounted, and there was much alleged plotting of, and counter-plotting against, the Council of Generals. Then in September 1965 a Palace Guard colonel staged a pre-emptive coup, murdering six generals. The details are obscure; but it is likely that Sukarno was at least partially implicated in the coup, and that it was either

---

20. *Keesing's*, 19718–19; the UN investigation seems more cursory than that of the earlier Anglo-Malay Cobbold Commission: *Keesing's*, 18937. Brunei finally decided to remain aloof after disagreement over the future of its oil revenues

21. Macmillan, *Memoirs* vi chap. 8; D.P. Mozingo, *Chinese Policy toward Indonesia* (Ithaca, NY, 1976) pp.201–2; *Keesing's*, 20576, 20591 ff

associated with, or triggered the parallel plans of, the PKI.[22] The coup failed, as General Suharto rallied the army. He then proceeded (with some American help)[23] to root out communists – the CIA later reported that 250,000 people were killed during their repression – and more gradually down-graded Sukarno. Suharto thus secured special powers in March 1966 and took over the presidency himself a year later. The army had never much liked the confrontation with Malaysia; once firmly in power, it readily accepted Thai mediation to end it, a process formally completed (despite Sukarno's opposition) in August 1966. The following August Indonesia, Malaysia, the Philippines, Singapore,[24] and Thailand came together to form the Association of South-East Asian Nations (ASEAN) – an amorphous grouping, but one that has proved, at a political level, surprisingly successful. In 1965 the outlook had seemed very different; Khrushchev comments wistfully

> Indonesia might have chosen the correct course and become a socialist country. It would have been one of the most powerful socialist countries in the world, occupying a strategic position in the struggle against imperialism.[25]

INDO-CHINA

In the troubles we have recounted, external superpower involvement was only indirect, or at most limited and clandestine. In Indo-China large numbers of US combat troops were to be committed in the 1960s and early 1970s. The USSR did not reciprocate, but (with China) it poured in, albeit surprisingly inconspicuously, the weapons and supplies without which North Vietnam's ultimate victory would have been impossible. Accordingly the 'Vietnam War' developed a far greater hold on international consciousness and public opinion than did, for instance, the

---

22. A.C.A. Dake, *In the Spirit of the Red Banteng: Indonesian Communists between Moscow and Peking 1959–1965* (The Hague, 1973) pp.326–420; Mozingo, *Chinese Policy toward Indonesia* esp. pp.221–6, 234 ff.

23. This took the form of passing on lists of several thousand communist cadres and then checking on their arrest: *Washington Post*, 21 May 1990 p.A5

24. Singapore had seceded from Malaysia in August 1965, following an irremediable dispute as to the freedom to be accorded to political action outside the Malay-dominated ruling coalition

25. *Khrushchev Remembers* ii p.330 – typically he blames the PKI's disasters on following Chinese advice

Indonesian turmoil of 1965–6, even though it could be argued that Indonesia's destiny was of more geopolitical importance than Indo-China's.

As we have seen (see pp. 104–5), the USA first came to feel the need to contain South-East Asian communism in 1949 (after the collapse of Kuomintang rule in China). There were prophecies that, if Indo-China went communist, Thailand and Burma would also fall.[26] The USA accordingly provided increasing financial support for the French war effort. When this was on the verge of major defeat at Dien Bien Phu in 1954, the USA did not intervene militarily. However, it was also unhappy with the French decision, reached during the 1954 Geneva conference, to pull out, and it sought to prevent any more countries following North Vietnam to communism by intrusively offering economic support and political training to South Vietnam and Laos. Trouble first developed in Laos.

LAOS

The Geneva conference had provided for Laos to become a non-communist neutral state, but it faced the problem of integrating the communist Pathet Lao forces that had ended the war controlling (with Vietminh backing) substantial areas in the east of the country. Prince Souvanna Phouma irritated the USA by his conciliatory stance towards the Pathet Lao. Although by mid-1958 he had become disillusioned with it, he encountered opposition from right-wing parties, lost his parliamentary majority, and was replaced (probably with CIA encouragement) by a strongly anti-communist premier – who in turn was ousted in December 1959 by a coup led by Phoumi Nosovan. When, from mid-1959, these rightist governments faced a Pathet Lao rebellion, the USA supported them and established a military training mission. In August 1960 a further coup by a young neutralist captain, Kong Le, reinstated Souvanna Phouma. Phoumi Nosovan took up arms, with Thai and CIA assistance. So Souvanna Phouma turned to the Pathet Lao, and by December was also receiving airlifted Soviet supplies.

This open external support for rival sides in the civil war was extremely ominous; the USA was under strong Thai and some

---

26. *Pentagon Papers* (Boston, Mass., Senator Gravel edn, 1971) i pp.361–2

Filipino pressure to intervene militarily to keep the communists at a safe distance. Eisenhower contemplated a SEATO intervention, but he did not wish one. Kennedy, too, was deeply suspicious of the communists; Congressmen were briefed that 'if Laos goes Communist' it would probably infiltrate guerrillas into Thailand. In March 1961 Kennedy secured SEATO agreement to the defence of western Laos, and in April (after rumours of a neutralist–Pathet Lao offensive) he seriously considered intervention. Unlike Eisenhower, however, Kennedy was ready to accept Laotian neutrality: 'If in the past there has been any possible ground for misunderstanding of our support for a truly neutral Laos', he announced in March, 'there should be none now'.[27] He accordingly supported British efforts to gain Soviet cooperation in reconvening a Geneva conference on Laos; in April 1961 the UK and USSR, as co-chairmen of the 1954 conference, jointly called for a cease-fire and conference. The conference duly convened; and the three Laotian factions (rightist, neutralist, and Pathet Lao) met periodically to discuss the formation of a unified government. The difficulty came over who should get which portfolios; in 1962 the USA began exerting financial pressure on the rightists to induce them to cooperate. The policy of backing Laotian neutralism alarmed Thailand, which had to be reassured (in early 1962) by guarantees of its security and promises that the USA would prevent a communist take-over of Laos.[28] The occasion to redeem these undertakings appeared to have come in May 1962, when the Pathet Lao routed the rightist army. The United States duly sent further troops to Thailand, but it was made plain that they would not support Phoumi. Thus weakened, he finally agreed to a coalition. The Pathet Lao, too, were restrained from further exploiting their – or more probably North Vietnam's – military victory. So in June 1962 a united neutralist government under Souvanna Phouma came into being, and the Geneva conference was able to conclude with a Declaration on the Neutrality of Laos.

Inasmuch as the civil war had been prevented from escalating into major conflict between outside communist and anti-communist powers, this was a great success, but in Laos itself not much had changed. By late 1962 cooperation between Pathet Lao troops and Kong Le's 'neutralist' forces had broken down, and the USA began supplying the latter. In April 1963 the Pathet Lao left

27. Martin E. Goldstein, *American Policy toward Laos* (Cranbury, NJ, 1973) p.236
28. Blechman and Kaplan, *Force without War* p.141

the government, and sporadic fighting resumed. The USA now supported Souvanna Phouma's 'neutralist' government, and success-fully blocked the attempted 'rightist' coups in 1964 and 1965. Outside involvement steadily deepened in response to the intensification of the war in Vietnam. In June 1962 Hanoi had told Souvanna Phouma that, though happy to see him lead a united Laotian government, it insisted on continued freedom to use the trails through Laos to South Vietnam; so the 1962 Geneva provision prohibiting such use was bound to be a dead letter. By the end of the decade Hanoi had 67,000 troops in Laos to operate and defend the trails, and this led to the gradual extension of the area under Pathet Lao control. From 1965 the USA, with Souvanna Phouma's permission, embarked on massive bombing in an attempt to cut the trails. It had already been drawn into air strikes to bolster the government in the north, to which end it later came to finance small numbers of Thai 'volunteers'. Finally the CIA came during the 1960s to recruit a private army (at its peak, 15,000 full time, 40,000 in all) from the minority Hmong (or Meos). This was, all too probably, partly financed by drug trading; although it at first brought great prosperity, in the end Pathet Lao counter-offensives killed or drove into exile an alarmingly high proportion of the Hmong.[29] The Laos civil war accordingly remained very much alive. It was conducted largely clandestinely, however, and attracted little international attention; partly because for both the Americans and the North Vietnamese (who provided most of the fighting power of the rival parties) it was essentially subsidiary to the struggle for South Vietnam. Once that was over, the remainder of Laos fell (as Khrushchev had forecast in 1961)[30] to the Pathet Lao 'like a ripe apple'.

SOUTH VIETNAM 1954–64

When Kennedy became President he was prepared for trouble over Laos, but he was shocked by the condition of South Vietnam: 'This

29. Goldstein, *American Policy toward Laos* p.330; Prados, *Presidents' Secret Wars* pp.292, 296; Powers, *The Man who Kept the Secrets* pp.226, 451

30. Goldstein, *American Policy toward Laos* pp. 245–6. The previous paragraphs are drawn chiefly from Goldstein, from David Hall, 'The Laotian War of 1962 and the Indo-Pakistani War of 1971' in Blechman and Kaplan, *Force without War*, and from Prados, *Presidents' Secret Wars* chap. 14

is the worst yet. You know, Ike never briefed me . . .'.[31] From 1954 South Vietnam was controlled by what had previously been a (theoretically independent) French puppet government. This was headed by Ngo Dinh Diem, a non-communist nationalist of the kind that the USA had been looking for; despite some initial hesitations, the USA proceeded from late 1954 to back him in the hope of building a viable state that would keep communism north of the parallel. In so doing the USA and what we can now call South Vietnam were disregarding the Geneva Agreements, which prescribed the holding of elections in 1956 to reunite Vietnam. This perhaps sat ill with US advocacy of elections to reunite Germany and Korea, but it was not otherwise remarkable. Neither the USA nor South Vietnam were a party to the agreements. China (which had negotiated them) apparently favoured Vietnam's continued partition, provided that South Vietnam did not become a vehicle for US influence (see pp. 137–8). North Vietnam itself broke the provision that any civilians who wished to leave for the other part of the country 'shall be permitted and helped to do so'; for the resulting exodus might, as Ho and Giap admitted, have tilted the numerical balance from North to South Vietnam.[32] Diem's refusal to contemplate elections cannot be said to have harmed his legitimacy in the short run. But the general assumption had been that the communists would have won elections in 1954;[33] Diem's refusal to hold them did much, in the 1960s and 1970s, to undercut his state's appeal in the West.

Initially both North and South Vietnam concentrated on internal consolidation. In the North, attacks on 'landlords' and 'rich peasants', together with anti-Catholic policies, sparked a revolt, which was firmly put down. In 1956–7 there was a change of Party Secretary, some backtracking, and a pause before the country proceeded to collectivisation.[34] Consolidation in the South was a good deal harder. Diem was at first unexpectedly successful, purchasing, coopting, and out-manoeuvring the religio-political sects in 1955 and staging a referendum that converted the state into a Republic under his presidency. Diem did attempt a land reform, but a very

31. Schlesinger, *Thousand Days* p.291
32. D.A. Ross, *In the Interests of Peace: Canada and Vietnam 1954–73* (Toronto, 1984) p.111 and chaps. 4, 5
33. *FRUS,* 1952–4 xiii Part 2 pp.1,794, 2,191, 2,407–8
34. William S. Turley, *The Second Indochina War* (paperback edn, 1987) p.19; E.A. Moise, 'Land Reform and Land Reform Errors in North Vietnam', *Pacific Affairs* xlix (1976) esp. p.78; *Pentagon Papers,* i p. 246; Philip B. Davidson, *Vietnam at War* (Novato, Calif., 1988) pp.286–7

limited one.[35] Basically, though, he relied on the rooting out of subversives. Some say this led to more political executions in the South than in the North. It reduced Communist Party membership from about 55,000 in 1954 to 5,000 in 1959, but it also alienated a wide spectrum of unattached opinion. Hanoi had originally expected the Southern regime to collapse in a welter of faction fighting. By 1959 it feared the complete elimination of communist cadres if nothing were done, but it also judged conditions propitious for armed struggle. In May 1959 the Politburo authorised the resumption of armed struggle; that summer saw the start of the reinfiltration south of cadres evacuated in 1954 and the creation of rudimentary facilities to supply them. Late in 1960 local colouring was provided by the creation of an ostensibly non-communist National Liberation Front for South Vietnam (NLF).[36]

In considering Vietnam, Kennedy was much influenced by Moscow's proclaimed support for 'wars of national liberation' and strategy of overcoming capitalism by first detaching the Third World. As we have seen, he was prepared to pull back from earlier US policies and accept the neutralisation of Laos. But this made firm action elsewhere all the more important, both to impress Khrushchev (who had reactivated the question of Berlin) and to reassure pro-American Asians (whose concerns had been forcefully put to Vice-President Johnson during a rapid tour in May 1961).[37] Few people advised Kennedy against increasing US involvement. Of these the most notable was President de Gaulle, who urged Kennedy to take a tough line on Berlin at the Vienna summit, but to keep clear of Indo-China: 'Once a nation has been aroused, no foreign power, however strong, can impose its will upon it'; 'you will sink step by step into a bottomless military and political quagmire, however much you spend in men and money'.[38] De Gaulle was no doubt thinking of French experience in Indo-China and Algeria, but Americans were apt to regard this as irrelevant, since they were both stronger than France and free from the taint of old-fashioned imperialism. William Bundy saw the danger 'that we would wind up like the French in 1954; white men can't win this kind of fight'; but

35. Landlords were allowed to keep as much as 100 hectares, and though rents were reduced, the state made possible their collection in many areas where they had lapsed during the anti-French insurgency

36. Turley, *Second Indochina War* pp. 19–20, 24, 33; *The Pentagon Papers as published by the New York Times* (paperback edn. 1971) pp.76–7, (hereafter, *Pentagon Papers*) (NYT)

37. *Pentagon Papers*, ii pp.57–9

38. Charles De Gaulle, *Memoirs of Hope* (1971) p.256

he nevertheless believed that early and forceful action had a 70:30 chance of success.[39] The military, who had opposed involvement in Laos, favoured sending troops to South Vietnam since they did not believe this would provoke major external intervention of the kind that had occurred in Korea.

Kennedy felt otherwise: open US troop commitments could upset the Laos cease-fire; he feared, too, that they might convert Vietnam 'into a white man's war, [which] we would lose as the French had lost a decade earlier'. There were also presentational problems, since, in contrast to Korea, there had been no overt aggression.[40] So in November 1961 Kennedy took a middle course, rejecting (for the time being) direct military participation, but increasing aid and providing South Vietnam with training, helicopter transport and 'combat advisers'. This was less than President Diem had asked for; perhaps for this reason, the USA did not insist on anything like the degree of control over his government that it had originally requested, and greatly watered down its demand for 'real administrative political and social reform' and a sharing 'in the decision-making process in the political, economic and military fields'.[41]

Providing Diem with enhanced resources but still leaving him essentially in control was not a success. Indeed it is remarkable how rapidly his government's position declined. In 1959, as we have seen, he seemed to have the communists on the run and to have gone far in recovering control over the countryside: in the province of Long An only 6 per cent of assessed land taxes had been collected in 1955 but 82 per cent in 1959.[42] However, when the communists resumed the offensive, things rapidly went into reverse. Government forces increasingly withdrew into the safer areas; the percentage of land tax collected in Long An (which may be taken as a proxy for other aspects of control) fell steadily to 21 per cent in 1964.[43]

Diem's 1962 recipe for stopping the rot was a 'strategic hamlets' programme modelled on British actions in Malaya. In Malaya, however, the British had had to deal only with the Chinese minority, not with the entire population; although the compulsory relocation of the rural Chinese had been harsh, it did provide an

39. *Pentagon Papers* (NYT) p.98
40. ibid, pp.106, 108 (unsigned notes of 15 Nov. 1961 NSC meeting); *Pentagon Papers* ii p.117
41. ibid, pp.120, 126
42. Jeffrey Race, *War Comes to Long An* (Berkeley, Calif., 1972) p.284
43. Race, *War Comes to Long An* esp. pp.113–16

immigrant community with the right to remain in Malaya, with land, and with amenities. Most of these inducements were not applicable to indigenous Vietnamese peasants; these were, if anything, more likely to feel indebted to the insurgents (whom it will be convenient to call Vietcong). Diem's land reforms had been very limited, while his restoration of order had enabled landlords to return to areas from which they had been driven by the Vietminh. By contrast the Vietcong reduced rent and redistributed landlords' lands, while carefully avoiding antagonising the peasants. In any case the strategic hamlets programme was, despite warnings, pushed through far too fast, with the result not only that amenities were lacking but also that their fortifications left much to be desired. Even so the hamlets posed problems for the Vietcong, but they would work only if they could be defended; given the political turmoil that set in in mid-1963, this ceased to be the case.[44]

This turmoil stemmed from a collision between the Roman Catholic-dominated government and the Buddhists, who constituted the overwhelming majority of the population. In May 1963 the government chose to enforce a generally ignored ban on the display of religious flags. The army dispersed festival crowds in Hué, killing nine people, which sparked a Buddhist campaign for the punishment of those responsible, freedom to celebrate and an end of arrests. In June a monk, Thich Quang Duc, alerted the press and burnt himself to death by way of protest, an action that had enormous impact on both national and American public opinion. As time went on Buddhist protest was aimed increasingly at the Diem regime and sought a neutralist and nationalist state. The USA urged tolerance on Diem, but his entourage saw the movement only as subversive. The last straw came in August when, shortly after Diem had promised the USA to be conciliatory, his brother Nhu sent troops into the pavilions and arrested 1,400 monks. Washington's response was to cable its ambassador that

> Diem must be given the chance to rid himself of Nhu and his coterie and replace them with best military and political personalities available.
>   If . . . Diem remains obdurate and refuses, then we must face the possibility that Diem himself cannot be preserved.[45]

Diem's position had never been completely secure – a 1960 coup had nearly unseated him – and the Kennedy administration had

---

44. ibid. pp.132–4 and pictures; Turley, *Second Indochina War* pp.49–50; Truong Nhu Tang, *A Vietcong Memoir* (New York, 1985) pp.46–7
45. *Pentagon Papers*, ii pp. 226–8, 235

always had at the back of its mind the possibility of switching support elsewhere if Diem proved a failure. In August 1963, after the pagoda raids, it began to listen approvingly to Vietnamese generals who were preparing another coup. Diem and Nhu, who had preserved some contacts with Hanoi, responded to US pressure by opening discussions on ditching the Americans and taking the National Liberation Front into a coalition government. It is unclear whether this was a serious initiative or simply an attempt to blackmail the USA.[46] In any case nothing had come of it by the time the presidential palace was attacked in early November 1963. Diem unwisely rejected Ambassador Lodge's offer of personal protection, and he and Nhu were shot.

In countenancing a coup, the USA had deepened its commitment. Indeed in August 1963 Lodge had been authorised to 'tell appropriate military commanders we will give them direct support in any interim period of breakdown [of] central government mechanism'.[47] In December 1963 the North Vietnamese Central Committee concluded, though from different premises, that the USA faced a choice between accepting defeat and introducing its own troops. The second course might well enable the Saigon government to develop into a neocolonial dependency able to withstand a purely Southern revolution. So the North would have to increase its involvement and build up 'main force' units capable of annihilating their regular Southern army (ARVN) counterparts. Accordingly 1964 saw preparations for escalation on both sides; in April North Vietnamese units started training to move south, and their infiltration began in October.[48] Even before then Washington was convinced that Hanoi controlled the southern insurgency and could call a halt if it wished. So in 1964 a number of low-key sabotage operations were launched against the North and plans made for major bombing, which, it was felt, would require a congressional resolution of support. Against this background a warning was sent to Hanoi in June that, unless the insurgency in the South was halted, the USA 'would carry the war to the north'. The North Vietnamese premier rejected it,[49] and President Johnson took no immediate action, perhaps for domestic political reasons.

46. Stanley Karnow, *Vietnam: A History* (New York, 1983) pp.291–2; Ross, *In the Interests of Peace* pp.276, 441

47. *Pentagon Papers*, ii p. 734

48. Hitherto the infiltration had been chiefly of communist cadres of Southern origin: Turley, *Second Indochina War* pp.44, 57–61

49. Ross, *In the Interests of Peace* pp.275–6; *Pentagon Papers* (NYT) p.256

THE 'GULF OF TONKIN' INCIDENT AND CONGRESSIONAL RESOLUTION, 1964

The situation was transformed by a naval incident in early August 1964. A US electronic intelligence destroyer, patrolling close to North Vietnam in the aftermath of a South Vietnamese commando raid, was attacked by Northern torpedo boats but emerged unscathed. Two days later radar and sonar indicated another attack.[50] Whether or not the episode was a false alarm, Johnson responded by bombing North Vietnamese naval bases in August 1964, and by securing a near-unanimous congressional resolution that authorised the President not only to repel any further attacks on US forces but also 'to take all necessary steps, including the use of armed force, to assist any member or protocol state of the Southeast Asia Collective Defense Treaty requesting assistance in defense of its freedom'.[51] This was later to be known as the 'Gulf of Tonkin Resolution'. It resembled that passed during the 1954–5 Chinese offshore islands crisis and that launching the Eisenhower Doctrine for the Middle East in 1957. These could have had even more serious consequences, but no real trouble transpired, and neither congressional nor public opinion was therefore upset. By contrast, Johnson was to act on the Gulf of Tonkin Resolution, treating it – controversially – as *carte blanche* for US military participation in the Vietnam War.

USA BOMBS NORTH VIETNAM AND COMMITS GROUND TROOPS TO SOUTH VIETNAM 1965

Johnson wanted to contest the November 1964 presidential elections as the peace candidate, so he initially did little more than send a second (and equally unavailing) warning to Hanoi; but the expectation was that sustained air attacks on North Vietnam would probably have to be launched 'early in the new year'.[52] In January 1965 Johnson approved retaliatory bombing of North Vietnam 'immediately following the recurrence of a spectacular enemy action'. The opportunity came in February with a Vietcong attack

---

50. Karnow, *Vietnam* pp. 366–76
51. *Pentagon Papers* (NYT) pp. 257, 264–5
52. ibid, p.307

on a US special forces camp at Pleiku; by March retaliatory raids had escalated into the continuous but controlled bombing of the North. Johnson had, however, already expressed doubts as to whether the war would be won from the air, and his belief that actual US participation on the ground would be needed. From February to July 1965 the presidential circle debated the wisdom and nature of such a commitment. Given Johnson's inclinations, commitment was always likely. The combination of major Vietcong victories and of the sixth governmental coup since the fall of Diem probably made it inevitable. · The US Commander, General Westmoreland, a strong partisan of intervention, reported in June that 'The South Vietnamese armed forces cannot stand up to this pressure without substantial U.S. combat support on the ground', and asked for 180,000 men; on 28 July 1965 Johnson announced his approval.[53]

On paper this decision had been reached after an impressive weighing of the options. Doubts were expressed both as to American staying power and as to whether 'an army of westerners can successfully fight orientals in an Asian jungle'. The more usual view was that 'If the communist world finds out we will not pursue our commitments to the end, I don't know where they will stay their hand'. It was generally accepted that Vietnam was a test case for the strategy of wars of national liberation. If South Vietnam were allowed to collapse, McNamara doubted the possibility of holding Thailand, and added 'Laos, Cambodia, Thailand, Burma, surely affect Malaysia. In 2–3 years communist domination would stop there, but ripple effect would be great [in] Japan, India. We would have to give up some bases. Ayub [Khan of Pakistan] would move closer to China. Greece, Turkey would move to neutralist positions'. And so on. In any case Johnson privately feared that failure in Vietnam would unleash a right-wing backlash, comparable to that occasioned by the 'loss' of China in 1949, which would prove fatal to all he stood for in domestic politics.[54] So it can be argued that the real debates were those over the extent of US intervention. The military would have liked a more rapid and intensive bombing of the North; Johnson preferred gradual escalation as less likely to upset US domestic opinion or to push

53. Karnow, *Vietnam* chap. 9; *Pentagon Papers* (NYT) chaps. 6, 7

54. ibid, p.326; G.McT. Kahin, *Intervention: How America Became Involved in Vietnam* (New York, 1986) pp.360–1, 374 ff; Charles De Benedetti in R.A. Divine (ed.) *Exploring the Johnson Years* (Austin, Texas, 1981) p.31

China into intervention.[55] Westmoreland wanted US troops to play a major role in fighting the Vietcong; Maxwell Taylor (formerly Chairman of the Joint Chiefs of Staff) and others felt they should be used only to hold enclaves, releasing ARVN forces to fight the Vietcong but not relieving them of the principal responsibility for the conduct of the war. After some wavering, Johnson decided for Westmoreland.

It can be argued not only that the decision to escalate was mistaken, but also that the wrong strategy was adopted. More bombs were supposedly dropped on North Vietnam than on Germany in the Second World War, and the spectacle placed the USA in a very bad light. Damage, and civilian casualties,[56] was naturally considerable, but no attempt was made to bomb the North 'back into the stone age'. Johnson chose targets (personally at first) with considerable restraint so as not to provoke Chinese intervention – to avoid which he quietly promised in 1965 not to destroy the vital Red River dams or attack the Chinese border. Even so there might have been scope for mining the North Vietnamese ports, as Nixon did in 1972. In the absence of such actions, and given that it was safeguarded by China from direct invasion, Hanoi was under no overwhelming pressure to discontinue its Southern interventions. Nor did the USA do all it could to prevent supplies and troops coming down from the North. The Ho Chi Minh Trail in Laos was bombed repeatedly, but no major attempt was made to cut it on the ground until 1971. The USA also acquiesced in the dispatch of supplies via Cambodia, and allowed the Vietcong to use Cambodian territory as a sanctuary. Finally, within Vietnam itself the Americans tended to concentrate on conventional search-and-destroy operations against major enemy units, and to neglect local protection, reconstruction and the winning of 'hearts and minds'.[57] It was, indeed, not until May 1967 that US civil and military pacification programmes were brought together under a single director.

US intervention nevertheless staved off collapse in 1965; by 1966 US operations were apparently inflicting heavy casualties. Stable

55. Gradual escalation also increased US losses by allowing time for the installation of anti-aircraft missiles

56. Nobody really knows their dimensions; the USA put them in 1969 at 52,000 (Turley, *Second Indochina War* p.202), Karnow at 100,000 (*Vietnam* p.458). That Vietnam has not claimed higher totals is confirmation that (unlike the Second World War Allies) the USA was not practising obliteration bombing

57. For a critique of this policy, see Race, *War Comes to Long An* chap. 5

government followed, though more slowly and after much political infighting and a final Buddhist rebellion in 1966.[58]

THE TET OFFENSIVE (JANUARY 1968) AND ITS CONSEQUENCES

None of this discouraged Hanoi. It had decided in 1963–4 to increase its involvement in the South and was unmoved by Soviet counsels of caution. Nor did it have any use for Chinese advice to fight a prolonged guerrilla war. It looked to an ultimate 'general offensive and general uprising', and apparently hoped for one in 1965. US intervention supervened, but Hanoi still decided late that year 'to win a decisive victory on the southern battlefield in a relatively short period'.[59] The campaign began in January 1968 with an assault on Khe Sanh that Washington took to be an attempt to repeat Dien Bien Phu; this diverted US attention and troops, but was inexplicably prolonged until April despite some 10,000 communist losses. Meanwhile, in late January, during the agreed truce for the Tet festival, the communists flung 70,000–80,000 troops against 100 towns all over the country, with audacious attacks on the US embassy, the Presidential Palace, and the Saigon radio station. Surprise was complete: half the ARVN was on leave. But the attacks failed to spark any sympathetic rising. Now that they had come out of hiding, communist forces were cut down in large numbers by superior firepower. By March the USA reported 2,000 American, 4,000 ARVN and perhaps 50,000 insurgent deaths.[60] But the effort was continued with renewed attacks on cities in May and August 1968, both (lacking surprise) repulsed fairly easily.

In military terms the Tet offensive was a disaster; as one of its planners later wrote, 'we suffered heavy losses of manpower and material, especially of cadres . . ., which caused a distinct decline in our strength'.[61] Major communist attacks accordingly declined

58. General Thieu became President in 1965, was confirmed in office by imperfect (but not completely fraudulent) elections in 1967, and thereafter progressively consolidated his power

59. W.R. Smyser, *The Independent Vietnamese: Vietnamese Communism between Russia and China, 1956–1969* (Athens, Ohio, 1980) pp.73–94; Turley, *Second Indochina War* p.101; D. Pike in P. Braestrup (ed.) *Vietnam as History* (Washington, DC, 1984) p.71; Karnow, *Vietnam* p. 453

60. Karnow, *Vietnam* p. 534

61. Turley, *Second Indochina War* p.116

sharply until 1972. As a disproportionate number of the Tet casualties had been Southerners (since General Giap had sought to husband his Northern regulars), growing numbers of Northerners had to be sent to take their places. These were less familiar with the territory. Countermeasures, too, were now more effective in that, since 1967, Vietcong cadres were being deliberately sought out for arrest or elimination by counter-intelligence. This CIA-sponsored Operation Phoenix was morally dubious; like much else in the South it was corrupt, with 70 per cent of those arrested supposedly able to buy back their freedom. But subsequent Vietcong testimony suggests that it was still distinctly damaging, though the claim that it accounted for 60,000 authentic agents cannot be tested.[62] After Tet, too, more emphasis was placed on 'rural construction', while in 1970 Thieu recognised the land redistribution effected by the Vietcong and embarked on a further programme that halved tenancy in the populous Mekong delta.[63]

There would, then, have been a case for *increasing* the US war effort after the Tet offensive. Instead Tet broke the American will to fight. This had been eroding for some time. Even in 1965 Johnson had worried about the question, 'Are we starting something that in two or three years we simply can't finish?'[64] Tet contradicted the official optimism about the course of the war, and public confidence in Johnson fell sharply. It also raised the question of dispatching more troops. To do so would have meant mobilising the reserves. This was something Johnson had always been reluctant to contemplate; and it became clear that even congressional hawks opposed significant troop increases. Then on 12 March 1968 Johnson almost lost the New Hampshire primary to the previously insignificant peace campaigner, Senator Eugene McCarthy. This convinced him that he needed 'a peace proposal'. The last straw came in late March, when the group of elder statesmen whom Johnson periodically consulted on foreign affairs reversed their previous stance and advised disengagement.[65] On 31 March Johnson finally decided to send only 13,500 more troops to

---

62. Karnow, *Vietnam* pp.601–2

63. Turley, *Second Indochina War* pp.135–6. It is not clear how far these reforms benefited Thieu's government, but they left a landowning peasantry that resisted later communist exactions and attempts at collectivisation: Nguyen Van Cahn, *Vietnam under Communism 1975–82* (Stanford, Calif., 1983) pp.30–3, 38, 139

64. Kahin, *Intervention* p.383

65. The State Department's Philip Habib briefed them, and later Johnson himself, that South Vietnam was in such a state that real progress might take five to ten years

Vietnam. He also announced his intention not to seek re-election, discontinued the bombing of most (later all) of North Vietnam, and proffered unconditional peace negotiations – which, to his surprise, Hanoi promptly accepted.[66] Talks began in Paris in May 1968. Although they made absolutely no progress, the US administration was to come under increasing pressure from an anti-war movement convinced that just one more concession would get them off the ground.

NIXON'S PLANS TO END THE WAR 1968–9

The three main US presidential candidates in 1968 all held out hopes of ending involvement in Vietnam. Nixon looked partly to intimidating North Vietnam into negotiating, and partly to enlisting the good offices of the Soviet Union. Unfortunately the latter no longer felt very forthcoming. Khrushchev had discouraged Hanoi from escalation in 1964, arguing that its forces were unprepared for modern war. On taking over, Brezhnev switched to endorsing the 'heroic liberation struggle', while Kosygin went to Hanoi in early 1965 promising the resumption of the aid Khrushchev had cut. While he was there, US bombing of the North started. The Kremlin responded by denouncing it, by instructing West European Communist parties to protest, and by increasing its aid to North Vietnam. The USSR also rushed in missiles, which were (in due course) to shoot down appreciable numbers of US bombers. But it was worried about growing US involvement, which (Brezhnev told the Hungarians) might change the current favourable military situation in the South. So Kosygin seems also to have talked in Hanoi and Beijing of de-escalation and of helping the USA 'find a way out' of Vietnam – to no effect. The Russians continued to worry about the possibility of major US escalation. So Kosygin jumped at the chance (which appeared to present itself when he was in London in February 1967) of arranging the discontinuance of US bombing against a secret promise by Hanoi not to send any more troops South (see pp. 303–4). The ending of the bombing of North Vietnam in 1968, and the obvious US eagerness to disengage, probably stilled many of these fears. Soviet military aid to North Vietnam switched increasingly to the kind of equipment that would

66. Karnow, *Vietnam* pp.545–66; *Pentagon Papers* (NYT) pp.607–23

enable it to launch a major conventional offensive (as it did in 1972).[67] By contrast Egypt was to be deliberately starved in the early 1970s of the weapons it needed to attack Israel.

The Nixon administration, however, initially hoped that the USSR could be brought to coerce Hanoi. Dobrynin was sounded out in April 1969, and in October Nixon sought to make the Soviet response a test case: 'If the Soviet Union found it possible to do something in Vietnam, and the Vietnam war ended, then we might do something dramatic to improve our relations . . . But until then . . . real progress will be very difficult'.[68] Given Hanoi's dependence on the USSR (inter alia for all its petroleum), the USSR could, in theory, have brought considerable pressure to bear (at the risk of driving Hanoi into Beijing's arms).[69] The USSR has been known to deal very abruptly with its clients,[70] but on this occasion it did not choose to do so; and unless subjected to intense pressure, Hanoi (like Israel) would go its own way. Nor, as things transpired, did the USSR have any reason to intervene. Nixon's threats notwithstanding, US–Soviet relations later improved dramatically, with a summit conference being arranged for May 1972. In April 1972 North Vietnam staged a long-awaited offensive even larger than that of 1968, despite US warnings of its possible impact on the summit. The Soviet Union had provided the where-withal, but equally it reacted very mildly when the USA resumed bombing and also mined North Vietnamese harbours, a step that Johnson had never dared to take. Despite a certain amount of bluster neither Nixon nor Brezhnev was prepared to let the episode prevent or spoil the summit. In short US–Soviet relations could not be 'linked' to events in Indo-China.

The other arm of Nixon's strategy was to threaten North Vietnam with terrible destruction unless it negotiated a

67. *Pentagon Papers* (NYT) esp. pp.38–40, 151, 167, 189–90, 204; Smyser, *The Independent Vietnamese* esp. pp.73–4,76–7, 88, 94; Douglas Pike, *Vietnam and the Soviet Union* (Boulder, Colo., 1987) esp. chap. 5 and pp.120–2, 139; Wilson, *The Labour Government 1964–70* chap. 19; Karnow, *Vietnam* pp.495–6

68. Nixon, *Memoirs* pp.391, 399–400, 405–7; Kissinger, *Memoirs* i pp.267–8

69. China could, presumably, have provided (lower quality) substitutes for all Soviet military aid except, perhaps, missiles. Whether it would have greatly increased its aid to Hanoi at a time when it was seeking US support against Moscow is less certain

70. In 1967–9 the USSR successfully pressed Cuba to revert to the Soviet line by holding oil deliveries constant despite the 8% per year growth in Cuban demand and by imposing other economic sanctions: Szulc, *Fidel* pp.678, 681, 684, 689. There was at least talk of its having forced Castro to accept the resolution of the 1962 missile crisis by threatening to cut off his oil: Radvanyi, *Hungary and the Superpowers* pp.135–6

compromise. But if there was ever a time for this approach, it had passed. There had been divisions within the North Vietnamese Politburo in the early 1960s as to how far it was right to put the country at risk by open intervention in the South. Probably hardliners like Le Duan were firmly in control by 1965, but Johnson might just possibly have been able to bargain for Northern restraint by making sufficiently convincing threats of all-out air attack. In fact his bombing lost much of its impact through gradual escalation, and was so far limited that Hanoi may by 1969 have come to believe that it could live with the worst that the USA could do. Be this as it may, Nixon issued threats, telling Ho Chi Minh in July that, in default of a breakthrough by November, he would have recourse 'to measures of great consequence and force'. Many similar warnings were given, and 1 November 1969 was built up as a deadline. But to no purpose. Nixon's threats were not entirely empty since he had commissioned plans for intensive bombing ('Duck Hook'). Rather than further stir the cauldron of internal US unrest, however, Nixon allowed his bluff to be called and confined himself to a firm speech for domestic consumption.[71]

VIETNAMISATION

If US forces were to be cut, the South Vietnamese would have increasingly to take over the fighting (whereas since 1965 they had been regarded largely as auxiliaries to the better equipped and more effective Americans). This policy of 'Vietnamisation' began early in 1969 while Nixon still hoped to bring North Vietnam to accept mutual troop withdrawal. When these hopes evaporated, only Vietnamisation remained. At one level it was quite effective. Troop cuts enabled the USA to reduce the draft, and the call-up machinery was also reformed. This did much to quieten US campuses; but the progressive reduction of US troops (from a peak of 543,000 in April 1969 to 157,000 by the end of 1971) opened up the possibility of their soon becoming militarily insignificant. An acute dilemma presented itself in early 1972 when a communist offensive seemed on the cards, but the compulsion to continue withdrawals was so strong that Nixon decided to halve US forces by May. However, if troops departed, US air power could still be used:

71. Nixon, *Memoirs* pp.393–411; Hersh, *The Price of Power* pp.120–34

it cost relatively few US casualties and was much less sensitive politically than a conscript army. Still, as Nixon noted in 1972, 'all the air power in the world' would not save Saigon 'if the South Vietnamese aren't able to hold on the ground'. So Vietnamisation also demanded the further strengthening of the ARVN. Quantitatively this was easy; qualitatively the picture was more mixed. Some ARVN units were indeed good, and South Vietnamese forces sometimes did well; in other circumstances (especially when deployed away from their home bases) they simply collapsed. 'The real problem', Nixon noted, 'is that the enemy is willing to sacrifice in order to win, while the South Vietnamese simply aren't willing to pay that much of a price in order to avoid losing'.[72] This must be qualified: ARVN deaths in battle (admittedly defending what was supposed to be their own country) were by late 1972 more than four times as high as the 46,000 the USA found unacceptable. But they pale before 'Vietcong' and North Vietnamese losses.[73]

THE LON NOL COUP IN CAMBODIA 1970

A disastrous side-effect of the policy of Vietnamisation was the extension of the war in Cambodia. Cambodia had after 1954 been successfully governed by its former King, Prince Sihanouk, whose chief ambition had been to keep the country out of trouble. In the 1960s this involved leaning verbally towards China, which he judged the predominant power in the region, condemning US intervention, and not contesting the Vietcong presence in his country. By December 1967 Sihanouk was having his doubts (the China of the 'Cultural Revolution' looked less impressive); so he suggested that US 'hot pursuit' raids 'in uninhabited areas', which 'would be liberating us from the Vietcong'.[74] Johnson would not undertake them, but in early 1969 Nixon started bombing in border areas, seeking not only to destroy or dislodge the Vietcong headquarters (COSVN) situated in Cambodia but also to 'signal' his determination to Hanoi. Although Nixon told some leading Congressmen, he otherwise kept the operation secret from the American public; both Cambodia and North Vietnam also preferred

72. Karnow, *Vietnam* pp.642–3; Nixon, *Memoirs* p.595; Braestrup, *Vietnam as History* (chronological table)
73. See *The Post-Imperial World* chap.6
74. Karnow, *Vietnam* p.590

to keep quiet about the bombing. North Vietnam did, however, begin to support the small communist resistance to Sihanouk, the Khmer Rouge.

As 1969 proceeded Sihanouk looked increasingly to the Americans, but others were more impatient. On 18 March 1970, while Sihanouk was on holiday in France, he was formally deposed and a new regime constituted under General Lon Nol. Sihanouk proceeded to Beijing where, in late April, China arranged a meeting, under his chairmanship, of North Vietnam, the Southern NLF, Pathet Lao and the Khmer Rouge, which provided legitimation for the continued 'Vietcong' use of Cambodia and for both North Vietnamese and Chinese support for the Sihanouk–Khmer Rouge coalition. There has been controversy as to how far the United States was responsible for Lon Nol's coup. He was probably acting independently, albeit in the belief that he was bound to get US support; both Nixon and Kissinger seem to have been taken by surprise.[75] Be that as it may, the effect was disastrous since it removed the constraints that had hitherto shielded Cambodia from full involvement in the Indo-Chinese struggle.

The North Vietnamese and Khmer Rouge were first off the mark, capturing or attacking several towns in April 1970 and cutting communications to the capital Phnom Penh. Official Washington was deeply divided as to whether to help Lon Nol militarily, but Nixon clearly felt that something should be done: 'They are romping in there, and the only government in Cambodia in the last twenty-five years that had the guts to take a pro-Western and pro-American stand is ready to fall'. US action, however, was geared chiefly to the needs of its existing war in South Vietnam: Cambodian developments provided a tempting opportunity to take out the Vietcong bases on the border, and in particular COSVN. So on 30 April Nixon announced joint South Vietnamese and US attacks on the 'sanctuaries', justifying them chiefly in terms of protecting US forces in Vietnam and guaranteeing 'the continued success of our withdrawal and Vietnamization programmes'. Then, to placate fears of getting bogged down in yet another Indo-Chinese war, he gave assurances that US troops would go no more than twenty-one miles into Cambodia and that they would leave by the end of June – which obviously limited their

75. Karnow, *Vietnam* pp.603–7; Kissinger, *Memoirs* i pp. 457–70; Hersh, *The Price of Power* chap. 15; Chang, Pao-Min, *Kampuchea between China and Vietnam* (Singapore, 1985) pp.27–33

effectiveness. South Vietnamese forces penetrated further and stayed longer, but they too had to be withdrawn to cover for US troop withdrawals from Vietnam. Thereafter the only combat assistance provided to Lon Nol was from the air – at grave cost to Cambodian civilians.[76]

Although the 1970 incursion did little to save Lon Nol, it did relieve pressure on South Vietnam by capturing quite sizeable stocks of Vietcong weapons and equipment; however, it narrowly failed to intercept the bulk of COSVN personnel, who had begun to withdraw into the interior immediately after Sihanouk's deposition. So perhaps the USA's chief gain from the 1970 Cambodian developments was that they diverted enemy forces into fighting Lon Nol – 'If those [40,000] North Vietnamese weren't in Cambodia', Nixon declared, 'they'd be over killing Americans' – and prevented Vietcong supplies using Cambodian ports.[77]

THE 1971 SOUTH VIETNAMESE ATTEMPT TO CUT THE HO CHI MINH TRAIL, AND THE 1972 NORTH VIETNAMESE OFFENSIVE

With these supplies cut off, the Ho Chi Minh Trail down through Laos became correspondingly more important. The trail had originally been a collection of jungle paths that took six months to travel and carried a considerable risk of malaria. From mid-1964 it was constantly upgraded, eventually finishing as paved roads, supply depots, and even an oil pipeline.[78] The USA sought to block (or at least damage) the route by bombing. But it had not tried to cut it on the ground, since permanent blocking would have required large numbers of troops and since Johnson in any case did not want cross-border forays. Now Nixon decided to seize the staging-point of Tchepone in February 1971 and destroy as many trail facilities as possible before withdrawing – but to do so using only the ARVN, since (in the aftermath of Cambodia) Congress had forbidden the

---

76. Precisely how grave has become a matter of controversy; in the Appendix to *Years of Upheaval* Kissinger defends himself against charges of indiscriminate bombing. The Cambodian civil war cost about half a million lives, but we cannot reliably apportion these as between bombing, fighting and Khmer Rouge atrocities

77. *Keesing's*, 24145; Truong, *Vietcong Memoir* pp.176 ff; Hersh, *The Price of Power* p.303

78. Karnow, *Vietnam* pp.331–4, 659–60, 663

use of US troops in either Cambodia or Laos. The operation was badly planned and executed. Tchepone was ultimately captured, but by late March the ARVN had pulled out in headlong and disorderly retreat. The incursion did delay the communist build-up, but its chief effect was to confirm North Vietnam's belief that it could beat the ARVN in conventional warfare.[79] The attempt was first made in June 1972, with the commitment of ten of North Vietnam's thirteen combat divisions. It almost succeeded: some cities were taken (provoking panic-stricken civilian flights), and guerrillas were able to return to 'pacified' regions when government troops withdrew to resist attacks elsewhere. But the communists, too, made mistakes and encountered logistic difficulties; they were battered by US air power, losing perhaps some 50,000 dead. Hanoi now decided the time had come to bargain seriously.[80]

SECRET NEGOTIATIONS AND THE CEASE-FIRE AGREEMENT 1973; US INABILITY TO ENFORCE IT; THE COMMUNIST OFFENSIVE OF 1975 AND THE FALL OF SAIGON

The Paris peace talks that started in 1968 achieved nothing but propaganda. They were supplemented in 1969 by secret North Vietnamese meetings with Kissinger (also in Paris). Initially these fared no better. As a precondition for a cease-fire and the return of US prisoners-of-war, the North Vietnamese demanded that the USA remove President Thieu and his regime. This Washington would not accept. The United States no longer pursued its pre-1968 goal of a unilateral suspension of Northern infiltration, but it still sought mutual US–North Vietnamese withdrawal. Hanoi objected on principle, since it regarded Vietnam as a single country and rejected the equation of US and North Vietnamese troops as being both aliens in the South. It also knew that, whatever the situation had been in the mid-1960s, Saigon could now defeat the Southern insurgents if Northern forces withdrew. So there was little progress till late 1972; then both sides wanted to settle before the November

79. Kissinger, *Memoirs* i pp.987–1010; Turley, *Second Indochina War* pp.141–3
80. US interdiction of its railways and mining of its ports may also have been a factor: Turley, *Second Indo-China War* pp.143–9; Karnow, *Vietnam* pp.639–47

US elections, the communists probably fearing that a re-elected Nixon would be stronger and more obdurate, the Americans that the new Congress might legislate to bar even the use of air power in Indo-China. In October 1972, therefore, a deal was nearly reached on the basis of a cease-fire, the return of prisoners, an American – but *not* a North Vietnamese – troop withdrawal, and an interim arrangement in South Vietnam that (should it not lead to mutually agreed elections) would leave the government and the NLF to control whatever territory they occupied. At this point Thieu, who had not expected earlier negotiations to succeed and so had raised no objections, became seriously worried and demanded changes. This led to a stiffening of the North Vietnamese position. To break the deadlock, and demonstrate his resolution, Nixon launched the 'Christmas bombing', which was suspended when Hanoi accepted his timetable for negotiations in early January 1973. These soon proved successful; Thieu's acquiescence was secured by the promise (which the 'Christmas bombing' made appear more credible) that the USA would again punish Hanoi if it broke the agreement, plus the carrot of further aid and the threat that if Saigon proved obdurate the USA would settle without it.

The cease-fire was concluded in January 1973. The chief lever the USA had to enforce it was the possibility that it might resume bombing in the event of violations. Kissinger may not always have been confident of Saigon's prospects,[81] but in March–April 1973 he certainly urged air strikes in response to what he saw as continued Northern infiltration. Nixon was hesitant. Both then and later Kissinger blamed Watergate: 'If we didn't have this damn domestic situation, a week of bombing would put this Agreement into force'. Nixon had already been reluctant to continue in early January 1973, when he had insisted on an early settlement and noted 'war-weariness has reached the point that Option Two [involving continued bombing] is just too much for us to carry on'.[82] So even without Watergate he would have found bombing very difficult to renew.

Nixon's threats might still have had value as a bluff, but Congress largely undercut them. Once it had recovered US prisoners of war, it felt free to bolt the door against further military involvement. The immediate occasion was Cambodia, where no cease-fire had been

81. John Erlichman claims Kissinger said, on 23 January, 'if they're lucky they can hold out for a year and a half': *Witness to Power. The Nixon Years* (paperback edn, 1982) p.288
82. Kissinger, *Memoirs* ii esp. pp.318–26, 1,237; Nixon, *Memoirs* p.743

arranged since Hanoi claimed that it could not control the Khmer Rouge. US air support for Lon Nol therefore continued. Amendments to delete all funds for this were attached in June to appropriations and other financial bills for the coming fiscal year. Nixon sought at first to resist, but he was being badly damaged by Watergate, and he eventually compromised on a measure that permitted continued bombing until 15 August, then cut off funds for all US military activity throughout Indo-China. The extension of bombing helped break a Khmer Rouge assault on Phnom Penh, but its real purpose was to buy time for discussions with China on Lon Nol's departure and the reconstitution of a neutralist coalition government under Sihanouk. Kissinger claims that Zhou Enlai's support for such an outcome evaporated when Congress halted the bombing.[83]

In South Vietnam Thieu ignored the fig-leaf provisions of the January 1973 agreement for a Tripartite National Reconciliation Council, and sought, in fairly low-key fashion, to expand the territory under his control. Saigon claimed the take-over of 1,000 hamlets by mid-1974,[84] but it suffered economically from the withdrawal of US troops, from aid cut-backs, and (in 1974) from the oil price rise. By 1974 the country was in the grip of an inflation that did much to undermine the morale of the army, and also led people to view the endemic official corruption with growing hostility. Meanwhile, in March 1973, the Hanoi Politburo reaffirmed 'the path of revolutionary violence' in the South, but decided initially to concentrate on rebuilding its forces and only to fight where they had local superiority, so there was a relative lull in 1973–4. In October 1974, after some hesitation, Hanoi decided to try an offensive next year, though still in the belief that final success would probably not come until 1976. Communist troop strength in the South was supposedly increased (from 190,000) to 275,000 by March 1975.[85]

On paper the ARVN was the stronger force, but it was spread too thinly in an attempt to hold as much territory as possible. Though still probably the better equipped, it had been trained to fight American-style with prodigal use of ammunition and had difficulty adjusting to reductions in its supply. Nor could its air force really replicate the US air strikes that had done so much to stem the 1968

83. Kissinger, *Memoirs* ii pp.343, 349–55, 358–9, 362–9; Franck and Weisband, *Foreign Policy by Congress* chap. 1

84. Turley, *Second Indochina War* p.164

85. Karnow, *Vietnam* pp.659, 663–4; Chang, *Kampuchea* p.39

and 1972 offensives. But the primary mistakes were those of command. After the relatively minor town of Banmethuot fell on 11 March 1975, Thieu ordered the evacuation of the central highlands. In the process the troops, encumbered by dependants and panic-stricken civilians, disintegrated as a fighting force. A second communist offensive in the north first broke the ARVN around Hué, then isolated and shelled Danang, which was swamped by up to a million refugees and in no condition to face a siege. An attempt was made to withdraw the garrison by sea, but most troops deserted or were left behind. After taking Danang on 29 March, Hanoi decided to drive on Saigon before Southern morale recovered. Only once did it meet prolonged resistance; much of the ARVN command (like other high Southern officials) fled abroad. Saigon was taken on 29 April.[86] Phnom Penh, besieged since January, had already fallen to the Khmer Rouge. In Laos, after a symbolic Pathet Lao victory in May, rightist politicians fled and a gradual communist political take-over was complete by December 1975.

REASONS FOR THE US FAILURE; THE WAR'S IMPACT ON THE USA

In the 1960s the USA had increased its involvement in Indo-China to prove that communist insurgency could be resisted and to demonstrate the credibility of its guarantees to its allies. It had failed on both counts, not as a result of military defeat but because its will to fight had evaporated. There were many reasons for this. One was simply the length of the war. General Marshall had once doubted whether the USA could ever fight 'a seven years war'. The Korean War (with which the US involvement in Vietnam is most directly comparable) lasted less than three years; by November 1952 the United States electorate was clearly looking to see it ended. Arguably support for the USA's Vietnam involvement lasted nearly as long as that for the Korean War: it was not until mid-1967 that a majority came to see the Vietnam War as 'a mistake'. But from about that time, US administrations were operating against the background of a strident anti-war movement (which was joined by many former supporters of the war). This exposed official

---

86. A puppet Southern government was established, then in 1976 North and South Vietnam were formally united

explanations – the phrase 'credibility gap' dates from the Johnson era – and brought out the indiscriminate destruction occasioned by American use of bombing, defoliation and fire power. It broadcast the unsavoury nature of the Saigon regime, and tended to romanticise the NLF and deny (or excuse) Hanoi's actions beyond its borders. Its arguments clearly came to sway many people inside as well as outside government.

Opposition to the war was, though, a matter not only of argument, but also of demonstrations – 'Hey, Hey, LBJ, How many kids did you kill today?' – and indeed, especially for substantial sections of educated youth, of a new mood and life-style. This had other sources besides Vietnam, notably the civil rights and black activist turmoil that had by 1967 degenerated into a 'long hot summer' of ghetto riots. By 1968–9 the United States seemed in a bad way; Nixon's inaugural noted that 'We are torn by division', and in March 1969 he said of the endemic campus disorders 'this is the way civilizations begin to die. . . . None of us has the right to suppose it cannot happen here'.[87] Accordingly one constraint on US decision-makers was their reading of the likely domestic effects of their actions. The anti-war movement was clearly not strong enough to induce them simply to pull out of Vietnam; but it did have a significant effect, especially in 1969–70, in deterring or limiting escalation. The desire to restore domestic calm was one important factor in encouraging the policy of 'Vietnamisation' and the withdrawal of US ground forces. Another was the fear that, if the administration did not so withdraw troops, Congress would simply cut off funds – as indeed it did in 1973 (once US prisoners of war had been recovered), thus removing any possibility that Hanoi would be constrained by fear of US air power to observe the cease-fire agreement.

The USA's Vietnam experience was undoubtedly traumatic. It led to some questioning of Cold War orthodoxies, and to a more widespread reluctance to risk further entanglements that would impose constraints on subsequent administrations' diplomatic freedom of manoeuvre. It also tarnished the United States' international image. All this had an appreciable effect on world politics, especially in the 1970s. In the last resort, it chastened the USA yet did not turn it fundamentally from its former international course (as revulsion against the Afghan war was to do to Soviet foreign policy in the later 1980s).

87. *Keesing's*, 23135; Ambrose, *Nixon* p.263

SOUTH-EAST ASIA SINCE 1975

The effects in South-East Asia of the communist victories in Indo-China were less far-reaching than many had feared. Thailand, admittedly, went through a disturbed period in the mid-1970s, but the region as a whole had calmed down since the days of Sukarno and confrontation, when the initial commitment of US troops to South Vietnam had been made. The fall of Saigon led ASEAN members to seek to pull together by way of self-preservation. We do not know whether the Indo-Chinese communists had ever had ideas of destabilising their neighbours, domino-fashion. The Khmer Rouge in Cambodia (Kampuchea) did offer some assistance to Thai guerrillas. But their chief concern (apart from horrific domestic reconstruction) appears to have lain with Cambodia's traditional enemy, the Vietnamese. Vietnam fully reciprocated: Hanoi undoubtedly meant to be master throughout ex-French Indo-China. It also put itself on a collision course with its traditional enemy, China, expelling its ethnic Chinese and entering into border disputes. It professed no hostility towards the other South-East Asian countries, but it seems to have meant them to revolve around itself (China apart, it was the largest military power in the region). Vietnam also condemned ASEAN as simply the imperialist South-East Asia Treaty Organisation under another form, and declared that 'The policy of setting up such military blocs . . . has failed and passed for ever'. Instead the individual ASEAN countries should conclude bilateral pacts of friendship with Hanoi.[88]

The events of 1978–9 were to set the regional pattern for over a decade. Vietnam (after signing a treaty with the USSR) overran Kampuchea and installed a puppet government (a great improvement on the Khmer Rouge). China responded by casting its protection over Thailand, and by invading Vietnam to teach it a 'lesson'. The 'lesson' was militarily unimpressive. China also embarked on a long-run policy of forcing Vietnam to maintain high readiness on its northern border and of channelling support to Kampuchean guerrillas operating out of Thailand, in the hope that 'Vietnam will be tied down and its plan to realise an "Indochina Federation" – a direct menace to Southeast Asia – will be delayed. The longer the delay, the greater will be the consumption of the

---

88. M. Leifer, *Conflict and Regional Order in South-east Asia* (IISS, Adelphi Paper no. 162, 1980) pp.34–5

national strength of Vietnam'.[89] This was a high-risk strategy, since fighting in Kampuchea could easily have spilled over into Thailand; but (one or two episodes apart) Kampuchea and Vietnam showed considerable restraint.

Meanwhile conditions within Vietnam deteriorated. Refugees had been leaving ever since the fall of Saigon; by 1979 they had become a flood,[90] the product of anti-communism, pressure on the ethnic Chinese, and, increasingly, a flight from poverty and hunger. By late 1986 things were serious enough for the Party Congress to be dominated by depressing economic reports and to lead to a major clear-out of the top leadership.[91] Vietnam was now coming under increasing Soviet pressure to leave Kampuchea – something China was insisting on before it would normalise relations with the USSR. The process of withdrawal, and still more of the negotiation of transitional arrangements to succeed the Vietnam-imposed regime, was prolonged. But a settlement was reached in 1991 and UN-monitored elections held in 1993 (though whether these will in fact lead to peace remains to be seen). Another blow was inflicted on Vietnam by the economic difficulties of the Soviet Union, which decided in 1991 to end its subsidy of some 2 billion roubles a year.[92] This finally impelled Hanoi to make its peace with China, and it further underlined the need, which Hanoi had already appreciated, of so conducting itself as to attract investment from the capitalist countries of the rim of Asia. Some progress was made in this direction in 1992; the once-despised ASEAN invited Vietnam (and Laos) to accede to its 1976 Treaty of Amity and Cooperation as a first step towards full membership.[93]

89. Charles McGregor, *The Sino-Vietnamese Relationship and the Soviet Union* (IISS, Adelphi Paper no. 232, 1988) pp.47–8, 52

90. In May–June 1979 over 100,000 'boat people' reached land (while another 35,000 may have drowned in the attempt). In the 1980s some 1.5 million refugees were resettled: *Keesing's*, 30075–83, 36526

91. *Keesing's*, 35067–70, 35899–901

92. *The Independent*, 23 Feb. 1991 p.11

93. *Keesing's*, 38005, 38574, 38729, 1992 R86

CHAPTER NINE
Détente in Europe

In contrast to the bitter, if often clandestine, competition surveyed in the previous chapter, once the Berlin crisis had faded away East–West relations in Europe moved slowly towards accommodation. The running was first made by de Gaulle. His full motives, and in particular the lengths to which he was prepared to push his differences with the United States, remain controversial. Over Berlin, Cuba and the 1960 summit he sided very firmly with the United States; despite talk in 1967–8 about omni-directional defence (*défense 'tous azimuts'*) it is likely that he would always have done so in a crisis. After Cuba, however, he saw the United States as far stronger than the USSR and the threat from the latter as rapidly receding. In these circumstances he felt free to work to modify the international system, and probably enjoyed ruffling Anglo-Saxon susceptibilities while doing so. De Gaulle had always disliked French exclusion from the Yalta and Potsdam summit conferences in 1945; he was among those who saw Yalta as having divided Europe into two blocs, or (as he termed them) 'hegemonies'. French participation in the Western bloc might have been necessary at the time. But it threatened to destroy the independence and identity of the French nation-state, through NATO's supranational control of defence and through the way in which (de Gaulle believed) the international monetary system facilitated the take-over of European by US industry.

'EUROPE FROM THE ATLANTIC TO THE URALS'

Most of de Gaulle's efforts were devoted to extracting France from such dependence (see pp. 393–8). But he was also anxious to transform the Soviet bloc – in two potentially conflicting ways. He sought to improve relations with the USSR itself, recalling the Franco-Russian alliance of the beginning of the century, and talking much of a Europe that extended from the Atlantic to the Urals (and not simply the Elbe). He also cultivated individual East (or, as he preferred to term them, Central) European states, encouraging them to imitate French national self-assertion and evolution away from rigid bloc subordination. In de Gaulle's eyes these two policies were complementary; he sought a general atmosphere of European entente, perhaps reinforced by external US guarantees, within which it would be possible to resolve the difficulties, chiefly over German reunification, that now seemed so daunting. But there was always a danger that French-style self-assertion on the part of some East European states might instead seem a threat to the socialist commonwealth, hence to the security of the Soviet Union and its partners.

Initially, at least, the Soviet Union took a relaxed attitude towards Gaullism, fully appreciating the trouble it was causing in NATO. Brezhnev's 1967 judgement was:

> Have we not succeeded, at no risk to ourselves, in driving a breach through the imperialist camp? De Gaulle is our enemy and we are well aware of it. . . . But look at our achievements! We have weakened the American position in the heart of Europe and this weakening will continue. De Gaulle . . . is aiming for mastery in Europe for himself and in opposition to us. But here we must be flexible. De Gaulle has virtually no chance of realizing his concept because the other West European countries are too powerful and they would never allow it.[1]

Accordingly the USSR was happy to welcome de Gaulle for a most successful visit in 1966 – he was shown the highly secret Baikonur cosmodrome and the launching of a satellite – and to conclude an imposing Joint Declaration. This looked to the development of trade and of scientific and cultural exchanges; it provided for a 'hot line' telecommunications link and for a permanent Franco-Soviet Commission; it agreed 'that the problems of Europe should first of all be discussed within the limits of Europe' to secure the normalisation, and then the gradual development, 'of relations between all

1. Weit, *Eyewitness* p. 140

European countries on the basis of respect for the[ir] independence . . . and non-interference in their internal affairs'. Kosygin returned de Gaulle's visit in December and gained his acceptance of the idea of 'a general European conference to examine problems of security in Europe and the establishment of general European cooperation',[2] a project that bore fruit in the 1970s. There was also agreement on a joint Franco-Soviet standard for colour television, incompatible with that adopted by most of Western Europe. Otherwise it is hard to point to any very tangible consequences of the arrangements de Gaulle established;[3] they continued to operate, but the emphasis placed on them gradually diminished.

The East European aspect of de Gaulle's policy found expression in visits to Poland and Romania in 1967–8.[4] He recalled their historic links and interwar alliances with France, and talked of the need for the nations of 'West, Centre and East' to practise 'the détente, entente, and co-operation which alone will allow Europe to settle its own problems, notably the German problem, [and] to organize its security'. In Poland he emphasised the permanence of its new postwar frontiers, hailing Zabrze (formerly Hindenburg), where he was welcomed by a crowd of 1.5 million, as 'the most Polish of Polish towns'; he praised Romania for following a course in international relations exactly comparable with that of France, and suggested that the two countries 'together set the example for the union of our continent'.

De Gaulle was in fact going too fast for the countries he was visiting. Both stressed the need to recognise two German states, while de Gaulle talked of reunification; both, though more particularly Poland's Gomulka, insisted on the primary importance of their alliance with the USSR and other socialist countries. Later events in 1968 were to confirm the continuing reality of the two European blocs. De Gaulle had to leave Romania early, as the riots and strikes in Paris were getting out of hand; ultimately these were mastered, but they destroyed international confidence in the French currency. Since de Gaulle would not devalue, this became dependent on US and West German support, which restricted his

2. *Keesing's*, 21543–4, 21879
3. It could be that Moscow restrained the French communists during the 1968 riots and strikes, but their moderation may well reflect nothing more than a preference for securing pay rises rather than pushing to the limit and risking forcible repression
4. *Keesing's*, 22339 ff (Poland), 22805 ff (Romania)

diplomatic freedom of manoeuvre. Still more seriously, the Warsaw Pact showed – by invading Czechoslovakia in August 1968 to force the abandonment of its internal reform programme – that it did not share de Gaulle's vision of the dissolution of the blocs back into the sovereign states of which they were composed. Such factors led de Gaulle to moderate, though not abandon, his stance during his remaining time in office. His successors, while retaining the Gaullist legacy of a nuclear deterrent and armed forces not subject to any supranational command, edged slowly back into the main stream of the Western alliance.

WEST GERMAN *OSTPOLITIK* BEFORE 1969

Perhaps the chief consequence of the Gaullist opening towards Eastern Europe was the pressure that it brought on West Germany to follow suit. 'We could not', Brandt explains,[5] 'become the last of the Cold Warriors, the opponents of change and thus, perhaps, the world's leading trouble-makers (and whipping-boys)'. Also the DDR was growing in stature. West German policy under the 'Hallstein Doctrine' had been to break off relations with any country (other than the USSR) that recognised East Germany. Were too many countries to do so, West Germany would itself become isolated; as early as 1965 Ulbricht's visit to Egypt had led (through a vicious spiral dragging in other grievances) to ten Arab states breaking off relations with Bonn.[6] In March 1966 Erhard's CDU–FDP government (a coalition of the Christian Democratic Union and the Free Democratic Party) made overtures to Eastern Europe, offering to still any remaining fears of a West German attack by exchanging undertakings not to settle international disputes by force. But the pace was increased in December when the FDP was replaced, in the governing coalition, by the SPD (the Social Democratic Party, which had always been more favourable to exploring openings to the East). The new Chancellor, Kiesinger, promptly declared an interest in improving cooperation with 'our Eastern neighbours . . ., and even of opening diplomatic relations with them whenever the

5. Brandt, *People and Politics* p.167
6. *Keesing's*, 20737 ff; relations were also broken with Tanzania after it recognised the DDR in 1964: Mayall, *Africa: Cold War and After* p. 145

circumstances allow it'[7] – in other words of suspending the Hallstein Doctrine.

Romania took up the offer; and 1967 also saw a consular agreement with Czechoslovakia, but little further progress was made. One reason was opposition within the Warsaw Pact, notably from the DDR (which probably disliked the improvement of relations with West Germany in any event, and certainly did not wish to see itself isolated by a rush of its allies into Bonn's arms). The Soviet Union was also hostile. The Soviet ambassador had in fact sought out the SPD leader, Willy Brandt, before he entered the Kiesinger government as Foreign Secretary, but thereafter he kept his distance. Indeed in 1967–8 the USSR even claimed that the UN Charter gave it a right of intervention in West Germany to prevent the 'resumption of aggressive policies by a former enemy state'.[8] The claim reflected concern about the emergence of a (small) neo-Nazi National Democratic Party. But it also indicated a distaste for Bonn's new Eastern policy that is usually attributed to a feeling that West Germany was bypassing the USSR and seeking to deal direct with other East European states, thus weakening the Warsaw Pact. Brandt denies any such intention, but Soviet coolness was certainly a fact. When it became necessary to justify the 1968 invasion of Czechoslovakia, much play was made of its alleged penetration by West German revisionists.

There were real obstacles to proceeding further, however; Poland, for instance, was bound to insist on West German acceptance of its 1945 acquisition of Silesia and probably also of the existence of the DDR. But Kiesinger had made it clear that he could not go so far, explaining that only a reunited Germany (i.e. one that had absorbed the DDR) could embark on such border negotiations with Poland. Meanwhile Bonn's official position remained that, since there had been no peace treaty, Germany's frontiers were in international law still those of 1937, that is of the period before Hitler had gone on the rampage, but also before Poland moved to the Oder–Neisse line and expelled most of the local Silesian population. This view of the German question had been built into the Federal Republic's 1949 constitution: in enacting 'this Basic Law . . . for a transitional period' 'the German people in' what became West Germany

7. *Keesing's*, 21802
8. *Keesing's*, 23857

has also acted on behalf of those Germans to whom participation was denied.

The entire German people is called upon to achieve, by free self-determination, the unity and freedom of Germany. [Preamble]

And though the Basic Law had not been explicit on boundaries, it had referred, in the context of nationality, to 'the territory of the German *Reich*, as it existed on 31 December 1937' (Article 116). Departing from this mind-set was not easy – Brandt records that he had himself 'hoped that it might be possible to modify the Oder–Neisse frontier, at least in places'.[9] Although politicians in Bonn could see this was becoming ever less likely, they were under some pressure from refugee organisations, and had little to gain by renouncing the territories 'under Polish administration' unless they in turn received something clearly of benefit to the rest of Germany. Privately in an April 1968 *Foreign Affairs* article, and in his capacity as leader of the SPD, Brandt showed himself more flexible than his coalition partners. From late 1968 the USSR proved rather more forthcoming in official talks with him, in September 1969 proposing negotiations on mutual undertakings not to use force. Discussions through unofficial intermediaries probably went further, though how far subsequently became a matter of political dispute.

BRANDT'S *OSTPOLITIK* 1969–73

In October 1969 Brandt became Chancellor after forming a coalition with the FDP. He says he hoped to facilitate reunion 'by easing the relationship between the two parts of Germany out of its present rigid state',

> leaving open the door for the Germans – and the fact that this may take generations rather than years compels one to add the proviso: if they so desire – to . . . organize their coexistence otherwise than developments have so far enforced upon them.[10]

He immediately declared an interest in opening diplomatic relations with Poland and establishing a *modus vivendi* with the DDR,[11] and he signed the Nuclear Non-Proliferation Treaty (thus

9. Brandt, *People and Politics* p.401
10. Brandt, *People and Politics* pp.237, 238
11. *Keesing's*, 23618, 23701

laying to rest well-ventilated Warsaw Pact fears of a nuclear West Germany). Thereafter events moved fast. Negotiations started in December 1969, and by August 1970 Brandt was able to visit Moscow to sign a treaty promising to regard 'as inviolable' existing frontiers including the Oder–Neisse line and that between the East and West Germany.[12] This opened the way to the conclusion with Poland in December 1970 of a treaty confirming the Oder–Neisse line and renouncing all future teritorial claims; it was accompanied by a Polish promise of rather more generous treatment for members of the remaining German minority wishing to travel or emigrate.[13] The treaty would have been striking in any event; it was made the more so by Brandt's kneeling in silence before the memorial to the Warsaw Ghetto, 'to ask pardon in the name of our people for a million-fold crime which was committed in the misused name of the Germans'.

Equally notable were Brandt's visit as Chancellor in March 1970 to Erfurt in East Germany and the return visit to Kassell of the DDR premier, Stoph. But they were not so successful. In Erfurt Brandt's popularity proved embarrassingly greater than Stoph's, while the Kassell visit was marred by the fighting of right and left-wing extremists, 1920s style, and the ominous chant,

Volksverräter[14] Hand in Hand,
Willi Stoph und Willy Brandt!

Nor were their talks initially productive. That autumn, though, negotiations started at a lower level. The following spring (1971) saw the replacement of Ulbricht as leader of the DDR's ruling party by the more flexible Honecker – partly, it has always been assumed, through Soviet pressure. Discussions were still difficult; much time was spent determining whether the term 'ties' (between West Berlin and West Germany) in the September 1971 Four Power Agreement on Berlin should be rendered in German as *Bindungen* or *Verbindungen*. Probably after another intervention by Brezhnev, December 1971 saw the conclusion of a DDR–West German transit agreement governing access to West Berlin (in implementation of the Four Power Agreement), May 1972 a broader Traffic Treaty.

12. *Keesing's*, 24144. Next year, on the conclusion of the Four Power Berlin agreement, Brezhnev invited him again – to his Black Sea villa, a gesture of some warmth
13. *Keesing's*, 24346; C.C. Schweitzer and others (eds) (Detler Karsten, Robert Spencer, R. Taylor Cole, Donald Kommers, Anthony Nicholls), *Politics and Government in the Federal Republic of Germany, Basic Documents* (1984) p.410
14. Betrayers of the Nation

Meanwhile Honecker had indicated a readiness for a more general settlement, which took the form in December 1972 of a 'Treaty on the Bases of Relations' between the two states.[15] This provided, 'without prejudice to [their] differing concepts . . . on fundamental questions, including the national question', for the development of 'normal good-neighbourly relations . . . on the basis of equality of rights'; in 1973 both countries joined the United Nations, and in 1974 they established 'permanent representative missions' in each other's capitals.

In pushing these negotiations West Germany had been acting largely on its own initiative; in Kissinger's words, 'the new German government informed rather than consulted'. Kissinger was at first seriously concerned. The negotiations might give the Soviet Union leverage over German and hence European policy. But the chief dangers were longer range; Brandt should not (Kissinger wrote in February 1970) initially

> have any serious difficulty in maintaining his basic pro- Western policy . . .
>
> But assuming Brandt achieves a degree of normalization, he or his successor may discover that the hoped-for benefits fail to develop. . . . [Kissinger himself thought *Ostpolitik* more likely to lead to a permanent division of Germany than to promote ultimate reunion] Having already invested heavily in their Eastern policy, the Germans may at this point see themselves as facing agonizing choices . . . [and the 1950s] kind of debate about Germany's basic position [between East and West] could well recur in more divisive form, not only inflaming German domestic affairs but generating suspicions among Germany's Western associates as to its reliability as a partner.[16]

Eventually Kissinger did reach, and press on the more sceptical Nixon, the view that Brandt had been right to open negotiations (since a continuation of earlier policies would only have isolated the Federal Republic). But in any case to have tried to prevent Brandt would have been explosive, and the United States really had no option but to go along with his initiative and try to put it to good account.

As things turned out, its spillover effects were decidedly helpful. For most of the diplomatic questions of the day proved to be interlinked – Kissinger talks at one point of three-dimensional chess. From the West German point of view, the recognition of the Oder–Neisse line and of the DDR had been concessions, acceptable

15. *Keesing's*, 25621–2
16. Kissinger, *Memoirs* i pp.408–11, 529–30

only if they led to a satisfactory settlement of the Berlin question. Yet Berlin was not part of the Federal Republic; so agreement would have to be reached between the Four occupying Powers, more especially between the Soviet Union and the United States. The USSR needed a success to secure West German ratification of the *Ostpolitik* treaties and agreement to attend a European Security Conference (a gathering the Warsaw Pact had been advocating since 1966). The United States thus gained a degree of leverage, which it was able to use in its bilateral dealings with the Soviet Union (notably over the ABM and SALT negotiations). It derived further benefit, after mid-1971, from its sudden ability to get on terms with its former arch-enemy China, and from the desire of the USSR (now China's principal opponent) to present itself to the USA as a far more valuable partner.

Kissinger claims that the breakthrough came in January 1971.[17] Negotiations over Berlin had already started, but they were not making much progress. US–Soviet relations in 1970 were beset with many problems (crises in September over an apparent Syrian invasion of Jordan and the attempt to establish a Soviet SLBM base in Cuba, several lesser frictions, and a loss of momentum associated with the Moscow power struggle in which Brezhnev displaced Kosygin from the management of foreign policy). In December 1970 Brandt complained to Washington about the slow pace of the Berlin talks in terms that convinced the USA that something would have to be done. Next month Nixon secured Soviet acceptance of simultaneous negotiations (through the Kissinger–Dobrynin backchannel) on Berlin and on ABM/SALT with the aim of completion that summer. The Berlin talks, eased probably by West German and perhaps French initiatives of which Kissinger was unaware, more or less met this target. September 1971 saw a Four Power Agreement on Berlin that embodied minor Western concessions (a slight reduction of the Federal German presence in West Berlin and the opening there of a Soviet Consulate-General) and major Eastern ones (a *Soviet* guarantee that civilian access to Berlin would not be impeded, and acceptance of West German representation internationally of West Berliners).[18] Naturally the USSR had at first tried for more, but the basic premiss of the 1970–2 *Ostpolitik* settlement

17. ibid, pp.800 ff
18. Brandt's intercession with Brezhnev was needed to gain agreement that West Berliners might travel in the East on a (specially endorsed) West German passport: Brandt, *People and Politics* p.391

was the recognition of facts, and if the Oder–Neisse line and East Germany were 'Eastern' facts, West Berlin was a 'Western' one.

It remained to secure ratification of the treaties West Germany had signed. The incentives to ratify were considerable, as refusal would sink the Berlin Agreement and East–West détente, and would infuriate Germany's allies. So it is remarkable that Brandt's government encountered such difficulty. Indeed it almost collapsed as a result of parliamentary defections: in April 1972 a motion to overturn it failed by only two votes. There followed intensive negotiations, but the Opposition still abstained when the treaties were ratified in May, and the crisis led Brandt to the unprecedented step of forcing premature parliamentary elections. In November 1972 these gave the SPD its best ever result, which suggests that there was more support for *Ostpolitik* among the electorate than in the political class. In 1973 the ratification of the 'Basic Treaty' with East Germany was rather easier.

CONSEQUENCES OF *OSTPOLITIK*

Ostpolitik's human consequences are clear. As Brandt proudly claims, it again became possible for West Berliners to telephone and visit the Eastern part of the city, and the number of West Germans visiting the DDR doubled between 1970 and 1975, as did that travelling overland to Berlin; East Germany, however, maintained its controls on emigration. Trade with Eastern Europe also trebled in these years (though it still accounted in 1981 for only 5–6 per cent of all West German trade).[19] These gains gave West Germany a real stake in détente and contributed to a certain modification of its international stance. The prospect of such a modification may have represented one of *Ostpolitik's* attractions to the USSR. Just as Brandt reasoned that only in an atmosphere of détente could any progress be made towards German reunification, so Brezhnev may, after the failure of so much ferocious bluster, have been inclined to try the effect of a little sunshine in inducing West Germany to doff its Cold War coat.

Certainly in the Adenauer era Bonn had always favoured a resolute policy; it was usually dove-ish tendencies in the USA that had produced German–American friction. But when East–West

19. Schweitzer, *Politics and Government in Germany* pp.413–4

relations started to deteriorate in the later 1970s, the boot was on the other foot: in 1977 Chancellor Schmidt urged in Washington more responsiveness to the 'good Brezhnev who is promoting détente and who needs our help'. Much of the friction between Bonn and Washington at this time stemmed from the mutual dislike of the German and American leaders. But President Carter also related it to policy, commenting in 1980 that West Germany 'opposes any sanctions against Iran or Soviets, are continuing business as usual with S[oviet] U[nion], refuse to commit publicly to Olympic boycott, and privately and in press are very critical of us'.[20]

Probably the Americans exaggerated. Schmidt may have been reluctant to jeopardise good relations in Europe because of US–Soviet quarrels over extra-European issues, thus raising the question of whether détente was divisible. But West Germany was in fact one of the few countries to follow the USA in boycotting the 1980 Moscow Olympic Games in protest over the Russian invasion of Afghanistan. Schmidt had also taken very seriously the implications of the Soviet military build-up, being one of the leading promoters of the decision to deploy cruise and Pershing missiles to counter it.

This decision, however, was one of the factors that brought to a peak, in the early 1980s, the internal debate Kissinger had feared on where West Germany really stood. For leftist opposition to the missiles readily assumed a nationalist form – deployment was not in 'German interests' – and established contacts with a new autonomous Christian peace movement in East Germany. Such feelings, together with environmental concerns, contributed to the successful launching of a new (if small) 'Green' party hostile to continued membership of NATO. Similar tendencies grew within the SPD, aided by several senior politicians including Brandt himself; when the SPD–FDP coalition unravelled in 1982 (over economic issues), Schmidt was no longer able to check them. The parliamentary elections early next year were bitter, and were marked by US pressure to accept and Soviet to reject missile deployment. The CDU–FDP government was confirmed in office by a large majority, which ensured that deployment would go ahead.

Fortuitously 1983 was the fifth centenary of the birth of Martin Luther; there were celebrations in both Germanies, but more especially in the East where he had actually lived. These focused public attention on a common German heritage; and they must

---

20. Zbigniew Brzezinski, *Power and Principle: Memoirs of the National Security Adviser 1977–1981* (paperback, New York 1985) pp.461–3

have been very welcome to Chancellor Kohl, one of whose chief concerns was to remind the world of what he saw as the continuing unnatural division of a single German nation. The reminder was needed. For foreign opinion (which had always had reservations about German reunification) had come to expect that, now that both were internally consolidated and externally recognised, East and West Germany would gradually grow apart and come to see each other as distinct states – as do Germany and Austria. This expectation collapsed soon after the 1989 upheavals in East Germany and the opening of the Berlin Wall. Already in November Kohl was calling for free elections in the DDR, and he soon started to push for rapid reunion, not only (no doubt) by way of striking when the iron was hot, but also to prevent economic collapse in the East unleashing a flood of migrants into West Germany. Accordingly monetary union between the two states, mooted in February 1990 to take effect by the end of 1992, was in place by July 1990. Political unity was achieved by October 1990; in the December elections (before the full costs of the process were apparent) the SPD was punished for its persistent coolness towards it. However, if Kohl had forced reunion through (overruling Bundesbank advice as to its financial implications), he had also stood very firmly behind the other aspects of Adenauer's legacy, insisting that Germany remain in NATO and declaring that unification would 'accelerate, not constrain' the 'unstoppable current' towards the economic and political union of the European Community.[21] The sudden bursting of German reunion on to the international agenda had reawakened in a number of quarters fears that it was not politically correct to voice openly. It took a certain amount of pressure to extract from Kohl an unqualified acceptance of the Oder–Neisse line.[22] Otherwise German politicians did their best to set all such fears at rest by stressing the Federal Republic's unchanged orientation, and made a virtue of it domestically: 'Vote', the FDP exhorted in December 1990, 'for the Germany the world trusts'.

21. *Keesing's*, 37025, 37259–60, 37303, 37536, 37827, 37904
22. This was finally and definitively confirmed by the November 1990 Polish-German treaty – *Keesing's*, 37260, 37302, 37867, 38306, 38536–7

The United States, China and the World

US ATTITUDES TO CHINA 1950–68

If one of the most hopeful symbols of the 1970s was Brandt's visit to Warsaw, another was Nixon's 1972 journey to China and reception by Chairman Mao, 'the week', as Nixon immodestly put it, 'that changed the world'.

Sino-American relations in the 1950s had been very bad, and at the rhetorical level the Americans and the Chinese were each other's worst enemies. From the Chinese perspective this was natural enough: the United States was the world's leading imperialist power (in the Marxist sense of the word) and its fleet preserved the Kuomintang regime on Taiwan. The Americans too had their reasons. Much bitterness had been generated by the Chinese intervention in Korea and ill will towards the People's Republic ran deep: Eisenhower told Kennedy that the only development that would lead him to return to active politics after he had left office would be the prospect of Red China entering the UN.[1] Such hostility was not merely instinctive. Dulles believed that 'the best way to get a separation between the Soviet Union and Communist China is to keep the pressure on Communist China and make its way difficult as long as it is in partnership with Soviet Russia'. In December 1953 he briefed the Western Bermuda summit on his hopes that 'pressure and strain would compel' Beijing 'to make more demands on the USSR which the latter would be unable to meet and the strain would consequently increase'. For, as NSC 166/1 had just put it with Eisenhower's approval,

1. Schlesinger, *A Thousand Days* p.423

As the inevitable differences in interest, viewpoint, or timing . . . develop between the Russians and the Chinese; as the Chinese tend to become importunate in their demands for Russian assistance or support; or as the role of the Chinese as viceregents for international communism in the Far East becomes too independent and self reliant – there will be strong temptation for the Russians to attempt to move in the direction of greater disciplinary control over the Chinese Communists. If the time ever comes when the Russians feel impelled to contest with the Chinese Communist leaders for primacy in the domestic apparatus of control of the Chinese regime, the alliance will be critically endangered. For . . . the Chinese Communist leaders are Chinese as well as Communists.

This policy underlay the hard American line during the Chinese offshore islands crises (see pp. 139–41 and 209–10). By late 1958 intelligence reports were leading Eisenhower to wonder whether 'the Soviets were not really becoming concerned about Communist China as a possible threat to them in the future', while in 1959 Dulles felt that 'you could very well have a struggle between . . . Mao Tse-tung and Khrushchev as to who would be the ideological leader of International Communism'.[2]

But if the USA anticipated trouble between China and the USSR its ideas as to how this could be turned to its own advantage were less developed.[3] Gromyko says that in mid-1959 he was sounded as to the possibility of US–Soviet cooperation against the 'yellow peril', but refused to be drawn. In the early 1960s the Sino-Soviet split came into the open (see pp. 435–6): the Kennedy administration inclined towards the Soviet side. Even in 1961 briefing for the Vienna summit suggested that, by emphasising the Chinese threat to both countries, Kennedy might gain Soviet agreement to help restrain China within a 'stable viable world order'. Vienna, of course, produced no such meeting of minds. But, as US–Soviet relations improved in 1963, the idea returned. The US embassy in Moscow attributed Khrushchev's acceptance of the Test Ban Treaty to 'the outbreak of virtually undeclared war between Moscow and Peiping'. Harriman was directed to broach with Khrushchev during the negotiations (perhaps using the bait of concessions over Germany) 'means of limiting or preventing Chinese nuclear development and his willingness either to take Soviet action or to accept

---

2. Immerman, *Dulles and the Diplomacy of the Cold War* pp.60–3; Gaddis, *The Long Peace* pp.174–87

3. In 1955 Dulles hoped eventually for 'sufficient independence between Peiping [Beijing] and Moscow as to create the beginnings of a balance of power relationship'. Given such Sino-Soviet hostility and a gradual revival of Japanese power, the USA would no longer have to be quite so involved in the Far East

US action aimed in this direction' that might require 'use of military force'. Khrushchev did not respond, but the issue was revived in 1964 as it became clear that China was about to conduct its first nuclear test. In September the Johnson administration decided against unilateral US military action to prevent it, but felt there were 'many possibilities for joint action with the Soviet Government if that Government is interested. Such possibilities include a warning to the Chinese against tests, a possible undertaking to give up underground testing and to hold the Chinese accountable if they test in any way, and even a possible agreement to cooperate in preventive military action'. The question was to be explored with the Soviet ambassador, but nothing had come of it by the time of Khrushchev's dismissal, and his successors' first thought was rather to improve Sino-Soviet relations.[4]

The Kennedy administration had been obsessed with the importance of guerrilla warfare in the Third World. Mao had both written on and practised such warfare (against the Japanese and the Chinese Nationalists), and China certainly trumpeted these experiences as a model. The USA was determined to demonstrate otherwise. In South-East Asia, Rusk claimed, 'the international community confronts a question that affects . . . every continent: shall this form of external aggression be allowed to succeed?' In Korea the 'international community [had] proved that overt aggression was unprofitable'; now it was necessary to show in Vietnam that 'semi-covert aggression across international boundaries cannot succeed'. Were this done, he later told the Senate, the militant Chinese approach would be discredited and the correctness of Soviet-style peaceful coexistence confirmed. Then, when Beijing stopped using force and abandoned its stategy for achieving revolution, 'we would welcome an era of good relations'.

Rusk himself appears initially to have favoured tying China with 'little threads' that might eventually draw it back into the community of nations; but the only overture made – feelers about food relief for its disastrous 1961 famine – was rebuffed.[5] Other ideas of a possible route to reconciliation centred on a 'Two Chinas' policy, with UN membership for both China and Taiwan. This would actually have been anathema to Beijing, but it was not attempted since Kennedy adjudged it politically unacceptable in the USA. In the early 1950s the China lobby's resentment of Truman's

---

4. Gordon Chang, 'JFK, China and the Bomb', *Journal of American History* lxxiv (1987–8) esp. pp.1289, 1,296–1,308; Schlesinger, *A Thousand Days* pp.771–2, 775–6

5. Warren I. Cohen, *Dean Rusk* (Totowa, NJ, 1980) pp.164, 247, 287

'betrayal' of Chiang Kai-shek had been one of the strongest forces in Congress; both Kennedy and Johnson were fearful of reviving it.

Although mutual hostility ran very high, there were no serious Chinese–American clashes in the 1960s despite US involvement in Vietnam. Nobody wanted to repeat the Korean experience. So China approached the USA, via France, in 1965, and agreed not to provoke war provided the USA abstained from invading North Vietnam, from destroying its Red River dams, and from attacking the Chinese border. The understanding was signalled by apparently unilateral public statements on both sides early in 1966, and was adhered to even though five US planes were shot down over or near southern China in May 1967.[6] But neither side seems to have sought any overt rapprochement. From 1966 to 1968 China was absorbed in the internal power struggle of the 'Cultural Revolution', which spilled over into the rabbling of foreign embassies and other scenes that gave the rest of the world little reason to seek dealings with it.

SINO-AMERICAN RAPPROCHEMENT 1968–72

The end of the decade saw a startling transformation. On the American side this was partly due to Johnson's 1968 decision to begin winding down the Vietnam War (which led China to conclude that the USA was no longer an expanding power in Asia), but chiefly to the election that November of Richard Nixon. Nixon believed the USA to be overcommitted, and was anxious to recover freedom of manoeuvre by ending what he saw as unnecessary quarrels (whether with Gaullist France or with China). He also says that he was encouraged by a number of Asian leaders to regard a new Sino-American relationship as a prerequisite for lasting peace in Asia after the end of the Vietnam War. He signalled this, cryptically in an October 1967 *Foreign Affairs* article, more plainly in an interview after his nomination in 1968 as Republican presidential candidate.[7] In so doing, Nixon knew he had one great advantage: as a former hardline conservative he was much less likely

6. K. Ito and M. Shibata, 'The Dilemma of Mao Tse-tung', *China Quarterly*, xxv (July–Sept. 1968), p.67n; T.M. Gottlieb, *Chinese Foreign Policy Factionalism and the Origins of the Strategic Triangle* (Rand, Santa Monica, Calif., 1977) pp.5–6, 18n, 57
7. 'We must always seek opportunities to talk with' China; 'We must not only watch for changes. We must seek to make changes': Kissinger, *Memoirs* i p.164

to encounter opposition at home from the right. Nixon had already spoken to the Romanian leader Ceauşescu, who had close contact with China, about normalising relations with the People's Republic after the Vietnam War. Once elected, Nixon started putting out feelers through several channels, of which the most immediately effective was the French.

Chinese politics are more opaque. It seems that, by late 1968, both Mao and Zhou had concluded that the Soviet Union was more dangerous than the United States. The USA was apparently seeking to withdraw from Vietnam; the USSR had just intervened in Czechoslovakia to displace a communist government not of its liking, and might well interfere in China, if not by direct invasion (though this could not be excluded) at least by supporting Chinese political factions ready to 'take the fortress from within'. In October 1968 Mao is supposed to have referred to the USSR, for the first time, as China's primary enemy, and in November China proposed the resumption of the Warsaw ambassadorial talks with the USA in February to 'conclude an agreement on the Five Principles of Peaceful Coexistence'. By February 1969 Nixon would (just) have assumed office, and China perhaps looked for some spectacular gesture. None was forthcoming, and China cancelled the talks at short notice.[8] But for the rest of the year events went the United States' way.

In March 1969 the Chinese Army seems to have ambushed a Soviet patrol on the disputed border island of Chenbao/Damansky. A fortnight later the Russians retaliated. Kosygin then sought border negotiations, but was allegedly treated with deliberate rudeness, the Beijing hot line operator declaring, 'You are a revisionist, and therefore I will not connect you'.[9] Soviet pressure followed in the form of border incidents (whose geographical location convinced Kissinger that the USSR, not as he had previously believed China, was the aggressor). The summer saw, on the one hand, a number of US gestures and messages of goodwill to China, and, on the other, tough Soviet military speeches and manoeuvres. Soviet diplomats also conducted soundings – that were presumably intended to leak – about the possibility of a preventive attack on Chinese nuclear installations. It is not clear whether this was just meant to intimidate, or whether (like Eisenhower's similarly diffuse talk in 1953 of escalation were no Korean armistice reached) it was

---

8. Gottlieb, *Chinese Foreign Policy Factionalism* pp.26–7, 98, 114
9. Nixon, *Memoirs* p.568

a real threat. Certainly there is the view that the USSR sought US participation in (or sympathy for) a real nuclear attack.[10] The administration appears to have taken the possibility seriously, Nixon telling the National Security Council that it was not in US interests to let China be 'smashed', while lesser spokesmen said the same in public in more elliptical language. In September 1969 Kosygin managed, with great difficulty, to arrange talks with Zhou at Beijing airport (on his way back from Ho Chi Minh's funeral), but they did not go well: the Chinese say Kosygin flaunted Soviet superiority, while they declared that hostility would last for thousands of years. Tension remained high for the next month, with Victor Louis (a Soviet journalist with good official connections) speculating in the *London Evening News* on the possibility of war or of anti-Mao forces in China appealing for Soviet 'fraternal help'.[11] In October China finally accepted border talks, but these made absolutely no progress. In December 1969 Kissinger thought that the Russians would probably attack China by April, and he soon had his staff draft plans for that contingency.[12]

Against this background the Chinese asked in December for *public* ambassadorial contacts in Warsaw. By January 1970 Zhou was hinting that the USA should send a top official to Beijing for talks. Arranging such a visit was still far from easy, and was to be delayed by the US incursion into Cambodia in April (which China was bound to condemn). More seriously there was resistance within China to the idea of accommodation with the USA, which may have lain behind the attempt in July 1970 to shoot down an offshore US spy plane. Still by December–January 1970–1 the Chinese were indicating readiness to receive not merely a top official but Nixon himself; it was due largely to American caution that the first visit was made in secret by his Security Adviser, Henry Kissinger, in July 1971. It was a great success, Kissinger being much taken with Zhou's charm and intelligence, while the two found sufficient common geopolitical ground in their lengthy surveys of the inter-

10. The most dramatic account is in H.R. Haldeman with Joseph Di Mona, *The Ends of Power* (1978) pp.89 ff. Powers accepts it with qualifications (*The Man who Kept the Secrets* pp.267, 455) and Zhou Enlai gave a very similar account to Joseph Alsop, 'Thoughts out of China . . . – Go versus No Go', *New York Times* 11 March 1973 Magazine pp.31, 100–2. See also Barron, *KGB* pp.3–4, 179

11. Kissinger, *Memoirs* i chaps. 6, 18; H.C. Hinton, *The Sino-Soviet Confrontation* (New York, 1976) pp.16–21, 37; Clare Hollingworth, *Mao* (paperback edn, 1967) p.227

12. Haldeman, *The Ends of Power* p.89 (citing his 10 December log); Kissinger, *Memoirs* i pp.781–2

national scene. Kissinger's return was followed by the immediate announcement of a prospective Nixon visit.

This seems to have brought internal Chinese resistance to a head. In part it was simply a power struggle. Mao invariably fell out with his number twos: one purpose of the Cultural Revolution had been to liquidate the overpowerful and pragmatic Liu Shaoqui, and the Army chief Lin Biao (who had succeeded Liu as Mao's heir) seems to have sensed that this was about to happen again. Accordingly he attempted in September 1971 to assassinate Mao and take over, then when the plot failed fled towards the Soviet Union, dying in a plane crash on the way. After the event he was accused of having been in touch with the USSR for some time, and of having been ready to seek (and pay for) Soviet military intervention in support of the coup. He is also said to have included in his secret listing of Mao's failings the move away from the 'sane socialists in the Soviet Union' towards the 'corrupt capitalists and imperialists' in Washington. There may be an element of exaggeration in all this.[13] But the episode occasioned substantial upheaval – Taiwan reported 37,000 arrests in the armed forces – and had the effect of consolidating the tilt towards the USA, approval of which Mao was always careful to signal by personally receiving Kissinger and later Nixon. In October 1971 Kissinger returned to negotiate a communiqué,[14] which surfaced as the 'Shanghai Communiqué' in February 1972 when Nixon finally made his triumphant and much televised tour. It stressed the desirability of 'progress towards normalization of relations'. This did not imply immediate US recognition of the People's Republic, but in 1973 'liaison offices' were established in Beijing and Washington. The communiqué also brought US acceptance in principle that 'there is but one China and that Taiwan is a part of China', and an undertaking to reduce US forces on Taiwan. Finally the USA and China agreed to oppose efforts by 'any country' (i.e. the USSR) to establish 'hegemony' in the Asia–Pacific region; this was the common interest that had brought the two together.

---

13. The charges are based on reconstituted captured documents: – *Keesing's*, 25635–6, 30834–5; Hollingworth, *Mao* chap. 13

14. Text in Kissinger, *Memoirs* i pp. 1,490–2

CHINA'S NEW ALIGNMENT AND ITS CONSEQUENCES

Kissinger's original draft of the communiqué had, he says, been innocuous; it was immediately rejected, on Mao's instructions, as the sort of banality the Soviets would sign but never observe. Instead the communiqué – even after Kissinger had secured the excision of declarations like 'revolution has become the irresistible trend of history' – firmly stated the two countries' diametrically opposed views on a wide range of issues. This probably made it easier to explain within China, where the opening to the USA was justified in strictly tactical terms. Zhou's December 1971 report on the international situation began by declaring that the general aim was 'to promote war and further revolution', but explains that 'At this stage it is necessary to take full advantage of the contradiction between the U.S. and USSR and to magnify it'; in 1973 he cited, as authority for opposing 'chiefly the most direct, the most perilous and the most practical enemy, Soviet revisionist social-imperialism', Mao's dictum, 'We must not fight two-sidedly, it is better to fight one-sidedly'. In 1975 the Foreign Minister told cadres that one must

> carry out revolution continuously in stages. The former is . . . the goal, and the latter . . . the means . . . Just think, if we were to employ all the socialist force to combat the combined forces of imperialism, revisionism, and reaction, we would gain no more advantage than if an egg were used to strike a stone. But if the socialist force is united together to . . . swallow the enemies one by one, our strength will outdo any one of them individually.[15]

Nevertheless it seems that in moving towards the United States China did de facto shift towards the maintenance of the international status quo, albeit unevenly in different areas. In the developed world the shift, and China's subsequent internal evolution after Mao's death, gradually destroyed its appeal to the ultra-left (so strong in the later 1960s) as the mecca of revolution. Instead Beijing played host to rightist politicians and was prodigal with its advice:

> The Soviet Union, Mao said, wanted world domination, and if their drive was ever to be stopped, the United States would have to stand up to them. That was why the U.S. would have to remain strong in the Pacific basin. . . . Would we do anything to challenge the

15. Institute of International Relations, National Chengchi University, Republic of China, *Classified Chinese Communist Documents: A Selection* (Taipei, 1978) pp.477, 480, 491, 559

Soviet–Cuban threat in Africa? When was the United States going to strengthen ties with its NATO allies? Were we going to continue helping our traditional friends in Asia?

Once Mao had argued within the communist world that Khrushchev's soft policy towards imperialism was more risky than firm confrontation; now he stressed the dangers of détente and appeasement: 'As for the Soviet Union, they bully the weak, and are afraid of the strong'.[16]

In Africa (other than Rhodesia/Zimbabwe) and in West Asia China largely withdrew from the support of insurrectionary movements. In South-East Asia China was slower to discontinue support for subversion. During 1971–3 there was a substantial increase in the supply of arms to Thai guerrillas. Later this did fall away, and (as we shall see) China even moved to protect Thailand from Vietnam; but it felt moral difficulty in disengaging, and seems to have permitted South-East Asian Communist parties to broadcast from Chinese territory at least until 1980, which earned it the continuing suspicion of some (not all) ASEAN countries.[17]

As for the Vietnam War, détente with China gave Nixon confidence that he could, as part of his tortuous disengagement, bomb Hanoi far more ferociously in 1972 than Johnson had ever dared. China also encouraged Hanoi to conclude a cease-fire with the United States and so secure the withdrawal of US troops, and even advised a period of consolidation after the 1973 cease-fire before resuming the attack on the Thieu regime. China stepped up its economic aid, however, and (up till 1972) continued to offer help with the construction of the Ho Chi Minh Trail.[18] China also identified firmly with the Sihanouk–Khmer Rouge coalition opposing the Cambodian government. According to Kissinger it was in mid-1973 on the point of moving to secure a compromise settlement when Congress destroyed the American negotiating position by forcing an end to US bombing.[19] Be that as it may, China then

16. President Gerald Ford's account of an interview (after the fall of South Vietnam): *A Time to Heal* (1979) p.336; Kissinger, *Memoirs* ii p.694

17. J.L.S. Girling, *Thailand. Society and Politics* (paperback edn, 1985) p.269; A. James Gregor, *The China Connection. US Policy and the People's Republic of China* (Stanford, Calif., 1986) p.191; Mahathir Mohamad (Prime Minister of Malaysia) in *Far Eastern Economic Review*, 30 Oct. 1981 pp.34–5

18. Ministry of Foreign Affairs, Socialist Republic of Vietnam, *The Truth about Vietnam–China Relations over the Last Thirty Years* (Hanoi, 1979) pp.41–2, 46–9; Hoang Van Hoan, 'Distortion of Facts about Militant Friendship between Vietnam and China is Impermissible', *Beijing Review*, 7 Dec. 1979 p.19. The difference between the two accounts lies less in the realm of facts than in the attribution of motives. But the former does quote Haig to the effect that in October 1973 the Chinese advised Kissinger 'not to allow yourselves to be defeated in Vietnam'

19. Kissinger, *Memoirs* ii pp.349–69

reverted to a full endorsement of the Khmer Rouge, a position it maintained despite both the barbarity of their rule after they came to power in 1975 and their support for Thai guerrillas. But then the Khmer Rouge had what was by the later 1970s the cardinal virtue in Chinese eyes, that of being anti-Vietnamese.

In the more general power equation, détente with China helped the USA reduce its armed forces; to China's distress, American capacity was allowed to drop from a '2½' to a '1½ war' capability.[20] Meanwhile the USSR maintained up to one-third of its army on the Chinese border, and people often suggested that, had it not felt the need to do so, its military preponderance within Europe would have been still greater. Perhaps. But it is equally possible that, without the requirement to keep troops in the east, the overall Soviet defence effort would have been that much smaller. In any case the build-up of Soviet forces in Asia had been a feature of the 1960s, and had long antedated Sino-American détente. Nor arc the diplomatic consequences of the Chinese shift clear. The Nixon administration felt it derived considerable advantage from having better relations with both China and the Soviet Union than they had with each other. Certainly the Soviet Union which had been stalling on a summit up to July 1971 in the hope of extracting further concessions, started pressing for one as soon as Nixon's invitation to Beijing was announced.[21] For some time thereafter it sought to conciliate the USA to try to win it over to the joint management of the Chinese problem, but after 1974 the USSR must have realised that this would not work.

IMPLICATIONS FOR JAPAN

What can be said is that the new Sino-American relationship smoothed both China's emergence as a major diplomatic player and Japan's adjustment to this. In the long run non-recognition of the largest country in the world was bound to seem increasingly artificial. In 1964 'With' (in de Gaulle's words) 'the weight of evidence and reason making itself felt more and more every day',[22]

20. In response to Chinese criticism, Defense Secretary Brown 'pointed out that the other war plan had been designed for use against the People's Republic': Carter, *Keeping Faith* pp.192–3
21. Kissinger, *Memoirs* i pp.759, 766
22. *Keesing's*, 19878

France had decided to recognise the People's Republic, becoming the forty-eighth country to do so. The Cultural Revolution slowed the process down, but with the restoration of order it resumed, Canada, Italy, Ethiopia and Equatorial Guinea according recognition in 1970. The announcement that Nixon would visit China must have accelerated things; in the autumn of 1971 (against US wishes) the United Nations unseated the Nationalist and admitted a Communist Chinese delegation. Japan had every reason to be upset. It had not been consulted before the secret Kissinger visit to China; it had dutifully played a leading role in managing the anti-Beijing group in the UN. It now feared the improvement of Sino-American relations over its head, and moved rapidly to join in. In August 1972 the new Prime Minister, Tanaka, secured an invitation to Beijing, and in October the two countries issued a joint declaration and established diplomatic relations.

Historically much of Japanese culture had come from China, and the Japanese had felt (even in the 1930s, though its tangible manifestation had then been horribly skewed) a strong affinity with the Chinese. Since 1945 Japan had also established a special relationship with the United States, the provider of protection, the major market, and an important cultural model. The price of this relationship had been a breach with the People's Republic. Now the way was open for Japan to enjoy good relations with both countries at once. Indeed China's anxiety to contain the USSR led it to commend the US–Japanese alliance it had once so warmly attacked, to lecture Kissinger on how best to manage it, and to stress the dangers for Japan's politics of forcing it to choose between China and the USA.[23] (China also made itself useful to Japan by supplying oil at the time of the 1973–4 Arab embargo.)

The Sino-Japanese-American triangle was further consolidated by the heavy-handedness of the other major East Asian power, the USSR. Tanaka had initially intended to conclude peace treaties with both China and the Soviet Union at much the same time. But in 1972–6 Soviet–Japanese negotiations always bogged down over the Japanese demand for the restoration of four of the Kuril islands that the USSR had occupied in 1945. Nor did talks about Japanese development of Siberian oilfields go well.[24] In addition the Russians became, as the Japanese put it, 'obsessed' with the clause China

23. Kissinger, *Memoirs* ii p.293
24. G.L. Curtis, 'The Tyumen Oil Development Project and Japanese Foreign Policy Decision Making' in R.A. Scalapino (ed.), *The Foreign Policy of Modern Japan* (Berkeley, Calif., 1977) pp.147–73; *Keesing's*, 25625, 27384, 27599

insisted in putting into any Sino-Japanese peace treaty to the effect that neither state 'should seek hegemony in the Asia-Pacific region . . . [and] each is opposed to efforts by any other country . . . to establish such hegemony'.[25] Though this was undoubtedly meant to annoy, as Japan pointed out, it committed her to nothing, and the USSR was unwise to weigh in with heavy warnings. Japanese reluctance to sign the clause delayed the conclusion of a formal peace treaty with China until 1978. But in the absence of any Soviet counter-incentives, Japan then gave way (with US encouragement); the USSR retaliated by largely freezing relations.

CHINA AND VIETNAM IN THE 1970s; THE 1979 WAR

The later 1970s saw the deepening of China's links with the West. President Carter was anxious to establish full diplomatic relations (which necessarily entailed breaking off formal relations, and ending the defence treaty, with Taiwan). But his offer involved China's accepting the continuance both of arms sales to Taiwan and of de facto US–Taiwan relations through an 'American Institute'. Such acceptance was not easy, but was facilitated by the collapse of Chinese relations with Vietnam. Indeed the late 1978 Central Committee meeting that decided to accept US terms for the normalisation of relations also decided on military action to teach Vietnam a lesson.[26]

The collapse of Sino-Vietnamese relations is, with hindsight, unsurprising. Kissinger says the North Vietnamese generally began negotiations by recounting 'the epic of Vietnam's struggle for independence through the centuries . . . The heroic saga of how the Vietnamese defeated all foreigners'; most of these foreigners, as Hanoi's History Museum made clear, were Chinese.[27] During the war with South Vietnam, Hanoi naturally tried to keep on good terms with both its sources of aid, China and the USSR. But the USSR could give more, and the Vietnamese Politburo inclined increasingly towards it. By the end of the war friction with China was already evident: in 1974 China seized the Paracel Islands from South Vietnam and claimed the Spratlies (the area probably

25. *Keesing's*, 29279–80
26. Carter, *Keeping Faith* pp.197–8; King C. Chen, *China's War with Vietnam* (Stanford, Calif., 1987) pp.85–9
27. Kissinger, *Memoirs* i p.281, ii p.28

contains oil), while in 1975 Hanoi scrambled to garrison the Spratlies and then claimed the Paracels.[28] More seriously, as the non-communist governments in Laos and Cambodia fell, Vietnam made sure of its pre-eminence in the one, China in the other. Further trouble stemmed from the position of the ethnic Chinese in Vietnam. Initially they were perhaps persecuted as capitalists (most had lived in the South), but by 1978 simply as Chinese. June 1977 is supposed to have seen an unsuccessful Vietnamese attempt at a coup in Cambodia (now renamed Kampuchea); that autumn the Kampuchean leader Pol Pot was welcomed in Beijing, while a counter-visit by Vietnam's Le Duan proved fruitless. Border hostilities between Kampuchea and Vietnam began in December 1977; just as Kampuchea looked to China for aid, so Vietnam turned to the Soviet Union. In June 1978 it joined the Soviet economic bloc, becoming a member of CMEA; so all Chinese economic aid to it was stopped. November 1978 saw a Soviet–Vietnamese Treaty of Friendship that, like the 1971 Soviet–Indian treaty, was the prelude to a military solution. In December–January 1978–9 Vietnam conquered Kampuchea, installing a puppet government under Heng Samrin that was, at least in humanitarian terms, a vast improvement on that of Pol Pot.

China had decided not to send troops or ships to Kampuchea (which might draw it into a lengthy war of attrition), but nevertheless to teach Vietnam a lesson (as it had done India in 1962). The new Chinese leader, Deng Xiaoping, discounted the likelihood of direct Soviet intervention, but thought it wise to secure the USA's moral support or at least tacit acquiescence. He therefore cleared up the remaining obstacles to normalising relations and invited himself to Washington, where in January 1979 he privately briefed Carter as to his intentions. Carter voiced standard liberal objections, for which Deng thanked him politely but added 'that it was highly desirable for China that its arrogant neighbors know that they could not disturb it and other countries in the area with impunity'.[29] In February China invaded northern Vietnam. Its army lacked recent fighting experience and was generally antiquated. So, though it was opposed mostly by Vietnam's second-best forces (the best being in Kampuchea), the result was far from a walk-over. However, in a month's heavy fighting China managed to flatten four provincial capitals and 320

28. Chen, *China's War with Vietnam* pp.46–7
29. Carter, *Keeping Faith* pp.206–7

villages and then retire, declaring a victory and carrying off some 150,000 buffaloes and 250,000 pigs.[30]

In April 1979 the Chinese ambassador to Thailand stated that, 'Supported by the Soviet Union, Vietnam is dreaming of dominating the whole of the South-East Asia region . . . [as] a component part of the global strategy of the Soviet Union to dominate the world', while in June Deng proclaimed that 'Any threat to Thailand is a threat to China'.[31] China was obviously operating a containment policy. Like any such policy it was open to charges of being unnecessary – perhaps Vietnam had no designs on Thailand – or counter-productive – in that it led Vietnam to turn over to the USSR the valuable ex-US base at Camranh Bay. But it was broadly welcomed by the USA, and for a time it seemed that China and the USA were establishing an unwritten alliance.

CHINA'S RELATIONS WITH THE USA AND USSR IN THE 1980s

In April 1979 China accepted US electronic surveillance devices displaced from Iran by the Khomenei revolution. In January 1980 Defense Secretary Brown was extremely forthcoming during his visit in the immediate aftermath of the Soviet invasion of Afghanistan, undertaking to sell military equipment and declaring that if Chinese or US interests were threatened, 'we can respond with complementary actions in the field of defence as well as diplomacy'. Indeed the incoming Reagan administration in January 1981 was reportedly 'startled by the depth and breadth' of US–Chinese relations.[32] But thereafter they were gradually to cool; this was partly due to trouble over Taiwan. The 1979 Taiwan Relations Act had required the USA to treat it as a separate entity for immigration purposes and to sell it defensive arms; China was not pleased when Reagan complied. Moreover the Reagan administration did not need to be needled to contain the Soviet Union, so

30. Chen puts Vietnamese dead at 30,000, Chinese at 26,000 (over half of the USA's Vietnam War dead): *China's War with Vietnam* chap. 5; *Keesing's*, 29874

31. Girling, *Thailand* pp.246–7. Both China and the USA warned Vietnam during its June 1980 attack on Kampuchean refugee/guerrilla camps in Thailand: J.C. Hsiung and W. Chai (eds), *Asia and US Foreign Policy* (1981) p.109

32. *Keesing's*, 30239, 30387, 31621; Hsiung and Chai, *Asia and US Foreign Policy* p.112

China was able to relax its pressure and move to a somewhat less aligned position.

In the 1980s, too, the USSR at last realised the stupidity of its China policy and started to correct it, notably in Brezhnev's 1982 Tashkent and Baku speeches. A variety of friendly contacts ensued, for instance at Brezhnev's funeral. But in 1982 China identified three major stumbling blocks to improved relations: Soviet troop concentrations on its borders; the maintenance of Soviet troops in Afghanistan; and Soviet support for the Vietnamese occupation of Kampuchea. Accordingly the 'normalisation talks' then started made little real progress, whereas Reagan was welcomed to China in May 1984. After Gorbachev's advent to power, the USSR proposed both a non-aggression treaty and a summit – to no effect. So in a July 1986 speech at Vladivostok, Gorbachev hinted at both troop withdrawals and concessions on the border issue. Border talks resumed in 1987, reaching agreement in principle in August, but Gorbachev's calls for a summit were still not met. In April 1988 serious negotiations (between Afghanistan and Pakistan, mediated by their backers the USSR and USA) finally resulted in an unprecedented promise to withdraw all Soviet troops by February 1989. In December 1988 Vietnam was induced to announce some withdrawals – in April 1989 full withdrawal – from Kampuchea. Gorbachev obtained his long sought summit in Beijing in May 1989. As things turned out, it was largely overshadowed by China's domestic political crisis. But he announced further troop movements that would, by the end of 1990, reduce Soviet forces in the Far East to 120,000. He secured the restoration of full Sino-Soviet party as well as state relations, though the Chinese were careful to balance this with a US naval visit.[33]

CHINA SINCE 1979

Mao's initial rapprochement with the USA had been a matter of strategy, not economics. He had not actually been able to manage without grain imports, but in principle he was (especially after the 1960 shock withdrawal of Soviet aid) a great believer in self-sufficiency. Mao was also, in domestic affairs, strongly socialist. Although he allowed periodic spells of order and consolidation, he

---

33. *Keesing's*, 31818, 35064–6, 35840, 35970–2, 36377, 36448, 36588, 36641–2

was always concerned that they would lead, as in the USSR, to the emergence of a privileged 'new class' of officials and administrators. Hence the Cultural Revolution, and, in the closing years of his life, the support he seems to have given to his wife and the leftist 'Gang of Four'. A month after his death in September 1976 the Gang was arrested, after which power gradually fell into the hands of their former victim, the pragmatic Deng Xiaoping. Deng believed, above all, in modernising the economy to quadruple GNP to $1,000 billion between 1979 and 2000. China is primarily an agricultural country; in 1979–84 Deng essentially wound up collective agriculture, restoring the land to the peasants, raising prices, and encouraging sales on the open market with dramatic results. Industrial reform was less drastic, but China went considerably further than the Soviet Union in facilitating entrepreneurship and reducing controls. Above all Deng started to orient China towards the world market, by setting aside in 1979 four 'Special Economic Zones' where foreign capital (in practice mostly from Japan, Hong Kong and Taiwan)[34] was welcomed and state controls were drastically reduced, a process further extended in the 1980s. As a result the Chinese standard of living is reckoned by the World Bank to have doubled (albeit from a very low level) in 1977–87, a rate comparable with that achieved by South Korea in 1966–77 and much faster than most previous economic take-offs.[35]

There were, however, many problems, notably corruption (for which the Communist Party in the Hainan Special Economic Zone was particularly notorious) and inflation (unofficially said to be running at 20–30 per cent per year in the later 1980s). This was worrying, for inflation and corruption had contributed greatly to the collapse of the KMT in the later 1940s, and many hardliners did not wish to risk repeating the process. To appease them Deng sacrificed the Party Secretary Hu Yaobang in 1987, but did not really change course. In 1989 matters came to a head, with intellectuals demonstrating on ideological grounds for Western liberalism, and drawing support from a working-class alienated from the regime by an inflation that was squeezing their real wages. Hu Yaobang's death touched off sympathy demonstrations by Beijing students, who took over Tienanmen Square, demanded Deng's retirement, and erected a Goddess of Democracy (modelled on the

34. This had officially to be funnelled through Hong Kong, but Taiwanese investment is now prominent in the Special Economic Zone opposite the 'offshore island' of Quemoy
35. *The Independent*, 8 July 1991 p.21

Statue of Liberty). All this coincided with Gorbachev's visit, and so took place under the eye of the world media. The current Party Secretary, Zhao Ziyang, was conciliatory, but hardliners in the army, party and uneconomic state industry felt the country to be on the verge of chaos. So did Deng Xiaoping, who had once already imprisoned the 'Democracy Wall' activists of 1979, and who now backed the hardliners. On 4 June tanks drove straight in and cleared Tienanmen Square with considerable loss of life, a process followed up throughout the country by arrests and executions. Of the East European regimes similarly threatened later in the year, only that of Romania was prepared to use such force.[36]

Zhao was soon dropped, and the authorities turned back to stressing socialism (and even Maoism) as the cement of order and Chinese unity. In international affairs a certain coolness descended with the West, though, for geopolitical, economic, and Hong Kong reasons, the US, Japanese and British governments have tried to conciliate and limit the damage. One might have expected a strengthening of relations with the Soviet Union. But initially Chinese leaders tended to resent perestroika: in October 1989 Deng warned party officials of the infiltration from the USSR of ideas of political change and blamed events in Eastern Europe on Gorbachev's weak leadership, while in December an internal party document attacked him for having 'subverted' socialism there. Matters improved with his 1991 swing back towards the hardliners: China extended $730 million in food and other credits, Party Secretary Jiang Zemin visited Moscow, and Defence Minister Yazov Beijing. But the August 1991 collapse of communism in the Soviet Union left China both uncomfortably isolated ideologically and uneasy that in the early 1990s there is no Great Power to balance the United States.

Economically, however, China's problems have been less than one might have anticipated. The year 1989 was undoubtedly a set-back: growth dropped to about 4 per cent and foreign loans halved. But inflation was substantially reduced. Although the new stress on socialism was bound to protect some uneconomic state industries and so swell the already large budget deficit, growth (though also fears of inflation) returned in 1991. The hope is that it will rise at 6 per cent per year through the 1990s.[37] China's economic impact on the rest of the world is still slight – probably

36. Hsu, *The Rise of Modern China* chaps 37–8, 40
37. Keesing's, 37339–40, 38105, 38145–6, 38189

still less than Taiwan's. But if it proves able to replicate the take-off of other East Asian countries the results would be immense. Indeed a 1988 US long-range defence study projected trends to conclude that China would by 2010 overtake Japan to become the world's second largest economy.[38] Unlike postwar Japan, the People's Republic has always had the self-confidence to act like a Great Power in international relations. If, in due course, China also acquires the power, there could be a distinct shift in the world's centre of gravity.

38. *Washington Post*, 11 Jan. 1988 p.A13

CHAPTER ELEVEN

The Rise and Fall of Détente in the 1960s and 1970s

Nixon's 1972 visit to China had been impressive. But the climax of his travels that year was his journey to Moscow, which appeared to set the seal on a new relationship of détente between the super-powers. It had in a way been a long time in coming. For we have seen that, after Cuba, the Soviet leadership decided on 'a temporary relaxation of international tensions'. By the same token Kennedy (despite a memorable Cold War speech when he visited the Berlin Wall)[1] devoted much effort to trying to change attitudes, notably in his June 1963 address to the American University. For 'If this pause in the Cold War merely leads to its renewal and not to its end, then the indictment of posterity will rightly point its finger at us all'.[2] This phase of détente yielded the Moscow–Washington hot line, the 1963 Test Ban Treaty, and American agreement *in principle* to sell wheat to the USSR.[3]

STRAINED US–SOVIET RELATIONS 1964–7; THE GLASSBORO SUMMIT 1967

In 1963–4 both Kennedy and Khrushchev passed from the political scene. As far as the USA was concerned this made little difference. Johnson began by telling the UN that 'America wants to see the

---

1. 'There are many people . . . who do not understand what is the great issue between the free world and Communism. Let them come to Berlin. And there are some who say in Europe and elsewhere that we can work with the Communists. Let them come to Berlin': *Keesing's*, 19519
2. Schlesinger, *A Thousand Days* pp.785–6; *Keesing's*, 19537–8
3. For the reality, see p. 308

Cold War end', and soon arranged with Khrushchev a symbolic mutual reduction in the production of material for nuclear weapons. By 1969 he would say 'that his major mistake as President was in "trusting the Russians" too much' and that they created fewer difficulties for Presidents they feared.[4] In his memoirs he boasts of concluding 'more significant political agreements . . . than in the thirty' previous years of US–Soviet diplomatic relations. This may seem odd, since Johnson is chiefly remembered for expanding US anti-communist involvement in the Vietnam War until it surpassed (both in length and casualties) that in the Korean War. To Johnson the two policies were compatible: 'We were fighting in Vietnam to demonstrate that aggression should not, must not, succeed. . . . On the other hand, we had to show that there was an alternative to confrontation . . . to create a climate in which nations of the East and West could begin cooperating to find solutions to their worst problems'. Not everybody saw it this way; indeed Johnson blames 'Resentment against nations supporting Hanoi' for congressional refusal to remove the special tariff restrictions on East–West trade. The agreements he did achieve, while certainly an advance on what went before, now mostly appear rather minor.[5]

If Johnson wanted to continue the Kennedy–Khrushchev thaw, the new Soviet leaders had considerable reservations: 'The Americans', they told Nasser in 1967,

> are trying to cause trouble. They like to give the impression that their relations with us are continually improving, and that we and they consult together on everything. But this simply isn't true. . . .
> . . . The American aim is to isolate the Soviet Union from its friends and create an atmosphere of Soviet–American collusion, in the hope that this will damage the world communist movement and national liberation movements everywhere, and deepen the Sino-Soviet conflict by appearing to justify the Chinese claim that détente is simply another word for collusion, and weaken the fighting spirit of the Vietnamese.

4. Nixon, *Memoirs* pp. 430–1
5. Lyndon B. Johnson, *The Vantage Point* (1971) pp. 464–76. He cites: a cut-back on the production of fissionable materials; a ban on nuclear weapons in space, and the 1968 Nuclear Non-Proliferation Treaty; a treaty providing for the return of astronauts/space vehicles landing accidentally in the wrong country; a consular convention, the renewal of a cultural agreement, the inauguration of a direct air service; and fisheries agreements. He could have added the discovery (in 1967–8) of a mutual interest in free maritime passage that led the USA and USSR (both great naval powers) to cooperate during the 1970s international negotiations on the Law of the Sea

But in fact I can assure you that relations between us and the Americans are extremely tense.[6]

Some of this was designed to reassure the Egyptians that they would not be sacrificed to achieve a superpower condominium; but there had been a definite, if low-key, shift away from a number of Khrushchev's foreign policies. Although the new leaders' chief concerns were probably domestic, they also abandoned overtures to West Germany, briefly sought to conciliate China, and in November 1964 hailed the 'courageous people of South Vietnam engaged in a heroic liberation struggle'. They showed little interest in Johnson's New Year proposals for an exchange of visits.[7]

Brezhnev seems to have had no expectations of early gains in Western Europe: he was often loudly contemptuous of its Communist parties, which (he told the Czechs in 1968) 'won't amount to anything for fifty years'.[8] His chief hopes related to the Middle East, where he would soon 'be in a position to deal' the Americans 'a decisive blow'. His main East–West problems probably arose from the Vietnam War. The Soviet Union, he told the Hungarians in January 1965, wished

> to reestablish close contact with the Korean and Vietnamese Communists who had been greatly neglected by Khrushchev. In . . . Vietnam, . . . the N[ational] L[iberation] F[ront] forces had already liberated almost 75 per cent of the countryside and units of the . . . North Vietnamese army had joined the guerrillas. But an American intervention might change this favourable situation.[9]

It did. American reprisal bombing of North Vietnam started during Kosygin's February 1965 visit there, and escalated into a sustained operation in March. Kosygin was supposedly angry. The Kremlin certainly took the opportunity to organise, and tell West European Communist parties to organise, anti-American protests. It also, as time went on, profited enormously from spontaneous Western anti-war feeling. Indeed, by the end of the 1960s, revulsion against US involvement in Vietnam had probably done more than anything else to undermine both the favourable image the United States had previously enjoyed with European liberals and the confidence that American liberals placed in policies of containment.

6. Heikal, *Sphinx and Commissar* pp. 169–70
7. R.W. Stevenson, *The Rise and Fall of Détente* (1985) pp.127–8; Smyser, *The Independent Vietnamese* p. 77
8. Mlynar, *Night Frost in Prague* p. 241
9. Weit, *Eyewitness* p. 139; Radvanyi, *Delusion and Reality* pp. 38, 55

In the mid-1960s, however, the Kremlin was probably more conscious of possible costs and dangers: it failed to end Sino- Soviet hostility, and the USSR had therefore to do at least as much as China for North Vietnam. This came quite expensive: the USA put 1965–71 Soviet aid at $3.2 billion (as against China's $1.2 billion) and it was later to rise further.[10] More alarming was the danger that the war would escalate. China allegedly urged on Shelepin (the hardest-line candidate for the Soviet leadership in 1965) the idea of 'putting military pressure on the Americans in Berlin and West Germany'; in 1966 the USSR accused the Chinese of seeking 'to originate a military conflict between the USSR and the United States . . . so that they may, as they say themselves, sit on the mountain and watch the fight of the tigers'. This the USSR could quite easily avoid; but it could not control the US response to the open dispatch south of North Vietnamese regiments, and the worst case scenario certainly looked depressing:

> High party officials were seriously concerned that the Americans . . . would call up reserves and launch an all-out attack against North Vietnam. Soviet Defense Ministry officials even predicted that American marines would execute amphibious landings deep in North Vietnamese territory as they did during the Korean War . . . [and] thought the United States might use tactical atomic weapons if the Chinese intervened militarily. The gloom deepened when reports reached Moscow . . . that the Chinese had offered to help Hanoi, if necessary, with an army of a half-million men on the condition that the DRV [Democratic Republic of Vietnam] would launch simultaneous general attacks against South Vietnam and Laos. It was a great relief when Ho Chi Minh sidestepped that plan.[11]

To prevent such developments the Russians appear to have sought a negotiated settlement. Kosygin apparently took to Hanoi in February 1965 a proposal for a new international conference on Indo-China, and was accused of advocating in Beijing (on his way back) the need to help the USA 'find a way out' of Vietnam. A year later Shelepin carried a similar message. In February 1967 Kosygin served as an intermediary for transmitting to Hanoi proposals for an ending of US bombing of the North and of both US and North Vietnamese troop reinforcement in the South. But North Vietnam made its own decisions, playing the China card where necessary

---

10. Chen, *China's War with Vietnam* pp. 24, 187; Turley, *The Second Indo-China War* p. 168. Valuing the Chinese contribution is not easy since much was in the form of direct labour; the Chinese claim a total of $20 billion over 1950–78
11. Radvanyi, *Delusion and Reality* pp. 153, 167, 189–90, 235

(Shelepin was told that China was 'as close as lips and teeth' to the Vietnamese), and extracting increased Soviet aid in the process.[12] The Russians appear to have found the whole process infuriating, and to have feared it could 'damage the Soviet revolutionary posture all over the world'. Some of their frustration over this (and over set-backs in Indonesia and Ghana) seems to have been diverted on to President Johnson – 'He's more dangerous than Dulles', Brezhnev told U Thant.[13]

However, alarm and frustration did not lead to a complete breakdown of cooperation. Soviet and US policies in the Middle East were incompatible, and there are unanswered questions about the role of both countries in connection with the 1967 Arab-Israeli War. But on the brink both countries urged restraint. Once war had started, Kosygin for the first time ever activated the Moscow–Washington hot line; the two countries undertook to work for a cease-fire, but did not initially agree on its terms. When Israel strafed a US intelligence ship, the USA used the hot line to explain to the Soviet Union (and get it to explain to Egypt) that US overflights were solely to pick up the pieces. Finally, fearing that Israel might stretch its victory over Syria to the seizure of Damascus, Kosygin came on the line to say with some heat that, if Israel did not stop within the next few hours, the USSR would take 'necessary actions, including military'. He managed to alarm the Americans, who responded not only by directing their Sixth Fleet towards Syria to warn against such Soviet action, but also by insisting that Israel stop.[14]

This was, of course, exactly how the hot line was meant to be used. But coordinated crisis management implied only a very limited measure of agreement. Later in June 1967 the USSR, against US wishes, secured an emergency meeting of the UN General Assembly to discuss the Middle East.

Johnson took advantage of Kosygin's attendance at the UN to arrange a summit (though it seems the Soviet Politburo had been split on whether to accept). Their two days of talks at Glassboro, while quite amicable, produced no results.[15]

12. Smyser, *The Independent Vietnamese* pp. 87–9, 94; W.J. Duiker, *The Communist Road to Power in Vietnam* (Boulder, Colo., 1981) pp. 231–2, 240–1; Radvanyi, *Delusion and Reality* p.211; Harold Wilson, *The Labour Government 1964–1970* (1971) chap. 19; Johnson, *Vantage Point* pp. 252–5, 592–5

13. Heikal, *Sphinx and Commissar* pp. 154, 161, 164, 166–7, 172

14. ibid; pp. 176–7, 181–2; Johnson, *Vantage Point* chap. 13

15. Johnson later said that Kosygin had advanced a helpful proposal on Vietnam but that Moscow then dropped it: Nixon, *Memoirs* p. 431

THE SOVIET SHIFT TOWARDS DÉTENTE 1968

However, 1968 saw a considerable change in the US–Soviet relationship. The Soviets were pleased by Johnson's March decision to suspend bombing over most of North Vietnam, by the May start of peace talks in Paris, and by the final signature of the Nuclear Non-Proliferation Treaty in July 1968. They also changed their mind over ABMs and became anxious for negotiations (see pp. 169–70). A final catalyst was the Soviet decision to invade Czechoslovakia to stop what they saw as its dangerous reformist drift. Détente now seemed attractive as a way of limiting the resultant damage to the USSR's international image; and on 19 August 1968 (the day before the actual invasion) Johnson was invited to visit the USSR in early October to inaugurate talks.[16]

Czechoslovakia may also have had a more indirect effect on Soviet thinking. One of the currents contributing to the 'Prague Spring' had been that of the economic reformers; the political consequences of their experiments had proved unacceptable. The lesson was reinforced, in a different form, by the 1970 developments in Poland, where an economically rational increase in prices triggered rioting serious enough to lead to the dropping of the Party Secretary, Gomulka. There is a school of thought that attributes détente largely to Brezhnev's reluctance to risk such economic reforms in the Soviet Union, and determination instead to seek economic growth by tapping Western grain and industrial technology, which would be much facilitated by an improvement in the international climate. Finally, the Soviet Union was now approaching nuclear parity with the United States, enjoying in the 1970s a superiority in megatonnage and in numbers of strategic missiles, if not warheads. This undoubtedly made discussion psychologically easier; as the hitherto junior power, the Soviet Union undoubtedly welcomed symbolic acceptance as the United States' equal,[17] and was the keener of the two to press for the joint handling of problems like China or the Middle East by a superpower condominium.

On the invasion of Czechoslovakia Johnson cancelled his October visit to the USSR. At the end of the month he warned (in deliberately vague terms) that similar pressure on Romania could

16. Johnson, *Vantage Point* p. 487. Johnson had been suggesting a summit since July: Kissinger, *Memoirs* i p. 50
17. In the 1920s the United States had itself insisted on formal naval 'parity' with Britain for largely psychological reasons

unleash 'the dogs of war' and gave Yugoslavia some security assurances.[18] Brezhnev seemed pleased with Johnson's acquiescence in the invasion,[19] however, while in September Johnson declared that 'we hope – and we shall strive – to make this setback a very temporary one' and resumed his pursuit of a summit before the end of his administration. In November 1968 the Soviets seemed forthcoming, but President-elect Nixon poured cold water on the idea.[20]

THE APPROACH TO THE MOSCOW SUMMIT OF 1972

Once in office, Nixon's chief aim was an acceptable and face-saving disengagement from Vietnam, and he looked to Soviet mediation to achieve this. In theory Moscow's economic and military aid should have given it considerable leverage over Hanoi. In practice it would no more convert this into control of Hanoi's policy than would the United States later dictate to Israel in a similar situation. Accordingly US–Soviet relations stagnated, though the SALT process did formally begin in November 1969. In April 1970 Nixon started making overtures for a summit, and discussion proceeded throughout the summer, but to no avail. Kissinger thinks that Nixon hoped to upstage the anti-Vietnam War movement, but claims the Russians asked too high a price for the meeting (notably in terms of collusion against China) and so missed a promising opportunity of extracting ABM and other concessions.[21]

There followed an 'autumn of crises'. One was set off by King Hussein of Jordan's crack-down in September 1970 on the Palestine Liberation Organisation (PLO), which had been building a state-within-a-state inside his kingdom. The USA accorded him the

18. Karen Dawisha, *The Kremlin and the Prague Spring* (Berkeley, Calif., 1984) p.371

19. He told the semi-captive Czech leaders that he had asked 'if the American government still fully recognizes the results of the Yalta and Potsdam conferences' (i.e. the division of Europe into Eastern and Western spheres), and that *before* the invasion he had 'received the reply: as far as Czechoslovakia and Rumania are concerned, it recognizes them without reservation; in the case of Yugoslavia, it would have to be discussed': Mlynar, *Night Frost in Prague* p. 241. Dawisha knows of no specific evidence bearing on this claim: *The Kremlin and the Prague Spring* pp. 292–3

20. Johnson, *Vantage Point* pp. 489–90; Kissinger, *Memoirs* i p.50

21. Kissinger, *Memoirs* i pp. 552–7

support of a naval build-up in the east Mediterranean. This in turn drew a polite expression of Soviet hope that there be no external intervention in the Jordanian civil war. There soon followed an invasion by Syrian tank units (albeit without their Soviet advisers), leading Hussein to appeal desperately for US help. The United States persuaded Israel to ready itself for intervention if necessary, and ostentatiously continued its own preparations to provide air cover and reinforcements. Israeli mobilisation seems to have alarmed the Syrian military, and the tanks were first left unprotected against Jordanian air attacks and then withdrawn.[22] The USSR and Egypt helped diplomatically. While all this was going on, the United States discovered that, despite the Soviet re-affirmation in August of the Khrushchev–Kennedy agreements over Cuba, the USSR was in fact installing an SLBM base there. The USA waited until after the Jordan crisis had subsided, then insisted forcefully but privately that it desist.[23]

This was not a very promising background against which to discuss a summit, but on his return to Washington at the end of the Jordan crisis Ambassador Dobrynin brought a softening of the Russian position. He did, though, suggest that the summit await the next Soviet Party Congress in March 1971. The Congress, when it came, reflected Brezhnev's emergence as unchallenged leader and his take-over of foreign affairs from Kosygin. Brezhnev told it, albeit with many qualifications, that 'We proceed from the assumption that it is possible to improve relations between the USSR and the USA' – a position reached, Garthoff was later informed, only after overcoming the scepticism of many Central Committee and Politburo members.[24] If Brezhnev's ascendancy was one factor moving the Soviet Union towards détente, another was the need to head off the incipient rapprochement between the USA and China. Meanwhile Brandt was pressing Washington over the slow pace of the Berlin negotiations.

January 1971 brought US–Soviet agreement to negotiate seriously on both SALT and Berlin; in May the Soviet Union accepted US wishes for parallel negotiations on ABMs and on the limitation of

22. ibid, chap. 15; Nixon, *Memoirs* pp. 482–5; S. Posner, *Israel Undercover* (Syracuse, NY, 1987) pp. 184–90; M. Heikal, *The Road to Ramadan* (paperback edn, 1976) pp. 96–7; Blechman, *Force without War* pp. 260–86

23. Kissinger, *Memoirs* chap. 16; Nixon, *Memoirs* pp. 485–9; Garthoff, *Reflections on the Cuban Missile Crisis* pp. 94–6, 98–100

24. Garthoff, *Détente and Confrontation* p. 42; *Report of the CPSU Central Committee to the 24th Congress* . . . (Moscow, 1971) p. 34

strategic missile numbers. In June 1971 it became clear that the Berlin talks would succeed, but the Russians made the mistake of holding out on US proposals for an autumn summit, only to discover that this enabled Nixon's China visit to come first. Eventually May 1972 was fixed on, with the expectation that a SALT treaty be worked out by then. Both the May 1971 breakthrough on ABMs and the mid-summer progress on Berlin were sweetened by the withdrawal of US export controls on machinery for the Kama River truck factory. More secretly, talks began to induce the American trade unions to relax their restrictions on the loading and shipping of grain to the USSR; they were given to understand 'that there would be no SALT agreement unless the grain deal was worked out'.[25]

The attractiveness to the USSR of détente must have been further enhanced by the failure of its 1972 grain harvest, down to about 168 million tons from a target of 195 million tons. In 1972 there were both intensive negotiations with, and shrewd agricultural purchases (in all worth over \$1 billion) from, the United States; it appears that Brezhnev set more store by these than did some of his colleagues.[26] Also the Russians were concerned at the difficulties the West German Parliament was making about ratifying the *Ostpolitik* treaties, and so sought the USA's good offices.

Nevertheless the summit was nearly wrecked by events in Vietnam, where the North embarked on a major offensive in late March 1972. But Nixon was determined that the US response include the resumption of heavy bombing of North Vietnam. This did not prevent a visit by Kissinger to Moscow in April at which he settled many of the outstanding summit issues. But Nixon would have preferred him to concentrate on Vietnam and come home if he did not get satisfaction. Kissinger did arrange a meeting with the North Vietnamese on 2 May 1972, but it proved fruitless. Nixon decided to escalate the bombing; rather than risk the Soviets cancelling the summit by way of reprisal (as in 1960), he considered calling it off himself. From this he was dissuaded by Treasury Secretary Connally, who was well-placed to know how much the Russians wanted trade and credits. The onus was therefore put on the USSR to cancel the summit. Some Soviet leaders (notably the Ukrainian Party Secretary Shelest) would have liked to do so, but

---

25. Kissinger, *Memoirs* i chap. 20; Hersh, *The Price of Power* pp. 343–9

26. *Keesing's*, 25577–8; Garthoff, *Détente and Confrontation* pp. 305–6; Kissinger, *Memoirs* i p. 1,213

Brezhnev secured general agreement that it should go ahead even while Hanoi was being bombed. (Fortuitously Kissinger had been able to sugar the pill by passing on the news that the West German politicians had agreed to ratify the *Ostpolitik* treaties.)[27]

THE 'MOSCOW DÉTENTE'

The May 1972 summit was a success. The final details of the ABM treaty and the Interim Agreement on Strategic Arms Limitation were tied up. There were at least two sessions on Vietnam, and Brezhnev undertook to send Podgorny to Hanoi with the latest US proposals 'in the interest of peace'. The hopes expressed for a trade agreement 'in the near future' were realised by a July credit for Soviet grain purchases and an October trade agreement, settling the Soviet wartime Lend-Lease debt,[28] according the USSR 'Most Favoured Nation' status and credits,[29] and looking to at least $1.5 billion worth of trade over the next three years. There was agreement, too, on the desirability of an early conference on European security (a long-standing Soviet wish) and on that of reciprocal military reductions in Central Europe. The opportunity was taken to sign several worthy, but minor, agreements on US–Soviet cooperation in technical fields. The whole was rounded off with a statement of the 'Basic Principles of Relations' between the two countries,[30] but only the future could show what all this would amount to in practice.

Nixon was aware of this. 'The pattern of US–Soviet summit diplomacy in the cold war era is well known', he told Congress on his return; 'One meeting after another produced a brief euphoric mood – the spirit of Geneva, the spirit of Camp David, . . . – but without producing progress on the really difficult issues'. Naturally he implied that this summit had been different, and claimed that

---

27. Garthoff, *Détente and Confrontation* pp. 96–105; Nixon, *Memoirs* pp. 586–607; Kissinger, *Memoirs* i chaps. 26–7; Hersh, *The Price of Power* chap. 36 – the last three being works of advocacy

28 The USSR undertook to repay $722 million for deliveries of *civilian* goods; the terms roughly followed those arranged with Britain in 1945

29. This status implies only that there be no special tariff discrimination against the country in question. But according to it a centrally planned economy is necessarily a concession, since the latter's planning system cannot provide comparable non-discriminatory access

30. Garthoff, *Détente and Confrontation* pp. 305–8; *Keesing's*, 25313–14, 25585–6

there was now an 'opportunity to build a new structure of peace in the world'. Volumes have been written, first seeking to establish the characteristics of this new détente, later explaining why it soured. At the time it certainly seemed as if the international climate had been transformed. *Ostpolitik* had resolved the old Cold War disputes over Germany. The USA and China had buried the hatchet. The USA and the Soviet Union had apparently curbed their strategic arms race, and acquired (in the 'Basic Principles'[31] and through Kissinger's remarkable diplomacy) 'a solid framework for the development of better relations'. In January 1973 a Vietnam cease-fire was agreed. Some of these achievements ultimately proved more durable than others; but it is very natural that politicians should have taken credit for them all, and that public opinion (which was, of course, largely unaware of recent East–West crises) should have been delighted.

Nixon's speech to Congress also stressed 'that Soviet ideology still proclaims hostility to some of America's most basic values. The Soviet leaders remain committed to that ideology . . . they are and will continue to be totally dedicated competitors of the United States'. So 'the time-tested policies of vigilance and firmness which have brought us to the summit are the only ones that can safely carry us forward to further progress in reaching agreements to reduce the danger of war'; the USA should not unilaterally reduce defence spending. Defense Secretary Laird was blunter, supporting SALT, but saying it had been 'made possible only by the United States' determination to negotiate from a position of strength', and so announcing new strategic programmes.[32]

As for the USSR, Ponomarev had allegedly been unhappy that the joint communiqué contained nothing about Soviet support for national liberation movements. But the Central Committee plenum on the eve of the summit stressed that Soviet foreign policy responded to the vital interests of 'world socialism, [and] the national liberation movement, and it organically links decisions on immediate current tasks with a long-term perspective'. Such a perspective was provided when Brezhnev reportedly told East European leaders in February 1973 that détente was a tactical

31. To which was added at the 1973 Washington summit the 'Agreement on the Prevention of Nuclear War': *Keesing's*, 25999. This promised consultation if relations, either between the signatories and third parties or simply between third parties, appeared 'to involve the risk of nuclear war'. Critics were to claim that the USSR had breached it by not giving the USA advance warning of Egypt's 1973 attack on Israel

32. *Keesing's*, 25316–17; Garthoff, *Détente and Confrontation* pp. 194, 299–300

interim phase to be pursued while the socialist countries built up their strength for the next fifteen years or so.[33]

Fifteen years would, however, last out Brezhnev's own lifetime. Furthermore, there was a degree of personal rapport between the leaders of the day: the Russians took to Kissinger, and were anxious to have him over for frequent negotiating visits. They also clearly respected Nixon, though not his successors. They were good, if somewhat heavy-handed, hosts: arguably the high point of détente was Kissinger's May 1973 visit to the Kremlin dacha at Zavidovo and his excursions and boar-hunting with Brezhnev. The Americans, for their part, found Dobrynin, the Soviet ambassador, congenial, and 'back-channel' negotiations with him were a welcome contrast to the vicious bureaucratic infighting of Nixonian Washington. Dobrynin's standing in Washington was such that Brzezinski, the US National Security Adviser, was surprised to discover, at the 1979 Vienna summit, that he was not in the Soviet inner circle. Both Nixon and Kissinger also responded to Brezhnev's personal charm. After his 1975 heart attack, however, Brezhnev became a less impressive, indeed by 1979 a rather pathetic, figure. Gromyko, by contrast, grew steadily in stature; but though his professionalism was always admired, he proceeded on the basis of well-informed attrition, not flexibility or creativity. The Americans were more impressed by the subtlety and sophistication of the Chinese leaders, and by their freedom from the Soviet negotiating habit of constantly seeking petty (and frequently counter-productive) advantages.[34]

Although one should not underestimate personal factors, both countries naturally embraced détente in the belief that it would be in their own interests. Where these overlapped there was no problem. SALT I had been at the centre of the Moscow summit; despite all the strains generated by rival strategic calculations and practices, there was sufficient common ground to secure further agreements/treaties at the 1974 Vladivostok and 1979 Vienna summits. Even where interests diverged, détente might be a helpful adjunct to crisis management: Brezhnev said after the 1973 Arab–Israeli War that without it 'the situation would look entirely different. If the current conflict would explode in an environment of general international tensions . . ., the confrontation in the

---

33. ibid, pp. 102–3, 294, 317
34. The *American* negotiating vice was that of withdrawing, in response to domestic pressures, from positions already agreed with other countries

Middle East could become far more dangerous and be on a scale threatening the general peace'.[35] Still it was clear from the outset that both countries hoped détente would promote the type of international order they preferred. As it started to sour, increasing emphasis came to be placed on this theme, so that détente appeared more and more as Cold War by other means.[36]

The key American concept here was 'linkage'. It was both a policy[37] – that only if the Soviet Union was accommodating in some respects should it be allowed what it wanted in others – and a statement of the fact that Congress was unlikely to 'support an expanding economic relationship while our basic relations with the Soviet Union are antagonistic'.[38] To succeed it demanded a degree of politeness: in the words of a British diplomat, the long-range objective was to enmesh the Soviets in 'a less competitive relationship, and we cannot get there by telling them to go to hell'.[39] But it involved chiefly the ability to *deliver* rewards for 'good' Soviet behaviour and the possession of so clear a capability to counter 'bad' behaviour that it was not attempted. It is Kissinger's basic contention (as well as excuse) that, in the mood of the 1970s and the aftermath of Watergate, the US Congress wilfully destroyed the United States' capacity either to reward or to punish. So 'not even Brezhnev will ever know how much he might have been prepared to pay in restraint for a genuine peace after 1972, had we maintained the right balance between firmness and conciliation'.[40] But the policy was also open to two other dangers. One was the belief that certain goals (like SALT or – for Europeans – détente in Europe) were so desirable that they should be pursued for their own sakes, regardless of Soviet behaviour elsewhere; this belief became attractive later in the 1970s, when the Russians began to act on the basis that détente was divisible and should not be affected by contretemps in the Third World. The converse was to allow conflict in one aspect of the US–Soviet relationship to spill back to poison

35. D.K. Simes, 'The Death of Détente?', *International Security* v (1980) p. 3

36. W.G. Hyland, *Soviet-American Relations: A New Cold War*, (Rand, Santa Monica, Calif., 1981) illustrates this from Kissinger's changing definitions of détente (pp. 31–3) and touches on a similar Soviet process (pp. 38, 40)

37. Firmly laid down by Nixon at the outset of his administration: Kissinger, *Memoirs* i pp. 135–6

38. President's Foreign Policy report, 1973: Garthoff, *Détente and Confrontation* p. 308

39. Kissinger, *Memoirs* ii p. 281

40. Kissinger, *Memoirs* i pp. 1,143–4. Kissinger does not go into charges that the congressional mood was fed, in part, by the inevitable revelation of the news (and other) manipulations essential to his own negotiating technique

other fields where agreements could still be reached. Once serious difficulties started to be encountered, the line between these two pitfalls would obviously become very hard to tread.

Kissinger is no doubt right that we shall never know what Brezhnev would have been prepared to pay. Nor will we ever know how great Kissinger's own expectations really were. Sometimes he spoke in high-flying terms:

> The history of the post-war era has been a never-ending effort to maintain peace through crisis management. The structure of peace we envisage would instead be sustained by a growing realization on the part of all nations that they have a stake in stability, and that this stability is ensured by acting from a sense of justice and with moderation.[41]

In briefing Nixon just before the 1972 summit he professed only moderate expectations, however: 'The prospect for a fundamental change in Soviet–American relationships is not bright'. SALT, economic ties, and the implementation of the *Ostpolitik* treaties would 'add to elements creating a more permanent Soviet interest in stable relationships'; but for both ideological and internal political reasons 'Soviet foreign policy will remain antagonistic', and it was likely 'that the USSR will press their challenge to Western interests with increasing vigor and in certain circumstances assume [greater] risks . . . [than] heretofore'. On the eve of the next summit he suggested that Brezhnev

> sees the US at once as rival, mortal threat, model, source of assistance and partner in physical survival . . . he no doubt wants *to go down in history as the leader who brought peace and a better life to Russia*. This *requires conciliatory and cooperative policies toward us*. Yet, he *remains a convinced Communist who sees politics as a struggle with an ultimate winner;* he intends the Soviet Union to be that winner. His recurrent efforts to draw us into condominium-type arrangements . . . are intended both to safeguard peace and to undermine our alliances. . . .
>
> Almost certainly, Brezhnev continues to defend his détente policies in Politburo debates in terms of a historic conflict with us as the main capitalist country and of the ultimate advantages that will accrue to the USSR in this conflict. Brezhnev's *gamble* is that as these policies gather momentum and longevity, their effects will not undermine the very system from which Brezhnev draws his power and legitimacy. Our goal on the other hand is to achieve precisely such effects over the long run. . . .
>
> The major, *long term question is whether the Soviets can hold their own bloc together while waiting for the West to succumb to a long period of relaxation* and

---

41. Aug. 1973: Coral Bell, *The Diplomacy of Detente: The Kissinger Era* (1977) p. 32

the temptations of economic competition. Certainly our chances are as good as Brezhnev's, given the history of dissent in Eastern Europe.[42]

In short Kissinger suggested that the two sides were adopting similar tactics, but for opposite reasons, with the outcome in the lap of the gods.

THE HELSINKI FINAL ACT 1975

We naturally know less about Soviet calculations. The Soviet Union clearly hoped for economic gains (of which more later). It sought, with a good deal of success, a final legitimation of its position in Eastern Europe. The way had, of course, been cleared by Brandt's *Ostpolitik*. The 1972 summit referred to the desirability of a European security conference and of mutual force reductions in Central Europe; in 1973 Brezhnev secured the convocation of conferences to discuss these themes, in a way that (as we saw on p. 177) greatly helped the USA with its political problems over the Mansfield amendment. In August 1975 the heads of government of all European states, Canada and the USA signed the Helsinki Final Act; this accepted the territorial integrity of each participant and the right of each state to choose its own political system, and repudiated the changing of existing frontiers by force or economic coercion.[43] The Final Act had its problems: it was not compatible with the 'Brezhnev doctrine', and it was accompanied by a 'human rights' basket that proved mildly destabilising in the East since people wanted to take advantage of it and had to be stopped. But from the Soviet perspective, Helsinki endorsed the existing East European regimes, which were of course full participants. In that December 1975 US ambassadors were briefed that, though 'There are almost no genuine friends of the Soviets left in Eastern Europe, except possibly Bulgaria', 'it must be our policy to strive for an evolution that makes the relationship between the East Europeans and the Soviet Union an organic one. . . . We seek to influence the emergence of the Soviet imperial power by making the base

42. Kissinger, *Memoirs* i p. 203, ii pp. 243–4 (italics represent Nixon's underlinings)

43. *Keesing's*, 27301 ff. In deference to West Germany the possibility of change by 'peaceful means and by agreement' was left open

more natural and organic so that it will not remain [dangerously] founded in power alone.'[44]

SOVIET–AMERICAN COMPETITION IN THE MIDDLE EAST

The Soviet Union also sought to draw the USA into a joint management of the China and Middle East problems. It got no joy over China, but fared still worse with the Middle East where it gained nothing and lost the allegiance of the largest Arab state, Egypt. The Arab defeat in the 1967 Arab–Israeli War had made unlikely Brezhnev's original hope of driving out US influence; the USSR had then made the mistake of breaking off diplomatic relations with Israel, which disqualified it from acting as a mediator. In other respects things still went well. Nasser admittedly had to discontinue his (Soviet-funded) intervention in the Yemen Civil War. But the British attempt to transfer power in Aden to conservative sheikhs collapsed; instead the People's Republic of South Yemen came to independence in November 1967, and soon gravitated into the Soviet orbit. In January 1968 Britain unexpectedly announced that in 1971 it would withdraw its troops from the Arab sheikhdoms bordering the Persian Gulf, which appeared to open up prospects for their overthrow (though in the event Oman was able to repress a South Yemen-supported insurgency). In 1969 coups brought apparently leftist military governments to Sudan and Somalia. The latter's leader, Siad Barre, as Ethiopia's enemy, inclined sharply towards the USSR (which he accorded a naval base) and opted for scientific socialism – until in 1977 a similar figure, Mengistu Mariam, came to power in Ethiopia and the USSR shifted its support to the larger country.

Further north the 1967 defeat had made Egypt and Syria far more dependent than before on the USSR for the re-equipment and training of their armies. The Soviet Union did not find this an unmixed blessing: by 1970 Nasser was defenceless against Israeli air attacks; he therefore extracted from the USSR its most advanced

44. *Keesing's*, 27795 ff; there was, unsurprisingly, an outcry when this 'Sonnenfeldt Doctrine' leaked to the press. By 'organic' Sonnenfeldt meant that the East European states should develop sufficient autonomy and identity, but also sufficient ties of mutual interest with the USSR, to keep them content 'within the context of a strong Soviet geopolitical influence'

surface-to-air missiles by declaring that, were they to be refused, his policy would be revealed as bankrupt and he would have to make way for a pro-American President. Unfortunately the missiles could be operated only by Soviet forces, which were thus drawn into the fighting. So it was probably a relief when Nasser decided to accept a US-sponsored cease-fire in order to get the missiles properly established. But if there were flies in the ointment, Russian influence in Egypt seemed to be progressing satisfactorily, the Soviet fleet gained facilities on Egypt's Red Sea and Mediterranean coasts, and its air force later acquired free use of Cairo West airport.[45]

This position unravelled remarkably quickly. In May 1971 Nasser's successor, Sadat, resolved a power struggle by purging the police and displacing a pro-Russian grouping, some of whose members probably also worked for the KGB.[46] At the time Sadat was anxious to keep his lines to Moscow open; so he paralleled his consolidation of domestic power with the conclusion of a fifteen-year treaty of friendship and cooperation in which Egypt was described as 'having set itself the aim of reconstructing society along socialist lines'. But he put out several feelers to the United States, which was sending a series of messages to the effect that America and only America could deliver a settlement.[47] Sadat also got increasingly impatient with Soviet delays in supplying the weapons that he would need to renew war with Israel, suspecting – probably accurately – that the Russians (who took a low view of Arab military prowess) were determined to prevent him doing so.[48]

For the Egyptians, the Moscow summit in May 1972 represented the last straw. Sadat had repeatedly told the Russians they had done less for him than the USA had for Israel; now he urged them to talk firmly to Nixon. But the summit communiqué produced only the briefest and blandest of references to the Middle East. Sadat concluded that the USSR was not really interested; for a time he still kept up the pressure, then in July 1972 abruptly demanded the removal of the 21,000 Soviet military advisers. As he hoped, this did the trick. Marshal Grechko stressed the danger of losing the

---

45. Heikal, *Road to Ramadan* pp. 160, 165–6, 176–9, *Sphinx and Commissar* p. 238

46. *Keesing's*, 24653–4; Heikal, *Road to Ramadan* pp. 120 ff; Anwar el-Sadat, *In Search of Identity* (paperback edn, 1978) pp. 266–9; Barron, *KGB* pp. 51–3, 58–9. To this set-back there was added in July that of a communist coup in Sudan, which implicated the Russians, almost succeeded, but then collapsed

47. 'remember that the key to a solution is here': Heikal, *Road to Ramadan* pp. 118–19, 174, *Sphinx and Commissar* pp. 239–40

48. Ismail Fahmy, *Negotiating for Peace in the Middle East* (1983) chap. 1; Heikal, *Road to Ramadan* p. 163, *Sphinx and Commissar* p. 238

Egyptian alliance and argued successfully for providing all the arms the Arabs wanted: if they fought and won, the aid would be vindicated; if they lost they would have again to look to the USSR for rescue.[49]

The way was thus cleared for Sadat's military option, but in 1973 Brezhnev made one final attempt to forestall it. At the close of his visit to Nixon's San Clemente home, he roused his hosts (as they were going to bed) for a heated discussion of the Middle East. The two countries should agree principles to govern a settlement;[50] otherwise, he implied (as he had done at Zavidovo), there might be 'a resumption of the war'. The Americans were annoyed at this attempt to bounce them into imposing a settlement, stuck to the view that peace could come only from talks between the parties, and held that if the superpowers promulgated such principles, the parties would simply refuse to talk.[51] Nor were Sadat's attempts at secret negotiation with Washington any more successful. So in October 1973 Egypt and Syria struck at Israel to force the world to take them seriously.

Taken by surprise, Israel began badly, but soon shattered the Syrian army, then turned on Egypt, crossing the Suez Canal and all but encircling the Egyptian Third Army. The early stages of the war had not been marked by superpower agreement, and both mounted major military airlifts in support of their clients. But when satellite reconnaissance showed that Egypt faced major defeat, Kosygin persuaded Sadat to allow him to arrange a cease-fire. He then invited Kissinger to Moscow, and there (as the Egyptian military situation deteriorated) accepted his terms. A joint US–Soviet proposal at the UN speedily secured theoretical agreement on a cease-fire. But in practice Israel completed the Third Army's encirclement.

Sadat appealed with mounting desperation to the USSR, the UN, and the USA. Eventually Brezhnev requested that the USA join him 'without delay' in sending military contingents to enforce the cease-fire, warning that otherwise he would consider unilateral action; there were indications that some Soviet forces had been alerted. As

---

49. Heikal, *Sphinx and Commissar* chaps 14–15, *Road to Ramadan* pp. 166 ff; Kissinger, *Memoirs* i pp. 1,151, 1,246–8, 1,296–7

50. Israeli withdrawal to the 1967 borders in exchange for non-belligerence and the opening of the Suez Canal, guaranteed apparently by the superpowers; final peace would depend on negotiations with the Palestinians. (The Americans regarded these principles as biased towards the Arabs.)

51. Kissinger, *Memoirs* ii pp. 296–9; Nixon, *Memoirs* pp. 884–6

in 1956, the USA rejected joint action, not wishing to legitimise a Soviet presence on the Canal, and fearing that attempts at joint enforcement on the part of two countries whose outlook on the area differed so widely could lead to quarrels. It responded instead by demonstrative military preparations, including an increase in alert to DEFCON 3. It persuaded Sadat to withdraw his request for superpower intervention and substitute one for a UN force. It also insisted to Israel that the Third Army *must* be resupplied, while managing to arrange in exchange direct Israeli–Egyptian talks on disengagement. The net result was the establishment of a negotiating process that looked far more to Washington than to Moscow.[52]

The next few months were to see Kissinger flying around the Middle East, negotiating disengagement between the parties. Most of these negotiations were formally linked to an Arab–Israeli conference that met at Geneva for two days in December 1973 under joint US–Soviet chairmanship, then recessed. But by 1974 it was obvious that the USSR was being sidelined; the USA certainly wished this, but so did the Arabs.[53] There were to be attempts to restore the Soviet relationship with Egypt, but they were dogged both by importunate pressure for the repayment of Egypt's arms purchase debts and by bad luck (Brezhnev's 1974–5 illness forced the cancellation of a planned summit with Sadat). Basically, though, Sadat was determined for both personal and political reasons to turn to the USA, and in March 1976 he abrogated the 1971 treaty and withdrew facilities from the Soviet fleet.

Egypt would, until Sadat's murder in 1981, put all its eggs into the American basket. The USA also enjoyed the friendship of the oil kingdoms, notably the conservative and anti-communist Saudi Arabia, and (of course) of Israel. But if most major Middle Eastern powers were anti-Soviet, the Arab–Israeli dispute was deep enough to prevent them cooperating overtly (Egypt was generally ostracised after its 1979 peace treaty with Israel) and it provided the USSR with a way back into Middle Eastern politics. Even the 1974 and

52. Garthoff, *Détente and Confrontation* pp. 371–85; Kissinger, *Memoirs* ii pp. 575–611: their interpretations differ at a number of points

53. Sadat had told Kissinger at the outset that he was now looking to the USA. Assad of Syria also made it clear that he did not want Gromyko involved in the disengagement talks; Gromyko's plane was kept circling over Damascus for 45 minutes to demonstrate that he had no part in Syria's final offer to Israel, and next day he was left cooling his heels while the Syrian leaders, who had invited him to dinner, instead celebrated with Kissinger Israel's acceptance: Kissinger, *Memoirs* ii pp. 1,101, 1,104

1975 Israeli–Egyptian disengagement agreements had so alienated Libya that it abandoned its original hostility to godless Bolshevik Russia. When Sadat flew to Jerusalem in 1977, Syria reacted by mending its fences with the Soviet Union; which in return built it into a significant military power, thus enhancing its capability to dissuade other countries from following the Sadat line. In 1980 there was a Soviet–Syrian friendship treaty and, reportedly, over \$1 billion Libyan aid for Syrian arms purchases.[54]

US–SOVIET TRADE AND DÉTENTE; THE 'JACKSON-VANIK' AMENDMENT

If the Middle East constituted something of a disappointment for détente, so too did US–Soviet trade. Not, admittedly, as severe a one as is sometimes suggested, for the Soviet Union was able to buy US grain. In 1972 it skilfully concealed the size of its purchases and thus got them cheap. This helped raise prices by one-third, touched off bitter remarks about the 'Great Grain Robbery', and led in 1973–5 to some restrictions on US agricultural exports. But in October 1975 a five-year orderly marketing deal was reached for guaranteed annual Soviet purchases of between 6 and 8 million tons of grain and sales to the USA of up to 10 million tons of oil per year. This worked smoothly, and (as pressure on US supplies slackened) Soviet grain purchases were allowed to rise steeply. US farmers benefited so much that, when Carter cut sales in 1980 to punish the USSR for invading Afghanistan, they persuaded the otherwise strongly anti-communist Reagan to reinstate them next year.[55]

Non-agricultural trade was a different story. An agreement was reached in October 1972, and both trade and credits duly took off. (There is, indeed, a controversy as to whether or not such imports of high technology goods made a major contribution to the pace of the Soviet strategic build-up later in the decade.) But the concession to the USSR of 'most favoured nation' tariff status needed legislation, while credits could be blocked by Congress. The Soviet decision of August 1972, supposedly taken at quite a low level, to impose a tax on emigrants had already aroused a congressional

---

54. *Keesing's*, 30703; see also *The Post-Imperial Age* chap. 13
55. *Keesing's*, 25577–8, 25953–4, 26169–70, 26851–2, 27641–2, 30882

furore. So in October the hostile Jackson–Vanik amendments were tabled in both houses of Congress, Jackson's being sponsored by no fewer than 72 senators. Initially the administration, rightly confident that the USSR could be quietly persuaded to withdraw the tax, did not take the amendments seriously enough. Only in the spring of 1973 did it become clear that the issue would not be allowed to die, and that it had linked together an alarmingly broad coalition – conservative opponents of détente, liberal critics of the allegedly amoral Nixon-Kissinger *realpolitik*, the Jewish lobby, and anti-communist and protectionist labor. In 1974 Ford determined to settle the issue, and the Soviets helped him by undertaking privately to let Jewish emigration go on rising (even though it was already high enough to cause friction with Egypt). But Jackson demanded assurances that, in both scale and publicity, went well beyond what the Soviet Union would accept; his ally Byrd managed to place an overall ceiling of $300 million on official US credits. By November 1974 Brezhnev was already saying at the Vladivostok summit that Congress 'had fouled up the progress we thought we were going to make with the expansion of trade'; when the amended Trade Reform Act became law in January 1975 the Russians cancelled the 1972 agreement. Instead they turned increasingly towards Western Europe, deals with which probably served the same economic but not the same political purpose as those originally contemplated with the USA.[56]

SOVIET RESTRAINT AFTER THE 1973 'OIL SHOCK' AND THE 1974 PORTUGUESE REVOLUTION

Both sides insisted that the trade set-back did not mean the end of détente, but it did reduce the incentives on offer for Soviet restraint at a time when the temptations to probe were increasing. Unfortunately, though we are conscious of the occasions when the USSR did fish in troubled waters, we do not know whether there were occasions when it decided not to. Until the end of 1973 there had probably been little opportunity. But the then tripling of the price of oil administered an economic shock to Western Europe that in

56. Garthoff, *Détente and Confrontation* pp. 309–10, 325–7, 356–7, 453–63; Ford, *A Time to Heal* pp. 216–17

turn highlighted major political weaknesses.[57] On top of this the authoritarian regime of Portugal was overthrown in March 1974; for the next two years (but more especially between a failed rightist coup in March 1975 and an unsuccessful leftist/communist one that November) it seemed that communist-leaning officers in the army or security police might become dominant. All communists believe (in theory) in the capitalist order's ultimate collapse amid economic crisis; there is some evidence of debate in Moscow as to whether this had suddenly arrived, of exhortations to exploit it, and of impatience with the pusillanimous liberalism of the Italian communists. Certainly the USSR provided the Portuguese (and other) communists with financial aid (and presumably advice), as the West Germans did their Socialist competitors. But there is no evidence that they went much further. Perhaps they could not have done so in any case. Perhaps they were responsive to the warnings of Kissinger and Ford: the Soviet ambassador in Lisbon is reported to have told the pro-communist Prime Minister that the USSR had no interest in a confrontation with the USA over Portugal.[58]

SOVIET INTERVENTION IN ANGOLA 1975–6 AND ITS IMPLICATIONS FOR DÉTENTE

The liquidation of Portugal's overseas empire was different. The new Portuguese regime was chiefly concerned to secure a rapid exit. Guinea Bissau and Mozambique were turned over to their Marxist liberation movements. So presumably would East Timor have been had not Indonesia snapped it up, with the acquiescence of its anti-communist neighbours. But in Portugal's richest colony, Angola, liberation movements had made almost no military progress, and were indeed split both along tribal lines and

57. For Italy, see pp. 349–50, 356. In Britain the Conservative government's 1974 defeat in an election called over a miners' strike led to a great increase in real, and a still greater one in perceived, trade union power; it also coincided with a dangerous economic crisis. In France power remained in strong right-of-centre hands, but electorally the country was very evenly divided between these and a left coalition in which the Communists were, until 1977, the largest party. General Franco, who had ruled Spain since the 1930s, was ageing, and it was not expected that the transition from his regime would be as smooth as it in fact proved after his death in 1975

58. Bell, *The Diplomacy of Détente* chap. 9 and pp. 204–5; Garthoff, *Détente and Confrontation* pp. 485–7; Harry Gelman, *The Brezhnev Politburo and the Decline of Détente* (Ithaca, NY, 1984) pp. 163–4; *The Times*, 22 Jan. 1974 p. 14h, 24 June 1975 p.1c, 19 Sept. 1975 pp. 1, 15, 30 Oct. 1975 p. 5d

according to their outside patrons – China had aided UNITA and FLNA, the Soviet Union and Cuba the MPLA, the USA and Zaïre the FLNA. A power-sharing agreement of January 1975 disintegrated in March, and the fighting began. The MPLA had the advantage of tribal support around the capital and of control of the oil-producing enclave of Cabinda; both the FLNA and their Zaïrian sponsors seem to have been remarkably incompetent; and UNITA (though representing the largest tribe) took time to build any military capability. The USSR and USA both provided their clients with clandestine aid. Zaïre, Cuba and South Africa all committed troops, South Africa secretly but with encouragement from the USA, Zambia and other African states.[59] By late November (that is shortly after Angola's official independence) the MPLA had, with Cuban assistance, repulsed the FLNA and checked the South African/UNITA incursion. Meanwhile the USA had been raising the Angolan question diplomatically with the USSR, and it is just conceivable that this might have led to a deal – the USSR, though not Cuba, suspended arms deliveries between 9 and 25 December – had not Congress cut off US aid. In refusing to vote any more money (CIA funds were now exhausted) and banning further covert aid, Congress was determined to stop the USA from again being sucked into an unsavoury civil war in a not obviously essential area, as in Vietnam. But its decision, besides further discouraging South Africa, gave Cuba and the USSR *carte blanche*: Brezhnev simply refused to discuss Angola during Kissinger's January 1976 visit to Moscow. Cuban troops were openly flown in until by late January they numbered some 12,000. They rapidly extended MPLA rule over all the country except some UNITA territory in the far south-east, and then remained to protect it.[60]

The US administration was not prepared either to break off the (then promising) SALT negotiations or to stop grain sales to the USSR by way of sanction, but it did see Angola as an alarming precedent. The trouble was not that a Marxist government had come to power – this had been acceptable in Mozambique – but that it had been put there by open Soviet/Cuban military intervention. 'Angola represents the first time that the Soviets have moved

---

59. When their presence became known it served to swing official African sentiment behind the MPLA and to legitimise Cuban intervention

60. A.J. Klinghoffer, *The Angolan War: A Study in Soviet Policy in the Third World* (Boulder, Colo., 1980); Barber and Barratt, *South Africa's Foreign Policy* pp. 186–96; also Christoper Coker, *NATO, the Warsaw Pact and Africa* (1985) pp. 92–9, 144, and Garthoff, *Détente and Confrontation* chap. 15

militarily at long distance to impose a regime of their choice . . .
[and] that the United States has failed to respond to Soviet military
moves outside the immediate Soviet orbit'. So, lacking other
weapons, Kissinger resorted to rhetoric in an attempt to impress
both on the Russians and on American liberals that Angola must
not be repeated. In December 1975 he had warned that relations
were bound to be affected by Soviet military intervention in an area
'where there are no historic Russian interests'. It was, he later
declared, 'a pattern of behavior that the United States will not
accept – . . . if continued it will have serious consequences for
any possibility of easing relations with the Soviet Union'. For, he
added in March 1976, détente 'requires reciprocity' and 'cannot
survive a constant attempt to seek unilateral advantage';[61] it
'cannot, specifically, survive any more Angolas'.[62]

The Russians were unimpressed. Brezhnev had complained
bitterly to Kissinger in 1974 about the Soviet Union exclusion from
the Middle Eastern disengagement agreements,[63] and may well
have seen Egypt's shift from Soviet to US alignment as an American
acquisition of unilateral advantage. Again, though Angola may have
been the first Russian 'military operation thousands of miles from
Soviet territory', there had been many such US operations. The
USSR had only recently acquired a major airlift and long-distance
naval capability, and now wanted to use it. Marshal Grechko,
recently promoted to the Politburo, declared in 1974 that

> At the present stage the historic function of the Soviet armed forces is
> not restricted merely to . . . defending our Motherland and other
> socialist countries . . . the Soviet state . . . supports the national
> liberation struggle, and resolutely resists imperialist aggression in
> whatever distant region of our planet it may appear.[64]

Moreover, Suslov contended, détente 'is based precisely' on a
change in the world correlation of forces in favour of socialism.[65] If
so, it was absurd for the Americans to invoke it to try to restrict just

---

61. Kissinger was invoking the 1972 'Basic Principles': 'Both sides recognize that efforts to obtain unilateral advantage at the expense of the other are incompatible' with the summit's objectives

62. Garthoff, *Détente and Confrontation* pp. 524–5

63. Kissinger, *Memoirs* ii p. 1,022

64. Gelman, *The Brezhnev Politburo and the Decline of Detente* p. 47

65. ibid, p. 161. Brezhnev said much the same to the 1976 Party Congress; in 1975 an *Izvestia* commentator had observed that the 'purpose of detente was to make the process of international change as painless as possible' (Simes, 'The Death of Detente' pp. 9–10)

such a further change. In February 1976 Brezhnev decided to be blunt, telling his Party Congress that

> Our Party supports and will continue to support peoples fighting for their freedom . . .
> The Soviet Communists warmly acclaim the victory of the peoples of Guinea-Bissau and the Cape Verde Islands, Mozambique and Angola, which crowns many years of heroic struggle for independence. The CPSU has always sided with these peoples and rendered every possible support to these embattled patriots. . . .
> Some bourgeois leaders affect surprise and raise a howl over the solidarity of . . . the Soviet people . . . with the struggle of other peoples for freedom and progress. This is either outright naivety or more likely a deliberate befuddling of minds. It could not be clearer, after all, that detente and peaceful coexistence have to do with interstate relations. This means above all that disputes and conflicts between countries are not to be settled by war. . . . Detente does not in the least abolish . . . the laws of the class struggle . . .
> We make no secret of the fact that we see detente as the way to create more favourable conditions for peaceful socialist and communist construction.[66]

FURTHER STRAINS ON DÉTENTE: SHABA I AND II AND THE SOMALI-ETHIOPIAN WAR

This did not mean that the USSR was no longer interested in its relations with the USA; it continued to value SALT negotiations. But it was moving back towards Cold War practices – after a lull since 1972, its propaganda forgeries of Western official documents increased again in late 1976.[67] The incentives for restraint were by now very limited, while promising opportunities multiplied. Zaïre had been the enemy of the MPLA, and it was only natural that, once firmly established, the MPLA would seek to pay it back. So in 1977 it staged an invasion by former Katangese gendarmes (who had left Zaïre after Tshombe's fall) of their home province, now renamed Shaba. The Zaïrean army proved ineffective. But the new US administration did not react: we have seen that Carter doubted the USA's willingness ever again to undertake such missions (see pp. 46–7). So Morocco contributed 1,500 troops, who were flown in by France, and the invaders withdrew. Next year they returned,

---

66. I.I. Brezhnev, *Report of the CPSU Central Committee* (Moscow, 1976) pp. 16, 19, 39

67. Garthoff, *Détente and Confrontation* p. 317

again meeting little local resistance and now capturing the city of Kolwezi and posing a significant threat to the Mobutu regime. France and Belgium stabilised the situation by sending in some 2,900 of their own troops – this time airlifted by the USA. Later Moroccan and Senegalese units were substituted, and Angola and Zaïre officially normalised relations. The 1978 Shaba invasion occasioned a good deal of diplomacy and a proliferation of East–West accusations: but it surely constituted not only a move to consolidate earlier achievements in Angola but also an attempt to exploit them by mounting a further probe. If successful this could have been reinforced by Cuban units (that were according to some accounts readied for the purpose), and have greatly altered the configuration of Africa. It was, however, a low-cost, low-risk exercise, not pressed when it encountered opposition.[68]

The next flashpoint was the Horn of Africa. Here the pro-American Emperor of Ethiopia, Haile Selassie, had been toppled in 1974. There followed a period of confusion, from which the leftist Colonel Mengistu emerged (bloodily) the victor in 1977. The Soviet Union had already concluded an arms deal with him in December 1976, and both it and Cuba promptly welcomed his success. They also tried, but failed, to reconcile Ethiopia with their friend Somalia. However, Somalia turned out to be irredentist first and socialist only second; with Saudi assistance it made overtures to the USA, and may have derived more encouragement than was intended from the latter's agreement in principle to supply defensive weapons. Meanwhile the multinational Ethiopian state was falling to pieces. From June 1977 onwards Somalia attacked it, first under the guise of a 'West Somalia Liberation Front' and then openly. The invasion was initially successful, but faltered in front of the vital town of Harar. To the anger of America's friends (Saudi Arabia, Egypt, the Sudan and Iran), the Carter administration adopted the legally correct position that it would send Somalia no arms till it withdrew behind the international border; it also blocked the transfer to Somalia of Iranian Phantom jets that might have made all the difference. November 1977 saw a massive Soviet and Cuban re-supply of Ethiopia, January 1978 a counter-offensive (under Soviet command and using 10,000 Cuban troops) that had

68. ibid, pp. 623–30; Coker, *NATO, the Warsaw Pact and Africa* pp. 122–9, 198–9. The *Observer* (21 May 1978) reported that in 1976 East Germany had been allocated the major supporting role, and that it accordingly provided the Katangese with training and equipment, but only on the basis that it would not become directly involved even in the event of military failure

by March driven the Somalis back over the border. The USSR followed up by helping Mengistu's regime reconquer the province of Eritrea, the bulk of which had been in secessionist hands. For good measure Cubans were used in June 1978 to determine the outcome of a power struggle in South Yemen.[69]

None of this encountered significant US opposition: action to support Ethiopia was acceptable in international law, and, though Arabs backed Somalia, most African states (and Israel) did not; the South Yemen episode was both obscure and soon over. The US official most alarmed by the strengthening of the Soviet position at the mouth of the Red Sea, and by the way it had been effected, was National Security Adviser Brzezinski. He would have liked to signal concern by dispatching a naval force to the area and hinting that over-forceful Soviet action might endanger congressional ratification of SALT II, but he was overruled. Brzezinski came to believe that this US passivity emboldened the Soviets, against whose subsequent stances the Americans sometimes over-reacted; accordingly 'SALT lies buried in the sands of the Ogaden'.[70]

GROWING US CRITICISM OF DÉTENTE IN THE MID-1970s

Détente was already in a bad way in 1976; indeed President Ford, faced with a right-wing challenge for the Republican presidential nomination, stopped using the word. Angola suggested that the USSR remained expansionist. Sonnenfeldt's briefing on Eastern Europe (see pp. 314-15) leaked, and was not well received. Concern was mounting both at the way in which Kissinger negotiated and at SALT's implications for US defences (see pp. 171-3). A further dimension was that of human rights. Soviet suppression of dissent, surprisingly tentative in the years after Khrushchev's fall, began to gather way in the early 1970s. This may have been partly because of détente: a Central Committee conference warned of 'the increasing danger of bourgeois ideology in direct connection with the broadening of contacts with the imperialist

---

69. Garthoff, *Détente and Confrontation* pp.630–1; Coker, *NATO, the Warsaw Pact and Africa* pp. 103–12; Steven R. David, *Third World Coups d'Etat and International Security* (Baltimore, Md, 1987) pp. 87–92

70. Brzezinski, *Power and Principle* pp. 178–89

world'.[71] Such contacts, always important to dissidents, became more so with the suppression of *samizdat*, and they provided the West with a steady stream of information about Soviet brutalities. A further turn came with the Helsinki agreements; these included a 'human rights' basket, and dissident groups in the USSR and Eastern Europe sought to monitor its (non)application, a course that sooner or later led to their arrest.

The Nixon and Ford administrations took no official notice, believing overt interference likely to be counter-productive. Many critics viewed this as proof of Republican amorality, and saw no point in a détente that did not improve conditions in the Soviet Union but only strengthened its oppressive leaders. In this they were encouraged by dissidents like Sakharov, who had warned against pursuing détente on Soviet terms, endorsed the Jackson–Vanik amendment, and declared that Soviet leaders should be pressured into granting human rights as a price for détente. The issue spilt over into the 1976 presidential election. President Carter determined to give human rights a much higher priority. Accordingly his first months saw a string of criticisms of Soviet and Czech arrests and harassments, warnings that attempts to intimidate Sakharov would 'conflict with accepted international standards', the reception at the White House of the exiled Bukovsky, and a UN address affirming Carter's intention to press for human rights around the world.[72]

SOVIET CONTEMPT FOR CARTER

Carter's human rights campaign was by no means directed only against the USSR, but it was selective in that (for strategic reasons) it was not extended to either South Korea or China. Arguably the Soviets had no right to resent it, since they proclaimed that there can be no such thing as ideological coexistence, but resent it they certainly did. In a generally harsh letter to Carter in February 1977, Brezhnev protested about 'correspondence with a renegade [Sakharov] who proclaimed himself an enemy of the Soviet state', and declared roundly that he would not 'allow interference in our

71. Gelman, *The Brezhnev Politburo and the Decline of Detente* p. 159
72. Stevenson, *The Rise and Fall of Detente* p.162; Garthoff, *Détente and Confrontation* pp. 568 ff.

internal affairs, whatever pseudo-humanitarian slogans are used to present it'. As Carter naively remarked a few months later, 'There has been a surprising, adverse reaction in the Soviet Union to our stand on human rights . . . apparently that's provided a greater obstacle to other friendly pursuits of common goals, like in SALT, than I had anticipated'.[73]

Carter's opening moves on SALT had been ill received (see p. 179); as Arbatov later put it, they 'confirmed the impression in Moscow that Carter was not serious'.[74] Furthermore, his human rights initiatives were perceived as aggressive, but the low profile he maintained during the Shaba and Ethiopia affairs suggested that he was not to be feared. In short Carter lost Soviet respect. In time, of course, he might well have recovered it: SALT II was eventually steered through to a respectable deal, concluded at the June 1979 Vienna summit. However in August 1979 the Americans suddenly discovered a Soviet 'combat brigade' in Cuba, and a furore was set off when Senator Church revealed its presence and called for its withdrawal. Carter felt obliged to follow suit, and several senators made clear that its continued presence would jeopardise SALT's ratification. The Soviets regarded the whole issue as either bogus – the brigade had in fact been in Cuba since 1962 – or alternatively as a deliberate attack on détente. They declined to make face-saving adjustments to help Carter extricate himself. So he had, in effect, to climb down in October.[75] The episode certainly did not add to the credibility of US warnings about Afghanistan.

SOVIET INVASION OF AFGHANISTAN 1979; CARTER'S REACTION

In retrospect the Soviets' major Afghan mistake had been their over-enthusiastic response to the 1978 coup. Before then Afghanistan had been a non-aligned country in which the USSR, through aid and strategic road-building, had greater influence than any other power. President Daoud was seeking to forge countervailing connections with China and the Islamic world when he was killed by a communist coup, probably of local origin. The USSR then

73. Brzezinski, *Power and Principle* pp. 154–6; Garthoff, *Détente and Confrontation* p. 568
74. Garthoff, *Détente and Confrontation* p. 566
75. ibid, chap. 24

assumed a tutelary position, sending in a party official to mediate between the rival Afghan communist factions and building up its advisory presence. The result was a disaster, since the new regime's modernising and non-Islamic reforms quickly led to rebellions. One such rising (at Herat in March 1979) touched off the mutiny of an Afghan army division and the massacre of its Soviet advisers and their families. There followed an increase in the Soviet presence,[76] and a succession of visits by Soviet generals and diplomats to assess the deteriorating political and military scene. The upshot was the attempted murder in September 1979, with Soviet complicity, of the regime's strong man, Amin, who responded by eliminating the Soviet protégé President Taraki. Amin continued relations with the USSR, but would not visit it in person and seems in December 1979 to have been seeking contacts with Pakistan and Iran. Meanwhile Soviet forces in Central Asia were mobilised, and in early December started to occupy strategic positions within Afghanistan. Amin survived another assassination attempt on 17 December. But on the 27th Soviet airborne troops attacked his palace and other key positions in Kabul. Amin was killed, Babrak Kamal was brought from the USSR and installed as leader, and within a month 85,000 Soviet troops had moved in to consolidate the new regime.[77]

Carter had warned Brezhnev at the Vienna summit against intervention in Afghanistan; but he received only standard rebuttals: 'Revolutions, which the Soviets do support, emerge only within other nations. The instigation for them never originates with us'. There followed further (though deliberately low-key) US warnings (three in December). Then on the 28th, down the hot line, Carter demanded that the invasion be reversed: 'Unless you draw back . . ., this will inevitably jeopardize the course of United States–Soviet relationships throughout the world'.[78] But with President Amin dead, it may now have been too late for the USSR to turn back. Anyway the USSR took no notice, reasoning (one assumes) that Carter was likely to accept the consolidation of the revolution in Afghanistan as he had that in Ethiopia and South Yemen – but that, if he didn't, it did not much matter since the positive Soviet stake in détente had already evaporated. If so, the USSR was wrong. The US administration speedily determined, in Vance's words, that 'The

76. The USA put Soviet advisers at 350 in April 1978, 3,000–3,500 in March 1979 and 7,200 by December: ibid, p. 899

77. Garthoff, *Détente and Confrontation* chap. 26; David, *Third World Coups* pp. 88–9, 97–9

78. Carter, *Keeping Faith* pp. 247 ff, 472

Soviets must recognize that they are going to have to pay a cost as long as their troops stay in Afghanistan', and (in marked contrast to the 1968 Czech affair) imposed sanctions accordingly. Many of these, admittedly, were trivial; major ones, like the reduction of US grain sales, proved unsustainable. But Carter's own outlook had been transformed. The invasion 'has made a more dramatic change in my own opinion of what the Soviets' ultimate goals are than anything they've done in the previous time I've been in office'. 'We cannot be certain . . . if they seek colonial domination only in Afghanistan, or . . . other conquests as well. No President . . . can afford to gamble . . . upon wishful thinking about the present or the future intentions of the Soviet Union'. 'There is no doubt that the Soviets' move into Afghanistan, if done without adverse consequences, would have resulted in the temptation to move again and again' towards the control of warm water ports and oil supplies.[79] Carter never formally abandoned détente. But in practice he had re-embraced containment, enunciating in January 1980 the 'Carter Doctrine' that any 'attempt by any outside force to gain control of the Persian Gulf region will be regarded as an assault on the vital interests of the United States' and 'repelled by any means necessary, including military force'.[80] The rest of 1980 was spent in trying to reassure Saudi Arabia, improve relations with Pakistan, and acquire the staging posts and bases around the Arabian Sea that would make possible the projection of a Rapid Deployment Force into the Gulf.

79. Garthoff, *Détente and Confrontation* pp. 950, 972–3. The Carter administration now tended to link Afghanistan with earlier events in Ethiopia/South Yemen; together they seemed to give the USSR a strong position at both ends of an 'arc of crisis' that ringed the valuable but volatile oil world, where the USA's long-time friend, the Shah of Iran, had collapsed in January 1979

80. Garthoff, *Détente and Confrontation* p. 954

CHAPTER TWELVE

Tension and the Ending of the Cold War in the 1980s

EAST–WEST TENSION

By 1980 most of the components were in place for the United States' policy of the next few years. The USSR was perceived as internally repressive, externally expansionist, and engaged on a massive arms build-up. To meet this the USA had secured NATO agreement on a 3 per cent per year increase in real defence spending, and was practising what it preached. There had also been agreement on the deployment in Europe of cruise and Pershing missiles to counter Soviet SS-20s. Meanwhile a 'new' strategic doctrine, PD-59, had been adopted in 1980; in fact a development of earlier reforms, it stressed options (as opposed to an all-or-nothing response) – including that of fighting a limited nuclear war. West European public opinion took some time to assimilate this; but later the combination of Carter's strategy and Reagan's cowboy image was to give rise to visions of a United States happy to fight a nuclear war *in Europe*.

Many West Europeans wondered whether they were not bound in too closely with superpower rivalries in other parts of the globe. This in itself was not new: Europe had shown precious little sympathy for US containment policy in the Chinese offshore islands crises, and not much for its application during the Vietnam War. Since then, too, a central European settlement had been reached; was it worth endangering it to contest a fait accompli in Afghanistan? The West German government agreed in condemning Soviet expansion there, but feared an American tendency to over-react – at one point Chancellor Schmidt said 'We will not permit ten years of détente and defense policy to be destroyed'. Similarly

President Giscard d'Estaing of France declared that 'the balance of power in Europe is a separate problem'. In May/June 1980 both leaders travelled east to meet Brezhnev; later Schmidt did his best to persuade Carter to dismiss Brzezinski (who was commonly seen as the initiator of the new hardline). West European trade with the USSR also increased sharply, thus undercutting US economic sanctions.[1] The Russians encouraged such moves by making token military withdrawals from East Germany, and by proposing INF talks.

The 1980s were, therefore, clearly going to be a very difficult period for East–West relations, but to begin with they saw more talk than action. Neither Vietnam's 1978 conquest of Kampuchea (which had so alarmed China) nor the 1979 Soviet move into Afghanistan led to further expansion; very possibly neither had been directly intended to.[2] Perhaps too the containment inaugurated by Deng Xiaoping and Carter proved effective. Probably the most important factor was that there were no further vacuums like those produced by the Portuguese revolution and the collapse of the Haile Selassie and Daoud regimes in Ethiopia and Afghanistan. The Reagan administration worried deeply over the possibility of a new Cold War arena developing in Central America following the Nicaraguan revolution and adopted highly questionable tactics to prevent this.[3] However the USSR, far more cautious than it had been twenty years earlier, stayed largely on the sidelines. There were, therefore, no major East–West crises, and the contest largely took the form of rival defence build-ups and of a publicity war (often justifying these build-ups by alarming portrayals of the other side's capabilities).

As far as the US administration was concerned, the publicity was aimed largely at its own people, both to generate political support and as part of a wider strategy designed to restore US self-confidence and readiness to resume a world leadership role. In the Soviet case it was directed rather more towards Western Europeans, and designed to awaken their fears of US irresponsibility and so

1. Garthoff, *Détente and Confrontation*, pp. 978–80; Brezinski, *Power and Principle* pp.310, 462–3; Schweitzer, *Changing Western Analysis of the Soviet Threat* pp.246–7; P. Short, *The Dragon and the Bear* (1982) p.474

2. In retrospect, though, Brezhnev listed the Afhgan revolution, along with those of Ethiopia and Nicaragua and with the fall of the Shah, as 'new victories' for the 'revolutionary struggle of the peoples': *Report of the Central Committee of the CPSU to the XXVI Congress of the Communist Party of the Soviet Union* (Moscow, 1981) p.6

3. For a fuller discussion, see *The Post-Imperial Age* chap.16

discourage them from linking themselves to it by accepting INF missiles. Thus in January 1983, while on a visit to Bonn, Gromyko described the US administration as 'compulsive gamblers and adventurists who declare that they are ready to plunge mankind into a nuclear catastrophe for the sake of their ambitions'; in February KGB residencies in Western Europe were told to popularise the slogan 'Reagan means War'.[4] Reagan, for his part, invited an evangelical convention in Florida to pray 'for the salvation of those who live in totalitarian darkness', talked of 'the aggressive impulses of an evil empire', and described communism as 'another sad, bizarre chapter in human history whose last pages are even now being written'.[5]

More tangibly NATO issued warnings against Soviet intervention in Poland, where the 'Solidarity' trade union had suddenly emerged as a de facto competitor with the government (see pp. 453–4). The warnings may have been heeded; certainly the USSR adopted the more subtle course of demanding that the Polish goverment itself suppress Solidarity, which it did in December 1981. This NATO unsurprisingly condemned; the USA pushed for tough sanctions, short (however) of suspending its own grain sales to the Soviet Union. Little came of this apart from internal friction within the alliance, for the USA sought also to use the episode to force the cancellation of the projected Soviet gas pipeline to Western Europe (which it did not wish to see become energy-dependent on the East). But it met with refusal. Even pro-American leaders like Thatcher resented US attempts to forbid European companies including American parts in equipment they made for the pipeline; indeed British legislation was invoked to counter them. Eventually the USA was forced to give way, but in return Western Europe agreed to a further tightening of controls on high technology exports to the East.[6]

More harmony was achieved in condemning the USSR for

4. *Keesing's*, 33346; Andrew and Gordievsky, *KGB* p.494

5. Earlier, in a speech to the British Parliament boycotted by most Labour MPs, he had applied Marxist analysis to the USSR: 'a political structure that no longer corresponds to its economic base, a society where productive forces are hampered by political ones. The decay of the Soviet experiment should come as no surprise to us. Wherever the comparisons have been made between free and closed societies – West Germany and East Germany, Austria and Czechoslovakia, Malaysia and Vietnam – it is the democratic countries that are prosperous and responsive to the needs of their people'; in the long term he had looked to 'the march of freedom and democracy which will leave Marxism-Leninism on the ash-heap of history': *Keesing's*, 31639, 33347

6. *Keesing's*, 31458–9, 31965–8; Garthoff, *Détente and Confrontation* pp.1,033–5

shooting down, in September 1983, a Korean airliner that had gone off course and strayed over military installations in the Soviet Far East. Whether because it really did not care about the loss of life, or because it had decided to brazen things out, the USSR stuck to its story that the plane was a spy. The USA played (or over-played) the disaster for publicity advantage. Soviet leaders reiterated their depressing warnings, Gromyko asserting that 'The world situation is now slipping towards a very dangerous precipice', Andropov that 'The Reagan administration, in its imperial ambitions, goes so far that one begins to doubt whether Washington has any brakes at all preventing it from crossing the mark before which any sober-minded person must stop'.[7] Worse still, Gordievsky maintains, Andropov actually believed it, having held since 1981 that the USA was actively preparing for nuclear war. In October 1983 the USA took advantage of murders within the communist leadership of the Caribbean islet of Grenada to invade and liberate it. There were fears in Moscow that this might be the prelude to greater things, even – during the simulated NATO exercises in November – that the count down for an attack might have started.[8] These fears, of course, were not generally known, but the USSR did respond to the deployment that month of cruise and Pershing missiles by pulling out of the arms limitation talks, the last remaining relics of super-power détente.

REAGAN'S SEARCH FOR A SUMMIT; GORBACHEV AND SHEVARDNADZE; THE 1985 GENEVA SUMMIT

In fact Reagan had always hoped for talks with the USSR, albeit from a position of renewed US confidence. Even the 'Evil Empire' speech had included passages to the effect that seeing the Soviets as they really were 'doesn't mean we should isolate ourselves and refuse to seek an understanding with them. I intend to do everything I can to persuade them of our peaceful intent'. Such passages had been overlooked, partly because of the climate of the times, partly in view of the attitudes of some of Reagan's administration – he himself noted (in April 1983) that

7. *Keesing's*, 32513 ff; Andrew and Gordievsky, *KGB* p.501
8. Andrew and Gordievsky, *KGB* pp.488–503

Some of the N.S.C. staff are too hard line and don't think any approach should be made to the Soviets. I think I'm hard line and will never appease. But I do want to let them see there is a better world if they'll show *by deed* they want to get along with the free world![9]

To this end he had first written to Brezhnev in April 1981, expressing hopes that his recent lifting of Carter's grain embargo 'will contribute to creating the circumstances which will lead to the meaningful and constructive dialogue which will assist us in fulfilling our joint obligation to find a lasting peace': Brezhnev's replies, Reagan says, were unforthcoming. In July 1983 he approached Andropov: 'our predecessors have made better progress when they communicated privately and candidly'. Andropov agreed. But both this exchange, and the attempt (in progress since the beginning of the year) to improve relations by 'quiet diplomacy' (initially in connection with the emigration from the USSR of Pentacostalists who had taken refuge in the US embassy in Moscow), were stopped in their tracks by the fracas over the shooting down of the Korean airliner.[10] In any case, deployment of cruise and Pershing missiles was imminent, and Reagan felt 'the Soviets won't really negotiate on arms reductions until we deploy Pershing II's and go forward with the MX'. After the Pershing deployments, Reagan made another – albeit this time public and therefore propagandistic – appeal to Andropov, 'The fact that neither of us likes the other system is no reason to refuse to talk'. He was told in reply that, by deploying, 'the United States has destroyed the very basis on which it was possible to seek such an agreement'. Andropov then died, thereby giving Reagan another chance; and he was soon writing of Chernenko,

> I have a gut feeling I'd like to talk to him about our problems man to man and see if I could convince him there would be a material benefit to the Soviets if they'd join the family of nations, etc. . . . considering an invitation to him to be my guest at the opening of the Olympics, July [1984] in L.A. Then he and I could have a session together in which we could start the ball rolling for an outright summit on arms reductions, human rights, etc.

Chernenko's answer to Reagan's first approach was not unpromising; but Washington was soon told that he did not wish a summit, nor indeed a dialogue without acts of 'concrete, weighty substance' (the discontinuance of cruise and Pershing deployment

---

9. Ronald Reagan, *An American Life* (1990) pp.569, 572

10. ibid, pp.272–3, 302, 576–82; George P. Shultz, *Turmoil and Triumph. My Years as Secretary of State* (New York, 1993) chap. 12

and of US work on S.D.I.).[11] Still Gromyko did, in the course of 1984, visit the White House; and in January 1985 he and Shultz agreed in Geneva to resume arms control talks.

When, in March 1985, 'George Bush went to Moscow for Konstantin Chernenko's funeral, he took an invitation from me to Gorbachev for a summit conference in the United States'. This time things were different. For in December 1984 Gorbachev (then Chernenko's most likely successor) had come to London at Thatcher's invitation'. The two had hit it off – 'I like Mr Gorbachev. We can do business together' – in the course of a long discussion that seems to have focussed chiefly on the arms race, but that left her with hopes that Gorbachev might mark a break with previous expansionist Soviet leaders; she had conveyed her favourable impressions to Reagan. Gorbachev's first letter to Reagan, on 24 March 1985, was cool and firm, but expressed 'a positive attitude to the idea' of a personal meeting. He spelt this out further in June:

> an improvement in the relationship between the USSR and the US is possible. There is objective ground for this. Of course, our countries are different. This fact cannot be changed. There is another fact, however: when the leaders of both countries, as the experience of the past shows, found in themselves enough wisdom and realism to overcome bias caused by differences in social systems, in ideologies, we cooperated successfully . . .[12]

In July Gorbachev made a further change by replacing Gromyko (known to the Americans as 'Grim Grom') as Foreign Minister with his own friend and confidant, Eduard Shevardnadze. Shevardnadze proved an altogether different figure; he began by summoning his ambassadors and telling them that the diplomacy of exporting revolution was over and the time of constructive thinking had come – 'We must stop being perceived as Mr Nyet'.[13]

A summit was arranged for November 1985 in Geneva. Both sides were anxious that it should succeed, and it did. Reagan and Gorbachev struck up a mutual rapport, through a combination of jokes and plain speaking, though this was *not* the case with their wives. If Reagan remained immovable on SDI, Gorbachev (as the sequel was to show) clearly did not give up hope. They readily agreed on the desirability of further summits in 1986 and 1987; and though Gorbachev's personal intervention was required to make his

11. Reagan, *An American Life* pp.586, 591–601
12. ibid, pp.609, 612–14, 617–19, 635; Sheehy, *Gorbachev* pp.186–90
13. *The Independent,* 6 Sept. 1991 p.9

subordinates more flexible over the terms of the press release, the two sides called for further talks on a range of subjects, notably a 50 per cent cut in strategic weapons and an 'interim INF agreement' on the SS–20, cruise and Pershing missiles that were causing so much acrimony.[14]

GORBACHEV'S POLICIES 1985–8

Of what Gorbachev really wanted in 1985, we have as yet no hard evidence. He gave Westerners the impression of being more flexible and open-minded than his predecessors, but as still seeing things through marxist eyes: at Geneva (despite earlier explanations from Thatcher and Shultz) he told Reagan 'he believed American munitions makers were the principal obstacle to peace on the American side. They were our ruling class, he suggested, and they kept our people fired up against the Soviets simply because they wanted to sell more weapons'.[15] His 1987 book *Perestroika* is self-consciously humane, and Leninist. He told writers in 1986 that what 'our adversaries' really feared was not Soviet military power but the success of Soviet domestic reform; 'if we can do it, we shall win'.[16] It seems most unlikely that he had, at first, any intention of leading the USSR where it in fact went; but if he had, he would of course have been careful to conceal it. All we can do here, therefore, is briefly to summarise successive threads of his policies. In so doing, however, we should be careful not to think that, because agreements were achieved, they came easily. Shevardnadze recalls that 'Almost at the finish line, the [INF] negotiations in Moscow were very nearly broken off'. Shultz prepared to go home in frustration, but was intercepted at the airport with suggestions for a solution. Over Afghanistan, he did go home; the USA then thought better of it and next day decided that it could after all accept the final Soviet offer.[17] Had such talks broken down, it would – on past East–West form – have seemed the entirely natural

---

14. Reagan, *An American Life* chap.78; Shultz, *Turmoil and Triumph* chap. 30; Sheehy, *Gorbachev* pp.224–8

15. Nor was he aware, until the 1987 summit, that unemployment benefits and welfare programmes existed in the USA: Sheehy, *Gorbachev* pp.190, 224; Shultz, *Turmoil and Triumph* p.590; Reagan, *An American Life* pp.635, 698

16. *La Repubblica*, 7 Oct. 1986 p.13

17. *The Future Belongs to Freedom* pp.97–8

consequence of their having aimed impossibly high in the first place. With different people involved, this could easily have happened.

In the course of a major stock-taking shortly after he took over, Gorbachev says, the leadership concluded 'that the situation in the world was too dangerous to allow us to miss even the slightest chance for improvement and for more durable peace'. In September 1985 he told Reagan that

> Since . . . preventing nuclear war and removing the threat of war is our mutual and, for that matter, primary interest, it is imperative . . . to use it as the main lever which can help to bring cardinal changes in the nature of the relationship between our nations, to make it constructive and stable and thus contribute to the improvement of the international climate in general.[18]

Gorbachev therefore started by focussing on arms control and on the elimination of SDI. As we have seen (pp. 184–5), he gradually decided that he would have to make concessions to secure progress. This eventually brought him in December 1987 to the milestone INF treaty, which set a precedent (later followed over conventional forces) for both 'intrusive' inspection such as no previous Soviet leader would have contemplated (including the 'open skies' Eisenhower had sought in the 1950s) and *asymmetrical* reductions to achieve a position of East–West parity.

Another strand was his wish to have the Soviet Union accepted by other European powers, which crystallised in 1987 into his slogan, 'Europe is our common home'. In itself this was not new: the Soviets had always contended that they were internal to Europe and that the Americans were not, and the acceptance of Canada and the USA as parties to the Helsinki 'Final Act' had represented a concession. But unlike his predecessors, Gorbachev came gradually to the belief that the USSR could not really become part of Europe unless it mended its ways internally – hence the 1987–8 release of dissidents (which Gorbachev had appeared still to oppose when talking to Sakharov in December 1986). Already in 1986 he had proposed the holding in 1991 of a human rights conference in Moscow, as a symbol of the USSR's new acceptability; this gave the Western powers a lever over his internal policies, something he had furiously rejected on his first visit to London. By December 1988 he had done enough to secure an Anglo-American promise to attend

18. Gorbachev, *Perestroika* p.225; Reagan, *An American Life* pp.624–8

his conference;[19] this could, of course, always have been called off again (as might indeed have happened had his hardline policies of early 1991 continued).

The policy of reconciliation with China was not new, nor indeed were the concessions Gorbachev offered in 1986 on border demarcation. But one of the 'obstacles' whose removal China demanded was Afghanistan. After the Soviet invasion, Carter had arranged for the insurgents to receive ex-Soviet (and therefore deniable) weapons from Egypt and China. Reagan took this further by making it financially worth Pakistan's while to support the guerrillas. In 1984 the USA received intelligence to the effect that the Kremlin feared becoming bogged down, and had therefore decided to escalate the war in an attempt to win it within two years. In 1985 the USA countered by drastically increasing its support for the insurgents, supplying them (inter alia) with superior US missiles that had a devastating effect on Soviet helicopters, and feeding them the products of its satellite and communications intelligence, in the hope that high Soviet casualties would lead to a withdrawal.[20] Soviet losses eventually came to well over 15,000,[21] and the war was both expensive and unpopular. In 1979 Gorbachev had seen the original invasion as a 'fatal error that would cost the country dearly'; at the 1985 Geneva summit he talked of withdrawing 'as part of a general political settlement between us' and hinted that the USA could 'help' the Soviets to leave; at the 1987 summit he promised to try to end the USSR's military presence.[22] The agreement in April 1988 on a Soviet withdrawal (which was completed in February 1989) was nevertheless remarkable, for it meant that the fall of a communist government was conceivable, though previously it had been axiomatic that the wheel of history turned only one way. (Actually, with the hated Russians removed – but still supplying equipment – and the insurgents bitterly divided, the Afghan government did not collapse until 1992.)

By late 1988 Gorbachev appeared to have reached quite a favourable position. He was internationally popular, and he built on

19. Sheehy, *Gorbachev* pp.185, 242, 248–9, 284–5; *Keesing's*, 35471–2, 36413, 36440, 36490

20. US supplies to the guerrillas apparently cost $2 billion over the 1980s, but the USA did draw the line at the Pakistani idea of extending guerrilla action to installations in Soviet Central Asia: *International Herald Tribune*, 21 July 1992 pp.1–2

21. 14,453 were killed in action (Radio Free Europe-Radio Liberty, *Daily Report* 29 Dec. 1992), and there were also many thousands of incidental deaths

22. Shevardnadze, *The Future Belongs to Freedom* p.26; Shultz, *Turmoil and Triumph* p.601

this by cultivating the UN (which the USA was then heavily cold-shouldering). Thus in December 1988, in a striking address to the General Assembly, he called for an international approach to the world debt problem (whereas the USA insisted on country-by-country deals) and announced a new era in which progress would be 'shaped by universal human interests'.[23] He probably hoped that the USSR would be able to function as a major international player, no longer disadvantaged by the suspicions of the Cold War, with a leading voice in settling world problems both through the UN Security Council and bilaterally with the USA. To some extent this happened. The Security Council had earlier in 1988 taken a more prominent role than heretofore in connection with the Iraq–Iran cease-fire; this continued, helped by quiet prior discussions between the five Permanent Members. December 1988 also saw Angola, Cuba and South Africa agree, thanks largely to Soviet and US brokerage, on a settlement of the linked problems of Namibian independence and Cuban withdrawal from Angola; later US–Soviet pressure plus participation in peace talks helped to bring about a May 1991 Angolan cease-fire and agreement to hold elections.[24]

GORBACHEV'S WEAKENING POSITION 1989–91

In 1989 Gorbachev's position was deeply undercut by the collapse of communist rule in Eastern Europe, while growing economic difficulties at home began to convert him, in some respects, into something of a suppliant. On the surface his diplomatic response was brilliant, but it led to settlement of most European Cold War issues on Western terms (see pp. 452, 454–64). Elsewhere these changes reduced the appeal of the Soviet model; thus in March 1990 Mengistu of Ethiopia suddenly discovered that socialism had been a mistake. They also reduced Soviet ability to support former clients. In 1990 aid to Ethiopia was first scaled down and then stopped; aid to Vietnam was similarly cut, with all trade being placed on a hard currency basis;[25] deliveries to Cuba were erratic, while planning started for the gradual phasing out of Soviet subsidies.[26]

23. *Keesing's*, 36779
24. *Keesing's*, 36076 ff, 36380, 38041–2, 38277; *The Post-Imperial Age*, chap.4
25. *Keesing's*, 37310, 37368, 38053 (Ethiopia: Mengistu's regime collapsed in 1991); *The Independent*, 23 Feb. 1991 p.11 (Vietnam)
26. In 1991 these were put at some $2 billion per year, perhaps half the level of the mid-1980s; after the failed coup in the USSR Gorbachev announced his wish to withdraw 11,000 Soviet troops: *Keesing's*, 37813–14; *Daily Telegraph*, 12 Sept. 1991 p.1

This growing weakness did not destroy the value the Bush administration set on cooperation with the USSR. Indeed Secretary of State Baker enjoyed an excellent relationship with Shevardnadze until the latter's resignation in December 1990, and at least a correct one with his successor. During the crisis triggered by Iraq's August 1990 seizure of Kuwait, Soviet support was needed if the USA was to respond through the UN; it was forthcoming, the USSR always voting favourably (whereas China abstained on, though it carefully did not veto, the resolution authorising Iraq's expulsion by force). Not everybody in Moscow was pleased with this ganging up on a former client; when fighting actually started in 1991, Moscow (where hardliners were back in the ascendant) showed itself distinctly uncomfortable, but there seems to have been some sort of tacit understanding. The USSR would not break with the Gulf War coalition; the USA would not, at least overtly, press it over actions taken to bring the Baltic Republics to heel.

Most Western countries also showed a marked reluctance to deal with Yeltsin and the other republics' leaders for fear of under-cutting Gorbachev, with whom they now felt very comfortable. They were, however, divided on how far they should go towards bailing him out economically. Germany (which was anxious that nothing should upset the agreements for the withdrawal of Soviet forces from its territory) and France were favourable. Japan, in fact the only country in a position to make massive loans, was hostile (at least until Soviet concessions were forthcoming on the disputed islands). The USA and UK took the line that aid would be useless unless Gorbachev introduced real economic reforms. As so often before, he recoiled from this, and in July presented the Western G7 leaders with a fudged plan. In return they resolved to recommend the USSR for associate, not full, membership of the International Monetary Fund, a status that would enable it to receive guidance but not to borrow from the Fund. Another set-back was Gorbachev's apparent wish to join the G7.[27] Though he again encountered some sympathy, the final compromise decision was that, at least for 1991, he should meet the Western leaders, but only after the completion of their formal summit.

In these dealings, Gorbachev had shown a desire to join the leading Western institutions, but, by doing so from a position of

---

27. The seven economically largest capitalist countries, whose heads of government hold annual summits and whose finance ministers and central bankers meet more often and inconspicuously

economic weakness, he had assumed the role of a 'demandeur' and had made the USSR to some extent the subject of international diplomacy. In August 1991 hardliners sought to depose him and turn the clock back. That they failed was due entirely to developments within the Soviet Union, and their failure prompted an internal upheaval, the banning of the Communist Party and the assumption of sovereignty by the Republics. For some time to come, the process of working out relationships between them is likely to occupy most political energies in what was formerly the Soviet Union. Meanwhile the West is being assailed with demands for ever greater quantities of economic help. In due course one would expect some strong country to re-emerge, as it did from the upheavals following the 1917 revolutions. (Certainly the Russian Republic alone is the most populous country in Europe, and has enormous resources.) At the time of writing little is left of the postwar structure of East–West rivalry chronicled in previous chapters; the real question is whether the new post-communist order (both in the former USSR and in Eastern Europe) can make good, or whether it will – like the optimistic liberal east European order of 1919 – collapse under economic, political and nationalist stresses.

PART III

Western Europe and the Communist World

CHAPTER THIRTEEN

Western Europe I: The Political Order

THE LIBERAL POLITICAL ORDER

As we have seen, the Cold War assumed global dimensions. It began in Europe (apart from the 1946 developments in Iran) and it ended with the transformation of Eastern Europe in and after 1989. So it is appropriate, in chronicling it, to devote rather more space to Europe than to any other continent. In fact Europe enjoyed remarkable stability from 1945 to 1989, but within the framework of a division into communist and capitalist halves. Chapters 15 and 16 will consider the USSR's attempts to organise and transform its half of Europe; in this chapter we must discuss the more complicated, though less dramatic, evolution of Western Europe. Some of its problems resembled those of its Eastern counterpart, notably the creation of viable political systems and the establishment and maintenance of an acceptable relationship with 'its' superpower. But it also needed to find ways of preventing the recurrence of the national rivalries that had had such dreadful consequences during the twentieth century, while still building on the sovereign states that had been restored with Liberation and that were joined within a decade by the ex-enemy countries of the Second World War. It proved remarkably successful. Western Europe has not, in modern history, known so long a period of peace, nor so great a measure of prosperity. Naturally there were many causes. As these have been mutually reinforcing, they cannot be ranked in any definite order of importance; probably, indeed, a general harmony could have been achieved even had one or two of them been absent. One can say, though, that there has (so far) been no such unravelling as befell the European system of the later 1920s, a system that had seemed, with the Locarno treaties, to have crossed 'the real dividing line between the years of war and the years of peace'.

Very possibly the chief factor in Western Europe's post-1945 success has been the prevalence of an internal liberal political order. Certainly in no major state has such an order, once established, collapsed, as it did in Italy in 1922 and in Germany in 1933. (Rather the process has been the other way, with Portugal making a tortuous and Spain a surprisingly easy transition to liberal democracy in the 1970s.[1]) We have space for only the most cursory glance at domestic politics, but one influence after 1945 was a determination not to repeat earlier mistakes. This did not always work: French politics soon returned to a Third Republican mould, but the Federal Republic did not go back to the ways of Weimar Germany; in Austria the Socialists and the People's Party, instead of literally fighting like their interwar predecessors, shared power in order to recover national sovereignty. We should also note that two great political forces, Catholicism and socialism, that had, in important countries, been ambivalent about the earlier liberal political order, now embraced it. In Italy and West Germany, indeed, the Christian Democrats had by the 1950s become the ruling party, while their counterpart, the Popular Republican Movement (MRP), featured in virtually all French governments. The Socialists' evolution was less dramatic: the German SPD had already strongly supported the Weimar Republic, while the SFIO (French socialist party) had between the wars formed part of French electoral alliances of the Left, though only rarely of subsequent co-alition governments. In Italy, where the socialists had never really been incorporated into the pre-fascist liberal order, during the Cold War they initially sided with the communists against the system; it was not until 1963 that the 'opening to the left' brought them into the governmental coalition.

THE CHALLENGE OF COMMUNISM; THE FRENCH AND ITALIAN COMMUNIST PARTIES

Mention of the communists, of course, points up another challenge to the liberal order. It is, admittedly, arguable that, for at least the first two postwar decades, the perceived threat from 'international

1. John W. Young, *Cold War Europe 1945–89: A Political History* (1991) chap. 6

communism' was a stabilising factor, reminding those of other per-
suasions how much they had in common despite differences that
had once seemed all-engrossing. Experience of communist rule in
East Germany also cut the party's appeal in the rest of the country.[2]
More generally, Western Communist parties were upset by the
developments of 1956, so much so that when the French leader
heard that Khrushchev meant to rehabilitate Bukharin and
Zinoviev, he rushed to Moscow to warn that, 'After the 20th
Congress and the Hungarian events we lost almost half our Party. If
you were formally to rehabilitate those who were tried in the open
trials, we could lose the rest'.[3] Still the communists were the largest
party in France and the second largest in Italy; to begin with both
behaved as arms of the Soviet Union, reversing their domestic
policies in 1947 in accordance with Cominform dictates (see p. 93).
In neither country did they seem likely to gain power (though the
US ambassador to Italy worried about the long-run implications of
the Christian Democrats' decline from their 1948 electoral peak).
But in both they contributed greatly to governmental instability, for,
given their constant opposition plus that of the far Right,[4] it
needed only a few extra critics to bring an administration down.

The French Communist Party (PCF) remained remarkably loyal
to Moscow: a brief attempt to distance itself by such moves as
abandoning its commitment to the 'dictatorship of the proletariat'
in 1976 ended in 1980 with the party's endorsement of the Soviet
intervention in Afghanistan. Its domestic support fell sharply. It
dropped 1.5 million votes on the first ballot of the 1958 elections,
and was trounced by the Gaullists on the second. In 1969 its
candidate (though outvoting the socialist) managed only third
place in the presidential elections; it was clear that the Left could
compete only if it came together. This was achieved in 1972 when
the communists, socialists and Left Radicals settled on a 'Common
Programme' of government and agreed to campaign together. In
this alliance the communists could hope for influence as the largest
party. But the socialist leader Mitterand soon stated that his aim was
to overtake the PCF and 'rebuild a great Socialist Party on the
terrain occupied by the Communist Party itself and thus to show
that of five million communist voters three million can be brought

---

2. They won only fifteen seats in 1949, none in 1953, and were declared
unconstitutional in 1956
3. Johnson, *Long March of the French Left* p.51
4. In France Gaullists and then Poujadists, in Italy Monarchists and Fascists

to vote Socialist'.[5] By 1981 he had largely achieved this, helped by the PCF's return to the Soviet line and by its attacks on himself, which had the effect of convincing the electorate that he was not a communist puppet. At the first ballot of the 1981 presidential elections the communist candidate polled only 15 per cent. The PCF then rallied to Mitterand, pinning its hopes on being accorded ministries in a socialist-led administration. Mitterand went on to win both the presidency and an absolute Socialist majority in the National Assembly. Only then were four communists taken into the government. They had little influence: Mitterand surprised everybody with the firmly anti-Soviet tone of his foreign policy. Domestically too the communists were squeezed, and their electoral decline continued for most of the 1980s.

The Italian Communist Party (PCI) was more lively than the French. It had followed the Soviet Union into the Cold War, condemning Marshall Aid perhaps against the better judgement of its leader, Togliatti. But Togliatti used Khrushchev's acceptance of different roads to socialism (and his revelations about Stalin) to float ideas of 'polycentrism', and of a distinctive 'Italian way' that would use parliamentary forms and involve collaboration with other political parties and the search for both peasant and middle-class support. The practical implications were still slight: the PCI accepted Soviet suppression of Hungary in 1956, and next year condemned Italian membership of the European Economic Community (EEC). The early 1960s brought further softening; in 1962 the PCI endorsed EEC membership, and it was cool towards Khrushchev's campaign against the Chinese Communist Party. Togliatti had no sympathy with the Chinese, but he held by the autonomy of individual Communist parties. In 1964 he died in Yalta on his way to confront Khrushchev on the subject, and the PCI published his 'testament'. This stressed that all was not well even with the Soviet Union, and that western parties needed to liquidate 'old formulae which no longer correspond to present realities', make overtures to 'the religious masses', and think more about a peaceful transition to socialism.[6] In 1968 Togliatti's successors proclaimed the long-run objective of a pluralist socialist democracy to be achieved through a union of all progressive forces, both secular and Catholic. They were both shocked and frightened by the Warsaw Pact intervention, later that year, to suppress 'socialism with a human face' in Czechoslovakia. This much reduced their hostility to the NATO alliance that protected them from such action.

By the early 1970s the PCI was becoming alarmed by the possibility that the internal disturbances then multiplying in Italy would play into the hands of the Far Right, as in the early 1920s; it sought to enter the circle of accepted constitutional parties through a 'historic compromise' with the Christian Democrats (DC). This was brought nearer when, in 1974, an old-fashioned Catholic and anti-communist campaign flopped in a referendum on divorce. Later that year the socialists pulled out of the government. The country seemed to be moving left, a view confirmed by the 1975 regional elections when the PCI greatly narrowed the gap between itself and the DC. Against this background the PCI asked to enter the government as a party whose support would be needed to overcome political instability, domestic violence, and economic crisis. Its secretary, Berlinguer, was free with assurances of devotion to democracy and liberalism, while as to NATO he publicly declared (though *not* in the party newspaper), 'I feel safer on this side'. He acted as patron to the emergent, and ostentatiously liberal, Spanish Communist Party; and he repeated his unwelcome 'Euro-communist' pronouncements at the 1976 Soviet Party Congress.[7]

By no means everybody believed them. The PCI still contained instinctively pro-Soviet elements. Its entry into the Cabinet might trigger defections from, or even a collapse of, the DC, hitherto the indispensable party of government. It could have had even wider consequences: one commentator observed that it was 'almost impossible to see right-wing Republican congressmen tolerating for long a situation in which American servicemen were stationed in Europe to protect Communist-dominated governments'.[8] There was a tradition of external intervention in Italian politics, which Kissinger was determined to continue. In 1975 he told US ambassadors that 'We cannot encourage dialogue with Communist parties within NATO nations. . . . The extent such a party follows the Moscow line is unimportant . . . the impact of an Italian Communist Party that seemed to be governing effectively would be devastating – on France, and on NATO too'; indeed the alliance, as now constituted, 'could not survive'. In 1976 there were further

---

7. *Keesing's*, 27694–6, 27736; Norman Kogan, *A Political History of Italy: The Postwar Years* (New York, 1983) p.296
8. Bell, *Diplomacy of Detente* p.229

elaborations, and also an agreement (soon revealed by Chancellor Schmidt) that if the PCI entered the government, the USA, UK, France and Germany would withhold financial assistance. The policy was continued by the Carter administration: Brzezinski wrote that the drift to the left in Italy was 'potentially the gravest political problem we now have in Europe'.[9]

Given the conflicting pressures, the DC adopted a step-by-step approach. After the 1976 elections a purely DC government was formed, but only after agreement on policy with the other moderate parties *including the communists*, who all then abstained from voting against it. The 1977–8 winter saw a renewed crisis over demands, backed by some of the DC and most of the other parties, for the PCI's inclusion in a government of national emergency; this prompted public US condemnation of the idea. The leading Christian Democrat, Aldo Moro, eventually worked out a compromise whereby the government would remain DC, but accept the communists into the ranks of its parliamentary majority. Left-wing terrorists then murdered him, thus removing the most influential proponent of dialogue with the PCI. This triggered demonstrations of national solidarity. But the communist position of support for, but not full membership of, the system became uncomfortable, and they were in danger of losing votes to the left. In 1979 they again demanded entry into the government and, when refused, withdrew into opposition. New elections showed the PCI to have passed its peak; in 1980 the socialists, who had for some time been squabbling with the communists, stopped advocating their entry into government and decided themselves to rejoin it. Despite a poor DC electoral performance in 1983–4, the 1980s were to see comparative political stability, based on broad moderate coalitions that excluded the communists. They also witnessed a decline in terrorism and considerable economic growth, though also the ballooning of budget deficits. Against this background the communist vote fell gently to 27 per cent in the 1987 parliamentary elections. Two years later came the collapse of communism in Eastern Europe. After considerable discussion, the PCI was refounded in 1991 as the Democratic Party of the Left (PDS), with hardliners breaking away to form a rival splinter group. At the 1992 elections the ex-communist vote continued to fall, the PDS gaining only 16.1 per cent. The decline of communism was to rock the structure that had

---

9. *Keesing's*, 27796–7, 27926; Garthoff, *Détente and Confrontation* p.488; Brzezinski, *Power and Principle* pp.311–12

been built over the previous four decades to contain it, however, for people now no longer felt it so necessary for the tarnished parties of the political establishment. In the 1992 elections the DC too fell below 30 per cent, while the governing coalition only just secured a majority.[10] Later that year there followed a wave of arrests for corruption, the advent of new faces in the existing parties, and a surge of support for new ones promising to clear up the mess. In 1993 the PDS appeared likely to prove the chief beneficiary.

MILITARY TAKE-OVERS IN GREECE AND TURKEY

During the early Cold War the most obvious threat to the liberal system was from the communists. But it was from the Right that take-overs had come between the wars. One such take-over did occur in Greece, when the army seized power in 1967 rather than risk the electoral victory of the Centre Union (a fairly moderate party, but one backed by the communists and thought likely to purge rightist officers). However, military rule collapsed in 1974 after a rash adventure in Cyprus had brought Greece to the brink of war with Turkey. In Turkey, too, the army took over from 1960–1 and 1980–3, voluntarily restoring power to civilians under conditions meant to prevent a recurrence of the developments it disliked.[11] There have been no other such upsets, but it is again worth touching briefly on events in France and Italy, both of which were ruled in the 1950s by a succession of short-lived governments.

ALGERIAN SETTLERS AND THE ARMY OVERTHROW OF THE FOURTH REPUBLIC; DE GAULLE RE-ESTABLISHES PARIS'S CONTROL

The French Fourth Republic's constitution had been meant to turn over a new leaf and provide stronger government. That Republic had its successes, but public perception was rather of inflation, strikes, and international humiliation. This last went back to the defeat of 1940. Since then Britain had blocked the restoration of

10. Kogan, *History of Italy* esp. chap. 21; *Keesing's*, 37786, 38021
11. On the former occasion the rightist Menderes government's revival of appeals to religion and tough ways with opponents, in the second extremism and violence of both left and right

351

French control over Syria in 1945. France had lost its war in Vietnam in 1954. Repression had failed in Tunisia and Morocco, and they became independent in 1956. Revolt broke out in Algeria;[12] in 1957–8 'the Anglo-Saxons' appeared to be intervening diplomatically, with the prospect of what the Minister for Algeria called a 'diplomatic Dien Bien Phu'. The army had had enough; as a 1958 broadcast put it, 'no more "strategic withdrawals"; no more "peace with honour"; no more "internal autonomy" . . .; no more "representative negotiators"; no more "good offices" '.[13]

There appear to have been extremist plotters in Algiers since at least 1956, and the idea grew of using a settlers' rising to prompt a change of regime in Paris. The ex-Gaullist Minister of Defence and his aides started establishing contacts in order to turn the anticipated explosion to the General's advantage. This explosion was touched off by a political crisis that saw the failure of the hardliner Bidault's bid for the premiership and its replacement by that of Pflimlin, who was suspected of wanting negotiations with the Algerian resistance movement (the FLN). On 13 May 1958 a demonstration in the predominantly European city of Algiers developed into a take-over of government offices; the army commander, General Salan, went along with calls for a Committee of Public Safety, and on the 15th was induced to declare for de Gaulle. In response de Gaulle announced his readiness 'to assume the powers of the Republic'. From then on he appears to have played a double game, in touch with at least some of the rebels' moves while simultaneously negotiating with the existing political leaders a peaceful accession to power that would head them off. On 24 May paratroopers from Algiers seized Corsica, and there were known to be plans for an early take-over of the mainland. Army leaders and the Paris police were sympathetic; despite a large pro-Republican demonstration in Paris, calls for strikes in support of the government failed outside the northern coalfield. What proved decisive was the determination of most leading politicians not to risk a confrontation in which any government opposing the insurgents would have to place itself in the hands of the (largely communist) organised workers. 'It would', Mollet is quoted as saying, 'have been the [1936] war in Spain – without the republican army' – or, in de Gaulle's later words, an 'adventure leading to civil war in the presence, and soon with the participation on different

12. See *The Post-Imperial World* chap.1
13. P.M. Williams and M. Harrison, *De Gaulle's Republic* (1961 edn) p.61

sides, of foreign powers'. Negotiations were still not easy, but de Gaulle was eventually induced to make enough concessions to secure his legal investiture as Prime Minister.[14]

There were fears that, in power, de Gaulle would be prisoner of the right-wing forces that had brought him there. When this was put to him, he is said to have replied, 'Prisoners escape'. Certainly he succeeded in so doing. He began by securing massive endorsement in a referendum for a new constitution, followed by parliamentary elections; for the rest of his life he seems psychologically to have needed regular repetitions of such votes of confidence. He was careful to promote most of the soldiers involved in the Algerian rising to positions where they would be less dangerous; he moved obliquely to disengage from *Algérie Française,* in September 1959 promising a choice between integration, association and independence. This led to the revival of earlier plots and to a plan for a coup in October, though it had to be dropped for lack of support. In January 1960 the army was ominously inactive when militants occupied the centre of Algiers for a week. In 1961 things were worse. De Gaulle's statement in April that France should disengage from Algeria prompted an army take-over there, organised by a network of colonels but attracting the support of retired generals like Salan and Challe (who had been in command in Algeria during the January 1960 affair). In response de Gaulle assumed emergency powers, and massive (and well-supported) preparations were made against any military move on the mainland. De Gaulle again broadcast, and prompted demonstrations of loyalty from conscript servicemen in Algeria. Within three days General Challe decided to call things off to avoid bloodshed, and the revolt collapsed. He had in 1960 declared that 'if a defeated French army were to return home accompanied by half a million furiously angry Algerians, France would be under dictatorship before three months were up'. In 1962 such an exodus did occur, but without the effects he had anticipated. As an Algerian senator had observed in 1959, de Gaulle 'has an enormous popular appeal. . . . The 13 May [1958 rising] succeeded because of a miracle, a conjuncture which brought Algiers, the army and the mainland together with the same aims at the same time. This conjuncture will not be repeated. A new 13 May will find no echo on the mainland'. Nevertheless the OAS terrorist resistance that mushroomed in Algeria in 1961 spilt over

14. Philip Williams, *Wars, Plots and Scandals in Post-War France* (Cambridge, 1970) chap. 7; Larkin, *France since the Popular Front* pp.263–9; de Gaulle, *Mémoires* p.22

into France, with no less a figure than Bidault eventually assuming the leadership. During 1961–3 there were several plots against de Gaulle's life, one of which nearly succeeded; but such troubles died down as events in Algeria gradually receded into the past.[15]

CONSOLIDATION OF FRENCH POLITICAL STABILITY UNDER THE FIFTH REPUBLIC

Until Algeria had been resolved de Gaulle was widely regarded as indispensable. Thereafter he was expected to be much weaker. Instead he confounded the prophets by pushing through a further constitutional change, announcing (shortly after an attempt on his life) a referendum to make the presidency directly elective, and threatening to resign if he did not get a good majority. His action was by normal criteria unconstitutional; and almost all the non-Gaullist deputies joined in censuring the government. Both de Gaulle and the idea of directly choosing a President were clearly popular, and 'the parties of the past' found they had put themselves in the wrong with the electorate: this not only voted for the referendum but also gave the Gaullists and their allies an unprecedented absolute majority in the parliamentary elections that followed. From then on, French administrations have (in marked contrast to experience since the 1870s) proved durable and have been able to count on parliamentary support. Some of the greater strength and decisiveness of Fifth Republican diplomacy must be attributable to these changes in the political system.

Initially, though, the system was still fragile. In May 1968 student demonstrations, caused chiefly by a recent university reform but reflecting also an international wave of leftist sentiment, touched off strikes and factory occupations (wages had been squeezed since 1967). By some accounts de Gaulle panicked and contemplated flight. Both Mitterand and Mendès-France offered to form provisional governments in what would have been a mirror image of 1958. Prime Minister Pompidou kept his nerve, bought off the strikers with wage increases, and persuaded de Gaulle to dissolve Parliament and campaign on an anti-communist law-and-order platform; the result was an electoral triumph. This did not resolve

---

15. Larkin, *France since the Popular Front* pp.272–8; Williams, *Wars, Plots and Scandals* chap. 10; Williams and Harrison, *De Gaulle's Republic* pp. 209, 227

all problems. Strong government was re-established; but there was much nervousness as to what would replace first the elderly de Gaulle, then (in the early 1970s) his successor Pompidou, who proved to have cancer. As we have seen, Mitterand joined forces with the communists and made strong speeches: 'I have to say that anyone who does not accept a rupture with the established order, with capitalist society, cannot be a member of the Socialist Party'.[16] In the mid-1970s France was electorally very evenly divided, and the Right both played up and genuinely believed in the red peril. Perhaps for this reason, they did not lose power until it had become quite clear that Mitterand controlled the communists rather than vice versa. Then in 1981 *alternance* happened remarkably smoothly, and Mitterand settled comfortably into the presidential system that he had once opposed. So well entrenched, indeed, did the constitution prove that it could accommodate the return of a rightist majority in the 1986 parliamentary elections. Mitterand appointed its leader, Chirac, Prime Minister and left government largely to him; then in 1988 he secured re-election as President, dissolved Parliament and won his socialists a working majority.

THREATS FROM THE RIGHT TO THE ITALIAN POLITICAL SYSTEM; THE TROUBLES OF THE 1970s

Events in Italy were less dramatic. In the late 1950s, however, there were fears that the DC's hegemony might collapse if international détente had the effect of legitimising the communists,[17] and bitter controversy as to whether the DC should look for allies to the left or the right. In late 1959 a DC congress decided to seek socialist support, and the Liberals responded next February by pulling out of the government. This led to a long political crisis, with the Church and employers' and peasant proprietors' organisations seeking to block any opening to the left. The socialists made the mistake of asking too high a price; and the outcome was a DC government, headed by Tambroni, that could attract votes from no other party except the fascists (MSI). That summer the MSI insisted

16. MacShane, *Mitterand* p.141
17. Earlier, French opposition to Churchill's pressure for a summit had been based partly on the fear that it would legitimise, and so strengthen, the PCF: Pierre Hassner, 'Perceptions of the Soviet threat in the 1950s and 1980s: the case of France', in Schweitzer, *The Changing Western Analysis of the Soviet Threat* p.176

on holding a congress in fiercely hostile Genoa; it touched off a wave of riots. Tambroni would have liked to respond forcefully, but the disturbances were bad enough to enable his rivals to organise an alternative DC government of 'democratic restoration' that was opposed only by the fascists and communists.[18]

The experience ruled out any further possibility of a parliamentary evolution to the right (which had been feared as leading imperceptibly to the return of the fascist 'regime'). But some people were tempted to achieve it by other means. The Carabinieri commander, General de Lorenzo, made unauthorised preparations to suppress disturbances and arrest a broad list of potential opponents; during a mid-1964 political crisis President Segni contemplated installing an emergency government of technicians, while perhaps readying the Carabinieri to put these preparations into effect in the event of trouble – which would have amounted to a 'Gaullist' coup. Any such development was forestalled by the hurried reassembly of a centre-left government.[19] The temperature rose again at the end of the 1960s, with violent student demonstrations (which evolved over the 1970s into small-scale but murderous left-wing terrorism) and the labour disputes of the 1969 'hot autumn'. Ultra-rightists thought this propitious: Mussolini had gained power by utilising similar if more extensive threats to order and property. So they stoked things up through the so-called 'strategy of tension', beginning in 1969 with a Milan explosion that they represented as the work of an anarchist. In 1970 there was an actual coup attempt by Prince Valerio Borghese; there were further plots in 1973–4 to kidnap the Cabinet and to establish a Fascist republic, in some of which the security service does seem to have been compromised.[20] The Republic was probably in no danger, but then failed coups generally look ridiculous in retrospect. The threat was taken seriously at the time, while rightist explosions (like leftist terrorism) continued for over a decade before they were gradually brought under control.

18. Kogan, *History of Italy* pp.151–62; Elizabeth Wiskemann, *Italy since 1945* (1971) pp.38–9; *Keesing's*, 17713–14

19. It should also be remembered that the 1967 Greek coup took the form of an unauthorised activation of an official counter-insurgency plan: Richard Collin, *The De Lorenzo Gambit: The Italian Coup Manqué of 1964* (1976, Sage Research Papers, Contemporary European Studies Series, no. 90–034)

20. The Far Right was encouraged by the Greek 'colonels' take-over, and probably received funds from them: *Keesing's*, 26410–12, 26821, 28494, 29057, 29224; Kogan, *History of Italy* p.287; Wiskemann, *Italy since 1945* p.88

POSTWAR ECONOMIC GROWTH

We have discussed France and Italy. More generally we may note that earlier issues of strident nationalism and of Church versus state were in relative decline, while economic questions assumed greater prominence. These last are perhaps politically easier to handle, at least as long as the economic cake is growing – as it has done to an unprecedented extent in all West European countries. Economic success does not cure all problems: although Italy's postwar growth rate has been higher than Britain's, Britain has generally been politically the more stable country. But economic set-backs – especially those accompanying the mid-1970s' 'stagflation' – could cause serious difficulties.[21] So it is worth speculating briefly as to why they were so few.

From the perspective of 1990 it looks as if economic growth is to be expected where governments provide a reasonably secure environment and a functioning infrastructure, but leave business exposed, and fairly free to respond, to market signals. Certainly Europe's 'economic miracle' has been more than matched by the capitalist countries of the west Pacific, which have operated broadly on this principle. But at the end of the 1920s the United States had been hit by the Slump despite the presence of such conditions; Europe had followed (with devastating political results in Germany), partly through contagion and partly through its own internal weaknesses. Happily there has been no postwar parallel in Western Europe;[22] states have generally sought to avoid the possibility by stimulating their economies when serious downturns threatened,[23] and by fighting shy of 1930s beggar-thy-neighbour tariff and currency policies. Beyond this, several interlocking factors have together constituted a strong 'virtuous circle'. They would include: the acceleration and diffusion of technological discoveries; a historically high investment ratio, cheap oil (from 1957 to 1973 and again from the mid-1980s); rapidly rising trade bringing the benefits of specialisation and comparative advantage; the spreading

21. Including, in Britain, a 1974 election over 'who governs' the country (the government, with its incomes policy, or the National Union of Mineworkers), and an economy where successive cycles seemed to be becoming so much more extreme that one influential *Times* journalist proclaimed that they would soon precipitate an authoritarian solution

22. The recession of the early 1990s had not (by late 1993) approached the scale of the interwar USA or German – or the contemporary Russian – slumps

23. Perhaps too readily, with the result that inflation has been a distinctive feature of the period

of prosperity to Mediterranean countries through tourism; increasing managerial efficiency; and (except in Britain) the movement of workers out of agriculture into industry and services with higher productivity. In West Germany this last was supplemented first by people from the East and later by 'guest-workers' from Italy and subsequently Turkey. Many other areas have also thus replenished their labour force from abroad, even Sicily drawing on North African labour in the late 1980s – though elsewhere the decline of old industries and the resultant rise in unemployment has rendered this less necessary, and the attendant social problems have made it generally unwelcome. Beyond such generalities it is not easy to go, since states have differed considerably in their economic policies, nor have these always had the effects one would have anticipated.[24]

MARSHALL AID 1947–52

At first, though, the question was not one of degrees of economic success but of recovery from disaster. In 1947 the US Under-Secretary of State for Economic Affairs, William Clayton, could report that 'Millions of people in the cities are slowly starving. More consumer's [*sic*] goods and restored confidence in the local currency are absolutely necessary if the peasant is again to supply food in normal quantities to the cities'. The present position 'represents an absolute minimum standard of living. If it should be lowered, there will be revolution'.[25] In fact the problem was more one of bottlenecks and transport difficulties; although agriculture was generally down on prewar levels, industrial production was up.[26] But further recovery would have run into a balance of payments crisis had it not been for Marshall Aid, since (in the absence of German industrial and of East European agricultural products) Western Europe had a collective deficit of $7.4 billion, mostly with the USA. Marshall Aid (and after it offshore military procurement) bridged the gap until exports could be expanded. Growth could thus continue, with the result that by 1951 per capita incomes were above prewar levels in most countries (though not West Germany).[27] Marshall Aid had thus excluded the risk of

24. D.H. Aldcroft, *The European Economy 1914–1980* chap. 5
25. *FRUS*, 1947 iii p.230
26. Except in the Netherlands (95%), France (92%) and the ex-enemy countries
27. Aldcroft, *European Economy* pp.148–57

'economic, social and political deterioration of a very grave character' and enabled Western Europe to proceed in the 1950s to self-sustaining growth.

What it did not do was to enable the Americans to impose their views on how Western Europe should be organised. The State Department had been clear that it sought 'a European economic federation' on the Benelux model, but divided as to how this could best be approached:

> Balancing the dangers of appearing to force 'the American way' on Europe and the danger of failure if the major responsibility is left to Europe, Mr Bohlen suggested that the alternative is to place strong pressure on the European nations to plan by . . . making it clear that the only politically feasible basis on which the US would be willing to make aid available is substantial evidence of a developing overall plan for economic cooperation by the Europeans themselves, perhaps an economic federation to be worked out over 3 or 4 years.

This was done, sometimes rather bluntly,[28] but it did not work. In 1947 sixteen states readily formed a Committee of European Economic Cooperation to produce a response to Secretary Marshall's offer. Few wished it to become permanent, but the USA was able to persuade them, though only after concluding a package deal with France on German questions. So in April 1948 an Organisation for European Economic Cooperation (OEEC) came into existence. But Britain and France (with considerable support from smaller countries like Norway) were determined that it should not assume supranational dimensions; by 1949 Harriman was to remark that 'the British had prevailed in setting the pattern of an organization whose impotency was now becoming alarming'.[29]

By dint of earmarking $600 million of Marshall Aid, the USA did secure the establishment in 1950 of a 'European Payments Union' (EPU), in effect a clearing house for currency settlements between OEEC members (plus their colonies and the sterling area) that also provided conditional loans of the kind now associated with the International Monetary Fund (IMF). This saw Germany through its unexpectedly high 1950–1 deficit,[30] and (after interruptions due to the Korean War) edged its members back towards the abandon-

---

28. *FRUS*, 1947 iii pp.232, 234–5, 317–18; congressional support for European economic integration was expressed in the preamble of the Act authorising Marshall Aid

29. *FRUS*, 1949 iv p.489

30. Fortunately German deficits coincided with sterling area surpluses and vice versa

ment of quantitative trade restrictions.[31] By 1955 Europe was beginning to look to the return of convertibility; the process was slowed by the disruptions attending the Suez affair; but in December 1958 de Gaulle (who was determined to secure a hard currency) devalued the franc in a move that was synchronised with the adoption by major countries of external convertibility. This rendered the EPU superfluous, and it was wound up.[32] It is generally regarded as having done an excellent job, but it did not fulfil American hopes (at the time of its creation) that it would lead to the establishment of a European central bank and common currency.

THE SCHUMAN PLAN (1950) AND THE ESTABLISHMENT OF THE ECSC; THE EDC

Instead the creation of a significant European entity is now usually traced to the 'Schuman Plan'. French policy towards Germany had since 1918 been a compound of cooperation and coercion, with the latter predominant. In 1945 France told the Americans that, 'With the aim of military security we prefer to increase French steel production . . . to the detriment of the Ruhr'.[33] There was, of course, international agreement that Germany's steel production should be curbed to prevent any revival of its military potential; and the Monnet Plan envisaged a great expansion of French steel output so that France could displace Germany as the heartland of continental industry. This had not worked: French steel had to be smelted with German coke. But production of this was, up to 1950, well short of prewar levels – the French believed because of the incompetence with which Britain managed the Ruhr; also, to save imports, German steel plants had to use not Swedish but inferior

31. By 1959 major countries had lifted over 90% of those on trade with other OEEC members. But France had scrapped the whole process in 1952–3 and 1957–8, while the restrictions that remained were, of course, the important ones: W.M. Scammell, *The International Economy since 1945* (Basingstoke, 1983 edn) p.34; *Keesing's*, 16606, 16610

32. This left the OEEC with little to do. In 1960 it was reconstituted as the Organisation for Economic Cooperation and Development with more global interests; in 1964 Japan joined as a symbol of its acceptance as an advanced industrial state. But the OECD has been extensively bypassed, and become largely a body for monitoring economic trends

33. A.S. Milward, *The Reconstruction of Western Europe 1945–51* (1984) p.129

domestic ore that took twice as much coke to smelt. Against this background France fought hard to secure a lien on German coal production. A sliding-scale entitlement was agreed in 1947, followed in 1948 by the excision of the Saar's output from calculations of 'German' coal. Also, at the price of abandoning its insistence that a reconstituted West German state be only of a minimalist nature and subject to prolonged – Bidault spoke of permanent – occupation, France managed in 1948 to secure agreement on an international Ruhr Authority. However, as London noted, 'the Ruhr document is full of sound and fury but signifying practically nothing'; in 1949 France could no more than dent the dual pricing system whereby such German coal as was exported cost considerably more than coal for German domestic consumption.[34]

Repeated demonstrations that France could not prevent a reconstruction of Germany along US lines inspired an important change of tack. As civil service appreciations put it in the 1948–9 winter, there was 'only one solution: to abandon . . . our malthusian policy with respect to Western Germany and to establish a common ground of economic and political association with' it.

> That is why the French government has come to the conviction that the guarantees it is seeking will only be capable of being validly secured in a kind of association of Germany in a larger framework, that of Europe . . . steel made in the Ruhr would no longer be German steel but a part of European steel. France would be associated on equal terms with Germany in the control of this steel cartel. In this way she would have her word to say, better than by international controls, in the question of the [capacity of] the German steel works.[35]

By late 1949 the time was propitious for trying out such an approach, for the USA was starting to soft-pedal its earlier policy of using Britain to bring about European integration. Acheson now felt France was the 'key':

> France needs, in the interests of her own future, to take the initiative . . . if the character of West Germany is to be one permitting healthy development in Western Europe . . . France and France alone can take the decisive leadership in integrating Western Germany into Western Europe. . . .
> Inability of the US and possibly of the UK and of other countries to join in actions involving some merger of sovereignty should not debar other countries from such progress.

34. ibid, esp. pp.134–6, 154, 157, 378, 386–7
35. ibid, pp.162–3

So Acheson wrote to the French Foreign Minister, imploring him to take the lead.[36]

The upshot was the 'Schuman Plan', secretly prepared by the French technocrat Jean Monnet, bounced through the French Cabinet, and released with a flourish in May 1950:

> A united Europe was not achieved [after 1918]; and we had war. Europe will not be made all at once or according to a single general plan. It will be built through concrete achievements, which first create a *de facto* solidarity. The gathering together of the nations of Europe requires the elimination of the age-old opposition of France and Germany. The first concern in any action taken must be these two countries.
>
> With this in view, the French government proposes to take action immediately on one limited but decisive point . . . to place Franco-German production of coal and steel under a common higher authority, within the framework of an organization open to the participation of the other countries of Europe.[37]

For Germany the offer, promising the end of discriminatory control by the Ruhr Authority and the lifting of restrictions on plant capacity, proved irresistible. Adenauer at once agreed in principle, later explaining that he had advanced similar proposals in 1923; at one point in the subsequent negotiations he reminded German steel manufacturers that 'the political aim was in the foreground and economic aims were more or less subordinate'.[38] So 1951 brought agreement on a European Coal and Steel Community (ECSC) to consist of France, Germany, Italy, the Netherlands, Belgium and Luxembourg.

If this seemed a success for the 'European idea', a major set-back soon followed. For, faced in late 1950 by strong US pressure for German rearmament, France proposed a 'European Defence Community' (EDC), partly to delay the unwelcome day, partly in the hope that it would permit German mobilisation for Western defence while still precluding a national German army. Unfortunately it would also weaken the French army. The EDC soon became exposed to the criticisms of opposites – it went too far, or not far enough, in a European direction – but above all to residual fears of the revival of the *Wehrmacht* and of the old Germany. When the treaty was, after much foreign pressure, eventually put to the National Assembly in 1954, it was rejected, thus derailing the agreed restoration of sovereignty to West Germany. That things were

36. Oct. 1949: *FRUS*, 1949, iv p.470, iii pp.622–5
37. C. Tugendhat, *Making Sense of Europe* (Harmondsworth, 1986) p.31
38. Milward, *Reconstruction of Western Europe* p.413

eventually straightened out, this time in the context of NATO and its predecessor the Western European Union, was due chiefly to British and US diplomacy.

A EUROPEAN COMMON MARKET 1955–8

The next moves came in the spring of 1955 from Benelux, whose Foreign Ministers (with the backing of the ECSC Assembly) called for economic integration in a variety of sectors (including nuclear energy) and for a 'Common Market'. This resulted in a Foreign Ministers' conference at Messina, which endorsed these goals and established a committee to draw up plans under the guidance of the Belgian Foreign Minister Henri Spaak. In the 'Spaak Report', this called for the creation by stages of a European Common Market, modelled institutionally on the ECSC, and also for a European Atomic Community. Its efforts were reinforced by the lobbying of European federalists – notably the 'Action Committee for the United States of Europe', founded in October 1955 by Monnet (now retired after a rather unsuccessful term as first President of the ECSC High Authority) and containing an impressive international range of politicians and union leaders. The French political situation had been altered by the decline of Gaullism and shift to the socialists at the 1956 elections. France still had serious reservations; but it decided, at the Venice Foreign Ministers' conference, to accept the Spaak Report as a basis for discussion while negotiating for a wide range of changes and safeguards, a process that lasted until March 1957. In November 1956 key concessions were made by Adenauer in a meeting with Mollet: there should be harmonisation of social security (though this never really came about) so that France should not be competitively disadvantaged by its more generous arrangements, and France could continue to subsidise exports and tax imports until its balance of payments improved. Later it was agreed that after the treaty had come into effect a Common Agricultural Policy (CAP) should be worked out. Finally French and Belgian colonies should be associated with, and receive development aid from, the European Economic Community for five years, after which the arrangements should be renegotiated. On Euratom (European Atomic Energy Community) possible disputes over the military application of nuclear energy were shelved by a decision to exclude this for the time being. In 1957 the EEC and Euratom were created by the Treaties of Rome, to take effect in March 1958. The negotiations had succeeded as a result of commitment and a disposition to compromise, but they had also shown the strength of France's position, despite its apparently fragile economy. For the other large countries, Italy and Germany, both felt a political need that France did not share for European integration as an escape from the past. As (in the absence of the UK) such integration seemed impossible without it, France could bargain strongly to protect its economic interests.[39]

Euratom never amounted to much, and nuclear energy programmes remained essentially national (partly, in the French case, because of their military implications). But the EEC made unexpectedly rapid progress. This was helped by de Gaulle's firm devaluation of the franc, accompanied by the lifting of most quota restrictions on OEEC trade and by a readiness to risk implementing the agreed initial tariff cuts in January 1959. There had been no certainty that French industry could face the resultant competition, but in fact it responded remarkably well – helped by a generally favourable trade environment.[40] A further stimulus came from the foundation of the rival European Free Trade Association (EFTA), of which more below; to avoid being overtaken, the EEC decided to speed up the removal of quota restrictions on internal trade (abolished by late 1961) and the construction of internal free trade and a common external tariff (completed by mid-1968).[41]

DE GAULLE AND THE WORKING OF THE EEC; THE 'LUXEMBOURG COMPROMISE' 1966

Some of these negotiations had been difficult, but the real problems came over the Community's decision-making processes and over agriculture, the two topics being linked as France had strong views on each. For enthusiasts, economic cooperation had been the way to political union, a slow route perhaps but the only

39. F. Roy Willis, *France, Germany and the New Europe 1945–1967* (1968 edn) chap. 9

40. Intra-EEC trade rose by 19% in 1959, 25% in 1960–1

41. Willis, *France, Germany and the New Europe* pp.282–6; W.O. Henderson, *The Genesis of the Common Market* (1962) p.164; Scammell, *International Economy since 1945* pp.137–8

possible one since the failure of the European Defence Community had shown that the high road was not available. As Monnet's Action Committee had explained in 1958:

> Tomorrow's political unity will depend on making the economic union effective in the everyday activities of industry, agriculture and government. Little by little the work of the communities will be felt, and the already distinguishable bonds of common interest will be strengthened. Then, the everyday realities themselves will make it possible to form the political union which is the goal of our Community, and to establish the United States of Europe.

In 1960 it became clear that de Gaulle thought otherwise:

> What are the pillars on which [Europe] can be built? In truth, they are the States . . . the only entities with the right to give orders and the power to be obeyed. To fancy one can build something effective in action, and acceptable to the peoples, outside or above the States, is a chimera.

The machinery of the European Communities was for fair weather only: 'So long as nothing serious happens, they work without any commotion, but as soon as a crisis occurs . . ., it becomes apparent that a high authority like that has no authority over the different national affairs'.

In 1961–2 de Gaulle sought to reorient the conduct of business around regular meetings of heads of government and Foreign Ministers (aided by a political secretariat), that would also harmonise foreign and defence policies. Italy and Germany were prepared to accept this, but Belgium and the Netherlands would not.[42] The real showdown came in 1965, when the EEC Commission unveiled a plan that would complete the Common Agricultural Policy, but strengthen the powers of the Commission and the European Parliament as against the Council of (Foreign) Ministers of the member states; the latter would also in some circumstances proceed on the basis of majority voting. The Commission had expected France to accept for the sake of the agricultural benefits; but deadlock was reached in July, and France responded by boycotting all but routine EEC workings – the policy of the 'empty chair'. In January 1966 the French position was accepted in practice, if not in so many words, by the 'Luxembourg compromise'. The Commission would in future work much more closely with representatives of the member states and with the

---

42. The scheme was known as the Fouchet plan: Jean Lacouture, *De Gaulle* pp.347–50; Willis, *France, Germany and the New Europe* pp.293–7

Council of Ministers, and the Council would, when faced with important matters, try to secure unanimity: 'The French delegation considers that, when very important issues are at stake, discussion must be continued until unanimous agreement is reached'.[43]

Countries tended to treat this as a licence to hold up business until they were satisfied, indeed to veto one item until they were reassured about another. Decisions continued to be made, but slowly and collegially; the key body came to be not the Commission but the Council of Ministers. In other ways, too, things evolved as de Gaulle would have wished. In the early years of the EEC, conferences of heads of government had been rarities. But Pompidou summoned one in 1972 to discuss future policies in the light of the accession of new members, and next year proposed regular meetings. In 1974 it was agreed that these should constitute a new body, the Council of the Communities. (They are now twice-yearly affairs, arranged by the country currently presiding over the Council of Ministers.) Although no attempt was made to take the Community into the field of defence, in the course of the 1970s the European Council began to make foreign policy pronouncements and the meetings of Foreign Ministers to seek to coordinate national policies – while still leaving the states as the primary actors.[44]

THE COMMON AGRICULTURAL POLICY

De Gaulle's other requirement, a Common Agricultural Policy (CAP), went less smoothly. Almost all developed countries protect their farmers, so it is not surprising that the EEC did so too, especially as one-fifth of its working population (more in France and Italy) was still engaged in agriculture in 1958. But the Netherlands and France were also anxious to profit by their competitive advantage in farming, and saw this as quid pro quo for the opening of their markets to industrial imports: 'We have', de Gaulle once remarked, 'already done a lot for Germany: ECSC, Euratom, EEC. It is really up to her to do something for us'.[45] In any case his

43. *Keesing's* 21591–5; France subsequently forced the retirement of the Commission's President, Walter Hallstein
44. Community members generally vote together at the UN (though the socialist government of Greece proved something of an exception); the Community has occasionally imposed economic sanctions (though not always unanimously)
45. Willis, *France, Germany and the New Europe* p.287

farmers were demanding remunerative outlets for the surpluses earlier modernisation had called into being; he pressed his colleagues accordingly. What resulted is conceptually simple. The Community aims at self-sufficiency in temperate agricultural products. It sets prices at which key commodities should trade throughout the Community;[46] variable duties prevent cheaper imports, while, as a safety net, the Community will buy and store surplus production, and, if this gets burdensome, subsidise its sale abroad.

The system painfully negotiated in the 1960s soon got out of hand. The price explosion that began in 1972 with the advent of Soviet grain purchases (see p. 319), and the attendant fears of a world shortage of food, made the goal of maximising Community production look attractive. Since prices were set by a Council of Ministers *of Agriculture*, they were naturally high – especially as German farmers were both high cost and politically powerful, with the result that the country that (as the largest contributor to the Community budget) had the chief interest in keeping prices down often took the lead in raising them. High prices called forth high production, which then had to be taken off the market, stored at great cost, and dumped abroad with the aid of further subsidies. By 1984 the enterprise had generated 'grain mountains' and 'wine lakes', and was consuming 70 per cent of the Community budget.[47] It had not created a true internal market, however: this had started to unravel before its construction was quite finished. In 1969 France devalued and Germany revalued its currency. Given that agricultural prices were now fixed in terms of a notional 'European unit of account', the French should have raised prices payable in francs and the Germans lowered those in marks, but both were allowed to keep their old prices and to impose countervailing border taxes to stop these being undermined by trade at the new exchange rates. Much the same happened when the Dutch and German currencies floated upwards in 1971–2. As floating became general in the 1970s this developed into a system of politically determined national 'green currencies', differential payments, and border controls. (It used to pay to land French grain in Hamburg, then instantly reload and export it with the 'German' subsidy.)[48]

---

46. Choice of key products depends on political pressure. Thus in 1970 Italy insisted on a Community regime for wine, but there is none for poultry

47. Tugendhat, *Making Sense of Europe* p.48

48. *Keesing's* 23522–3, 23682, 24972, 25250; Dick Leonard, *Pocket Guide to the European Community* (1988) p.95; *Daily Telegraph* 19 July 1990 p.14

ATTEMPTS AT EXCHANGE RATE STABILITY; THE COMMUNITY IN THE EARLY 1980s

The Community would in any case have sought a single currency as a symbol of unity, and had in 1969–70 started to plan towards it: the experience of the 1970s showed that the CAP would not really work without one. Achieving it, however, was not easy. In 1972 there was an arrangement (the 'snake in the tunnel') whereby participant currencies were to fluctuate within much narrower limits than those permitted under the Smithsonian agreement: Britain, Italy and others left fairly soon; France left in January 1974, went back in March, then finally pulled out in 1976, leaving the snake in effect only a deutschmark bloc. But disquiet with the effects of floating currencies produced a new effort to secure, as from 1979, a 'zone of monetary stability' in the form of a 'European Monetary System' (EMS). Here, as under Bretton Woods, participant currencies could fluctuate (against a notional 'European Currency Unit' or écu) only within narrow limits. Agreed realignments were permitted – with the ironic result that, despite its considerable short-term instability, the pound sterling (a non-member) was in 1986 the currency that had diverged least from the écu.[49]

In the Community's first decade,[50] it had achieved the removal of tariff barriers on manufactured goods and the legal framework for the free movement of labour, though *not* its third desideratum, the free movement of capital. To this was added a Common Agricultural Policy that had, by the early 1980s, degenerated into a fraud-ridden bureaucratic mess,[51] whose cost precluded any very considerable development of other policies. Important fields of economic activity, like financial services and air transport, were kept outside the Community's purview. Frontiers remained a reality, as illustrated by massive tailbacks of lorries when Italian customs officials went on strike; indeed it was not until 1988 that the seventy different national forms were replaced by a standardised border declaration for goods. There were, of course, some supranational elements, and many instances of inter-governmental harmonisation

---

49. Leonard, *Guide to the European Community* p.86; C.P. Kindleberger, *A Financial History of Western Europe* (1985 format) pp.456–62

50. The EEC, ECSC, and Euratom merged in 1967 into a single body, then styled the European Communities but later the European Community (EC)

51. Sometimes picturesquely so; in three areas of Germany, the European Parliament found, 80% of all cattle were officially slaughtered more than once: *Keesing's*, 36493, 37209

and cooperation, but in the early 1980s the Community remained very much an *Europe des patries*. Thereafter, as we shall see, it shook off some of this 'Euro-sclerosis' and began again to develop.

ADENAUER AND FRANCE

For many years the European concept's chief contribution to stabilisation was the framework it provided for the conduct of Franco-German relations. We have seen that the Schuman Plan represented a new approach to an old problem, as did the ill-starred European Defence Community. The resolution (albeit by other means) of the German rearmament question encouraged Adenauer and Mendès-France to agree on the 'Europeanisation' of the Saar as an autonomous entity, but one within the French economic system.[52] After a violent campaign the Saarlanders rejected this solution in a referendum, then voted in a new administration that in January 1956 demanded to accede to Germany. Fortunately the French government did not want the Saar to wreck the discussions then in progress to create the EEC. So it agreed to the Saar's joining Germany in 1957, securing in exchange continued coal deliveries plus a German contribution to the canalisation of the Mosel to reduce the costs of shipping Ruhr coal to Lorraine.

Adenauer was obsessed with the need for Western unity in the face of godless Soviet communism, and the fear that this could not be preserved unless France and Germany were locked together in a European framework. In 1954, after the collapse of the EDC, *Der Spiegel* reports him as telling the Belgian and Luxembourg Foreign Ministers

'When I am no longer there, I do not know what will happen to Germany if we have not yet succeeded in creating a united Europe . . .'
'The French nationalists are just as ready as the German to repeat the old policies, in spite of past experience. They would rather a Germany with a national army than a united Europe – so long as they can pursue

52. To offset wartime destruction of French mines, the Saar had, from 1919–35, been detached from Germany and its mines placed under French control. In 1947 France (the local occupying power) transferred the territory to its own currency and customs zone; in the treaty establishing the ECSC France signed on the Saar's behalf. The Saar was accorded some political autonomy; but in its 1952 elections, pro-German candidates were banned. Official policy, confirmed by the 1954 Adenauer-Mendès-France agreement, came to be that it should enjoy a special 'European' status but remain within the French economic zone. This the Saarlanders rejected in Oct. 1955

their own policy with the Russians. And the German nationalists think
exactly the same way; they are ready to go with the Russians.'
  Adenauer seemed completely possessed by the fear of a revival of a
cynical, narrow German nationalism . . .
  Again and again, he used the words 'when I am no longer there'.
'Make use of the time while I am still alive, because when I am no more
it will be too late – my God, I do not know what my successors will do if
they are left to themselves: if they are not obliged to follow along firmly
preordained lines, if they are not bound to a united Europe.'

Adenauer continually returned to this theme. Thus in 1962 he
descanted to de Gaulle on the communist danger and continued:

> But if the French and German people were to be so strongly clamped
> together that neither a French nor a German government could go with
> the Soviet Union, then these two countries would accomplish a historic
> task in building a firm European dam against communism.[53]

In late 1955, when Britain again seemed to be contemplating
security concessions to the Russians to achieve German unification,
Adenauer secretly indicated his dissent.

> The bald reason was that Dr. Adenauer had no confidence in the
> German people. He was terrified that when he disappeared from the scene
> a future German Government might do a deal with Russia at the
> German [*sic*] expense. Consequently he felt that the integration of
> Western Germany with the West was more important than the
> unification of Germany. He wished us [the British] to know that now he
> would bend all his energies towards achieving this in the time which was
> left to him.[54]

In January 1956 he issued a directive to his ministers in connection
with the discussions then proceeding on the creation of the EEC:
Soviet concessions would come only through an integration that
would both destroy Soviet hopes of winning over Western states one
by one and enable the weight of a united Europe to be thrown
behind German reunification at the crucial moment; 'furthermore,
a permanent ordering of our relations with France is possible only
on the basis of European integration. Should integration fail through
our hesitations or reluctance, the results would be incalculable'.
Adenauer was therefore ready to make the concessions that France
demanded, and to override the hostility of his economics minister,
Erhard, to the dirigiste and inward-looking elements that resulted.[55]

---

53. Richardson, *Germany and the Atlantic Alliance* pp.13–4; Adenauer, *Erinnerungen 1959–63* (Stuttgart, 1967) p.166
54. Minute by Sir Ivone Kirkpatrick, 16 Dec. 1955: printed in J. Foschepoth (ed.) *Adenauer und die Deutsche Frage* (Göttingen, 1986) pp.289–90
55. Adenauer, *Erinnerungen 1955–9* pp.253–4; Willis, *France, Germany and the New Europe* pp.265 ff

The decline of the Fourth Republic presented a problem; during its final crisis in May 1958 Erhard went on record as saying that Germany would not extend credit within the EEC framework to an undemocratic Gaullist France. Adenauer also had his worries about de Gaulle; but he decided to bury them. In September 1958 he visited de Gaulle at his country home in Colombey-les-deux-Eglises. There may be an element of hindsight in the two leaders' later accounts – de Gaulle in particular would have us believe that a detailed deal was struck to cover the range of European, German, and NATO questions – but the meeting was clearly a great success.[56] De Gaulle then almost spoilt things by leaking his proposals for a Franco-British-American NATO directorate, to which Germany would be clearly inferior (see p. 393). Adenauer was distinctly displeased. Macmillan hoped that this would induce him to help establish an industrial free trade area between the EEC and neighbouring states. At a second meeting with de Gaulle in November 1958, however, Adenauer agreed to the termination of the negotiations, 'which sought to drown the Community of the Six at the outset, by plunging them into a vast free trade area including England, and, soon, the whole West'. This meeting was held at a time when Adenauer was still soliciting British diplomatic intervention over Berlin. But the Berlin crisis (see pp. 211–15) soon provided a further reason for preferring France to Britain. Adenauer, who had not been consulted in advance, deplored Macmillan's February 1959 visit to Moscow: he assumed it had been undertaken for purely electoral reasons, and asked the British ambassador if he realised what it would mean for Britain if the Federal Republic was lost to the West. This made all the more welcome de Gaulle's declaratory position that the West should simply refuse to negotiate under Soviet pressure. So in March 1959, when Erhard gave a talk favouring a European free trade zone, Adenauer dashed off a rebuke: 'It is quite impossible for you to make a speech that insults France and approves of Britain's behaviour just at the moment when Britain is injuring us most severely . . . and we are absolutely dependent on French help. Such performances are in glaring contradiction with the lines of my policy which are well-known to you.'[57] Adenauer had never liked Erhard, and was already manoeuvring to block his succession to the

56. Adenauer, *Erinnerungen 1955–9* pp.424 ff, 518; De Gaulle, *Mémoires* pp.184 ff
57. Adenauer, *Erinnerungen 1955–9* pp.469–70, 518–19; De Gaulle, *Mémoires* p.190; Horne, *Macmillan* ii pp.110–19

chancellorship. Now he had all the more reason to stay on in politics; he devoted his remaining time, until he was finally pushed out of office in 1963, to the consolidation and institutionalisation of his relationship with de Gaulle.

This relationship was certainly close: by mid-1962 the two had had fifteen meetings and exchanged forty letters. De Gaulle was the dominant partner: not only did Adenauer's language (as recorded in his *Memoirs*) become increasingly 'Gaullist',[58] but also, when necessary, de Gaulle could crack the whip; when Adenauer's government was making difficulties over agriculture during crucial negotiations in 1961, de Gaulle got his way by telegraphing to Adenauer that he would break up the EEC unless Germany changed course.[59] De Gaulle certainly found the relationship very convenient, for with German support he could usually dominate the EEC. But his attitude towards Germany was always rather ambivalent. On resuming power in 1958 he is said to have asked how much remained of his policy for dismembering Germany, and received the reply, 'Nothing'. Courtship of Adenauer was an adaptation to this; it was pursued with a degree of cynicism. In March 1959 de Gaulle agreed with the British that 'one could not have a nuclear war' on the question of whether a Soviet or an East German sergeant 'signed the pass to go along the autobahn . . . to West Berlin'. German reunion, too, was impossible without war, though 'the "idea" of reunion should be kept alive in order to give some comfort to the German people', and there should be practical cooperation between the two German states: 'What Dulles had called *con*federation should be pressed'. But he had not told Adenauer this: 'It would depress him'[60] – and, no doubt, inhibit his tendency to look to France not Britain.

58. Some 'Gaullist' themes were already visible in his remarks to the French during the Suez crisis. US protection was unreliable since the USA would never start an atomic war; and as no West European country would ever again be of stature comparable to the USA and USSR, 'There remains to them only one way of playing a decisive role in the world; that is to unite to make Europe. England is not ripe for it but the affair of Suez will help her prepare her spirits for it. We have no time to waste: Europe will be your revenge': Kyle, *Suez* pp.466–7

59. De Gaulle, *Mémoires* pp.193, 198

60. Macmillan, *Memoirs* iv p.637. Macmillan, who genuinely feared that Berlin could lead to war, always thought that de Gaulle, too, really hoped for a negotiated *modus vivendi* to prevent this but preferred that the odium attached to it should fall on the Anglo-Saxons. De Gaulle apparently told the Soviet ambassador in 1961 that he did not want German reunion (Cold War International History Project *Bulletin* 3 (1993) p.60)

De Gaulle's policy was also designed to forestall disillusion that might lead West Germany to an independent deal with the Soviet Union. In 1959–60 he said he was more confident than some of his advisers that they would not be tempted:

> The only thing that might make them desperate would be their abandonment by the West. Thus in the economic field it was very important that West Germany should be tied in with France. There must be no more economic '*Drang nach Osten*'. It was for this reason that he had approved the Common Market, although he had no real liking for it.

'As regards Berlin, etc., his chief object is to support Adenauer, because – if he is let down – more dangerous sentiments may begin to develop in Germany.' Indeed de Gaulle told Macmillan in November 1961 that 'even if the present weak and incapable German Government accepted' the need for negotiations, he would still feel 'it his duty to be the protector of German interests . . . *plus royaliste que le roi*' so that 'the Germany of the future will know that France was true'. De Gaulle was by then looking with some apprehension towards the post-Adenauer era. Adenauer (he had told Sulzberger) would never deal with the Russians, but later things might change, as German industry was attracted by the Soviet market and a deal over Berlin plus a federation of the two Germanies was not inconceivable, hence the need to wall Germany in within a united Europe.[61]

De Gaulle's policy meshed well with that of Adenauer, who was also keen to exclude any possibility of a *French* deal with Moscow; their work found its apparent culmination in the January 1963 Treaty of Franco-German friendship. This, according to Couve de Murville (then French Foreign Secretary), was meant to establish 'a sort of permanent concertation' or even interpenetration 'between everybody, heads of state and government, ministers and senior civil servants, in the areas covered . . ., foreign affairs, defence, education and youth'. Unfortunately it coincided with de Gaulle's veto of the British application to join the EEC. Adenauer did not mind, but the West German Parliament did, and ratified it only with an anti-Gaullist preamble looking to the integration of NATO members' armed forces, British accession to the EEC, and negotiations for the removal of trade barriers between the EEC and

61. Macmillan, *Memoirs* v pp.110–11, 181, 426; C.L. Sulzberger, *The Last of the Giants* (1970) p.45

other members of GATT.[62] In October 1963 Adenauer was finally forced to retire, and his successor, Erhard, had very different views.

FRANCO–GERMAN RELATIONS SINCE 1963

De Gaulle rapidly lost enthusiasm for the treaty; and though the stipulated regular meetings continued, they were the occasion for quarrels over the EEC,[63] NATO (whose integrated command structure France withdrew from in 1966), and France's new policy of entente with Eastern Europe. For if reconciliation and partnership with France was one of the goals of West German foreign policy, the other fixed point was good alliance relations with the United States (whose protection was in the last resort more important). In this context Erhard was an Atlanticist, though he continued to be sniped at by Adenauer and a group of German 'Gaullists'. In 1966 he fell (for more domestic reasons); the new Kiesinger-Brandt government sought a more even balance between Washington and Paris, and also launched its own East European policy. Germany was becoming increasingly self-confident, while de Gaulle's position was badly damaged by the 'events' of 1968 and the resultant weakness of the franc. That autumn Germany resisted considerable international pressure to ease the pressure on the franc by revaluing, something Couve said would have been unimaginable a few years earlier. De Gaulle seems to have become worried by this German recovery, to the point of saying privately that an alliance with the USSR (or war) could prove necessary to contain it; as for Western Europe, he was in February 1969 apparently contemplating a loosening of the EEC and a political association between the four major West European Powers, France, Germany, Britain and Italy. In December 1969 the new West German Chancellor, Brandt, touched on this concern when advocating British membership of the EEC; the next year Pompidou told Nixon that it had been fear of a revival of German nationalism (triggered by Brandt's *Ostpolitik*) that had caused him to lift the ban on British entry.

62. Maurice Couve de Murville, *Une Politique étrangère 1958–1969* (Paris, 1971) p.256; RIIA, *Documents 1963* pp.54–5

63. One of de Gaulle's worries about the supra-national structure Hallstein proposed in 1965 was that in it Germany would 'acquire the preponderant weight that its economic capability would undoubtedly bring', then use it to promote German reunification (*Mémoires* p.195)

Even if the 1963 treaty had not realised all the hopes invested in it, it had, as Couve says, 'created habits by establishing procedures and demonstrated that France could keep up dialogue with Germany without intermediaries'.[64] These 'habits', too, were reinforced by a network of lower level Franco-German exchanges and associations that had been deliberately fostered since the 1950s and that did much to make cooperation seem natural. At the summit the relationship has fluctuated. It was not especially close in the early 1970s; when Britain joined the Community there seemed some prospect of its developing into a triangle, but in 1974 Britain turned instead to renegotiating the terms of its entry. France and Germany also acquired new leaders, Giscard D'Estaing and Schmidt, both former Finance Ministers and fluent English speakers; they proved personally extremely close, meeting regularly and demonstratively and ringing each other up frequently. They claimed a joint leadership, with Giscard once remarking that France and Germany 'never forgot that they had in their charge to a great extent the progress of Europe', and Schmidt explaining that 'Italy is notorious for its lack of government. Britain is notorious for governments, Labour and Conservative, that think the Atlantic is narrower than the Channel. That leaves only the French and the Germans'. There are, in fact, some divergent national interests even within the EC; but a former British Commissioner has observed that 'when they are at one they can carry everything in the Community before them – except Mrs Thatcher when she digs in . . . if Paris and Bonn are in agreement on something it is well on its way to being accomplished. If they are not, no other combination has yet shown itself capable of achieving remotely similar results'.[65] However (gestures apart) this combination could not really be carried into the field of security, partly because French protection was no substitute for American, partly because France cut itself off by withdrawing from the main forums of NATO. This requires some qualification of the picture painted above of Franco-German

64. Couve de Murville, *Une Politique étrangère* pp.276, 284, chap. 7; C.L. Sulzberger, *An Age of Mediocrity: Memoirs and Diaries 1963–1972* (New York, 1973) pp.507–10; Kissinger, *Memoirs* i pp.110, 422; *Keesing's* 23267, 24168. De Gaulle's February 1969 overtures developed into a major diplomatic fracas with Britain (the Soames affair), and the details are correspondingly disputed

65. J.R. Frears, *France in the Giscard Presidency* (1981) p.107; Tugendhat, *Making Sense of Europe* pp.92, 104

relations: as Schmidt put it to Vance, 'the United States was our most important ally but France was our closest one'.[66]

Giscard lost office in 1981, Schmidt in 1982; their successors, Mitterand and Kohl, were less close. For one thing Mitterand began by worrying about the advances neutralist sentiment was making in the SPD, and adopting a strongly pro-USA line during the general East–West tension of the early 1980s; for another Mitterand and Kohl had no language in common. Later in the decade they drew rather closer, around the issue of the construction of Europe. For Kohl placed greater emphasis than his predecessors on German reunification, and sought to balance it by stressing European integration: 'Our passionate advocacy of European unification', he had said in 1984, 'stems to a great extent from awareness that a peaceful settlement of the German question is only conceivable within a greater European framework'.[67] With the advent of German reunification, Kohl hoped that simultaneous progress with European integration would allay fears of an over-mighty Germany or one again tempted to look East away from its recent European partnerships. France sometimes seemed distinctly worried by such prospects; but talk of Franco-German tension repeatedly evaporated into demonstrative moves like Mitterand and Kohl's joint appearance at an emergency European Parliament debate in November 1989 or the Franco-German call in April 1990 for immediate preparations for a conference on political unity.

66. Helmut Schmidt, *Men and Powers: A Political Retrospective* (1990) p.205. Schmidt was telling Vance not to play Bonn against Paris, but Bonn also always resisted French attempts to make it choose between Paris and Washington

67. Tugendhat, *Making Sense of Europe* p.99

CHAPTER FOURTEEN

Western Europe II: Britain, France and the USA

BRITAIN AND EUROPEAN INTEGRATION 1945–58

If the development of the European Communities helped the reintegration and revival of West Germany, it played a role in Britain's diplomatic decline. At bottom, of course, this decline stemmed from relative economic weakness and loss of empire, but the decision to stand aloof from the early stages of Western European economic integration imposed appreciable costs. Bevin had initially been attracted by a European Customs Union, not least because of the possibility it held out that the European states and their colonies 'would form a bloc which, both in population and in production capacity, could stand on an equality with the Western hemisphere and Soviet blocs'. So in September 1947 Britain both joined in a European 'Customs Union Study Group' and established its own Cabinet committee to look into the idea. The Customs Union Study Group moved only very slowly, largely because it came to feel that tariffs were not the real problem and that a gradual lifting of trade restrictions under the aegis of the OEEC was more promising. This was consonant with the ideas of the British Treasury, which did not like customs unions (whether European or Commonwealth) and which saw the exercise as a diversion from the immediate need to earn hard currency.[1] Over the course of 1948, Bevin seems to have been gradually won over to the Treasury viewpoint. At the outset he had sought, in his call for a Western Union, a British-led Europe that could (once it had recovered) 'be independent both of the United States and of the

1. British trade with Europe then resulted in an appreciable loss of dollars

Soviet Union'.[2] As the Cold War deepened, his interests shifted towards closer involvement with the United States on the basis of NATO and other security cooperation. In January 1949 an inter-departmental conference agreed to look rather to

> the Atlantic Pact. We hope to secure a special relationship with the U.S.A. and Canada within this, for in the last resort we cannot rely upon the European countries . . . we must in practice establish the position that U.S. will defend us, whatever happens to the Europeans.
>   . . . Our policy should be to assist Europe to recover as far as we can. . . . But the concept must be one of limited liability . . . [not extending] beyond the point at which the assistance leaves us too weak to be a worth-while ally for U.S.A. if Europe collapses – i.e. beyond the point where our own viability was impaired. . . . Nor can we embark upon measures of 'co-operation' which surrender our sovereignty and which lead us down paths along which there is no return.

In February 1949 the Cabinet confirmed that its plans should be coordinated with those of other OEEC members, but only 'so long as' British 'economic recovery was not thereby prejudiced'. In October it accepted that 'We must remain, as we have always been in the past, different in character from other European nations and fundamentally incapable of wholehearted integration with them'.[3]

This was less negative than it sounds: Britain did much to organise West European response to the offer of Marshall Aid, and contributed both to functional cooperation within the OEEC and to the establishment of the European Payments Union (which in combining Western Europe, its colonies and the sterling area had much in common with Bevin's 1947–8 vision). But it resisted federalist and supranational proposals, in 1948–9 this led to a contest with France as to whether the 1948 Brussels treaty should lead on to a real European Parliament. Bevin was determined that it should not. He had in 1949 to concede a Consultative Assembly attached to the new 'Council of Europe', but he ensured that it should remain 'as little embarrassing as possible'; with the important exception of the 1950 European Convention on Human Rights,[4] it has never amounted to much. In 1950, as we have seen,

2. cf. e.g. CAB 129/23, CP(48) 6 (4 Jan. 1948), and the 'Confidential Annex' to the Cabinet Conclusions of 5 March
3. John W. Young, *Britain, France and the Unity of Europe 1945–51* (Leicester, 1984) esp. pp.68–9 and chap. 13; Milward, *Reconstruction of Western Europe* chap. 7; Bullock, *Bevin* esp. pp.517–20, 733–4; Sir Richard Clarke (ed. Sir Alec Cairncross), *Anglo-American Economic Collaboration in War and Peace 1942–9* (Oxford, 1982) pp.208–9; Cabinet Conclusions, 24 Feb. 1949 p.81
4. Several states have incorporated this into their domestic legislation; some others (including Britain) allow their nationals to take them to the European Court of Justice, and so de facto expose themselves to a degree of external judicial review

France was more insistent; come what may, it would secure a supranational High Authority over coal and steel. Schuman does not seem to have sought to exclude Britain, were it to accept this, but he was quite prepared to go forward without it.

This is often seen as the point at which Britain 'missed the bus' – experience of the ECSC clearly accustomed its members to working together. But staying outside the ECSC imposed no obvious economic costs; and the next 'European' venture, the Defence Community, never got off the ground. The general British view, often expounded by Churchill, was that the UK was strategically placed at the intersection of three circles, the United States, the Commonwealth, and continental Europe: for both sentimental and power-political reasons, the first two were the more important. Accordingly Britain rejected an invitation to join in the elaboration of the EEC, even though France appeared flexible on policy and very anxious for British collaboration. The decision was influenced (as Macmillan later put it) by two considerations, both mistaken: 'We thought they would not succeed [a view shared, at least in some moods, by Spaak[5]] – or if they did that we could work out a satisfactory association'.[6] In the course of 1956 Macmillan persuaded his colleagues at least to consider association; by July he was able to propose that the OEEC study plans for a free trade area between the EEC Six and other member states. Elaborating these plans took time, partly because of the need to square the Commonwealth and partly because of Suez; the Six were not disposed to wait the outcome, or to contemplate further negotiations until the Treaties of Rome had been ratified. What Britain ideally sought (though it was increasingly prepared to make concessions) was that the EEC should be surrounded by an area with which there should be free trade in *industrial* products; this would square the circle, permitting Britain to continue to allow Commonwealth goods free access and subsidise its own farmers (an important political interest whose vulnerability to continental competition was much exaggerated). France had other ideas, and negotiations were slow. They were further interrupted by the French May 1958 political crisis (see pp. 352–3); but in October it was agreed to push them forward with a view to conclusion before the first EEC tariff cuts took effect in

5. cf. Spaak's very gloomy prognostications of Feb. 1956 and his appeal to Britain 'to take the lead in the creation of a united Europe': – Macmillan, *Memoirs* iv p.76

6. Macmillan, *Memoirs* vi p.15; S. Burgess and G. Edwards, 'The Six plus One: British Policy-Making and the Question of European Economic Integration, 1955', *International Affairs* xliv (1988) pp.101–2

January. By then de Gaulle had privately made it clear to Macmillan that he was hostile, provoking the anguished plea, 'The Common Market is the [Napoleonic] continental blockade. England will not accept it. I beg you to give it up. Or we shall enter a war that will doubtless only be economic to start with, but that may later extend itself by degrees to other areas.' Macmillan had always looked, not without some encouragement, to Germany to overcome French opposition; after the uproar engendered by de Gaulle's proposals for a Three Power NATO directorate, he was still hopeful in November. But on the 14th, while a meeting was in progress, Paris announced that 'it is not possible to create a Free Trade Area as wished by the British'; despite Benelux attempts to mediate, this brought matters to an end.[7]

BRITAIN'S DECISION TO APPLY FOR EEC MEMBERSHIP; DE GAULLE'S 1963 VETO

The seven excluded countries responded by adopting a Swedish plan for a European Free Trade Association of their own (with effect from 1960).[8] After some British and Swedish concessions on agriculture, this was negotiated easily. EFTA worked fairly smoothly, and proved unfounded some of the technical objections raised against the original Free Trade Area plan; but its members' economies were, for geographical reasons, not really complementary. Macmillan, however, can hardly be said to have given it a fair trial. For in July 1960, depressed by the collapse of the Four Power summit, he asked himself

> Shall we be caught between a hostile (or less and less friendly) America and a boastful powerful 'Empire of Charlemagne' – now under French but later bound to come under German control? Is this the real reason for 'joining' the Common Market (if we are acceptable) and for abandoning a) the Seven b) British agriculture c) the Commonwealth? It's a grim choice.

Eventually he decided to make it. For, as he told ministers in 1961, 'If we stand aloof, we shall find ourselves in a position of growing weakness. Europe under France could well wield more

7. Macmillan, *Memoirs* iv chaps 3, 14; Horne, *Macmillan* i pp.349–51, 362–3, 385–6, ii pp.31–4; de Gaulle, *Mémoires* p.199; *Keesing's*, 15098, 15394–5, 17613–14
8. Sweden, Norway, Denmark, the UK, Austria, Switzerland, Portugal

power than the UK both with the Americans and some Commonwealth countries'.[9] The process of reaching a final decision,
sounding out (unhappy) Commonwealth partners, and convincing
colleagues and party took until August 1961.

Macmillan had asked Kennedy to prepare the ground for
Britain's application by talking to de Gaulle. After his visit to Paris
(on the eve of the Vienna summit), Kennedy told Macmillan that
'The general has no wish whatever to see the United Kingdom join
the Common Market'. During a visit in November 1961 de Gaulle
made this plain in person. Macmillan countered by forecasting a
dangerous and unpredictable response if Britain were rebuffed; it
might, for instance, junk its expensive troop commitments to
European defence 'if the Europeans did not want her in Europe'.
De Gaulle was unmoved; one of the things he had found most
attractive about the EEC in 1958, his biographer judges,[10] was the
concern it occasioned across the Channel: 'if his British neighbours
were so very much alarmed by it, it must be of benefit to the
Continent'. Now he explained that if Britain came in with its
Commonwealth connections, the USA would want to join too. 'In
short, if Europe let the rest of the world in, it would lose itself;
Europe would have been drowned in the Atlantic'.[11]

Serious negotiation could not begin until the Six had resolved
their own deep differences over agriculture in January 1962. Even
then talks went very slowly, partly because the British wished to tie
up every detail and to minimise the impact of entry on the
Commonwealth. The original hope that most points would be
settled by the summer holidays proved unfounded; in December
Macmillan thought the crunch would come in February 1963.
These delays must have reinforced the French contention that
Britain would not easily be assimilated. More importantly, de
Gaulle's domestic position strengthened enormously in the course
of 1962 with the ending of the Algerian war and his remarkable
referendum and electoral victories, and he may have felt freer to
act as a result. That summer Adenauer seconded his suspicions –
'England could not bear it that France was the leading power [in
the EEC]. It was the old English game with the continent, divide
and rule' – and advised him to 'negotiate toughly'. A meeting

9. Horne, *Macmillan* ii p.256; *The Times*, 1 Jan. 1992 p.5. Macmillan also looked to
US investment to rejuvenate the economy, and knew that this was less likely if Britain
remained outside the EEC
10. Lacouture, *De Gaulle* p.213
11. *The Times*, 1 Jan. 1992 p.5; *The Independent*, 2 Jan. 1992 p.6

between Macmillan and de Gaulle in June 1962 had not gone too badly. For Macmillan made concessions on both Commonwealth preferences and the need for an EEC Common Agricultural Policy, though de Gaulle expressed some doubt as to whether he would be politically able to deliver them. When Macmillan returned in December, claiming that he had done so (though privately expecting a 'great battle' with the General), the result was a disaster. The details of their conversations at Rambouillet are controversial.[12] De Gaulle's primary concerns seem to have been those of power: at present 'France could say "no" even against the Germans; she could stop [EEC] policies with which she disagreed, because of the strength of her position. Once Britain and all the rest joined the organisation things would be different'. More generally, contrary to the pattern of much recent history, Britain was now the supplicant, and de Gaulle wished to take advantage of this: 'I want her naked'.[13] In January 1963 he put an end to the formal negotiations on EEC entry, a decision Adenauer tacitly endorsed by concluding the Franco-German treaty.

BRITAIN JOINS THE EUROPEAN COMMUNITY 1973; WILSON AND THATCHER RENEGOTIATE TERMS

In 1967 de Gaulle vetoed another British application to join the EEC. In 1969 de Gaulle's successor was induced to allow serious negotiations by the promise that the Six would in the mean time press on with European construction and in particular the completion of the CAP. British accession in 1973 was expected to lead to something of a Bonn–Paris–London triangle within the. Community. But in Opposition the Labour Party had reverted to its initial hostility to EC membership. Wilson's strategy for containing this was to demand renegotiation of British entry terms, declare the result a success and then get it legitimised by a domestic referendum. In his own terms he succeeded, though Labour's hostility to membership re-emerged even stronger after its loss of office in 1979. The episode strained the patience of other EC members,

12. See notes 36, 32 below

13. Without Britain's US guardians and Commonwealth cousins: – Lacouture, *De Gaulle* pp.347–60; Horne, *Macmillan* ii pp.256–8, 326–9, 428 ff; Macmillan, *Memoirs* vi chaps 1, 5, 11; Adenauer, *Erinnerungen 1959–63* pp.160, 165, 178

however, and returned Britain to the role of *demandeur*. Nor did it really tackle the issue of Community taxation; and as a result partly of its pattern of imports, partly of the way the CAP had developed, Britain found itself the only net contributor to Community funds apart from Germany. The sums involved were not enormous, but they were burdensome to pay over the exchanges and, given the UK's comparative poverty, clearly unjust. Since there had already been one 'renegotiation', there was little disposition to reopen the question; when Mrs Thatcher did so in 1979 she was apparently subjected to sexist bullying by the Schmidt–Giscard axis. This proved a mistake, and led to much thumping of the table on her part before the question was resolved (at least for the time being) by the 1984 Fontainebleau compromise;[14] it also confirmed Thatcher's naturally combative style. Subsequently she turned to constructive, though not always popular, pressure to create a true internal market and to reform the CAP. But towards the end of the decade she again painted herself into a corner, this time by opposing the revival of momentum towards political and monetary union and the harmonisation of social security. In the end this contributed greatly to her political downfall at home.

NATO'S SURVIVAL

If the Community had emerged as an increasingly important element in the politics and horizons of Europeans, in 1991 it still had no military component. For Western Europe that aspect of security was provided by the Atlantic alliance, which, while directed against the threat from the East, simultaneously provided reassurance against the wrong kind of German revival; as its first Secretary-General rather undiplomatically put it, NATO existed to keep the Americans in, the Russians out, and the Germans down. NATO now appears to have been more securely based than its East European counterpart. Since it survived intact throughout the period of this book, we shall not spend too long discussing the threats to its cohesion. These have sometimes overlapped, but basically they came from two directions; NATO might have disinte-

14. This still left the net British contribution disproportionately high, but both reduced and capped it by providing a 66% rebate: Tugendhat, *Making Sense of Europe* pp.120–5; *The Economist*, 28 July 1990 p.42. By 1992, however, the rebate was again coming under attack from other EC members

grated because the people in one or more countries would stand it no longer; or it might have collapsed as a result of the mutual suspicions of governments.[15] Unsurprisingly both the French and the Italian Communist Parties opposed NATO (though the latter eventually came round to accepting it). In Germany the SPD, though well disposed towards the West, saw Adenauer's foreign policy as sealing their country's division and campaigned against military alignment, conscription, and (most strongly) in 1958 against 'Atomic Death' and the stationing of nuclear weapons on German territory. In 1959–60 the party changed course; for twenty years it stood firmly behind military integration with the West, and it was an SPD-led government that procured the 1979 NATO agreement on the deployment of cruise and Pershing missiles. This was meant to reassure West Europeans that they would remain linked to the US strategic deterrent; but as East–West relations froze after the invasion of Afghanistan, many came to see it as preparation for fighting a nuclear war on German (or European) soil. The SPD veered sharply towards a policy of disengagement and the dissolution of blocs; Schmidt managed, with increasing difficulty, to contain this trend, but after he lost the chancellorship in 1982 his policy was ditched (with the support of his predecessor, Brandt). Practically, however, the SPD's change had little effect, since the new CDU–FDP government continued with the previous policy and was sustained by the 1983 election.

In Britain, too, the Labour Party, though it had done much to create the US alliance in the first place, twice came to query it. In 1960 there was increasing East–West tension with the failure of the Paris summit, and a number of moves (like the decision to base US Polaris submarines in Scotland) that emphasised British involvement with the US deterrent and consequent exposure to Soviet attack. At the same time attempts to modernise Britain's own nuclear forces were much in the news. The result was the sudden upsurge of the Campaign for Nuclear Disarmament (CND). Meanwhile the Labour Party was reeling from a third electoral defeat, and rejecting its leader's attempts to steer it towards a different domestic policy. In this context the 1960 Party Conference resolved in favour of scrapping British and expelling US nuclear weapons; in

15. War between Greece and Turkey, though not between any other NATO members, has certainly been thinkable on a number of occasions, though in the event they have always drawn back from such a catastrophe. In 1974 the Greek military regime (then *in extremis*) is said to have been stopped by the USA from launching what would have been a suicidal attack

other respects the insurgents were less successful, and in 1961 the leadership managed to reverse Conference's decision on American weapons. Thereafter the issue gradually died down, aided by the recovery in Labour's electoral fortunes and its desire to present itself as 'the natural party of government'. Twenty years later Labour's loss of office and violent swing to the left coincided with decisions to deploy US cruise missiles and to replace British Polaris with Trident submarines. CND revived from the dead; this time Labour's attachment to it ran considerably deeper, with the adoption of two unilateralist leaders (Foot and Kinnock) in succession and of a fully unilateralist programme. As in Germany, the 1983 and 1987 elections decided otherwise. No country, therefore, has yet broken with NATO as a result of popular disillusion.

There have been, however, some near misses. Iceland let it be understood that it might leave if the 'Cod War' with Britain was not settled to its satisfaction (for a fuller discussion, see *The Post–Imperial Age*, chap. 19). After the 1974 revolution Portugal adopted a generally leftist and Third-World stance, but it did not seek to expel the crucial US bases from the Azores, for fear that this would bring the islands to declare their independence with the USA's blessing; in late 1979, elections brought into office a government anxious to mend its fences with NATO. Turkey's 1974 intervention in Cyprus led the US Congress to impose an arms embargo, so Turkey closed US bases in retaliation; the quarrel, however, was not of Turkey's seeking, and some were reopened when the embargo was lifted in 1978, while the position was regularised in 1980 after Congress had voted to restore military aid. In 1981 Greece elected a government (under Papandreou) with considerable sympathy for the Soviet point of view and a mandate to set a timetable for the closing of US bases.[16] In office, it was checked partly by the loss of dollars that this would entail, partly by fear of the consequences if Turkey continued to receive US military aid while Greece did not. Negotiations over the bases were therefore very leisurely; a settlement was reached in 1990 after Papandreou's fall. The 1980s also saw difficulties with Spain: defence agreements with the USA in the 1950s had helped restore international respectability to the Franco regime, but had not endeared the Atlantic connection to his opponents. In 1986 the Socialist government nevertheless brought

16. The USA was widely blamed for not having distanced itself from the 1967–74 military regime, and for not protecting Cyprus from Turkey

Spain into NATO by referendum, to strengthen both its European credentials and its claims to recover Gibraltar; to balance this, it then put pressure on the USA to abandon its great air base near Madrid; in late 1988 the USA at last gave way, though only after Spain had undertaken not to inquire too closely into the presence of nuclear weapons in other US facilities.

Mostly, though, disputes within NATO, while sometimes intense, were deliberately conducted in low key, and revolved around questions of strategy often incapable of resolution as long as peace held. So, if the alliance has sometimes been 'troubled', there has been little disposition to push things to extremes, and a general preference for accepting assurances in which only one half believed, rather than so rocking the boat as to destroy entirely the alliance's credibility and utility.

THE 'SPECIAL RELATIONSHIP' 1949–92

For two European countries, Britain and France, questions relating to the alliance assumed a much higher profile. Indeed its 'special relationship' with the USA was an important component of Britain's postwar claims still to be a Great Power: 'It was clear', reported the British ambassador (Sir Oliver Franks) after successful talks in 1949, 'that the Americans decided to regard us once more as their principal partner in foreign affairs, and not just as a member of the European queue'. From a British perspective, such a relationship offered the prospect of making 'use of American power for purposes which we regard as good', or (in Bevin's words) exerting 'sufficient control over the policy of the well-intentioned but inexperienced colossus on whose co-operation our safety depends. . . . It can only be done by influencing the United States Government and people, not by opposing or discouraging them'.[17]

There has been much debate as to how special this 'special relationship' really was. No cut-and-dried answer is possible: it varied from time to time, person to person and issue to issue. Thus during Truman's administration the two governments did *not* see eye to eye on Mossadegh's Iran, but the great US oil companies

---

17. Kenneth O. Morgan, *Labour in Power 1945–51* (Oxford, 1984) p.385; David Reynolds, 'Rethinking Anglo-American Relations', *International Affairs* lxv (1989) pp.96–7

instinctively took Anglo-Iranian's side. Dulles abandoned his predecessor's policy and had the CIA join the British in covert action to topple Mossadegh. But he (and the CIA) initially so inclined towards the Egyptians in their disputes with Britain as to prompt Eden's outburst, 'they want to replace us in Egypt . . . they want to run the world'. When national interests diverged there could be considerable asperity, but the relationship rested on similar (though not identical) world-views, and had a strong core of perceived mutual self-interest. The more obvious benefits came to Britain, as the weaker partner; Americans sometimes found embarrassing the way in which the British stressed the relationship, Eisenhower once remarking that Churchill was 'just a little Peter Pan' who would not adjust to Britain's changed position in the world. But US resources were not unlimited: the United States has generally found it desirable to work with partners (or 'proxies') and for two decades after 1945 no other friendly country matched the British range of international positions or involvements. Indeed subsequent critics have claimed that, partly through delusions of grandeur, the British functioned as US mercenaries, and also risked Soviet retaliation by accepting so many US nuclear facilities as to become, in effect, an unsinkable American aircraft carrier.

Institutionally the relationship gave rise to the 1947 agreement (still operative) for sharing the collection of electronic intelligence on a worldwide basis between the USA and the Commonwealth (UK, Canada, Australia, New Zealand), and the arrangements made from 1957 for nuclear cooperation between the USA and UK. Its essence lay rather in the habit of mutual consultation and the access this gave each country to the decision-making processes of the other: the legacy, in part, of being (in Churchill's words) 'mixed up together' in the combined planning of the Second World War, but one reinforced by a range of personal friendships and collaboration that spread well beyond the official sphere. Acheson recalls that, during his time as Secretary of State (1949–53) he invited Franks to talk

> regularly, and in complete personal confidence, about any international problems we saw arising. Neither would report or quote the other unless he got the other's consent. . . . We met alone, usually at . . . at the end of the day before or after dinner. No one was informed even of the fact of the meeting.
>
> Later, comparing the relations between our governments during our time with those under our successors, we concluded that whereas we thought of those relations and their management as part of domestic affairs, they had regarded them as foreign affairs.

A similar picture was given in late 1962. Acheson then fluttered the dovecots by pronouncing that, with the loss of its empire, Britain's 'attempt to play a separate power role – that is, a role apart from Europe, a role based on a "special relationship" with the United States . . . – this role is about to be played out'. In reply, though perhaps also to soothe hurt British feelings, the White House instructed the State Department to tell the press that

> US–UK relations are not based only on a power calculus, but also on a deep community of purpose and long practice of close cooperation. Examples are legion: nuclear affairs, Sino-Indian crisis, in which Sandys and Harriman missions would have been ineffective without each other, Berlin, and also Cuba, where . . . President and Prime Minister were in daily intimate consultation to a degree not publicly known.[18] 'Special relationship' may not be a perfect phrase, but sneers at Anglo-American reality would be equally foolish.[19]

Since it is so intangible and lies so much in the eye of the beholder, attempts to chart the rise and decline of the 'special relationship' can only be imprecise. That said, it would seem that in 1945 neither the Truman administration nor Congress was particularly inclined to continue it. From 1946 onwards, though, the administration came increasingly to see the Soviet Union as an adversary, and to back (or shore up) Britain against it. Certainly this did not extend to all policy areas: the USA cut off the wartime collaboration on the atom bomb, and Britain went it alone – Bevin observing that, to save future Foreign Secretaries from being talked at by their US counterparts as he had just been by Byrnes, Britain needed a bomb with 'the bloody Union Jack flying on top of it' 'whatever it costs'.[20]

---

18. Macmillan did indeed phone Kennedy frequently during the crisis, and held a distinctly grouchy Cabinet to public support of the American position. Ambassador Ormsby-Gore, too, was able to persuade Kennedy to locate the blockade far closer to Cuba than the US Navy would have liked, so as to give Khrushchev more time to back off (though it is not clear that the Navy did in fact comply: Allison, *Essence of Decision* pp.129–32); and he was trusted with early thoughts on the missiles in Turkey that he did not believe 'the president would repeat . . . to any member of his administration except his brother Bobby'. But the British input was essentially marginal. On the 22nd Macmillan asked Ormsby-Gore what 'the President is really trying to do', adding that 'Since it seemed impossible to stop his action, I did not make the effort, although in the course of the day I was in a mind to do so' – though also that, if things looked like escalating into war, he would try 'by calling a conference of my own, or something of the kind, to stop it': The *Independent*, 2 Jan. 1993 p.7; *The Times*, 1 Jan. 1993 pp.1, 6

19. Reynolds, 'Rethinking Anglo-American Relations' p.109; Acheson, *Present at the Creation* p.323; Ambrose, *Eisenhower* p.146

20. *The Times*, 30 Sept. 1982 p.10

But NATO developed out of secret US–UK–Canadian talks, and many other Cold War developments followed this pattern.

In his early years President Eisenhower felt Britain was trying to push things too far: he noted that Churchill

> has fixed in his mind a certain international relationship he is trying to establish. . . . This is that Britain and the British Commonwealth are not to be treated just as other nations would be treated by the United States. . . . On the contrary, he most earnestly . . . intends that those countries shall enjoy a relationship which will recognize the special place of partnership they occupied with us during World War II. . . .
>
> In those days he had the enjoyable feeling that he and our President were sitting on some rather Olympian platform . . . and directing world affairs from that point of vantage. . . .
>
> In the present international complexities, any hope of establishing such a relationship is completely fatuous.[21]

This was, of course, far from the end of close Anglo-American cooperation: Eden's triumphant settlement in 1954 of the Italo-Yugoslav dispute over Trieste (that had led to Italian threats to leave NATO) was underpinned by quiet US aid to Yugoslavia.[22] At the 1954 Geneva conference on Indo-China, however, Eden did not let himself be unduly deflected by Dulles's wishes; and in 1956 Britain and France went it alone in their invasion of Egypt. US action in blocking this was bitterly received by much of the Conservative Party, but the episode had the improbable effect of tightening Anglo-American relations. Drawing on their wartime friendship, Eisenhower and Macmillan met in Bermuda in March 1957 determined to put Suez behind them. They there arranged for US IRBMs to be deployed in the UK; and in October 1957 in Washington Eisenhower promised to seek repeal of the 1946 McMahon Act ban on the exchange of nuclear information. Thereafter Macmillan enjoyed excellent relations with the Eisenhower administration, and showed considerable skill in continuing these with its successor – helped by the remarkable personal popularity of the British ambassador, David Ormsby-Gore, with both President Kennedy and Bobby Kennedy.

It was, however, perhaps unfortunate that a major symbol of the post-1957 relationship was nuclear cooperation, since this was bound to appear exclusive. The McMahon Act amendment permitting exchanges of nuclear information restricted them to

21. Carlton, *Britain and the Suez Crisis* pp.5–6
22. Cook, *The Declassified Eisenhower* pp.193–4

countries that had 'made substantial progress in the development of atomic weapons', a condition then met only by Britain.[23] In 1960 Britain afforded basing facilities to US Polaris submarines; and Eisenhower offered Macmillan cheap access to US strategic delivery systems then under development. Of these Macmillan unwisely chose the air-launched rocket 'Skybolt', since it fitted better with the existing British bomber force. Development proved difficult, and in December 1962 McNamara made clear his intention to cancel it. He was no doubt acting chiefly on cost and technical grounds, but he thought small nuclear forces served only to invite Soviet pre-emptive strikes, and probably did not regret the prospect of the British force being squeezed out of existence. Macmillan, however, saw this as a devastating blow, and (at his Nassau meeting with Kennedy) pulled out all the stops and persuaded him to allow Britain to switch to Polaris. (The rockets were offered also to France, but as it could not then manufacture warheads to fit them, this was a deliberately empty gesture.) Implementation of the Nassau agreement proved remarkably smooth, and the life of the national British deterrent was thus prolonged at minimum cost. By the late 1970s, when it became time to think about a replacement, US opinion had shifted to the Gaullist view that the uncertainties inherent in there being more than one centre of nuclear decision would tend to deter an aggressor. Both the Carter and Reagan administrations were happy to allow Britain to replace Polaris with the current submarine-launched missiles, Trident, on the same terms. All the controversy attending the decision to take up this option has so far (1993) been internal to the UK.

But if the 1960s saw the preservation of the British deterrent with US assistance, they also bought a sharp decline in the importance of the special relationship. In part this was for personal reasons – President Johnson was offended by the lack of British support for his Vietnam War. It reflected, too, the British decision to withdraw from East of Suez. The British Defence Secretary had been told in 1964 that the USA wanted the UK 'not to maintain huge bases but to keep a foothold in Hong Kong, Malaya, the Persian Gulf, to enable us [Britain] to do things for the alliance which they can't do . . . they think that our forces are much more useful to the alliance outside Europe than in Germany'. In 1967, despite pleas to

---

23. Horne says this had been agreed between Eisenhower and Macmillan (*Macmillan* ii p.109), Ullman that it was insisted on by Congress ('The Covert French Connection', *Foreign Policy* 1989 p.6)

the Foreign Secretary of 'Be British, George, be British – how can you betray us?',[24] the government decided to pull out of Malaysia and – more worryingly from the US point of view – the Gulf. Actually the vacuum there was to be filled quite smoothly, for a time, by America's friend the Shah of Iran. As the recession of its power left Britain less and less to offer, so such relationships with regional powers became ever more important to the USA; they too could be 'special', notably that with Israel (which had always possessed great political clout and an excellent intelligence service, to which was added from the mid-1960s rapidly growing military connections). The 1970s also brought better US relations with France (the only Western ally besides Britain with significant out-of-area capabilities), and indeed at least an adversary-partnership with the Soviet Union.[25]

Of course the attitudes underlying the British 'special relationship' did not simply vanish. Nixon prided himself on having forecast Heath's election victory of 1970, and often sought to re-establish the old relationship with personal telephone calls and bilateral joint working parties. Heath, however, seemed scarred by de Gaulle's judgement that Britain was not 'European' enough to be allowed to enter the EEC, and was determined to forestall any further complaints on this score. He

> not only accepted that Britain's future lay with Europe, he preferred it that way. And so paradoxically . . . when the other European leaders strove to improve their relations with us . . . Heath went in the opposite direction. His relations with us were always correct, but they rarely rose above a basic reserve that prevented – in the name of Europe – the close coordination with us that was his for the asking.

Despite this, Kissinger says, as National Security Adviser, he kept the Foreign Office 'better informed and more closely engaged than I did the State Department' – which was, admittedly, not difficult. Some previous patterns continued: 'most of the actual drafting' of the 1973 US–Soviet Agreement on the Prevention of Nuclear War was done by a Foreign Office team invited to Washington to advise on the negotiations.[26] However, this did not prevent the 1973

24. Reynolds, 'A "special relationship"? America, Britain and the International Order since the Second World War', *International Affairs* lxii (1985–6) pp.14–15

25. Though basically very different, this had features in common with the 'special relationship'; thus until Reagan's inauguration Ambassador Dobrynin had privileged and inconspicuous access to key foreign policy-makers not unlike that earlier enjoyed by Sir Oliver Franks

26. For Kissinger's views on the 'special relationship' see e.g. his *Memoirs* i pp.89 ff, 421, 610, 964, ii pp.140–3, 191–2, 278, 281–6, 920–1, and 'The Special Relationship', *The Listener* 13 May 1982 p.16

Arab–Israeli War and oil shock from severely straining US relations with Britain, as with other West European countries, until Heath's fall brought improvement next year.

By the mid-1970s the leaders of the major Western countries (barring of course the USA) had, for most diplomatic purposes, become a group of equals, meeting each other (from 1975) at annual summit conferences. Accordingly the USA's choice of partners was coming to depend chiefly on the policy areas in question and on the personal preferences of policy-makers. Thus it offered Britain support over Rhodesia (as a second, except briefly in 1976 when Kissinger personally took command of the negotiations); the US and British ambassadors worked closely together in urging the appeasement of the Iranian revolution in 1978–9 – with National Security Adviser Brzezinski dissenting. Brzezinski did not share Kissinger's partiality for the UK; rather he admired France and 'consulted more frequently with my French colleagues than with either the British or the Germans'.[27] He was, however,

> amazed how quickly Callaghan succeeded in establishing himself as Carter's favorite, writing him friendly little notes, calling, talking like a genial older uncle, and lecturing Carter in a pleasant manner on the intricacies of inter-allied politics. Callaghan literally coopted Carter in the course of a few relatively brief personal encounters.[28]

This pattern continued in the 1980s. Thatcher made great play of supporting American leadership (and in 1986 allowed the use of British-based US planes to bomb Ghadaffi, at some political risk and in sharp contrast to the rest of Europe). She had herself profited greatly, during the 1982 Falklands War, from logistic support accorded by Defense Secretary Weinberger (a strong Anglophile, unlike UN ambassador Jeane Kirkpatrick, who doubted the wisdom of risking US relations with Latin America for the sake of satisfying what she saw as British pride). Thatcher got on remarkably well with President Reagan, thereby reviving international perceptions of the 'special relationship' and acquiring a certain amount of diplomatic leverage (especially during Gorbachev's early years when she was his preferred Western interlocutor).

The next US administration (Bush) at first laid much more stress on European unity (where Thatcher appeared as an obstacle) and seemed (at the instance of Secretary of State Baker) to cultivate West Germany as the USA's preferred European partner. In 1990

27. He was suspicious of the revival of German power, and got on badly with Schmidt
28. *Power and Principle* pp.291, 313

this greatly eased reunification, a process that seemed yet further to reinforce German economic pre-eminence in Europe. Over the Gulf crisis, though, Germany proved a broken reed: its constitution prevented it from sending troops outside the NATO area, and, since it was habituated to consume, not provide, security, it made remarkably heavy weather even of sending planes to reassure Turkey. Both Britain and France were more attuned to geopolitics, and both made useful military contributions. Despite some US irritation with France's ostentatiously independent diplomacy on the eve of the actual fighting, their standing in Washington rose accordingly. Both continued to derive diplomatic weight from their permanent seats on the UN Security Council.

DE GAULLE AND THE ANGLO-SAXONS – 1958–68

Franco-American relations have been more uneven. Fourth Republican governments were predominantly Atlanticist, though their domestic weakness, procrastination on German rearmament, and entanglement in colonial wars prompted a mixture of US concern and exasperation. From 1958 de Gaulle sought to transform France from a courtesy to a real Great Power. For this he needed nuclear weapons. The Fourth Republic already had a nuclear programme, and had indeed just concluded a secret deal for joint French, German and Italian funding of the development of both atom bombs and delivery systems. De Gaulle promptly ditched this,[29] and pursued with great vigour a purely national deterrent. He also, in September 1958, sought to define France's status by proposing a new Franco-British-American body responsible for 'taking joint decisions on all political matters affecting world security, and . . . [for] drawing up, and if necessary putting into action, strategic plans, especially those involving the use of nuclear weapons'.[30] This, French diplomats usually confirmed, implied a French veto on the use of *any* US weapons, not just of those based in France.

Opinion differs as to whether this proposal was serious, or just put forward to provide a pretext for the gradual disengagement of French forces from supranational NATO command that began in

29. Hans-Peter Schwarz, *Adenauer. Der Staatsman: 1952–1967* (Stuttgart, 1991) pp. 394–401.
30. The text was leaked but never officially published – Brian Crozier, *De Gaulle. The Statesman* (1973) p. 525

1959. Though no American president would ever promise more than prior *consultation*,[31] some effort was made to devise diplomatic arrangements that would satisfy French aspirations without grating on the susceptibilities of countries like Italy and West Germany. The years 1958–9 saw more discussion than action, but in December 1959 Eisenhower agreed, to the State Department's annoyance, that there should be regular, if 'clandestine', Three Power discussions in London on 'matters of common interest, outside and transcending NATO'. By March 1960, however, he was telling Macmillan of his 'amazement' that de Gaulle seemed 'unable to fathom the methods by which our three governments could easily keep in close touch on main issues. I explained to him how you and ourselves used both normal diplomatic exchanges, personal communications, and, in acute cases, ad hoc committees to keep together'. It is unclear how far French difficulties in plugging into the Anglo-American relationship were cultural. There were language barriers;[32] but France may also have been uneasy with informal arrangements and preferred structure for its own sake. Eisenhower briefed Kennedy about de Gaulle's 'obsession' with a 'triumvirate of the United States, France, and Great Britain . . . organized on a joint staff concept' (which, Eisenhower thought, 'would break up NATO immediately'). Macmillan felt that 'de Gaulle attaches more importance to the *fact* of the Tripartite talks than to the substance of them', a view consistent with the very limited French contribution to those discussions that were arranged at the official level.[33]

Still Macmillan was increasingly anxious to satisfy France, provided this was not 'at the cost of our arrangements with the Americans', in the hopes of reciprocal concessions over British trade relations with the EEC: 'The future of British trade in Europe is far more important than whether a few French fighters are or are not to be put under the command of SACEUR'. In May 1960 he proposed frequent meetings of the three Foreign Ministers under cover of the various international gatherings they would have attended anyway. Eisenhower was agreeable both to this and to military discussions in Washington on questions outside the NATO area, but insisted on maintaining existing NATO arrangements for

31. ibid, p. 543

32. Kennedy's attempts at telephone calls broke down for this reason (Sorenson, *Kennedy* p.561); although Macmillan spoke excellent and Dulles passable French, there have been suggestions that important points were sometimes missed

33. Ambrose, *Eisenhower* p.615; John Newhouse, *De Gaulle and the Anglo-Saxons* (1970) pp.88–9; Horne, *Macmillan* ii p.295; Macmillan, *Memoirs* v pp.106, 246

Europe. De Gaulle initially pressed for a summit to take matters further; but he then cooled, possibly offended by differences of policy over the Congo (which he was far quicker than Britain to voice in public) and by US reluctance to see France as speaking for the whole of continental Western Europe.[34] So further developments were left to the next US President, Kennedy.

With his eye on Britain's European relations, Macmillan sought to persuade Kennedy to take Tripartism further and to offer France help in developing nuclear weapons. Kennedy was delighted to intercede with de Gaulle for a British move into 'Europe' (though the attempt may well have been counterproductive), happy with Tripartism, but unwilling 'to assist France's efforts to create a nuclear weapons capability. . . . If we were to help France . . ., this could not but have a major effect on German attitudes'. The subjects were discussed during Kennedy's June 1961 visit to Paris, but to little effect.[35] De Gaulle was by now placing more emphasis on the Fouchet proposals for the coordination (inevitably under French leadership) of EEC defence and foreign policies; the Tripartite Foreign Ministers' meetings became increasingly acrimonious, and were not continued into 1962. Macmillan, though, was becoming really anxious about the progress of Britain's EEC application, and began to cogitate offering France nuclear aid if Britain was admitted. He discussed the idea with colleagues before meeting de Gaulle at Champs in June 1962, but found no way of overcoming US objections to passing on American technology. So at Champs and (in December) Rambouillet, he probably did no more than speculate about a possible 'European' (i.e. Anglo-French) deterrent and promise such nuclear cooperation as did not involve US technology, though the French ambassador was convinced that a definite offer was made of collaboration in exchange for EEC entry.[36] But in late December 1962, when a

34. Macmillan, *Memoirs* v pp.112–14, 245–6; Crozier, *De Gaulle* pp.536–41. Chaban-Delmas was later to explain that France represented Europe just as Britain represented the Commonwealth, and that it therefore had as much right to be admitted to US counsels

35. Macmillan, *Memoirs* v p.325; Horne, *Macmillan* ii pp.295, 301; Schlesinger, *Thousand Days* pp.319–23; Crozier, *De Gaulle* p.543

36. Some say that, at Rambouillet, Macmillan promised to replace Skybolt through nuclear collaboration with France, and that when instead he later arranged the exclusive purchase of US Polaris missiles, this proved to de Gaulle that Britain was not really European and precipitated his EEC veto. But de Gaulle subsequently confirmed that he had been told at Rambouillet of the British intention to seek Polaris; he also made it plain before Nassau that he had turned Macmillan down over the EEC: Horne, *Macmillan* ii pp.430 ff, 673; Lacouture, *De Gaulle* pp.355–7

French EEC veto seemed likely, Macmillan did ask the USA to allow Britain to offer France Polaris warheads in exchange for entry. Kennedy refused – though next summer he was to offer France nuclear data and underground test facilities in a vain attempt to get de Gaulle to accede to the treaty banning atmospheric testing.[37]

De Gaulle's EEC veto went down extremely badly in both Washington and London; his relations with the Anglo-Saxons deteriorated rapidly. The post-Cuba détente gave his foreign policy more scope. He had unhesitatingly backed the US stance over Cuba, and during the Berlin crisis he advocated a firm Western front. But he had told Kennedy that, while France would do nothing to disrupt NATO during the Berlin crisis, it would seek a different organisation for the future. De Gaulle was never attracted by the various US schemes designed to head off this trouble: a French SACEUR, a multilateral nuclear force where all participating countries would possess vetoes, or even the commitment of some Polaris submarines to NATO to be controlled by a 'Tripartite' authority.[38] Now his public pronouncements about NATO became increasingly hostile; in early 1966 he declared that, though France would continue to accept the obligations of the original 1949 treaty to 'fight on the side' of any member subject to 'unprovoked aggression', it would withdraw from the subsequent supranational military arrangements and resume sovereign control over all armed forces on its territory. Accordingly 1966–7 saw the departure of foreign forces and support facilities from France, and the relocation of NATO headquarters to Brussels. In many ways the alliance worked more smoothly without France, but the loss of logistic depth, and uncertainty as to what French forces would do in the event of war, could have had serious military consequences. The French action was seen as rather cynical sabotage: President Johnson said it raised 'grave questions regarding the whole relationship between the responsibilities and the benefits of the alliance'; in protecting West Germany, NATO would inevitably protect France even though France had ceased to contribute much to it.[39]

Nor were de Gaulle's other policies widely appreciated. With hindsight one might judge that they usually incorporated a real insight and voiced feelings quite widely held in Europe, but that no

37. Horne, *Macmillan* ii pp.326–9, 440–5; Schlesinger, *Thousand Days* pp.780–1
38. Schlesinger, *Thousand Days* pp.320, 322; *New York Times*, 9 Apr. 1990 p.A9
39. *Keesing's*, 21604 ff., 22123 ff.; Don Cook, *Charles De Gaulle* (1984) p.383

other country would countenance the extremes to which they were carried. Thus de Gaulle's fears that the USA would not put itself at risk, now that the USSR had nuclear weapons too, were not unreasonable – US Secretary of State Herter had once suggested as much – and de Gaulle's view that even small national deterrents contributed to overall stability by increasing a potential aggressor's uncertainty as to the likely response was later adopted by official London and Washington. However, successive US presidents resented his questioning of America's determination to honour its obligations, while most Europeans thought it counter-productive. De Gaulle's denunciation of the 1963 Test Ban Treaty was widely seen as unhelpful; the final progression, whereby it was declared in 1967 that France needed to be able to defend itself against attacks 'from all points of the compass', appeared gratuitously offensive.

There was, too, much to be said for de Gaulle's attempts to open up Eastern Europe diplomatically (see pp. 271–2), and they were ultimately adopted and developed by West Germany. However, his constant lumping together of the US and Soviet hegemonies was more debatable, especially after the 1968 Soviet intervention in Prague. Similarly de Gaulle had warned the USA privately against getting involved in Vietnam, but his 1966 visit to Cambodia, and his denunciations of the US war apparatus, were not appreciated. French recognition of Communist China in 1964, and dissociation from Israel in 1967–8, can be regarded as in advance of their time, but then seemed more like disengagement from the West. His 1964 tour of Latin America looked like an attempt to woo it away from its Yankee affiliations, and his 1967 cry in Montreal of 'Vive le Québec libre' (and possibly deeper involvement with Québécois, and Biafran, separatism) appear simply mischievous. For the most part, though, these were words only. In economic matters de Gaulle proceeded to deeds. Here too he was voicing widely felt fears of a take-over of Europe by technologically superior US multinationals, financed (in effect) by the United States' ability, in virtue of the dollar's reserve status, simply to print internationally acceptable money. He was also correct in observing that the system rested on US ability to keep gold at an artificially low price.[40] But there was less enthusiasm for his call for a new gold exchange system that would benefit chiefly South Africa, the USSR – and France. De Gaulle's conversion, between 1965 and 1968, of large quantities of French dollars into gold, while well calculated to squeeze the USA,

---

40. For a fuller discussion, see *The Post-Imperial Age* chap.20

was seen also as risking the collapse of the international monetary system with incalculable consequences. To the Cold War was added the Franco-US 'Gold War'.

US–FRENCH RELATIONS 1969–83

Although it was not easy to accommodate Gaullist France within the Western alliance, the US–French rift was to be healed far more easily than the contemporary Sino-Soviet one. The process may be said to have begun with the weakening of the franc by the 1968 'events'. Thereafter France needed foreign help, especially as de Gaulle refused to devalue. In 1969 Nixon became President. He was well disposed towards de Gaulle, who had been gracious to him when his political career seemed finished (after his defeat in the California gubernatorial elections), and anxious to end what he saw as the unnecessary and constraining quarrel with France (as also that with China). His visit to de Gaulle went well. Then de Gaulle was succeeded by Pompidou, a more cautious man who valued his predecessor's achievements but worried about Germany and sought to edge back towards Atlanticism. US–French relations were mostly smooth, if unremarkable, though they were nearly marred when Pompidou and his wife were jostled and sworn at by demonstrators in Chicago. In 1971 the USA was able to use France's position in Europe to negotiate with Pompidou the package of currency realignments that became known as the Smithsonian agreement, instead of seeking a general monetary summit that would probably have collapsed into mutual acrimony. More friction developed, however, from Pompidou's view that 'while it would be absurd to conceive of a Europe constructed in opposition to' the USA, 'the very closeness of these links requires that Europe affirm its individual personality with regard to the United States'.[41] During 1973–4, with Pompidou enfeebled by terminal illness, this requirement was pushed strongly by the extremely prickly French foreign minister Jobert. Kissinger had, perhaps unwisely, launched an attempt to rethink the Atlantic relationship in the very year that the European Community had expanded from six to nine members and had to adjust its own functioning accordingly. The result was much stiffness and misunderstanding, subsequently exacerbated by

41. Kissinger, *Memoirs* i pp.958–62, ii p.132

the combination of European refusal to back the USA during the 1973 Arab–Israeli War and a most uncollective scramble for oil by its individual countries. Not until things had settled down again, and governments changed in France, Germany and Britain, did transatlantic relations return to a more even keel; then 1975 saw the institution (at French initiative) of annual gatherings of the leaders of major Western countries (including Japan) that, though very far from the Three Power directorate that de Gaulle had been seeking, do go some way towards providing a loose framework for discussion and coordination, without however denting US pre-eminence in any but the economic field.

Nixon and Kissinger had always regarded doctrinaire opposition to the French nuclear deterrent as unwise; it had certainly created considerable anti-American feeling. Accordingly they held out hopes of collaboration as a carrot to improve relations, and in 1973 are supposed to have offered it to still French fears (after the Nixon–Brezhnev summit) of a US–Soviet condominium.[42] Setting up the collaboration proved difficult, as both countries required secrecy for domestic reasons; the transfer of information proved patchy – France was given advice on miniaturising warheads, but not on silencing submarines. As intended, the exercise seems to have tightened links, especially those running through military and presidential channels bypassing the two countries' diplomatic services. It may have encouraged Giscard to oblige the USA by, for instance, keeping French troops in Djibouti. Under Mitterand, it is claimed, cooperation grew to the point where detailed arrangements were worked out for the placing of French forces under SACEUR's command in time of war, and for integrating French nuclear targeting, like British, into SACEUR's plans.[43] Certainly though France continued to adhere to the Gaullist posture of sovereign national defence, it surprised the world, in the early 1980s, by the depth of its suspicion of the Soviet arms build-up and by its support for (though not participation in) the deployment of cruise missiles to counter it. French public opinion was then (at least for a time) far more pro-American than British or West German; observers sometimes wondered whether this was not

---

42. This paragraph is derived from Ullman, 'The Covert French Connection', *Foreign Policy* lxxv (1989). His narrative is consistent with some points in the public record, but given its subject matter it inevitably rests on unattributable interviews

43. Both countries have two sets of targets, those assigned by NATO, and those they would attack if they were to fight alone

precisely because (as a result of de Gaulle's activities) it had no US weapons on its soil.[44]

DEVELOPMENT OF THE EC SINCE 1985

Since the early 1980s, the European scene has been transformed both by the collapse of communist rule in the East and by the development of the EC in the West. By 1984 the Community was running out of money; it needed unanimous consent to raise its VAT levy, and this provided the final stimulus for a compromise resolution of the problem of British financial contributions that had bedevilled its politics since 1979. Change was also promoted by the expansion of EC membership, with Greece joining in 1981, Spain and Portugal in 1986. More members, on the old system, would have meant more vetoes and even slower decision-making. Such considerations meshed with pressure from the European Parliament for a full-scale political union and an upgrading of its own position. The outcome was a new treaty, the Single European Act (signed in 1985, effective in 1987). This made weighted voting in the Council of Ministers the norm in most (but not all) areas, while slightly increasing the Parliament's powers. It also extended the legal scope of the Community to areas like the environment, social policy, and technical cooperation. It made new declarations in favour of monetary union, and it set a deadline of January 1993 for the establishment of what came to be called the 'Single European Market'. This had, in theory, been an aim of the original EEC. Although tariff barriers had been abolished, non-tariff ones certainly had not. Largely under British pressure, the 'Single Market' had been blessed by the 1985 Milan summit. With the settlement of other problems, it was to be strongly forwarded not only by the British Commissioner Lord Cockfield but also by the Commission President (since 1985) Jacques Delors; serious plans to achieve it were adopted in 1987–8. Thatcher, as an economic liberal, would have been happy to realise it and then stop. European federalists were determined to go further. Among them was

44. For the evolution of French attitudes, see Hassner, 'Perceptions of the Soviet threat . . . : the case of France' in Schweitzer, *The Changing Western Analysis of the Soviet Threat.* With the end of the Cold War, however, France has been readier than Britain to contemplate a US military withdawal from Europe, and to prepare for (or risk precipitating) it by pushing the EC towards a military role

Delors, who (as a socialist) felt too that harmonisation of social policy should accompany the opening of markets. He was also not averse to enhancing his own position, declaring in 1988 that, within a decade, '80 per cent of economic legislation, and perhaps tax and social legislation' in member states would be determined in Brussels. The prospect alarmed Thatcher, who countered that it would be folly to try to fit the individual nation states 'into some sort of Identikit European personality'.[45]

She was to find herself isolated. In 1989 the Commission proposed a 'Social Charter'. More fundamentally it began to promote monetary union. The European Monetary System (and its Exchange Rate Mechanism – ERM) had witnessed repeated currency realignments up to 1987, but they then stopped. This emboldened people to push for further convergence and ultimately a single currency managed by a European central bank. This raised major issues of sovereignty. Thatcher claimed that it would work only if there were a European government rather than twelve national states: 'That being not on the cards, I see no point in having anyone study a European central bank'. Despite Kohl's initial coolness towards the project, it was widely taken up. At the 1989 Madrid summit Thatcher's ministers forced her to agree in principle to join the ERM (as was done in 1990); it was resolved that 1990 should see serious planning for monetary union. The process was eventful. In October Thatcher was unexpectedly presented with a timetable worked out at a meeting of Christian Democrat leaders; the virulence of her later assertion that she would never, never consent to the abolition of the pound ('the most powerful expression of sovereignty you can possibly have') set off a chain of events that led to her political downfall in November 1990. Delors took credit for this, and threatened another crisis if her successor, John Major, again tried to stall.[46] Major was in general treated far more gently by his European colleagues, partly because he adopted a warmer tone towards the EC and partly because he established much better relations with Chancellor Kohl. The outcome was agreement at Maastricht in December 1991 on a new treaty intended to come into force in 1993 and constitute a 'European Union'. Among much else, the agreement provided that

45. *Keesing's*, esp. 33159 ff, 34106–8, 36153, 36306, 36194; *Keesing's UK Record* (1988) pp.171, 187. Equally the idea of recovering via Brussels the ground it had lost domestically to 'Thatcherism' so attracted the British Labour Party that it finally dropped its hostility to EC membership
46. *Keesing's*, 36307, 36740–1, 37782, 37905

a single currency might be launched in 1996, failing which the states that met the agreed criteria of economic convergence would definitely go ahead in 1999. Britain and Denmark secured undertakings that they would not have to participate without their explicit consent. [47]

Among the issues underlying the debate was the role of Germany. Kohl had always held Bonn's traditional view that Germany needed to be anchored and integrated into Europe; he returned from Maastricht announcing that the 'German dream has been fulfilled' and that European unity was now 'irreversible'. Another perspective, voiced eighteen months later (as he thought off-the-record) by a close associate of Thatcher's, saw monetary union as 'a German racket designed to take over the whole of Europe'.[48] A variant, towards which France seemed sometimes to incline, was that Germany was either actually (especially in economic matters)[49] or potentially dominant, and that it should be contained by transferring policy-making, not simply to the Community level, but to the kind of Community institutions where Germany would have only one voice among many. Accordingly in 1991 France opposed the idea of an independent European central bank lest it prove to be only the Bundesbank under another name, and pushed instead for one managed by the political appointees of member states. After Maastricht the possibility that its inflation-free deutsch mark might thus, through monetary union, be swapped for a laxer écu occasioned such concern in Germany that in 1992 Kohl felt he had to promise the Bundestag that this would not happen without its consent.

Nor was this by any means the Community's only set-back. For Denmark unexpectedly voted, in a referendum, to reject Maastricht. When Mitterand sought to restore confidence in the treaty by putting it to a referendum, he almost lost. All this emboldened other critics, notably in Britain (which, by the end of 1992, had still not ratified Maastricht). It demonstrated that the EC Commission was far more widely unpopular than it had realised. Nor was this all: the ERM was also to be badly dented. In the period of exchange

47. Britain also insisted that harmonisation of social policy should proceed under a separate protocol (the 'Social Chapter') to which it would not be a party: *Keesing's*, 38657–9; *The Independent*, 12 Dec. 1991 p.8

48. *The Independent*, 12 Dec. 1991 p.8 (Kohl); *Keesing's*, 37623: publication of these anti-German remarks made Nicholas Ridley's ministerial resignation inevitable

49. Germany's centrality was illustrated when, for domestic reasons, the Bundesbank increased interest rates in December 1991 and almost all ERM members had to follow suit, even though this probably hurt their economies

rate stability after 1987, the feeling had grown up that countries should live with their existing parities as part of their preparation for the future single currency. Accordingly Germany was not allowed to fight the inflationary pressures that had stemmed from reunification by revaluing the mark. So the Bundesbank kept interest rates high instead, with the side-effect of attracting hot money.[50] In September 1992 market surges (partly encouraged by fears over the oncoming French referendum) blew the Italian lira and British pound out of the ERM; a devaluation of the peseta followed; in August 1993 the franc was driven down, and the ERM's operation, in effect, suspended. The pieces will no doubt be picked up in due course, but the EC's momentum has undoubtedly been slowed.

EC policy-making is, then, a slow, and not always edifying or successful, process. Viewed from outside, however, the Community is more impressive, the largest trading bloc in the world, and it has strong attractive power. In 1961 Britain decided that it could not afford to stay out. In 1973 it finally managed to join, accompanied by Denmark and Eire (though not, as had been expected, Norway). There followed a period of Mediterranean extension designed, in part, to stabilise the new democracies of Greece, Spain and Portugal. This in turn led to other membership applications (notably that by Turkey in 1987), consideration of which has been stalled until after the completion of the Single Market. Even more impressive is the Community's recent appeal to countries like Austria and Sweden that appeared to be getting on quite successfully without membership. One factor here was the downfall of the USSR, which would have been upset by Sweden's membership, and would have vetoed Austria's as incompatible with its promised neutrality. Another was a fear of being left outside the Single Market. This fear led initially to EFTA–EC negotiations to create a common free-trading 'European Economic Area',[51] but it was followed by a flood of applications for EC membership. Those from economically developed countries should present the EC with comparatively few problems. More controversial is the question of relationships with the former communist countries of Eastern

50. Almost no income was lost by investing in Germany, and the exercise would become very profitable if other currencies devalued. Moreover matching German interest rates damaged the economies of countries that had moved earlier into recession, and reduced their readiness to defend their currencies by moving their own interest rates yet higher

51. This was finally agreed in Feb. 1992, though the Swiss subsequently voted, in a referendum, against participation

Europe. Some at least of these look to the Community for not only immediate assistance but also ultimate membership. President Havel of Czechoslovakia claimed, 'It is in the West's own interest to seek the integration of eastern and central Europe into the family of European democracy because otherwise it risks creating a zone of hopelessness, instability and chaos, which could threaten Western Europe every bit as much as the Warsaw Pact tank divisions of old'. Britain is particularly keen on EC membership for east European states (and perhaps even Russia) 'as soon as they are ready, politically and economically'; Major has cautioned against developments that would make this more difficult. This raises the old dispute between broadening and deepening: Mitterand replied that he did 'not want the Community to become a vague free trade area, as certain . . . countries wanted from the very beginning'. The issue assumed some prominence in Denmark's EC presidency, inaugurated in January 1993 under the slogan of 'The Open Europe'.[52]

Whatever the outcome, it is clear that the EC accounts for most of Europe's economic activity. With the decline of the 'bipolar world' its future relationship with the other main centres of economic power, the USA and Japan, is inevitably problematical. The question presents itself chiefly in terms of trade (to which we shall soon turn). But, as regards the USA, it is intertwined also with considerations of foreign policy and security. The EC has made collective foreign policy pronouncements since the early 1970s. Before 1991 they cannot be said to have had much impact, but when in June 1991 Yugoslavia fell apart into secession and civil war, the Community's time seemed to have come; it seized hold of the problem and sought to broker a solution. But it would not contemplate using force; by the end of the year its diplomatic efforts had been unsuccessful and the initiative was passing to the UN. A further question-mark was posed in December 1991 over its ability to take meaningful collective action when Germany decided to defer no longer to French and British hesitations but to recognise the independence of Slovenia and Croatia on 15 January 1992 come what may. The episode suggests that, despite the Maastricht pronouncement for a measure of majority voting on foreign policy, the EC still has some way to go before it is a major actor in high politics. However France and Germany were pressing it in 1991 to start acquiring a capability in the defence field. Britain and Italy

52. *Keesing's*, 381125; *Financial Times*, 13 Sept. 1991 p.1; *The Independent*, 2 Jan. 1993 p.10

were more cautious, not opposing the idea in principle but being anxious to do nothing that would undermine the USA's commitment to NATO. Maastricht gave some satisfaction to both sides, and held out the possibility of the Community's absorbing the Western European [defence] Union in 1999.

The more immediate problem with the United States, however, comes in the field not of defence but of trade. Trade negotiations fall within the Commission's competence, and the EC has, since the 'Kennedy' round of GATT tariff talks in the 1960s, operated as a single unit. In this sphere, at least, it is a Great Power. There have been periodic minor skirmishes with the USA ever since the 1963 'chicken war'(see *The Post-Imperial Age*, chap. 20). Until the 1980s such disputes were no more than storms in teacups. Frictions then increased, in large part as a by-product of American-European inability to compete industrially with Japan. One alternative, to think instead in terms of regional trading blocs, commends itself particularly to France and to Delors:

> Japan is spinning its spider's web over large areas of the Pacific. The US and Canada are closing together in a free-trade zone, with doubtless Mexico to follow. This means that the world is beginning to build large regional ensembles.

Another response, pushed particularly by the USA, was to seek through the GATT 'Uruguay' round, a general settlement that would inter alia facilitate freer trade in agriculture (where the USA believed it had a comparative advantage).[53] In this field the EC was less protectionist than Japan or Korea, but, given its subsidised exports, possibly more disruptive. In any case the CAP emerged as a major obstacle in 1988. In 1990 talks broke down over a call to cut EC farm support by 70 per cent. In preparation for their resumption, the Community tried to introduce its own CAP reforms, and in mid-1992 it appeared (after many set-backs) to have done so.[54] Thus fortified, the Commission proceeded in cliff-hanging negotiations that autumn to strike an agricultural deal with the USA, only to encounter ferocious opposition from France (which talked of invoking the 'Luxembourg Compromise' to veto it). The issue was pursued throughout 1993; and though an agreement was ultimately reached, the effort distracted GATT negotiators from areas like financial services and shipping, where the original Uruguay aims had accordingly to be scaled back.

53. For a fuller discussion, see *The Post-Imperial Age*, chap.20
54. *Keesing's*, 36508, 37930, 38352, 38943

CHAPTER FIFTEEN

Splits in the Communist World

The Western half of the developed world has enjoyed considerable success. We have seen that this has rested on the consolidation or creation of political systems incorporating its general values, on its economies' ability to grow and to overcome without really serious damage those strains and shocks they have been subjected to, and on the ability of the United States to avoid fundamental rifts with its allies. The communist world has failed in each of these respects: first Yugoslavia and then China broke with the Soviet Union. Despite a promising start, the economies of the Soviet Union and of a number of East European countries slowed down in the 1970s, stopped altogether (or otherwise ran into major difficulties) in the 1980s; their shortcomings in comparison with those of the West were then driven home by the Soviet policy of glasnost and the increasing openness of East European society. In most of Eastern Europe, too, communism was imposed, not indigenous; there was always a danger that it would simply collapse if the Soviet Union did not maintain it, by force if necessary. Admittedly there was also the possibility that communist governments would eventually acquire national roots, and would come to be accepted by their subjects as inevitable since there was apparently no way in which they could be changed. We can now see that this seldom happened, and that they lost further ground with the economic strains of the 1980s. Attempts at reform proved destabilising. The Soviet Union, itself in grave economic trouble, lost the will to intervene. The upshot was the collapse of communist regimes, first in East Europe, then in the Soviet Union itself.

EAST EUROPEAN COMMUNIST PARTIES AND THE SOVIET UNION TO THE AFTERMATH OF THE WAR

In the 1930s almost all communists had accepted that the interests of foreign parties were identical with those of the Soviet Union since these parties could not prosper without the support of the 'socialist motherland'. They also believed that there were 'objectively correct' doctrines and policies, and that the Communist Party of the Soviet Union (CPSU) – and more especially its leader, Stalin – was an infallible guide to these. As a result they had followed the current Moscow line with remarkable discipline, opposing first Germany (until the Nazi-Soviet pact), then during 1939–41 the anti-German war effort that they were to back strongly as soon as Germany invaded the USSR. Stalin naturally hoped that these attitudes would continue after victory, as for the most part they did. But since, with the take-over of Eastern Europe, there would now be other 'communist' states besides the Soviet Union,[1] a new pattern of relationships would have to be worked out. For this there was no clear model. Marxist *theory* stressed ideological not nationalist alignments. Between the wars, however, communist and USSR patriotism had been fused through the doctrine of 'socialism in one country'. Similar developments could potentially occur in other countries; indeed *some* communists showed solicitude for the national interests of the countries they had returned to rule, at least where these did not clash with those of the USSR. 'Thus the Polish and East German communists were soon making discrepant statements about the permanence of the Oder–Neisse frontier, the Polish and Czechoslovak ones about their states' respective border claims in the Teschen . . . and Glatz . . . districts, the Czechoslovak and Hungarian ones about the treatment of the Magyar ethnic minority in Slovakia', etc.[2] Nor is this at all surprising; even foreign occupiers, like the US Army in Germany, came to identify with the interests of 'their' areas.

At the same time the state structure of Eastern Europe was perceived to be fluid. This view was not exclusively communist: the area's interwar history had been disappointing, and in 1943 Britain had toyed with ideas of an Eastern, or at least Danubian, Fed-

---

1. Outer Mongolia had had a Soviet-supported regime since 1922 and had formally become independent in 1942, but it had been too small and dependent to pose problems

2. Joseph Rothschild, *Return to Diversity: A Political History of East Central Europe since World War II* (New York, 1989) p.125

eration. Stalin did not like them. But he allowed the canvassing, after the war, both of various Balkan federations and of a more ambitious extension of the Soviet Union, merging 'the Ukraine with Hungary and Rumania, and Byelorussia with Poland and Czechoslovakia, while the Balkan states were to be joined with Russia'.[3] Interestingly, in 1945 Kardelj, a prominent member of the Yugoslav leadership that broke with Moscow three years later, told the Soviet ambassador

> he would like the Soviet Union to regard them, not as representatives of another country, capable of solving questions independently, but as representatives of one of the future Soviet Republics, and the C[ommunist] P[arty of] Y[ugoslavia] as a part of the CPSU. . . . For this reason they would like us to . . . give them advice which would direct the internal and external policy of Yugoslavia along the right path.[4]

TITO'S BREAK WITH STALIN

In the early postwar years Yugoslavia was to cast itself as Moscow's leading ally. This is not surprising. Tito had emerged from the war in full control, whereas in all other East European countries except Albania the communists were to take two to three years to consolidate their power. Tito loved power, and the perquisites and palaces that went with it, and looked to extend his rule; as early as 1943 he had written, 'In our opinion, and also in that of . . . [Comintern], we should be in the centre for the Balkan countries, both in the military and in the political sense'. He had been

3. Djilas, *Conversations with Stalin* p.137. In Nov. 1941 Maisky had sketched a scheme for a Balkan federation centred on Yugoslavia, a federation of Poland, Czechoslovakia and Hungary, and another of the Baltic states, all to lean economically and militarily on Russia (*FRUS*, 1941 i pp.337–8). In 1948 Gottwald suggested to Stalin that Czechoslovakia accede to the Soviet Union (*Khrushchev Remembers* iii p.131); a high SED leader told Wolfgang Leonhard it was quite possible, though not inevitable, that in due course all the People's Democracies would join 'as new Union Republics': *Child of the Revolution* (1957) p.403. As late as 1972 Zhivkov agreed with Brezhnev to create conditions for Bulgaria to do so, something he continued to hope for until the advent of Gorbachev: *Keesing's*, 37745
4. S. Clissold (ed.) *Yugoslavia and the Soviet Union 1939–1973* (1975) pp.166–7. The ambassador reported Kardelj as saying (in the context of Tito's anger at the absence of Soviet support over Trieste) that Tito 'was inclined to regard Yugoslavia as a self-sufficient unit outside the general development of the proletarian revolution and socialism', whereas he himself hoped the USSR would regard it as a future Soviet Republic: Ivo Banac, *With Stalin against Tito. Cominformist Splits in Yugoslav Communism* (Ithaca, NY, 1988) p.17

instrumental in founding and backing the Albanian Communist Party; after the war he extended the Yugoslav presence through the Soviet-style dispatch of advisers and formation of joint-stock companies; in 1946, Enver Hoxha claims, Tito dangled before him the carrot of the transfer of the primarily Albanian-inhabited province of Kosovo when Albania federated with Yugoslavia.[5] Yugoslavia had also been discussing federation with Bulgaria since 1944, in the hope that Bulgaria would first cede its sector of Macedonia (an object of dispute since the beginning of the century), then become a seventh republic within Yugoslavia. It took the lead in helping the communist insurgency in Greece, partly out of what Djilas was later to describe as 'revolutionary idealism', partly with the aim of securing Greek Macedonia in return.[6] Finally Yugoslavia had territorial claims on Italy and Austria.

We do not know how Stalin really viewed all this. Occasional sharp words were exchanged, notably in May 1945 when the USSR took Tito's nationalist speech over Trieste as an 'unfriendly attack' and threatened to reply in public.[7] But Yugoslavia mostly seemed to be in high favour, if possibly seen as a little too impetuous. Tito had been accorded a triumphal tour of the USSR in April 1945. In 1946 Stalin singled him out for distinction at a state funeral, and declared that 'Tito must look after himself. I won't live long, and Europe needs him'. Stalin also cited him as a model when rebuking the Poles for their mild treatment of political offenders: 'Tito is a tower of strength . . . he wiped them all out'.[8] When in September 1947 Stalin decided to revive the Communist International, under the name of Cominform, and to realign the policy of the French and Italian parties, the Yugoslavs were cast in a star role as their accusers.[9] This is not to say that there were no

5. Clissold, *Yugoslavia and the Soviet Union* pp.46, 105; Nora Beloff, *Tito's Flawed Legacy: Yugoslavia and the West: 1939–84* (1985) p.192; cf. also Djilas, *Conversations with Stalin* p.112

6. Clissold, *Yugoslavia and the Soviet Union* pp.46–8; Djilas, *Rise and Fall* pp.277–8. During 1946–8 Yugoslavia arranged for the supply of untraceable Wehrmacht weapons, provided food, clothing and medical assistance, and gave (bad) military advice; almost half the insurgent fighting forces, too, were Slav Macedonians: Banac, *With Stalin against Tito* pp.35–6

7. 'We do not wish to be petty cash used in bribes; we do not wish to be involved in a policy of spheres of interest'; 'We will not be dependent on anyone ever again'

8. Djilas, *Rise and Fall* p.105; Djilas, *Tito. The Story from Inside* (1981) p.39; Beloff, *Tito's Flawed Legacy* p.142

9. This may have led Tito to think Stalin had put caution aside and was now fully endorsing his own uninhibited sponsorship of revolutionary take-over: Geoffrey Swain, 'The Cominform: Tito's International?', *Historical Journal* xxxv (1992) pp.641–63

frictions: Stalin resented Yugoslav criticism of the Red Army's propensity to loot and rape. The Yugoslavs, too, saw the Soviet approach to commerce as hard-nosed and exploitative. In 1947 Stalin tried to mend this by backing away from joint companies: 'Clearly, this isn't a good form of collaboration with a friendly ally like Yugoslavia. . . . Such companies are appropriate for satellites'.[10] When relations worsened both issues were paraded, but they probably reflected rather than caused the breach.

Two matters were more serious – Yugoslav expansionism, and the Soviet propensity to recruit agents and intervene directly in the working of Yugoslav government. In retrospect Djilas felt that conflict with the USSR was bound to come some time, but that it was touched off by events in Albania. Yugoslav encroachment had divided the Albanian party, and driven its director of economic affairs to suicide in protest. It also seemed to be encountering increasing opposition from the Soviet Mission in Tirana. In late 1947 Tito sent two divisions into Albania, ostensibly to protect it from Greece, but chiefly to pre-empt any Soviet inclination to shoulder Yugoslavia aside and 'grab' the country.

Stalin had not been consulted; he summoned Djilas to Moscow in January 1948 for an explanation, then jovially told him (on arrival) to go ahead and swallow the country. Djilas, however, suspected a trap, and relations continued strained. Later in the month Tito was himself invited to come and clear up 'complications', but prudently sent his deputy Kardelj instead. Though the Yugoslavs may not have realised it, Stalin was very much on edge over Czechoslovakia, being determined to complete the communist take-over and apprehensive about possible Western intervention (see pp. 68, 121); this may have reinforced his natural disposition not to tolerate independent initiatives by his satellites. On 10 February 1948 (the Czech crisis came to a head on the 20th) the Soviet leadership staged an intimidating session in which the Yugoslav leaders were attacked, and their Bulgarian counterparts humiliated, for taking initiatives (in their relations with each other, Albania and Romania) without first consulting Moscow.[11] They were also not

10. Djilas, *Rise and Fall* p.97. Accordingly only two such companies were established, but after the rift Yugoslavia did denounce them to the UN as exploitative

11. Dimitrov had exposed himself by advocating a customs union with Romania and an eventual Balkan federation, but the Yugoslavs felt Stalin's abuse of the Bulgarians was really directed at them. Embarrassingly the Bulgarians and Yugoslavs were both able to show that Molotov *had* been informed of some of the initiatives of which Stalin complained

invited to the customary dinner that evening at Stalin's dacha. The next day Kardelj was intimidated into signing a treaty pledging Yugoslavia to consult before taking any initiative in international affairs. Nevertheless Stalin's attitude may not have been entirely negative, since he enjoined the rapid consummation of a Yugoslav–Bulgarian–Albanian federation. But, in the context of Stalin's other behaviour, Tito saw this as a Trojan horse, designed to dilute his own control of Yugoslavia.[12]

The other cause of the rift was the USSR's attempt, in Yugoslavia as elsewhere, to recruit agents at all levels in the political machine – by means ranging from sexual entrapment to appeals to socialist loyalty – and to give orders directly, bypassing the formal Yugoslav leadership. As early as 1945 one such recruitment had led Tito to exclaim, 'A spy network is something we will not tolerate! We've got to let them know right away'. The process did not stop, however, Soviet penetration being particularly obtrusive in the army. By 1947–8 the Yugoslavs seem to have countered by subjecting Soviet officials and advisers to police surveillance. In March 1948 the USSR suddenly withdrew its advisers, and an exchange of accusations ensued. Moscow was clearly taking the initiative, and its tone was undignified (dredging up incidents from the distant past and throwing in touching complaints about the undemocratic nature of the Yugoslav party and its supervision by the secret police). Belgrade continued to protest its loyalty, but it insisted it was 'improper' for Soviet agents

> to recruit in our country, which is moving towards socialism, our citizens for their intelligence service. . . .
> . . . such recruiting is not done for the purpose of a struggle against some capitalist country, and we must inevitably come to the conclusion that this recruiting is destroying our internal unity, that it kills confidence in the leadership, . . leads to the compromising of leading people and becomes a channel for the collection of false information. . . .
> We cannot allow the Soviet Intelligence Service to spread its net in our country. We have our state security and intelligence service . . .

To Stalin this accusation seemed to be 'made solely for the purpose of justifying the [Yugoslav police] in placing the Soviet workers in Yugoslavia under surveillance'. Similarly when Tito and Kardelj complained that the Soviet ambassador had no right to pry

12. Djilas, *Rise and Fall* p.145, *Conversations with Stalin* pp.104–6, 111–14, 132–43; Clissold, *Yugoslavia and the Soviet Union* pp.51, 106; Beloff, *Tito's Flawed Legacy* p.144; Rothschild, *Return to Diversity* p.130; Banac, *With Stalin against Tito* pp.39 ff

into the conduct of Yugoslav party business, Stalin replied that this was to equate him with 'an ordinary bourgeois ambassador'; did they not understand 'that the Soviet ambassador, a responsible communist, who represents a friendly power which liberated Yugoslavia from the German occupation, has not only the right but the duty . . . to discuss with the communists of Yugoslavia all questions which may interest them?'[13]

By May, not having secured a Yugoslav surrender, the USSR referred the decision to Cominform. Though protesting 'that we are resolutely building socialism and that we remain loyal to the Soviet Union, loyal to the doctrine of Marx, Engels, Lenin, and Stalin', the Yugoslavs declined to attend; and on 28 June 1948 – tactlessly the historic Serbian national day – Cominform announced their excommunication: they had

> taken the path of seceding from the united socialist front against imperialism, have taken the path of betraying the cause of international solidarity of the working people, and have taken up a position of nationalism. . . .
> The Information Bureau considers that, in view of all this, the Central Committee of the Communist Party of Yugoslavia has placed itself and the Yugoslavia Party outside the family of the fraternal Communist Parties, outside the united Communist front and consequently outside the ranks of the Information Bureau.

It then appealed to 'healthy elements' within the Yugoslav party to 'compel their present leaders to recognize' and rectify their mistakes, or 'to replace them' with 'a new internationalist leadership of the Party'.[14]

Khrushchev claims that Stalin expected an easy victory – 'I will shake my little finger – and there will be no more Tito'. But Tito had his country well in hand. With most of his subjects, indeed, external abuse probably made him more popular; few will have been influenced by Soviet propaganda stories of a miraculous image of Lenin that had wept tears over his apostasy.[15] Tito's chief problems were with the army (perhaps as a result of recent Soviet training) and the party (which had been raised in a climate of uncritical enthusiasm for the USSR). He was careful to associate the party with replies to Soviet letters, convening Central Committee

---

13. Djilas, *Rise and Fall* p.83; Beloff, *Tito's Flawed Legacy* p.144; Clissold, *Yugoslavia and the Soviet Union* pp.170 ff

14. RIIA, *Documents on International Affairs 1947–8* pp.396–7

15. *Khrushchev Remembers* i p.544 (the 'Secret Speech'); D.L. Larson, *United States Foreign Policy toward Yugoslavia, 1943–1963* (Washington, DC, 1979) p.195

plenums and even a Party Congress in a way he had never done before – *but* against the background of the arrest of two leading pro-Soviet politicians. By good luck, too, the now pro-Soviet former army commander was shot by a border patrol while escaping to Romania, perhaps with the intention of creating a government-in-exile. Police surveillance of the party, already intimidating in 1947, was stepped up. In the summer of 1948 there was a sweep of pro-Cominform suspects, who were dispatched to a deliberately unpleasant island concentration camp. Probably the chief danger that Tito faced was assassination; apparently Soviet agents in his bodyguard planned to shoot the top leadership while it was playing billiards. More conventional pressure came from a Soviet and East European trade embargo. As a result partly of this, partly of drought, and partly of agricultural collectivisation, conditions were extremely difficult for several years; – indeed there was a small peasants' revolt in Bosnia in 1949.[16]

The effect of such pressure was to turn Yugoslavia towards the West. The process took time, since its leaders were at first determined to disprove Soviet charges by demonstrating the purity of their socialism (farm collectivisation was stepped up after the breach with Moscow) and their continued foreign policy alignment with the East (there was no interference in 1948 with the airlift of Czech arms via Yugoslavia to Israel). Tito clearly hoped for Western support should it prove necessary; 'The Americans are not fools', he remarked in mid-1948, 'They won't let the Russians reach the Adriatic'. Overtures were made to the effect that Yugoslavia was ready to discontinue its aid to the Greek insurgents.[17] The first tangible assistance came from Britain in the form of a £30 million trade agreement in December 1948. In May 1949 Yugoslavia promised to abandon the insurgents and close its Greek border, and it sought a $250 million loan from the USA. The administration thought this too much to ask of a strongly anti-communist Congress, but it moved gingerly to provide aid in dribs and drabs: $150 million by August 1951 (plus about another $60 million from Britain and West Germany). This was matched by more open diplomatic support; the USA and Britain warned in September 1949 that a Soviet attack on Yugoslavia could have serious consequences, and shortly afterwards secured Yugoslavia's election to the UN Security Council in preference to the Soviet candidate, Czecho-

16. Djilas, *Tito* pp.71–2, 79–90, *Rise and Fall* pp.227, 235–6
17. Djilas, *Tito* p.125; *FRUS* 1948 iv pp.1,084–5

slovakia. In 1950 the Yugoslav leadership began to worry about its military equipment; that autumn it at last criticised the Northern invasion of South Korea; and in January 1951 Attlee was sounded out over arms and found sympathetic. The USA was then approached; its Chief of Staff visited Belgrade, and by the end of the year some $60 million of military supplies had come through. The trend continued in the early 1950s, with Tito visiting London and the Yugoslav secret service obliging the CIA. It culminated in the 1954 Balkan mutual defence Pact between Yugoslavia, Greece and Turkey (the two latter being NATO members).[18]

All this led Yugoslavia to distance itself ideologically from the USSR, which (Tito declared) had 'long since diverged from socialist development into state capitalism and an unprecedented bureaucratic system'.[19] To distinguish itself, Yugoslavia experimented from 1950 with workers' self-management: 'The factories belonging to the workers', Tito exclaimed, 'something that has never been achieved'. In practice it was not achieved, and the system eventually proved economically disastrous.[20] But it helped Yugoslavia claim to be pioneering an original form of socialism, and enhanced its standing with the European Left. In 1953 self-management was complemented by de-collectivisation, though this was no more than a belated reaction to agricultural disaster. By now the swelling criticism of centralised bureaucracy and political monopoly was beginning to worry Tito; it was carrying the ideologue Djilas towards the conclusion that the governing elite under 'socialism' constituted a 'New Class'. Stalin's death in March 1953 stilled Tito's fears of a Soviet invasion and provided an occasion to call a halt. In June Tito insisted that a Central Committee plenum be held on ideology. In 1954 he turned on Djilas, who was dropped from the leadership and forced into (temporary) self-criticism, in a move probably intended to open the door to a reconciliation with the USSR.

On breaking with Belgrade Stalin had moved successfully to prevent its contagion from spreading. He hoped to secure Tito's collapse without overt recourse to force. By 1949 this seemed unlikely. So pressure was increased by troop concentrations on the

18. Acheson, *Present at the Creation* pp.332–3; Larson, *US Policy toward Yugoslavia* pp.201, 205, 210, 212, 240–1, 255; Djilas, *Rise and Fall* pp.257, 273–4; Ranelagh, *The Agency* pp.255, 302

19. Clissold, *Yugoslavia and the Soviet Union* p.246

20. It had sufficient substance to add to inflationary wage pressure and prevent the closure of uneconomic plants; but it did not motivate the work force, and central planning remained in being

borders, which prompted Tito to proclaim in August that Yugoslavia would defend itself (presumably by reverting to the guerrilla tactics of 1941–4). Incidents mounted to nearly 4,000 over 1949–51, with 40 Yugoslavs killed. And it has been claimed, by a defecting Hungarian general, that plans were drawn for an invasion (probably in 1951), but abandoned when the Korean War suggested that an American response could not be ruled out. Moscow would then seem to have turned to other means. Planning to poison Tito was apparently well advanced in 1952–3, but was cancelled by Beria after Stalin's death. Beria indeed made secret overtures to Belgrade, and bawled out the author of a study that took the traditional Stalinist line on Yugoslavia.[21] His fall limited any rapprochement to the restoration of diplomatic relations.

SOVIET–YUGOSLAV RELATIONS 1953–74

The question of how much further to go proved controversial. Molotov, in particular, had participated in the original rift, and in 1955 still defended it. He did not mind an improvement in inter-state relations, but thought it unwise to chase after Yugoslavia to restore party-to-party relations. (As we have seen – pp. 145, 196 – Molotov favoured a policy of holding tightly what USSR already held, rather than risking it in pursuit of wider gains.) Khrushchev took the more adventurous line, at any rate once he no longer needed support against Malenkov. He had a committee examine Yugoslavia and conclude that it was still a socialist state, cleared with other Communist parties the goal of restoring party-to-party relations, and invited himself to Belgrade. His visit in May 1955 was only a limited success, since Yugoslavia would not go beyond inter-state relations. But he did not give up. His efforts are chronicled at great length in the memoirs of the Yugoslav ambassador, Micunovic, who was sent in 1956 with a brief neither to quarrel with the Russians nor to 'give in to them on matters of major political importance'.[22]

Many forces pulled the Yugoslavs back towards 'the camp',

21. Clissold, *Yugoslavia and the Soviet Union* pp.247, 252; M. Charlton, *The Eagle and the Small Birds* p.78; *The Independent*, 12 June 1993 p.15; Zubok, *Soviet Intelligence and the Cold War: the 'Small' Committee of Information* pp.16–17

22. Bialer, 'Ich wahlte die Warheit', *Hinter dem Eisernen Vorhang* x (Oct. 1956) pp.23–4, 27–8; *Khrushchev Remembers* i chap. 12; Micunovic, *Moscow Diary* p.13

notably their communism and a nostalgia, probably felt most strongly in police and army circles, for past relationships. Also Yugoslavia had, in 1954–5, struck out as a founder-member of the Third World 'non-aligned' movement, whose stance – especially as evidenced at their 1961 Belgrade summit – was much closer to the Soviet vision of anti-imperialist change through competition and 'peaceful coexistence' than to Western interests; in particular, until the mid-1970s, Yugoslavia served as a useful bridge between Egypt and the Soviet Union, and is praised accordingly in Khrushchev's memoirs.[23] On the other hand the Yugoslav economy could not easily dispense with what had become a significant level of Western aid; in the 1960s it deepened this dependence by permitting the migration of *Gastarbeiter* (guest workers) to Western Europe, thus easing its unemployment and securing valuable income from remittances. There were, too, occasional reminders that Yugoslav sovereignty had been more obviously threatened from the East than from the West. In any case Tito was probably too attached to his uncommitted position – 'Without an independent foreign policy there is no true independence'[24] – to opt irrevocably for either East or West. On the Soviet side, even Khrushchev was remarkably touchy, and some of the recurrent Soviet–Yugoslav flare-ups seem to have been over quite minor points. Nor did Khrushchev have a free hand: Molotov's opposition, reinforced by the East European crisis of 1956, continued until the final 'Anti-Party Group' showdown of 1957. By 1958 Yugoslav–Soviet relations had got caught up in the growing Sino-Soviet rift.

The result was something of a see-saw. Relations improved in 1955–6, with Tito consulted on the management of Eastern Europe and approving the 1956 Soviet invasion of Hungary. In 1957 there was first renewed friction, then mutual visits by Defence Ministers and Yugoslav recognition of East Germany, and finally further trouble over the version of recent history presented in the Yugoslav party's draft programme. Coolness deepened in 1958, as China attacked Yugoslavia, and the USSR thought it politic to join in. By 1962 the Sino-Soviet rift was past healing, so good Yugoslav–Soviet relations were restored, and Tito was fêted when he demonstratively visited Moscow after the Cuban missile crisis. Relations continued warm for most of the 1960s, Tito apparently sympathising in 1964

23. These themes are (perhaps slightly over) developed in Beloff, *Tito's Flawed Legacy* chap. 5
24. Djilas, *Rise and Fall* pp.319–20

with Khrushchev's plans for a general anti-Chinese gathering of world Communist parties and later adopting positions on Vietnam and the Middle East that were close to Brezhnev's. In 1968, however, the Czech crisis came as a rude shock; this time Tito condemned the Soviet intervention, conferred with Ceauşescu of Romania (who also seemed threatened), and mobilised his own armed forces.[25] In due course, however, things mended again. 1971 saw Sino-Yugoslav rapprochement, and, perhaps to limit the spread of Chinese influence, Brezhnev again visited Belgrade. Thereafter there were occasional frictions, but no serious rifts.

By 1970, however, Yugoslavia's importance was much reduced. After the Second World War, Tito had aspired to be Stalin's leading ally; the way in which the USSR first quarrelled and then sought reconciliation with him had, as we shall see, an important influence on the rest of Eastern Europe. Tito had played a major role, too, in supporting the communists in the Greek civil war; his need for Western assistance led him to disengage in 1949, and accelerated their defeat. Yugoslavia's Western orientation also facilitated the settlement in 1954 of its border dispute with Italy. Although its relations with the USSR then improved, the fact that Yugoslavia stayed outside the Warsaw Pact saved Italy from the pressures borne by Norway, West Germany and Turkey as militarily frontline states.

Yugoslavia continued to play a conspicuous role on the international stage, partly as a leading member of the 'non-aligned' movement, partly as a stalking-horse in the Sino-Soviet dispute. From the 1960s its salience diminished. The cause of 'non-alignment' became no longer remarkable, or coherent, enough to secure international prominence. Yugoslavia's position as a communist state with an independent foreign policy seemed less unusual; indeed by the end of the 1960s Romania had come to overshadow it. Also the Soviet Union came, in its European policy, to place increasing emphasis on the consolidation, recognition, and legitimation of existing alignments. It was, admittedly, still tempted to dabble: there was talk of links with Croatian separatists and of a 'Revolutionary Communist Party of Yugoslavia in Exile' in 1970, and in 1974 some Montenegrins founded a secret pro-Soviet party with encouragement from Kiev.[26] But serious action along these lines would have been fatal to détente. The usual view, from both East and West, was probably of support for Tito and fear of the

25. Clissold, *Yugoslavia and the Soviet Union* pp.77–82
26. ibid, pp.86, 93, 111, 112

consequences should he – or more probably his successors – fail to keep his heterogeneous country together. A struggle, whether over the succession or between rival national groups within Yugoslavia, could have led to appeals for external assistance and so drawn in rival outside Powers.

'TITO-ISM' AND EAST EUROPEAN PURGES

In the 1940s many East Europeans were attracted to the idea of building states that, though both 'socialist' and aligned with the USSR, did not slavishly follow its example or obey its orders. As Leonhard makes clear, several East German and Czech communists privately sympathised with Yugoslavia. At a higher level, the Polish Party Secretary Gomulka had, in 1947, opposed agricultural collectivisation and appeared unenthusiastic about the foundation of Cominform. In 1948 he declared that Polish communism had suffered politically between the wars as a result of its ambivalent attitude towards Poland's national independence; he may even have sought to negotiate with Tito a face-saving exit from his confrontation with Stalin. Worse still, the Bulgarian leader Dimitrov had, while passing through Belgrade, secretly urged the Yugoslavs to 'hold firm'. Stalin did not propose to risk the further spread of 'Tito-ism', and laid down that 'the attitude towards the Soviet Union is now the test of devotion to the cause of proletarian internationalism'.[27] He insisted that there be purges, had his police chief for Eastern Europe (General Belkin) help arrange them, and contributed Soviet interrogators. Implementation, however, differed from country to country. In Albania Hoxha moved very rapidly after the Cominform denunciation of Tito to break off economic relations (with Soviet compensation) and expel Yugoslav advisers. His pro-Yugoslav rival Xoxe was arrested in October 1948 and executed next June. Hoxha probably saw Tito's defection as a golden opportunity and required no prompting to take it. In Bulgaria Dimitrov denounced the Yugoslavs, but in fairly moderate terms. He may have been protected by the reputation he had established before the war in Comintern, but he conveniently died

---

27. Leonhard, *Child of the Revolution* chap. 9; Nicholas Bethell, *Gomulka* (paperback edn, 1972) pp.138–43; Djilas, *Rise and Fall* p.199; Clissold, *Yugoslavia and the Soviet Union* p.55; Bullock, *Bevin* p.599

when visiting the USSR in July 1949. Party Secretary Kostov, who had clashed with the USSR in defence of Bulgaria's economic interests, was arrested in March, tried and executed in December 1949 – though at his trial he repudiated his confession of having worked for the prewar Bulgarian police, the Trotskyists, the West, and Tito. In Hungary the tough Interior Minister, Rajk, was moved sideways in August 1948, arrested next June, and executed in the autumn. This puzzled the Yugoslavs, since they had had little to do with him,[28] but he was induced (by appeals to party loyalty and the promise of a new life in the USSR) to admit to working for Horthy-Himmler-Dulles-Tito. The Czech secretary, Slansky, then declared 'We need a Czechoslovak Rajk' and set about finding one. The security services kept changing their minds as to quite what conspiracy they wanted to unmask, and in 1951 turned on Slansky himself. In 1952 he was tried and executed – for Zionism as well as Tito-ism. In Poland the process was milder. Gomulka was expelled from the Politburo in 1948; in 1949 several of his associates were arrested, and he was dropped from the party. There seems to have been Soviet pressure to do more, but he was not arrested until 1951, and even then treated gently. His associates were less fortunate; but they too were imprisoned not executed, presumably because the Polish leader, Bierut, was more restrained than his counterparts elsewhere in Eastern Europe.[29]

These cases were, of course, only the tip of the iceberg. Matters were perhaps worst in Hungary, where 2,000 communists were executed, 150,000 imprisoned, and 350,000 expelled from the party, and Czechoslovakia, where 136,000 were imprisoned or executed.[30] *Some* purges were unsurprising as Communist parties that had recruited everybody they could during the period of forceful take-over were reduced to the more disciplined Stalinist model. Tito's defection, and the deepening Cold War, made matters worse. Certainly overt hankering for national routes to socialism was suppressed. It is, too, generally true that the process removed from the leadership men who had (like Gomulka or Rajk) lived in their countries before or during the war. They were replaced by exiles trained in the USSR in the 1930s and brought home in the wake of the Red Army, who might be expected to be more docile. Romania

28. Djilas, *Rise and Fall* pp.252–3
29. Rothschild, *Return to Diversity* p.121, chap. 4; Andrew and Gordievsky, *KGB* pp. 336 ff; François Fejtö, *A History of the People's Democracies* (1971), Introduction; Bethell, *Gomulka* chaps 10–12
30. Fejtö, *History of the People's Democracies* p.8; Rothschild, *Return to Diversity* p.137

provides something of an exception. The purge of local communists began in 1948, before Tito's defection, with the imprisonment of the Justice Minister (and founder-member of the party) Patrascanu. Power was thus securely in the hands of the three 'Muscovites', Bodnaras, Luca and Ana Pauker. In 1952 the Party Secretary, Georghiu-Dej, an ethnic Romanian who had spent 1933–44 in local prisons, coalesced with Bodnaras to ditch Luca and Pauker and inaugurate a second purge of the party. Tito was duly denounced and Stalin praised, but the net effect was to make the regime rather more indigenous.[31] Perhaps the fact that Luca and Pauker were Jewish helped keep Stalin happy; anti-Semitism certainly played a major role in the Slansky trial in Czechoslovakia later that year. But it was not really extended to either Poland or Hungary, where much of the leadership was Jewish, though it might have been had Stalin lived longer.

CHANGES IN SOVIET POLICY 1953–6

Stalin's death was soon followed by a disorganised workers' rising in East Germany (see pp. 131–2). With hindsight we can see that this pinpointed two major weaknesses in the structure of communist Eastern Europe. One source of the explosion was the squeeze on workers' living standards (as a result of rearmament and of Ulbricht's insistence on the construction of socialism). The other was the wavering in the regime's determination, the result partly of its leaders' rivalries and partly of a shift in Soviet policies (linked, probably, in this case to Beria's machinations). Order was restored by Soviet tanks; Ulbricht was always to see the timely application of force as the most reliable prophylactic, and to commend it accordingly to his colleagues in other countries.

In East Germany the Kremlin was now prepared to back Ulbricht. Elsewhere in Eastern Europe its approach, from 1953–6, was more ambiguous. To a considerable extent this was a function of Soviet politics; thus Nagy's installation in 1953 as Hungarian premier, and his dismissal in 1955, seem linked to Malenkov's fortunes in the USSR. Still the Soviet Union appears in this period to have been attempting a controlled relaxation and a distancing of itself from the day-to-day running of East European countries. At a

31. ibid, pp.113, 138, 231, 233

secret 1955 Central Committee plenum, Khrushchev and Kaganovich (in the course of attacking Molotov) criticised the pro-consular intervention in Polish affairs of ambassadors Lebedev (1945–51) and Popov (1953–4).[32] Nevertheless they kept on, as Polish Defence Minister, the Soviet Marshal Rokossovsky, a Pole by origin but a man whose heart was very much in the USSR. In economic matters the USSR was more forthcoming, selling almost all its 'joint' companies back to their host countries over the period 1953–6, but it continued to collect coal from Poland at negligible prices.[33] The chief tension, however, lay between the position, accepted as part of the process of wooing Tito, that 'the ways of socialist development vary in different countries', and the instinctive Soviet feeling that their allies should do as they did in domestic as well as foreign policy.

REVOLUTIONARY FERMENT IN POLAND 1953–6; GOMULKA COMES TO POWER

Such interference proved destabilising in Poland (and, more seriously, in Hungary). In 1953 the Polish leadership embarked, probably quite readily, on a 'New Course' parallel to the slow thaw in the USSR. In 1954 a former leading secret policeman, Swiatlo, started telling all on Radio Free Europe. The revelations damaged Bierut's prestige and prompted an outburst of criticism within the party that left the leadership, as Ochab later put it, 'in complete isolation'; it also led to the subdivision of the security services (as in the USSR) and to Gomulka's release from prison, though not his rehabilitation. By his own confession, Khrushchev continued to needle Bierut. Bierut attended the Soviet Twentieth Party Congress, and the 'Secret Speech' came as a further shock to him. Indeed he died a fortnight later, probably from a heart attack, though subsequent Warsaw gossip said he committed suicide when Khrushchev told him to go home and dismantle Stalinism.[34] His successor,

---

32. Bialer, 'Ich wählte die Warheit' pp.28–9. To the end, however, Soviet ambassadors continued to be personally chosen by the Politburo, largely from high Party officials, and to go 'directly to the top . . . ignoring the foreign ministries' of the countries to which they were accredited': Shevardnadze, *The Future Belongs to Freedom* p.113

33. M.C. Kaser (ed.) *The Economic History of Eastern Europe 1919–1975* ii (Oxford, 1986) pp.253–4; *Khrushchev Remembers* ii pp.208–9

34. *Khrushchev Remembers* ii p.197; Erwin Weit, *Eyewitness* p.37

Ochab, proceeded to open the gaols (pardoning 28,000 people by June 1956), and accepted the resignation of the Politburo member responsible for security, Berman. Censorship collapsed, and a critical muck-raking journalism ensued. Then in late June 1956 riots broke out in Poznan. They originated in a minor pay grievance in an enormous local factory. Workers demonstrated, then, when ignored, boiled over into looting, the demolition of a radio jamming station, and attacks on the police. The army restored order, shooting fifty-three people.

The Poznan riots seem to have set alarm bells ringing in Moscow, but not in Warsaw. For though initially Polish leaders condemned the riots as of foreign provocation, they soon changed their tone to stress the limited and justified nature of the original grievances.[35] In July 1956 Ochab told his Central Committee that he meant to press ahead with reform, and managed to exclude from its deliberations a Soviet delegation headed by Bulganin and Zhukov. Bulganin, however, denounced those who 'on the pretext of demo-cratization are undermining the power of the people' and declared that 'We must not permit a weakening in the international links of the socialist camp through an appeal to national determinism'. Most Polish leaders were unmoved; they readmitted Gomulka to the party and placed some of his former associates in influential jobs. Other signs of the times were the pilgrimage in late August of nearly a million Catholics to the shrine of Czestochowa and the emergence in Warsaw factories of workers' councils assisted by intellectuals and students. Outside Warsaw, however, local party secretaries often soft-pedalled reform and kept more control. The hardline minority of the leadership, known as the Natolin group, conducted a rearguard action and fed alarming reports to Moscow.

Gomulka seemed the key to the situation. The Russians tried to come to terms with him by inviting him (in vain) to holiday in the Crimea. Ochab negotiated, hoping to coopt him into some high office short of the Party Secretaryship (for which Gomulka held out). In early October 1956 Ochab decided, perhaps on Chinese advice, to give way, and called a central committee meeting for the 19th. The Natolin group planned a pre-emptive coup, but the plot was blown. So the top Soviet leadership, accompanied by the Pact commander and eleven generals, invited itself to Warsaw, and Soviet troops started to move on the city. In extremely tense talks it

---

35. Z.A. Pelczynski, in R.F. Leslie (ed.) *The History of Poland since 1863* (Cambridge, 1983 edn) pp.346–51; Bethell, *Gomulka* pp.202–4

was made clear that they would be resisted (ferociously, if the city's performance during the Second World War was anything to go by). But though Gomulka insisted that the Polish party alone should choose its leaders, he also assured the Russians that he would continue their ally: 'Poland needs the friendship of the Soviet Union more than the Soviet Union needs the friendship of Poland'. Eventually Khrushchev decided to withdraw his troops and accept Gomulka on these terms. Events in Hungary were to show that the Russians could have done much worse; they were soon ready to buttress his position by providing credits and by cancelling all outstanding Polish debts in compensation for past inequitable Soviet trade practices.[36]

Gomulka took control of the situation. There was a range of national and popular measures. The Defence Minister, Marshal Rokossovsky, was sent back to the Soviet Union for which he had worked in October 1956. The Catholic primate, Cardinal Wyszcynski, was freed from detention. Collective farms were dismantled and land restored to the peasants. Foreign travel was permitted, though in practice limited by the absence of hard currency; the censorship and police were so remodelled that, for a decade, Poland was the freest country in Eastern Europe. But Gomulka was not about to scrap the communist rule he had done so much to institute after 1944. His initial speech as General Secretary had declared that

> At the head of the democratization process stands our Party, and our Party alone. . . . We must give a decisive rebuff to all voices . . . that aim at weakening our friendship with the Soviet Union. . . . We shall not allow harm to come to the vital interests of the Polish state and of the building of socialism in Poland.

And he insisted that Soviet troops would have to stay in Poland as long as NATO bases remained in West Germany; their position was regularised by agreements reached in November 1956.

Above all, Gomulka confronted the hurdle of parliamentary elections in January 1957. In Poland (as elsewhere in Eastern Europe) the ruling party was flanked by the relics of non-communist former parties, and reforms of October 1956 had provided that there be more candidates than seats: so there could have been trouble had the electorate taken the opportunity to vote systematically against communist candidates (as it was to do in 1989). Gomulka therefore employed both the stick –

36. Fejtö, *History of the People's Democracies* pp.64–73; Bethell, *Gomulka* pp.206–12; *Khrushchev Remembers* ii pp.198–205; Leslie, *History of Poland* pp.321, 358

What is at stake in the elections is not whether . . . our Party will go on keeping power. A revolutionary party of the working class . . . will never surrender power to reaction and the restorers of capitalism in Poland. . . . What is at stake is whether we shall be able to go on widening the democratisation of our life or whether we shall be forced to restrict it

– and an implicit warning of possible Soviet intervention (as in Hungary): 'Crossing off our Party's candidates means crossing out the independence of our country, crossing Poland off the map of European states'. He also turned the elections into a personal vote of confidence; he was rewarded with massive support. In due course Gomulka's rule was to deteriorate and his image to sour; for the time being he had secured great improvements in Poland's autonomy and condition, while reconciling its people to the constraints still imposed by its geopolitical situation.[37]

THE HUNGARIAN RISING 1956; SOVIET INTERVENTION AND INSTALLATION OF KADAR; REPRESSION 1956–61

Hungary provides an unhappy contrast. 'Stalinist' repression under Rakosi had been perhaps the worst in Eastern Europe. After Stalin's death the Kremlin moved rapidly to effect a change, summoning Rakosi to Moscow and dressing him down severely. Perhaps because of the fall of Beria (in this context a liberal), Rakosi managed to limit the damage to a separation of the Party Secretaryship (which he kept) from the Premiership, which went to the reformist Imre Nagy. Nagy followed a policy of pushing light industry and consumer goods, slowing collectivisation, winding down the prison camps, and general liberalisation. Rakosi sought to check it, and the two seem to have been at loggerheads until 1955, when Rakosi managed to extrude Nagy first from his offices and then from the party. The experience may have radicalised Nagy, who wrote a long defence of his position including reflections of a rather Tito-ist bent.[38] It also upset much of the communist intelligentsia, whose

37. Bethell, *Gomulka* pp.223–34; Z.A. Pelczynski, 'Poland 1957', in D.E. Butler (ed.), *Elections Abroad* (1959) esp. pp.159–60, 165
38. Thus, 'the five basic principles [of Bandung, including respect for the sovereignty and equality of all countries] cannot be limited to the capitalist system or the battle between the two systems, but must extend to the relations between the countries within the democratic and socialist camps': – *On Communism: In Defence of the New Course* (1957) p.22

eyes had been opened to Rakosi's earlier doings by contact with prisoners released in 1954. Writers, in particular, came to constitute a liberal and nationalist pressure group through clubs like the Petöfi Circle, which in 1956 progressively broke from official party supervision. After Khrushchev's Secret Speech, Rakosi tried to pre-empt trouble by blaming other people for Rajk's execution and announcing his rehabilitation. But this did not succeed in calming things. In June 1956 Rajk's widow asked the Petöfi Circle to campaign for the punishment of those responsible for his death, and soon there were calls for Rakosi's resignation. He countered by expelling critics from the party and closing the Circle down. In July the Kremlin at last decided that Rakosi had become a liability, so Mikoyan and Suslov visited Budapest and forced his resignation – despite his warnings that this might bring down the whole political system. But his replacement, Gerö, had been too closely associated with Rakosi to convince the Hungarians that things had really changed.[39]

By mid-1956 the Kremlin was seriously worried. At a summit in late June Khrushchev had warned that counter-revolution was possible, notably in Poland (though Ochab denied this).[40] In July Khrushchev was stressing, for Yugoslavia's benefit, that 'If the situation in Hungary gets still worse, we here have decided to use all means at our disposal to bring the crisis to an end . . . the Soviet Union could not at any price allow a "breach in the front" in Eastern Europe'. But he bent his chief efforts to securing Yugoslav endorsement of Gerö (Tito's antipathy having been a factor in undermining Rakosi's position).[41] Pressures continued to mount within Hungary: in September a writers' conference demanded 'complete freedom for literature'; the Petöfi Circle resumed meeting and sparked off imitators in other towns. The regime did little to prevent this, and on 6 October accorded Rajk a state funeral, which drew a huge procession, headed by Nagy. To the Yugoslav ambassador in Moscow it seemed that 'The initiative is slipping out of the hands of the authorities and into the hands of the people'.[42] Gerö spent 14–23 October 1956 on a visit to

39. Fejtö, *History of the People's Democracies* pp.23–6, 53–4, 61, 74–5; Rothschild, *Return to Diversity* pp.154–7

40. Z.A.B. Zeman, *The Making and Breaking of Communist Europe* (Oxford, 1991) p.273

41. Tito was particularly set against Chervenkov (who resigned the Bulgarian Party Secretaryship in April 1956) and Rakosi; although this may have influenced the Kremlin against them, they were not simply sacrificed to secure Tito's good will since both survived the 1955 reconciliation with Tito for some considerable time

42. Micunovic, *Moscow Diary* pp.87–8, 121

Yugoslavia; by the time he returned things were out of control. Stimulated, no doubt, by Gomulka's advent to power in Poland, the Petöfi Circle called for Nagy's promotion and extensive reform (albeit within the system). Students went much further, demanding multi-party elections and the withdrawal of Soviet troops, and arranging a major demonstration for 23rd October. This was first banned, then authorised. It swelled into a nationalist movement (destroying the Stalin monument, displaying a Hungarian flag with the communist insignia removed, and occupying the radio building) that proved beyond the capacity of the police to disperse. That evening Gerö responded with the dual tactic of making Nagy Prime Minister and of appealing to Soviet troops to restore order.

Since the Hungarian army would not help, their attempts to do so on 24 October proved a complete failure, serving only to touch off a general strike in Budapest. Mikoyan and Suslov flew in, accepted Nagy's view that military intervention had been a mistake, and dismissed Gero. He was replaced as Party Secretary by Kadar, who had been imprisoned during the Rakosi purge and stood to attract sympathy accordingly. However the strike still spread, provincial towns were taken over by workers' councils, and there were attacks on, and lynchings of, the secret police, which disintegrated. Nagy responded with successive concessions, endorsing the national uprising, announcing a return to the 1945 pattern of multi-party coalition government, and promising free elections. He also secured a cease-fire, and sought the withdrawal of Soviet troops, which Mikoyan and Suslov apparently promised on 30 October.

By now it looked as if, failing external intervention, communism was doomed in Hungary. Other countries were worried: Czechoslovakia and Romania warned of the possible effect on their own Hungarian minorities, while Tito and Gomulka remonstrated with Nagy over the restoration of multi-party government. Ulbricht had long regarded the entire policy as crazy: he had told a leading Hungarian, 'Just keep on going the way you are. First you depose Rakosi, then you institute reforms, and the end result is collapse'.[43] The Soviet Union had, as we have seen, come close to using force in Poland, and had often said it would do so if necessary in Hungary. While in Budapest Mikoyan and Suslov were endorsing the principle of Soviet troop withdrawal, the Soviet Praesidium apparently decided on intervention (see pp. 195–6). It then sought

---

43. Fejtö, *History of the People's Democracies* pp.76–9; Radvanyi, *Hungary and the Superpowers* pp.6–13; Zeman, *Making and Breaking* p.276; Carola Stern, *Ulbricht* p.160

the approval of China, which had opposed intervention in Poland. According to Khrushchev, China was reluctant but ultimately accepted the decision; the Chinese were to claim that they had pressed for it, fearing Soviet 'capitulationism'. Anyway Marshal Konev was ordered to make preparations, while the Soviet leaders proceeded to brief their East European allies, including Gomulka and Tito.

Meanwhile the Soviet troops pulling out of Budapest regrouped around the airport, and others began moving into Hungary from Romania. Nagy repeatedly warned the Soviet ambassador that, if these movements did not stop, Hungary would pull out of the Warsaw Pact; on 1 November 1956 he announced that it had done so and appealed to the UN.[44] This was a Cabinet decision, but the party leader, Kadar, fled to the Soviet Union; on 4 November (when Soviet troops were ready) he announced the formation of a rival government and appealed to the USSR to crush the forces of reaction. The Red Army then broke into Budapest, and in a week had extinguished armed resistance throughout the country. There followed a general strike, orchestrated by the Budapest Central Workers' Council. Initially Kadar was prepared to negotiate with this. But in early December he lost patience, restored the old secret police, and in February 1957 sealed the borders and ended the exodus of refugees. This was accompanied by executions (including that of Nagy in June 1958) and internments. By 1960 Kadar felt secure enough to begin amnesties, close the internment camps, and in 1961 to announce that only active opponents would be repressed: 'Those who are not against us are with us'.[45]

---

44. McCauley, 'Hungary and Suez, 1956', *Journal of Contemporary History* (1981) pp.789, 797. As the Hungarian decision to leave the Warsaw Pact was a response to alarming Soviet troop movements, and one not announced until 8.15 p.m. Moscow time, it seems most unlikely that it was (as is often claimed) the *cause* of Soviet intervention. This began at dawn on 4 November, and had (*Khrushchev Remembers* i p.382) required three days' preparation. At his meeting with Tito, arrangements for which were made on 1 November (McCauley, p.799), Khrushchev talked much more generally of the murder of communists in Hungary and of the unacceptability of a return to capitalism (Micunovic, *Moscow Diary* p.133). In any case the initial Praesidium decision to intervene had been made while Mikoyan and Suslov were in Budapest (*Khrushchev Remembers* i p.380), well before Hungary's departure from the Pact

45. F.A. Vali, *Rift and Revolt in Hungary* (Cambridge, Mass., 1961) pp.438–41; Paul Ignotus, *Hungary* (1972) pp.254, 263–4; Csaba Békés, 'New Findings on the 1956 Hungarian Revolution', Cold War International History Project *Bulletin* 2 (1992) pp. 2–3

SINO–SOVIET RELATIONS TO 1956

The year 1956 is the first in which we are aware of the exertion of Chinese influence in Eastern Europe. It was soon to become more visible, with Zhou Enlai touring Hungary and Poland in January 1957 and Mao himself attending the Moscow conference of Communist parties in November. Admittedly the Chinese were, at least overtly, strongly supportive of the CPSU, stressing its position as 'head' and 'leader' of the socialist camp. But the Chinese Party's stature was evident in the care taken to settle with it the terms of the declaration of ruling Communist parties, which was then presented as a joint Soviet–Chinese draft.[46] Over the next three years the two parties' 'monolithic unity' collapsed, with important repercussions for both the socialist and the wider world.

Many hold that, to understand this breach, we need to go back to the origins of the Chinese Communist Party. For (unlike those of their European counterparts) these were strongly tinged with nationalism; they also proved that Soviet advice could be disastrous. Lenin had proclaimed his readiness to give up Russia's special rights in China, and some Chinese intellectuals were attracted to communism by this marked departure from standard Western behaviour. Others were disillusioned by the 1919 Paris Peace Conference's refusal to return to China the former German concession in Shandong. This sparked major student protests, and drew people towards direct action to rebuild China independently of Western liberalism. The Chinese Communist Party (CCP) was founded in 1921 and soon steered by Comintern agents into alliance with the nationalist Kuomintang (KMT). At the time the KMT looked towards Russia; General Chiang Kai-shek went there in 1923 to study its army, and was then commissioned to establish the Whampoa Military Academy, where the young communist Zhou Enlai taught and many others (including Lin Biao) studied. By 1926 much of the KMT was worried by the extent of communist penetration and began to clamp down. Stalin encouraged the communists to stay within the KMT the better to manipulate it: it was 'to be utilized to the end, squeezed out like a lemon, and then thrown away'. Two could play at this game; in 1927 the communists were hopelessly handicapped by Stalin's mistaken orders, first to

46. John Gittings, *Survey of the Sino-Soviet Dispute* (1968) pp.70, 73–8; Micunovic, *Moscow Diary* pp.319 ff

allow Chiang's army into Shanghai, after which it promptly turned on them, then to stage take-overs and risings in central China, which were duly suppressed, and finally to establish a 'Canton commune', which lasted three days. Meanwhile the attempts of Mao Zedong and Gao Gang to establish rural resistance movements of a more traditional Chinese kind were cold-shouldered: 'a purely peasant uprising without the leadership and help of the working class cannot achieve conclusive victories'. Successive disasters drove the party leadership to Mao's territory, but did not bring it to accept his tactics. Eventually Mao was, with Comintern assistance, first downgraded and then placed under house arrest in 1934. That year also brought crushing defeats, partly as a result of the orthodox communists' dislike of guerrilla warfare, and the Red Armies were forced into the devastating flight of the Long March. Mao then turned on their directors for military ineptitude, and managed to resume control. What remained of the communists found refuge in Yenan; KMT pressure was relaxed in response to the need for all Chinese to unite against mounting Japanese aggression. Mao used his time well, and emerged from the 1937–45 war far stronger than he had been at its start. Nevertheless Stalin discouraged him from attacking the KMT; in February 1948 he confessed to the Yugoslavs that he had urged the CCP to reach

> a *modus vivendi* with Chiang Kai-shek. They agreed with us in word, but in deed they did it their own way when they got home: they mustered their forces and struck. It has been shown that they were right and we were not.[47]

Of course Stalin may simply have been mistaken: until well into 1947 most people thought the KMT the stronger force. But the suspicion has been voiced that Stalin did not want the communists to succeed, whether because he feared that a communist China could become a rival to the USSR or simply because he felt that the Soviet Union would be better served by a KMT regime kept weak and pliable by pressure from a sizeable communist minority. Certainly the USSR had been actively pushing its interests in the Chinese borderlands. For despite having in 1924 recognised Outer Mongolia as an integral part of China, Stalin had developed it into a 'sovereign' but satellite state. From 1934 he had intervened on occasion to distance Sinkiang from the rest of China. In 1945, as his price for entering the war against Japan, Stalin had stipulated for

---

47. Djilas, *Conversations with Stalin* p.141. For a fuller discussion of the Chinese civil war, see *The Post-Imperial Age* chap. 5

the recovery of the Port Arthur naval base lost to Japan in 1905, and of control over the railway through Manchuria; he extracted from the KMT a treaty confirming both this and the independence of Outer Mongolia. If the CCP came to power in China all might be reopened; indeed Mao was to declare in 1949 that 'Ours will no longer be a nation subject to insult and humiliation. We have stood up'.[48]

Alternatively Stalin's policy may have stemmed from caution. Zhou Enlai was later to attribute it to an 'erroneous assessment' of international relations:

> The Soviets were worried that the civil war in China might overturn the established sphere of influence set up by the Yalta conference, thus leading to an American intervention and making the Soviet Union suffer. Stalin was also scared by the prospect of the Third World War. The point of departure of Stalin's policy was to appease the United States so that the Soviet Union would be guaranteed time necessary for their peaceful reconstruction. The Soviet Union had a strong reservation upon our ability to liberate the whole of China.[49]

Whatever Stalin's motivation, Soviet conduct during the Chinese civil war was distinctly ambiguous. In Manchuria the communists were allowed to capture a plentiful supply of Japanese weapons; one of their armies was reformed and equipped after being driven out into North Korea; North Korean 'volunteer' units were allowed to join in Manchurian fighting; Soviet logistic and engineering support contributed substantially to the victories of 1948. There were rumours that Stalin sought to mediate between the CCP and KMT in both December 1947 and July 1948; and it was later to be claimed that even in 1949 'there were some well-meaning friends . . . who said that we should be content with separate regimes in North and South China and should not provoke the intervention of . . . American imperialism'. Meanwhile the USSR was still concluding agreements with the KMT government to extend its mining concessions in Sinkiang. When the KMT capital fell in April 1949 the Soviet ambassador was the only one to follow the government south.[50]

Once China and the Soviet Union had quarrelled, all this was to be recalled in anger. At the time it had little impact on Mao's decision to side with the USSR in the Cold War. He had, admittedly, been saying in 1945 that the USA was 'the only country

48. D. Wilson, *Mao: The People's Emperor* (1979) p.259
49. Chen, *The Sino-Soviet Alliance and China's Entry into the Korean War* p.5
50. Gittings, *Survey* pp.13–14

fully able to participate' in China's economic recovery, and seeking
an invitation to Washington. But even if this was sincere, he had
since changed his mind, and by 1948–9 feared US military
intervention to salvage the KMT or (on the analogy of imperialist
intervention during the Russian civil war) to upset his new regime.
A Chinese judgement is that it was this perception of 'the possibility
of military intervention from imperialist countries that decided the
necessity of China allying itself with socialist countries'.[51] Already in
1948 Mao was anxious to visit Moscow. Although Stalin initially put
him off, 1949 saw successful mutual visits by senior Soviet and
Chinese politicans – in preparation for one of which, and to show
that he was not Tito-ist, Mao praised the USSR as the undisputed
leader of international progressive forces and insisted that 'all
Chinese without exception must lean either to the side of imperialism or the side of socialism. Sitting on the fence will not do,
nor is there a third road'. Eventually the stage was set for Mao to
visit Moscow in December 1949 to clear up all oustanding questions
and, if possible, secure a defence treaty. Though he was warmly
received, subsequent negotiations were not easy, not only because
of the two sides' differing negotiating tactics, but also because Stalin
was upset by a report he received on the currency of anti-Soviet
attitudes in the Chinese Communist Party. Eventually China had to
reaffirm Mongolia's independence and accept 'joint stock' companies on the usual Soviet model for the exploitation of Sinkiang.
The USSR was to give up the rights it had acquired in 1945 in
Manchuria, though not immediately, and to lend China the trivial
sum of $300 million. The two countries also concluded a trade, and
far more importantly a defence, treaty: Soviet fighters were sent to
China to provide cover against the KMT air force; the impression
was certainly given that the USSR would protect China against US
attack.[52] (For the half decade after the outbreak of the Korean War
such a contingency did not appear unlikely, and China had every
reason to value this Soviet pledge.)

Mao was to say that Stalin did not really begin to trust him until
after China's intervention in the Korean War, but he himself
cannot have been pleased by Stalin's decision to withhold the air
cover he had promised for this (see p. 111). Khrushchev was to

(see p. 111)

51. Quoted by Chen, *The Sino-Soviet Alliance and China's Entry into the Korean War*
p.3
52. ibid, pp.6–18; Gittings, *Survey* pp.14–17, 43–5; Hsii, *Rise of Modern China*
pp.674–5. The USSR had already started (in Oct. 1949) to deliver planes and help
establish a Chinese air force

contend that 'tenseness in relations continued right up to the time of Stalin's death'. Indeed the Soviet ambassador sent back reports of anti-Russian attitudes in the Chinese leadership, derived from the Manchurian boss Gao Gang. Stalin's response was to turn these over to Mao; they may have been a factor in a political struggle that culminated in Gao Gang's defeat and suicide in 1954. Later that year Khrushchev visited Beijing 'to remove causes of tension', with mixed results. The 'joint stock' companies were wound up, and the USSR arranged to give up its naval base in Port Arthur (though it was too mean to present China with the guns that had defended this). Mao also sought in vain to recover Outer Mongolia. On the surface the visit was a success, but there were a number of sources of friction (including the indigestibility of the green tea liberally pressed on the Soviet delegation). Khrushchev claims that, on his return, he told his colleagues that 'Conflict with China is inevitable'. In 1955 he spoke to Adenauer of China as one of his greatest problems: 'Just think of it. Red China now has more than 600 million people, with every year another twelve million. All people who can live on a handful of rice. What will become of it?'[53]

THE GROWTH OF SINO-SOVIET FRICTION 1956–60

These, however, were only premonitions. Relations between the two great communist Powers at the 1954 Geneva conference on Indo-China had been excellent. The Chinese economy was oriented towards the Soviet model; Mao appeared to be happy discussing Marxist philosophy with the Soviet ambassador Yudin. In retrospect the Chinese were to say that major disagreements started with Khrushchev's condemnation of Stalin without prior consultation (in the 1956 Secret Speech), while the Russians saw the Chinese policy later in 1956 of letting 'a hundred flowers bloom, a hundred schools of thought contend' as providing the seed-bed for chauvinist anti-Soviet sentiments. As we have seen (pp. 422, 427, 428) China was beginning to make its presence felt in Eastern Europe. Still in 1957 it was careful not to rock the boat but rather to insist on Soviet primacy within the communist movement. The USSR

---

53. Gittings, *Survey* p.57; *Khrushchev Remembers* i p.429, ii pp.243–50; J. Guillermaz, *The Chinese Communist Party in Power 1949–1976* (Boulder, Col., 1976) pp.99–105; Adenauer, *Erinnerungen* ii pp.527–8. In due course the Chinese were to stress the racial implications of this exchange with Adenauer; but they themselves invoked anti-European sentiment against the Soviet Union

reciprocated, promising in October 'to provide China with a sample of an atomic bomb and technical data concerning its manufacture', and then concerting with it the declaration presented to the November meeting of communist parties in Moscow. However, the Yugoslav ambassador had his suspicions that all was not well, and they were soon to be amply borne out.[54]

One problem was that Mao seems to have swallowed Soviet propaganda claims as to the military significance of the launching that autumn of the sputnik, and to have concluded that 'the forces of socialism are overwhelmingly superior to the forces of imperialism'. Given both this technical ascendancy and Sino-Soviet numerical superiority, it would be wrong to take too soft a line (as could easily result from Khrushchev's doctrines of 'peaceful co-existence'), and better to 'resist imperialism firmly and bury it' than 'to be afraid of sacrifice and to capitulate'. Mao did not think this would lead to war; but if it did, 'and half of mankind died, the other half would remain while imperialism would be razed to the ground and the whole world would become socialist' – mostly, indeed, Chinese.[55] The Russians, on the other hand, were well aware that they were *not* stronger than the West; they were also shocked by the levity with which Mao appeared to contemplate nuclear war.

In 1958 these issues got entangled with others. China appeared to favour a tougher line on the Middle East crisis than did the USSR. It may also have been offended by Khrushchev's call for a summit meeting to be attended by China's rival, India, but not by China itself (see p. 208). This constituted the backdrop for an unscheduled visit by Khrushchev to Beijing after he had received a long telegram from his ambassador about Mao's bitterness towards the USSR. In his *Memoirs* Khrushchev relates the friction chiefly to a Soviet wish to obtain radio and submarine basing facilities on Chinese soil; but the Chinese were later to suggest that he had advocated a 'joint fleet' and advanced 'unreasonable demands designed to bring China under military control', presumably through a supranational command like that of the Warsaw Pact (and NATO). The USSR could well have sought this to curb China's apparent belligerence. More than once in that summer of 1958 Mao floated the idea of luring the Americans deep into the interior where they could then be trapped and annihilated.[56] China then

54. Gittings, *Survey* chaps 7, 8, 12; Micunovic, *Moscow Diary* pp.228, 243, 322
55. Gittings, *Survey* pp.74, 76, 79–84, 307–9; *Khrushchev Remembers* ii p.255
56. Gittings, *Survey* pp.89–91, 103–4; *Khrushchev Remembers* i pp.428, 431–2, ii pp.256–61; Gromyko, *Memories* pp.321–3

went ahead with the shelling of Quemoy and Matsu, which the USSR was later to describe as reckless and deliberate provocation. At the time the USSR kept rather quiet until the crisis seemed to be subsiding, then weighed in with face-saving expressions of solidarity. China was not impressed, and may have felt that it was getting distinctly less from its superpower than was the KMT from the United States. Worse still, in 1959 Khrushchev suggested that China drop the idea of forcibly liberating Taiwan, and adopted no more than a neutral attitude towards its border clash with India. He also decided not to send China the sample atom bomb promised in 1957.[57] His final visit to Beijing that autumn was not a success.

Another major bone of contention was China's style of development. Until 1957 this had been broadly along the Soviet model, and quite successful. In 1958 China embarked on the 'Great Leap Forward', a grandiose scheme for boosting production with cheap decentralised plant (like 'backyard' steel furnaces) and for regrouping existing collective farms into 'communes', which were – in Marxist-Leninist terms – a more advanced form of social organisation than any the USSR had achieved. As a 1964 Soviet analysis put it,

> Instead of the approximately 15 years that had been envisioned for setting up the base of socialism in China, in 1958 a period of only three years was proclaimed to be adequate even for the transition to communism . . . the slogan was proclaimed of the 'people's communes', which formed the basis of the attempt to leap over the natural stages of socialist construction in the countryside, tested by the experience of other socialist countries, [in] the effort to get 'ahead of progress' here.

The Russians did not appreciate this implicit challenge to their leadership, which they found all the more worrying in that it had some appeal in Eastern Europe: Khrushchev says he had to talk the Bulgarians out of their enthusiasm for the 'Great Leap Forward'. In 1959 he also encouraged the Chinese Defence Minister, Peng Dehuai, to attack it, which cost Peng his job. The Great Leap Forward was indeed a disaster – some 20 million are supposed to have died of hunger in what Vice-Chairman Liu Shaoqi described as a primarily man-made calamity[58] – and Mao was forced to tone it down.

---

57. China's standing in Moscow had not been improved by its reluctance to let the USSR examine an unexploded Sidewinder missile acquired during the 1958 Quemoy fighting: Gittings, *Survey* chaps. 10, 14; *Khrushchev Remembers* i pp.433–4, ii pp.269, 307–9, 270, iii pp.150–2; Gromyko, *Memories* pp.323–4

58. Gittings, *Survey* pp.93–7, 99, 101; *Khrushchev Remembers* ii pp.275–7; Hsii *Rise of Modern China* pp.692–3; Short, *The Dragon and the Bear* pp.165–6

THE SINO-SOVIET RIFT AND ITS IMPACT ON THE WORLD COMMUNIST MOVEMENT

Perhaps by way of diversion, the Chinese decided to take the initiative in their dispute with the USSR, publishing (in the run up to the 1960 summit) *Long Live Leninism,* an attack on the Soviet policy of peaceful coexistence. Khrushchev picked up the gauntlet, announcing at the June 1960 Congress of the Romanian Party that he did not intend 'to yield to provocation and to deviate from the general line of our foreign policy' and circulating a letter rebutting the Chinese positions. China replied in kind. In July 1960 the Soviet Union abruptly pulled its technical advisers and aid personnel out of China.

The gloves were now off, but there was agreement that the dispute should be referred to a conference of eighty-one communist parties that met in Moscow in November. Its proceedings were tense, with Deng Xiaoping refusing to accept the right of the majority to bind the minority and recalling that Lenin had himself 'formed what was at first a minority fraction' within the Social Democratic Party 'in order, successfully in the end, to win a majority'. In the event the dispute was patched up, partly by condemning both revisionism (to which China saw the USSR as inclining) and dogmatism (China's error in Soviet eyes), and partly by emphasising the national liberation struggle of colonial peoples against imperialism – on which, in the abstract, both countries could agree. The quarrel was kept up by proxy, however, using Albania. This had come out in 1960 (after an internal power struggle) on the Chinese side, and was exposed to Soviet economic pressure and perhaps a coup attempt. In 1961 China supplied it with money and grain, while Soviet submarines evacuated their base there. At the Soviet Party Congress in October 1961 Khrushchev took as his chief theme de-Stalinisation and threw in a strong denunciation of Albania for opposing it (the charge could also have been levelled against China). Zhou Enlai responded by observing that 'open unilateral condemnation of a fraternal party does not make for unity', laid a wreath on Stalin's tomb 'to the memory of a great Marxist-Leninist', and flew home. Khrushchev then had Stalin's body removed from the Lenin mausoleum in Red Square and reburied elsewhere.[59] Thereafter, despite some attempts at mediation and negotiation,

---

59. Gittings, *Survey* chaps 15–19; Rothschild, *Return to Diversity* p.174; *Keesing's,* 18042, 18302, 18479

Sino-Soviet polemics became endemic. Initially they were still disguised as attacks on Yugoslavia and Albania respectively, but when the USSR concluded the Nuclear Test Ban Treaty in 1963, all inhibitions evaporated, and the breach was openly acknowledged.

The Sino-Soviet dispute was to prove singularly impervious to political changes within the two countries. When it began, Mao's domestic position had been damaged by the Great Leap Forward and more pragmatic forces were in the ascendant. In 1962 he began to reassert himself, and in late 1965 launched what was to become the 'Cultural Revolution', to prevent Liu Shaoqi and other pragmatists from taking China away from socialism down the 'revisionist' trail originally blazed by Khrushchev. Unsurprisingly the feud with the Soviet Union was continued, the road to the Soviet embassy being renamed 'Anti-revisionist Lane'. But 1969, when the internal tumult in China was subsiding, saw not reconciliation with the USSR but the beginnings of the opening to the USA (see pp. 286–8). This opening was personally blessed by Mao, but chiefly conducted by Zhou Enlai, who became heir-apparent after the 1971 defeat and death of Lin Biao. Mao, however, never tolerated his prospective heirs for long, and from 1974 Zhou and his protégé Deng Xiaoping were under attack by the radical 'Gang of Four'; this in no way damaged relations with the United States. Mao then died in 1976, and by the end of the 1970s Deng had achieved pre-eminence (using criticism of Mao as a political weapon, much as Khrushchev had used de-Stalinisation). In 1979 he visited the USA, attacked Vietnam, and took advocacy of the containment of Soviet influence to a very high pitch. In the 1980s he gradually modified this posture; in 1989 Deng at length allowed Gorbachev a summit meeting in Beijing, healing the Sino-Soviet rift, though not breaking with the USA.

On the Soviet side, the rift began under Khrushchev. Indeed, after Khrushchev's fall, he was accused of reducing the ideological dispute to the level of a personal feud between himself and Mao. Such signals brought a Chinese delegation to Moscow in November 1964, but it had no great expectations, and returned home in a huff after Marshal Malinovski suggested that China should ditch Mao as Russia had Khrushchev.[60] Polemics resumed in 1965, and China refused to attend the 1966 Soviet Party Congress. In response the USSR built up its troops on the Chinese border; in the early 1970s Brezhnev angled for US support in dealing with China. For

---

60. *Sunday Times*, 7 Feb. 1988 p.1; Heikal, *Sphinx and Commissar* p.139

most of his rule he thus let Sino-Soviet relations go from bad to worse, but he eventually started to change his tune, and called for improvement in a major speech in March 1982. Relations warmed gradually under both Andropov and Chernenko, though it may be that no leader but Gorbachev would have made all the concessions that China required as the price of reconciliation. Of course it is unlikely that the Sino-Soviet rift never figured in domestic politics: both Liu Shaoqi and Lin Biao were to be accused of looking to the Soviet Union. However, in both communist giants the policy to be adopted towards the other seems to have been surprisingly uncontroversial, which suggests that their 'cold war' commanded in its day a consensus comparable with that generated by US–Soviet rivalry.

The dispute was initially conducted in terms of ideology, sometimes indeed at quite a high theoretical level. Perhaps one should not take this too seriously. Chinese leaders may temperamentally have favoured a hard line, whether against US imperialism in the 1950s or Soviet 'social imperialism' in the 1970s. But their earlier revolutionary rhetoric did not stop them turning to the USA, clearly a status quo Power, and showing a marked preference for the more conservative Western politicians. Also, though it suited them to denounce Khrushchev's doctrine of peaceful coexistence and his cultivation of non-socialist Third World leaders, they had themselves embraced peaceful coexistence at the 1955 Bandung conference and had urged the USSR, in terms remarkably close to Khrushchev's own thinking, to arm Nasser and non-communist Arab nationalism since their victory over the colonialists 'would be in the interest of the socialist camp'.[61] Even in the 1960s the major country that China drew closest to was Ayub Khan's Pakistan; this was neither socialist nor revolutionary, but was impeccably anti-Indian and therefore welcome (on the principle that the enemy of my enemy is my friend). Ideology, then, was as much a convenient weapon in the Sino-Soviet dispute as a deep-seated conviction.

Other issues soon arose, notably over borders. One school of thought sees border incidents as consequential on the souring of Sino-Soviet relations, and notes that similar (though far worse) Soviet-Japanese fighting had occurred in the same areas in 1937–9 (when relations between the two countries were bad) but ended when they improved. It is also true that the issues in dispute

---

61. Heikal, *Sphinx and Commissar* pp.58–9; come the Sino-Soviet quarrel, China showed Cairo the text to disprove Soviet charges that it wished to confine aid to communists

between the Soviet Union and China on the ground were comparatively minor, and capable of being cleared up quite quickly in 1986–7.[62] However, for long periods border negotiations were stalled by Chinese insistence that, even if the current border were to be taken as a point of departure, the Russians should first accept that the treaties establishing it had been imperialist and 'unequal'. So no doubt they had; but for the USSR to accept this would, as the Chinese were well aware, have had embarrassing implications for several of its other borders, and conceivably have opened the door to much wider Chinese claims. In any case the USSR did not concede territory easily: witness the four diminutive islands in dispute between it and Japan (whose claims Mao endorsed in 1964). Equally China's border claims have precipitated hostilities not only with the USSR but also (on a larger scale) with India and Vietnam. Indeed of the countries large enough to stand up to China, only Pakistan has adjusted its borders amicably – almost certainly because it sought Chinese support in its more important dispute with India over Kashmir. Perhaps border troubles were initially only a manifestation of a prior deterioration of relations, but they soon assumed a dynamic of their own. The Soviet defence build-up of the later 1960s, followed by the 1969 fighting over Chen-pao island, raised Sino-Soviet friction to a new plane in which war was by no means inconceivable, and provided an added reason for China's turn towards the United States.

In the 1960s the Soviet Union was not the only superpower to have trouble with a major ally: the decade also witnessed de Gaulle's revolt against the US 'hegemony'. Of course several of the issues in contention in the two alliances were different: France had no borders with the USA; Western beliefs did not provide the same scope as Marxist-Leninism for polemics as to their correct interpretation; nor, equally, did the socialist camp possess an international monetary structure capable of being contested along

62. One was whether the boundary ran, as usual, down the middle of rivers (the *thalweg*) or, as the USSR contended, down the Chinese shore leaving all islands as Soviet territory. Khrushchev says he accepted the Chinese claim in principle, but insisted on retaining control of Bear Island opposite Khabarovsk (where there are believed to be nuclear installations) and confining Chinese shipping to the western channel. This was impassable in summer. It could have been dredged, but that would have meant conceding the Soviet case. Instead in 1977 the USSR agreed to allow Chinese shipping to use the eastern channel in summer. In 1986 Gorbachev, like Khrushchev before him, accepted China's claim to the *thalweg*; in 1987 agreement on the demarcation of the border was announced, though *Keesing's* does not record the decision over Bear Island: *Khrushchev Remembers* ii p.288; *Keesing's*, 31599, 35840, 36320

the lines of the French 'gold war' with the USA. But both sides shared the problem of nuclear weapons. The USA's initial instinct had been to disregard Britain's wartime share in the development of nuclear weapons and keep them to itself. Admittedly Eisenhower changed course, but in the 1960s US doctrine was again hostile to other national deterrents. Although special factors preserved US assistance to Britain, it was – at considerable political cost – withheld from France. At first the USSR had seemed readier than the USA to share nuclear technology; but in 1959 it abruptly changed its mind, partly because China was more resistant than NATO countries to the idea of integrated military structures that would necessarily be dominated by the presiding superpower. China proceeded to build its own bomb, as Britain had done after 1946 and France from 1958.

Given the levity with which Mao appeared to treat nuclear war, this was worrying. President Kennedy seems always to have hoped that the Soviet Union would be so concerned that it would join the USA in putting a stop to it. Khrushchev was slow to respond, but by 1963 the deterioration of Sino-Soviet relations was plain enough for the Americans to think it worth broaching the question. Khrushchev would not then be drawn, but discussions may perhaps have been resumed in September 1964, when the first Chinese nuclear test was clearly imminent (see pp. 283–4). Of the USSR's attitude, however, we know only that its unofficial Pugwash delegates suggested sanctions against any power conducting nuclear tests, and that a Belgian communist adherent of Beijing claimed in the *People's Daily* that Khrushchev had made a 'threat of military aggression against' China. It has been surmised that this claim was true, and that Khrushchev's colleagues' concern led them to depose him; but this never featured among the explanations they gave.[63] Khrushchev's fall ended any question there may have been of Soviet action against China's nuclear plants, but, as we have seen (pp. 286–7), there are grounds for believing that Brezhnev was weighing something of the kind in 1969.

Be this as it may, the Sino-Soviet rift proved more serious than de Gaulle's dissent. This was partly because it lasted longer, and partly because China loomed distinctly larger in the communist world than France in the Western alliance. Also whereas other countries

63. Chang, 'JFK, China, and the Bomb', *Journal of American History*, lxxiv (1987–8) pp.1,287–310 (McGeorge Bundy's Sept. 1964 memorandum was 'sanitized' before declassification); Harold Hinton, *Communist China in World Politics* (1966) pp.478–82, 502

were little moved by French attacks on US hegemony, a number of communist parties sought to turn the Sino-Soviet split to their own advantage. We have already seen that it precipitated a break with Moscow on the part of Albania, a country that could not easily be disciplined since it did not border on Warsaw Pact territory.[64] Khrushchev's pressure to secure a general condemnation of China prompted the Italian party to publish Togliatti's 'Testament' and thus accelerated its drift into revisionist 'eurocommunist' unorthodoxy. Romania, too, managed in 1963–4 to establish itself as a mediator between Moscow and Beijing, reassuring Moscow through its own domestic conservatism, but declaring eirenically that 'no party must label the fraternal party with which it differs anti-Marxist and anti-Leninist', and pronouncing for 'a qualitatively new system of relations' based on 'the principles of independence and national sovereignty' and of 'non-interference'.[65] Later in the 1960s this was broadened into a diplomacy that departed from the Soviet line not only over China but also over Israel, and that sought to set itself up as a bridge between East and West.

Meanwhile both the Soviet Union and China were competing for the support of Communist parties throughout the world. This had its ridiculous side; the tiny New Zealand party did not really deserve the attentions China bestowed on it. But then China was not directly very successful. In the end the only ruling party to choose the Chinese side was the Khmer Rouge (1975–9), with North Korea balancing between its two great neighbours. Cuba's advocacy of romantic insurrection inclined it towards China, but in 1968 the USSR so restricted its oil deliveries and other economic aid that by 1970 Castro had returned to the Soviet fold.[66] As the Cuban example suggests, the competition was unequal, since the USSR had so much more to give both economically and militarily; even parties like that of Mozambique that had won power through Chinese-style rural guerrilla war tended to align with the USSR. Such considerations weighed less with non–ruling parties, and here China had more success, especially with those of Asia.

As Soviet propaganda stressed, the most important effect was probably the 'splitting' of many communist movements, largely over

64. Albania saw itself as threatened by Yugoslavia and Greece. It may have found China's anti-Yugoslav rhetoric attractive, and been upset by Khrushchev's readiness in May 1960 to discuss with a visiting Greek politician the possibility of autonomy for its Greek minority

65. Fejtö, *History of the People's Democracies* pp.109–10, 183

66. Szulc, *Fidel* pp.671–5, 678, 681–5, 689

the issue of whether a peaceful and constitutional evolution to socialism was possible (as the Russians claimed) or whether socialism could come only through violent struggle. In Latin America the outcome was 'the withdrawal of the more militant members from the pro-Moscow parties, . . . a swing to the right . . . of the more orthodox Communist parties in favour of legality, and [their] abandonment of the armed struggle',[67] which (given the disturbed state of the continent) may have been a factor of some importance. In Western Europe a similar stress on organisation and order distanced the orthodox parties from the surge of *Marxisant* revolutionary sympathies that was so evident in and after 1968. Some sought to put this to good account by turning to a liberal 'eurocommunism', some (notably the PCF) fell between two stools. Many of the leftist groups (*groupuscules*, the French derisorily called them) saw themselves as 'Maoist', but they never followed Beijing's direction in the disciplined way in which communist parties had clung to the Moscow line down to the 1950s; once China had turned to the right after Mao's death, it lost any particular claim on their allegiances.

67. Gott, *Rural Guerrillas in Latin America* p.44

CHAPTER SIXTEEN

Eastern Europe Since 1957

In 1957 the break-up of 'international communism' lay in the future. Khrushchev had still to find a way of managing Eastern Europe which would, without counter-productive repression, keep in power communist governments that (unlike Tito's) saw themselves as part of the 'camp' led from Moscow. 1956 seemed to have established ground rules: the USSR would allow local parties some internal autonomy, accept leaders like Gomulka (in Poland) whom it would not itself have chosen, and allow them to adapt the Soviet model (by, for instance, de-collectivising agriculture), provided they stayed within the Warsaw Pact and the Soviet alliance system; but if, like Hungary, they tried to go neutral, the USSR would intervene. Defence arrangements were no doubt crucial; the Warsaw Pact functioned far more successfully as a supranational structure than did NATO. Khrushchev recognised that keeping troops abroad was both expensive and liable to irritate the local population. Accordingly he himself proposed partial withdrawal from Poland and Hungary, and in 1958 he eventually accepted Romania's desire for all Soviet troops to leave its soil. East Germany he says he regarded as a special case, where the Red Army would have to remain in force at least until the state was internationally recognised.[1] From 1958 to 1962 he pressed hard for such recognition, using the vulnerability of West Berlin as a lever, but did not achieve it. He did, however, put an end to the outflow of the East German population, by building the Berlin Wall; this enabled the regime to consolidate, and to secure general recognition a decade later.

---

1. *Khrushchev Remembers* ii pp.219–230

FAILURE TO SECURE ECONOMIC INTEGRATION THROUGH CMEA (1961–3); EAST EUROPEAN TRADE WITH THE USSR; HUNGARIAN ECONOMIC REFORMS

Khrushchev was, however, far less successful in securing economic integration. In copying Stalinist Russia, the East European countries had created their own centrally planned systems, all oriented towards self-sufficiency in heavy industry. In 1961, partly to counter the EEC (which Moscow always strongly denounced), the USSR sought to revive the moribund 'Council for Mutual Economic Assistance' (CMEA or 'Comecon'). It therefore proposed 'Fundamental Principles of Socialist Division of Labour', aimed at coordinating individual countries' national plans to permit specialisation and cooperation in economic production. East Germany and Czechoslovakia approved, since their developed industries stood to benefit. Romania did not; it was industrialising hard, and felt that it was being invited to give up and concentrate on agriculture. Nor did it relish the suggestion that it sell its oil within Eastern Europe rather than for hard currency on the world market. So, with some Polish and Bulgarian support, it took its stand on national sovereignty, and sniped at CMEA for the rest of Khrushchev's time in office.[2] It made its point. For in 1963 CMEA agreed to shelve plans for supranational integration and to concentrate instead on agreed, and generally bilateral, deals.[3] These were not wholly ineffective; Hungary, for instance, came to forgo car manufacture and concentrate on buses, while Bulgaria specialised in fork-lift trucks. But CMEA as a whole never moved much beyond the facilitation of inter-state barter, partly because (despite some Hungarian pressure) it never established a currency genuinely transferable between its members. The integration of centrally planned systems must always be harder than that of market economies, since it is more of an all-or-nothing process dependent on high-profile supranational intervention, and less can be left to the piecemeal operation of the 'invisible hand'.

Eastern Europe was, therefore, not as economically integrated as

2. 'The idea of a single planning body for all Comecon countries has the most serious . . . implications. The sovereignty of the Socialist State requires that it should hold in its hand all the levers for managing economic and social life'

3. *Keesing's*, 18896–7, 19911, 20365; R. Medvedev, *Khrushchev* (Oxford, 1982) p.242; Fejtö, *History of the People's Democracies* pp.107–9; Kaser, *Economic History of Eastern Europe* pp.236–43

the EEC, but it did share a common orientation towards the Soviet Union, which offered a large and undemanding market for manufactured goods and which became the major supplier of oil and gas. Initially the USSR still used its political power to drive hard bargains (which led to the 1965 suicide of the chairman of the East German planning commission); in 1968 Czechoslovakia was unable to transmute its favourable balance on Soviet trade into hard currency with which to deal with the West.[4] After the 1973 oil price rise, Eastern Europe derived real benefits from Soviet supplies at below world market rates. They were, however, not sufficient to compensate in the public mind for the overall costs of an economic system that was manifestly not keeping pace with that of Western Europe, and that was widely perceived to be falling behind precisely because it was communist.

With hindsight, it is clear that economic failure undermined East European systems that had anyway never put down much in the way of roots. At the time it was hoped that problems could be overcome by 'economic reforms' that would strengthen rather than endanger these systems; the 1960s saw a rash of such reforms. They seemed most successful in Hungary, whose experiments (Shevardnadze says)[5] some Russians saw as a model for their own economy, but others 'derailed'. By the 1970s Hungary had permitted a measure of individual economic enterprise, and introduced into the still heavily preponderant state sector some proxy for market forces. The result was the plentiful availability of goods and the emergence of a degree of affluence. Eventually this prosperity proved delusive: it was based on foreign borrowing, and on widespread 'moonlighting' by individual workers to supplement the exiguous earnings from their official, but undemanding, employments. For the time being, though it was appreciated; and Kadar's policy of 'he who is not against us is with us' provided considerable scope for the unpolitical, while never endangering ultimate party control. So he achieved some popularity, it being felt that he had gained as much for Hungary as was feasible without again provoking Soviet intervention.

---

4. *Keesing's*, 21156; Galia Golan, *The Czechoslovak Reform Movement* (Cambridge, 1971) pp.281–2

5. Kaser, *Economic History of Eastern Europe* pp.160 ff; Shevardnadze, *The Future Belongs to Freedom* p.114

THE PRAGUE SPRING 1968

Czechoslovakia was less fortunate. Its leaders had maintained a hard line throughout the 1950s, but then ran into trouble on several fronts. The economy went into deep recession: there were food shortages, and in 1962 the current five-year plan had to be scrapped. This gave scope to a group of economic reformers who advocated moving towards supply and demand; one of their leaders, Ota Sik, who became a Deputy Premier in 1968, was later to say that, though he had naturally kept quiet about it, he had also believed that political pluralism would have to accompany economic. In 1961 Khrushchev had renewed his support for de-Stalinisation, and pressed for a re-examination of the 1949–54 Czech trials. This encouraged jurists to seek the establishment of a genuine rule of law to preclude any further repetitions. Rehabilitations also entailed the dropping of the charge that the Slovak, Slansky, had been guilty of 'bourgeois nationalism'. Slovaks used this to press for more autonomy. For some time the Party Secretary, Novotny, managed to live with, even to derive advantage from, this ferment. In 1967 he seems to have decided that it had gone far enough. An economic reform was introduced, but its practical implementation blocked. Writers were warned to respect the party's doctrinal primacy; as elsewhere in Eastern Europe, the 1967 Middle Eastern war prompted an official anti-Zionist campaign that spilt over into anti-Semitism. This was denounced at a writers' congress, and Novotny moved towards repression. The Slovak Party Secretary, Dubcek, then took up the intellectuals' cause, especially after Novotny had unwisely attacked him as a 'bourgeois nationalist'. Novotny had managed to fuse all the currents of discontent, and his position looked shaky. In December 1967 Brezhnev visited Prague, and Novotny appealed for help. He had, however, earlier blotted his copybook by criticising the ouster of Khrushchev, so Brezhnev declined to intervene. There followed a Central Committee meeting that recessed without agreement over Christmas. As a last throw, Novotny sought a coup d'état, but it failed (perhaps partly because of Moscow's opposition). When the Central Committee resumed in January, it replaced Novotny by Dubcek as Party Secretary.[6]

Dubcek had expressed his opposition to 'coercive and despotic measures'; in April 1968 the party propounded a new 'Action

---

6. Fejtö, *History of the People's Democracies* pp.115–18, 146–9; Rothschild, *Return to Diversity* pp.167–9; Mlynar, *Night Frost* pp.68–71, 91–3; Golan, *The Czechoslovak Reform Movement passim*

Programme', declaring that it did not 'wish to assert its leading role by bringing pressure to bear on society, but by serving it devotedly with an eye to its free, progressive, socialist development. The party cannot impose its authority; it must earn it continually'. The Action Programme also repudiated 'the false thesis that the party is the instrument of the dictatorship of the proletariat'. In August 1968 new draft statutes were produced that would have shattered the traditional model whereby communist parties were controlled from the top downwards: elections should be by secret ballot, and dissent (though not the operation of minority factions) was to be permitted. With this went separation of party and state, with government responsible to Parliament – in which there were other parties besides the communists, albeit only within the context of a single 'National Front'. Opinions differed. Dubcek, at least, does not seem to have contemplated abandoning power: reconstitution of the Social Democrats was banned, and Dubcek said that the parties of the National Front should not 'struggle for the repartition of power' and that the communists should continue to exercise a leading role, though by proving the merits of their programme. In short he favoured a return to the communist-led postwar coalitions, much as Nagy had done in Hungary in 1956. This would probably have worked for a time, as most of the reformers came from within the party and (opinion polls suggested) the party commanded 70 per cent support. But the reform movement fed on itself, particularly after censorship was tacitly dropped in March 1968. Mlynar (in 1968 himself a leading politician) describes the Prague Spring as 'snowballing' into a 'nationwide democratic and humanitarian movement'; he believes Dubcek 'did not perceive the . . . potential political consequences of the radical democratic criticisms he had more or less set free in February and March', or 'that a mechanism had been introduced capable of forcing change on the system . . . a kind of public lobby backed by a free press and the free expression of opinions outside the power structure'.[7]

We cannot tell where all this would have led, but it is not surprising that other communist countries proved apprehensive. An analysis produced for party members in the DDR claimed that

> The Czechoslovak Communist Party is, in fact, powerless. Loyal Communists have been expelled from top governmental bodies, and their positions taken over by secret enemies of the party. . . .

7. Fejtö, *History of the People's Democracies* pp.150, 154; R. Rhodes James (ed.) *The Czechoslovak Crisis 1968* (1969) p.20; Golan, *The Czechoslovak Reform Movement* pp.300–1, 303, 305, 308; Mlynar, *Night Frost* pp.101–3, 117, 169

Counter-revolution is getting a grip, and the elements of a return to the bourgeois system have seeped into the party's programme of action. . . . On the pretext of granting freedom to the press, freedom has been given to the counter-revolution. This policy has already driven countless honest Communists to suicide. . . . Assurances given by Czechoslovak representatives of their friendship for the U.S.S.R. and the socialist allies are worthless, since these people are no longer in control of internal developments in their country.

Poland, then engaged in a clamp-down on intellectuals, saw things in the same way. Newspapers spoke of 'neutralist and anti-Soviet tendencies' in Czechoslovakia, and of pressures 'to introduce a "dictatorship of the intelligentsia" and to minimise the influence of the working class'; they said that some Czech Central Committee members feared the country would be pushed 'off the path of socialist development'.[8] The DDR and Poland seem accordingly to have pressed particularly strongly for intervention to curb the Prague Spring before it spread.

The Soviet Union was slower to reach a decision. Brezhnev was to say that military intervention had been approved in principle in May 1968, but 'Then it seemed that it wouldn't be necessary'. One way of avoiding it was to pressure Dubcek to rein things back, as was done in bloc meetings in March and early May. In July 1968 the USSR, DDR, Poland, Hungary and Bulgaria met to express concern that reactionary forces were threatening to push Czechoslovakia 'off the road to socialism'; the Second World War had advanced socialism's frontiers to the Bohemian Forest, and they 'would never agree to these historic gains being placed in jeopardy'. The Czech Central Committee rejected this advice to mount 'a decisive offensive against right-wing and anti-socialist forces'. Meetings were arranged between first the Czech and Soviet Politburos, then (at Bratislava) all the six parties concerned. Dubcek represented them as a success; Soviet troops, who had entered Czechoslovakia for Warsaw Pact exercises and shown an ominous indisposition to leave, did now go, though perhaps only to lull fears. But no real agreement had been reached. Kadar, by far the most sympathetic of the foreign leaders, privately hinted that if the Czechs did not themselves clamp down, somebody else would do so for them. A fortnight later he sought another meeting with Dubcek, and left

8. Fejtö, *History of the People's Democracies* p.157 (some Czech communists had indeed committed suicide); *Keesing's*, 22745

him with the words, 'Do you *really* not know the kind of people you're dealing with?'[9]

Dubcek, however, and many of his colleagues, expected to get by without intervention, partly because they did not think that the Soviet Union would risk the resultant odium, but chiefly because they could see no reason for it. Whereas the 1956 intervention in Hungary was generally (though – it is argued above on pp. 427n. – inaccurately) attributed to its decision to leave the Warsaw Pact, Czechoslovakia was profuse and sincere in its assertions of loyalty. This attitude ruled out preparations to oppose intervention, whether by armed resistance (the likelihood of which had in 1956 weighed with Khrushchev in the Polish, though not the Hungarian, case) or by attempts (such as were to be made by Romania) to enlist the support of outside Powers. In 1948 the Yugoslav leadership, though it had not wanted to quarrel with Stalin, had put its own safety first and had not drawn back from a rupture. But, Mlynar concludes, the Czech leadership would never have accepted

> a position knowing it might lead to a break with Moscow. The only point on which they could unite and which would avoid creating ungovernable domestic political conflicts . . . was the one on which they actually did unite: that the reform was achievable even while maintaining all the relationships and commitments between Czechoslovakia and the Warsaw Pact bloc.[10]

SOVIET REPRESSION IN CZECHOSLOVAKIA 1968–9

On 20–1 August 1968 Soviet, DDR, Polish and Hungarian troops moved in, encountering much passive but little overt resistance. Dubcek's comment was, 'So they did it after all – and to *me!*' Militarily the operation was a success, but politically it nearly miscarried. It had apparently meant to establish an emergency government, like Kadar's in Hungary in 1956, that would appeal for intervention and then try Dubcek as a saboteur of socialism; he was whisked off as a prisoner to the Soviet Union. No such government could be created; and the Czech Party held a defiant emergency

9. *Keesing's*, 22885 ff; Mlynar, *Night Frost* pp.152–7, 161–2. Mark Kramer offers some refinements to this picture in 'The Prague Spring and the Soviet Invasion of Czechoslovakia: New Interpretations', Cold War International History Project *Bulletin* 3 (1993), and other scholars are working on the topic. We can probably expect a much fuller history fairly soon

10. Mlynar, *Night Frost* pp.172–5. Mlynar thinks the wooing of Yugoslavia, Romania, China, and major Third World and Western countries *might* have given the USSR pause, but says he did not contemplate it at the time. Sik has said that he urged approaches to China on Dubcek, but to no effect

Congress and elected an alternative leadership. The situation was resolved by President Svoboda, who sympathised with Soviet aims but not methods. He led to Moscow a leadership delegation that eventually signed a protocol disowning the emergency Congress and promising to reintroduce censorship and sack people 'whose further activities would not conform to the needs of consolidating the leading role of the working class and the Communist party'. In return Dubcek was allowed to return, still Party Secretary but now to adhere much more closely to Soviet wishes.

A further crisis developed in March 1969, when a Czech ice-hockey victory over the USSR touched off widespread anti-Soviet riots. There followed the descent on Czechoslovakia of the Soviet Defence Minister, Marshal Grechko, and Dubcek's replacement as First Secretary by the turn-coat reformer Gustav Husak.[11] Husak presided over a clamp-down euphemistically known as 'normalisation'. It was far less drastic than that which Kadar had imposed after 1956. Perhaps as a result, Husak never managed to create the feeling that Kadar later generated in Hungary that conditions were again improving. What remained was stasis. The Prague Spring was rolled back. Communist control was not threatened. Most people were sullenly acquiescent. A few, mainly philosophers, writers, and former politicians, bravely protested despite persecution and exile (but not physical elimination). They included a dissident playwright, Vaclav Havel, who helped launch the human rights manifesto 'Charter [19]77', was arrested in 1978, and was repeatedly in and out of prison until May 1989.

THE BREZHNEV DOCTRINE AND THE HELSINKI FINAL ACT (1975)

The 1968 intervention destroyed both long-standing Czech affection for the Soviet Union and the popularity the Prague Spring had brought to the Czech Communist Party. It shocked many Western communists, notably the Italians. It also alarmed the Chinese, whose fears that they too might be subjected to intervention under

11. Mlynar, *Night Frost* chap. 3 and pp.282–6; *Keesing's*, 23301–2

12. The generic term given by the West to explanations (in *Pravda*, and by both Gromyko and Brezhnev himself) that when socialism was threatened, 'it becomes not only a problem of the people of the country concerned, but a common problem and concern of all socialist countries', justifying (in extreme cases) 'military assistance to a fraternal country'. For 'The sovereignty of each socialist country cannot be opposed to the interests of the world of socialism': *Keesing's*, 23027; Rhodes James, *Czechoslovak Crisis* p.114

the 'Brezhnev Doctrine' helped them decide to bury their quarrel with the USA.[12] It had surprisingly little direct effect on East–West relations, however, and it seemed to establish clear ground rules for the division of Europe. During the Moscow negotiations with Dubcek in August 1968, Brezhnev had uttered a number of home truths. On the one hand, 'the Communist movement in Western Europe . . . won't amount to anything for fifty years'. On the other, the USSR's sacrifices during the Second World War had gained it security. The guarantee of that security was the postwar division of Europe, and in particular the fact that Czechoslovakia was linked to the Soviet Union 'forever'. 'For us the results of the Second World War are inviolable, and we will defend them even at the cost of risking a new war'. Nor indeed would there be any such risk, since President Johnson had confirmed that he accepted the results of Yalta and Potsdam.[13]

Over the next few years Brezhnev proceeded to consolidate and develop this vision. After 1968 little more was heard of Gaullist hopes of the gradual dissolution of the Soviet and US 'hegemonies' over Europe. By 1969 the West Germans had recognised that *Ostpolitik* could not bypass the USSR but would have to be conducted through it. Brezhnev then proved forthcoming, engineering the removal of Ulbricht as East German Party Secretary in 1971 so as to secure DDR acceptance of the new policies.[14] In return for confirming the status quo in West Berlin, Brezhnev secured full international legitimation and UN membership for East Germany. Building on this, and on détente generally, he gained recognition in the 1975 Helsinki 'Final Act' of the Conference on Security and Cooperation in Europe (CSCE) that 'The participating states regard as inviolable all one another's frontiers as well as the frontiers of all states in Europe'. This, to the Soviets, meant the long-delayed acceptance by the West of the new order in Eastern Europe created at the end of the war.

The United States does seem to have seen it as unchallengeable, if unattractive. In December 1975, in what became known as the 'Sonnenfeldt Doctrine', Kissinger's aide briefed US ambassadors:

> it must be our policy to strive for an evolution that makes the [present 'unnatural'] relationship between Eastern Europeans and the Soviet Union an organic one. . . .
> our policy must be a policy of responding to the clearly visible

13. Mlynar, *Night Frost* pp.239–41
14. Martin McCauley, *Marxism-Leninism in the German Democratic Republic* (1979) pp.174–5

aspirations of Eastern Europe for a more autonomous existence within the context of a strong Soviet geopolitical influence.

This has worked in Poland. The Poles have been able to overcome their romantic political inclinations which led to their disasters in the past. They have been skilful in developing a policy that is satisfying their needs for a national identity without arousing Soviet reactions. It is a long process.

A similar process is now going on in Hungary. Janos Kadar's performance has been remarkable in finding ways which are acceptable to the Soviet Union, which develop Hungarian roots and the natural aspirations of the people. . . . To a considerable degree he has been able to do this because the Soviets have four divisions in Hungary and, therefore, have not been overly concerned. . . .

We seek to influence the emergence of the Soviet imperial power by making the base more natural and organic so that it will not remain founded in sheer power alone. But there is no alternative open to us other than influencing the way Soviet power is used.[15]

It was not good domestic politics to say such things; instead the West was subsequently to focus more sharply on human rights in Eastern Europe. The Helsinki 'Final Act' had also contained a human rights 'basket' that had encouraged Soviet and East European activists, not least those of 'Charter 77'. A crack-down resulted; at subsequent CSCE conferences (held to monitor implementation of the 'Final Act'), Western delegations sought to probe this in ways the USSR saw as subversive and inimical to détente. But that Eastern Europe would for the foreseeable future remain both 'communist' and aligned with the USSR was scarcely doubted.[16] Few Western politicians hoped for more than its internal softening and the establishment of non-antagonistic relationships between the two halves of Europe. The chief exception was Helmut Kohl, West German Chancellor from 1982, who made it his business constantly to remind the world that the partition of Germany was cruel and unnatural, and therefore unacceptable. Even he never suggested that it could, under existing circumstances, be reversed.

15. *Keesing's*, 27302, 27795–6

16. Indeed the once notable Romanian breach with the Soviet Union gradually healed. Romania had felt threatened after 1968 and responded by raising its international profile and welcoming visitors like President Nixon. In 1971 the USSR accused it of organising a Balkan bloc under Chinese and US patronage, and staged intimidatory Warsaw Pact manoeuvres. But Romania later ran into economic difficulties, partly because its distinctive pro-Israeli stance had not endeared it to Arab oil producers; accordingly it took a more positive view of CMEA and became increasingly dependent on Soviet energy exports. Its internally repressive regime seemed no threat to 'socialism'; and though it kept up contacts with the West, Brezhnev is said to have hoped to use them to acquire Western technology. In 1976 he and Ceauşescu exchanged visits to seal their reconciliation: *Keesing's*, 24934, 25209, 26887–8, 27786, 28163–4

GORBACHEV'S CATALYTIC REFORMS 1985–9

In 1989 the East European system suddenly collapsed. There seem to have been two main reasons – economic troubles, and political developments in the USSR. In 1985 Gorbachev became General Secretary and soon inaugurated a period of major domestic reform. By March 1989 this had led to partially free elections to the new Congress of People's Deputies, in which several leading politicians were defeated and a number of reformers triumphed. Gorbachev greeted the result with words reminiscent of the Prague Spring: 'socialist democracy and people's self-government give vast opportunities for all to express their opinions, interests and attitudes'. The joke ran that to save socialism, Czech tanks would have to move on Moscow; and it was not easy to maintain that what was done in the USSR was unacceptable in Eastern Europe. All this was peculiarly upsetting in East Germany, which eventually came to censor Soviet publications, and Czechoslovakia, whose leaders were not pleased when their Warsaw Pact colleagues (bar the East Germans) began to condemn the 1968 intervention that was their raison d'être.[17]

POLAND 1970–89

The destabilising effects of economic troubles had by now become endemic in Poland. They had first been apparent in 1970, when sudden price increases sparked rioting in cities like Gdansk. Order was restored by force (those killed being later regarded as the precursors of 'Solidarity'), but the episode prompted Gomulka's forced retirement, and his replacement as First Secretary by Gierek. The Soviet Union welcomed the change, and provided economic aid to help the new government. All went fairly well until 1976, when Gierek again sought to raise prices, encountered demonstrations, and backed off. An important development was the formation by intellectuals (many of whom had become deeply alienated by various clamp-downs in the later 1960s) of a 'Committee for the Defence of Workers' (KOR) to help those punished for their part in the demonstrations. A further dimension was added when the Archbishop of Krakow became Pope (as John

---

17. *Keesing's*, 36513, 36624, 36831, 36856, 36982

Paul II) in 1978 and made a triumphant return visit the following year. Poland had always been strongly Catholic, and religious enthusiasm had further increased as an expression of popular attitudes towards the communist regime. Meanwhile the economy was kept afloat only by massive borrowing: Poland's hard currency debt went from $7.4 billion in 1975 to over $21 billion in 1980.

July 1980 saw another attempt to increase prices. Poland was already in ferment; the increases touched off widespread strikes, increasingly orchestrated by unofficial 'workers' committees' that elbowed aside the puppet official trade unions. In mid-August 1980 the Lenin shipyard in Gdansk was occupied by its workers, who demanded not only the rolling back of price increases but also the establishment of freely elected independent unions, and managed to get these demands broadcast. A week later 150,000 people were on strike around Gdansk, panic buying had led to food shortages, and the Church was calling for restraint to avoid bloodshed. Its advice was eventually taken. Negotiations ensued; on 31 August the government concluded an agreement with the Gdansk strike leader, Lech Walesa, that provided not only for wage increases but also for the right to establish independent unions, for the revision of censorship, the broadcasting of Catholic services, and the review of sentences passed on civil rights activists over the previous decade. In September 1980 Walesa went on to found an independent trade union, Solidarity, with the support both of KOR intellectuals and of the Church. The authorities were initially reluctant to register it, but gave way after a threatened strike; by January 1981 it had 8 million members, and the official unions had to be wound up.[18]

That a communist regime should allow such autonomy to the workers, or such a political role to the Church, was unprecedented. Solidarity sought to avoid trouble by incorporating (in an annex to its statutes) a recognition of the leading role of the Communist Party; manifestly the USSR, DDR, and Czechoslovakia were extremely unhappy about developments, but it was hoped that this would stop them claiming, under the Brezhnev doctrine, that socialism was endangered. In practice the party's leading role could not easily be reconciled with the free operation of a massive trade union of very different outlook, and there was much friction, especially as the economy deteriorated and shortages increased. In the autumn of 1981 Solidarity's Congress rejected government proposals for economic reform and demanded round-table negotiation

18. *Keesing's*, 30565 ff, 30717ff

of an 'anti-crisis' agreement that would incorporate revision of the economic system and the democratisation of many public institutions. In effect Solidarity was seeking a position of co-determination with the communist authorities. Meanwhile the party had been running through its leaders. Gierek gave place to Kania in September 1980; in October 1981 the Prime Minister and Defence Minister, General Jaruzelski, also took over the Party Secretaryship. Things could run no further. In December he formed the 'Military Council for National Salvation', proclaimed martial law, and managed to arrest most of the Solidarity leadership. There has since been debate as to whether he acted to avert Soviet intervention, or whether he sought promises of Soviet aid in the event that his move was unsuccessful.[19]

Jaruzelski's actions were well planned, and he established control using only Polish forces and without provoking the massive resistance that many had anticipated. A year later he felt that he was in a position to relax; in November 1982 he negotiated with the Pope, agreeing to release Walesa in exchange for a papal visit in the summer of 1983 that would imply acceptance of the new order. Martial law was lifted shortly after this visit, though repression (both official and unofficial) continued in lower key. An informal dialogue was established with the Church (which was itself in touch with Walesa and other activists); Solidarity preserved a restricted and clandestine existence. A certain normality had returned; what Jaruzelski could not do was restore the economy. After strikes in mid-1988 official contact was resumed with Walesa. Foreign leaders, notably Mrs Thatcher in November 1988, appeared to suggest that external aid would be conditional on the re-establishment of freedom and 'real dialogue with representatives of all sections of society, including Solidarity' (which was, officially, still banned). Much of the party remained extremely hostile to any revival of Solidarity, but Jaruzelski pushed the idea through the Central Committee in January 1989. By April a deal had been struck: Solidarity would be relegalised; outline economic reforms were agreed, while Walesa offered his assistance in securing foreign aid; and there would be a new constitution.[20]

This was meant to preserve communist leadership for the time

19. *The Times*, 13 Dec. 1991; *The Independent*, 4 Dec. 1990 p.8; *Keesing's*, 31218–19, 31389, 32018; Leslie, *History of Poland* pp.458–62; The Observer, *Tearing down the Curtain: The People's Revolution in Eastern Europe* (1990) pp.15–18; CWIHP *Bulletin* 3 (1993) p.78

20. Observer, *Tearing down the Curtain* pp.18–23; *Keesing's*, 36298–302, 36400–1

being, but to open up prospects of gradual development. There would be a strong President – Jaruzelski – a freely elected Senate, and a predominant lower chamber (the *Seym*) where (for the first elections only) the government parties were to be guaranteed 65 per cent of the seats, other parties 35 per cent. What had not been anticipated was the election results: Solidarity candidates won all but one seat in the Senate and all the non-government seats in the *Seym*; and thirty-three members of the government, though unopposed, failed to get enough votes to secure election to the *Seym*. Solidarity then refused invitations to join a broad coalition government; previously docile satellite parties began to break with the communists; in August 1989 Walesa proposed a non-communist coalition. Jaruzelski wondered whether the Warsaw Pact would accept it, but Walesa reassured him by pledging adherence to the Pact and offering the communists the Interior and Defence ministries. With Gorbachev's encouragement, the communists eventually agreed to participate, but haggled over terms and eventually secured four Cabinet places. Potentially they still seemed strongly placed, and may have hoped for support from the President. Jaruzelski behaved as a non-political head of state, however, and Solidarity dominated the government and embarked on a rapid and radical free market reform.[21]

HUNGARY 1987–90

Hungary's evolution was less eventful. Its regime seemed solid and opposition slight, but its economy faltered slightly in 1985–6, and its net debt was the highest per capita in Eastern Europe. In 1987 the hitherto orthodox Karoly Grosz became Prime Minister to devise an austerity programme. This was adopted, but only after sparking a debate in which intellectuals urged the need for more general reform. They were joined, from within the party, by Imre Pozsgay, who called for a new constitution and cultivated the new intellectual activists. The now elderly Kadar seems to have been uneasy, and is said to have contended that he would have to stay on in office as a guarantee that reforms would not get out of control. However in May 1988 he was toppled by an alliance between Grosz (who replaced him as Party Secretary) and Pozsgay. Reform continued apace: in October a law permitted medium-sized private joint stock

21. *Keesing's*, 36722–3, 36838–9, 36896–7; Observer, *Tearing down the Curtain* pp.25 ff

companies; in November the government promised to allow competitive political parties, and these started to be formed even before the requisite legislation was passed. Pozsgay still warned that two subjects remained taboo – the rehabilitation of Imre Nagy and withdrawal from the Warsaw Pact – but his inhibitions were soon eroded. Early in 1989 a party commission under his patronage declared that 1956 had been not a 'counter-revolution' but a popular uprising; it added a strong condemnation of the Stalinist system of 'dictatorship, bureaucratic centralism, fear and retribution' that had been imposed on Eastern Europe. March 1989 saw a massive opposition demonstration on the newly revived National Day commemorating the 1848 revolution, June the formal reburial (attended by 250,000 people) of Nagy and other heroes of 1956. Grosz had for some time been muttering about counter-revolution, but he could never bring himself to a showdown with the reformers, only to attempts to delay and water down the transition to a multi-party system. At a June 1989 Central Committee meeting, he effectively lost control; the party began roundtable talks with opposition politicians on a new system. In September these produced agreement, though only with part of the Opposition, on the basis of direct presidential elections – which Pozsgay expected to win – followed by free parliamentary elections. On this basis the 'Communist' Party reconstituted itself as the Hungarian Socialist Party (HSP), with Pozsgay as its presidential candidate. Pozsgay's personal appeal might well have enabled him to win a direct election. But other reformers managed to force a constitutional referendum; as a result the choice of president was transferred to Parliament. When parliamentary elections finally came in March–April 1990 the HSP was pushed into fourth place. Victory went to the Hungarian Democratic Forum, whose leader was moved to claim that 'after decades of dictatorship the political reflexes of the Hungarian people have not changed' since his coalition had together 'achieved the same result as the Smallholders in 1945'.[22]

GERMAN REUNIFICATION 1989–90

Meanwhile Hungary's evolution had helped set off an avalanche. In September 1989 it declared that it would no longer stop East Germans crossing its border with Austria. It was then full of DDR

22. Observer, *Tearing down the Curtain* chap. 3; *Keesing's*, 36164, 36468, 36746, 36960–1, 37048, 37380

tourists, and by the end of the month 24,000 had crossed on their way to West Germany. Hungary was roundly denounced for this breach of Warsaw Pact obligations; Czech guards began to stop East Germans going there. As a result would-be migrants swamped the West German embassy in Prague. It was eventually agreed that they might leave too, but by train through East Germany; there followed riots in Dresden as people tried to board these trains to the West. The East German regime already seemed isolated by its refusal to countenance Soviet-style reforms: 'If your neighbour wallpapered his flat', asked its ideological spokesman, 'would you feel the need to decorate yours?' In September 1989 intellectuals had illegally established a 'New Forum' to press for pluralist reforms, albeit without challenging the party's 'leading role'. Also there had for some time been small 'peace' movements and demonstrations, sponsored by the Lutheran Church. In October 1989 they mushroomed, partly in consequence of developments abroad (East Germans could watch West German TV), partly as a response to the fortieth anniversary of the DDR. The authorities, who had applauded the Chinese suppression that summer of the democracy movement in Tiananmen square, initially dispersed demonstrations with some violence. Honecker seems to have been ready to shoot up the 9 October mass meeting in Leipzig, but to have been stopped by local SED party leaders and perhaps also by his heirapparent Egon Krenz. Honecker's line was that 'everything will collapse if we give an inch'. The party decided to replace him with Krenz, who, though previously a hardliner, sought a controlled relaxation. After flying to Moscow, Krenz brought in, first to the Politburo and then as Prime Minister, the Dresden party chief, Hans Modrow, who had marched with a demonstration in early November. Honecker had been right. The demonstrations redoubled in size, as did the exodus through Czechoslovakia. On 8 November 1989 it was announced that the border would be opened at midnight. There ensued a massive surge of sightseers into West Berlin and an extraordinary celebration and street party on the Wall.[23]

It had been hoped that this would satisfy pent-up curiosity about the West, and that things would then settle down. When presenting his new government, Modrow talked of a reformed but still 'socialist' state, with 'no dangerous speculation about reunification'. New Forum also deplored reunification and felt Krenz should be given a chance; leading intellectuals joined him in looking 'to develop

---

23. *Keesing's*, 36894; Observer, *Tearing down the Curtain* chap. 4

a socialist alternative to the Federal Republic'.[24] Initial opinion polls suggested a good deal of support for this, but it did not last. The demonstrations continued, and the working class in southern industrial cities came increasingly to display an unreconstructed nationalism – 'We are one people!' By January 1990 they had turned to attacks on the secret police, while Modrow lost face by seeking to establish a substitute. There was a flood of revelations of corruption, environmental pollution, and economic crisis; in January the government admitted to a serious budget deficit, a balance of payments deficit, and a higher per capita foreign debt than Poland's. West German prosperity became ever more appealing. Modrow had originally thought of elections in May, but, faced with a disintegrating system, brought them forward to March. He had wished to exclude foreign participation, but in fact West German parties largely took over the campaign. Kohl made six electioneering visits; his hastily created 'Alliance for Germany' won a remarkable victory with nearly half the vote, more than double the SPD, on a platform of rapid monetary union to be followed by accession to the Federal Republic.

Kohl had always denounced the partition of Germany; he now pressed unification hard, both from conviction and in the belief that it was the only way to stop West Germany being swamped by an exodus from the collapsing East. To smooth his path he was prepared to override the Bundesbank's objections to the inflationary conversion of East into West marks at par.[25] Officially West Germany's allies had always supported reunion, but partition had suited them quite well; neither the British nor the French government was pleased by the sudden re-emergence of the 'German question'. They could, however, do no more than hope that Soviet objections – which were promptly and repeatedly voiced – would prove insuperable.[26] In fact Gorbachev seems to have decided quite early to trade German unification for security concessions. In

24. Observer, *Tearing down the Curtain* pp.74–5, 80; *Keesing's*, 37026

25. For the purpose of calculating wages, pensions and savings of below 4000 marks, i.e. for the concerns of the average elector (*Keesing's*, 37379). The result was an inflationary reunification boom, especially as Kohl also refused to raise taxes (claiming that reunion would cost nothing); the Bundesbank jacked up interest rates to control it, resolutely ignoring complaints as to the effects on the ERM and on other European economies

26. Gorbachev was to suggest that both had urged him to prevent reunification: Gail Sheehy, *Gorbachev* p.263. Margaret Thatcher sought in Dec. 1989–Jan. 1990 to arrange a common front with Mitterand to block or slow reunification; but Mitterand, though apparently sharing her fears, decided that it was unstoppable and returned instead to tying Germany into a federal Europe – *Downing Street Years* (1993) pp. 792–8, 813–15

February 1990, after a lightning visit to Moscow, Modrow suddenly reversed himself and proposed a unified, but neutral, Germany – which had been official Soviet policy in the early 1950s. Kohl then visited Moscow and gained a declaration from Gorbachev that 'the unity of the German nation must be decided by the Germans themselves'. Soon afterwards the Americans steered the parties to an agreement that the two Germanies should first negotiate their union and then discuss external security aspects with the four occupying Powers of 1945 (whereas Britain and France had wanted prior Four Power discussions).

There were two main security problems – the status of the Oder–Neisse line, and German adherence to NATO. Presumably for electoral reasons, Kohl proved worryingly slow to confirm the Oder–Neisse line as Germany's definitive eastern border, but was eventually brought to provide reassurances for Poland. As for NATO, the West German government and its allies agreed that Germany should remain a member. The USSR did not, but it found itself isolated at a Warsaw Pact meeting in March: Poland declared that neutrality was likely to foster German 'tendencies to become a great power acting on its own' and Hungary stated that NATO membership was 'the only way to keep Germany under control'. Subsequently the USSR floated several other alternatives – unification subject to a continuing Four Power (hence Soviet) troop presence and rights, German membership of both NATO and the Warsaw Pact, or a diluted membership only of NATO. The deadlock broke in July 1990, when NATO undertook to conclude a treaty limiting armed forces in Europe (including those of a united Germany), and Gorbachev invited Kohl and his Foreign Minister Genscher to his home town of Stavropol. There, just as Brandt had settled *Ostpolitik* with Brezhnev, Kohl concluded a deal. Germany should be free to decide 'to which bloc it wants to belong' (as the West had insisted in 1952–3); Soviet troops would stay for a further three or four years in eastern Germany, during which time there would be no NATO presence there; and the forces of a united Germany would be cut to well below current West German levels, with a continuing renunciation of nuclear, chemical or biological weapons. Kohl had smoothed the path with economic aid for the USSR, and, after a last-minute hitch in September, Gorbachev was able to extract more.[27] Reunification finally took effect on 3 October 1990.

27. $9.5 billion to support the maintenance and relocation of Soviet forces in eastern Germany: *Keesing's*, 37259, 37466, 37599, 37659, 37717–18; Sheehy, *Gorbachev* p.264

CZECHOSLOVAKIA 1989–90

The opening of the Berlin Wall on 9 November 1989 had been dramatic, but more was to come. On the 17th the Czech police roughed up a students' march that sported anti-communist and pro-perestroika banners; rumours were spread that they had murdered a participant. This touched off mounting demonstrations, organised by Vaclav Havel's newly created 'Civic Forum', and joined on the 24th by the once persecuted Dubcek. Amazingly (as it seemed on the surface) General Secretary Jakes resigned; on 26 November Prime Minister Adamec joined Havel and Dubcek in addressing a final rally, having already opened discussions with Civic Forum. These were not easy: Civic Forum saw his initial broadening of the government as inadequate, but agreement was reached on 10 December 1989; on the 29th Parliament elected Havel as President; in June 1990 Civic Forum duly won the elections.

BULGARIA 1989–90

Meanwhile things had also been moving in Bulgaria. 'Ecoglasnost' (ecology and glasnost) demonstrations prompted a Politburo meeting at which the Foreign Minister, Mladenov, apparently with Moscow's backing, replaced the long-serving Party Secretary, Zhivkov. Mladenov then cleared out his predecessor's supporters and opened talks with the opposition. These failed, however, and February 1990 saw the installation of a purely communist government under Lukanov. In June the former communists, reconstituted as the Bulgarian Socialist Party, won the elections convincingly on the basis of their support outside the capital. But the Opposition did not accept the results as fair. In July Mladenov was brought to resign by the revelation that he had at one point favoured calling in the tanks to deal with an opposition demonstration; by the end of the year Lukanov's government had been forced out by strikes against its economic measures.

ROMANIA 1989–90

In Romania Ceauşescu's rule had degenerated into a personal dictatorship (derided as 'socialism in one family') of an unpleasant and megalomaniac character. Ruthless priority was given to repaying foreign debt by squeezing consumption. There had been strikes, but they had been firmly suppressed; the Securitate cultivated an image of omnipresence and violence. The Party Congress in late November 1989 gave no hint of change. Disturbances broke out on 17 December in a Hungarian minority area, which Ceauşescu placed under a state of emergency. When he addressed a staged rally in Bucharest on the 21st, he was heckled; next day he was shouted down, and fled. Much of the army came out in support of the demonstrators, and something calling itself the National Salvation Front (NSF) took over the television station. During 23–5 December 1989 there was a fierce counterattack, represented as coming from the Securitate. The army (with massive popular support) gradually got the upper hand, assisted by the capture and execution of Nicolae and Elena Ceauşescu. By the end of the year the NSF had rescinded the most obnoxious practices of their regime, permitted the formation of political parties, and promised elections and a free enterprise economy. It also improved living standards by distributing food reserves and cutting exports. Initially billed as a caretaker regime, it decided in January 1990 to continue as a political party. In May it easily won elections that were marred by violence and some official harrassment of the Opposition, but were regarded by international observers as acceptable. The Opposition did not accept them, and saw the NSF as a continuation of the Communist Party under another face. They occupied University Square in Bucharest from April to June 1990, when police moves to clear it provoked attacks on official buildings akin to those of the previous December. The NSF responded by bringing in 10,000 miners, who beat up the demonstrators and smashed Opposition parties' offices; they were then thanked by President Iliescu.[28]

ALTERNATIVE EXPLANATIONS OF THE COMMUNIST COLLAPSE

This sudden collapse of overt communist rule in the Warsaw Pact countries (other than the USSR) prompts the question, 'did it fall or was it pushed?' One view is that the fall was entirely natural.

28. Observer, *Tearing down the Curtain passim*; *Keesing's*, 37027, 37544, 37619, 37745 (Bulgaria), 37104–5, 37441–2, 37545 (Romania)

Communist rule had been imposed by force after the war. Its achievements had been few. Its idealistic appeal, which had been quite real in the 1930s and 1940s despite Stalin's actual behaviour, had evaporated, partly because of the suppression of earlier communist reform movements like the Prague Spring. Further some of the rulers, Kadar in Hungary and Honecker in East Germany, were old and ill, others (notably Grosz) indecisive, while Ceauşescu overconfidently left on a foreign visit as the Romanian troubles broke. Also, in one important way, they had softened. For most leaders (the exceptions being Ceauşescu and probably Honecker) were no longer ready to use force on the scale of their predecessors – or of the Chinese suppression of the democracy movement in Tiananmen Square. Mention of that movement – which erected a 'Goddess of Democracy and Freedom' modelled on the New York Statue of Liberty – reminds us that the attraction, both moral and economic, of Western free-market liberal capitalism, then stood very high. Undoubtedly there was a widespread hope that its adoption would bring massive Western assistance and a quick resolution of problems. Moreover though individual communist regimes had sought to sink local roots, they had generally failed, and were often vulnerable to the appeal of nationalism. This was most obviously so in the rump state of East Germany, which had not managed to create a German socialist nation and which lasted less than a year after the fall of communism. Elsewhere the nations had more substance, but the regimes were potentially vulnerable to their invocation. Thus Hungary was, until 1989, forbidden to celebrate its 1848 revolution, suppressed by tsarist Russia. This year 1956 was even more taboo; the rehabilitation and reburial of Imre Nagy proved a turning-point. The new post-communist Republic was formally inaugurated on 23 October 1989, the anniversary of the start of the 1956 rising. One could continue . . .

So it could be argued that communism's roots were very shallow, and that once things were allowed to slip they would soon get out of control. This was the view of hardliners like Ulbricht and Honecker. Certainly in 1956 communist rule would have collapsed in Hungary in less than a month, but for outside intervention. One cannot be so sure about Czechoslovakia in 1968; events were moving very fast there, with its neighbours clearly fearing that they would spread. In 1980–1 Solidarity, though not ostensibly aiming at government, managed to transform the way in which Poland was run. In these cases the situation was controlled by Soviet intervention, actual or threatened. But in 1989 the Brezhnev Doctrine was repudiated, and though, when matters actually came to the crunch, there were calls for the use of force as in 1956 and 1968, things were allowed to take their course.[29] Moreover the collapse of communism in the countries we have discussed was part of a broader phenomenon. Thus 1990 saw Opposition election victories in the Yugoslav republics of Slovenia and Croatia, which next year proceeded to secession. Within the USSR communists lost (through the ballot box) both major Russian cities like Moscow and Leningrad and a number of union-republics. In 1991 communist control of Albania progressively disintegrated (despite an initial election victory).

These developments cannot all be laid at Gorbachev's door; he had no direct influence in Yugoslavia or Albania, and though his electoral reforms opened the way for nationalists to take over the Baltic states, Georgia and Moldavia, this was clearly contrary to his wishes. It has, though, been suggested that there was more to the communist débâcle in Eastern Europe than met the eye. A soft formulation would be that Gorbachev, like Khrushchev before him, could not conceive that the policies he devised for the USSR might not be suitable elsewhere, and insisted that they be generally adopted. 'Those who delay', he told Honecker, 'are punished by life itself'; Honecker expressed doubts,[30] and might well now reply that those who concede too much come unstuck.

At the other extreme, it has been argued that Gorbachev was positively anxious to get rid of the political and economic liability of Eastern Europe, preferably in exchange for the dismantling of NATO. As early as 1984 he had quizzed Thatcher on the way in which Britain had exchanged its Empire for a Commonwealth. In 1985, Shevardnadze says, 'we' ruled out the possibility of further military intervention in Eastern Europe. In 1987 there were hints of the need to 'reassess' the 1968 intervention; proposals were even made in private for a gradual withdrawal of Soviet troops from Eastern Europe, though they seem to have been buried quite easily. Shevardnadze already had a feeling that the issue of German reunification would soon resurface, though it was not one that could yet be addressed given the conviction that 'the existence of two Germanys maintained the security of the Soviet Union and the whole continent'. In 1989, the case continues, Gorbachev received an assessment that, if Honecker went, no other communist could

---

29. *Keesing's*, 36982; Shevardnadze, *The Future Belongs to Freedom* p.120
30. Observer, *Tearing down the Curtain* p.68. There had been similar confrontations with other leaders, that with Ceauşescu being so stormy as to bring the security guards running in: Shevardnadze, *The Future Belongs to Freedom* p.117

pick up the pieces, but he ignored it. In 1990, in response to the charge that East European changes had constituted 'the collapse of socialism' (with the USSR 'leaving the field without fighting'), Gorbachev replied that what had collapsed was not socialism but Stalinism; Shevardnadze added that 'we predicted all the events in Eastern Europe' and that the outcome had improved the USSR's financial and defence position.[31]

A third possibility is that Gorbachev saw the East European structure was weakening and tried to push forward reform communists in a pre-emptive attempt to limit the damage. Generally he made matters worse. In Bulgaria, for a time, and Romania, former communists – without themselves altering very much – succeeded in taking charge and controlling the process of change. This conspiracy theory is widely accepted in Eastern Europe, but there are only snippets of evidence. The *Observer* was told at the time that Gorbachev personally asked Kadar to step down in 1988; he may have given Pozsgay some support in 1989. Similarly a Central Committee member said Gorbachev told the DDR leadership that Honecker's health was not good enough to continue; it is likely that Moscow later advised Modrow's appointment as Premier. In Bulgaria, Mladenov apparently secured Soviet backing for his displacement of Zhivkov from the leadership. In Czechoslovakia a parliamentary inquiry suspected that both the Czech and the Soviet secret services had had a hand in creating the initial incident in order to bring about a change in party leadership; a leading Czech secret policeman claims that he had earlier been seeking a new leader, but that he did not find anybody satisfactory and so held off suppressing Civic Forum and turned his attention to 'preventing civil war'. Finally, though the Romanian revolution claimed to be spontaneous, it has since been conceded that there had been a long-standing plot against Ceaușescu involving several generals and a section of the Securitate. I know of no evidence of Soviet involvement, though it may be suggestive that, at the height of the fighting, the National Liberation Front appealed to Moscow for assistance. We have probably not heard the last on the subject.[32]

31. Shevardnadze, *The Future Belongs to Freedom* pp.121–2, 126, 131–2; Sheehy, *Gorbachev* pp.188, 239, 264; *Keesing's*, 35516, 37615

32. Observer, *Tearing down the Curtain* pp.45, 49, 70–1, 96–7; *Keesing's*, 37027, 37737, 37745; *The Independent*, 15 May 1990 p.8, 24 Aug. p.11, 27 Oct. p.11. The CPSU continued to support East European post-communist parties, lending the Poles $1.2 million interest free in Jan. 1990 and in March 1991 discussing plans to finance the East European parties with cash from private companies (*Keesing's*, 38586)

THE BREAK-UP OF YUGOSLAVIA

The collapse of communism has been followed by, or associated with, the break-up of the multi-national states of the USSR itself, Yugoslavia and Czechoslovakia. The process has ranged in civility from the 'velvet divorce' (as of January 1993) between the Czech Republic and Slovakia to the wars of the Caucasus and Tadzhikistan. Recent events in ex-Yugoslavia are less horrific than the two last-named, or than several wars in Africa. But, because they take place in central Europe, with easy access and TV coverage, they have attracted more attention and diplomatic activity. A brief outline may accordingly be in order.

The 'south' ('Yugo') slav peoples differ from each other as a result of history, religion, and – though less markedly, save in the case of the Slovenes – language. It was, however, the proclaimed mission of Serbia before 1914 to unite them as Piedmont had united Italy in the *risorgimento*. This was achieved in 1918; but for most of its inter-war history the new state was torn by Serb-Croat rivalry. After its destruction by Germany in 1941, there ensued a complex of civil wars, with the Fascist regime imposed on Croatia seeking to expel, convert or exterminate all non-Roman Catholics, and the principal resistance movement in Serbia, the Chetniks, aspiring to the ethnic cleansing of Serb lands. The conventional figure for war-time deaths is 1.7 million. This may be exaggerated; but the inter-communal killings left a legacy of mutual fear and hatred that was to resurface almost half a century later.

The victorious communists' solution was a combination of exclusive party control and the gratification of national sentiment by the creation of Soviet-style republics for the Serbs, Croats, Slovenes, Macedonians and 'Bosnians', plus autonomous provinces within Serbia for Kosovo (with its large Albanian population) and the Vojvodina (with its Magyar minority). Initially the centre was firmly in control. But the 1960s saw a general devolution of power to the republican level and the curbing of the security apparatus. In Croatia this opened the way to pressure for the use in schools of the Croatian rather than the 'Serbo-Croat' language and for the elimination of Serb over-representation in the republic's economic and political life. The Serb minority was alarmed; and in 1971 Tito warned that 'in some villages . . . the Serbs are drilling and arming themselves . . . Do we want to have 1941 again?' That December he forced the resignation of the Croatian leadership, declaring that it had been moving 'little by little towards a separatist line'; 'if we had not stopped that, . . . perhaps in six months it would have come to shooting, to a civil war'.[33]

Surprisingly Tito did not re-assert institutionalised central control. Rather the 1974 constitution provided for a collective 'presidency' consisting of a delegate from each republic *and autonomous province*, plus a weak and rotating federal executive, with the understanding that after Tito's death the formal office of president would rotate too. The system appeared to survive Tito's death in 1980. But the economy deteriorated and grievances mounted – with Serbia upset by the weight the richer Slovenia and Croatia enjoyed in economic decision-making, worried about the position of Serbs in Croatia, and alarmed by the situation in the province of Kosovo. This lay at the heart of Serbs' self-consciousness, their national day commemorating defeat there by the Ottomans in 1389. But by the 1980s it had a large and growing Albanian majority, the product partly of differential birth-rates, partly of Serb emigration that may have reflected economic forces but that Serbs blamed on 'terror' and on discrimination by the province's Albanian leadership. In 1987 the new party leader of Serbia, Slobadan Milosevic, visited Kosovo and promised its Serbs that 'nobody would ever beat them again'. Over the next couple of years he played the national card – staging huge patriotic rallies that topped the leaderships in Vojvodina and in Montenegro (which has always been ultra-Serb in sentiment), using force in Kosovo and intimidating its assembly into accepting a new constitution that in effect restored Serbia as a unitary state.

None of this went down well in Slovenia or Croatia; accordingly Milosevic was to talk of 'fascist hatred' by Slovenes of Serbia, and his press of an 'anti-Serbian coalition' of Croats and Slovenes. For its part Slovenia was, in 1989, moving towards liberalism and nationalism, permitting the formation of independent parties, and in September declaring itself to be a 'sovereign and autonomous state' with the right to veto the application of federal legislation and, *in extremis*, to secede. Milosevic had pressed for an extraordinary congress of the League of Communists of Yugoslavia to address the political crisis, but it backfired. Unable to halt its convocation, the Slovenes campaigned for the legitimation of 'multiparty pluralism' and the division of the League into eight independent parties, while Serbia stressed the need for 'democratic centralism' and warned that the Slovenes were creating a climate

---

33. Dennison Rusinow, *The Yugoslav Experiment 1948–1974* (1977) Chaps. 7, 8

for 'internecine war'. In January 1990 the congress endorsed the abolition of the party's guaranteed leading role, but refused to permit its division along national lines; whereupon the Slovenes walked out.[34] Then in April–May 1990 opposition nationalists won elections in Slovenia and Croatia.

Both Slovenia and Croatia said they wanted to stay in 'Yugoslavia', but in a very loose confederation. In December 1990, a Slovene referendum called for independence unless such a confederation was agreed to within six months. The omens were not good. Serbia and Slovenia had been imposing escalating mutual sanctions ever since Belgrade had ordered a cutting of industrial links in December 1989. In December 1990 Serbia helped itself to the equivalent of $1.4 billion from the Yugoslav National Bank. In May 1991 Serbia blocked the accession of the Croat Vice-President to the office of President of Yugoslavia (which, by convention, it was his turn to hold by rotation) despite his warning that this would lead to immediate Croat moves to secession. Last minute talks failed, despite the European Community's diplomatic intervention and attempt to use its economic power to promote a continued, but loose, Yugoslav state; in late June both Croatia and Slovenia declared their independence.[35]

There had been informal intimations that Yugoslavia might accept a Slovene but not a Croat secession. In fact there were air raids on, and some fighting in, Slovenia. But Slovenia had acquired arms (probably from Austria) and managed to trap Yugoslav troops ignominiously in their barracks. After it had undertaken in early July to release its prisoners, it was basically left alone; and in October the Yugoslav army agreed to leave.

Croatia was another matter: it was far more central to the continued existence of a meaningful Yugoslavia; and (unlike Slovenia) it had a Serb minority, 12 per cent in numerical terms but occupying nearly a third of its territory. The victorious party in the 1990 elections had fought a strongly nationalist campaign. In office, President Tudjman excluded any possibility of 'a state within a state', and he did not come round to offering the Serb regions autonomy until July 1991. There is, though, no certainty that Serbs could ever have been persuaded to live as a minority in a Croat state. In July 1990 Serb leaders had asserted their sovereignty and autonomy and called a referendum for August; Croat attempts to

---

34. *Keesing's* 36398, 36899, 37155, 37172–3
35. *Keesing's*, 37130, 37867, 37294, 37973–4, 38203–4, 38274–5

ban this led to a Serb rising in Knin; in October the 'Serbian National Council' proclaimed an 'autonomous region', with clear support from Belgrade. In 1991 clashes became more frequent, with the federal Yugoslav army sometimes intervening to protect Serb insurgents; and Croatia's moves towards secession from Yugoslavia were paralleled by Serb votes either to remain in it or to accede to Serbia in accordance with 'the principle that all Serbs should live in one state'. Croatia had made fewer military preparations than Slovenia; and by September it had lost a third of its territory to local insurgents backed by the federal army. By January 1992, 15 cease-fires had been negotiated through the good offices of the European Community, later reinforced by the United Nations. The last, brokered by the UN, proved rather more lasting than its predecessors; Serbia insisted in February on its acceptance by the self-proclaimed autonomous regions, and the UN went ahead from April with the full deployment of a 10,000 strong 'Protection Force'. As Croatia had feared, its chief effect was to stabilise the existing partition of the country; and the UN's inability to unblock the north-south highway led in January 1993 to a partially successful Croat offensive to do so.[36]

But if Croatia quietened down in 1992, a worse flare-up succeeded in Bosnia. In December 1991 Germany tired of the EC's policy of trying vainly to halt the fighting while keeping Yugoslavia together as a unit. At the Maastricht summit it brought the EC to agree in principle to recognise Slovenia and Croatia, and to invite any other republics that wished to apply for recognition. Macedonia and Bosnia did so. Macedonia then declared its independence in January 1992; and, though Greek hostility in fact blocked EC recognition, no catastrophic consequences have so far (1993) followed. Bosnia was persuaded to hold back until after a referendum. In this the Moslems (44 per cent of the population) and Croats (17 per cent) voted overwhelmingly for independence, while the Serbs (31 per cent, but occupying considerably over a third of the territory) abstained, their leader declaring that 'we are not going to accept an independent Bosnia-Hercegovina'. Independence was proclaimed on 3 March 1992. The EC then brokered an agreement to divide the country into ten provinces, of which all (bar the capital, Sarajevo) would, though containing important

36. *Keesing's*, 37381, 37622, 37666, 37789–90, 38204, 38275, 38375, 38704, 38778–9, 39279, 39471–2, 1993 R103; the Jan. 1993 fighting was ended by a May cease-fire brokered by Russia

minorities from other groups, be designated as Serb, Moslem or Croat. But the (Moslem) President Izetbegovic, an advocate of a unitary and non-racial state, reneged. Serb leaders then proclaimed the 'Serbian Republic of Bosnia-Hercegovina'. As forecast by UN representatives on the ground, fighting mounted rapidly. The international community readily recognised Bosnia; but the Bosnian Serbs, armed by the former Yugoslav federal army, soon secured the greater part of the country. By November it was being claimed that 100,000 people had been killed and 800,000 displaced – with Serb forces carrying through a policy of 'ethnic cleansing' of their conquests by expulsion, murder and systematic rape. The UN deployed a protection force of 21,000 and busied itself with the distribution of humanitarian aid that did much to ward off starvation in the winter. But, as in Croatia, negotiated cease-fires long proved meaningless.[37]

1993 appeared to bring a change when patient diplomacy by EC and UN mediators secured Moslem and Croat acceptance of the 'Vance-Owen' plan for ethnic provinces (adapted from that briefly agreed in March 1992). In April Serbia itself (following pressure from the Orthodox countries closest to it, Greece and Russia) advised the Bosnian Serbs to accept 'Vance-Owen'. They refused; and there was considerably less than met the eye in Serbia's closing of its borders to induce them to think again. There then followed a reversal of alliances, both on the ground and diplomatically. The Bosnian Croats had initially allied with the Moslems against the Serbs; but as early as July 1992 they had (despite President Tudjman's apparent disapproval) formed a Croat state of 'Western Bosnia'. There had subsequently been sporadic Croat-Moslem clashes; then in the summer of 1993 both groups, having been taught that possession is nine-tenths of the law, started to scramble for territory in central Bosnia (with the Serbs moving towards the sidelines, or extending minor assistance towards the Croats). Meanwhile in June, Presidents Milosevic and Tudjman (who had long been rumoured to be negotiating secretly) tabled a plan for the subdivision of Bosnia into three autonomous ethnically–based states. Owen, and Vance's replacement, Stoltenberg, managed to rework it somewhat in the Moslem interest, then put it in August to Izetbegovic as the best that could be obtained by a group that had

37. *Keesing's*, 38684–5, 38832–3, 1993 R101-2; *The Annual Register. A Record of World Events* (ed. A.J. Day) *1991* p.173, *1992* pp. 123–5

469

clearly lost the war. After some thought he rejected not the principle but the geographic details.[38]

The 'Yugoslav' tragedy is the product of local factors. But outside attempts to calm it have had a melancholy history. The EC stepped in diplomatically in 1991 with some enthusiasm, hoping to demonstrate that it was now an actor in foreign as well as economic policy and that it could manage a crisis on its doorstep. It could not; and the manner of its switch from trying to keep Yugoslavia together as a unit to recognising the seceding Republics laid it open to charges of having encouraged the Bosnian secession and consequent civil war. The UN has fared slightly better. Its achievement of a cease-fire in Croatia in January 1992 may only have reflected the fact that Serbs had now made all the conquests they felt they really needed. But the UN has the machinery for deploying peace-keeping troops on a scale far exceeding the EC's civilian 'observers'. Its 'Protection Force' has, however, confined itself to the roles of negotiating, neutralising strategic territory, and above all delivering humanitarian aid. The UN's more coercive actions have so far (1993) proved largely ineffective. Indeed the ban on arms deliveries has worked to the advantage of Serbs, who have access to the munitions of the former federal army. But repeal has been opposed by Britain and France, who fear that it would escalate the level of violence and conceivably even lead to offsetting Russian counter-supply to Serbia. The US has accordingly failed to carry repeal through the Security Council; and there is a possibility that it could be vetoed there. The UN's 'no-fly zone' in Bosnia, declared in December 1992, has simply not been enforced. Economic sanctions, imposed on Serbia in May 1992, have been more successful in grinding down an already ailing economy than in altering Milosevic's behaviour. They may, indeed, have inclinded him to urge peace on the Bosnian Serbs in April, and then again in the summer, of 1993; but they have not so far (1993) induced him to bring pressure to bear on the scale applied to Croatian Serbs in 1992.

There have, accordingly, been many calls for military intervention by outside powers (especially as the quality of the forces fighting in Croatia and Bosnia appears to have been low). But some of the countries best placed to intervene (Germany, Italy, Turkey) are estopped for historical reasons. Britain and France, on whom

38. *Keesing's*, 39425–7, 39471, 39517; *Annual Register 1992* pp.123–5. The pattern of three way (though previously Croat-Muslim) fighting on the ground, and continued mediation (and refinement of the offers by Serbia and Croatia) in Geneva continued for the rest of 1993

much of the burden would fall, are reluctant to incur casualties in a Balkan war that they believe would develop into a major and messy operation. Also, like the other countries with troops deployed in the UN peace-keeping force, (and like the UN secretariat), they do not wish to endanger their people on the ground – and end their relief activities – by military action that would alienate one (or more) of the contending communities. In 1993 the USA emerged as a strong advocate of intervention from the air. But this would have been simpler in Croatia in 1991 (when Dubrovnik and Vukovar were being attacked by recognisable conventional military units) than in the diffuse fighting and mountainous terrain of Bosnia. Moreover the USA has been handicapped diplomatically by the fact that it does not have troops on the ground, and that (in the spring of 1993) it backed out even from contributing them to supervise the implementation of the Vance-Owen plan when this seemed likely to be accepted locally. Accordingly, though the USA has managed to secure planning for (and threats of) NATO air strikes in certain contingencies, by December 1993 none had been made. Instead the predominant line of policy, agreed by the USA, Russia, France, Britain and Spain in the aftermath of the Vance-Owen plan's rejection, has been to work to 'contain' the fighting to Bosnia, while trying pacifically to mitigate its effects there.[39]

39. *Keesing's*, 39469, 39517

PART IV
Conclusion

CHAPTER SEVENTEEN

Perspectives on the Cold War

We are still too close to the Cold War for it to be really possible to distinguish the wood for the trees. It seems unexceptionable to conclude that the contest resulted from an admixture of ideology and geopolitics, both being necessary prerequisites. Had Stalin, after 1945, confined himself to the borders of the USSR (even as enlarged by the war) but continued to rule within them in his evil prewar style, he would probably not have been perceived as a major threat; it is most unlikely that the USA would have mobilised itself (through the Long Telegram, Truman Doctrine, Marshall Aid, and so on) to provide sustained, expensive, and burdensome leadership to a 'Free World' coalition – or that it would have been pressed to assume such a role.[1] It would, however, presumably have concluded with the Soviet Union, and the rest of the victorious alliance, the twenty-five (or more) year treaties of guarantee against renewed German or Japanese aggression that it offered in 1945–6 and, in contrast to 1920, would probably have ratified them. The United States would still have disliked communism intensely, and there might have been an internal Red Scare reminiscent of the early 1920s. But Soviet ideology alone, had it been effectively confined to the USSR as in the interwar period, would not have generated the Cold War as we know it. The war, however, had shattered the geopolitical constellation that had kept the Soviet Union and its purportedly universal ideology so constrained; Soviet and communist advance (the two being, in the Europe of the 1940s, initially indistinguishable) met United States containment. Here one can

---

1. cf. Geir Lundestad, 'Empire by Invitation? The United States and Western Europe, 1945–1952', *Journal of Peace Research* xxiii (1986) pp.263–77

see the consequences of the 'power vacuum' in Central Europe created by the defeat of Germany. Although the USA was certainly averse (as it showed in two world wars) to the dominance of the continent by a Power it distrusted, had events in the later 1930s led instead to an Anglo-French coalition toppling the Fascist Powers and restoring the imbalance of the 1920s, it would almost certainly have applauded. The world would then have continued safe for an 'isolationist' USA; it is most unlikely that the United States' theoretical anti-imperialism would have brought serious conflict with the 'liberal' empires of Britain and France, any more than it had done earlier. Both ideological and geopolitical considerations, then, featured in the first phases of the Cold War.

As time went on, the USSR came, especially under Brezhnev, to seem an increasingly 'normal', even conservative, state, paying no more than lip-service to 'communism' at home, and behaving like a restrained and cautious Great Power abroad. As far as Europe was concerned, this was probably true – Brezhnev may well have antici- pated no change for the foreseeable future; and even in the Middle East he was strongly attracted to a settlement to be jointly imposed by the two superpowers. However Brezhnev seems never to have wavered in his commitment to Soviet military build-up and when, in his later years, opportunities occurred in the Third World, he not only took them but also justified the process by a Khruschevian invocation of *competitive* 'peaceful coexistence' and the ineluctable advance of socialism. US anti-communists, for their part, picked up both these developments and used them to discredit détente (which they had already done much to damage by refusing the USSR 'most favoured nation' trade status, ostensibly on human rights grounds). So the stage was set for the 'Second Cold War' of the early 1980s. There then followed a quite unexpected denouement: Gorbachev decided to transform the Soviet Union and its international posture. This meant, in the first place, ending its antagonistic stance towards the United States (and the 'West' generally); then reducing defence expenditure and switching military doctrine from the offensive to the defensive; and finally accepting the collapse of communism in Eastern Europe, a remarkable exercise in self- abnegation to which the USSR could certainly not have been compelled. This collapse ended the adversary relationship of East and West (as was formally recognised in, for instance, the 1990 Charter of Paris). In 1991, however, in combination with his own domestic reforms, it also destroyed Soviet communism, the unity of the USSR, and Gorbachev's own domestic position. In these transformations, ideological shifts within the Soviet Union played the primary role, though of course they had (in Soviet economic retardation) an important non-ideological cause, and they led to major geopolitical consequences.

Historians are unlikely to abandon some such picture of the interweaving of ideology and geopolitics, but future developments may influence the weight they give to each. Were, for instance, Russia to revert to an étatiste authoritarianism, not communist but (in the tsarist sense of these terms) slavo-phile and 'Eastern', friction with the United States and Western Europe would again mount: in December 1992 the Russian Foreign Minister gave a 'hoax' speech by way of warning of what might be expected from a regime of this nature. Although such a Russia would, at least for a time, be weaker than the old USSR, one might come to see an essential continuity in which seventy years of 'communism' would appear merely the temporary vehicle for a more deep-rooted geopolitical division between Russia and most of the rest of Europe.

It is possible to sketch many other possible interpretations of the Cold War. One would be the fairy story: the evil empire vanished, and everybody lived happily ever after. This vision was explicitly invoked by the Prague demonstrations that brought down communist rule in the 1989 'velvet revolution'.[2] It was widely shared at the time in both Eastern Europe and the Soviet Union. The West would extend massive aid, and so soon help to create in the rest of Europe prosperous free-market democracies. Alas, this was too simple. There was Western assistance,[3] but not on a Marshall Aid scale. Nor was the creation either of market economies or of stable and secure democracies easy. Both may yet be achieved (though probably not universally). Even in the former East Germany, which was incorporated into a strong democracy and given massive economic aid, the process has generated unemployment and anomie and been disfigured by outbreaks of xenophobic and nationalist violence. Elsewhere it could be that the collapse of communist stability will lead, especially in multinational states, to inter-ethnic violence. This indeed happened in 'Yugoslavia' after 1991 (though the rise of nationalism there was only partly due to the collapse of communism)[4] and also in what had been Soviet Central Asia and

2. Observer, *Tearing down the Curtain* p.111
3. Symbolically, the food stockpiled in West Berlin as insurance against a second blockade was sent east to help the USSR
4. Slobodan Milosevic began to bid for real power as the exponent of Serbian nationalism in 1987–8, well before the collapse of communism: *Keesing's*, 35795 ff, 36374–6

the Caucasus. The process could spread widely enough to make mature communism (as distinct from the earlier Stalinist variety) appear comparatively benign.

The Cold War was by no means unique in being largely an ideological contest, nor was it the longest period of bipolar international rivalry; and it ended peacefully with the two sides embracing like teams after a football match, not with the fire and sword of (say) the duel between Rome and Carthage. As it recedes in time, the Cold War is bound to be seen increasingly in the context of earlier parallels. But of which will depend partly on developments still in the future. In the early seventh century the Byzantine Empire was more strenuously beset, and more nearly brought down, by Persia than ever the USA was by the USSR. It broke back and imposed peace on its long-standing rival, which then collapsed into civil war. However the real victors were the hitherto unconsidered Arabs, who burst in from the south, inspired by a new religion, swallowed Persia, drove back Byzantium, and lapped the southern Mediterranean (eventually) as far as the Pyrenees. In much the same way, future historians could come to view the Cold War chiefly as the prelude to the rise of China in the twenty-first century.

Of course the Cold War took place in a far larger geographical theatre than did the Roman(Byzantine) Persian conflict. Indeed it touched almost all continents, though some of them only fairly lightly. But its spread was not much wider than that of some of its predecessors, for instance the mid-eighteenth-century contest between Britain and France, of which Macaulay wrote that the European peace of 1748

> had not even been an armistice in other quarters of the globe. In India the sovereignty of the Carnatic was disputed between two great Mussulman houses; Fort St. George had taken one side, Pondicherry the other; and in a series of battles . . . the troops of Lawrence and Clive had been opposed to those of Dupleix. A struggle less important in its consequences, but not less likely to produce irritation, was carried on between those French and English adventurers, who kidnapped negroes and collected gold dust on the coast of Guinea. But it was in North America that the emulation . . . of the two nations was most conspicuous. The French attempted to hem in the English colonists by a chain of military posts, extending from the Great Lakes to the mouth of the Mississipi. The English took up arms. The wild aboriginal tribes appeared on each side mingled with the Pale Faces. Battles were fought; forts were stormed; and hideous stories . . . reached Europe, and inflamed that national animosity which the rivalry of ages had produced. The disputes between France and England came to a crisis at

the very time when the tempest which had gathered was about to burst on Prussia. . . . France became the tool of Austria; and Frederic was forced to become the ally of England.

So perhaps the only way in which the Cold War was unique was that its chief protagonists – unlike any of their predecessors – had weapons capable of destroying all civilised human life. It may be that this leap in destructive power has produced a fundamental change in the international environment, excluding head-on war between Great Powers. If so, future rivalries may take the form of trade wars, or be decided – as the Soviet–American one was in the 1980s – by the perceived superiority of one economic and socio-political system. Trade wars did not feature much in our story: there was not enough East–West trade. But ever since Stalin's first Five Year Plan, the Soviet system had prided itself on delivering economic growth. Khrushchev had been confident that socialism would triumph through its ability thus to surpass the United States; in practice the reverse proved the case. Economic prowess had, of course, long been recognised as a factor in international politics. But that quite so much should turn on the relative performance of rival systems (as opposed to the ability of one to do the other direct harm)[5] was new. In this sense the Cold War could come to be seen as a transitional stage in the evolution of international competition away from the more conventional power politics typical of earlier periods.

Finally, though the Cold War was projected into the Third World (and all the fighting that it entailed took place there), it was essentially a competition between two 'developed' Northern blocs. The 'North' may well continue to determine the parameters of the international system and to provide its chief players. It is also possible to see the axis of politics moving, after the end of the Cold War, to North–South relationships, whether of relatively amicable mutual development (along the lines of the explosion of Pacific-rim and trans-Pacific trade in the 1970s and 1980s) or of a more hostile and Malthusian confrontation. Were this to happen, we could well look back on the Cold War as a hold-over, or even (metaphorically) as a dinosaur surviving some way into a radically new political environment.

---

5. As in the case of e.g. the confrontation between Napoleon's 'Continental System' and the counter-blockade of the British 'Orders in Council'

Guide to Further Reading

While there are many things that we do not know, there is no quantitative shortage of secondary – or even primary – sources. It has, indeed, been calculated that 20 per cent of all US doctoral theses on US foreign relations submitted in 1979–82 covered topics within the years 1945–50, while nearly half the Society for Historians of American Foreign Relations' *Guide to Diplomatic History since 1700* (ed. R.D. Burns, Santa Barbara, Calif., 1982) related to the period since 1945. Admittedly our sources have a serious bias towards the United States: not only has the USA been the most important single actor in international affairs since 1945, but it also has led the way in the release, publication, and (some would say) multiplication of historical documents. Scholars have tended to give it if anything disproportionate attention, partly for these reasons, partly (in some cases) from sheer insularity, and partly because, where space is short, it is easier to structure one's writing around an American or a 'bipolar' USA–USSR, than around a multilateral, framework. There is also a question of national perspectives. Most scholars underplay the appreciable Canadian contribution to international diplomacy in the first two postwar decades; some Canadians err in the opposite direction; the result is a distinctive Canadian historiography. The same is true, to a lesser extent, in connection with Britain and France.

Postwar, like earlier, historiography has proceeded on the basis of a voluminous public record (of official documents and statements, parliamentary debates, press releases and comment, and the like). This is shaped and built on by memoirs, biographies, 'instant histories' (often by able and well-informed journalists), and comment and analysis by students of the contemporary scene. Even

such recent events as the 1989 collapse of communism in Eastern
Europe, the 1990 reunification of Germany, and the 1991 Gulf War
have been so covered. But the blanket release of the confidential
documents shaping and recording government deliberations and
decisions takes much longer. The UK (whose archives are among
the better organised and more accessible) operates a thirty-year rule
(with derogations), which means that the frontier of classic
document-based history now lies in the 1960s, with what one might
term cultivated territory not extending quite so far. Much the same
is true of the USA: study of the Truman and Eisenhower administrations is qualitatively different from that of their successors. But
our knowledge of these is much expanded by a combination of:
presidential libraries (each President is entitled to one, and, though
security classification still applies, they make available documents
that would in most other countries remain confidential); widespread declassification under the Freedom of Information Act; and
massive leaks, plus investigations into the Central Intelligence
Agency, in the 1970s.

At the opposite extreme, until recently, lay the communist bloc,
where archives were closed and information went little beyond the
public record; most memoirs have been fairly uninformative, with
the significant exception of Khrushchev's taped reminiscences
unofficially published in the West. With the collapse of communism
there has been an opening up. However (with the exception of the
former East Germany, whose archives have been opened wide after
unification) this has mostly meant the extraction of nuggets of
information – for specific conferences (like those on the Cuban
missile crisis), for political reasons (material on the 1968 intervention was turned over by the Russian to the Czech government in
1991–2), for general interest, and indeed for money – rather than
an orderly opening of the archives as a whole. Nevertheless these
revelations have altered our picture of a number of episodes
(notably the Cuban missile crisis) and, indeed, prompted the
declassification of some related US material; they have settled some
controversies (notably on the origins of the Korean War); and they
have strongly impacted on others. It is likely, too, that, over time,
our perceptions of the Cold War will be substantially changed by
the availability of such new material, just as the focus of interwar
history (originally set largely by captured German documents)
shifted markedly with the opening of the British documents and is
now shifting again to take account of French ones.

For documents in the public domain, two convenient sources are

J.A.S. Grenville, *The Major International Treaties 1914–1973: A History and Guide with Texts* (1974), and the series of *Documents on International Affairs* (nearly one volume for each year down to 1963) produced for the Royal Institute of International Affairs. The RIIA also published a companion series, *Survey of International Affairs* (whose last volume also covers 1963). An enormous amount of material is contained in *Keesing's Contemporary Archives* – since 1987 *Keesing's Record of World Events* – (until 1973, Keynsham, Bristol, thereafter London), a well-indexed press digest with (in recent years) annual updates of developments by country (especially useful for small countries) and international organisation. Also valuable are the (London) International Institute for Strategic Studies' (IISS) annual *Strategic Survey*, and its series of *Adelphi Papers* (short monographs on issues and developments of recent or current interest). A similar series is *The Washington Papers* (Praeger, with the Center for Strategic and International Studies, Washington). *The World Today* (London) contains academic articles on recent events that emerge more rapidly than do their counterparts in heavyweight publications like *Foreign Affairs* (New York) and *International Affairs* (London); these in turn are less conventionally historical than *Diplomatic History* (Wilmington, Del.) or other scholarly journals.

By far the most extensive published collection of primary sources is the Department of State's *Foreign Relations of the United States* (*FRUS*) (Washington, DC). Publication up to 1957 is nearly complete; a start has been made on later years, with the 1964–8 sub-series just beginning. Even *FRUS* cannot include everything, and the more recent sub-series are noticeably thinner than their predecessors. There is, too, a certain bias towards US State Department documents, which are not necessarily the most useful; of those bearing on the Middle East in 1956 it has been noted that the editor '"did not have access to the full range of documentation on US intelligence operations and the diplomacy of the Suez crisis". Those interested in the CIA-MI6 plot to overthrow the Syrian government . . . will have to look elsewhere'; they also contain nothing on the US Treasury's crucial dealings with the IMF. Nevertheless *FRUS* constitutes an enormous quarry, useful for the history of many countries besides the USA. The trouble, for most people, is that *FRUS* is too large. This prompted Geoffrey Warner's review of 'twelve massive volumes of American diplomatic documents for 1945' – 'The United States and the Origins of the Cold War', *International Affairs* xlvi (1970) – and its sequels: 'The Truman Doctrine and the Marshall Plan', ibid, l (1974); 'The Division of

Germany 1946–1948', ibid, li (1975); 'The United States and the Rearmament of West Germany, 1950–4', ibid, lxi (1985); 'The United States and Vietnam 1945–1965', two articles in ibid, xlviii (1972) surveying the leaked *United States–Vietnam Relations 1945–1967* based, as its common title *The Pentagon Papers* implies, on Defense Department documents, plus 'The United States and Vietnam: Two Episodes', ibid, lxv (1989) reviewing the *FRUS* coverage of the decision to extend aid to France in 1950 and the debate over US military intervention in April 1954; 'The United States and the Suez Crisis', ibid, lxvii (1991); and 'Eisenhower, Dulles and the Unity of Western Europe, 1955–1957', ibid, lxix (1993). Supplementing *FRUS*, and often extending to a later date, are documents released under the Freedom of Information Act, which have been published on microfiche (initially by Carrolton Press Inc., Washington, DC, currently by its new owners Research Publications Inc. (Woodbridge, Conn., and Reading, England). Unlike *FRUS*, these documents are not edited into orderly volumes, but Carrolton and (from July–Sept. 1981) Research Publications have produced indexes in the form of *The Declassified Documents: Retrospective Collection* (3 vols, Washington, DC, 1976) and *Declassified Documents Quarterly Catalog* (Washington, DC, then Woodbridge, Conn. 1975–).

Both Britain and France have begun publishing their postwar documents, but neither has anything comparable in scope with *FRUS*. Such collections simply do not exist for the USSR or other ex-communist or communist countries. A *Cold War International History Project* was established in late 1991 with a three-year grant, to disseminate information now emerging from communist sources; operating from the Woodrow Wilson International Center (1000 Jefferson Drive, SW, Washington, DC), it publishes a *Bulletin* and periodic Working Papers. The result is inevitably rather bitty, but both interesting and useful.

As for secondary sources, 'of the making of books there is no end'; new and valuable ones are continually emerging. Most of the works that I have used are referred to in my footnotes, but both that choice and the suggestions that follow here should be seen only as indicative rather than in any way comprehensive or exclusive.

Writing on the origins of the Cold War has gone through many phases, classified by John L. Gaddis in 'The Emerging Post-Revisionist Synthesis on the Origins of the Cold War', *Diplomatic History* vii (1983) as 'orthodox', 'revisionist' and 'post-revisionist' (though some scholars have resisted such classification, preferring to class themselves as 'honest eclectics'). Gaddis's own *The United States and the Origins of the Cold War, 1941–1947* (New York, 1972) had been broadly 'orthodox'. Such basically benign interpretations of US foreign policy were challenged, especially in the 1960s and 1970s, by writers (frequently of the New Left) who portrayed it as driven by the search for economic profit and expansion abroad (often under the impact of pressures inherent in the USA's own internal economic structure), and as using the fear of communism to effect repressive changes in US domestic society and politics. 'Revisionists' tended also to doubt whether Soviet communism was expansionist, to portray Stalin's actions as essentially fearful and defensive responses, and so to see the Cold War as, at best, an inevitable process of action and reaction, at worst as primarily the product of US initiatives. Moderate versions of this approach would include Walter LaFeber, *America, Russia and the Cold War* (New York, 1967, with many later editions), extreme versions Joyce Kolko and Gabriel Kolko, *The Limits of Power: The World and United States Foreign Policy, 1945–54* (New York, 1972). As the domestic US scene calmed down, so did its polemic. In Gaddis's view this led to a 'post-revisionist synthesis' that accepted the concept of an American 'empire', albeit (he thought) one that was both 'defensively' motivated and often welcomed abroad; it also conceded that US diplomacy had used economic instruments and pressures, that there had been some exaggeration of external dangers to achieve domestic political goals, and that Stalin had been an 'opportunist' with no 'ideological blue-print for world revolution'. Gaddis continued, however, to reject much 'revisionist' writing; some critics have termed 'post-revisionism' 'orthodoxy plus archives'. There was, then, no monolithic unity. Most of the general accounts one would now recommend come from this period, however, notably Daniel Yergin, *Shattered Peace: The Origins of the Cold War and the National Security State* (Boston, Mass., 1977), and William Taubman, *Stalin's American Policy: From Entente to Detente to Cold War* (New York, 1982), which is unusual, among the works we have been considering, in its use of such communist sources as were then available. These were, of course, relatively few and of much lower quality than the Western documents. They still are. But we can expect important new material, which will eventually lead to a 'post-post-revisionist' phase in Cold War studies. There will presumably be some surprises, and some radical displacements of focus. On the basis of what has emerged so far, the new material seems more likely to strengthen the 'orthodox' than the 'revisionist' case.

'Revisionism' as such was an American phenomenon, but it is not only in connection with the US that the 'official' and/or traditional views of postwar developments can be challenged. Anne Deighton (ed.) *Britain and the First Cold War* (Basingstoke, 1990) not only presents the claim that British policy in the period was of far more importance than many US historians have recognised, but also demonstrates that in 1946 Britain (and especially the Foreign Office) gave up on cooperation with the USSR in Germany – and that thereafter it was chiefly concerned so to play things that the breakdown should appear to be the USSR's fault and redound to the advantage of the West. Of course the impact of this finding depends largely on what Stalin's German intentions really were; there is now some material, noticed in R.C. Raack, 'Stalin Plans his Post-War Germany', *Journal of Contemporary History* xxviii (1993), to suggest that already by June 1945 he was, though aspiring to a united communist-dominated country, immediately projecting the existence of two Germanies.

The 1945–55 handling of Germany has always been controversial. From a Western perspective, the greater part of the country was 'saved' from communism, rehabilitated, and erected into a successful state well integrated into a new and peaceful Europe. This story is told in, for instance, John Gimbel, *The American Occupation of Germany: Politics and the Military, 1945–49* (Stanford, Calif., 1968), Avi Shlaim, *The United States and the Berlin Blockade, 1948–1949: A Study in Crisis Decision-Making* (Berkeley, Calif., 1983), Michael J. Hogan, *The Marshall Plan: America, Britain and the Reconstruction of Western Europe, 1947–1952* (Cambridge, 1987), and, of course, in Hans-Peter Schwarz's biography of Adenauer (*Adenauer: der Aufstieg, 1876–1952* and *Adenauer: der Staatsman, 1952–1967*, Stuttgart, 1986 and 1991). Social Democrats at the time saw some, at least, of these policies as needlessly sealing the division of Germany (at least until 1990). Revisionist historians returned to this perspective, and also demonstrated that, despite official rhetoric, the outcome was by no means necessarily unwelcome in London and Paris. In this tradition are Josef Foschepoth (ed.), *Adenauer und die deutsche Frage* (Göttingen, 1988) and Rolf Steininger, *Eine Chance zur Wiedervereinigung? Die Stalin-Note von 10 März 1952* (*Archiv für Sozialgeschichte*, Beiheft 12, 1985 – abbreviated translation, *The German Question: The Stalin Note of 1952 and the Problem of Reunification* – New York, 1990). Now, however, there are indications (though not as yet categoric proof) that the Stalin note was not a genuine offer; and James Richter, *Reexamining Soviet Policy towards Germany during the Beria*

Interregnum (*Cold War International History Project* Working Paper no. 3, Washing- ton, DC, 1992) shows that though Beria, in 1953, advocated readiness to negotiate East Germany away, he was unable to persuade his colleagues, and that Soviet policy hardened after his fall.

Deighton's *Britain and the First Cold War* did not, of course, confine itself to the German question; it also contains (inter alia) John Kent's suggestion that Britain's efforts to redefine its Medi- terranean position and global role 'were a prime cause of growing contention in 1945, and therefore an important element in the origins of the cold war'. Evaluating this claim demands a detailed study of these frictions. It has been argued that the origins of the Cold War should now be approached through the investigation of a series of discrete issues. Judgements appropriate to one may not always fit another: there can be little doubt, for instance, that the great majority of Turks welcomed US support against Soviet pressure, but Greece, as its civil war shows, was more divided. Many books could be listed in connection with such case studies. Perhaps it is enough to refer the reader, as a starting-point, to R. Jervis and J. Snyder (eds) *Dominoes and Bandwagons: Strategic Beliefs and Great Power Competition in the Eurasian Rimland* (New York, 1991).

The Korean War, however, may deserve a little more attention here in view of its remarkable impact on developments in a wide and disparate range of contexts. It is covered in, for instance, Peter Lowe, *The Origins of the Korean War* (1986), in Rosemary Foot, *The Wrong War: American Policy and the Dimensions of the Korean Conflict, 1950–1953* (Ithaca, NY, 1985), and in her review article, 'Making Known the Unknown War: Policy Analysis of the Korean Conflict in the Last Decade', *Diplomatic History* xv (1991). Such coverage is, however, inevitably affected by the fact that we know far more of the imperfections of what became South Korea over the period 1945–50 than we do of those of North Korea, far more about American than Soviet or Chinese decision-making. New light is, however, cast both on North Korea's original invasion and on Mao's eagerness to intervene in the subsequent fighting by Kathryn Weathersby, *Soviet Aims in Korea and the Origins of the Korean War, 1945–1950: New Evidence from Russian Archives* and Chen, Jian, *The Sino-Soviet Alliance and China's Entry into the Korean War* (*Cold War International History Project* Working Papers nos. 8, 1 Washington, DC, 1992).

One of the side-effects of the Korean War was the extension of US protection to Taiwan, and the USA's precipitation into a policy of massive rearmament and the geographical extension of 'containment' that had been advocated in the famous policy paper NSC-68. J.L. Gaddis's survey of shifting conceptions of the idea of containment, *Strategies of Containment: A Critical Appraisal of Postwar American National Security Policy* (New York, 1982) has been extremely influential, though I personally prefer his less schematic and more primary-source-based collection of studies, *The Long Peace: Inquiries into the History of the Cold War* (New York, 1987). Both works bear on the comparison between the policies of the Truman and Eisenhower administrations. The latter have recently been receiving enormous historical attention – mostly favourable. Stephen E. Ambrose, *Eisenhower: The President* (1984 – the second part of a two-volume biography) gives a useful overview, while Richard H. Immerman (ed.) *John Foster Dulles and the Diplomacy of the Cold War* (Princeton, NJ, 1990) examines a Secretary of State who (like Eisenhower) was more complex and thoughtful than he seemed. 'Covert action' played a major role in Eisenhower's diplomacy, though it was (of course) by no means confined to his presidency: John Ranelagh, *The Agency: The Rise and Decline of the CIA* (1986) is perhaps the best of many CIA histories, while Nigel West, *The Friends: Britain's Post-war Intelligence Operations* (1988) more briefly describes its UK counterpart. Although historians have recently been intensively mining seams from the Eisenhower era, they have only just begun to move over the border into the Kennedy years. These we have always known quite well from, in particular, Arthur M. Schlesinger's brilliant – if selective – *A Thousand Days: John F. Kennedy in the White House* (Boston, Mass., 1965). Camelot has now faded, and Kennedy's reputation has been heavily discounted: Thomas G. Paterson (ed.) *Kennedy's Quest for Victory: American Foreign Policy, 1961–1963* (New York, 1989) is still, arguably, written on the rebound, but draws on new material.

Khrushchev was Eisenhower and Kennedy's opposite number. In switching our attention to him, we move into a historiographically far dimmer and more uncertain world. J.L. Nogee and R.H. Donaldson, *Soviet Foreign Policy since World War II* (Oxford, 1981) provides a general narrative, Paul Dibb, *The Soviet Union: The Incomplete Superpower* (1986 and 1988 edns) a perceptive (though inevitably dated) analysis. Khrushchev himself was, unlike other Soviet leaders, deposed, and so had time to dictate, and smuggle to the West, bundles of recollections, which have been edited into three volumes of *Khrushchev Remembers* (Boston, Mass., 1971, 1974 and 1990). Inevitably there are episodes, notably his own involvement in Stalin's purges, that he does not dwell on; he is, in any case, only reminiscing without access to documents. But a number of his claims (such as those on the origins of the Korean War or the state of Vietminh disarray in 1954) would seem to have been confirmed, and his account should be treated with respect. Further light is shed on his attitudes in and after 1956 by his lengthy conversations with the Yugoslav ambassador, recorded in V. Micunovic, *Moscow Diary* (1980). There are also interesting vignettes of Khrushchev, and still more of his 1960s successors, in works by Nasser's confidant Mohamed Heikal, notably *Sphinx and Commissar: The Rise and Fall of Soviet Influence in the Arab World* (1978) and *The Road to Ramadan* (1975). Relaxation in and after the Gorbachev era has produced in the Moscow press a flood of reminiscences and memoirs from lesser Soviet officials that have not yet been fully digested by historians.

Khrushchev's years were, 'not by accident', marked by major crises, the most serious (in an East–West context) being the Berlin and the Cuban missile crises. On Berlin the best account may still be Jack M. Schick, *The Berlin Crisis, 1958–1962* (Philadelphia, Pa, 1971), supplemented by William Burr, 'New Sources on the Berlin Crisis, 1958–1962', Cold War International History Project (CWIHP) *Bulletin* ii (1992); important material from the communist side is used by Hope M. Harrison, *Ulbricht and the Concrete 'Rose': New Archival Evidence on the dynamics of Soviet–East German relations and the Berlin Crisis, 1958–61* and Vladislav M. Zubok, *Khrushchev and the Berlin Crisis (1958–62)* (Cold War International History Project Working Papers nos. 5, 6, Washington, DC, 1993). On the Cuban missile crisis, the parameters are well set out in R.L. Garthoff, *Reflections on the Cuban Missile Crisis* (Washington, DC, 1987); even this has been overtaken by a flood of new revelations (both Soviet and American) and declassifications, summarised in Garthoff's 'The Havana Conference on the Cuban Missile Crisis', Cold War International History Project *Bulletin* ii (1992), and there may be more to come.

If, however, Soviet foreign policy lies in half darkness, defence concerns are even more obscure. Crude facts and figures as to spending and hardware are produced annually, for all countries, in the International Institute of Strategic Studies' *The Military Balance.* But inevitably there are secrets: South Africa recently revealed, to the general surprise, that it had in the 1980s possessed nuclear weapons. Nor is it easy to translate into a common currency the defence efforts of very dissimilar countries; this occasioned a major and long-running debate on the true scale of Soviet defence spending. Fortunately the Third World War was never fought, so we can neither tell how appropriate preparations for it were, nor assess the voluminous literature compiled by people seeking to 'think [rationally] about the unthinkable' (much of which has been termed by its detractors 'nuclear theology' – very subtle, but unverifiable and quite possibly remote from reality). We cannot always even distinguish between declaratory and actual policy. A guide to the evolution of US nuclear doctrine is provided by A.L. Friedberg, 'The Evolution of U.S. Strategic Doctrine, 1945–80' in S. P. Huntington (ed.) *The Strategic Imperative: New Policies for American Security* (Cambridge, Mass., 1982) and by D.A. Rosenberg, 'The Origins of Overkill: Nuclear Weapons and American Security, 1945–1960', *International Security* vii (1963). There are interesting sidelights on NATO's actual targeting policy in Richard Ullman, 'The Covert French Connection', *Foreign Policy* lxxv (1989). A.H. Cordesman, *Deterrence in the 1980s: Part 1, American Forces and Extended Deterrence* (IISS Adelphi Paper no. 175, 1982) provides not only valuable tables but also a good expression of the fears that the US 'strategic' deterrent would soon become vulnerable, with important political consequences. These fears came to impinge strongly on the Strategic Arms Limitation Talks and Treaties that lay at the heart of the 1970s US–Soviet détente, and that are well described in R.L. Garthoff, *Détente and Confrontation: American–Soviet Relations from Nixon to Reagan* (Washington, DC, 1985). Commentary on Soviet defence policies is even more a matter of making bricks without straw, but the task has been well attempted by David Holloway, *The Soviet Union and the Arms Race* (New Haven, Conn., 1984 edn), whose focus is chiefly nuclear, and by Michael MccGuire, *Military Objectives in Soviet Foreign Policy* (Washington, DC, 1987), while J. Van Oudenaren uses lightly classified Soviet military journals to write on *Deterrence, War Fighting and Soviet Military Doctrine* (IISS Adelphi Paper no. 210, 1986). 'Warsaw Pact Military Planning in Central Europe: Revelations from the East German Archives', *Cold War International History Project Bulletin* ii (1992) confirm the offensive nature of the Pact's planning but cast doubt on whether there was the degree of interest some have imagined in a non-nuclear offensive.

Of wars fought, as opposed to merely projected, one of the longest was the struggle (nearly continuous, save for the second half of the 1950s) by Ho Chi Minh and his successors for the liberation, control and unification of Vietnam. Direct US participation in this war in the 1960s and 1970s proved traumatic, and has generated a mountain of literature. Other aspects are less well covered; developments in the area after the fall of Saigon are often ignored. Stein Tønnessson, 'The Longest Wars: Indochina 1945–75', *Journal of Peace Research* xxii (1985) has much to say on the origins of the conflict. R.E.M. Irving, *The First Indochina War: French and American Policy 1945–54* (1975) covers events up to the temporary settlement at the 1954 Geneva conference. US interest in Indo-China is also explored in Geoffrey Warner's 1972 and 1989 *International Affairs* articles (cited on p. 483), and in Michael Schaller, 'Securing the Great Crescent: Occupied Japan and the Origins of Containment in Southeast Asia', *Journal of American History* lxix (1982) and J.W. Dower, 'The Superdomino in Asia: Japan in and out of the Pentagon Papers', *Pentagon Papers* (Senator Gravel edn, vol. 5). (These last, by illustrating the perceived connection between the rehabilitation of a Western-oriented Japan and the keeping of Indo-China non-communist and open to Japanese trade, go far to undermine the distinction historians often make between an initial 'selective' and a post-NSC 68 universal containment policy.) Lawrence S. Kaplan, Denise Artaud, Mark R. Rubin (eds.), *Dien Bien Phu and the Crisis of Franco–American Relations, 1954–5* (Wilmington, Del., 1990) describes the ending of the 'First' Vietnam War and the USA's move to become patron of the Dien regime in South Vietnam. The 'Second' War is covered in (among *many* other books): Stanley Karnow, *Vietnam: A History* (1984); William S. Turley, *The Second Indochina War: A Short Political and Military History, 1954–1975* (Boulder, Colo., 1986), which seeks to pay 'special attention to the view-points and strategies of the ultimately victorious parties, particularly the Vietnamese Communists'; and Jeffrey Race, *War Comes to Long An* (Berkeley, Calif., 1972), a study of a single province. International attention shifted away from Indo-China after the fall of Saigon in 1975, but events did not therefore stand still. Some account of subsequent developments is to be found in: King C. Chen, *China's War with Vietnam, 1979* (Stanford, Calif., 1987); Charles McGregor, *The Sino-Vietnamese Relationship and the Soviet Union* (IISS Adelphi Paper no. 232, 1988); and Michael Leifer, *ASEAN and the Security of South-East Asia* (1989).

The Vietnam imbroglio was one of the factors that led Nixon to reverse the hostile US attitude towards China. This attitude had in fact been more sophisticated (at least at the highest level) than it had seemed in the 1950s, as is shown in Gaddis's *The Long Peace* (cited on p. 487). The fullest overall picture is, perhaps, Gordon H.

Chang, *Friends and Enemies: The United States, China and the Soviet Union 1948–1972* (Stanford, Calif., 1990). See also Nancy Bernkopf Tucker, 'China and America: 1941–1991', *Foreign Affairs* lxx (1991) for further reflections on the Sino–American relationship.

Détente with China came to form one half of Nixon's foreign policy, détente with the Soviet Union the other. US–Soviet relations have attracted the more attention. An overall view is given in R.W. Stevenson, *The Rise and Fall of Détente: Relaxations of Tension in U.S.–Soviet Relations, 1953–84* (Basingstoke, 1985), while Brian White, *Britain, Detente and Changing East–West Relations* (1992) argues that the UK contribution has been unduly overlooked. The rise and fall of the 1972 'Moscow' détente is recounted far more fully in Garthoff's massive *Détente and Confrontation* (cited on p. 489); a more Kremlinological analysis, painting a darker portrait of Soviet dynamics, is Harry Gelman, *The Brezhnev Politburo and the Decline of Detente* (Ithaca, NY, 1984). On the American side, assessments of the 'Moscow' détente meld with more general discussion of the Nixon, Kissinger and Carter foreign policies. One source is R.M. Nixon, *The Memoirs of Richard Nixon* (1978); Nixon's presidency is covered more fully in Stephen E. Ambrose, *Nixon: The Triumph of a Politician, 1962–1972* and *Nixon: Ruin and Recovery, 1973–1990* (New York, 1989 and 1991). As time proceeds, greater emphasis will probably be laid on Nixon's personal foreign policy input. At the moment this appears overshadowed by the tour de force of Henry Kissinger (National Security Adviser, then Secretary of State, 1969–77). Kissinger has given us two enormous, and beautifully written, volumes of memoirs, *White House Years* (1979) and *Years of Upheaval* (1982), taking the story up to 1974. Even his enemies would admit that these cite and print copious quantities of documents. But Kissinger certainly has enemies – one useful hatchet job (for the period 1969–73) is Seymour M. Hersh, *The Price of Power: Kissinger in the Nixon White House* (New York, 1983). More detached assessment is to be found in Coral Bell, 'Kissinger in Retrospect: The Diplomacy of Power Concert?', *International Affairs* liii (1977); Hedley Bull, 'Kissinger: The Primacy of Geopolitics', ibid, lvi (1980); and (Sir) Michael Howard, *The Causes of Wars and Other Essays* (1983). Disputes over the Carter administration are less ferocious. But Carter, Vance and Zbigniew Brzezinski have all written their memoirs, with Brzezinski's *Power and Principle: Memoirs of the National Security Adviser 1977–1981* (New York, 1983) being perhaps the most useful. Elie Kedourie offers a devastating review of all three in 'Disastrous Years When US Foreign Policy Fumbled and Stumbled', *Encounter* lxiii (Nov. 1984). Détente, however, was not – especially in Europe – a matter for the United States alone. In the 1960s de Gaulle had spoken (possibly with prescience) of a 'Europe from the Atlantic to the Urals', and had launched overtures towards the East, for which see Jean Lacouture, *De Gaulle: The Ruler* (1991). West Germany followed with what developed into Willy Brandt's *Ostpolitik.* This is described in his *People and Politics: The Years 1960–1975* (1978); for a broader canvas, see also Wolfram Hanrieder (ed.), *West German Foreign Policy 1949–1979* (Boulder, Colo., 1980), and Timothy Garton Ash, *In Europe's Name: Germany and the divided continent* (1993).

The 1980s were a remarkable decade, beginning with talk of a 'Second Cold War' and concluding with the transformation of Eastern Europe and general declarations of amity. Early accounts include Don Oberdorfer, *The Turn: How the Cold War Came to an End. The United States and the Soviet Union 1983–1990* (1992) and Michael J. Hogan (ed.) *The End of the Cold War: Its Meaning and Implications* (Cambridge, 1992). Ronald Reagan, *An American Life* (1990) quotes extensively from his correspondence with Soviet leaders, while George P. Shultz, *Turmoil and Triumph. My Years as Secretary of State* (New York, 1993) is both solid and lengthy. It is clear, though, that the changes stemmed chiefly from developments within the USSR. The Soviet Foreign Minister from 1985 to 1990, Eduard Shevardnadze, has produced his memoirs, *The Future Belongs to Freedom* (1991), but they are more philosophical and less informative than Khrushchev's. Gorbachev, who shifted the levers and set off the process of political change, is still (1993) writing his memoirs; although he has attracted many 'instant' biographies, including Gail Sheehy, *Gorbachev: The Making of the Man who Shook the World* (1991), we await (probably from A.H. Brown) a more substantial and detached study.

It is clear, though, that the Soviet alliance was both more fissiparous and less firmly based than the American. John Gittings produced an excellent *Survey of the Sino-Soviet Dispute: A Commentary and Extracts from Recent Polemics, 1963–1967* (1968), based on exchanges of public criticism. The subject is also covered in Chang's *Friends and Enemies: The United States, China and the Soviet Union 1948–1972* (cited on p. 490), while H.J. Ellison reflects on a longer span of 'Changing Sino-Soviet Relations' in *Problems of Communism* xxxvi (May–June 1987). Immanuel C.Y. Hsü gives us, in *The Rise of Modern China* (New York, 1990 edn), a substantial textbook history of China in and before the twentieth century, which is complemented by Harrison E. Salisbury, *The New Emperors. China in the Era of Mao and Deng* (paperback edn, New York, 1993). J.W. Lewis and Xue, Litang, *China Builds the Bomb* (Stanford, Calif., 1988) sheds light on an important theme in Sino-Soviet relations, using Chinese sources; and Chen, Jian, *The Sino-Soviet Alliance and China's Entry into the Korean War* (cited on p. 486) has much new to say on the 1948–50 period.

None of the USSR's other allies ever aspired to equality with it. Most remained loyal as long as their communist regimes lasted, but Yugoslavia (and later Albania) broke away. On the Tito–Stalin rift, see: Geoffrey Swain, 'The Cominform: Tito's International?', *Historical Journal* xxxv (1992); S. Clissold (ed.) *Yugoslavia and the Soviet Union 1939–1973* (1975); Ivo Banac, *With Stalin against Tito: Cominformist Splits in Yugoslav Communism* (Ithaca, NY, 1988), which, as its title suggests, seeks to emancipate the story from the Titoist canon; and Nora Beloff, *Tito's Flawed Legacy: Yugoslavia and the West 1939–84* (1985). More general surveys of East European developments are to be found in Joseph Rothschild, *Return to Diversity: A Political History of East Central Europe since World War II* (New York, 1989) and Charles Gati, *The Bloc that Failed: Soviet–East European Relations in Transition* (1990). The Observer, *Tearing Down the Curtain: The People's Revolution in Eastern Europe* (1990) provides a good 'instant history' of the remarkable events of 1989; the transformation is further analysed in Alex Pravda (ed.) *The End of the Outer Empire: Soviet–Eastern European Relations in Transition 1985–90* (1992). Mark Almond, *Europe's Backyard War* (1993) addresses the tragic sequel to the collapse of communism in Yugoslavia.

Western Europe is covered in John W. Young, *Cold War Europe 1945–89: A Political History* (1991) and Derek W. Urwin, *Western Europe since 1945* (1989 edn). Postwar developments are discussed in Beatrice Heuser and Robert O'Neill (eds), *Securing Peace in Europe, 1945–62: Thoughts for the Post-Cold War Era* (Basingstoke, 1992). Alfred Grosser, *The Western Alliance: European–American Relations since 1945* (1980) offers a broader overview of the Atlantic relationship. This is further discussed, as it affected Britain, in William R. Louis and Hedley Bull (eds) *The 'Special Relationship': Anglo-American Relations since 1945* (Oxford, 1986) and in David Reynolds, 'A "Special Relationship"? America, Britain and the International Order since the Second World War' and 'Rethinking Anglo-American Relations', *International Affairs* lxii (1985–6) and lxv (1989). Material on the more prickly relationship with France will be found in Jean Lacouture, *De Gaulle: The Ruler* (1991), in Richard Ullman, 'The Covert French Connection', *Foreign Policy* lxxv (1989), and – indirectly – in Pierre Hassner, 'Perceptions of the Soviet Threat in the 1950s and the 1980s: The Case of France', in C.-C. Schweitzer (ed.) *The Changing Analysis of the Soviet Threat* (1990). A general view of Western European integration is given by D.W. Urwin, *The Community of Europe: A History of European Integration since 1945* (1991). There is a marked difference between the archive-based studies now appearing on the postwar decade and accounts of more recent developments. The densest of the former studies is A.S. Milward, *The Reconstruction of Western Europe, 1945–51* (1984); non-specialists may prefer John W. Young, *Britain, France and the Unity of Western Europe 1945–51* (Leicester, 1984). The actual foundation and early development of the EEC was well described, albeit from the public record, by F. Roy Willis, *France, Germany, and the New Europe: 1945–1967* (Stanford, Calif., 1968). Further insights are provided by Jean Monnet's *Memoirs* (1978), and by biographies of Adenauer and de Gaulle (cited on pp. 485, 492). The subsequent Franco-German entente is considered in Haig Simonian, *The Privileged Partnership: Franco-German Relations in the European Community, 1969–1984* (Oxford, 1985). A picture of the EC's operation towards the end of that period is given by a former Commissioner in C. Tugendhat, *Making Sense of Europe* (Harmondsworth, 1986). On the eve of Maastricht, William Wallace reflected on *The Transformation of Western Europe* (1990), while material on the turbulent European Monetary System is to be found in David Marsh, *The Bundesbank: The Bank that Rules Europe* (1993).

Finally, maps are almost indispensable: 'where you stand' often, though not always, 'depends on where you sit'. A good atlas should suffice, since topography does not change rapidly. Economic and population statistics do, and are in any case less trustworthy; but those presented in, for instance, the annual World Bank *Atlas* are both interesting and useful, provided they are taken with a pinch of salt.

Index